Dale and Appelbe's Pharmacy and Medicines Law

Dale and Appelbe's Pharmacy and Medicines Law

THIRTEENTH EDITION

By

David H Reissner LLB (Hons), Hon LLD
Solicitor, Honorary Professor of Pharmacy and Medicines Law,
University of Nottingham, Deputy District Judge

Christopher A Langley BSc (Hons),
LLM, PhD, FRPharmS, MRSC, PFHEA, FRSB
Professor of Pharmacy Law and Practice, Aston University, UK

PHARMACEUTICAL PRESS
Essential Knowledge

Published by Pharmaceutical Press
66-68 East Smithfield, London E1W 1AW

PHARMACEUTICAL PRESS
Essential Knowledge
is a trade mark of Pharmaceutical Press. Pharmaceutical Press is the publishing division of the Royal Pharmaceutical Society

First published 1976
Second edition 1979
Third edition 1983
Fourth edition 1989
Fifth edition 1993
Sixth edition 1997
Seventh edition 2001
Eighth edition 2005
Ninth edition 2009
Tenth edition 2013
Eleventh edition 2017
Twelfth edition 2021
Thirteenth edtion 2025

Printed in Great Britain by TJ Books, Padstow, Cornwall

ISBN 978-0-85711-493-8

A catalogue record for this book is available from the British Library.

Table of Contents

Preface to the Thirteenth Edition

In writing this book, we have built on and revised the work of past contributors including, of course, the original editors whose names the book still bears, Joe Dale and Gordon Appelbe, and the subsequent editorship of Joy Wingfield. In the twelfth edition, we were assisted by the contributions to specific chapters by Sarah ME Cockburn, Ann Godsell, Gordon Hockey, Edward Mallinson and Helen Root. In this edition, we have aimed to build on their contributions which we wish to acknowledge. This book seeks to cover in one volume the many laws that govern medicines and the practice of pharmacy in Great Britain. We hope that the book will prove useful not only to pharmacy undergraduates, foundation training students and pharmacists in all branches of the profession, but also to others in Britain and overseas who may need some knowledge of current law in Great Britain relating to medicines and the practice of pharmacy, including the members of healthcare professions who, since the last edition, have been granted the right to prescribe and supply medicines.

Just as in the intervals between previous editions, the period between the publication of the twelfth edition, and this edition has seen many changes in almost all areas of law and regulation addressed by this book. When the last edition was written the UK had voted to leave the European Union. The basis on which the UK would leave was unclear for a long time after the referendum and the UK reached an agreement with the EU only days before we were due to deliver the final text of the twelfth edition to the Pharmaceutical Press. We had a busy time between Christmas and New Year's Eve 2020, making changes to reflect the agreement. Things have moved on again in the intervening period, necessitating many changes to the text, not least because of the Windsor Framework agreed between the UK and the EU. Many other changes have also been necessary. These changes include new legal duties for superintendent pharmacists and responsible pharmacists; the role of chief pharmacists; extensive amendments to the Veterinary Medicines Regulations; extending the right to prescribe and to supply medicines to pharmacists and other healthcare professionals; the broadened roles of pharmacy technicians; original pack dispensing; and a defence to prosecutions for dispensing errors made in hospitals and prisons. Other changes and case law that are covered in this edition bring into play topical issues involving puberty blockers, Wegovy and Ozempic, valproate, cannabis and Botox, all of which feature in the following pages.

The twelfth edition featured six new chapters. In this edition, several chapters have been extensively updated and, in addition, we introduce two new chapters: Online pharmacy; and Hospital pharmacy (and other relevant pharmacy services). In the case of the former, although much of the law is the same as for bricks and mortar pharmacies, there are growing differences in the law as well as different risks which we discuss. The chapter on hospital pharmacy will, we hope, be helpful to the pharmacists and other healthcare professionals who practise in hospital and allied settings.

In addition to the many changes in the law that have taken place since the last edition, there are still many proposed changes that have been announced, but not yet brought into force. These include changes to the law on pharmacist supervision, changes to broaden the opportunity to use hub and spoke dispensing (which is relevant to no fewer than five chapters in this book), amendments to the regulations governing clinical trials, and to the regulations governing medical devices. We have done our best to future-proof this edition by including details of the proposals in boxes that also provide details of how readers can check whether the respective proposals have been brought into force.

As well as changes in the law and changes in pharmacy practice, British society has continued to change. As in the twelfth edition, we have endeavoured to reflect societal changes by using gender-neutral language except when quoting from a document that does not use such language. We have also made editorial decisions concerning other terminology. Legislation does not recognise the term *community pharmacy*, so we refer to *retail pharmacy* throughout the book. For similar reasons, although it is commonplace to refer to pharmacies that provide NHS services as *pharmacy contractors,* this term does not appear in any legislation and there is no contract between such pharmacies and any NHS body[1] (except in relation to commissioned services). We therefore refer to *pharmacy owners*, especially in Chapter 3. We have also in places used the term *pharmacy professionals* to refer collectively to pharmacists and pharmacy technicians registered with the General Pharmaceutical Council. We are aware that this term is not one that is universally accepted within the profession but as the term used by the regulatory body for pharmacy in Great Britain, it seemed appropriate to adopt it within this book.

The laws are those of Great Britain except where otherwise stated in the text. It is important to emphasise this because the law in Northern Ireland has significantly diverged from that in the rest of Great Britain. Our aim has been to state the law as concisely as accuracy permits, but it should be borne in mind that only the courts can give a legally binding decision on any question of interpretation..

We have been greatly assisted in our efforts by our two Consulting Editors, Louise Wilson and Noel Wardle. The responsibility for the text and any views expressed there lie with us, and any errors in this work are our responsibility alone.

Except to the extent that we have reflected in outline changes in the law that were not in force at the time of going to print, the law is stated as at 7 April 2025.

David H Reissner
Christopher A Langley
April 2025

1. Roy v Kensington and Chelsea and Westminster Family Practitioner Committee [1992] 1 AC 624.

Foreword

The pharmacy regulator and the pharmacy professions we work with share a common purpose: the health, safety and wellbeing of patients and the public. The professionalism and skill of pharmacists and pharmacy technicians keeps patients and members of the public safe. We support, facilitate and assure the public protection role of the pharmacy professions, in all the sectors and environments where they are caring for people.

The pharmacy professions are evolving rapidly, and they are reshaping how care is delivered. These advancements present significant opportunities but also bring new challenges in maintaining safety, quality, and public trust.

Pharmacists in Great Britain have greater scope to prescribe medicines, enabling wider opportunities to provide care, as well as new potential risks that need to be managed. Likewise, the role of pharmacy technicians has widened, with the profession being added to the list of professions legally enabled to supply and administer medicines under Patient Group Directions.

Health services across Great Britain are increasingly encouraging visits to pharmacies for a wider range of conditions, enhancing access to medicines expertise and reducing pressure on General Practice and other health services.

As online prescribing and supply services become more common and convenient, pharmacists and pharmacy technicians must ensure they meet the same high standards for public safety, albeit through new and rapidly changing service delivery models. Digitally-enhanced clinical services have the potential to benefit patients and also to create risks which need to be managed and regulated.

Healthcare integration in various countries aims to create a more cohesive, efficient, and patient-centred system by breaking down barriers between providers, leveraging technology, and fostering collaborative governance.

One constant amidst so much change is the pharmacy professions' expertise in all aspects of the law relating to medicines and pharmacy practice. Pharmacy has an honourable tradition as keeper of the health professions' body of knowledge and professional conscience when it comes to medicines and the complex laws governing their safe and effective use. This new, 13th edition of Dale and Appelbe's Pharmacy and Medicines Law provides essential underpinning for this unique and enduring aspect of the pharmacy professions' vocation. The distinguished editors and contributors are once again to be thanked and congratulated on their signal achievement.

Duncan Rudkin
General Pharmaceutical Council
April 2025

About the contributors

Authors

David H Reissner LLB (Hons) was admitted to the Roll of Solicitors in 1978 and shortly afterwards joined the law firm now known as Charles Russell Speechlys LLP where he was Head of Healthcare. He specialised in pharmacy law including professional conduct, fitness to practise and market entry cases. He retired as a partner in the firm in 2018. He was appointed Honorary Professor of Pharmacy and Medicines Law by the University of Nottingham in 2022 and was awarded an honorary Doctor of Laws degree by the University of Hertfordshire in 2024. He is chair of the Pharmacy Law & Ethics Association, a consultant to Community Pharmacy Northern Ireland, a Trustee of the Commonwealth Pharmacists Association, and is a regular contributor to the pharmacy press on legal and ethical issues. He is a Deputy District Judge.

Christopher A Langley, BSc (Hons), LLM, PhD, FRPharmS, MRSC, PFHEA, FRSB is Professor of Pharmacy Law and Practice and Deputy Dean of the College of Health and Life Sciences at Aston University. He qualified as a pharmacist in 1997 before returning to university to complete a PhD in medicinal chemistry. He joined the academic staff at Aston University in 2000 undertaking a number of roles before taking over as Head of Pharmacy in 2016, a role he undertook until 2022. In 2012, he completed a Master of Laws in the Legal Aspects of Medical Practice. Chris is a team leader of the General Pharmaceutical Council's Accreditation and Recognition Panel, and a former member of the Board of Assessors. Chris sat as a registrant member of the General Pharmaceutical Council's Fitness to Practise Committee for eight years between 2014 and 2022. He is a Fellow of the Royal Pharmaceutical Society and a Principal Fellow of the Higher Education Academy.

Consulting Editors

Noel Wardle LLB (Hons) was admitted to the Roll of Solicitors in 2001. Since 2005 he has specialised in pharmacy law including professional conduct, fitness to practise and market entry cases. Noel is currently a partner at Temple Bright LLP.

Louise E Wilson MPharm (Hons), FHEA, MRPharmS is Assistant Professor in Pharmacy Practice and School of Pharmacy Lead for Pharmacy Law at the University of Nottingham. She joined the register as a pharmacist in 2004 and practised in community pharmacy for 15 years undertaking a variety of branch management roles. In 2017 she began working at the University of Nottingham supporting pharmacy practice teaching, initially alongside her practice role. In 2022 she was appointed to her current full academic position and has overseen the development of the pharmacy law curriculum and assessment for the reaccredited MPharm programme. In 2023 she established the Professor Joy Wingfield Annual Memorial Lecture in pharmacy law and ethics. She is also currently completing a PhD in pharmacy practice.

Introduction

Development of the law in relation to pharmacy, medicines and poisons

Before the middle of the 19th century, there were no legal restrictions in England on the sale of poisons or drugs, and anyone could describe themselves as a pharmaceutical chemist. Statutory control over sales was first applied to arsenic because, as the preamble to the Arsenic Act 1851 stated, the unrestricted sale of arsenic facilitates the commission of crime. The first statute relating to pharmacy followed the next year. The Pharmacy Act 1852 confirmed the charter of incorporation of the Pharmaceutical Society of Great Britain, which had been granted in 1843. The 1852 Act established the framework of the Society and gave it power to hold examinations and to issue certificates. It also restricted the use of the title pharmaceutical chemist to members of the Society, although it did not restrict the use of the titles *chemist* or *druggist*. The Society received its Royal prefix in 1988. In 2010, the Society was wound up to be replaced by two bodies: a new regulator, the General Pharmaceutical Council, and a professional leadership body, the Royal Pharmaceutical Society. References in this book to the Pharmaceutical Society or to the Royal Pharmaceutical Society that relate to the period before the establishment of the General Pharmaceutical Council, are to the body that was the professional regulator at the relevant time.

The Pharmacy Act 1868 brought new developments. It introduced a Poisons List (with 15 entries) and empowered the Society to add other substances to it, subject to the approval of the Privy Council. A poison was defined as any substance included in the Poisons List. Articles and preparations containing poisons could be sold by retail only by pharmaceutical chemists or by a new legal class of chemists and druggists. Both titles were protected by the Act. The class of chemists and druggists comprised (a) all those who before the passing of the Act had been engaged in the keeping of open shop for the compounding of the prescriptions of duly qualified medical practitioners, and (b) all those persons who had been registered as assistants under the provisions of the Pharmacy Act 1852.

The Registrar of the Society was thereafter required to keep registers of pharmaceutical chemists, of chemists and druggists, and of apprentices or students. The qualification of chemist and druggist became the statutory minimum for persons carrying on a business comprising the sale of poisons. Chemists and druggists were eligible to be elected members or associates of the Pharmaceutical Society but did not have all the privileges of a member who had qualified as a pharmaceutical chemist. That state of affairs continued – slightly modified by a statute of 1898 – until the Pharmacy Act 1953 combined the two qualifications in one Register of Pharmaceutical Chemists. The profession of pharmacy was now regulated by the Pharmacy Act 1954, which absorbed the 1953 Act. The 1954 Act was subsequently repealed by a section 60 Order under the Health Act 1999, which paved the way for specific legislation establishing the General Pharmaceutical Council.

The 1868 Act had not only introduced the first list of poisons but also regulated the manner in which they could be sold, specifying more stringent restrictions on sale for the more dangerous poisons. Fixed penalties, recoverable in the civil courts, were prescribed for breaches of the Act. The list of poisons was extended by the Poisons and Pharmacy Act 1908, which also stipulated that poisons for agricultural and horticultural purposes could be sold by licensed dealers as well as by pharmacists. This Act also prescribed conditions under which corporate bodies could carry on the business of a chemist and druggist (such as having a superintendent pharmacist). This had become necessary because it had been held in the High Court in 1880 that an incorporated company was not covered by the word *person* as used in the 1868 Act and was, therefore, not liable for penalties under the Act (*Pharmaceutical Society v London and Provincial Supply Association Ltd*, see earlier editions of this book).

Under the Pharmacy and Poisons Act 1933, a Poisons Board was established to advise the Secretary of State on what should be included in the Poisons List. Poisons in Part I of the list could be sold by retail only at pharmacies; poisons in Part II could be sold also by traders on a local authority list. Poisons were further classified by means of the Schedules to the Poisons Rules made under the Act. Schedule 4, for example, comprised a class of poisons which could be supplied to the public only on the authority of a prescription written by a practitioner. A Register of Premises was set up under the Act, and all registered pharmacists were required to be members of the Pharmaceutical Society.

One of the main features of the 1933 Act was the establishment of a disciplinary body (the Statutory Committee), which had authority not only over pharmacists who committed misconduct but also over pharmacists and corporate bodies convicted of offences under the Pharmacy Act. The Society was placed under a duty to enforce the Act and was authorised to appoint inspectors for the purpose. These enforcement powers and the creation of an inspectorate made pharmacy the most highly regulated of all the healthcare professions (because no other healthcare profession was subject to inspection in the same way, at least until the creation of what is now the Care Quality Commission). Proceedings under the Act were to be taken in criminal courts and not, as previously, in the civil courts. The Pharmacy and Poisons Act 1933 was repealed by the Medicines Act 1968. The Poisons Act 1972 dealt only with non-medicinal poisons. The Statutory Committee was replaced by a Disciplinary Committee in 2007 and then by the current Fitness to Practise processes of the General Pharmaceutical Council in 2010.

Pharmacy and poisons were firmly linked together by statute, but the sale and manufacture of medicines was not regulated in any way except for medicines containing poisons. Some control over quality was provided by a series of Food and Drugs Acts, culminating in the Food and Drugs Act 1955. Under those Acts, it was an offence to sell adulterated drugs, or to sell, to the prejudice of the purchaser, any drug not of the nature, substance or quality demanded. The effectiveness of those provisions was limited by the fact that most drugs were of vegetable origin and there were no precise standards for many of them. Furthermore, a manufacturer of a proprietary medicine did not have to disclose its composition, provided that they paid the appropriate duty by way of fixing the appropriate excise stamps to each bottle or packet as required by the Medicine Stamp Acts. That state of affairs was changed by the Pharmacy and Medicines Act 1941, which abolished medicines stamp duty and required, instead, a disclosure of composition of each container. It also restricted the sale of medicines to shops (as distinct from market stalls etc.) and made it unlawful to advertise any article for the treatment of eight named diseases, including diabetes, epilepsy and tuberculosis. This was the first statute in which pharmacy and medicines were directly linked. The 1941 Act, however, did not apply to animal medicines.

The Therapeutic Substances Act 1925 controlled by licence the manufacture (but not the sale or supply) of a limited number of products the purity or potency of which could not be tested by chemical means, for example vaccines, sera, toxins, antitoxins and certain other substances. The list was greatly extended when antibiotics came into use. It had not been held necessary to restrict the retail sale or supply of vaccines, sera and antitoxins, but penicillin and most other antibiotics were found to be substances which were capable of causing danger to the health of the community if used without proper safeguards. Consequently, the Penicillin Act 1947 and the Therapeutic Substances (Prevention of Misuse) Act 1953 permitted the supply of antibiotics to the public only by practitioners, or from pharmacies on the authority of practitioners' prescriptions. The Therapeutic Substances Act 1956 replaced the earlier Acts, so bringing under the control of one statute both the manufacture and the supply of therapeutic substances. It could be regarded as the precursor to the Medicines Act 1968, which replaced it.

Legislation relating to medicines developed in a piecemeal manner, each problem, scandal or tragedy being dealt with as it arose, and the law was scattered throughout a number of pieces of legislation. However, rapid developments in pharmaceutical research after the Second World War made available an increasing number of potent substances for use in medicine, and a working party was set up by the government in 1959 to examine the need for new controls. The thalidomide tragedy in 1961 almost certainly precipitated proposals for new legislation, which were published in 1967 in a White Paper entitled Forthcoming Legislation on the Safety, Quality and Description of Drugs and Medicines (Cmnd.3395). The Medicines Act 1968, which was designed to replace all earlier legislation relating to medicines, was based on the proposals in the White Paper.

European Community legislation has had, and still has, a large impact on UK law. This impact has not disappeared following the UK's exit from the EU because, under the European Union (Withdrawal) Act 2018, law introduced into the UK from the EU remains in effect unless changed by subsequent legislation in the UK. The Treaty of Rome and the issue of regulations, directives, decisions and recommendations by the Council of Ministers in Brussels led to amendments of pharmacy and medicines law in Great Britain, particularly with regard to the mutual recognition of pharmaceutical qualifications and the manufacture and distribution of medicines. However, the UK's withdrawal from the EU has led to some immediate changes that make certain processes domestic in nature, such as the recognition of qualifications and the arrangements for marketing authorisations. In 2005, veterinary (animal) medicines were removed from the 1968 Medicines Act and consolidated under the European Communities Act 1972, with a view to annual updating. By 2012, the need to maintain compliance with European directives precipitated a consolidation and review of all the human medicines (but not pharmacy) regulations issued under the Medicines Act and to issue a single consolidated set of regulations, again under the European Communities Act 1972. The Medicines Act 1968 currently still contains the substantive provisions covering registered pharmacy businesses.

International agreement about the control of narcotics began with the International Opium Convention signed at The Hague in 1912, although the Convention was not implemented until after the First World War. A series of Dangerous Drugs Acts, beginning with the Dangerous Drugs Act 1920, brought the various international agreements into force in Great Britain. The Single Convention on Narcotic Drugs 1961 replaced all the earlier international agreements and was reflected in the Dangerous Drugs Act 1965.

The misuse of amphetamines and other psychotropic drugs widened the problems of abuse, and a Convention on Psychotropic Substances was signed in 1971. In Great Britain, however, the Drugs (Prevention of Misuse) Act 1964 had provided a measure of control by making the unlawful possession of amphetamines, and certain other drugs, an offence. As problems of drug abuse continued to increase, the law was extended and recast in the Misuse of Drugs Act 1971, which repealed the various Dangerous Drugs Acts and the 1964 Act. The provisions of the 1971 Act and a series of regulations continue to apply to all aspects of dealings in controlled drugs.

The National Health Service Act 1946 and the National Health Service (Scotland) Act 1947 provided for a comprehensive health service across Great Britain, including the provision of pharmaceutical services. By 1999, both Scotland and Wales secured devolution of power in matters of health, and their legislation, organisation and practice within the NHS now differs considerably from that of England. In 1991, Crown immunity was removed from NHS services provided in hospitals and elsewhere such that medicines licensing legislation applies equally to services within the managed sector and the private sector. However, the supply of medicines within hospitals remains exempted from the legislation unless those hospitals have chosen to register their pharmacies or, as in the case of some hospitals, their out-patient pharmacies are now run by registered pharmacy businesses.

Many important changes to pharmacy and medicines law have taken place in the first quarter of the twenty-first century. Amongst them:

- In 2005, significant changes were made to the NHS regulations in England. Until then, NHS pharmaceutical services were focussed entirely on dispensing. Amongst other things, the changes introduced advanced and enhanced services and permitted the opening of 100-hour pharmacies and distance selling pharmacies.
- In 2008, a requirement for a pharmacist to be in personal control of every pharmacy was replaced with the requirement for a responsible pharmacist with statutory duties.
- In 2010, the General Pharmaceutical Council (GPhC) replaced the Royal Pharmaceutical Society of Great Britain as regulator of the pharmacy profession. The

GPhC has different and wider powers than those of its predecessors, some of which were acquired as recently as 2018.
- In 2012, the Human Medicines Regulations 2012 replaced most of the Medicines Act 1968, although the law in relation to the registration of pharmacy professionals and of premises, the requirement for responsible pharmacists and their statutory duties are still in the Medicines Act.
- In 2022, the statutory duties of responsible pharmacists in the Medicines Act were amended, and a new statutory duty for superintendent pharmacists was introduced.
- In 2022, when a defence was created for someone who is prosecuted for making a dispensing error in a hospital, the Medicines Act created the role of chief pharmacist. The GPhC published standards for chief pharmacists in January 2025.
- In 2024, the Veterinary Medicines Regulations 2013 were subject to considerable change, including a focus on antimicrobial stewardship.

As explained in the Preface to this edition, and in the following chapters, further significant changes to pharmacy and medicines law are likely to be made in the foreseeable future.

Legislation

Table of international treaties and conventions

Title	Chapter(s)
Convention on Psychotropic Substances	Introduction, 19
Convention on the Elaboration of a European Pharmacopoeia	20
Convention on the International Trade in Endangered Species of Wild Fauna and Flora	17
European Convention on Human Rights	1, 14, 23, 24, 25
International Opium Convention	Introduction
Single Convention on Narcotic Drugs	Introduction, 19
United Nations Convention against Illicit Traffic in Narcotic Drugs and Psychotropic Substances	14

European law

Directives

Reference	Title	Chapter(s)
85/374/EEC	Directive on the approximation of the laws, regulations and administrative provisions of the Member States concerning liability for defective products	26
88/378/EEC	Directive on the approximation of the laws of the Member States concerning the safety of toys	21
96/98/EC	Directive on marine equipment	21
2001/82/EC	Directive on the Community code relating to veterinary medicinal products (known as *the Veterinary Medicines Directive*)	15
2001/83/EC	Directive on the Community code relating to medicinal products for human use (known as *the Medicines Directive*)	1, 4, 5, 20
2003/63/EC	Directive amending Directive 2001/83/EC of the European Parliament and of the Council on the Community code relating to medicinal products for human use	20
2003/94/EC	Directive laying down the principles and guidelines of good manufacturing practice in respect of medicinal products for human use and investigational medicinal products for human use (known as the *Good Manufacturing Practice Directive)*	5
2011/62/EU	Directive amending Directive 2001/83/EC on the Community code relating to medicinal products for human use, as regards the prevention of the entry into the legal supply chain of falsified medicinal products	5
2014/40/EU	Directive on the approximation of the laws, regulations and administrative provisions of the Member States concerning the manufacture, presentation and sale of tobacco and related products and repealing Directive 2001/37/EC	5

Regulations

Reference	Title	Chapter(s)
(EEC) 2309/93	Regulation laying down Community procedures for the authorisation and supervision of medicinal products for human and veterinary use and establishing a European Agency for the Evaluation of Medicinal Products	15
(EC) 141/2000	Regulation on orphan medicinal products	18
(EC) 1907/2006	Regulation concerning the Registration, Evaluation, Authorisation and Restriction of Chemicals (REACH), establishing a European Chemicals Agency, amending Directive 1999/45/EC and repealing Council Regulation (EEC) No 793/93 and Commission Regulation (EC) No 1488/94 as well as Council Directive 76/769/EEC and Commission Directives 91/155/EEC, 93/67/EEC, 93/105/EC and 2000/21/EC	21
(EC) 1272/2008	Regulation on classification, labelling and packaging of substances and mixtures, amending and repealing Directives 67/548/EEC and 1999/45/EC, and amending Regulation (EC) 1907/2006	21
(EC) 470/2009	Regulation laying down Community procedures for the establishment of residue limits of pharmacologically active substances in foodstuffs of animal origin, repealing Council Regulation (EEC) No 2377/90 and amending Directive 2001/82/EC of the European Parliament and of the Council and Regulation (EC) No 726/2004 of the European Parliament and of the Council	15
(EU) 98/2013	Regulation on the marketing and use of explosives precursors	21
(EU) 122/2013	Regulation amending Regulation (EC) No 1950/2006 establishing, in accordance with Directive 2001/82/EC of the European Parliament and of the Council on the Community code relating to veterinary medicinal products, a list of substances essential for the treatment of equidae	15
(EU) 2016/161	Regulation supplementing Directive 2001/83/EC of the European parliament and of the Council by laying down detailed rules for the safety features appearing on the packaging of medicinal products for human use (known as *the Falsified Medicines Directive*)	5

Table of Statutes

Title	Chapter(s)
Abortion Act 1967	12
Access to Health Records Act 1990	1, 23
Adults with Incapacity (Scotland) Act 2000	24
Arsenic Act 1851	Introduction, 21
Botulinum Toxin and Cosmetic Fillers (Children) Act 2021	12
Care Standards Act 2000	2, 3
Civic Government (Scotland) Act 1982	2
Civil Liability (Contribution) Act 1978	26
Communications Act 2003	12

Title	Chapter(s)
Companies Act 2006	7
Competition Act 1998	26
Consumer Protection Act 1987	5, 22, 26
Consumer Rights Act 2015	26
Coroners and Justice Act 2009	1
Corporate Manslaughter and Corporate Homicide Act 2007	26
Criminal Attempts Act 1981	14
Criminal Justice (International Co-operation) Act 1990	14
Criminal Justice and Courts Act 2015	26
Customs and Excise Act 1952	14
Customs and Excise Management Act 1979	14, 21
Dangerous Drugs Act 1920	Introduction
Dangerous Drugs Act 1965	Introduction
Data Protection Act 1998	23, 26
Data Protection Act 2018	1, 23
Dentists Act 1984	13
Deregulation Act 2015	21
Disclosure (Scotland) Act 2020	2
Drugs (Prevention of Misuse) Act 1964	Introduction
Environmental Protection Act 1990	26
Equality Act 2010	1, 3, 24, 26
European Communities Act 1972	Introduction, 1
European Union (Withdrawal) Act 2018	Introduction, 4, 15
Family Law Reform Act 1969	25
Fatal Accidents and Sudden Deaths etc. (Scotland) Act 2016	1
Female Genital Mutilation Act 2003	23, 24
Finance (No. 2) Act 2023	21
Food and Drugs Act 1955	Introduction
Food Safety Act 1990	13, 14
Freedom of Information (Scotland) Act 2002	23
Freedom of Information Act 2000	7, 23
Health (Tobacco, Nicotine etc. and Care) (Scotland) Act 2016	5
Health Act 1999	Introduction, 1
Health Act 2006	14
Health and Care Act 2022	3
Health and Safety at Work etc. Act 1974	1, 14, 26
Health and Social Care (National Data Guardian) Act 2018	23
Health and Social Care Act 2008	2, 3, 8, 13

Title	Chapter(s)
Health and Social Care Act 2012	1, 3, 23
Health Service Commissioners Act 1993	3
Health Service Medical Supplies (Costs) Act 2017	3
Human Rights Act 1998	1, 23, 25
Legal Aid, Sentencing and Punishment of Offenders Act 2012	18
Limited Liability Partnerships Act 2000	7
Local Government and Public Involvement in Health Act 2007	3
Medicines Act 1968	Introduction, 1, 2, 4, 5, 6, 7, 9, 10, 11, 12, 14, 17, 18, 21, 23, 24, 25, 26
Medicines and Medical Devices Act 2021	1, 4, 22, 26
Mental Capacity Act 2005	7, 24
Mental Health Act 1983	13
Merchant Shipping Act 1995	14
Mineral Workings (Offshore Installations) Act 1971	14
Misuse of Drugs Act 1971	Introduction, 1, 3, 7, 9, 14, 26
National Health Service (Scotland) Act 1947	Introduction, 3
National Health Service (Scotland) Act 1978	2, 3, 9, 12, 13, 14
National Health Service (Wales) Act 2006	3, 9, 12, 13
National Health Service Act 1946	Introduction, 3
National Health Service Act 1977	3, 14
National Health Service Act 2006	1, 3, 6, 9, 12, 13, 23, 25
National Health Service Reform and Health Care Professions Act 2002	2, 25
Occupiers' Liability Act 1957	26
Offences Against the Person Act 1861	12, 26
Opticians Act 1989	13
Partnership Act 1890	7
Patient Rights (Scotland) Act 2011	3, 23
Penicillin Act 1947	Introduction
Pharmacy Act 1852	Introduction
Pharmacy Act 1868	Introduction
Pharmacy Act 1953	Introduction
Pharmacy Act 1954	Introduction, 7
Pharmacy and Medicines Act 1941	Introduction
Pharmacy and Poisons Act 1933	Introduction, 11, 21
Poisons Act 1972	Introduction, 2, 21, Appendix 4
Poisons and Pharmacy Act 1908	Introduction
Police (Scotland) Act 1967	Appendix 3

Title	Chapter(s)
Police Act 1996	Appendix 3
Police and Criminal Evidence Act 1984	21
Police Reform and Social Responsibility Act 2011	14
Postal Services Act 2011	14
Proceeds of Crime Act 2002	14
Protection of Vulnerable Groups (Scotland) Act 2007	2
Psychoactive Substances Act 2016	4, 14
Public Health (Control of Disease) Act 1984	2
Public Health (Wales) Act 2017	2
Public Health etc. (Scotland) Act 2008	2, 14
Public Interest Disclosure Act 1998	24
Public Services Ombudsman (Wales) Act 2019	3
Public Services Reform (Scotland) Act 2010	3, 9
Regulation of Investigatory Powers Act 2000	2
Rehabilitation of Offenders Act 1974	25, 26
Retained EU Law (Revocation and Reform) Act 2023	1
Safeguarding Vulnerable Groups Act 2006	25
Scottish Public Services Ombudsman Act 2002	3
Sentencing and Punishment of Offenders Act 2012	18
Social Action, Responsibility and Heroism Act 2015	26
Social Security Administration Act 1992	25
Therapeutic Substances Act 1925	Introduction
Therapeutic Substances Act 1956	Introduction
Therapeutic Substances (Prevention of Misuse) Act 1953	Introduction
Value Added Tax Act 1994	11
Wildlife and Countryside Act 1981	14

Table of Statutory Instruments, Orders of Council and Directions

Title	SI no.	Chapter(s)
Act of Sederunt (Fatal Accident Inquiry Rules) 2017	2017 SSI no.103	1
Alcoholic Products (Excise Duty) Regulations 2023	2023 SI no.806	21
Anaesthesia Associates and Physician Associates Order 2024	2024 SI no.374	13
Branded Health Service Medicines (Costs) Regulations 2018	2018 SI no.345	3

Title	SI no.	Chapter(s)
Civic Government (Scotland) Act 1982 (Licensing of Skin Piercing and Tattooing) Order 2006	2006 SI no.43	2
Civil Procedure Rules 1998	1998 SI no.3132	25
Consumer Contracts (Information, Cancellation and Additional Charges) Regulations 2013	2013 SI no.3134	26
Consumer Protection from Unfair Trading Regulations 2008	2008 SI no.1277	26
Control of Explosives Precursors and Poisons Regulations 2023	2023 SI no.63	21
Control of Poisons and Explosives Precursors Regulations 2015	2015 SI no.966	21
Control of Substances Hazardous to Health Regulations 2002	2002 SI no.2677	15, 21, 26
Controlled Drugs (Drug Precursors) (Community External Trade) Regulations 2008	2008 SI no.296	14, 21
Controlled Drugs (Drug Precursors) (Intra-Community Trade) Regulations 2008	2008 SI no.295	14, 21
Controlled Drugs (Supervision of Management and Use) (Wales) Regulations 2008	2008 SI no.3239 (W. 286)	14
Controlled Drugs (Supervision of Management and Use) Regulations 2013	2013 SI no.372	14
Controlled Waste (England and Wales) Regulations 2012	2012 SI no.811	26
Coroners (Investigations) Regulations 2013	2013 SI no.1629	1, 8
Denatured Alcohol Regulations 2005	2005 SI no.1524	21
Deregulation Act 2015 (Poisons and Explosives Precursors) (Consequential Amendments, Revocations and Transitional Provisions) Order 2015	2015 SI no.968	21
Food and Drink, Veterinary Medicines and Residues (Amendment etc.) (EU Exit) Regulations 2019	2019 SI no.865	15
Food Supplements (England) Regulations 2003	2003 SI no.1387	17
Food Supplements (Scotland) Regulations 2003	2003 SSI no.278	17
Food Supplements (Wales) Regulations 2003	2003 SI no.1719 (W. 186)	17
General Pharmaceutical Council (Appeals Committee Rules) Order of Council 2010	2010 SI no.1614	2, 25
General Pharmaceutical Council (Constitution) Order 2010	2010 SI no.300	2
General Pharmaceutical Council (Continuing Professional Development and Consequential Amendments) Rules 2011	2011 SI no.1367	2
General Pharmaceutical Council (Fitness to Practise and Disqualification etc. Rules) Order of Council 2010	2010 SI no.1615	1, 24, 25

Title	SI no.	Chapter(s)
General Pharmaceutical Council (Registration Rules) Order of Council 2010	2010 SI no.1617	2, 25
General Pharmaceutical Council (Statutory Committees and their Advisers) Order of Council 2010	2010 SI no.1616	25
Health and Safety (First-Aid) Regulations 1981	1981 SI no.917	13
Health and Safety (Sharp Instruments in Healthcare) Regulations 2013	2013 SI no.645	26
Health and Social Care Act 2008 (Regulated Activities) Regulations 2014	2014 SI no.2936	2, 3, 8, 13
Health Care and Associated Professions (Indemnity Arrangements) Order 2014	2014 SI no.1887	2
Health Care and Associated Professions (Knowledge of English) Order 2015	2015 SI no.806	2
Health Protection (Notification) (Wales) Regulations 2010	2010 SI no.1546 (W. 144)	2
Health Protection (Notification) Regulations 2010	2010 SI no.659	2
Health Service Products (Provision and Disclosure of Information) Regulations 2018	2018 SI no.677	3, 5
Herbal Medicines Advisory Committee Order 2005	2005 SI no.2791	17
Human Medicines (Amendment) (No. 2) Regulations 2014	2014 SI no.1878	6
Human Medicines (Amendments Relating to Naloxone and Transfers of Functions) Regulations 2024	2024 SI no.1125	13
Human Medicines Regulations 2012	2012 SI no.1916	Introduction, 1, 2, 4, 5, 6, 7, 8, 9, 10, 11, 12, 13, 14, 15, 16, 17, 18, 19, 20, 21, 23, 26, Appendix 2, Appendix 3
Ionising Radiation (Medical Exposure) Regulations 2017	2017 SI no.1322	12
Local Authority Social Services and National Health Service Complaints (England) Regulations 2009	2009 SI no.309	3
Manual Handling Operations Regulations 1992	1992 SI no.2793	26
Medical Certificate of Cause of Death Regulations 2024	2024 SI no.492	1, 23
Medical Devices Regulations 2002	2002 SI no.618	1, 4, 5, 22
Medical Examiners (England) Regulations 2024	2024 SI No.493	1
Medicines (Aristolochia and Mu Tong etc.) (Prohibition) Order 2001	2001 SI no.1841	17, 21
Medicines (Bal Jivan Chamcho Prohibition) (No. 2) Amendment Order 1997	1997 SI no.856	21

Title	SI no.	Chapter(s)
Medicines (Bal Jivan Chamcho Prohibition) (No. 2) Order 1977	1977 SI no.670	21
Medicines (Chloroform Prohibition) Order 1979	1979 SI no.382	21
Medicines (Collection and Delivery Arrangements - Exemption) Order 1978	1978 SI no.1421	12
Medicines (Cyanogenetic Substances) Order 1984	1984 SI no.187	21
Medicines (Gonadotrophin-Releasing Hormone Analogues) (Emergency Prohibition) (England, Wales and Scotland) Order 2024	2024 SI no. 727	12
Medicines (Gonadotrophin-Releasing Hormone Analogues) (Restrictions on Private Sales and Supplies) Order 2024	2024 SI no. 1319	12, 21
Medicines (Pharmacies) (Responsible Pharmacist) Regulations 2008	2008 SI no.2789	7, 11
Medicines (Pharmacy and General Sale – Exemption) Order 1980	1980 SI no.1924	13
Medicines (Products Other Than Veterinary Drugs) (General Sale List) Order 1984	1984 SI no.769	10
Medicines for Human Use (Clinical Trials) Regulations 2004	2004 SI no.1031	4, 5, 21
Medicines for Human Use (Kava-kava) (Prohibition) Order 2002	2002 SI no.3170	17, 21
Medicines for Human Use (Prohibition) (Senecio and Miscellaneous Amendments) Order 2008	2008 SI no.548	17, 21
Misuse of Drugs (Amendment) (No. 2) (England, Wales and Scotland) Regulations 2015	2015 SI no.891	14
Misuse of Drugs (Safe Custody) Regulations 1973	1973 SI no.798	12, 14, 15, 26
Misuse of Drugs (Supply to Addicts) Regulations 1997	1997 SI no.1001	14
Misuse of Drugs Act 1971 (Amendment) Order 2024	2024 SI no.190	14
Misuse of Drugs and Misuse of Drugs (Designation) (Amendment) (England, Wales and Scotland) Regulations 2021	2021 SI no. 897	14
Misuse of Drugs and Misuse of Drugs (Designation) (England and Wales and Scotland) (Amendment) (No. 2) Regulations 2024	2024 SI no. 1369	14, 15
Misuse of Drugs and the Misuse of Drugs (Supply to Addicts) (Amendment) Regulations 2005	2005 SI no. 2864	14
Misuse of Drugs Regulations 2001	2001 SI no.3998	1, 3, 7, 9, 12, 13, 14, 15, 26
National Health Service (Charges for Drugs and Appliances) Regulations 2015	2015 SI no.570	3

Title	SI no.	Chapter(s)
National Health Service (Concerns, Complaints and Redress Arrangements) (Wales) Regulations 2011	2011 SI no.704 (W. 108)	3
National Health Service (General Medical Services Contracts) (Prescription of Drugs etc.) (Amendment) Regulations 2024	2024 SI no.728	3
National Health Service (General Medical Services Contracts) (Prescription of Drugs etc.) Regulations 2004	2004 SI no.629	3
National Health Service (General Medical Services Contracts) (Prescription of Drugs etc.) (Wales) Regulations 2004	2004 SI no.1022 (W. 119)	3
National Health Service (General Medical Services Contracts) (Scotland) Regulations 2004	2004 SSI no.115	12
National Health Service (General Medical Services Contracts) (Scotland) Regulations 2018	2018 SSI no.66	12
National Health Service (Pharmaceutical and Local Pharmaceutical Services) Regulations 2013	2013 SI no.349	1, 3, 7, 12, 20, 23, 25, 26
National Health Service (Pharmaceutical Services) (Scotland) Regulations 2009	2009 SSI no.183	3, 7, 12, 18
National Health Service (Pharmaceutical Services) (Wales) Regulations 2020	2020 SI no.1073 (W. 241)	3, 7, 12
National Health Service (Scotland) Act 1978 (Independent Health Care) Modification Order 2024	2024 SSI no.172	2
National Health Service (Tribunal) (Scotland) Regulations 2004	2004 SSI no.38	3
National Health Service Litigation Authority (Functions relating to Pharmaceutical Services and Local Pharmaceutical Services) (England) Directions 2012	N/A	3
National Health Service Litigation Authority (Pharmaceutical Remuneration – Payment Disputes) (England) Directions 2022	N/A	3
Nicotine Inhaling Products (Age of Sale and Proxy Purchasing) Regulations 2015	2015 SI no.895	5
Nursing and Midwifery (Amendment) Order 2017	2017 SI no.321	9, 14
Nursing and Midwifery Order 2001	2002 SI no.253	9, 14
Personal Protective Equipment at Work Regulations 1992	1992 SI no. 2966	26
Pharmaceutical Services (Advanced and Enhanced Services) (England) Directions 2013	N/A	1, 3
Pharmaceutical Services (Advanced and Enhanced Services) (Wales) Directions 2005	N/A	3

Title	SI no.	Chapter(s)
Pharmacy (Premises Standards, Information Obligations, etc.) Order 2016	2016 SI no.372	2, 25
Pharmacy (Preparation and Dispensing Errors – Hospital and Other Pharmacy Services) Order 2022	2022 SI no.851	26
Pharmacy (Preparation and Dispensing Errors – Registered Pharmacies) Order 2018	2018 SI no.181	26
Pharmacy (Responsible Pharmacists, Superintendent Pharmacists etc.) Order 2022	2022 SI no.849	1, 7, 10
Pharmacy Order 2010	2010 SI no.231	1, 2, 7, 9, 24, 25, 26
Poisons Act 1972 (Explosives Precursors) (Amendment) Regulations 2018	2018 SI no.451	Appendix 4
Prescription Only Medicines (Human Use) Order 1997	1997 SI no.1830	12
Provision and Use of Work Equipment Regulations 1998	1998 SI no.2306	26
REACH Enforcement Regulations 2008	2008 SI no.2852	21
REACH etc. (Amendment etc.) (EU Exit) Regulations 2019	2019 SI no.758	21
Registration of Private Dentistry (Wales) Regulations 2017	2017 SI no.201 (W. 56)	13
Regulation of Investigatory Powers (Authorisations Extending to Scotland) Order 2007	2007 SI no.934	2
Rehabilitation of Offenders Act 1974 (Exceptions) Order 1975	1975 SI no.1023	25
Rehabilitation of Offenders Act 1974 (Exclusions and Exceptions) (Scotland) Order 2013	2013 SSI no.50	25
Safeguarding Vulnerable Groups Act 2006 (Miscellaneous Provisions) Order 2012	2012 SI no.2113	26
Safeguarding Vulnerable Groups Act 2006 (Miscellaneous Provisions) Regulations 2012	2012 SI no.2112	26
Special Procedures Exempted Individuals (Wales) Regulations 2024	2024 No. 1247 (W. 207)	2
Supply of Relevant Veterinary Medicinal Products Order 2005	2005 SI no.2751	15
Veterinary Medicines (Amendment etc.) Regulations 2024	2024 SI no.567	15
Veterinary Medicines and Animals and Animal Products (Examination of Residues and Maximum Residues Limits) (Amendment etc.) (EU Exit) Regulations 2019	2019 SI no.676	15
Veterinary Medicines Regulations 2013	2013 SI no.2033	Introduction, 1, 11, 15, 21
Waste (England and Wales) Regulations 2011	2011 SI no.988	26

Cases

AB v CD [2021] EWHC 741 (Fam) (ch. 24)
Abdul-Razzak v General Pharmaceutical Council [2016] EWHC 1204 (ch. 7 and ch. 11)
Abdullah v General Medical Council [2012] EWHC 2506 (ch. 25)
Abrahaem v General Medical Council [2008] EWHC 183 (Admin) (ch. 25)
Aga v General Dental Council [2025] EWCA Civ 68 (ch. 25)
Akodu v Solicitors Regulation Authority [2009] EWHC 3588 (Admin) (ch. 25)
Albert et Le Compte v Belgium (1983) 5 EHRR 533 (ch. 1)
Alberts v General Dental Council [2022] EWHC 2192 (Admin) (ch. 25)
Ali v Luton Borough Council [2022] WEHC 132 (ch. 26)
Allan v New Mount Sinai Hospital (1980) 109 D.L.R. (3d) 635 (ch. 26)
Allergycare (Testing) Limited v Commissioners of Customs and Excise [2002] Lexis Citation 980 (ch. 11)
Appleby v Sleep [1968] 1 WLR 948 (ch. 3)
Ashraf v General Dental Council [2014] EWHC 2618 (ch. 25)
Ashton v General Medical Council [2013] EWHC 943 (Admin) (ch. 25)
Barclays Bank plc v Various Claimants [2020] UKSC 13 (ch. 26)
Basson v General Medical Council [2018] EWHC 505 (Admin) (ch. 25)
Bawa-Garba v General Medical Council [2018] EWCA Civ 1879 (ch. 1)
Bayer PLC and Novartis Pharmaceuticals UK Ltd v NHS Darlington CCG and others [2020] EWCA Civ 449 (ch. 3, ch. 5, ch. 9 and ch. 12)
Beckwith v Solicitors Regulation Authority [2020] EWHC 3231 (Admin) (ch. 1, ch. 24 and ch. 25)
Blackbay Ventures Ltd v Secretary of State for Health [2012] EWHC 2635 (Admin) (ch. 6)
Blakely v General Medical Council [2019] EWHC 905 (Admin) (ch. 25)
Bolam v Friern Barnet Hospital Management Committee [1957] 2 All E.R. 118 (ch. 26)
Bolton v Law Society [1994] 1 WLR 512 (ch. 25)
Bradshaw v General Medical Council [2010] Med L.R 323 (ch. 25)
Burrows v General Pharmaceutical Council [2016] EWHC 1050 (Admin) (ch. 25)
Caelham v General Medical Council [2007] EWHC 2606, [2008] LS Law Medical 96 (ch. 25)
Campbell v MGN Limited [2004] UKHL 22 (ch. 23)
Carlill v Carbolic Smoke Ball Co [1893] 1 QB 256 (ch. 26)
Cattley v St John's Ambulance Brigade [1988] Lexis Citation 1703 (ch. 26)
Central Liverpool Primary Care Trust v Charles S Bullen Stomacare Ltd [2005] EWCA Civ 1514 (ch. 3 and ch. 11)
Cheatle v General Medical Council [2009] EWHC 645 (Admin) (ch. 25)
Clarke v General Optical Council [2017] EWHC 521 (Admin) (ch. 25)
Cohen v General Medical Council [2008] EWHC 581 (Admin) (ch. 25)
Customs and Excise Commissioners v Wellington Private Hospital Ltd [1997] STC 44 (ch. 5)
Darnley v Croydon Health Services NHS Trust [2018] UKSC 50 (ch. 26)
Davey v General Dental Council 2015 WL 6757832 (ch. 25)
Dickson v Pharmaceutical Society of Great Britain [1970] AC 403 (ch. 3)
Diggins v Bar Standards Board [2020] EWHC 467 (Admin) (ch. 24)
Donoghue v Stevenson [1932] AC 562 (ch. 1 and ch. 26)
Doorstep Dispensaree Ltd v Information Commissioner [2023] UKUT 132 (AAC) and [2024] EWCA Civ 1515 (ch. 23)
Dwyer v Roderick, Jackson and Cross Chemists (Banbury) Limited [1982] Lexis Citation 703, [1983] Lexis Citation 725, The Times 12November 1983, 127 SJ 805 (ch.26)
E Moss Ltd v HMRC (2006) VAT Decision 19510 (ch. 11 and ch. 12)

Elder Home Care Ltd v Customs and Excise Commissioners (1993) VAT Decision 11185 (ch. 11 and ch. 12)
Exelogen v University of Birmingham [2023] EWHC 1523 (Comm) (ch. 5)
Fletcher and Lucas v Pharmaceutical Society of Great Britain, Pharm J, July 1978 p. 93 (ch. 25)
General Medical Council v Dr Raied Haris [2020] EWHC 2518 (Admin) (ch. 25)
General Medical Council v Hiew [2007] 1 W.L.R. 2007 (ch. 25)
General Medical Council v Nwachuku [2017] EWHC 2085 (Admin) (ch. 25)
General Medical Council v Shekhar Chandra [2018] EWCA Civ 1898 (ch. 25)
General Pharmaceutical Council v (1) Kellett and (2) Gamble [2020] EWHC 2401 (Admin) (ch. 25)
General Pharmaceutical Council v Abdullah [2022] EWHC 180 (Admin) (ch. 25)
General Pharmaceutical Council v Khan [2021] EWHC 3212 (Admin) (ch. 25)
General Pharmaceutical Council v Mann [2021] EWHC 3217 (Admin) (ch. 25)
George v General Medical Council [2016] EWHC (ch. 25)
Gillick v West Norfolk and Wisbech Area Health Authority [1986] AC 112 (ch. 3 and ch. 24)
Griffiths v Peter Conway Ltd [1939] 1 All ER 685 (ch. 26)
Gulamhusein v General Pharmaceutical Council [2014] EWHC 2591 (Admin) (ch. 25)
HA v University of Wolverhampton [2018] EWHC 144 (Admin) (ch. 25)
Harris v Registrar of Approved Driving Instructors [2010] EWCA Civ. 808 (ch. 25)
Horton v Evans and Lloyds Pharmacy Ltd [2006] EWHC 2808 QB (ch. 26)
Hughes v Rattan [2022] EWCA 107(Civ) (ch. 26)
Hunter v Hanley [1955] SC 200 (ch. 26)
Ibrahim v General Medical Council [2022] EWHC 2936 (Admin) (ch. 25)
IB v General Medical Council [2024] CSIH 4 (ch. 25)
Ivey v Genting Casinos UK Ltd (trading as Crockfords Club) [2017] UKSC 67 (ch. 25)
J & J Franks Limited v Shotter and others [2023] EWHC 1080 (KB) (ch. 15)
Jideofo v The Law Society [2007] EW Misc 3 (ch. 25)
Judicial Review of a decision of the Senate Fitness to Practise Appeal Committee of a Scottish university [2023] CSOH 52 (ch. 25)
Karwal v General Medical Council [2011] EWHC 26 (Admin) (ch. 25)
Khan (Habib) v General Pharmaceutical Council [2016] UKSC 64 (ch. 25)
Land v Customs and Excise Commissioners (1998) VAT Decision 15547 (ch. 12)
Lawrence v GMC [2012] EWHC 464 (Admin) (ch. 25)
Layne v Attorney General of Grenada [2019] UKPC 11 (ch. 25)
Lewis v Secretary of State for Health [2008] EWHC 2196 (QB) (ch. 23)
LH v Latvia [2014] ECHR 453 (ch. 23)
Lister v Romford Ice and Cold Storage Limited [1957] AC 555 (ch. 26)
Lloyd v Google LLC [2021] UKSC 50 (ch. 23)
Lloyds Pharmacy Ltd v National Appeal Panel [2012] CSOH 22 (ch. 3)
Mahoney v Prestatyn Magistrates' Court [2009] EWHC 3237 (Admin) (ch. 26)
Marcheselli v (1) the Information Commissioner and (2) the General Medical Council [2023] UKFTT 00076 (GRC) (ch. 23)
Marland v DPP [2023] EWHC 1046 (Admin) (ch. 26)
Meadow v General Medical Council [2007] 2 W.L.R. 286 (ch. 25)
Monji v General Pharmaceutical Council [2014] EWHC 3128 (Admin) (ch. 25)
Montgomery v Lanarkshire Health Board [2015] UKSC 11 (ch. 24)
Norbrook Laboratories Ltd v Veterinary Medicines Directorate [2010] NICA 21 (ch. 15)
Norris v Weeks (1970) (*The Times Law Reports*, 6 March 1970) (ch. 7)
Nursing and Midwifery Council v Persand [2023] EWHC 3356 (Admin) (ch. 25)
Pepper v Hart [1992] UKHL 3 (ch. 1)

Petition of Community Pharmacy Scotland [2023] CSOH 65 (ch. 3)
Pfizer Corporation v Ministry of Health [1965] AC 512 (ch. 3, ch. 12 and ch. 26)
Pharmaceutical Society of Great Britain v Boots Cash Chemists (Southern) Ltd [1952] 2 QB 795 and [1953] 1 QB 401 (ch. 11 and ch. 26)
Pharmaceutical Society of Great Britain v Storkwain Ltd [1986] 1 WLR 903 (ch. 12, ch. 14 and ch. 26)
Pharmaceutical Society v London and Provincial Supply Association Ltd (1880) 5 App Cas 857 (Introduction)
Pharmaceutical Society v Wright (1981) (unreported) (ch. 12)
Preiss v General Dental Council [2001] 1 W.L.R. 26 (ch. 25)
Prendergast v Sam & Dee Ltd [1988] 3WLUK 198 (ch. 26)
Professional Standards Authority for Health and Social Care v General Pharmaceutical Council and Ali [2021] EWHC 1692 (Admin) (ch. 24)
Professional Standards Authority v General Medical Council and Igwilo [2016] EWHC 524 (Admin) (ch. 25)
Professional Standards Authority v General Medical Council and Uppal [2015] EWHC 1304 (ch. 25)
Professional Standards Authority v General Pharmaceutical Council and Ali [2024] EWHC 577 (Admin) (ch. 25)
Professional Standards Authority v General Pharmaceutical Council and Onwughalu [2014] EHC 2521 (Admin) (ch. 25)
Professional Standards Authority v General Pharmaceutical Council and R2 [2024] EWHC 3005 (Admin) (ch. 25)
R (on the application of Actegy Ltd) v Advertising Standards Authority Ltd Authority [2019] EWHC 2374 (Admin) (ch. 19)
R (on the application of Alami) v Health and Care Professions Council [2013] EWHC 1895 (Admin) (ch. 25)
R (on the application of British Homeopathic Association) v National Health Service Commissioning Board [2018] EWHC 1359 (Admin) (ch. 16)
R (on the application of Eisai Ltd) v National Institute for Health and Clinical Excellence [2008] EWCA Civ 438 (ch. 3)
R (on the application of Fraser) v National Institute for Health and Clinical Excellence [2009] EWHC 452 (Admin) (ch. 3)
R (on the application of Hexpress Healthcare Ltd v Care Quality Commission [2022] EWHC 2943 (Admin) (ch. 8)
R (on the application of Maughan) v HM Senior Coroner for Oxfordshire [2020] UKSC 46 (ch. 1)
R (on the application of Napp Pharmaceuticals Ltd) v Secretary of State for Health (acting as licensing authority) and Sandoz Ltd [2016] EWHC 1982 (Admin) (ch. 5)
R (on the application of Pharmacy Care Plus Ltd) v Family Health Services Appeal Unit [2013] EWHC 824 (Admin) (ch. 3)
R (on the application of Remedy UK Ltd) v General Medical Council [2010] EWHC 1245 (Admin) (ch. 25)
R (on the application of RRR Manufacturing Pty Ltd) v British Standards Institution and MHRA [2024] EWCA Civ 530 (ch. 22)
R (on the application of Rycroft) v Royal Pharmaceutical Society of Great Britain [2010] EWHC 2832 (Admin) (ch. 25)
R (on the application of Scholten) v General Medical Council [2013] EWHC 173 (Admin) (ch. 25)
R (on the application of Sheikh) v General Dental Council [2010] Med L. R. 323 (ch. 25)
R (on the application of Smeaton) v Secretary of State for Health [2002] EWHC 610 (Admin) (ch. 12 and ch. 26)

R (on the application of Squier) v GMC [2015] EWHC 299 (Admin); QBD (Admin); 13 February 2015 (ch. 25)
R (on the application of Thilakawardhana) v Office of the Independent Adjudicator for Higher Education [2018] EWCA Civ 13 (ch. 25)
R (Redgrave) v Commissioner of Police for the Metropolis [2003] 1 W.L.R. 1136 (ch. 25)
R (Westminster City Council) v National Asylum Support Service [2002] UKHL 38 (ch. 1)
R v Adomako [1995] 1 AC 171 (ch. 26)
R v Chapman (Sonny) [2017] EWCA Crim 1743 (ch. 4 and ch. 14)
R v Department of Health, ex parte Source Informatics Limited [2001] QB 424 (ch. 23)
R v Family Health Services Appeal Authority, ex parte Elmfield Drugs Limited [1999] 46 BMLR 191 (ch. 3, ch. 10, ch. 11 and ch. 12)
R v Guy's & St Thomas' NHS Trust [2008] EWCA Crim 2187 (ch. 26)
R v Lee (Elizabeth) [2010] EWCA Crim 1404 (ch. 7, ch. 18 and ch. 26)
R v Maginnis [1987] AC 303 (ch. 3)
R v Medicines Control Agency Ex p. Rhone Poulenc Rorer Ltd (C94/98) [2000] All ER (EC) 46 (ch. 5)
R v North Yorkshire Family Health Services Authority, ex p. Wilson [1997] 33 BMLR 12 (ch. 3)
R v Quayle; Ditchfield; Lee; Taylor; Kenny; Wales [2005] EWCA Crim 1415 (ch. 14)
R v Rebelo [2021] EWCA Crim 306 (ch. 26)
R v Rochester (Kirk) [2018] EWCA Crim 1936 (ch. 14)
R v Rose (Honey Maria) [2017] EWCA Crim 1168 (ch. 26)
R v Secretary of State for Health Ex p. Pfizer Ltd [1965] AC 512 (ch. 3)
R v St George's Healthcare Trust, ex parte S [1998] 3 WLR 996 (ch. 26)
R v Statutory Committee of the Pharmaceutical Society of Great Britain and Martin and Shutt Ex p. Pharmaceutical Society of Great Britain [1981] 1 W.L.R. 886 (ch. 25)
R v Statutory Committee of the Royal Pharmaceutical Society of Great Britain, ex parte Boots the Chemists Limited [1997] Lexis Citation 2670 (ch. 12)
Rasool v GPhC [2015] EWHC 217 (Admin) (ch. 25)
Registrar of Restrictive Trading Agreements v W.H Smith & Son Ltd [1969] 1 WLR 1460 (ch. 7)
Roberts v Littlewoods Mail Order Stores Ltd [1943] KB 269 (ch. 11)
Roy v Kensington and Chelsea and Westminster Family Practitioner Committee [1992] 1 AC 624 (Preface, ch. 3)
Scott v LGBT Foundation [2020] EWHC 483 (QB) (ch. 23)
Shaikh v General Pharmaceutical Council [2013] EWHC 1844 (Admin) (ch. 25)
Shakoor v Situ (trading as Eternal Health Co) [2001] 4 All ER 181 (ch. 26)
Solicitors Regulation Authority v Wingate Evans [2018] EWCA Civ 366 (ch. 24)
Spl (2004) Ltd v Secretary of State for Health [2013] EWHC 4520 (Admin) (ch. 6)
Stocker v Stocker [2019] UKSC 17 (ch. 24)
Stuewe v Health and Care Professions Council [2022] EWCA Civ 1605 (ch. 25)
Summers v Congreve Horner & Co [1992] 7 WLUK 105 (ch. 11)
The Council for the Regulation of Healthcare Professionals v General Medical Council and Saluja [2006] EWHC 2784 (ch. 2)
The King (on the application of (1) Transactual CIC and (2) YY v Secretary of State for Health and Social Care and another [2024] EWHC 1936 (Admin) (ch. 2 and ch. 21)
The Queen (on the application of Chemistree Homecare Ltd and Blackbay Ventures Ltd) v Medicines & Healthcare Products Agency [2013] EWHC 4491 (Admin) (ch. 6)
The Queen (on the application of Evgeniy Kuzmin) v GMC [2019] EWHC 2129 (ch. 25)
The Queen (on the application of Ngole) v The University of Sheffield [2019] EWCA (Civ) (ch. 24)

The Queen (on the application of Pitt and Tyas) v General Pharmaceutical Council [2017] EWHC 809 (Admin) (ch. 24)
The Queen (on the application of The Good Law Project) v Secretary of State for Health and Social Care [2019] EWCA (Civ) 1211 (ch. 12 and ch. 26)
The Queen (on the Application of *Zygmunt) v General Medical Council* [2008] EWHC 2643 (Admin); [2009] LS Law Medical 219 (ch. 25)
The Queen v Royal Pharmaceutical Society of Great Britain, ex parte Association of Pharmaceutical Importers and others [1990] 1 Q.B. 534 (ch. 5 and ch. 12)
The Queen v Statutory Committee of the Pharmaceutical Society, ex parte Sokoh, The Times, 4 December 1986 (ch. 25)
The Queen v The Statutory Committee of the Pharmaceutical Society of Great Britain, ex parte Lewis & Jeffreys Limited, Berg and others (unreported) (ch. 1, ch. 7 and ch. 25)
The Republic (France) v Jean-Marie Delattre [1993] CMLR 445 (ch. 4)
The Upjohn Company and Upjohn NV v Farzoo and Kortmann C-112/89 [1991]; [1993] 1 CMLR 657 (ch. 4)
Underwood v Bounty UK Limited [2022] EWHC 888 (QB) (ch. 23)
Vali v General Optical Council [2011] EWHC 310 (Admin) (ch. 25)
VI v KRONE – Verlag Gesellschaft mbH & Co KG (C-65/20) (ch. 26)
Vidal-Hall v Google Inc [2015] EWCA Civ 311 (ch. 23)
Vision Dispensing Limited v Revenue and Customs Commissioners [2023] UKFTT 991 (TC) (ch. 11)
W v Edgell [1990] Ch. 359 (ch. 23)
W, X, Y and Z v the Secretary of State for Health and the Secretary of State for the Home Department [2014] EWHC 1532 (Admin) (ch. 23)
Warner-Lambert Company LLC v Generics (UK) Ltd [2018] UKSC 56 (ch. 26)
Warren v DSG Retail Ltd [2021] EWHC 2168 (QB) (ch. 23)
Watt v Lothian Health Board [2015] CSOH 117 (ch. 16)
White v General Medical Council [2021] EWHC 3286 (Admin) (ch. 25)
Whitechurch v Royal Pharmaceutical Society of Great Britain (1998) 41 BMLR 46 (ch. 2 and 26)
Wilkes v Depuy International Ltd [2016] EWHC 3096 (QB) (ch. 26)
Wingate v Solicitors Regulation Authority; and Solicitors Regulation Authority v Malins [2018] EWCA Civ 366 (ch. 25)
Wm Morrison Supermarkets plc v Various Claimants [2020] UKSC 12 (ch. 23 and ch. 26)
Yasin v General Medical Council [2018] EWHC 677 (Admin) (ch. 25)
Yeong v General Medical Council [2009] EWHC 1923 (ch. 25)
YSL v Surrey and Borders Partnership NHS Foundation Trust [2024] EWHC 391 (KB) (ch. 23)
Zoan v Rouamba [2000] 1 W.L.R 1509 CA (ch. 14)

Abbreviations and acronyms

Abbreviation or acronym	Meaning
Admin	The Administrative Court (part of the King's Bench Division of the High Court of England and Wales)
AHSN	Academic Health Science Network
AIS	Accessible Information Standard
All ER	All England (Law) Reports
ALL ER (EC)	All England Reports (European Community)
AUR	Appliance Use Review Service
AVM-GSL	Authorised Veterinary Medicine – General Sales List
BNF	British National Formulary
BP	British Pharmacopoeia
BPC	British Pharmacopoeia Commission
CA	Court of Appeal
CAP	Centrally Authorised Product
CAP	Committee of Advertising Practice
CCG	Clinical Commissioning Group
CD	Controlled drug
CE	Conformité Européenne (EC approval symbol for medical devices)
CFTP	Continuing Fitness to Practise
CHIP	Chemicals (Hazard Information and Packaging for Supply) (legislation)
CHRE	Council for Healthcare Regulatory Excellence (superseded by the PSA – see below)
Civ	Civil
CJEU	Court of Justice of the European Union (also known as the European Court of Justice)
CLP	Classification, Labelling and Packaging of Substances and Mixtures (legislation)
COSHH	Control of Substances Hazardous to Health (regulations)
CPD	Continuing Professional Development
CPE	Community Pharmacy England
CPW	Community Pharmacy Wales
CQC	Care Quality Commission
CRB	Criminal Records Board
Crim	Criminal
CSU	Commissioning Support Unit
DBS	Disclosure and Barring Service
DEFRA	Department for Environment, Food and Rural Affairs
DHSC	Department of Health and Social Care

Abbreviation or acronym	Meaning
EAMS	Early Access to Medicines Scheme
EC	European Commission
ECJ	European Court of Justice (also known as the Court of Justice of the European Union)
ECR	European Court Reports
EEA	European Economic Area
EEC	European Economic Community
EHCR	European Court of Human Rights
EMA	European Medicines Agency
EPS	Electronic Prescription Service
EU	European Union
EWCA	Court of Appeal of England and Wales
EWCA (Civ)	England and Wales, Court of Appeal: (Civil Division),
EWCA (Crim)	England and Wales, Court of Appeal (Criminal Division)
EWHC	England and Wales High Court: Admin (Administrative Court)
Ex	Exchequer Law Reports
FtP	Fitness to Practise
GDC	General Dental Council
GDP	Good Distribution Practice
GMC	General Medical Council
GMP	Good Manufacturing Practice
GP	General Practitioner
GPC	General Practitioners Committee
GPhC	General Pharmaceutical Council, also "the Council"
GSL	General Sales List (medicines)
HL	The Judicial Committee of the House of Lords
HMR	Human Medicines Regulations 2012
HSE	Health and Safety Executive
HWB	Health and Wellbeing Board
IRME	Ionising Radiation Medical Exposure
ISA	Independent Safeguarding Authority
JSNA	Joint Strategic Needs Assessment
LETB	Local Education and Training Boards
LLP	Limited Liability Partnership
LPC	Local Pharmaceutical Committee
LPS	Local Pharmaceutical Services
LS Law Medical	Law reports published by Informa
Ltd	Limited (referring to a private limited company)

Abbreviation or acronym	Meaning
MA	Marketing Authorisation or (depending on the context) the Medicines Act 1968
MD	Maximum Dose
MDA	Misuse of Drugs Act
MDD	Maximum Daily Dose
MHRA	Medicines and Healthcare products Regulatory Agency
ML	Manufacturer's Licence
MPharm	Master of Pharmacy (accredited degree)
MPTS	Medical Practitioners Tribunal Service
MRL	Maximum Residue Limit
MSO	Midwife's Supply Order
MUR	Medication Use Review
NFA-VPS	Non-Food Animal medicine prescribed by a veterinary, pharmacist or suitably qualified person only
NHS	National Health Service
NHSCB	NHS Commissioning Board (known as NHS England or NHS England and Improvement)
NICE	National Institute for Health and Care Excellence
NMS	New Medicines Service
NSAID	Non-Steroidal Anti-Inflammatory Drug
OHCS	Outer House Court of Session
ona	on the application of
OSPAP	Overseas Pharmacist Assessment Programme
P medicine	Pharmacy medicine
PALS	Patient Advice and Liaison Service
PCT	Primary Care Trust
PGD	Patient Group Direction
Pharm J	Pharmaceutical Journal
PHE	Public Health England
PI	Parallel Import
PL(PI)	Product Licence for Parallel Import
Plc	Public Limited Company
PLR	Product Licence of Right
PNA	Pharmaceutical Needs Assessment
POM	Prescription Only Medicine
POM Order	Prescription Only Medicines Order (legislation)
POM-V	Prescription Only Medicine prescribed by a veterinary prescriber only
POM-VPS	Prescription Only Medicine prescribed by a veterinary, pharmacist or suitably qualified person only
PSA(HSC)	Professional Standards Authority (for Health and Social Care)

Abbreviation or acronym	Meaning
PSNC	Pharmaceutical Services Negotiating Committee
PSUR	Periodic Safety Update Report
QB	Queen's Bench
QBD	Queen's Bench Division of the High Court
QC	Queen's Counsel
QPPV	Qualified Person responsible for Pharmacovigilance
RCVS	Royal College of Veterinary Surgeons
Reg	Regulation
RMP	Reference Medicinal Product
RP Reg	Responsible Pharmacist Regulation
RPS	Royal Pharmaceutical Society
RPSGB	Royal Pharmaceutical Society of Great Britain (the regulator of the pharmacy profession until the creation of the GPhC)
S or s	A section number in an Act of Parliament
SARSS	Suspected Adverse Reaction Surveillance Scheme
Sched	Schedule
SCR	Summary Care Record
SI	Statutory Instrument
SmPC	Summary of Product Characteristics
SQP	Suitably Qualified Person
STP	Sustainability and Transformation Plan
TDA	Trust Development Authority
THR	Traditional Herbal Remedy
UK	United Kingdom
UKCA	UK conformity assessed
UKFTT	UK First Tier Tribunal
UKPC	UK Judicial Committee of the Privy Council
UKSC	UK Supreme Court
VAT	Value Added Tax
VMD	Veterinary Medicines Directorate
VMR	Veterinary Medicines Regulation
w/v	weight per volume
w/w	weight per weight
WDA(H)	Wholesale distribution authorisation for human medicines
WDA(V)	Wholesale distribution authorisation for veterinary medicines
WDL	Wholesale dealer's licence
WLR	Weekly Law Reports

CHAPTER 1

Introduction to the law in Great Britain

This chapter has been written to assist readers of the book who are not familiar with the legal systems in Great Britain to understand the laws that are described in the following chapters.

Introduction

This book covers the law in Great Britain, namely England, Scotland and Wales. However, there is no such thing as "British law". Although reference is often made to the United Kingdom, and much of the relevant law is the same in England, Scotland and Wales, as health law has been devolved to the Scottish Parliament and the Welsh Parliament (or Senedd Cymru – formerly the Welsh Assembly), there are some differences. Also, England and Wales share the same legal system – the same system of courts – whereas Scotland has its own legal system. Northern Ireland is part of the United Kingdom, but not part of Great Britain, so, Northern Ireland is outside the scope of this book.

Legislation may be amended from time to time by later legislation. In this book, unless the context requires us to refer to an Act or regulations that amend an existing Act or regulations, we will only give references for legislation in its amended form. In other words, for example, when the Human Medicines Regulations 2012 have amended a section in the Medicines Act 1968, we refer only to the section of the Medicines Act 1968 in its amended form.

Acts of Parliament and statutory instruments usually end with an Explanatory Note. Some also have a more detailed Explanatory Memorandum. These aim to explain the contents of the document in plainer English. It is important to bear in mind that Explanatory Notes and Explanatory Memoranda are not part of the Act or statutory instrument. Indeed, if a court is asked to interpret the meaning of words in an Act or statutory instrument, the Explanatory Notes can be used as an aid to interpretation, but only in so far as they cast light on the objective setting or contextual scene of the Act, and the mischief at which it is aimed.[1] A judge will not even take into account what a minister has said in Parliament about the intention behind a proposed Act unless the judge finds the wording of the Act to be ambiguous.[2]

Box 1.1 explains some of the terminology used in relation to legislation.

---

1. *R (Westminster City Council) v National Asylum Support Service* [2002] UKHL 38.
2. *Pepper v Hart* [1992] UKHL 3.

Box 1.1: Terminology

Act of Parliament – the law passed (or "enacted") by Parliament (also referred to as "primary legislation"). An Act of Parliament is also known as a *Statute*.

Assimilated law – previously referred to as *retained law*, this is law introduced because the UK was a member of the European Union and is retained as part of UK law even though the UK has left the EU.

Common law – the law as declared by judges and found in decided cases rather than in legislation.

Damages – compensation.

Domestic legislation – law passed by Parliament or the Scottish or Welsh Parliament rather than the EU.

EU Directive – a law the UK, as an EU member state, was required to adopt into domestic law.

Legislation – laws made by a public body such as the EU, the UK Parliament or the Scottish or Welsh Parliament.

Quash – to overturn a decision, usually in judicial review cases.

Repeal – the abolition of a law so that it ceases to be a law. For example, most of the Medicines Act 1968 was repealed by the Human Medicines Regulations 2012, and some laws introduced into UK law as a result of membership of the European Union have been repealed and replaced by new laws.

Revoke – this word has a similar meaning to *repeal*.

Secondary legislation – laws made by Ministers, Government Departments or the Privy Council pursuant to powers in an Act of Parliament. These are usually in the form of Regulations, but are occasionally Orders, Orders in Council and sometimes Directions.

Statute – usually an alternative word for an Act of Parliament.

Statutory instrument (or "SI") – a document that creates detailed laws, usually in the form of Regulations – made under powers given in an Act of Parliament or a national Parliament. A statutory instrument is a form of secondary legislation.

Sue – bring a claim in a court for damages or for some other legal remedy.

Tort – a civil wrong, such as negligence, for which one person may sue another and claim damages.

Tribunal – a body that has been given power to make judicial decisions, such as the First Tier Tribunal in England.

European law

From 1973 until 2020, the United Kingdom (UK) was a member of the European Union (EU). As such, the UK was required to introduce into the law across the UK many laws that were also introduced in all other EU member states. EU laws were brought into effect in different ways. When the EU brought into force a Directive, such as the Medicines Directive,[3] member states including the UK were required to introduce legislation to give effect to the Directive. Some other EU laws came into force in the UK without new laws having to be introduced separately. Questions regarding the meaning

3. Directive 2001/83/EC.

of EU laws were decided by the European Court of Justice (ECJ). These decisions remain binding on the UK's domestic courts. Decisions of the ECJ took precedence over the decisions of courts in the UK. Following the UK's exit from the European Union, the UK Parliament has passed (amongst other legislation) the Retained EU Law (Revocation and Reform) Act 2023. Under this Act many laws derived from the EU have been revoked. Laws that have not been revoked are treated as "assimilated law" and in making any decisions on assimilated law following the UK's departure from the EU, the courts of the UK take precedence over any decision of the ECJ.

Domestic legislation

The word *domestic* refers to England, Scotland or Wales. The easiest way to find domestic legislation is to go to www.legislation.gov.uk.

Domestic legislation operates mainly at two levels: *primary legislation*, mainly Acts of Parliament or Acts passed by the parliaments of Scotland and Wales, and *secondary legislation* (also referred to as *subordinate legislation*). Secondary legislation consists of laws that are made under powers in primary legislation. Secondary legislation often sets out detailed provisions implementing the broad provisions of an Act. An Act will often give a minister the power to make regulations that contain detailed rights and obligations. Typically, secondary legislation takes the form of regulations that have been laid by ministers before Parliament. The UK Parliament may pass legislation that applies to the whole of the UK, or only to parts of it. The Scottish and Welsh parliaments may also pass legislation in relation to health and other matters that have been devolved to them.

Acts of Parliament and parliamentary sovereignty

Acts of Parliament contain laws that have been decided on by the UK Parliament. Parliament is often referred to as sovereign. The courts of law cannot overturn an Act of Parliament, although disputes may arise as to the meaning of an Act, and a judge may be asked to decide on the interpretation of an Act. The judge's decision will be based on what Parliament intended, not on whether the judge agrees or disagrees with the Act. Such decisions become precedents to be followed in subsequent cases (see below).

The parliamentary process for creating legislation is outlined in **Box 1.2**.

Box 1.2: Acts of Parliament

Unless otherwise stated, *Parliament* refers to the UK Parliament at Westminster. An Act of Parliament starts as a Bill which is usually presented by a Minister in the House of Commons or the House of Lords. Similar processes are followed when Bills are introduced into the Scottish or Welsh Parliaments. A Bill may have separate numbered parts for each subject area it deals with. Within each part, the Bill is divided into numbered clauses.

The Bill goes through various stages in each House, including stages at which the Bill is considered in detail and debated.

After all stages have been completed, the Bill receives the Royal Assent by being signed by the monarch. By constitutional convention, the monarch has no choice in the matter and must sign.

Box 1.2: Acts of Parliament (cont.)

At this point, the Bill becomes an Act. The numbered clauses referred to when the Bill was going through Parliament are now known as sections.

In this book, we refer to relevant sections of an Act. We do not refer to Parts of an Act unless this would be helpful to the reader. For example, Part III of the Medicines Act is entitled *Further provisions relating to dealings with medicinal products*. This Part contains sections 51 to 68 (not all of which are still in force). We refer to section 64 of the Act, for example, not to Part III, which is less precise.

If section 1 has a sub-section, it will appear like 1(1) or 1(2). Then there are paragraphs which will appear as 1(1)(a), and sub-paragraphs which will appear as 1(1)(a)(i).

If the Act contains many details or lists or rules, these often appear in a Schedule to the Act. Some Acts, like the National Health Service Act 2006, have many Schedules.

An Act may state the date on which it will become law, or it may say it will come into force (in other words, that it will become law) on a day to be appointed. If it says it will come into force on a day to be appointed, then a future statutory instrument will specify the date when the Act or sections of it will become law.

Following devolution and the creation of the Scottish and Welsh Parliaments, Acts of Parliament state whether the laws they contain apply to Scotland and/or Wales and/or Northern Ireland as well as to England.

The European Convention on Human Rights

In 1950, in the light of the atrocities committed during the Second World War, the UK and many European nations signed the European Convention on Human Rights. The signatories guarantee certain fundamental freedoms. The UK played a leading role in drafting the Convention, which has the status of an international treaty and, since signing it (the UK was one of the original signatories), the UK has been bound by the Convention. However, the Convention was not formally incorporated into domestic law in the UK until the passing of the Human Rights Act 1998.

Some of these rights may at times be relevant to pharmacy practice or to the conduct to be expected of pharmacy professionals (see **Chapter 24**). **Box 1.3** contains extracts from the European Convention on Human Rights.

Box 1.3: Extracts from the European Convention on Human Rights

Article 2 – Right to life

1. Everyone's right to life shall be protected by law ...

Article 5 – Right to liberty and security

1. Everyone has the right to liberty and security of person. No one shall be deprived of his liberty save in the following cases and in accordance with a procedure prescribed by law: ...
   (e) the lawful detention of persons for the prevention of the spreading of infectious diseases, of persons of unsound mind, alcoholics or drug addicts or vagrants ...

Article 6 – Right to a fair trial

1. In the determination of his civil rights and obligations or of any criminal charge against him, everyone is entitled to a fair and public hearing within a reasonable time by an independent and impartial tribunal ...

Box 1.3: Extracts from the European Convention on Human Rights (cont.)

Article 8 – Right to respect for private and family life

1. Everyone has the right to respect for his private and family life, his home and correspondence.
2. There shall be no interference by a public authority with the exercise of this right except such as is in accordance with the law and is necessary in a democratic society in the interests of national security, public safety ... for the protection of health or morals, or for the protection of the rights and freedoms of others.

Article 9 – Freedom of thought, conscience and religion

1. Everyone has the right to freedom of thought, conscience and religion ... to manifest his religion or belief, in worship, teaching, practice and observance.
2. Freedom to manifest one's religion or beliefs shall be subject only to such limitations as are prescribed by law and are necessary in a democratic society in the interests of public safety, ... health or morals, of for the protection of the rights and freedoms of others.

Article 10 – Freedom of expression

1. Everyone has the right to freedom of expression. This right shall include freedom to hold opinions and to receive and impart information and ideas without interference by public authorities ...
2. The exercise of these freedoms, since it carries with it duties and responsibilities, may be subject to such formalities, conditions, restrictions or penalties as are prescribed by law and are necessary in a democratic society, in the interests of national security ... or public safety, for the prevention of disorder or crime, for the protection of health or morals, for the protection of the reputation or rights of others, for preventing the disclosure of information received in confidence ...

First Protocol – Article 1 – Protection of property

Every natural or legal person is entitled to the peaceful enjoyment of his possessions. No one shall be deprived of his possessions except in the public interest and subject to the conditions provided for by law ...

Section 6 of the Human Rights Act 1998 says that it is unlawful for a public authority to act in a way which is incompatible with a Convention right. The definition of a public authority includes not only governmental bodies such as the Department of Health and Social Care, but also Integrated Care Boards and any person whose functions are of a public nature. Indeed, the definition covers anyone providing NHS services, such as pharmacy owners and pharmacy professionals.

Issues that may arise in relation to the Article 2 right to life include when life begins, assisted conceptions, assisted dying and end-of-life.

Article 6 issues arise from time to time in fitness to practise cases, for example because of delays by the General Pharmaceutical Council (GPhC) in bringing cases (see **Chapter 25**).

Article 8, concerning the right to respect for private life creates a tension with the obligation in standard 6 of the *Standards for pharmacy professionals* (see Appendix 1) which stipulates that the standards must be met at all times, not only during working hours, and requires pharmacy professionals to behave in a professional manner. In a case involving a senior solicitor who was found by the Solicitors Disciplinary Tribunal to have acted "inappropriately" by having a consensual "sexual encounter" with a junior colleague after an event at which they had both had too much to drink, the High Court[4] overturned a decision of the Solicitor's Disciplinary Tribunal and held that professional rules:

> *"may reach into private life only when conduct that is part of a person's private life realistically touches on her practise of the profession ... or the standing of the profession ... Any such conduct must be qualitatively relevant. It must, in a way that is demonstrably relevant, engage one or more of the standards of behaviour which are set out in or necessarily implicit from the [professional standards]. In this way, the required fair balance is properly struck between the right to respect for private life and the public interest in the regulation of the ... profession. Regulators will do well to recognise that it is all too easy to be dogmatic without knowing it: popular outcry is not proof that a particular set of events gives rise to any matter falling within a regulator's remit."*

Article 8 has also been relevant to cases involving confidentiality and data protection (see **Chapter 23**).

Article 9 may be an issue when, for example, a pharmacist is unwilling to supply emergency hormonal contraception because they view it as incompatible with their religious beliefs.

Articles 9 and 10 have come up in fitness to practise cases after a registrant has made a public statement or posted on social media something that reflects their genuinely held beliefs but which some people have found offensive (see **Chapters 24** and **25**).

In addition to the rights in the Convention, Article 1 of the First Protocol to the Convention gives protection to possessions. A possession includes professional practices of someone who has built up a clientele[5] and it includes a licence to run a business, such as the inclusion of a pharmacy owner in a pharmaceutical list (commonly referred to as an *NHS contract* – see **Chapter 3**).

Section 19 of the Act requires the minister in charge of a Bill in the House of Commons or House of Lords to make a written statement "to the effect that in his view the provisions of the Bill are compatible with the Convention rights"; or a statement to the effect that "although he is unable to make a statement of compatibility the government nevertheless wishes the House to proceed with the Bill". For example, during the COVID-19 pandemic of 2020, the Coronavirus Bill, which included sweeping emergency powers, included in a preface a Minister's statement that the provisions of the Bill were compatible with the Convention Rights.

The courts cannot overturn UK legislation that is found to be in breach of the Convention, but the High Court in England and Wales and the Court of Session in Scotland can declare that legislation is incompatible with the Convention. The European

4. *Beckwith v Solicitors Regulation Authority* [2020] EWHC 3231 (Admin).

5. *Albert et Le Compte v Belgium* (1983) 5 EHRR 533.

Court of Human Rights (ECHR) can also rule on whether the Convention has been breached, but references to the ECHR have been less frequent since the UK passed the Human Rights Act.

Statutory Instruments

An Act of Parliament often creates powers that may be exercised by ministers. These are typically powers to make regulations, rules or orders, and these regulations or rules are also part of the law. For example, section 7 of the Misuse of Drugs Act 1971 gives the Secretary of State (the Home Secretary) power to make regulations to authorise things that would otherwise be unlawful, such as supplying controlled drugs. The Misuse of Drugs Regulations 2001 were made pursuant to this power (see **Chapter 14** for further details of the Act and Regulations). Other regulations that are referred to throughout this book include the Human Medicines Regulations 2012 which were made pursuant to powers in the European Communities Act 1972. Although the European Communities Act was repealed following the UK's exit from the European Union, regulations made under powers in that Act remain in force unless those regulations are also repealed.

The Medicines and Medical Devices Act 2021

Following the repeal of the European Communities Act, the powers to make or amend existing laws are in the Medicines and Medical Devices Act 2021. Section 2 of the Medicines and Medical Devices Act creates a power to make regulations about human medicines with the overarching objective of safeguarding public health. Section 10 creates a power to make regulations about veterinary medicines with the overarching objectives of promoting the health and welfare of animals; the health and safety of the public; or the protection of the environment. Section 15 creates power to make regulations about medical devices with the overarching objective of safeguarding public health. For example, the powers in the Act have been used, or their use was under consideration at the time of publication, to amend:

(a) the Human Medicines Regulations 2012 in relation to hub and spoke dispensing (see **Chapter 5**) and supervision (see **Chapters 11** and **12**);
(b) the Veterinary Medicines Regulations 2013 (see **Chapter 15** where extensive amendments made in 2024 are reflected); and
(c) the Medical Devices Regulations 2002.

The Health Act 1999 and section 60 Orders

Section 60 of the Health Act 1999 provided that an Order in Council could be made regarding the regulation of health professions. An Order in Council is made by the Privy Council (which is usually composed of ministers). It was pursuant to this power that the GPhC was created by the Pharmacy Order 2010 (see **Chapter 2**); and the Medicines Act 1968 was amended in 2022 in relation to the legal duties of responsible pharmacists and superintendent pharmacists (see **Chapter 7**).[6]

---

6. Pharmacy (Responsible Pharmacists, Superintendent Pharmacists etc.) Order 2022.

The Pharmacy Order 2010 gave the GPhC the power to make rules for various purposes. In relation to fitness to practise, the GPhC made the General Pharmaceutical Council (Fitness to Practise and Disqualification etc. Rules) Order of Council 2010. This Order of Council has a Schedule which contains the rules that govern all fitness to practise proceedings – the General Pharmaceutical Council (Fitness to Practise and Disqualification etc.) Rules 2010.

The Human Medicines Regulations 2012

Until 2012, most legislation governing medicines and pharmacy practice was in the Medicines Act 1968 or in numerous regulations made under powers in that Act. The Human Medicines Regulations (HMR) consolidated and replaced most of the Medicines Act in relation to medicinal products for humans. The HMR leave parts of the Medicines Act 1968 in force, principally Part IV of the Act, which deals with the registration and conduct of pharmacies (see **Chapter 2** and **Chapter 7**). Future amendments to the HMR will be made under powers in the Medicines and Medical Devices Act 2021.

The HMR provide that medicines may be supplied to the public only from pharmacies,[7] except those medicines which can with reasonable safety be sold without the supervision of a pharmacist.[8] The HMR also cover matters relating to the labelling of medicines, the containers in which they are supplied and the manner in which their sale is promoted, whether by advertisement or oral representation.

Other examples of secondary legislation and referencing

In addition to regulations, orders may be made under section 62 of the Medicines Act to prohibit the sale, supply and importation of products containing particular substances (see **Chapter 21**).

Another, less common type of statutory instrument takes the form of Directions. For example, the authorisation for advanced and enhanced pharmaceutical services under the National Health Service in England is in the Pharmaceutical Services (Advanced and Enhanced Services) (England) Directions 2013.

Statutory Instruments have a formal reference that includes the year and a number. For example, the Human Medicines Regulations 2012 has the unique reference 2012 no. 1916. This may also be shown as 2012 SI no. 1916. SI numbers are included in the list of statutory instruments at the beginning of this book but, since statutory instruments can be identified and found by reference to their titles and year, SI numbers are not included in individual chapters unless there is a reason to do so.

The terminology of individual statutory instruments varies according to the type of document. Where the title of a document contains the word Regulations, each individual provision will be a *regulation*. Where the title contains the word Rules, each individual

---

7. Subject to exemptions – see Chapters 6 and 15.
8. At the time of going to press, the Department of Health and Social Care proposes to amend the HMR to additionally allow supervision to be carried out by pharmacy technicians – see Chapter 11.

provision will be a *rule*, e.g. rule 1. Where a statutory instrument is an Order, each individual provision is an *Article*, e.g. Article 1.

Codes of Practice and other legislation

Some legislation refers to other documents or enables guidance to be given. For example:

- The National Health Service Act 2006[9] requires the Secretary of State to publish a Drug Tariff which sets out the details of how pharmacy owners are remunerated for providing NHS pharmaceutical services and how they are to be reimbursed with the cost of drugs they have supplied.
- The Health and Safety Executive (HSE) is responsible for enforcing the Health and Safety at Work etc. Act 1974 (see **Chapter 26**). The HSE publishes a number of Approved Codes of Practice which describe preferred or recommended methods that can be used (or standards to be met) to comply with regulations and the duties imposed by the Health and Safety at Work etc. Act. Although the Codes are not mandatory, in the event of prosecution for breaching the Act, if it is proved that the defendant did not follow a relevant Code, the defendant will be found guilty unless the defendant can show that they complied with the law in some other way. This is a change to the usual requirement that the prosecution must prove that an offence has been committed.
- The Medicines and Healthcare products Regulatory Agency (MHRA) has published Good manufacturing practice (GMP) and Good distribution practice (GDP). These set out respectively the minimum standards that medicines manufacturers must meet in their production processes; and that wholesalers and distributors must follow when storing, transporting and handling medicinal products. Compliance is a requirement of a marketing authorisation (see **Chapter 5**), so a failure to comply may lead to the imposition of sanctions and/or involve the commission of a criminal offence.

Common law

The easiest way to find cases that form part of the *common law* – the law that is not found in legislation – is to go to www.bailii.org or to use a subscription service like Westlaw. Until recent years, judgments of the High Court and more senior courts were reported with references (known as *citations*) that included the year, court and page number. Although such citations are still used, since 2001, the primary reference is now a neutral citation that gives the year, court and an identifying number. For example, cases that begin UKSC refer to the United Kingdom Supreme Court, and EWCA refers to the Court of Appeal of England and Wales (the case of *Bawa-Garba v General Medical Council* is cited as [2018] EWCA (Civ) 1879). Abbreviations Civ, Crim or Admin indicate whether the case was a civil one, a criminal one, or whether the case involves administrative law.

Common law (sometimes also referred to as *case law*) has developed through rulings by judges over the centuries. In theory, judges do not make the law: they decide what

9. Section 127(4) and, in England, regulation 89 of the National Health Service (Pharmaceutical and Local Pharmaceutical Services) Regulations 2013.

it always has been. For example, the law of contract[10] and the law of negligence are not based on Acts of Parliament but on what judges have decided over the years.

The common law covers both civil law and criminal law.

Civil law

Civil law usually regulates rights between citizens or, in the case of Administrative Law (see below) concerns rights that citizens seek to exercise against the State. A civil wrong is known as a *tort* and the most common tort is negligence. The tort of negligence is based on the decision of the House of Lords in *Donaghue v Stevenson*[11] and has been developed in later cases. One person, for example a patient, may sue another person, such as a pharmacist who is alleged to have made a dispensing error causing injury. The claim will be for damages (compensation). Other torts include breach of confidentiality, battery, libel, slander and trespass. (Specific torts are discussed further in **Chapter 26**.) A person who brings a civil claim in England and Wales was known as a *Plaintiff* up to 1998 and is now known as a *Claimant*; and is known as a *Pursuer* in Scotland. The person against whom a claim is made is known as a *Defendant* in England and Wales and as a *Defender* in Scotland. A person who commits a tort is sometimes referred to as a *tortfeasor* but a more modern expression is *wrongdoer*.

Importantly, fitness to practise proceedings are part of the civil law (see **Chapter 25**). In contrast, the criminal law involves the State taking action against citizens.

Administrative law

Administrative law is a part of civil law concerning the supervisory role that courts exercise in relation to the activities of public bodies. Such bodies include ministers, government and NHS bodies such as Health Boards (in Scotland) and Local Health Boards (in Wales). Every NHS body and Integrated Care Board is created by legislation (such as the National Health Service Act 2006). Bodies created by an Act of Parliament must act within the statutory powers given to them. Decisions of public bodies must be arrived at through a lawful process that is fair and observes the rules of natural justice. Sometimes, before a decision is made, certain people or organisations will have a legitimate expectation of being consulted.

All public bodies must comply with the *Public Sector Equality Duty*. Specifically, section 149 of the Equality Act 2010 says that a public body must, in the exercise of its functions, have due regard to the need to:

a. eliminate discrimination, harassment, victimisation and any other conduct that is prohibited by or under this Act;
b. advance equality of opportunity between persons who share a relevant protected characteristic and persons who do not share it;
c. foster good relations between persons who share a relevant protected characteristic and persons who do not share it.

---

10. Subject to certain exceptions, including consumer rights legislation that incorporates certain conditions into contracts between traders and consumers.

11. [1932] AC 562.

If a public body exceeds its powers or otherwise acts unlawfully, for example by making a decision without acting fairly or consulting when it should have done so, or if it fails to comply with its duties such as the Public Sector Equality Duty, any party wronged may apply to the High Court (England and Wales) or the Court of Session (Scotland) for judicial review of the decision of the body in question. Sometimes, government departments or NHS bodies issue written guidance. Someone who believes that such guidance does not accurately reflect the law may apply for judicial review (see for example, the cases in **Box 3.5** in **Chapter 3**). A judge who decides that the guidance is unlawful may make a declaration to that effect and the guidance would be overturned or "quashed".

In addition to judicial review cases, appeals in most fitness to practise cases, including those involving the GPhC, are heard in the Administrative Court, which is part of the King's Bench Division of the High Court in England and Wales and, in Scotland, in the Court of Session. Judicial review cases are brought in the name of The King. Sometimes, the law report citation in a judicial review case refers to *The King (or the Queen,* depending on who the Sovereign was at the time the case was heard) and sometimes as *Rex* or *Regina* which are often abbreviated to *R*. Older cases may be reported as *The Queen v The Statutory Committee of the Pharmaceutical Society of Great Britain, ex parte Lewis & Jeffreys Limited, Berg and others*. This means that the case was brought against The Statutory Committee of the Pharmaceutical Society of Great Britain (which was the disciplinary body for the pharmacy profession at the time the case was brought); and the applicant was Lewis & Jeffreys Limited. More recent judicial review cases have a different form of citation, such as *R (Westminster City Council) v National Asylum Support Service*. This indicates that Westminster City Council was the applicant for judicial review and that it challenged a decision of the National Asylum Support Service. Sometimes, the case is also cited as *R (on the application of Westminster City Council) v National Asylum Support Service*. The words *on the application of* in the citation of judicial review cases are often abbreviated to *ona*.

Sometimes, an Act of Parliament will specify a legal process for challenging decisions made by public bodies. For example, market entry decisions made under the National Health Service (Pharmaceutical and Local Pharmaceutical Services) Regulations 2013 may be appealed to NHS Resolution (see **Chapter 3**). Some other decisions may be appealed to the First Tier Tribunal. The doctrine of "binding precedent" means that lower courts are bound to accept statements of law decided by higher courts. A hierarchy of civil courts is given in **Box 1.4**.

Box 1.4: Hierarchy of UK civil courts in descending order

Supreme Court – created in 2009, the judges are known as *Justices of the Supreme Court*. This is the highest court in the UK and hears appeals from the Court of Appeal, Inner House and sometimes from the High Court in cases across all of the UK. It only decides the law, not disputes of fact. Usually, five justices hear each case and the outcome depends on the decision of the majority.

Box 1.4: Hierarchy of UK civil courts in descending order (cont.)

The House of Lords – this was the highest court in the UK before the role was superseded by the Supreme Court. The judges were informally referred to as *Law Lords*.

The Privy Council – this is a judicial committee of the Privy Council made up mostly of Supreme Court (or, before 2009, House of Lords) judges. For historic reasons, some cases including appeals in fitness to practise cases for some healthcare professions, have been heard by the Privy Council. This judicial function of the Privy Council must be distinguished from occasions when the Privy Council is composed of ministers to exercise a political or executive function such as making regulations.

The Supreme Court, House of Lords and Privy Council are not bound by the decisions of law made by lower courts and are also free to change earlier decisions made by the same court.

The Court of Appeal in England and Wales, and the **Court of Session (Inner House)** in Scotland – these courts hear appeals from the High Court in civil cases. They usually only deal with questions of law, including the meaning of legislation. Their decisions are binding on judges in future appeal cases and on lower courts. Usually, three judges hear each case and the outcome depends on the decision of the majority.

Court of Appeal Judges have the title *Lord Justice* or *Lady Justice* followed by their surname.

The High Court in England and Wales, and the **Court of Session (Outer House)** in Scotland – amongst other functions, the High Court and Outer House hear the most important cases and the judges decide the facts and the law. Usually, only one judge hears a case. Decisions on what the law is are binding in future High Court cases and also on the decisions of lower courts.

In the High Court, judges have the title *Mr Justice* or *Mrs Justice* followed by their surname.

The County Court in England and Wales, and **the Sheriff Court** in Scotland – these courts hear the less important or lower value civil cases.

Tribunals – among the tribunals referred to in this book is the First Tier Tribunal.

It can be illustrated by the 1932 case of *Donaghue v Stevenson* ([1932] AC 562). Mrs Donaghue's friend bought her a bottle of ginger beer. Mrs Donaghue alleged that after consuming some of the ginger beer, she found the bottle contained a decomposed snail. She claimed to have suffered gastroenteritis as a result of consuming some of the snail. She sued the ginger beer manufacturer, Mr Stevenson, claiming that he owed her a duty of care which he had breached by failing to take sufficient care to ensure that the bottle would not be contaminated. These were issues that had not previously been authoritatively decided in the UK. The case was decided by the UK's then highest court, the House of Lords. In the leading judgment, Lord Atkin said:

> *"The rule that you are to love your neighbour becomes in law, you must not injure your neighbour; and the lawyer's question, Who is my neighbour? receives a restricted reply. You must take reasonable care to avoid acts or omissions which you can reasonably foresee would be likely to injure your neighbour. Who, then, in law is my neighbour? The answer seems to be – persons who are so closely and directly affected by my act that I ought reasonably to have them in contemplation as being so affected when I am directing my mind to the acts or omissions which are called in question."*

All courts in the UK are bound by the precedent set in this case and must apply the law as stated by the House of Lords (whose role has now been superseded by the Supreme Court).

Criminal law

Some of the terminology used in criminal cases is explained in **Box 1.5**.

Box 1.5: Terminology in criminal proceedings

Accused – the accused is a person or group of people charged with (accused of) criminal offences by a prosecutor. (In Scotland, this is equivalent to the use of the word *Defendant* in England and Wales.)

Breach – a failure to comply with a legal requirement, usually in an Act of Parliament or in Regulations.

Burden of proof – what a court has to be satisfied about in order to find a defendant guilty.

Conviction – a decision of a court that a defendant is guilty of an offence either because the defendant has pleaded guilty or because a judge or a jury has found that the defendant is guilty.

Defendant – in England and Wales a person accused of committing an offence.

Duty, obligation, requirement – these words are generally interchangeable.

Offence – a crime.

Prosecution/Prosecutor – the person responsible for bringing a case to court and presenting the case in court (see also **Chapter 26**).

The criminal law includes the processes for the investigation of crime, for dealing with suspects, and the court procedures when someone is formally accused of an offence – a crime – and brought to court.

Investigation is usually carried out by the Police or other investigators, such as GPhC inspectors, MHRA investigators or local authorities (such as trading standards officers).

Most prosecutions are brought in England and Wales by the Crown Prosecution Service and in Scotland by the Crown Office and Procurator Fiscal Service. Other bodies have the power to bring prosecutions for breaches of specific statutory provisions. These include the GPhC and the MHRA. The principal regulators follow a code[12] that dictates whether a prosecution will be brought. The key features are that there must be sufficient evidence to provide a realistic prospect of a conviction and that bringing a prosecution is in the public interest.

In England and Wales, most cases (other than the most serious cases) start in a Magistrates Court; in Scotland, the Sheriff Court. Some cases in England and Wales may only be dealt with in a Magistrates Court or, in Scotland, the Sheriff Court. In other cases, the magistrates may decide, or the accused person – the defendant – may choose to have the case dealt with in the Crown Court in England and Wales; the High Court of

---

12. For example, the Code for Crown Prosecutors https://www.cps.gov.uk/publication/code-crown-prosecutors (accessed 29 December 2024), published by the Crown Prosecution Service, and the Prosecution Code in Scotland https://www.copfs.gov.uk/publications/prosecution-code/html/ (accessed 29 December 2024).

Justiciary in Scotland. The most serious types of cases must be dealt with in the Crown Court in England and Wales, the High Court of Justiciary in Scotland.

Legislation often says that doing something or failing to do something is an offence. If so, the legislation will say what the maximum penalty is for someone who is convicted – someone who pleads guilty or who is found guilty. For example, many breaches of the Human Medicines Regulations 2012, the Misuse of Drugs Act 1971 and the Misuse of Drugs Regulations 2001 are offences.

In addition to offences that are created by legislation, some offences have roots in history that pre-date modern legislation. Such offences are part of the common law and include murder and manslaughter (see **Chapter 26**).

Distinguishing between criminal law and civil law

The distinction between criminal law and civil law is important because different rights exist for criminal and civil matters, for example under Article 6 of the European Convention on Human Rights. Moreover, a criminal conviction may give rise to a criminal record and an obligation to report the conviction to the GPhC (see **Chapters 25** and **26**).

One of the key differences between criminal cases and civil cases is that in civil cases the person bringing the case has to prove their case on the balance of probabilities. This means that the court or tribunal has to be satisfied that the claimant or pursuer is probably right – in percentage terms, this means 51 per cent. In a criminal case, in order to convict a defendant, the prosecution must prove its case beyond reasonable doubt. This means that the decision-maker – a magistrate or a judge in the lower courts and, usually, a jury in the Crown Court in England and Wales or in the High Court of Justiciary in Scotland – must be satisfied so that it is sure that the prosecution has proved its case.

Sometimes, especially in modern regulation, a failure to comply with a requirement, may result in a civil enforcement process (see Civil law above and **Chapter 26**) or a financial penalty being imposed without involving a court hearing. For example, a breach of the UK General Data Protection Regulation (UK GDPR; see **Chapter 23**) may result in a financial penalty being imposed by the Information Commissioner. These are civil processes and may not mean that a crime has been committed.

Investigations into deaths

England and Wales

Coroners

Coroners exercise an ancient jurisdiction in England and Wales. This jurisdiction is separate from the jurisdiction of the civil or criminal courts. Coroners' powers have been modernised by the Coroners and Justice Act 2009 (*the 2009 Act*).

When a coroner's investigation is required

Under section 1 of the 2009 Act, a senior coroner who is made aware that the body of a deceased person is within that coroner's area must as soon as practicable conduct an investigation into the persons death if the coroner has reason to suspect that:

a. the deceased died a violent or unnatural death,
b. the cause of death is unknown, or
c. the deceased died while in custody or state detention.

An investigation involves obtaining evidence and the holding of an inquest, which is a formal hearing in a Coroner's Court. The purpose of an investigation (section 5 of the 2009 Act) is principally to ascertain:

- who the deceased was, and
- how, when and where the deceased came by their death.

Pharmacy owners and anyone who works in a pharmacy may be involved in a coroner's investigation if it is suspected that medication caused or was a contributory factor in a death, whether as a result of suicide, an overdose that was accidental or involving a possible dispensing error. NHS Resolution has published *Inquests: a guide for health providers*.[13]

Coroner's powers

Schedule 5 to the 2009 Act gives a senior coroner powers to require a person to attend at a time and place. These powers are exercised by giving notice to the person concerned. The UK GDPR and the Data Protection Act 2018 will not apply if such a notice is given.[14] A notice from the coroner overrides any duty of confidentiality the recipient of a notice may otherwise have.

In conducting an investigation (generally before an inquest takes place), a notice may require a person to:

- provide evidence to the coroner about any matters specified in the notice, in the form of a written statement,
- produce any documents in the custody or under the control of the person which relate to a matter that is relevant to the investigation, or
- produce for inspection, examination or testing any other thing in the custody or under the control of the person which relates to a matter that is relevant to the investigation.

Coroner's inquests

An inquest will open to record a death, ensure the deceased is identified and for a body to be released for burial or cremation. In more complex cases, the coroner may also hold a pre-inquest hearing where the scope of the inquest will be considered, including possible timeframes and directions to be set.

Although a notice from a coroner can require a person to give evidence, a person cannot be compelled to give or produce evidence that would involve incriminating themselves or which they could not be required to provide in civil proceedings in a court in England and Wales.

---

13. https://resolution.nhs.uk/resources/inquests-a-guide-for-health-providers/ (accessed 29 December 2024).
14. Paragraph 5(2) of Schedule 2 to the Data Protection Act 2018 disapplies the provisions of UK GDPR when disclosure of data is required by an enactment, a rule of law or an order of a court or tribunal, to the extent that the application of those provisions would prevent the controller from making the disclosure.

Inquests are held in public unless the coroner considers that it is in the interests of justice or national security to exclude the public. The procedure is known as an *inquisitorial* one in which the coroner questions witnesses first and then additional relevant questions may be asked by any interested person or their legal representative.[15] A pharmacy owner or employee may apply to the coroner to have legal representation if they have an interest in the outcome of the inquest, for example if there is a possibility that a claim for compensation may be made by the family of the deceased or there is a possibility of prosecution for a criminal offence (see **Chapter 26**).

In most cases the coroner sits alone but the coroner must sit with a jury if, amongst other reasons, the coroner has reason to suspect that the death was caused by an accident or poisoning which must be reported to a government department or inspector or if the coroner thinks there is sufficient reason to sit with a jury. The word *poisoning* is not defined but, for these purposes, deaths caused by ingestion of medicines or drugs, such as overdoses, are not treated as *poisoning*. The position may be different if a medicine or drug is administered by a third party with the intention of causing death (but not in the case of what is known as assisted suicide), or if death results from the ingestion of an adulterated medicinal product.

Coroner's inquest conclusions

The outcome of an inquest is recorded in the form of a conclusion (the word *verdict* has been replaced but is still in popular use). The main conclusions of relevance to pharmacy practice are:

- accident or misadventure;
- alcohol/drug related;
- lawful/unlawful killing;
- natural causes;
- open;
- suicide.

An open conclusion means that the coroner or jury has not been able to decide which of the possible conclusions is applicable or that unlawful killing is possible, but the evidence was insufficient to meet the standard of proof. A conclusion must be reached using the civil standard of proof, namely the balance of probabilities.[16] To avoid prejudicing the outcome of a possible future criminal trial, if a conclusion of unlawful killing is reached, the suspected offender must not be named.

As an alternative or in addition to what is known as a short-form conclusion, the coroner or jury may record a brief narrative conclusion. A narrative conclusion should be a brief, neutral, factual statement that should not express any judgment or opinion which should probably avoid judgmental words such as "missed opportunities" or "inadequate

---

15. The inquisitorial procedure is in contrast to court proceedings or fitness to practise proceedings (see Chapter 25) in which competing parties seek to persuade the court to reach a particular decision – though there are currently proposals to change the adversarial nature of fitness to practise proceedings.

16. In *R (on the application of Maughan) v HM Senior Coroner for Oxfordshire* [2020] UKSC 46, the Supreme Court held that the standard of proof is the balance of probabilities, including cases of murder and suicide.

failures"; but rather should say just as effectively: "The evidence leads me to find that the written standard operating procedure was not followed". The conclusion may refer to *neglect*. Neglect has a narrower meaning than the duty of care in the law of negligence (see above and **Chapter 26**). It is limited to cases in a medical context where there has been a gross failure to provide basic medical attention.[17]

Coroners have a duty not just to decide how somebody came by their death but also, where appropriate, to report about that death with a view to preventing future deaths. As the Chief Coroner has put it[18] "A bereaved family wants to be able to say: 'His death was tragic and terrible, but at least it shouldn't happen to somebody else' ". As such, Schedule 5 to the 2009 Act requires a coroner who has a concern that circumstances creating a risk of further deaths will occur, or will continue to exist in the future, to report the matter to a person or organisation who the coroner believes may have power to take action prevent those circumstances happening again or to reduce the risk of death created by them. The report must also be sent to the Chief Coroner. The arrangements for making reports are set out in regulation 28 of the Coroners (Investigations) Regulations 2013. Examples of regulation 28 reports in recent years are set out in **Box 1.6**.

Box 1.6: Examples of coroners' reports

In each of the cases described below, the Coroner who conducted the inquest expressed the opinion that action should be taken to prevent future deaths.

It is notable that the Coroner did not specify in each case what action should be taken. The variation in the recipients of these reports, all of which are relevant to pharmacy practice, is also notable, suggesting that Coroners are not always aware of whom the appropriate recipient of a report should be.

Recipients of reports are required to respond. Where a response is available online, this is indicated below.

Deceased: Steven Fone[19] – inquest 23 March 2017
Mr Fone died on 31 October 2016 following the consumption of a fatal "cocktail" of tramadol, cocaine, amitriptyline, methadone, pregabalin and heroin.

The Coroner expressed concern about evidence given at the inquest that Adams Pharmacy permitted three separate customers to interchangeably collect each other's prescriptions. The Coroner sent his report to Adams Pharmacy and asked if the practice of allowing different people to collect each other's prescriptions was approved of by the pharmacy regulator. The coroner considered that the practice "could be open to abuse and facilitate stockpiling, leading to an increased risk of harm or death to those prescribed medicines which have the propensity to be fatal if taken outside the recommended guidance".

19. https://www.judiciary.uk/wp-content/uploads/2017/05/Fone-2017-0101.pdf (accessed 31 December 2024).

---

17. Chief Coroner Guidance No.17 https://www.judiciary.uk/wp-content/uploads/2021/09/GUIDANCE-No-17-CONCLUSIONS-7-September-2021.pdf (accessed 29 December 2024).
18. Guidance No.5 Reports to prevent future deaths https://www.judiciary.uk/wp-content/uploads/2013/09/guidance-no-5-reports-to-prevent-future-deaths.pdf (accessed 29 December 2024).

Box 1.6: Examples of coroners' reports (cont.)

Deceased: Michael Lobban*[20] *– inquest 10 September 2019

Mr Lobban had prescriptions for methadone tablets 5 mg, which he collected regularly from a branch of Boots where he was well known. On 19 October 2017, he collected 68 tablets. Four days later, Mr Lobban was found dead in his home. He was found to have an excessive amount of methadone in his blood (0.56 ug/mL in his blood). As well as what amounted to a significant overdose of methadone, other drugs were found in Mr Lobban's body.

Three days after Mr Lobban's body was found – a week after the most recent methadone tablets had been collected – a running balance audit check was carried out at the Boots branch and 51 methadone tablets 5 mg were missing.

The Coroner found the following matters of concern:

1. The investigation into the disparity of methadone tablets was slow, and efforts to contact patients who had regular prescriptions for methadone were not followed through.
2. The audit checking of controlled drugs was not robust in that there was no double check in place in relation to the audit checking procedure at the branch.
3. There appeared to be no physical check of the contents of boxes when the running balance was audited.
4. The GPhC did not have any reporting requirements for pharmacies when discovering a discrepancy in schedule 2 controlled drugs; and the GPhC appeared to have no investigative powers when a disparity in controlled drugs was discovered; nor sanctions when a pharmacy "mislaid" controlled drugs.

The Coroner sent a report to the GPhC, Boots UK Ltd and the Senior Clinical Advisor for controlled drugs at NHS England, proposing that the following actions should be taken to prevent future deaths:

1. The GPhC should implement industry-wide policies and reporting requirements in relation to discrepancies in controlled drugs;
2. Boots should review its processes and procedures in dealing with occurrences in disparities in controlled drugs, including:
   a. making robust rules to ensure contact was made with patients or third parties who could be affected by disparities in controlled drugs;
   b. ensuring the physical checking of the contents of boxes of controlled drugs was robust and secure; and
   c. implementing a second check in relation to the controlled drugs in the controlled drugs register.

Deceased: Debbie Headspeath*[21] *– 11 November 2019

Ms Headspeath died suddenly at her home as a result of inflammation of the pancreas. The inflammation was "a direct result of the uncoordinated availability of codeine medication which she sourced from [different pharmacies]".

Ms Headspeath had a long-standing dependence on codeine. She had developed a tolerance that led to much higher quantities being prescribed than is "normal". Ms Headspeath supplemented prescribed codeine by buying over-the-counter medication containing codeine. She also obtained prescriptions from online suppliers. In the six months before her death, Ms Headspeath obtained significant quantities of codeine from 16 online suppliers in addition to the codeine prescribed by her GP.

In a report to the Secretary of State for Health, the Coroner expressed the following matters of concern:

1. There is no single database that allows a prescriber to identify what prescription only medication has been prescribed to any particular patient.

---

20. https://www.judiciary.uk/wp-content/uploads/2020/02/Michael-Lobban-2019-0489.pdf (accessed 31 December 2024).
21. https://www.judiciary.uk/wp-content/uploads/2019/12/Deborah-Headspeath-2019-0387.pdf (accessed 31 December 2024).

Box 1.6: Examples of coroners' reports (cont.)

2. Evidence was given at the inquest by the Care Quality Commission and pharmacists providing online services that opiate-based medicines should no longer be supplied unless the patient in question gives permission for their GP to be contacted. However, online pharmacies that did not wish to adopt such an arrangement were changing their business model (primarily by using prescribers based overseas). Although such a practice would no longer be consistent with the GPhC's *Guidance for registered pharmacies providing pharmacy services at a distance, including on the internet,*[22] some witnesses highlighted that the GPhC's guidance was "advisory" and not mandatory, leaving uncertainty as to what sanctions would be available if a pharmacist chose not to follow the guidance.
3. The use of overseas prescribers overseas meant in some cases that the online pharmacies were able to avoid the need to register with the Care Quality Commission (CQC) and thereby remove themselves from regulation by the CQC. As a result, patients remain able to access uncoordinated quantities of prescription only medication from unregulated online pharmacies.

In a response[23] to the Coroner, the Department of Health and Social Care said it was aware of the problem relating to medicines obtained online and said, amongst other things, that the Department was working closely with the CQC and relevant professional regulators to look at how they can better regulate online prescribers and close loopholes in legislation that allow a small number of online organisations to operate without the necessary oversight. Reference was made to guidance published by the GPhC and by the General Medical Council, and the Department also pointed to the obligation in section 251(b) of the Health and Social Care Act 2012 to share information about a patient where it will facilitate that patient's care and is in their best interests.

Deceased: Brenda Anne Drew[24] – 27 November 2019

Ms Drew, who was partially sighted, fell at her home and was hospitalised. On discharge, she was prescribed Oramorph (morphine sulfate) for pain relief. Repeat prescriptions for Oramorph were dispensed at a branch of Lloyds Pharmacy in November and December 2018 and January, February and March 2019. On 29 March 2019, she was advised by her GP to stop taking it. The Coroner received evidence at the inquest that Ms Drew had not requested the repeat prescriptions. On 6 April 2019, she was found at home in a collapsed and unresponsive condition. She died, and a fatal level of morphine was found in her blood.

The Coroner wrote to the Chief Executive of the Royal Pharmaceutical Society to express the following concerns:

1. Repeat prescriptions were requested by pharmacists without consultations and without requests from patients.
2. Consideration should be given to advising all pharmacists in England and Wales that when requesting prescriptions from GPs, they should ensure that the wishes of the patient are ascertained except when this is not possible, such as when the patient lacks capacity.

In its response[25] the Royal Pharmaceutical Society explained that the regulator was the General Pharmaceutical Council and that the RPS had published guidance covering the points raised in the Coroner's report, including advising that consideration should be given to:

- confirming with the patient or carer whether medicines were needed before re-ordering, and
- considering whether medication prescribed was still clinically appropriate at the time of supply.

---

22. https://assets.pharmacyregulation.org/files/2024-01/guidance-for-registered-pharmacies-providing-pharmacy-services-at-a-distance-including-on-the-internet-march-2022.pdf (accessed 31 December 2024) – see chapter 8.
23. https://www.judiciary.uk/wp-content/uploads/2019/12/2019-0387-Response-from-The-Department-of-Health-and-Social-Care.pdf (accessed 31 December 2024).
24. https://www.judiciary.uk/wp-content/uploads/2019/12/Brenda-Drew-2019-0421_Redacted.pdf (accessed 31 December 2024).
25. https://www.judiciary.uk/wp-content/uploads/2019/12/2019-0421-Response-by-RPS_Redacted.pdf (accessed 31 December 2024).

Medical examiners

Under the Coroners and Justice Act 2009, it is legal requirement in England and Wales for all deaths that are not investigated by a coroner to be reviewed by a medical examiner before the death can be registered. The functions of medical examiners include confirming or establishing the cause of death.

Under section 3 of the Access to Health Records Act 1990, medical examiners in England and Wales may apply for access to a health record, or to any part of a health record, made by or on behalf of a health professional. The definition of *health professional* includes pharmacists and pharmacy technicians.

In England, under the Medical Examiners (England) Regulations 2024, a medical examiner who is seeking to confirm or establish the cause of a death may obtain and consider such information as is reasonably available to them in respect of trends and unusual patterns of certified causes of death, public health surveillance, patient safety and clinical governance for the purpose of informing their professional judgement as to the cause of death in a particular case. A supply of such information to the medical examiner will not breach any obligation of confidence owed by the person supplying the information.[26] However, there is no obligation to disclose information which would contravene data protection legislation.

Scotland

Fatal accident inquiries

In Scotland, there is no equivalent system to coroners' inquests. Under the Fatal Accidents and Sudden Deaths etc. (Scotland) Act 2016 (the 2016 Act), a Fatal Accidents Inquiry may be held into the death of a person which occurred in Scotland if the Lord Advocate considers that the death was sudden, suspicious or unexplained, or occurred in circumstances giving rise to serious public concern, and decides that it is in the public interest for an inquiry be held into the circumstances of the death.

Inquiries are conducted by the sheriff who must make a determination under section 26 of the 2016 Act:

a. when and where the death occurred;
b. when and where any accident resulting in the death occurred;
c. the cause or causes of the death;
d. the cause or causes of any accident resulting in the death;
e. any precautions which:
    i. could reasonably have been taken, and
    ii. had they been taken, might realistically have resulted in the death, or any accident resulting in the death, being avoided;
f. any defects in the system of working which contributed to the death or any accident resulting in the death; and
g. any other facts which are relevant to the circumstances of the death.

26. Medical Certificate of Cause of Death Regulations 2024.

A spouse or civil partner of the deceased may participate in inquiry proceedings as well as a person living with the deceased at the time of death (cohabitee), and the deceased's nearest known relative if the deceased did not have a spouse, civil partner or cohabitee.

The procedure is governed by the Act of Sederunt (Fatal Accident Inquiry Rules) 2017. The sheriff sends out notice of the inquiry to the persons who may participate. A person who has not been given notice but who wishes to participate in an inquiry may apply to the sheriff to participate (rule 3.5). The sheriff determines the procedure at an inquiry. Unlike the system in England and Wales where the Coroner leads the questioning, in Scotland, the facts are presented to the Sheriff by the Procurator Fiscal. The strict rules of evidence do not apply in inquiries (rule 4.1).

Witnesses may be compelled to appear at the inquest (rule 4.3), but witnesses may not be required to give evidence that would incriminate themselves.

The 2016 Act replaced an Act of 1976 with more modern provisions. However, the matters which the sheriff has to determine under the 2016 Act are broadly similar to the matters which had to be determined under the earlier legislation and an example of a case[27] is described in **Box 1.7**.

Box 1.7: Fatal accident inquiry held in the Sheriffdom of Grampian, Highlands and Islands at Inverness

Sheriff Margaret M Neilson conducted an inquiry in 2016 into the death of Margaret Ann Forrest. The deceased had been in good health except for some age-related conditions for which various medications were prescribed. She lived independently. She had become confused about her medication and her GP decided that it would be helpful for her to receive her medication in a dosette box (a monitored dosage system). This was supplied by a branch of Boots UK Limited in Kingussie. On an occasion in November 2013, Mrs Forrest was handed a dosette box intended for a different patient. That medication included gliclazide for diabetes. Mrs Forrest did not have diabetes.

Mrs Forrest was found later in an unconscious state. She did not regain consciousness. It was not possible to identify which member of staff had made the mistake. Reference was made by the Sheriff to Boots' written Standard Operating Procedures (SOP). It was clear that if specific steps in the relevant SOP had been followed, Mrs Forrest would not have received the incorrect medication.

After identifying the name of the deceased and the date and place of death, the sheriff determined the cause of death as including probably gliclazide-induced hypoglycaemic brain injury.

As to the reasonable precautions, if any, whereby the death and any accident resulting in death might have been avoided, the sheriff determined that had the staff member who handed the dosette box to Mrs Forrest followed the relevant steps in the SOP, then the death would have been prevented.

The sheriff did not identify any defect in the system of working which contributed to the death or any accident resulting in the death.

27. [2016] FAI 7.

SUMMARY

- The UK Parliament is sovereign. The Courts cannot overturn laws that Parliament makes, though the courts can decide whether regulations come within the scope of powers that an Act of Parliament has given. Also, the courts can declare that the provisions in an Act are not compatible with the European Convention on Human Rights which was formally brought into law in the UK by the Human Rights Act 1998.
- Acts of Parliament – laws made by a parliament – are known as legislation. Acts made by a parliament are also known as statutes. Some laws introduced as a result of the UK's former membership of the European Union are now assimilated into the law in Great Britain. Acts of Parliament or Acts passed by the Scottish or Welsh Parliaments are known as *primary legislation*. Primary legislation may give powers for ministers and others to make regulations, rules, orders, and directions. These are known as secondary legislation and are set out in statutory instruments.
- A key Act is the Medicines and Medical Devices Act 2021 which gives powers to amend the Medicines Act 1968, the Human Medicines Regulations 2012 and the Veterinary Medicines Regulations 2013. Section 60 of the Health Act 1999 gives powers to amend the law governing the regulation of the healthcare professions. It was used to create the Pharmacy Order 2010 which established the General Pharmaceutical Council and to create the rules which the GPhC uses to regulate the profession.
- The High Court and Court of Session can review the administrative decisions of government departments and other public bodies, and can decide that a decision was unlawful, for example because an unfair process was followed.
- The common law is not contained in legislation. It is based on decisions of judges going back many years. Decisions on the law made by higher courts are binding on lower courts.
- Civil law regulates rights between citizens. Criminal law involves the State taking action against an individual who is accused of breaking the law. For example, many Acts and Regulations say that a person who does a specific thing commits an offence.
- The decisions of public bodies may be challenged in the courts by a process known as judicial review.
- Violent or unnatural deaths are investigated by Coroners at inquests in England and Wales; and by Sheriffs at Fatal Accident Inquiries in Scotland.

FURTHER READING

- Crown Office Guide to Fatal Accident Inquiries **https://www.copfs.gov.uk/services/bereavement-support/guide-to-fatal-accident-inquiries/** (accessed 29 December 2024).
- House of Commons Library briefing paper no.03981 (10 February 2020) Coroners' investigations and inquests **https://commonslibrary.parliament.uk/research-briefings/sn03981/** (accessed 29 December 2024).
- Judicial review in Scotland: **http://archive2021.parliament.scot/ResearchBriefingsAndFactsheets/S5/SB_16-62_Judicial_Review.pdf** (accessed 29 December 2024).
- Reissner DH. Judicial review: be aware of the time limits and make sure you act quickly, *The Pharmaceutical Journal*, Oct 2008, Vol 281, p424.
- The Chief Coroner's Guide to the Coroners and Justice Act 2009 **https://www.judiciary.uk/wp-content/uploads/JCO/Documents/coroners/guidance/chief-coroners-guide-to-act-sept2013.pdf** (accessed 29 December 2024).

CHAPTER 2

The regulation of pharmacy and other healthcare professions

The pharmacy profession is highly regulated. In particular, pharmacists and pharmacy technicians and pharmacy premises are regulated by the General Pharmaceutical Council (GPhC), which has its own inspectorate. The GPhC and other healthcare regulators are overseen by the Professional Standards Authority.

Regulation of the pharmacy profession

The General Pharmaceutical Council (GPhC) was created by the Pharmacy Order 2010 (the Order).[1] It is the independent regulator for pharmacists, pharmacy technicians and pharmacy premises in Great Britain. Prior to this, the Royal Pharmaceutical Society of Great Britain (RPSGB) was both the regulator and the professional leadership body. The creation of the GPhC resulted in the separation of the regulatory and professional leadership roles.

The Professional Standards Authority for Health and Social Care (PSA), oversees the work of the GPhC and nine other healthcare regulators and promotes the health and wellbeing of patients and the public in the regulation of health professionals (the PSA is more fully discussed below and in **Chapter 25**).

Structure of the GPhC

The GPhC has a chair and 13 other members of the Council appointed by the Public Appointments Commission. Seven members are registrants and seven are lay members. This structure was formalised by the Pharmacy Order 2010 and the General Pharmaceutical Council (Constitution) Order 2010.

There are limitations on the period for which members may serve on the Council (Art.3). The GPhC must make provision with regard to the education and training of Council members in standing orders (Art.4). Certain categories of people, for example people who have been convicted of certain types of offences, are disqualified from being members of the Council (Art.5) and once members have been appointed, there are certain circumstances in which they may be removed (Art.6) or suspended from office

1. The Pharmacy Order is divided into 8 Parts and, within each Part, separate numbered provisions are referred to as *Articles*, abbreviated here to *Art*.

(Art.7). Provisions relating to the chair (including powers to appoint a deputy chair) of the Council can be found in Articles 8 and 9. There are also provisions relating to the proceedings of the Council including its quorum, which is eight members (Arts.11 and 12). Members of Council are appointed by the Appointments Commission to ensure a balance of qualities, skills and experience, and to reflect the diversity of the public and of the pharmacy profession.

The GPhC has a Great Britain rather than a UK jurisdiction; that is, it has regulatory powers in England, Scotland and Wales. It has appointed a director in each of Scotland and Wales, recognising the divergence in Great Britain health policy and delivery.

Role and principal functions of the GPhC

Article 6 of the Pharmacy Order 2010 stipulates that the GPhC's overarching objective in exercising its functions is the protection of the public. The role of the GPhC (also referred to as the Council) is to protect, promote and maintain the health, safety and wellbeing of members of the public by upholding standards and public trust in pharmacy. Article 4(3) of the Pharmacy Order 2010 identifies the principal functions of the GPhC. These are set out in **Box 2.1**.

Box 2.1: Principal functions of the GPhC

a. to establish and maintain a register of pharmacists, pharmacy technicians and premises at which a retail pharmacy business is, or is to be, carried on;
b. to set and promote standards for the safe and effective practice of pharmacy at registered pharmacies;
c. to set requirements by reference to which registrants must demonstrate that their fitness to practise is not impaired;
d. to promote the safe and effective practice of pharmacy by registrants (including, for example, by reference to any code of conduct for, and ethics relating to, pharmacy);
e. to set standards and requirements in respect of the education, training, acquisition of experience and CPD that it is necessary for pharmacists and pharmacy technicians to achieve in order to be entered in the Register or to receive an annotation in the Register and to maintain competence; and
f. to ensure the continued fitness to practise of registrants.

The GPhC has broad powers to make rules.[2]

Education and training of pharmacists

Article 42 of the Pharmacy Order requires the GPhC to produce standards for the initial education and training of pharmacists.

The standards[3] are in two parts. Part 1 comprises learning outcomes, which describe what a student/trainee pharmacist must be able to demonstrate upon successful

---

2. Section 84A of the Medicines Act 1968.
3. https://assets.pharmacyregulation.org/files/2024-01/Standards%20for%20the%20initial%20education%20and%20training%20of%20pharmacists%20January%202021%20final%20v1.4.pdf (accessed 29 December 2024).

completion of their initial education and training. The learning outcomes are presented in four domains:

- Person-centred care and collaboration.
- Professional practice.
- Leadership and management.
- Education and research.

Part 2 comprises standards for all organisations involved, which describe the requirements for anyone providing initial education and training. The standards for providers are split into two sections, and set out the requirements for the:

- MPharm degree.
- Foundation training year.

If a UK MPharm degree or an Overseas Pharmacists' Assessment Programme (OSPAP) (see below) is not accredited (or is not provisionally accredited) by the GPhC, then this means that the graduates will not be eligible to be registered as a pharmacist. The GPhC accreditation process involves peer review, site visits, provider self-assessment and public reports.

Foundation training

In addition to approval of qualifications, the GPhC is required to set out the conditions for a period of training, together with successful completion of a registration assessment, to be undertaken prior to registration. An integrated course combining four years of academic study with the equivalent of 12 months of training in practice is an alternative approach. Foundation training must be managed by an approved pre-registration designated supervisor at an approved training site, and a designated prescribing practitioner to oversee the period of learning in practice specifically relating to prescribing (which may be the same person as the designated supervisor). All trainees are required to achieve a number of learning outcomes, grouped within four domains of study, during their training, namely personal-centred care and collaboration, professional practice, leadership and management, and education and research.

Pharmacists qualified in Northern Ireland[4]

There are reciprocal arrangements between the GPhC and the Pharmaceutical Society of Northern Ireland for the registration with the GPhC of pharmacists who qualified in Northern Ireland (Art.20(4)).

Pharmacists who have trained outside the UK

A person who has qualified as a pharmacist outside the UK is entitled to be entered in Part 1 of the Register if their qualification has been approved by the Council as attesting

---

4. The Pharmaceutical Society of Northern Ireland is the pharmacy regulator for Northern Ireland. The law in Northern Ireland is outside the scope of this book.

to a standard of proficiency for the safe and effective practice of pharmacy that, in the Council's opinion, it is necessary for a person to achieve in order to be registered (Art 21). For this purpose, a qualification granted in an EEA country or Switzerland is normally treated as having been approved. Evidence of competence in the English language will be required. This arrangement is currently in place until September 2028.

In the case of someone holding a qualification from outside the EEA or Switzerland, if that qualification on its own is not considered to attest to the relevant standard of proficiency, that person may nevertheless be entitled to entry in the Register if they have undertaken additional education, training or experience that the Registrar requires. This is an Overseas Pharmacists' Assessment Programme (known as OSPAP).[5]

Registration

A pharmacist or pharmacy technician is not permitted to practise unless they are registered with the GPhC. Article 3(2) of the Pharmacy Order states that:

> *"a person practises as a pharmacist or a pharmacy technician if, while acting in the capacity of or purporting to be a pharmacist or a pharmacy technician, that person undertakes any work or gives any advice in relation to the preparation, assembly, dispensing, sale, supply or use of medicines, the science of medicines, the practice of pharmacy or the provision of healthcare."*

The term *registrant* is used to refer to someone who is registered. Parts 4 and 5 of the Pharmacy Order set out the obligations of the GPhC to appoint a Registrar (and one or more Deputy Registrars to whom the Registrar's functions may be delegated) (Art.18), to establish, maintain and ensure access to the Register and to maintain the Register in the appropriate form and content (Art.19). The Register is in three parts:

- Part 1 relating to pharmacists.
- Part 2 relating to pharmacy technicians.
- Part 3 relating to premises.

Part 5 of the Pharmacy Order requires the GPhC to set the requirements for appropriate qualifications, to hold assessments and to appoint examiners (Art.44). In connection with all aspects of education and training, the GPhC may appoint visitors to inspect any site at which relevant education or training is provided and to examine the associated assessments or tests of competence (Art.45). Education and training providers must provide the Council with relevant information when required (Art.46) and the GPhC may refuse or withdraw approval of a course, qualifications and institutions as a result of any visitor's report (Art.47).

Parts 3, 4 and 5 of the Pharmacy Order should be read in conjunction with the Registration Rules[6] which provide the detail in relation to registration issues. Part 2 of

---

5. https://www.pharmacyregulation.org/pharmacists/registering-pharmacist (accessed 29 December 2024).
6. General Pharmaceutical Council (Registration) Rules 2010 which can be found in the Schedule to the General Pharmaceutical Council (Registration Rules) Order of Council 2010.

the Registration Rules requires the Register to be kept in writing and securely, although certain information is also available online in a searchable format. Part 2 also contains provisions relating to the recording of fitness to practise matters in the Register, for example if conditions have been imposed by the Fitness to Practise Committee (**Chapter 25**). Registrants are required to notify the Registrar in writing of any changes to their name or contact details. Part 3 of the Registration Rules makes detailed provision in respect of the form and manner of various applications in relation to entries in the Register and include annotations in respect of specialisations (so far, the only annotations are as a pharmacist independent prescriber or a pharmacist supplementary prescriber). Provision is made for the voluntary removal of entries (including annotations) in the Register for pharmacists and pharmacy technicians. Applications for the voluntary removal of an entry from the Register will generally be refused where there is an ongoing investigation or there are outstanding proceedings relating to a registrant's fitness to practise.

If the Secretary of State advises the Registrar of an emergency, for example involving loss of human life or human illness,[7] the Registrar has the power to enter temporarily in Part 1 or 2 of the Register persons whom the Registrar considers are fit and proper and suitably experienced. During the COVID-19 pandemic, the Secretary of State took such a step and a temporary register was created in order to register pharmacy professionals who had voluntarily removed themselves from the register (for example on retirement) or who had been removed because of non-payment of fees.[8]

In 2022, when administrative delays and technical issues caused problems for students taking the pre-registration exam, the GPhC offered affected students provisional registration, subject to meeting certain criteria.[9]

Part 4 of the Registration Rules contains a procedure to be followed by the Registrar for dealing with Register entries relating to registrants that may have been fraudulently procured or incorrectly made, or where the fitness to practise of a registrant was impaired at the time of the registrant's entry in the Register but was not declared.

Registration as a pharmacy technician

Registration as a pharmacy technician requires applicants to complete:

- one of the approved knowledge and competency training programmes, and
- a minimum of two years relevant work-based experience in the UK under the supervision, direction or guidance of a pharmacist or pharmacy technician to whom the applicant was directly accountable for no less than 14 hours per week.

A summary of the current standards for the initial education and training of pharmacy technicians is set out in **Box 2.2**.

---

7. Article 34 of the Pharmacy Order 2010.
8. The register closed on 1 April 2023.
9. https://www.pharmacyregulation.org/about-us/news-and-updates/gphc-offer-provisional-registration-eligible-candidates-who-experienced-severe-delays (accessed 29 December 2024). It is not clear what power the GPhC had to provide provisional registration in these circumstances.

Box 2.2: Standards for the initial education and training of pharmacy technicians

The standards consist of two parts:

- Part 1: learning outcomes – includes the skills, knowledge, understanding and professional behaviours a trainee must demonstrate at the end of their initial education and training. The learning outcomes fall under four domains:
  1. Person-centred care.
  2. Professionalism.
  3. Professional knowledge and skills.
  4. Collaboration.

  All domains and learning outcomes have equal importance.
- Part 2: standards for initial education and training course providers – sets out the key features of courses that deliver the learning outcomes in part 1 of the standards. These standards fall under seven domains:

  Domain 1: Selection and entry requirements.
  Domain 2: Equality, diversity and inclusion.
  Domain 3. Management, resources and capacity.
  Domain 4: Monitoring, review and evaluation.
  Domain 5: Course design and delivery.
  Domain 6: Course assessment.
  Domain 7: Pre-registration trainee pharmacy technician support and the learning experience.

Student pharmacy technicians must abide by the *Standards for pharmacy professionals* (see below and Appendix 1). Applications for registration with the GPhC as a pharmacy technician can be made if the person has GPhC-approved qualifications and meets the work experience requirements, or if they are an EEA national with an EEA pharmacy technician qualification.

Other conditions for registration as a pharmacy professional

As well as completing the appropriate qualification, training and assessment requirements and paying the appropriate fee, the applicant must provide evidence of their identity, that their fitness to practise is not impaired by reason of physical or mental health (see also **Chapter 25**), and in certain cases, evidence as to their good character and good repute (Arts.20-23 of the Order). A registrant must have in force an adequate and appropriate indemnity arrangement (a form of insurance) that provides cover in respect of liabilities which may be incurred by that registrant when practising (Art.32).[10] Indeed, a failure to have professional indemnity cover has been found to be a ground for removal from the register on the ground of misconduct.[11] Registrants and applicants must also have the necessary knowledge of English for safe and effective practice.[12] The GPhC

10. Health Care and Associated Professions (Indemnity Arrangements) Order 2014.
11. *Whitechurch v Royal Pharmaceutical Society of Great Britain* (1998) 41 BMLR 46.
12. Health Care and Associated Professions (Knowledge of English) Order 2015.

may require evidence of English language skills and has issued guidance on how this requirement is interpreted.[13]

Registration appeals

Certain registration decisions are appealable, and these are set out in Article 39. The GPhC must operate an Appeals Committee to deal with these appeals (Art.40) and further appeal is permitted to the courts (Art.41). Further details of these processes are set out in GPhC Rules[14] and on the GPhC website (see also **Chapter 24**). The Appeals Committee must, as soon as is reasonably practicable, send the person bringing the appeal the Committee's decision and the reasons for it and of any right of appeal. Rule 10 provides that the burden of proof is on the appellant and that the civil standard of proof applies (**Chapter 1**). An example of an Appeals Committee case is provided in **Box 2.3**.

Box 2.3: Registration Appeal case: pharmacy technician

By virtue of Article 39(1)(b) of the Order, a decision by the Registrar not to enter a person in Part 2 of the Register is an appealable decision. The appellant appealed against a decision of the Registrar on 11 July 2011 not to enter her as a pharmacy technician in the Register. This was a meeting of the Appeals Committee, not a hearing, so it did not hear oral evidence.

On 5 December 2005, the appellant had pleaded guilty at Croydon Magistrates' Court to four offences of making a false representation with a view to obtaining a benefit under the social security legislation for herself. The offences were committed in the period 2001 to 2004. She was sentenced to a community punishment order for 100 hours in respect of each offence and was also sentenced to a fine. The appellant applied to the RPSGB for voluntary registration as a pharmacy technician in 2008. In her application dated 24 May 2008 she declared that she had been convicted of a criminal offence which related to the overpayment of benefit. On receipt of this information, the then RPSGB Registrar investigated the circumstances of the conviction and following that investigation decided on 2 October 2008 to refuse the appellant's application to be entered in the Register.

In February 2011, the appellant then made an application to be entered in the GPhC's Register. In that application at paragraph 3.1 she was asked "Have you ever applied previously for registration with the Royal Pharmaceutical Society of Great Britain (RPSGB) or the General Pharmaceutical Council (GPhC), either as a pharmacy technician ...?" The appellant ticked the "No" box.

She was also asked: "Have you previously been convicted or cautioned for a criminal offence in the British Islands or elsewhere ...?" The appellant ticked the "No" box.

Further on in the application the appellant made a number of declarations as follows:

> *"The information that I have provided in this application for registration is complete, true and accurate ..."*
>
> *"I understand that if I am found to have given false or misleading information in connection with my application for registration in the Register, this may be treated as misconduct, which may result in my removal from the Register."*

The Registrar wrote to the appellant on 11 July 2011 to notify her of his decision to refuse her application for registration as a pharmacy technician. In giving his reasons, he

---

13. https://assets.pharmacyregulation.org/files/document/guidance-on-evidence-of-english-language-skills-march-2021.pdf (accessed 29 December 2024).
14. General Pharmaceutical Council (Appeals Committee) Rules 2010 which can be found in the Schedule to the General Pharmaceutical Council (Appeals Committee Rules) Order of Council 2010.

Box 2.3: Registration Appeal case: pharmacy technician (cont.)

referred to the appellant's failure to declare her conviction and a previous application for registration with the Society; her declarations on the application form: and to her understanding of the consequences of giving false or misleading information referred to in the application form.

He also referred to the conviction in the following terms

"In your application of 24 May 2008 you disclosed your conviction at Croydon Magistrates' [sic] in December 2005 for making dishonest representations to obtain benefit. Following careful consideration by the Registrar of the former pharmacy regulator [the RPSGB], your application for registration was refused. You were notified of the Registrar's decision by letter dated 2 October 2008. Reasons for the decision to refuse included not only the serious nature of the offences and that they were committed whilst you were practising as a pharmacy technician but also:

i. your failure to provide evidence of your insight into the offences,
ii. your lack of understanding of the offences' relevance to the practice of pharmacy, and
iii. your decision not to provide supporting testimonials despite being given the opportunity to do so."

In concluding his reasons for refusing to register the Registrar wrote:

"The GPhC's standards of conduct, ethics and performance require registrants to act with honesty and integrity to maintain public trust and confidence in the profession. In all the circumstances, I consider that you have demonstrated a failure to meet this standard and that granting your application would undermine public confidence in the regulation of the pharmacy profession and may bring the profession into disrepute."

Rule 10 of the Appeal Rules establishes that the Appellant bears the burden of establishing that the appealable decision should be overturned and Rule 10(2) sets out that:

"If the appeal is against a decision to refuse to enter the appellant ... in the Register, the Committee may only decide to enter, or direct the Registrar to enter, the appellant ... in the Register if the appellant has proved that the appellant is ... entitled to be so entered."

Article 20(1)(a)(ii) of the Pharmacy Order states that a person is entitled to be entered in Part 2 of the register as a pharmacy technician if, amongst other matters, the Registrar is satisfied that the person's fitness to practise is not impaired. The applicant appealed to the Appeals Committee which said in its decision:

"Having carefully considered all the evidence submitted together with the submissions made by both the appellant and the respondent the decision of the committee is to dismiss the appeal. The committee noted that the Council had argued that both misconduct and a conviction, in fact four convictions, were present here triggering consideration of impairment of fitness to practise. The committee recognised that the convictions were in respect of behaviour several years ago and also noted that the offences did not, on the information supplied to it, require proof of dishonesty to establish a conviction. The committee therefore regarded the convictions as not establishing dishonest behaviour by the appellant in 2001, 2002 and 2004. The committee did however regard the appellant's behaviour in knowingly submitting an application for registration in 2011 that was wrong in a number of respects as dishonest, which the appellant accepts. The committee also noted that the appellant's behaviour both in relation to the matters for which she was convicted and in relation to her application in 2011 all involved her over a period of ten years in making false representations in order to secure an advantage to herself; benefits to which she was not entitled in the case of the convictions and to improve her chances of being registered in the case of the application this year."

The committee concluded that it was "not satisfied that the appellant has proved that her fitness to practice is not impaired".

Standards for pharmacy professionals

Under Article 4 of the Pharmacy Order, the GPhC must set and promote standards for the safe and effective practice of pharmacy at registered pharmacies.[15] The GPhC has published nine *Standards for pharmacy professionals*. These Standards are:

Pharmacy professionals must:

1. provide person-centred care;
2. work in partnership with others;
3. communicate effectively;
4. maintain, develop and use their professional knowledge and skills;
5. use professional judgement;
6. behave in a professional manner;
7. respect and maintain the person's confidentiality and privacy;
8. speak up when they have concerns or when things go wrong; and
9. demonstrate leadership.

The full Standards are in Appendix 1.

Guidance to support the standards for pharmacy professionals

The GPhC has published the following guidance[16] to support the *Standards for pharmacy professionals*:

- Guidance for pharmacist prescribers.
- Guidance on religion, personal beliefs and values.
- Guidance on consent.
- Guidance on maintaining clear sexual boundaries.
- Guidance on confidentiality (see data protection in **Chapter 23**).
- Guidance on raising concerns.
- Joint statement of healthcare regulators on the professional duty of candour.
- Joint statement with healthcare regulators on conflicts of interest.
- Demonstrating professionalism online.
- Female genital mutilation: mandatory duty for pharmacy professionals to report.
- Gender identity services for children and young people.
- Requirements for the education and training of pharmacy support staff (see below).

For more details of the Standards and guidance, see **Chapter 24**.

15. The Standards themselves suggest that they apply in all pharmacy settings, not just in registered pharmacies (see, for example, paragraph 5, under the heading *The standards for pharmacy professionals*. However, Article 4 of the Pharmacy Order specifically refers only to registered pharmacy premises.

16. https://www.pharmacyregulation.org/pharmacists/standards-and-guidance-pharmacy-professionals/guidance-pharmacy-professionals (accessed 29 December 2024).

Revalidation and continuing professional development

Part 5 of the Order contains powers to regulate training both before and after registration (Arts.42 and 43) through continuing professional development (CPD). Specific requirements are contained in the General Pharmaceutical Council (Continuing Professional Development and Consequential Amendments) Rules 2011.

CPD is now part of *revalidation*, which is seen by the GPhC as a means by which to show that the trust members of the public have in pharmacy professionals is well placed. It is a process through which pharmacists and pharmacy technicians:

- keep their professional skills and knowledge up to date;
- reflect on how to improve; and
- show how they provide the safe and effective care patients and the public expect, as set out in the GPhC's *Standards for pharmacy professionals*.

Under the General Pharmaceutical Council (Continuing Professional Development and Consequential Amendments) Rules 2011, the Registrar has a range of measures that can be taken if a registrant fails to submit appropriate records.

Non-registered support staff

The GPhC does not register pharmacy support staff such as dispensing assistants and medicine counter assistants, but it does accredit courses for them. Its *Requirements for the education and training of pharmacy support staff*[17] covers all staff involved in:

- all stages of the dispensing or supply of medicines and medical devices to individuals,
- advising individuals about the use of medicines and medical devices, and
- assisting pharmacy professionals to provide pharmaceutical services.

Support staff covered by these requirements must meet the GPhC's education and training requirements by demonstrating relevant knowledge, understanding, abilities and behaviours at minimum RQF level 2 or SCQF level 5 (in Scotland) or an equivalent level. Support staff must be enrolled on a training course as soon as practically possible and within three months of starting their role. They must complete the course promptly, normally within three years. There is an exemption for students on MPharm degrees and OSPAP programmes and pre-registration pharmacy trainees to work as support staff without further training. However, the supervising pharmacist must check the competency of the student or trainee and act on any learning needs they identify.

The GPhC has also reminded pharmacy owners of their responsibilities regarding pharmacy staff who provide a delivery service.[18]

Registered pharmacy premises

Certain activities by pharmacists (such as the sale of Pharmacy medicines (**Chapter 11**) and the sale or supply of Prescription Only Medicines (**Chapter 12**)) can only be

17. https://assets.pharmacyregulation.org/files/document/gphcrequirements-for-the-education-and-training-of-pharmacy-support-staff-effective-october-2020_0.pdf (accessed 29 December 2024).

18. https://www.pharmacyregulation.org/about-us/news-and-updates/regulate/training-and-responsibilities-pharmacy-staff-providing-delivery-service (accessed 29 December 2024).

conducted from registered pharmacy premises. Registration is dealt with in the Medicines Act 1968 and references to section numbers below are to this Act.

It is the duty of the GPhC Registrar to keep the Register of Pharmacy Premises and, subject to the provisions described below, to enter in the Register, on payment of the prescribed fee, any premises in respect of which application is made (s.74A). *Registered pharmacy* means premises entered for the time being in Part 3 of the GPhC Register (Arts.3 and 19). Where a business which concerns the retail sale or supply of medicinal products is carried on in one or more separate or distinct parts of a building, each part is taken to be separate premises (s.69(2)). A department store or supermarket, for example, might have a department or area which is a registered pharmacy and separate departments or areas (which are not a pharmacy) where general sale medicines (see **Chapter 10**) are sold.

Conditions for registration of pharmacy premises must be fulfilled in a prescribed manner (s.74B) and as in Part 5 of the Registration Rules.[19] An application for the registration of premises must be in writing and be given or sent to the Registrar with the prescribed fee. It must be made and signed by or on behalf of the person carrying on, or who intends to carry on, a retail pharmacy business at or from the premises to which the application relates. A separate application must be made in respect of each premises.

Change of ownership

Where a change occurs in the ownership of a registered pharmacy, the registration becomes void at the end of the period of 28 days from the date on which the change occurs unless the Registrar is notified in writing of the change prior to the end of the relevant period by the person who, as a result of the change, will be carrying on the business at or from the premises. If the change occurs on the death of the person carrying on the business (i.e. the death of a pharmacist owner or, in the case of a partnership, one of the partners), the period is three months from the date of the death (s.74H).

When the registration of pharmacy premises becomes void following a change of ownership, an application for restoration to the Register may be made by the new owner. The Registrar must restore the premises to the Register if reasonably satisfied that the new owner is a person lawfully conducting a retail pharmacy business or will be so at the time they commence business at or from the premises.

The GPhC may direct the Registrar to remove any premises from the Register if the person carrying on the retail pharmacy business fails to pay the prescribed fee within two months from the date on which a demand for it has been made to them. If, before the end of the year, or whatever period is permitted by the GPhC in any particular case, the prescribed fee is paid, together with any prescribed sum by way of penalty, the Registrar must restore the premises to the Register. If the GPhC so directs, the restoration shall be

19. General Pharmaceutical Council (Registration Rules) Order of Council 2010.

deemed to have had effect as from the date on which the premises were removed from the Register.

Standards for pharmacy premises

The GPhC has the power to make rules relating to the registration of pharmacies[20] and for setting the standards that are to be met in connection with carrying on a retail pharmacy business at a registered pharmacy (Art.7). It also has power to enforce certain provisions of the Medicines Act 1968 and the Poisons Act 1972. To carry out its functions effectively the GPhC works in close collaboration with other regulators and other organisations such as those representing patients and the public, professional bodies such as NHS England,[21] NHS Scotland, NHS Wales, the Royal Pharmaceutical Society (RPS), educators and employers. The GPhC also works with a number of government agencies to avoid duplication of effort and to improve patient safety; these include the Police, Healthcare Improvement Scotland, the Care Quality Commission (CQC) in England, Healthcare Inspectorate Wales, the NHS Counter Fraud Authority, the Crown Prosecution Service, His Majesty's Inspectorate of Prisons, the Medicines and Healthcare products Regulatory Agency (MHRA) and the Veterinary Medicines Directorate (VMD). Collaboration with other organisations is usually arranged through a Memorandum of Understanding.

The standards for registered pharmacies set out the requirements for the provision of pharmacy services at or from a registered pharmacy (Art.7).[22] The standards for registered pharmacies are designed to create and maintain the right environment for the safe and effective practice of pharmacy, and to improve the quality and safety of services provided to patients and the public.

The Pharmacy (Premises Standards, Information Obligations, etc.) Order 2016 (the Premises Standards Order):

- requires the GPhC to publish premises standards which, amongst other things, may relate to:
  - the working environment at and the condition of registered pharmacies;
  - the patient and public experience of pharmacy services provided at or from registered premises;
  - the condition of equipment and facilities used in the provision of pharmacy services;
  - the working environment at and condition of associated premises; and
  - training of staff;
- empowers the GPhC to publish reports of inspections and other visits to pharmacy premises; empowers the GPhC to serve improvement notices on the owners of pharmacy premises;

---

20. For example, in Article 19 of the Pharmacy Order.
21. Shortly before going to press the Prime Minister announced that NHS England would be abolished as a separate body, and its functions will be exercised by the Department of Health and Social Care.
22. https://assets.pharmacyregulation.org/files/document/standards_for_registered_pharmacies_june_2018_0.pdf (accessed 29 December 2024).

- provides that breach of an improvement notice is not a criminal offence and requires the Registrar, if there is a failure to comply with an improvement notice, to refer the matter to the Fitness to Practise Committee (see **Chapter 25**);
- gives the Fitness to Practise Committee power to impose an interim suspension on the use of premises pending a final hearing if this is necessary for the protection of the public or otherwise in the public interest;
- as an alternative to disqualification of the owner, gives the Fitness to Practise Committee power at a final hearing to direct the removal of specific premises from the register.

Premises standards

The standards for registered pharmacies set out five principles which are of equal importance:

- *Principle 1.* The governance arrangements safeguard the health, safety and wellbeing of patients and the public.
- *Principle 2.* Staff are empowered and competent to safeguard the health, safety and wellbeing of patients and the public.
- *Principle 3.* The environment and condition of the premises from which pharmacy services are provided, and any associated premises, safeguard the health, safety and wellbeing of patients and the public.
- *Principle 4.* The way in which pharmacy services, including the management of medicines and medical devices, are delivered safeguards the health, safety and wellbeing of patients and the public.
- *Principle 5.* The equipment and facilities used in the provision of pharmacy services safeguard the health, safety and wellbeing of patients and the public.

Guidance to support the standards for registered pharmacies

The GPhC has published guidance, summarised below, to support the standards for registered pharmacies. The guidance is covered in more detail in **Chapter 24**.

- Guidance to ensure a safe and effective pharmacy team[23]

  The guidance sets out what pharmacy owners are expected to do to ensure a safe and effective pharmacy team and meet the standards set out under Principle 2 of the standards for registered pharmacies. These standards focus on making sure staff are empowered and competent to safeguard the health, safety and wellbeing of patients and the public.
- Guidance for registered pharmacies providing pharmacy services at a distance, including on the internet[24]

23. https://assets.pharmacyregulation.org/files/document/guidance_to_ensure_a_safe_and_effective_pharmacy_team_june_2018.pdf (accessed 29 December 2024).
24. https://assets.pharmacyregulation.org/files/2025-02/gphc-guidance-registered-pharmacies-providing-pharmacy-services-distance-february-2025.pdf (accessed 2 March 2025).

This guidance, which was updated in February 2025, explains what pharmacy owners should consider before deciding whether any parts of their pharmacy service can be provided safely and effectively at a distance (including on the internet), rather than in the traditional face-to-face way. (See also **Chapter 8**.)

- Guidance for registered pharmacies preparing unlicensed medicines[25]
  This guidance sets out what pharmacy owners and superintendents of a body corporate should consider when a registered pharmacy prepares medicines, including the preparation of extemporaneously prepared methadone. It supports the standards for registered pharmacies.
- Equality guidance for pharmacies[26]
  Equality, including protected characteristics, is dealt with in **Chapter 24**.
- Other standards and guidance
  Much of the GPhC standards and guidance relates to the behaviour and conduct of registrants – pharmacists and pharmacy technicians – and these are covered in greater detail in **Chapters 24** and **25**. Some set out obligations on registrants and require owners and superintendent pharmacists to support registrants in achieving them. (The legal requirements for responsible pharmacists and superintendent pharmacists are covered in **Chapter 7**). At the time of going to press, the GPhC is expected to make rules regarding the presence of a responsible pharmacist at pharmacy premises.

Inspectorate

The pharmacy profession is unique among healthcare professions in having its own statutory inspectorate. The GPhC must establish an inspectorate (Art.8) and must make provision in Rules about the intervals at which inspectors may conduct routine inspections of registered pharmacies and the circumstances in which inspectors may conduct special inspections of, and visits to, registered pharmacies (Art.9).

Powers to enter premises, sampling and seizure

Powers under the Pharmacy Order 2010

Under Article 10, inspectors have the power, on producing evidence of their identity and appointment as an inspector, to enter any registered pharmacy or any other premises at a reasonable hour to enforce the GPhC's standards, to assist the GPhC in investigations or to enforce the provisions of the Pharmacy Order, including the restrictions on the use of the title *pharmacist* or *pharmacy technician* (under Art.38).

In the case of a residential property (the Pharmacy Order uses the technical term *private dwelling house*), an inspector must first give the occupier 24 hours' notice. A justice of the peace (usually a magistrate) can grant a warrant to enter premises if

25. https://assets.pharmacyregulation.org/files/document/guidance_for_registered_pharmacies_preparing_unlicensed_medicines_august_2018_0.pdf (accessed 29 December 2024).

26. https://assets.pharmacyregulation.org/files/2023-02/gphc-equality-guidance-for-pharmacies-december-2022_0.pdf (accessed 29 December 2024).

the justice is satisfied that entry is required for the exercise of an inspector's powers, but that admission has been or is likely to be refused, provided that notice has been given of the intention to apply for a warrant. A warrant can also be issued if asking for admission or giving advance notice would defeat the object of entry, for example because of a perceived risk that evidence would be removed or destroyed. A warrant can also be issued allowing entry without prior notice if the case is urgent or the premises are unoccupied, or the occupier is temporarily absent.

Article 11 sets out the powers of an inspector on entering premises. These include:

a. inspecting the premises and any plant, machinery and equipment;
b. searching the premises;
c. inspecting and removing from the premises any substance, article or product (not just medicinal products);
d. taking away any samples of any substance, article or product;
e. carrying out any examinations, tests and making any enquires (including any inquiries relating to the fitness to practise of a registrant who is or has been employed on the premises to provide pharmaceutical services); and
f. requiring any person holding or accountable for any documents or records (whether or not kept at the premises being inspected) to produce them for inspection at the premises. This power extends to any documents or records on a computer or other electronic device (such as a mobile phone) and the inspector can require the production of a printout which can be taken away. The inspector can also require someone in charge of a computer or other device to provide such assistance as the inspector may reasonably require. For example, the inspector may ask for passwords to access documents or data.

Any person who intentionally obstructs an inspector in exercising their powers, who fails to give assistance that is reasonably required, who provides false information, or who fails to provide a document or record when required by an inspector, is guilty of an offence (Art.12).

Powers under the Human Medicines Regulations 2012

In addition to powers of entry under the Pharmacy Order, inspectors also have rights to enter premises, to inspect, take samples and seize goods and documents (Human Medicines Regulations 2012 (HMR) Reg.325 and Reg.327) in order to ascertain whether there has been a contravention of the Regulations. *Inspector* means a person authorised in writing by an enforcement authority for the purposes of Part 16 (enforcement) of the HMR (Reg.8). In practice, inspectors will be authorised both under Art 8 of the Pharmacy Order and under Part 16 of the HMR.

An inspector, having produced their identification if requested to do so, is empowered Reg.327):

1. at any reasonable time, to enter premises (which includes any place and a ship, aircraft, hovercraft or vehicle) in order to determine whether there has been a contravention of any part of the Regulations which the enforcement authority is required or empowered to enforce;

2. to inspect any of the following to determine whether there has been a contravention of any provision of the Regulations which the enforcement authority must or may enforce:
   a. a substance or article appearing to the inspector to be a medicinal product;
   b. an article appearing to the inspector to be a container or package used or intended to be used to contain a medicinal product, or a label or leaflet used or intended to be used in connection with a medicinal product;
   c. plant or equipment, including computer equipment, appearing to the inspector to be used or intended to be used in connection with the manufacture, assembly, importation, sale, supply or advertising of, or wholesale dealing in, medicinal products;
   d. any process of manufacture or assembly of medicinal products;
   e. the way in which medicinal products, or the materials used in the manufacture of medicinal products, are tested at any stage in the process of manufacture or assembly;
   f. information and documents (including any that are stored electronically) relating to the manufacture, assembly, importation, sale, supply or advertising of, or wholesale dealing in, medicinal products; or
   g. information and documents (including any that are stored electronically) relating to the safety of medicinal products, including information and documents relating to compliance with specified parts of the Regulations;
3. to take or purchase a sample of a substance or article which appears to the inspector to be a medicinal product which is, or is intended to be, sold or supplied or a substance or article used, or intended to be used, in the manufacture of a medicinal product (there is a process for dealing with samples in Schedule 31 to the HMR);
4. to require a person carrying on a business which consists of or includes the manufacture, assembly, importation, sale, supply or advertising of, or wholesale dealing in, medicinal products, or a person employed in connection with such a business, to produce information or documents relating to the business which are in the person's possession or under the person's control;
5. to take copies of information or documents mentioned, above;
6. to seize and retain a substance or article appearing to the inspector to be a medicinal product, or an active substance, if the inspector reasonably believes that an offence under the Regulations is being or has been committed in relation to, or by means of, that substance or article;
7. to seize and retain any document (including any that are stored electronically) or anything inspected, or discovered in the course of an inspection, if the inspector reasonably believes that it may be required as evidence in proceedings; and
8. to require a person who has the authority to do so to open a container, package or vending machine or to allow the inspector to open a container, package or vending machine, for the purpose of enabling the inspector to seize a substance, article, document or other thing, as outlined above. The term *vending machine* is not defined

in the HMR, but *vending* involves a sale, so a machine for the retrieval of dispensed medicines would not be covered by this power.

Where an inspector seizes a substance, article, document or other thing, they must, where practicable, inform the person, if any, from whom it was seized, and the occupier of the premises from which it was seized. If the seizure is from a vending machine, they must inform the person whose name and address are stated on the machine to be those of the machine's owner or, if no name and address are stated, the occupier of the premises on which the machine stands or to which it is affixed (Reg.328).

Twenty-four hours' notice must be given to the occupier if an inspector intends to enter any premises used only as a private dwelling (Reg 325). In cases where admission is refused, or such refusal is anticipated and notice of the intention to apply for a warrant has been given to the occupier, or where a request for admission, or the giving of notice, would defeat the object of the entry or where the case is one of urgency or the premises are unoccupied or the occupier is temporarily absent, a justice of the peace may issue a warrant authorising an inspector to enter premises, by force if necessary (Reg.326). Regulation 326 goes into further detail regarding who may issue a warrant and its period of validity.

An inspector entering any premises by virtue of a right of entry (Reg.325) or of a warrant under Regulation 326 may be accompanied by such persons, and take such equipment, as the inspector thinks appropriate. Where an inspector enters premises in pursuance of a warrant under Regulation 326, the inspector must, if the property is unoccupied or the occupier is temporarily absent, leave the premises as effectively secured against trespass as they were before the inspector entered (Reg.334).

It is an offence either to intentionally obstruct an inspector or to fail to comply with a requirement relating to inspection, sampling or seizure properly made by them. It is also an offence, without reasonable cause, to fail to give an inspector any other assistance or information which they may reasonably require in order to perform a function under the HMR or to provide false information in relation to any such requirement (Reg.334). The Regulation goes on to say that "Nothing in this regulation is to be read as requiring a person to answer a question or to give information if doing so might incriminate that person or the spouse or civil partner of that person". However, the Pharmacy Order 2010 Article 49 makes it clear that failure on the part of pharmacists or pharmacy technicians to supply information or produce any document required for a fitness to practise investigation may lead to a court order to comply (**Chapter 24**).

There may be occasions when an inspector operates undercover (see the reference to the Regulation of Investigatory Powers Act under Enforcement of premises standards below). In some fitness to practise cases (see **Chapter 25**) proceedings have arisen from the activities of investigatory journalists acting undercover.

When inspectors investigate undercover, for example by making a test purchase, a fitness to practise committee is likely to allow such evidence to be given, as the case of *The Council for the Regulation of Healthcare Professionals v General Medical Council and Saluja*[27] in **Box 2.4** makes clear.

27. [2006] EWHC 2784. The Council for the Regulation of Healthcare Professionals is the former name of the Professional Standards Authority for Health and Social Care.

Box 2.4

The Council for the Regulation of Healthcare Professionals v General Medical Council and Saluja

Dr Saluja was a medical practitioner. In return for payment, Dr Saluja had offered to provide a fake sick note to a journalist posing as a patient. When the offer was exposed, Dr Saluja was referred to the General Medical Council. The doctor argued that the evidence of the journalist should have been rejected in fitness to practise proceedings because he was the victim of entrapment.

Typically, entrapment takes place when an undercover officer or informant encourages another person to commit an offence in order to obtain evidence of the offence committed by the other person. Under English law, where an accused can show entrapment, the court may stop the proceedings as an abuse of the court's process or it may exclude evidence.

The judge, Mr Justice Goldring, rejected the argument that for a journalist to go into a doctor's surgery and pretend to be a patient is similar to abuse of power by an agent of the state. The judge distinguished cases of entrapment of the kind that sometimes involve undercover police officers from proceedings brought against doctors by their regulator in order to protect the public, uphold professional standards and maintain confidence in the profession.

Inspection reports

The Premises Standards Order gives the GPhC the power to publish reports and ratings for registered pharmacies. The arrangements for publishing inspection reports and for pharmacy owners to seek a review of the overall outcome of the inspection process is described on the GPhC's website.[28] Following an inspection, the outcome a pharmacy will receive will either be "standards met" or "standards not all met". All of the standards will need to be met for a pharmacy to receive a "standards met" outcome, and any pharmacy not meeting all of the standards will need to complete an improvement action plan. The improvement action plan will be published alongside the report on an inspections website.[29]

The pharmacy will also receive one of four possible findings for each of the five principles listed above. The four possible findings are:

- "excellent practice";
- "good practice";
- "standards met"; and
- "standards not all met".

Enforcement of premises standards

The GPhC has reached agreement with the Care Quality Commission, the MHRA, NHS England, and NHS Protect (now the NHS Counter Fraud Authority) that it will be the

28. https://www.pharmacyregulation.org/inspections/reports (accessed 29 December 2024).

29. https://inspections.pharmacyregulation.org/ (accessed 29 December 2024).

principal regulator for inspections of registered pharmacies. Memoranda of agreement/understanding also exist between the GPhC and Health Inspectorate Wales, and NHS Scotland Counter Fraud Services.

The GPhC has published an enforcement policy for registered pharmacies.[30] The GPhC says it is "committed to using the minimum regulatory intervention required to achieve the desired result, known as 'right-touch' regulation". This means it "will use the minimum regulatory action required to ensure that pharmacy owners are meeting [its] standards". The factors taken into account when deciding on enforcement action are:

- the seriousness of the concerns;
- the risk of harm to patients or the public;
- compliance with other regulatory or enforcement requirements;
- the willingness and ability of the pharmacy owner to meet the standards, including any steps already taken to do this;
- the impact or potential impact of non-compliance;
- evidence of repeated or multiple failures to meet standards;
- the likely impact of the enforcement action on the registered pharmacy;
- the likely impact of the enforcement action on the wider patient community and public (for example, where a condition on premises registration is imposed that restricts the provision of a certain service);
- the wider public interest;
- the potential for wider learning points for pharmacy owners, so that enforcement sends a broader message to a sector and encourages improvements in the sector; and
- any other relevant considerations.

The enforcement policy refers to other powers that the GPhC has in England under the Regulation of Investigatory Powers Act 2000 (*RIPA*) and in Scotland under the Regulation of Investigatory Powers (Authorisations Extending to Scotland) Order 2007. An authorisation under RIPA provides the GPhC with a lawful basis to carry out covert (directed) surveillance and activity surveillance (for example, monitoring and observing movements or activities) in their investigations, where appropriate.[31] However, the legislation does not authorise the GPhC to use covert human intelligence sources. The GPhC says it will only consider using these powers in very limited cases and where all relevant criteria have been met. The use of directed surveillance for a specific investigation must be subject to prior authorisation by a relevant GPhC Director, as specified in Regulations made under RIPA. In all cases, the GPhC is required to ensure that any directed surveillance is proportionate, lawful, properly authorised and necessary, having considered relevant and practicable alternatives. The use of the GPhC's powers under RIPA is overseen by the independent Investigatory Powers Commissioner's

---

30. https://assets.pharmacyregulation.org/files/document/registered-pharmacies-enforcement-policy-updated-december-2022.pdf (accessed 29 December 2024).

31. At the time of publication, the GPhC had not used its powers of covert directed surveillance, and was considering relinquishing these powers - https://www.chemistanddruggist.co.uk/CD138115/Covert-surveillance-GPhC-may-abandon-never-used-spying-powers (accessed 29 December 2024).

Office (ICPO). The GPhC is subject to inspection by the ICPO in relation to the use of its powers.

Registration conditions

Under section 74D of the Medicines Act, the Registrar may make the entry of premises in the register subject to such conditions as the Registrar considers it is necessary to impose for the purpose of securing the safe and effective practice of pharmacy at those premises. This power may be exercised when entering the premises in the register or subsequently. There is no right of appeal against the imposition of conditions.

Before imposing a condition on a pharmacy already entered in the register, the Registrar must give reasonable notice to the person carrying on the business at the premises, except that reasonable notice does not have to be given if the Registrar is of the opinion that giving reasonable notice would prejudice the health, safety or well-being of members of the public. Examples of cases in which conditions of registration were imposed are set out in **Box 2.5**.

Box 2.5: Registration conditions imposed by GPhC

In 2019, following allegations in a newspaper[32] that a number of online pharmacies were involved in the inappropriate supply of opioids, the General Pharmaceutical Council (GPhC) carried out inspection of those pharmacies. Following those inspections, the reports of which listed failures to meet certain premises standards, the GPhC sent notices to some of the pharmacies, imposing conditions on the registration of the premises. In one case:

"That the dispensing service provided to overseas patients by the pharmacy is stopped until the pharmacy has demonstrated to the GPhC that there are adequate systems in place to:

- *manage the associated risks of this service to protect the safety and wellbeing of patients;*
- *comply with GPhC Standards for registered pharmacies and GPhC 'Guidance for registered pharmacies providing pharmacy premises at a distance, including on the internet'; and*
- *comply with UK law, with specific regard to record-keeping requirements for dispensed medicines, labelling of dispensed medicines, and supply of prescription-only medicines against lawful prescriptions."*

Other examples of conditions imposed after an inspection that found standards were not all met include:

- not to provide a prescribing service;
  not to sell or supply any codeine linctus preparations or medicines that contain promethazine except in accordance with NHS prescriptions.

32. https://www.thetimes.co.uk/article/online-opioids-scandal-dangerous-painkillers-sold-without-proper-checks-dgnh8jpfw (accessed 31 December 2024).

Improvement notices

Under Article 13 of the Pharmacy Order 2010, if an inspector has reasonable grounds for believing that there is a failure to meet the GPhC's standards in connection with the carrying on of a retail pharmacy business or a failure to comply with conditions of registration under section 74D of the Medicines Act, the inspector may serve an improvement notice on the person carrying on the business.

An improvement notice must set out the grounds of the inspector's belief that there is a failure, specify the measures that must be taken to rectify the failure and specify the period within which those measures must be taken. This period must be at least 28 days. The notice must state that there is a right of appeal to the magistrates' court (in England and Wales) or the sheriff's court (in Scotland).

Improvement notices have been served on some of the pharmacies investigated as a result of the newspaper report regarding online opioid sales referred to in **Box 2.5** above in relation to the registration of pharmacy premises. An example of the improvements required in one case is described in **Box 2.6**.

Box 2.6: Example of improvements required in an Improvement Notice served by the GPhC

a. You must provide confirmation from the prescribers' regulating authority that they are specifically authorised to prescribe remotely via online consultations to people who are resident in the UK.
b. You must ensure that the prescriber you work with is working within UK national prescribing guidelines and good practice guidance ... For example through clinical audits and/or risk assessments of the prescribing.
c. You must ensure that the indemnity arrangements of the prescriber you work with cover their remote prescribing activity and this cover extends to patients residing in the UK.
d. You must ensure that the pharmacy effectively monitors and reviews all prescriptions to prevent over-ordering or misuse. You must ensure that when requests are denied because a medicine is requested "early" for medicines liable to abuse, the prescriber will use this information to inform future prescribing decision.
e. The pharmacy website must not allow people to choose the medicines they want before they have had an appropriate consultation with a prescriber.

Article 14 says that failure to comply with an improvement notice is an offence unless the failure relates to conditions of entry into the register of premises.

If an inspector is reasonably satisfied that an improvement notice has not been complied with, the inspector must notify the Registrar of the GPhC; and the Registrar may remove the premises from the register or suspend the registration of the premises pending compliance with such requirements or conditions as the Registrar considers it necessary to impose. Notice must be given to the person carrying on the retail pharmacy business and the notice must include information about that person's right of appeal to the Appeals Committee. The Registrar's powers to remove premises from the register or suspend registration apply to the failure to comply with an improvement notice, not to a failure to meet standards at registered premises or a failure to comply with conditions of entry into the register. Instead, the Registrar must refer the latter types of case for consideration by the Fitness to Practise Committee (see **Chapter 25**). The Fitness to Practise Committee may direct that the owner be disqualified from running a retail pharmacy business if it is satisfied that the owner is unfit to carry on a retail pharmacy business safely and effectively so far as concerns the retail sale or the supply on prescription of medicines (including medicines subject to General Sale) (see also **Chapter 25**).

Regulation of healthcare professions – the catalyst for change

Changes in the regulation of healthcare professions have often followed the recommendations of inquiries that were set up following a scandal or a tragedy. These have included the Kennedy Inquiry,[33] which investigated a flawed system at Bristol Royal Infirmary, which led to around one-third of all the children who underwent open-heart surgery receiving less than adequate care. The Inquiry also led to the establishment of what is now the Professional Standards Authority (PSA) (see below), a super-regulator, which has provided increasing oversight of the regulators of health professionals (see below and also **Chapter 25**).

The Shipman Inquiry[34] followed the murders by Harold Shipman, an outwardly benign and caring GP who murdered at least 200 of his patients by injecting them with large doses of diamorphine. He had obtained stocks of diamorphine by presenting prescriptions and signed orders to a pharmacy. Key outcomes of the Shipman Inquiry included recommendations to modify the legislation regarding controlled drugs to limit the likelihood of such unnoticed misappropriation occurring again (see **Chapter 14**); and a series of changes to the regulation of doctors and subsequently all the health professions, so that regulators are independent of the professions they regulate. The role of the PSA was also strengthened to ensure regulation works in the public interest.

Details of Inquiries and the implementation of recommendations are set out in the Thirlwall Inquiry Review.[35]

Statutory duty of candour

In 2013, the Inquiry by Robert Francis QC, considered the appalling care Mid-Staffordshire NHS Foundation Trust provided to its patients between 2005 and 2008.[36] The Francis Inquiry concluded that the suffering of patients was due to a "serious failure on the part of the Trust Board ... to tackle an insidious negative culture involving a tolerance of poor standards and a disengagement from managerial and leadership responsibilities", which was compounded by a failure of the various NHS checks and balances and regulators to do something effective to remedy the situation. The report

33. https://webarchive.nationalarchives.gov.uk/20090811143822/http:/www.bristol-inquiry.org.uk/final_report/the_report.pdf (accessed 29 December 2024).

34. There were six reports written by Dame Janet Smith, each addressing different aspects https://webarchive.nationalarchives.gov.uk/20090808155110/http://www.the-shipman-inquiry.org.uk/reports.asp (accessed 29 December 2024).

35. https://thirlwall.public-inquiry.uk/wp-content/uploads/thirlwall-documents/Table-of-Inquiries-Reviews-and-Recommendations-made-and-whether-they-were-implemented.pdf (accessed 29 December 2024).

36. https://www.gov.uk/government/publications/report-of-the-mid-staffordshire-nhs-foundation-trust-public-inquiry (accessed 29 December 2024).

indicated that the Trust's care of patients was compromised by a desire to meet various targets and one of the key recommendations was to ensure a common culture shared by all in the NHS of putting the patient first, and that compliance with standards should be professionally led. Amongst other things, the Francis report recommended that all healthcare providers should observe a statutory duty of candour which involves:

> *"The volunteering of all relevant information to persons who have or may have been harmed by the provision of services, whether or not the information has been requested and whether or not a complaint or a report about that provision has been made."*

A statutory duty of candour was introduced,[37] requiring providers and managers registered with the CQC to act in an open and transparent way with service users, in relation to the care and treatment provided to service users in carrying on a regulated activity.

The legal duty means that as soon as a registered person becomes aware that a notifiable safety incident has occurred, the registered person must notify the service user or someone acting on their behalf that the incident has occurred, and provide a true account of all the facts known about the incident. The registered person must advise what further enquiries into the incident are appropriate, and give an apology. The information and apology must be repeated in writing.

A *notifiable safety incident* means any unintended or unexpected incident that occurred in respect of a service user that, in the reasonable opinion of a health care professional, could result in, or appears to have resulted in:

(a) the death of the service user, where the death relates directly to the incident rather than to the natural course of the service user's illness or underlying condition, or

(b) severe harm, moderate harm or prolonged psychological harm to the service user.

The statutory duty does not apply to pharmacy professionals who work in pharmacies that are registered with the GPhC. However, the GPhC has signed a statement on the professional duty of candour jointly with other regulators, and has adopted such a duty into its professional standards (see **Chapter 24** for further details). In addition, if a pharmacy professional were to make a dispensing error resulting in a prosecution, they would only have a defence if they acted consistently with the professional duty of candour (see **Chapter 24**).

Whistleblowing

In 2015, Sir Robert Francis' *Freedom to Speak Up* review considered the difficulties NHS and associated staff have raising concerns – *whistleblowing* – about standards of patient care or patient safety within the NHS. This resulted in a policy[38] to be adopted by all

37. Health and Social Care Act 2008 (Regulated Activities) Regulations 2014.

38. NHS Improvement and NHS England, Freedom to Speak Up: raising concerns (whistleblowing) policy for the NHS (April 2016).

NHS organisations as a minimum standard for raising concerns which includes Freedom to Speak Up Guardians and the appointment of a national guardian, to support NHS whistleblowers. In May 2017, the GPhC issued revised guidance[39] on raising concerns. Amongst other things, the guidance says:

> *"Pharmacy professionals have a professional responsibility to take action to protect the well-being of people receiving care and the public. Raising concerns about individual pharmacy professionals, the members of the pharmacy team they work with (including trainees), employers and the environment they work in is a key part of this."*

The health profession regulators publish annually a joint report on whistleblowing.

The Care Quality Commission

The CQC was established by the Health and Social Care Act 2008. It regulates health and social care in England through a process of registering, monitoring, inspecting and rating regulated activities. This includes the regulation of care homes, hospitals, GP services, mental health services and community-based health and care services. The CQC also has power to assess Integrated Care Systems.[40] The fundamental standards are:

- person-centred care, dignity and respect to those receiving care;
- consent before any care or treatment is given;
- safety (not being given unsafe care or treatment or put at risk of harm that could be avoided);
- safeguarding from abuse;
- food and drink (enough for good health while you receive care);
- premises and equipment that are clean, suitable and looked after;
- a complaints system;
- good governance (of the provider);
- enough suitably qualified, competent and experienced staff, who are fit and proper;
- a duty of candour (for the organisation, separate to the duty on individual professionals); and
- to display the inspection ratings of CQC (which are also on the CQC website).

Providers of health and care services must be registered if the services they provide are regulated. The CQC may require a hospital or service to be closed until safety requirements are met and may suspend or de-register services where necessary.

The definition of regulated services extends to the provision of treatment for a disease, disorder or injury where the treatment is under the supervision of a healthcare professional or a team that includes a health care professional. The definition of *health*

39. https://assets.pharmacyregulation.org/files/2024-01/in-practice-guidance-on-raising-concerns-november-2020.pdf (accessed 29 December 2024).
40. Health and Social Care Act 2008 (Regulated Activities) Regulations 2014.

care professional does not include pharmacists or pharmacy technicians. Services provided at or from registered pharmacy premises of a kind that are, or could be, pharmaceutical services are not regulated activities and, therefore, are not subject to CQC registration.[41] However regulated activities associated with pharmacy services must be registered, for example:

- the provision of associated medical services;
- hospital pharmacy services (see **Chapter 9**);
- pharmacies providing care to patients in their homes, places of work, or in the community;
- services provided under some Patient Group Directions (see **Chapter 13**); and
- services involving prescribing as part of online pharmaceutical services (see **Chapter 8**). However, because services that are provided at or from pharmacies are outside the scope of regulated activities, the CQC will not regulate prescribing that is done there, for example by a pharmacist.

Businesses run by pharmacists but not from registered pharmacy premises, such as prescribing services, will be regulated by the CQC.

The work of pharmacy professionals who work in GP practices as part of a multi-disciplinary team is also overseen by the CQC as part of its regulation of GP practices.[42]

Providing services without being registered is a criminal offence under section 10 of the Health and Social Care Act. For example, an independent ambulance service that transported patients without being registered was fined £4,000 in 2021.[43]

Examples of pharmacy-related reports by the CQC are given in **Box 2.7** below.

Box 2.7: Examples of pharmacy-related reports by the CQC

In 2017, the CQC found in the case of an online pharmacy run by Doctor Matt Ltd that risks to patients were not appropriately assessed or managed. For example, the CQC found patients being prescribed large quantities of inhalers for the treatment of respiratory disease but there was a lack of monitoring or follow up for these patients whose condition could put them at serious risk of harm.[44]

At Derriford Hospital in Plymouth in 2019, the CQC found that there were no safeguards to ensure medicines had been delivered to patients using the trust transport service and patients were adequately advised on their medicines.[45]

44. https://www.cqc.org.uk/location/1-615727353/inspection-summary (accessed 31 December 2024).
45. https://www.cqc.org.uk/news/releases/chief-inspector-hospital-requires-further-improvements-university-hospitals-plymouth (accessed 31 December 2024).

---

41. Schedule 2 to the Health and Social Care Act 2008 (Regulated Activities) Regulations 2014.
42. See, for example, https://www.chemistanddruggist.co.uk/CD138445/Excessive-GP-pharmacist-workload-leaving-safety-gaps-warns-CQC?utm_source=onesignal&utm_medium=web-push&utm_term=CD138201&s=03 (accessed 29 December 2024).
43. https://www.cqc.org.uk/news/releases/cqc-fine-independent-ambulance-company-%C2%A34000-providing-unregistered-services (accessed 29 December 2024).

Box 2.7: Examples of pharmacy-related reports by the CQC (cont.)

In 2022, Lloyds Pharmacy Clinical Homecare's service was rated inadequate overall. There "had been a significant decline in the service's performance between May and October 2021, resulting in significant delays in responding to contact from patients ... the service didn't have enough staff working in the medicine dispensary unit to deliver an effective service."[46]

46. https://www.cqc.org.uk/news/releases/lloyds-pharmacy-clinical-homecare-harlow-rated-inadequate-following-cqc-inspection (accessed 31 December 2024).

Chapter 8 deals with the role of the CQC, Health Improvement Scotland and Healthcare Inspectorate Wales in regulating the online sale and supply of medicines.

Health Improvement Scotland and Healthcare Inspectorate Wales

In Scotland, similar functions to those exercised by the CQC in England are exercised by Health Improvement Scotland under sections 10A and 10F of the National Health Service (Scotland) Act 1978; and in Wales under the Care Standards Act 2000, are exercised by Healthcare Inspectorate Wales. As an example of enforcement, in 2018, Health Inspectorate Wales prosecuted Online GP Services Limited and Dr Helen Webberley for unlawfully providing online healthcare services for transgender patients without being registered. She was convicted and fined £12,000.[47]

In Scotland, independent clinics where services are provided by a doctor, nurse, dentist, dental care professional or midwife have been regulated by Healthcare Improvement Scotland since 2016. However, independent clinics where services are provided by pharmacists and pharmacy technicians have not been regulated in Scotland unless those services are provided from premises registered with the GPhC or the services are provided under the NHS. Following a transitional period that ended on 18 June 2025, where pharmacists and pharmacy technicians provide services from unregulated clinics and in relation to providers of healthcare online, they will be regulated by Health Improvement Scotland. This regulation will not apply to services provided in registered pharmacies and/or under the NHS.[48]

Overseas practitioners

UK and Great Britain regulators such as the GPhC, General Medical Council (GMC) and the CQC have no jurisdiction to regulate practitioners who are not registered or who do not practise in the UK, such as prescribers who are registered overseas. This can cause difficulties if prescribing by overseas doctors gives rise to public health concerns in the UK. When claimants sought judicial review of a Prohibition Order that prohibited the sale or supply of puberty blockers prescribed by overseas-registered doctors, Mrs Justice Laing said: "In the past when attempts have been made by the Care Quality Commission

47. https://www.hiw.org.uk/healthcare-inspectorate-wales-prosecutes-online-gp and https://www.bbc.co.uk/news/uk-wales-46400184 (both accessed 29 December 2024).

48. The National Health Service (Scotland) Act 1978 (Independent Health Care) Modification Order 2024.

and GMC to report unsafe EEA prescribers to the relevant regulator, the report was met with a lack of engagement and resistance."[49]

Regulated roles in Scotland

Under section 44 of the Protection of Vulnerable Groups (Scotland) Act 2007, Ministers must maintain a scheme for collating and disclosing information about individuals who carry out, or wish to carry out, regulated roles with children or protected adults. The scheme allows pharmacy owners to check that their pharmacists are not on any barred list.

Individuals may apply to join the scheme and may not carry out regulated work unless they are members of it. It is an offence under section 45C of the Act to carry out any type of regulated role without being a member of the scheme.

Under section 45D of the Act, it is an offence for an organisation to offer any type of regulated role to an individual unless the organisation has requested and received disclosure under the Disclosure (Scotland) Act 2020.

Regulated roles include the activities of practising as a pharmacist where the activities give the opportunity to have unsupervised contact with children or the opportunity to have contact with protected adults. (Pharmacy technicians are not mentioned in the Act.) A person whose normal duties include the day-to-day supervision or management of an individual carrying out a regulated role is also to be treated as carrying out a regulated role.

Non-surgical cosmetic procedures

In Scotland, the Civic Government (Scotland) Act 1982 (Licensing of Skin Piercing and Tattooing) Order 2006 requires anyone who carries on a business which provides skin piercing or tattooing to have a local authority licence, and it is an offence under the Civic Government (Scotland) Act 1982 to do anything for which a licence is required without having a licence. However, the 2006 Order exempts from the need for a licence skin piercing or tattooing carried on by a regulated healthcare professional.

Pharmacy professionals in Scotland who provide non-NHS services (including non-surgical cosmetic procedures) from premises that are not registered pharmacies come within the definition of providers that are regulated by Health Improvement Scotland[50] in section 10F of the National Health Service (Scotland) Act 1978.

In Wales, the Public Health (Wales) Act 2017 provides that an individual who performs a special procedure on someone else in the course of a business must have a licence granted by the local authority. The licence must specify the premises where the procedure is performed.

The Act defines each of the following activities as "special procedure":

1. acupuncture;
2. body piercing;
3. electrolysis; and
4. tattooing.

---

49. *The King (on the application of (1) Transactual CIC and (2) YY) v Secretary of State for Health and Social Care and another*, [2024] EWHC 1936 (Admin).

50. From 19 June 2025.

When the Public Health (Wales) Act was passed, there was an exemption from the requirement for a licence in the case of procedures performed by members of regulated healthcare professions including pharmacists and pharmacy technicians. However, this exemption was removed by the Special Procedures Exempted Individuals (Wales) Regulations 2024.

In relation to non-surgical cosmetic procedures involving Prescription Only Medicines, see **Chapter 12**.

Professional Standards Authority for Health and Social Care

The PSA was established due to concern that healthcare regulators were regulating themselves, and lacked independence. Its overarching objective is the protection of the public and it is charged with providing assurances to Parliament that healthcare regulators are carrying out their legal functions and protecting the public. These regulators include the bodies that regulate the medical, dental, nursing, optical, chiropractic, osteopathic, pharmaceutical (GPhC and Pharmaceutical Society of Northern Ireland), health and care professions and Social Work England. The PSA's role is to review and scrutinise their regulatory systems, drive up standards and to foster harmonisation of regulatory practice and outcomes. The PSA may investigate and report on the performance of each regulatory body and may recommend changes to the way in which the body performs its functions. It has power to advise regulators.[51] It reviews every final decision made by the regulators' fitness to practise committees and may refer to the High Court in England and Wales or the Court of Session in Scotland a decision by one of the healthcare regulators that it considers is not sufficient for the protection of the public (see **Chapter 25**).

The PSA carries out annual reviews of the regulators for which it is responsible and publishes a report of each review. The PSA's Standards[52] set out the outcomes it expects from regulators and how they should approach to their work. The Standards prioritise the core role of regulators in:

- protecting patients and reducing harms;
- promoting professional standards; and
- maintaining public confidence in the professions.

The Standards are informed by the PSA's principles of good (right touch) regulation which state that regulators should act in a way which is:

- proportionate;
- consistent;
- targeted;
- transparent;
- accountable; and
- agile.

In addition to the healthcare professions listed above, for which the PSA has statutory responsibility, the PSA assesses other bodies and maintains accredited registers of

51. Section 25B of the National Health Service Reform and Health Care Professions Act 2002.
52. https://www.professionalstandards.org.uk/sites/default/files/attachments/The%20Standards%20of%20Good%20Regulation_0.pdf (accessed 29 December 2024).

its members. Such bodies are granted the PSA's *Quality Mark*. The aim is to provide the public with confidence in choosing a practitioner who is on an accredited register. Examples of bodies with an accredited register include:

- British Acupuncture Council;
- Complementary and Natural Healthcare Council;
- International Federation of Aromatherapists;
- Joint Council for Cosmetic Practitioners; and
- UK Public Health Register.

The PSA also advises the Secretary of State and Health Ministers in Scotland, Wales and Northern Ireland on regulatory policy and may be requested to carry out special reviews. These have included a 2018 Lessons Learned Review on the handling by the Nursing and Midwifery Council (NMC) of concerns about midwives' fitness to practise at the Furness General Hospital.

The future of healthcare regulation

In 2011, the Law Commission started a review of the regulation of health (in the UK) and social care professionals (in England) and proposed a single legal framework for all the regulators of health and social care professionals. The intention was to simplify and modernise the current complex arrangements for professional regulation and impose consistency across the regulators by giving government the power to make regulations for any of the regulators or merge or abolish existing regulators or establish a new regulator.

In 2015 the Government accepted the majority of the recommendations of the subsequent report[53] and, in 2017, consulted on the proposals, commenting that "regulators continued to be hampered by a legislative framework that is in parts more than 150 years old and with outdated procedures that have not kept pace with changes in the health and social care system".[54] The Government's proposals for the future of healthcare regulation are dealt with in **Chapter 25**.

The future structure of regulatory bodies

The UK Government and the devolved governments' intentions following the consultation on *Promoting professionalism, reforming regulation* include a further consultation on rationalising the 10 healthcare regulators.[55] Regardless of the outcome of the further consultation, there will be structural changes to all the healthcare regulators. Their councils will become boards which comprise executive and non-executive directors, appointed on the basis that they have the skills, knowledge and expertise to ensure the regulator discharges its functions effectively. The non-executive directors will always form the majority of the board. Current and former registrants

53. https://assets.publishing.service.gov.uk/government/uploads/system/uploads/attachment_data/file/399020/Response_Cm_8995.pdf (accessed 29 December 2024).

54. https://assets.publishing.service.gov.uk/media/5a81d78ce5274a2e8ab561e7/Regulatory_Reform_Consultation_Document.pdf (accessed 29 December 2024).

55. https://www.gov.uk/government/consultations/regulating-healthcare-professionals-protecting-the-public/outcome/regulating-healthcare-professionals-protecting-the-public-consultation-response-executive-summary (accessed 29 December 2024).

may be appointed to the board, but they will not form a majority. The governments have dropped a proposal for employers to be represented on the regulatory bodies' boards but expects regulatory bodies to actively seek and consider the views of employers.

Notifiable diseases

In addition to the professional duties imposed on pharmacists and healthcare professionals, and enforced by regulatory bodies overseen by the PSA, the law sometimes imposes positive legal duties. Of particular recent relevance, the Health Protection (Notification) Regulations 2010 were made under powers in the Public Health (Control of Disease) Act 1984. The Regulations apply to England only. Regulation 2 of the Regulations requires a registered medical practitioner to notify the proper officer of the relevant local authority if the medical practitioner has reasonable grounds for suspecting that a patient:

a. has a notifiable disease; or
b. has an infection which, in the view of the medical practitioner presents or could present significant harm to human health; or
c. is contaminated in a manner which, in the view of the medical practitioner, presents our could present significant harm to human health.

The notification must include, so far as the information is known to the medical practitioner, the patient's details, including name, date of birth, home address, telephone number, NHS number, relevant recent travel history and ethnicity, as well as disease details, date of onset of symptoms, date of diagnosis and the medical practitioner's own name and details. In Scotland, there are similar requirements under section 13 of the Public Health etc. (Scotland) Act 2008; and in Wales, under regulation 2 of the Health Protection (Notification) (Wales) Regulations 2010.

Examples of notifiable diseases include acute meningitis, acute infectious hepatitis, anthrax, leprosy, food poisoning, malaria, measles and COVID-19.

The regulations applicable to England impose a duty on the operators of diagnostic laboratories to notify the UK Health Security Agency of causative agents found in human samples and of SARS-CoV-2 or influenza tests processed. Notification must be made within seven days of the causative agent being identified unless the causative agent is SARS-CoV-2, in which case the notification must be made within 24 hours of the causative agent being identified.

The Regulations impose a duty on point of care test providers to notify results of tests for the detection of SARS-CoV-2 or influenza virus to the UK Health Security Agency. A point of care test is a diagnostic test which is not carried out in a diagnostic laboratory. A *test provider* is defined as a company, partnership, charity, corporation, unincorporated association, or other organisation or body, whether public or private, or sole trader, carrying out point of care tests for the detection of SARS-CoV-2 or influenza virus: this definition is wide enough to cover pharmacies that sell lateral flow tests for COVID-19. Notification must be made in writing within 24 hours of the time when a positive or indeterminate test result is received by the test provider in the case of the result of a test for the detection of SARS-CoV-2 or, if the test is negative or void, within seven days. In the case of influenza virus, notification must be made within seven days of the test result being received by the test provider.

The details to be notified include, insofar as they are known to the test provider, the patient's name, sex, date of birth, NHS number, ethnicity, current address (including postcode), and, in the case of a test for SARS-CoV-2 that is positive or indeterminate, a telephone number and email address. The test provider must notify its name, the nature of the establishment, specimen identification number (if applicable), specimen type, specimen date, test method, result of test, date on which the test was carried out, and the name of the testing equipment manufacturer.

Failure to notify in accordance with the Regulations without reasonable excuse is an offence.

SUMMARY

- The General Pharmaceutical Council was created under the Pharmacy Order 2010 to regulate the pharmacy profession. Its remit extends to England, Scotland and Wales.
- The GPhC:
  - has an overarching objective of protecting the public,
  - is responsible for the education and training of pharmacists,
  - maintains registers of pharmacists, pharmacy technicians and pharmacy premises,
  - publishes standards that include standards for pharmacy professionals,
  - publishes standards for pharmacy premises,
  - publishes guidance to support its standards,
  - is responsible for revalidation and CPD,
  - has enforcement powers,
  - appoints inspectors who have statutory powers to enter premises and to search for evidence,
  - publishes inspection reports,
  - checks the fitness to practise of pharmacy professionals, and
  - has fitness to practise procedures.
- Changes in regulation of healthcare professions generally have often followed scandals or tragedies.
- Healthcare providers registered with the CQC have a statutory duty of candour. This does not apply to pharmacy professionals, but they have a professional duty of candour.
- The CQC regulates health and social care, but not pharmacy, though some CQC regulation and inspection impinges on aspects of pharmacy practice.
- The PSA regulates and oversees healthcare regulators such as the GPhC.
- There are plans to reduce the number of healthcare regulators and to reform the structure of healthcare regulators.
- There is a legal obligation to notify the UK Health Security Agency of certain diseases.

FURTHER READING

- Gomez D (2019). *Regulation of Healthcare Professionals, Law, Principle and Process.* (2nd edition) London: Sweet & Maxwell.
- Government response to the consultation 'Promoting professionalism, reforming regulation', published July 2019: **https://www.gov.uk/government/consultations/promoting-professionalism-reforming-regulation** (accessed 29 December 2024).

CHAPTER 3

National Health Service law

Until the National Health Service was created in 1948, pharmacies mainly prepared and sold medicines. Retail pharmacies did not generally only sell medicines, but a wide range of other products such as perfumes, cosmetics and provided photographic services.[1] *Today, most pharmacies are dependent on income from providing NHS services that include clinical services as well as dispensing prescribed medicines. As the range of services has expanded, the regulation of pharmacies has increased. The law and regulation of NHS pharmacy has features common to England, Scotland and Wales, but there are also variations between the three countries.*

Introduction - NHS structure in Great Britain

Like the legislation that underpins it, the structure of the NHS undergoes constant change. Although the structures and titles vary significantly in England, Scotland and Wales, all have organisations that plan and commission local health services and primary care services, and organisations that plan and provide secondary (mostly hospital) care. NHS laws are devolved to the national governments within the UK. Although laws in England, Scotland and Wales are often the same or similar, there are some key differences.

The NHS bodies referred to in this chapter are *creatures of statute*, meaning that they have been created by an Act of Parliament or by secondary legislation. As such, they only have the powers that are given to them in an Act or in secondary legislation. The same applies to the powers of the Department of Health and Social Care and Secretary of State for Health and Social Care. Those powers are often very wide, but they are not unlimited.

Shortly before going to press, the Prime Minister announced that NHS England would be abolished as a separate organisation and its functions will be taken over by the Department of Health and Social Care.

England

The roles of the key NHS bodies for England are set out in **Box 3.1**.

1. This was still the case when the House of Lords heard the case of *Dickson v Pharmaceutical Society of Great Britain* in 1968, [1970] AC 403.

Box 3.1: Key NHS bodies for England

NHS England

NHS England has a duty concurrently with the Secretary of State for Health and Social Care to promote a comprehensive health service in England and has the function of arranging for the provision of services for the purposes of the health service except in relation to public health. NHS England must also ensure that Integrated Care Boards carry out their statutory roles. NHS England exercises its functions through Local Area Teams.

Each year, after public consultation, the Department of Health publishes a mandate[2] setting out objectives and a budget for NHS England. This helps ensure that the NHS remains accountable to Parliament and the public.

Integrated Care Boards, Integrated Care Systems, and Integrated Care Partnerships

Integrated Care Boards (ICBs – see above) have commissioning functions previously performed by Clinical Commissioning Groups. This includes assuming delegated responsibility for primary medical services and being able to take on delegated responsibility for pharmaceutical, dental and general ophthalmic services.

ICBs have a duty under section 14Z42 of the National Health Service Act 2006 to promote integration and ensure that health services are integrated with health-related social care services. In particular, section 116ZA of the Local Government and Public Involvement in Health Act 2007 requires ICBs and each local authority to establish a joint committee for the ICB's area and this committee is known as an integrated care partnership.

Under section 116ZB of the Local Government and Public Involvement in Health Act 2007, each integrated care partnership must prepare a strategy setting out how the assessed needs in relation to its area are to be met by the exercise of functions of: (a) the integrated care board for its area, (b) NHS England, or (c) the responsible local authorities whose areas coincide with or fall wholly or partly within its area.

Integrated Care Systems are the combination of NHS bodies, local authorities and others that have collective responsibility for planning services, improving health and reducing inequalities across geographical areas. There are 42 ICSs that cover England.

UK Health Security Agency

The UK Health Security Agency (UKHSA) was formed to take over the functions previously exercised by Public Health England. UKHSA is responsible for protecting members of the public from the impact of infectious diseases, chemical, biological, radiological and nuclear incidents and other health threats. UKHSA's functions include scientific and operational leadership at national and local level.

Health and Wellbeing Boards

Each local authority must establish an HWB for its area. The HWB consists of the director of adult social services, director of children's services and director of public health, a representative of the local Healthwatch organisation, a representative of each relevant ICB, at least one councillor of the local authority and other persons that the local authority thinks appropriate. These boards are intended to encourage local authorities to integrate health and local government services. The responsibility for preparing a "pharmaceutical needs assessment" (PNA) as a basis for awarding community pharmacy contracts (see below) now sits with the HWB and is a major influence on the commissioning of public health services locally. Local authorities also work with their HWB to commission local public health services such as smoking cessation or anti-obesity schemes from community pharmacies.

2. See, for example, https://www.gov.uk/government/publications/nhs-mandate-2023/the-governments-2023-mandate-to-nhs-england (accessed 30 December 2024).

Box 3.1: Key NHS bodies for England (cont.)

National Institute for Health and Care Excellence

The National Institute for Health and Care Excellence (NICE) was established by Part 8 of the Health and Social Care Act 2012. It is an advisory body that provides guidance and support to providers and commissioners to improve outcomes and describe what good care looks like. It develops quality standards and provides information services for commissioners and practitioners.

NICE's best known role is to decide whether to approve the use of new medicines in the NHS.

NICE has been the subject of a number of judicial review cases, typically over its recommendations not to approve the prescribing of certain medicines. For example, it did not approve certain drugs, vitamin supplements and complementary therapies for the treatment of chronic fatigue syndrome/myalgic encephalomyelitis on the basis that there was not enough evidence that they were effective. This led to an unsuccessful judicial review in *R (on the application of Fraser) v National Institute for Health and Clinical Excellence*;[3] and in *R. (on the application of Eisai Ltd) v National Institute for Health and Clinical Excellence*,[4] a challenge to its guidance in relation to the use of acetylcholinesterase inhibitors for the treatment of Alzheimer's disease, on grounds of procedural unfairness.

ICBs are expected to have regard to relevant NICE guidelines in their commissioning decisions (see the case of *Bayer v Darlington CCG* described in **Box 5.4** in **Chapter 5**).

National Health Service Litigation Authority (NHS Resolution)

The National Health Service Litigation Authority (NHSLA) operates under the name NHS Resolution. NHS Resolution has a wide range of activities in relation to pharmacy practice, NHS Resolution deals with appeals on behalf of the Secretary of State against decisions on market entry, remedial notices, breach notices, determinations of opening hours, and arising from determinations by NHS England regarding overpayments of remuneration.

Care Quality Commission

The Care Quality Commission (*CQC*) is the statutory body entrusted by Parliament under the Health and Social Care Act 2008 (*the 2008 Act*) with the responsibility for registering and reviewing the providers of health and social care services in England. The CQC plays an important role in the regulation of online pharmacy services (see **Chapter 2** and **Chapter 8**) and in the operation of Patent Group Directions (see **Chapter 13**).

1. Under section 3(1) of the 2008 Act the main objective of the CQC is protecting the health, safety and welfare of people who use health and social care services.
2. Under section 10 of the 2008 Act, it is an offence to carry on a regulated activity without being registered. Under section 8 of the 2008 Act, *regulated activity* means an activity of a prescribed kind. Under paragraph 4(1) of Schedule 1 to the Health and Social Care Act 2008 (Regulated Activities) Regulations 2014 (*the Regulations*) the provision of treatment for a disease, disorder or injury by a health care professional is a prescribed regulated activity. An activity which is ancillary to, or is carried on wholly or mainly in relation to, a regulated activity is treated as part of that activity. Note that, for the purposes of the Act, pharmacists and pharmacy technicians are not within the definition of *health care professional*.
3. Under the Regulations, certain activities are exempted from the need for registration. Exceptions from the definition of *regulated activities* that may be relevant to pharmacies include:
   (a) diagnostic and screening procedures;
   (b) services in slimming clinics;

3. [2009] EWHC 452 (Admin).
4. [2008] EWCA Civ 438.

Box 3.1: Key NHS bodies for England (cont.)

(c) the practice of alternative and complementary medicine;
(d) testing for the presence of severe acute respiratory syndrome coronavirus ("SARS-CoV-2") in an individual, or for the presence of antibodies to SARS-CoV-2, or is carried on for the purpose of processing, analysing or reporting the results of a test for the presence of SARS-CoV-2 in an individual, or for the presence of antibodies to SARS-CoV-2.

4. Under section 29 of the 2008 Act, if it appears to the CQC that a registered person has failed to comply with requirements imposed by it, the CQC may give that person a warning notice. Under section 33 of the 2008 Act, failure to comply with the warning is an offence.
5. Under section 46(1) of the 2008 Act, the CQC must (i) conduct reviews of the carrying on of regulated activities by service providers; (ii) assess their performance following each such review; and (iii) publish the reports of its assessments.
6. Under section 60(1)(a) of the 2008 Act the CQC may for the purposes of its regulatory functions carry out inspections of regulated activities. Under section 61, where such an inspection is carried out, the CQC must (i) prepare a report on the matters inspected; (ii) without delay send a copy of the report to the person who carries on the regulated activity in question; and (iii) publish the report.
7. Under Regulation 20A of the Regulations, where a report gives a rating, the service provider must display that rating conspicuously and legibly in each and every place where the regulated activity is delivered, and on its website, where people will be sure to see it.

In Scotland, equivalent functions are performed by Health Improvement Scotland under sections 10A and 10F of the National Health Service (Scotland) Act 1978.

In Wales, equivalent functions are performed by Healthcare Inspectorate Wales on behalf of the Welsh Parliament (Senedd Cymru) under the Care Standards Act 2000.

Legislative framework

The National Health Service Act 1946 created the National Health Service (NHS), making it the duty of the Minister of Health (now the Secretary of State for Health and Social Care) to:

- promote the establishment in England and Wales of a comprehensive health service designed to secure improvement in the physical and mental health of the people of England and Wales and the prevention, diagnosis and treatment of illness;
- provide or secure the provision of services to do this; and
- provide these services free of charge unless otherwise expressly provided in any other legislation. In England, Regulations require pharmacy owners to charge patients for the supply on prescription of drugs, appliances and elastic hosiery unless the patient is exempt from the charge.[5]

In Scotland, a similar health service was established by the National Health Service (Scotland) Act 1947.

5. National Health Service (Charges for Drugs and Appliances) Regulations 2015.

Health is now devolved to the home nations, and the law creating the structure of the NHS and the laws governing the arrangements to be made are to be found in the National Health Service Act 2006 for England, the National Health Service (Scotland) Act 1978 and the National Health Service (Wales) Act 2006.

National Health Service Act 2006 (the NHS Act)

In Part 1 of the NHS Act 2006, the Secretary of State has a duty to promote in England a comprehensive health service to secure improvement in the physical and mental health of the people of England, and in the prevention, diagnosis and treatment of physical and mental illness. In exercising this overarching duty, the Secretary of State also has other duties, including:

- acting with a view to securing continuous improvement in the quality of services provided to individuals;
- having regard to the NHS Constitution (see below);
- reducing inequalities with respect to the benefits that can be obtained from the health service;
- promoting the autonomy of anyone who exercises functions under the Act;
- promoting research;
- securing an effective system for the planning and delivery of education and training to NHS employees and prospective employees; and
- reporting on and reviewing treatment of providers.

Section 1H of the Act creates NHS England. NHS England has the same function as the Secretary of State to arrange for the provision of services and the same duty to promote a comprehensive health service (apart from the public health functions). The duty of the Secretary of State and NHS England is to promote, but not necessarily to provide, a comprehensive service (which seems understandable since resources are finite).

Section 14Z25 of the Act requires NHS England to establish integrated care boards (ICBs) for geographical areas that, together, cover the whole of England. ICBs replaced Clinical Commissioning Groups (CCGs). ICBs have the general function of arranging for the provision of services. Under section 13YB of the Act, NHS England may make directions that any of its functions, including functions relating to the provision of services that may be provided as pharmaceutical services or local pharmaceutical services, may be provided by one or more integrated care boards. All ICBs have assumed responsibility for primary health services including commissioning, complaints and pharmacy market entry. However, under the Act, NHS England retains overall accountability for the discharge of functions delegated to ICBs. Pharmaceutical services and local pharmaceutical services are dealt with in Part 7 of the NHS Act. In particular, section 126 of the Act says that NHS England must make arrangements for the provision of proper and sufficient drugs and appliances that are prescribed by a medical practitioner, a dental practitioner or other categories of prescriber (see **Chapter 12**), and the Secretary of State must make regulations that set out the arrangements. The Secretary of State has made the National Health Service (Pharmaceutical and Local Pharmaceutical Services) Regulations 2013.

In addition, the Secretary of State may give directions to NHS England requiring it to arrange for the provision of additional pharmaceutical services, namely enhanced services that are commissioned locally from specific pharmacies or from all pharmacies in an area, or advanced services that all pharmacies in England may provide.

Except in the case of local pharmaceutical services (LPS) (see below), arrangements for the provision of essential and advanced NHS pharmaceutical services do not involve a legal contract between NHS England, NHS Scotland or NHS Wales and the pharmacy owner who provides services.[6] Instead, the legal obligations between pharmacy owners and the relevant NHS body are based on the terms of service in the relevant Schedule to the Regulations[7] or, in the case of enhanced and advanced services, also in Directions.[8] However, the convention is to describe this arrangement as a *contractual framework* and to refer to *NHS contracts.*

When a medicine is supplied to a patient under the NHS, there is no sale, and therefore no contract between the pharmacy owner and the patient[9] (unlike the case of a private prescription where there is a contract of sale). This is why some pharmacy legislation uses the words *circumstances corresponding to retail sale* when an NHS supply is made, to distinguish between NHS and private prescriptions.

Part 9 of the Act contains the provisions for prescription charges to be paid by certain people presenting NHS prescriptions in the community. Part 10 makes a series of requirements concerning the protection of the NHS from fraud, such as compulsory disclosure of documents and information. Part 12 includes details of how the public and patients will have an input into NHS planning and operation.

Part 13 of the Act contains provisions enforcing controls on the maximum price of medicines. There is a Voluntary Scheme for Branded Medicines Pricing, Access and Growth which is in place until 2028.[10] The prices of medicinal products whose manufacturers have not agreed to include them in the voluntary scheme will be determined by a statutory scheme in accordance with the Branded Health Service Medicines (Costs) Regulations 2018. The Secretary of State has powers under the Health Service Medical Supplies (Costs) Act 2017 to require any person who manufactures, distributes or supplies health service medicines, medical supplies or other related products required (for the purpose of the health service), to record, keep and provide specified information.

---

6. *Roy v Kensington and Chelsea and Westminster Family Practitioner Committee* [1992] 1 AC 624 and *Appleby v Sleep* [1968] 1 WLR 948.
7. For example, in England, in Schedule 4 to the National Health Service (Pharmaceutical and Local Pharmaceutical Services) Regulations 2013.
8. In England, the terms of advanced services are set out in the Pharmaceutical Services (Advanced and Enhanced Services) (England) Directions 2013. (Enhanced services that are commissioned will be governed by a contract with the commissioner.)
9. *Pfizer Corporation v Ministry of Health* [1965] AC 512.
10. https://assets.publishing.service.gov.uk/media/657b2977095987001295e139/2024-voluntary-scheme-for-branded-medicines-pricing-access-and-growth.pdf (accessed 30 December 2024).

Pharmaceutical lists and market entry

Details of the arrangements for the provision of NHS pharmacy services are contained in the National Health Service (Pharmaceutical and Local Pharmaceutical Services) Regulations 2013. These are referred to below as *the Regulations*. There is not space here for comprehensive coverage of the Regulations, which are lengthy and complex. What follows are key points.

NHS England is required to prepare two pharmaceutical lists for each Health and Wellbeing Board (HWB) area. The first list comprises the names and addresses of all those persons who have undertaken to provide pharmaceutical services from premises in the area, in particular by way of the provision of drugs. Pharmacy owners whose names are included in such a list are commonly referred to as *pharmacy contractors*. The second list comprises the names and addresses of those persons who have undertaken to provide pharmaceutical services only by way of the provision of appliances, commonly referred to as *appliance contractors* (or *dispensing appliance contractors*).

Supply of drugs and appliances from listed premises

Only persons who are included in a pharmaceutical list are entitled to provide and be paid for providing NHS pharmaceutical services. Prescribed drugs and appliances must be provided from the listed premises in order to be eligible for payment. Even under a hub and spoke arrangement (see **Chapter 12**) in which a prescription is presented at one pharmacy (the spoke) and assembled at another pharmacy (the hub), the supply to the patient must be made from the spoke in order for that pharmacy to be eligible for payment for providing the dispensed medicine (see **Chapter 5** for the meaning of *assembled*). For the purpose of the Regulations, the words *provide* and *supply* have the same meaning. In *R v Family Health Services Appeal Authority Ex parte Elmfield Drugs Ltd*)[11] the word *supply* was held to mean the physical handing over of a medicinal product (see **Chapter 11**). However, in terms of the supply *from listed premises*, the Court of Appeal clarified in *Central Liverpool Primary Care Trust v Charles S Bullen Stomacare Ltd*[12] that supplying *from* listed premises requires more than handing over the medicinal product (see **Box 3.2**). It should be noted that in the context of the Misuse of Drugs Act 1971, the word *supply* has a different meaning when controlled drugs are unlawfully supplied.[13]

Box 3.2: The meaning of supply from listed premises

Charles S Bullen Stomacare Limited (Bullen) was an appliance contractor that was included in the pharmaceutical list of Central Liverpool Primary Care Trust (the PCT). Bullen had four listed premises, three of which were in the area of the PCT. Under the provisions of the Drug Tariff, the more listed premises from which prescribed appliances could be supplied, the higher the fees Bullen was entitled to claim.

---

11. [1999] 46 BMLR 191.
12. [2005] EWCA Civ 1514.
13. *R v Maginnis* [1987] AC 303.

Box 3.2: The meaning of supply from listed premises (cont.)

Bullen had a warehouse and an adjacent office building. A narrow alley ran between them at ground floor level, but they intercommunicated at first floor level. The warehouse and office had different addresses and separate entrances. One of those addresses was in the pharmaceutical list. There was found to be no relevant physical or operational separation between the two premises and the business was found to be conducted within them as if they were a single site. The PCT alleged all supplies had, in reality, been made from the warehouse and that other premises in the pharmaceutical list were no more than staging posts used transiently before supplies were made to patients.

The Court of Appeal rejected Bullen's argument that in order for supplies to be made from the listed premises, it was sufficient for the prescribed appliances to cross the threshold of the listed premises on the way to being delivered to patients' homes. Lord Justice Sedley (with whom Lord Justice Jonathan Parker agreed) said that in terms of whether a supply has been made from listed premises:

> *"more is required ... than transient presence in a building. They require ... the making there of some material contribution to the process of supply. For example, some modification or preparation of the appliances which it was reasonable not to make at source [i.e. in the warehouse], or some significant measure of availability not offered by the warehouse. Put another way, 'from' is not the same as 'through'."*

Part 2 of the Regulations deals with Pharmaceutical Needs Assessments (PNAs). Every three years, each HWB must publish a PNA for its area (and may publish supplementary PNAs between these three-year periods). Amongst other things, the PNA must identify:

- the services currently provided;
- services that are not provided but which need to be provided or which, in specified future circumstances, will need to be provided to meet a future need;
- services which, though not necessary to meet a need, have secured improvements or better access to pharmaceutical services, or affect the assessment;
- services that are not provided but which, if they were provided, would secure improvements or better access to pharmaceutical services; and
- services which would, in specified future circumstances, secure improvements or better access to pharmaceutical services.

Any person who wishes to be included in a list must apply to NHS England in the prescribed form for inclusion in a pharmaceutical list. Amongst other things, fitness to practise information must be supplied, and applicants not already included in a pharmaceutical list must provide references. The process and detailed requirements for applications are dealt with in Schedule 2 to the Regulations.

Directions provide that NHS Resolution will determine appeals concerning applications for entry onto pharmaceutical lists, and relevant determinations on core opening hours of NHS community pharmacies.[14] The appeals procedure is primarily in schedule 3 to the Regulations.

14. National Health Service Litigation Authority (Functions relating to Pharmaceutical Services and Local Pharmaceutical Services) (England) Directions 2012.

Routine applications

Part 3 of the Regulations deals with routine applications for inclusion in pharmaceutical lists. The main types of routine application are to meet a current or future need that has been identified in the PNA; to secure improvements or better access as identified in the PNA; or to secure improvements or better access to services that were not foreseen when the PNA was written (unforeseen benefits applications). Subject to certain conditions, an application to meet a need that has been identified in the PNA will normally be granted. An unforeseen benefits application will only be granted if, after taking into account the desirability of:

i. there being a reasonable choice of services in the HWB area,
ii. people who share a protected characteristic having access to services that meet their specific needs for pharmaceutical services that are difficult for them to access,[15] and
iii. innovative approaches to the delivery of services,

granting the application would confer significant benefits on persons in the HWB.

If an application falls within the express grounds for refusal in the Regulations (see below), the application must be refused.

Excepted applications

Part 4 of the Regulations deals with excepted applications - types of application that are not linked to PNAs. These excepted applications include:

- Relocations that do not result in a significant change to pharmaceutical services provision (no significant change relocations) – if, for the patient groups that are accustomed to accessing the pharmaceutical services at the existing premises, the location of the new premises is not significantly less accessible.
- Distance selling pharmacies – which must provide the uninterrupted provision of essential services during core opening hours to persons anywhere in England who request them, with no (physical) face to face contact between pharmacy staff and the patient or patient's representative. The applicant's premises must not be on the same site as those of a provider of primary medical services.
- Changes of ownership - which may be combined with an application for a no significant change relocation.
- Consolidation of two listed pharmacies into the premises of one of the pharmacies (a merger of two pharmacy businesses with one of the pharmacies then closing) – the consolidation must not create a gap in pharmaceutical service provision that could be met by a routine application. Distance selling pharmacies may not apply for consolidation.

Excepted applications will be granted if they satisfy certain conditions in the Regulations, subject to the express grounds for refusal in the Regulations.

Grounds for refusal

Part 5 of the Regulations deals with certain grounds for refusing applications. For example:

---

15. Protected characteristics are defined in Part 2 of the Equality Act 2010 and are set out in Chapter 24.

- an application for inclusion in the pharmaceutical list by a person not already included in it must be refused if the applicant is an individual who qualified as a pharmacist in Switzerland or an EEA state other than the UK, unless the applicant satisfies NHS England as to their level of knowledge of English.
- An application must be refused if a person is already providing or has undertaken to provide pharmaceutical services from the premises to which the application relates, or adjacent premises, and it is reasonable to treat the services that the applicant proposes to provide as part of the same services as the existing services. The purpose of this restriction is to prevent the duplication of NHS remuneration. In *R (on the application of Pharmacy Care Plus Ltd) v Family Health Services Appeal Unit*,[16] the question of whether the services to be provided by an applicant were part of the same services provided by an existing pharmacy was held to be primarily about the ownership and control of the two businesses.[17]

Part 6 of the Regulations deals with other grounds for refusing an application for inclusion in a pharmaceutical list. For example, an application must be refused if:

- the applicant has been convicted of murder or, after 1 April 2005, an offence which resulted in a sentence of imprisonment exceeding six months; or
- the applicant is the subject of a national disqualification.

An application may be refused if NHS England is not satisfied with the applicant's references or if:

- it considers the applicant unsuitable to be included in the pharmaceutical list;
- it considers refusal to be justified having regard to the facts of any past or current fraud investigation or proceedings (even if, for example, the applicant had been prosecuted and found not guilty); or
- it considers that granting the application would be prejudicial to the efficiency of the service that the applicant has undertaken to provide.

Applications (other than unforeseen benefits applications) must also be refused if granting them would result in an undesirable increase in the availability of essential services in the Health and Wellbeing Board area.[18]

The reasons for any decision to refuse inclusion in the list must be given.

Controlled localities

Part 7 of the Regulations deals with controlled localities. These are areas that are rural in character. In controlled localities, the Regulations include additional requirements. Among other provisions, an application will be refused if it would prejudice the proper provision of relevant NHS services (usually pharmaceutical services or primary medical services). This *prejudice test*, as it is known, typically involves an assessment

16. [2013] EWHC 824 (Admin).
17. See also the guidance published by NHS Resolution https://resolution.nhs.uk/wp-content/uploads/2024/08/NHS-Resolution-Regulation-31-Guidance-Note-August-2024.pdf (accessed 30 December 2024).
18. Regulation 21A of the Regulations.

of the financial impact granting the application would have on other pharmacies or GP practices (usually practices where the doctors have the right to dispense medicines (see below)) and whether the loss of NHS income would force a pharmacy or medical practice to close.

If a routine application is refused, a new application cannot be made in respect of premises within 1.6 kilometres of the proposed pharmacy for five years unless there has been a substantial and relevant change of circumstances affecting the controlled locality.

Performance related sanctions and market exit

Pharmacy owners (referred to in the Regulations as *NHS pharmacists* or *NHS chemists*) are required to comply with the terms of service that are primarily in Schedule 4 to the Regulations[19] (see below).

Part 10 of the Regulations gives NHS England a range of enforcement powers in relation to the terms of service.

If a pharmacy owner breaches a term of service and the term is capable of remedy, NHS England may serve a remedial notice specifying the breach, the steps to be taken to remedy it and the period within which such steps are to be taken. If a breach of the terms of service is not capable of remedy, NHS England may serve a breach notice, requiring the pharmacy owner not to repeat the breach. Examples of breaches include failing to open to provide services during listed hours, or incorrect claims for remuneration or reimbursement.

If a breach relates to the failure to provide a service, or a failure to provide a service to a reasonable standard, and is without good cause, a remedial notice or breach notice may provide that NHS England is to withhold all or part of the pharmacy owner's remuneration relating to the period of time in which the breach occurred. The amount of any withholding must be justifiable and proportionate having regard to the nature and seriousness of the breach and, generally, the reasons justifying both the withholding and the amount withheld must be stated in the remedial or breach notice.

Before issuing a breach notice, NHS England must usually make reasonable efforts to communicate with the pharmacy owner with a view to resolving the dispute relating to compliance with a term of service.

If a pharmacy owner fails to take the steps set out in a remedial notice, NHS England may remove the pharmacy owner or specific premises from the pharmaceutical list if this is necessary to protect the safety of any persons to whom the pharmacy owner may provide pharmaceutical services, or to protect NHS England from material financial loss.

NHS Resolution has published a guidance note that includes examples of its decisions on remedial notices and breach notices.[20]

NHS England also has power to remove a pharmacy owner or specific premises from the pharmaceutical list if it has repeatedly issued the pharmacy owner with remedial

---

19. Regulation 11.
20. https://resolution.nhs.uk/wp-content/uploads/2020/02/Primary-Care-Appeals-Breach-and-Remedial-Notices-March-2021-1.pdf (accessed 30 December 2024).

notices or breach notices; or if a remedial notice or breach notice has previously been issued and the pharmacy owner is likely to persist in breaching the term of service without good cause; or if the pharmacy owner has previously been issued with remedial notices or breach notices in relation to different terms of service and the pharmacy owner is likely to persist in breaching the terms of service without good cause. Removal from the pharmaceutical list is likely to be a very severe sanction in financial terms for the pharmacy owner and may also result in a loss of services to patients and the public. NHS England may only take such a step if it is justifiable and proportionate, having regard to the nature and seriousness of the breach or breaches and the reasons for them.

NHS England must remove a pharmacy from the pharmaceutical list if a pharmacist who is the owner dies, unless the legal representatives of the deceased pharmacist carry on the business.

NHS England must also remove a pharmacy owner from the pharmaceutical list if the pharmacy owner has ceased to carry on a retail pharmacy business (see **Chapter 7**). If a pharmacy owner has not, during the preceding six months, provided pharmaceutical services, the owner must be removed from the pharmaceutical list; or if the pharmacy owner owns more than one pharmacy, the removal will relate only to premises from which services have not been provided.

Remuneration for pharmaceutical services

Remuneration for pharmaceutical services is dealt with in part 12 of the Regulations which refers to the Drug Tariff. The Drug Tariff is published by the Department of Health and Social Care after consulting Community Pharmacy England (formerly called the Pharmaceutical Services Negotiating Committee or PSNC) and includes amongst other things the fees payable for services, the prices at which pharmacy owners will be reimbursed for the drugs and appliances they supply, and the directions that have been given for the provision of enhanced and advanced services.

Part 12 of the Regulations (regulation 94) also includes a procedure for the recovery of any overpayments made by NHS England to pharmacy owners with a right of appeal to NHS Resolution[21].

Terms of Service for pharmacy owners

Essential services

Part 2 of Schedule 4 to the 2013 Regulations sets out the terms for the essential services which must be provided by every pharmacy owner. This includes the dispensing of prescriptions and repeat dispensing.

Dispensing may be against a paper prescription or an electronically transferred prescription bearing the prescriber's advanced electronic signature (where the patient may have a hard copy token indicating that an electronic prescription has been issued).

---

21. The National Health Service Litigation Authority (Pharmaceutical Remuneration – Payment Disputes) (England) Directions 2022.

The pharmacy owner must supply any drugs except those *scheduled drugs*[22] which comprises medicines in certain categories that cannot be prescribed for supply at NHS expense. The categories were originally indigestion remedies, laxatives, analgesics for mild to moderate pain, bitters and tonics, vitamins and the benzodiazepine tranquillisers and sedatives. The list now includes many other medicines.[23] Some medicines may be prescribed only in specified circumstances.[24] A recent example concerns the puberty-suppressing hormone GnRH, following the Cass review of NHS gender identity services for children and young people.[25] Prescribing for the treatment of gender dysphoria or gender incongruence (or both) is not permitted in the case of patients aged under 18, except in the case of patients who had started treatment before 26 June 2024, or in the case of clinical trials run by NICE. Prescribing remains permitted for patients over the age of 18 and for patients aged under 18 if the treatment is for a purpose other than puberty suppression. (The prohibition on the sale or supply of puberty blockers on private prescriptions is covered in **Chapter 21**).

In a case of urgency, a pharmacy owner may (but is not required to) dispense a medicine (other than a controlled drug in Schedules 1, 2 or 3 to the Misuse of Drugs Regulations 2001) requested by a prescriber who is unable to issue a prescription without delay provided that the prescriber undertakes to supply a signed prescription or transmit an electronic prescription within 72 hours.[26]

Prescription charges

Prescriptions attract an NHS prescription charge which must be paid to the pharmacy owner, unless an exemption applies.[27] The exemption categories are to be found in Part XVI of the Drug Tariff. The most common exemptions are:

- persons who are exempt on age grounds;
- expectant mothers and women who have given birth in the last 12 months;
- owners of a range of exemption certificates;
- persons who receive, or are partners of someone receiving certain state benefits; and
- free of charge items including contraceptive substances and listed contraceptive appliances for women.

---

22. Schedule 1 to the National Health Service (General Medical Services Contracts) (Prescription of Drugs etc.) Regulations 2004.
23. See Drug Tariff Part XVIIIA.
24. See Drug Tariff Part XVIIIB.
25. The National Health Service (General Medical Services Contracts) (Prescription of Drugs etc.) (Amendment) Regulations 2024. The Cass review can be found at https://cass.independent-review.uk/ (accessed 30 December 2024).
26. Note that the Misuse of Drugs Regulations do permit the supply without prescription of phenobarbital or phenobarbital sodium for the treatment of epilepsy (see Chapter 14). The omission of phenobarbital and phenobarbital sodium from the NHS terms of service suggests that these products cannot be supplied in an emergency under the NHS. Such a supply would be lawful, but the pharmacy owner would not be entitled to be paid by the NHS.
27. National Health Service (Charges for Drugs and Appliances) Regulations 2015.

Where an exemption has been claimed other than on age grounds, pharmacy staff are required to check at the point of dispensing whether the patient has evidence of entitlement to the exemption (unless the exemption is confirmed by real time exemption checking).[28] Where the patient cannot produce satisfactory evidence, an *evidence not seen* box on the reverse of the prescription form must be marked with an X, but the prescription need not be refused. Where a patient does not provide, where required, evidence of entitlement to the exemption, the pharmacy must advise that checks are routinely undertaken to ascertain entitlement.[29] Any charges collected by the pharmacy owner are later offset against the payments due to the pharmacy owner.

Providing ordered drugs or appliances

When a prescription is presented in a pharmacy or the pharmacy receives an electronic prescription form from the Electronic Prescription Service (EPS), or a patient presents an EPS (hard copy) token, the pharmacy owner must, with *reasonable promptness*, supply the prescribed drugs and such appliances as are supplied in the normal course of business (paragraph 5). The pharmacy owner is expected to give an estimate of the time when drugs or appliances will be ready, if asked. The term *reasonable promptness* is not capable of precise definition and whether a supply is made with reasonable promptness is a question of fact and degree. For example, it is unlikely that a prescription must routinely be dispensed the instant that it is presented, whether a patient is on the pharmacy premises or not; but if the prescribed medication is available, circumstances may indicate that the medication should be supplied as soon as the prescription is presented, for example if it is for the treatment of a life-threatening condition or other cases of urgency, such as for the treatment of severe pain. There has also been debate about whether a pharmacy owner must immediately procure a prescribed medicine that is not in stock, even if the price of that medicine is significantly higher than the price the pharmacy owner will be reimbursed by the NHS for making the supply.[30]

The pharmacy must have constant and reliable access to the EPS, so far as this is within the owner's control, and if this fails, must supply prescribed drugs and relevant appliances within *a reasonable timescale* and take other steps for the patient as the circumstances require. It appears that the expression *a reasonable timescale* contemplates a longer period than *with reasonable promptness*. The latter expression requires promptness, but the former expression does not. In either case, whether something is reasonable will depend on all the circumstances.

---

28. See the NHS Business Services Authority website: https://www.nhsbsa.nhs.uk/help-nhs-prescription-costs/real-time-exemption-checking (accessed 30 December 2024).

29. Paragraph 7(3A) of the Terms of Service in Schedule 4 to the National Health Service (Pharmaceutical and Local Pharmaceutical Services) Regulations 2013.

30. https://www.pharmacy.biz/news/exclusive-drug-prices-what-contractors-need-to-be-aware-of/ (accessed 30 December 2024).

The pharmacy owner must only supply the drugs or appliances as ordered on the prescription (para. 8) but, provided they are not controlled drugs (other than those specified in Schedule 4 or 5 of the Misuse of Drugs Regulations 2001), pharmacists may exercise their professional skill and knowledge to remedy deficiencies on the prescription in dosage or strength, or where quantity is not stated, to supply treatment for up to five days.

Paragraph 8 also states that prescribed drugs must be provided by a pharmacist or under the direct supervision of a pharmacist. The meaning of *supervision* is discussed in **Chapters 11** and **12** where the difference between *supervision* and *direct supervision* is considered.

The following products must be supplied in a manufacturer's original pack even if the quantity supplied is different to the quantity prescribed: drugs that are sterile, effervescent or hygroscopic, a liquid preparation for addition to bath water, a coal tar preparation, a viscous preparation, or a drug that was packed at the time of its manufacture in a special container from which it is not practicable to dispense an exact quantity. The pack size supplied must be the nearest to the quantity prescribed. This provision does not apply to controlled drugs other than those in Schedule 5 to the Misuse of Drugs Regulations 2001. For reasons explained in **Chapter 12**, valproate products are designated by the Drug Tariff as *special containers*.[31]

Apart from valproate products which it is mandatory to supply in a manufacturer's original pack, the terms of service allow the supply of a different quantity (no more than 10% more or 10% less) than that prescribed, if the supply is in a manufacturer's original pack, subject to the conditions set out in **Chapter 12** (under the heading Supplies in original packs). In addition, the pharmacist must consider, in the exercise of their professional skill and judgement, whether it is reasonable and appropriate to supply a different quantity (but not more than 10% more or less than that prescribed), having regard to the benefits to patients when the drugs are provided in their manufacturer's original outer packaging.

A pharmacist may refuse to provide the items prescribed (para. 9), for example:

- where the pharmacist reasonably believes that the prescription is forged;
- where to supply would be contrary to the pharmacist's clinical judgement;
- where the pharmacist or others on the premises are subject to or threatened with violence;
- where the person presenting the prescription commits or threatens to commit a criminal offence;
- where drugs are ordered through EPS and access to EPS has failed; or
- where there are irregularities or there are other circumstances in a repeat dispensing service which mean that a repeat supply is not appropriate (in this case, the pharmacist must refuse to dispense).

31. Part II, clause 10B of the Drug Tariff.

The pharmacy owner must ensure that appropriate advice on use and information is given to patients about their drugs or appliances supplied (para. 10) to enable them to use them appropriately. This may include advice on safekeeping, returning unwanted drugs to the pharmacy owner for safe destruction, and providing guidance about only requesting repeats of items that are actually needed, and details of any items or part-items that are owed.

Patients who have a long-term stable medical condition and require regular medicine must be given appropriate advice about the benefits of repeat dispensing.

Pharmacy owners must keep and maintain records of drugs[32] and appliances provided in order to facilitate the continued care of the patient, and of any advice given and any interventions or referrals made (including clinically significant interventions in cases involving repeatable prescriptions). The pharmacy owner must notify the prescriber of any clinically significant issues arising in connection with a repeatable prescription and keep a record of that notification.

There are additional factors that apply to the essential dispensing service:

- If a pharmacy owner is presented with a prescription for a product which is the subject of a Serious Shortage Protocol (SSP) (see **Chapter 12**), the pharmacy owner must consider whether it is reasonable and appropriate to supply in accordance with the SSP instead of in accordance with the prescription form or repeatable prescription.[33]
- Pharmacy owners and dispensing doctors[34] must also make supplies in accordance with any Pandemic Treatment Protocol[35] (introduced during the COVID-19 pandemic) to allow for the supply of medicines for the prevention or treatment of diseases while a disease is pandemic or anticipated to be imminently pandemic.
- The terms of service for pharmacies (and also the respective terms of service of providers of Local Pharmaceutical Services, dispensing doctors and appliance contractors) enable NHS England during or in anticipation of a pandemic to require the provision of a home delivery service to eligible patients (likely to be those who are housebound) in the case of a medicinal product that is designated for pandemic treatment or is the subject of a SSP. This does not apply to distance selling pharmacies.
- An additional route to pandemic treatments is through a Listed Prescription Items Voucher (LPIV). A pharmacy owner must provide the item on a LPIV with reasonable promptness.

The pandemic provisions described above do not apply if the circumstances are already covered by a directed service.

---

32. The NHS legislation usually refers to *drugs* rather than to *medicines* or *medicinal products*.
33. Paragraph 5A of Schedule 4 to the Regulations.
34. Paragraph 3B of Schedule 6 to the Regulations.
35. Paragraph 5B of Schedule 4 to the Regulations.

Electronic prescription service

A pharmacy owner must have access at the listed premises to the electronic prescription service (EPS), which enables pharmacies to receive prescriptions electronically from any GP that has been authorised to issue them. So far as it is within the pharmacy owner's control, the access must be constant and reliable.[36] This places a responsibility on the pharmacy owner to ensure that, for example, appropriate hardware and software are in place, and that a reliable internet service provider is used.

Although medicines or appliances on an electronic prescription must be supplied with reasonable promptness, a pharmacy owner may refuse to provide the prescribed item if access to the EPS is not such as to enable the prescription to be dispensed promptly (or at all). If the pharmacy owner refuses to provide the item for this reason, the owner must take all reasonable steps to ensure that the product is supplied within a reasonable timescale. This may involve giving a patient the details of other pharmacies in the same area who may be able to provide the product in question. It may also involve making an urgent supply without a prescription.[37]

If the EPS is temporarily unavailable from a pharmacy, the owner of that pharmacy must provide any patient who requests with the details of at least two other pharmacies in the area at whose premises EPS is available.[38]

Summary Care Record

A pharmacy owner must have constant and reliable access at the listed premises to the Summary Care Record (SCR), which contains details from the GP's electronic records, including medicines prescribed, allergies and adverse reactions. Each pharmacy owner accessing the SCR must nominate a governance person who is responsible for auditing and reviewing access.

Pharmacy owners must access the SCR when providing pharmaceutical services, to the extent that a pharmacist in the exercise of their clinical judgement considers this to be appropriate.[39]

Other essential services

Paragraphs 13, 14 and 15 of the terms of service require that a pharmacy owner shall accept and dispose of unwanted drugs (returned from households) in the appropriate manner. NHS England provides a national framework agreement for clinical waste services for GPs and pharmacies for collection and disposal of any unwanted drugs collected at the pharmacy.

---

36. Paragraph 29B of Schedule 4 to the Regulations.
37. Paragraph 9(2A) of Schedule 4 to the Regulations.
38. Paragraph 11(1) of Schedule 4 to the Regulations.
39. Paragraph 29A of Schedule 4 to the Regulations.

The pharmacy owner must comply with the legislation applicable to waste (**Chapter 26**). Guidance on waste is available in *Safe management of healthcare waste* published by NHS England[40] (and see also **Chapter 26**).

Paragraphs 16 to 18 of the terms of service require the pharmacy owner to promote health messages to the public and to undertake prescription-linked interventions, backed up by leaflets and referral, if appropriate, for patients who have diabetes, are at risk of coronary heart disease, who smoke or who are overweight. Records of any clinically significant advice must be made in a form that facilitates audit and follow-up care. This service involves both opportunistic interventions as well as participating in up to six health campaigns a year as specified by NHS England. When requested, pharmacy owners must send relevant information on the health campaign to NHS England.

Paragraphs 19 and 20 of the terms of service set out the duty to provide information to users of the pharmacy about other health and social care providers and organisations ("signposting") where advice is requested which cannot be provided at the pharmacy.

Paragraphs 21 and 22 of the terms of service set out how the pharmacy owners shall also provide advice and support to people caring for themselves or their families. This includes providing advice on the purchase of appropriate over-the-counter medicines.

Paragraphs 22B and 22C set out the Discharge Medicines Service , to provide advice, assistance and support to patients recently discharged from a hospital or where care is transferred between different providers of NHS services.

Hours of opening

Pharmacies are required[41] to be open for the provision of pharmaceutical services for at least 40 core hours per week unless NHS England allows a lower number or directs a higher number. Change to the number or distribution of core hours requires a successful application to NHS England.

Pharmacies that had their applications for inclusion in the pharmaceutical list granted under an exemption in earlier Regulations for pharmacies undertaking to provide pharmaceutical services for at least 100 core hours per week may apply to reduce these hours, but not below 72 hours a week and any reduction cannot change core opening hours between 5pm and 9pm on Mondays to Saturdays or core opening hours between 11am and 4pm on Sundays (except that rest breaks of up to one hour during these times are permitted).

Except as mentioned below, core hours may only be changed if NHS England grants a formal application.

Pharmacies may open for longer periods than their core hours after notifying NHS England of these additional periods, which are known as *supplementary opening hours*. Supplementary opening hours may be changed after giving notice to NHS England.

---

40. https://www.england.nhs.uk/wp-content/uploads/2021/05/B2159iii-health-technical-memorandum-07-01.pdf (accessed 30 December 2024).

41. Paragraph 23 of Schedule 4 to the Regulations.

Core hours and supplementary opening hours can be changed to introduce a rest break not exceeding one hour, after notifying NHS England. This does not apply to pharmacies that had previously undertaken to open for at least 100 hours per week.

Where NHS England is satisfied that people in a particular area are experiencing, or are likely to experience, significant difficulty in accessing pharmaceutical services on a temporary basis for an identified period, NHS England may establish a local hours plan with the NHS pharmacists in that area that are willing to participate in a local hours plan for that area.[42]

Unless the pharmacy is a distance-selling pharmacy, a notice showing the hours when the pharmacy is open for the provision of pharmaceutical services must be exhibited.

At times when the pharmacy is closed, a notice must be displayed which lists the addresses of other pharmacies and their opening hours from which drugs and appliances may be obtained.

A pharmacy is not normally required to open on Good Friday, Easter Sunday, Christmas Day or on bank holidays, but NHS England has powers to direct a pharmacy to open on these days or indeed any other date or time where the needs of the people in the area are not being adequately met (subject to a right of appeal).

Where a pharmacy owner is prevented from opening by illness or other reasonable cause, if practicable, the owner must make arrangements with one or more other owners in the same area for the continued provision of services. Where such temporary suspension of services is beyond the owner's control, the owner must notify NHS England and use all reasonable endeavours to resume the provision of services.

Emergency provisions on temporary changes to opening days and hours were activated and extended by Directions during the COVID-19 pandemic.[43] In addition, further emergency provisions were introduced which allow NHS England to announce and notify pharmacy owners of changes to core and supplementary opening days or hours (including on bank holidays), while a disease is pandemic or anticipated to be imminently pandemic (which is not subject to any appeal process).[44]

Clinical governance and the promotion of healthy living

Paragraph 28 of the terms of service requires that the pharmacy owner shall "participate in an acceptable system of clinical governance and the promotion of healthy living", which must comprise:

- *A patient and public involvement programme.* This is met by means of a practice leaflet for the public giving information about the pharmacy services available from each premises, a requirement to promote the NHS services provided, the undertaking of an approved annual workforce survey, having arrangements for monitoring drugs or appliances that are out of stock, adopting monitoring arrangements to ensure

42. Paragraph 23A of Schedule 4 to the Regulations.
43. Paragraph 27 of Schedule 4 and regulation 2(5) and (6) of the Regulations.
44. Paragraph 27A of Schedule 4 to the Regulations.

compliance with the Equality Act 2010, an approved community engagement exercise in relation to healthy living, and co-operating with any statutory inspection or review.

- *A clinical audit programme.* The pharmacy owner must implement each year at least one pharmacy-determined clinical audit and one clinical or policy-based audit chosen by NHS England.
- *A risk management programme.* This includes the appointment of a clinical governance lead, arrangements to manage the quality of stock and maintenance of equipment, appropriate standard operating procedures including standard operating procedures in respect of the discharge medicines service, dispensing prescriptions and repeatable prescriptions, and providing advice and support to people caring for themselves or their families, appropriate safeguarding procedures for service users, an approved incident reporting system together with arrangements, including record keeping, for analysing and responding to critical incidents, arrangements for dealing with communications concerning patient safety such as MHRA drug alerts, waste disposal arrangements for confidential waste, and monitoring of compliance with health and safety legislation (**Chapter 26**). Incident reporting involves maintaining a patient safety incident log for all incidents. These, excluding near misses, must be reported to the Learn from Patient Safety Events Service. Pharmacies may report incidents anonymously if, for example, the error could constitute a criminal offence (see **Chapter 26**), or as part of staff "whistleblowing" in relation to unsafe dispensing practices.
- *A clinical effectiveness programme.* The programme would include having arrangements to ensure appropriate advice is given in respect to repeat dispensing and to people caring for themselves or their families.
- *A staffing and staff management programme.* This includes induction and training, checking of qualifications and references, any necessary certification or declarations in respect of the roles staff are asked to perform, addressing poor performance for all staff, identifying and supporting development needs of staff, and whistle-blowing procedures.
- *An information governance programme.* This provides for compliance with approved procedures for information management and security, and submission of an annual self-assessment of compliance via approved data submission arrangements.
- *A premises standards programme.* This includes a system for maintaining cleanliness at the pharmacy which is designed to ensure that the risk to people at the pharmacy of healthcare-acquired infection is minimised, and arrangements for compliance in the areas of the pharmacy in which patients receive NHS services with any approved particulars that are designed to ensure that those areas are an appropriate environment in which to receive healthcare. There must also be a dedicated health promotion zone (different requirements apply to distance selling pharmacies in relation to websites (see below)).

Premises requirements for consultation rooms

A pharmacy owner must ensure the pharmacy has a consultation room which is clearly designated as a room for confidential conversations where both the persons accessing and providing pharmaceutical services can be seated together and communicate effectively. An owner with an exempt pharmacy for these purposes (for example, because it is too small to have a consultation room), or a distance selling pharmacy, must ensure there are arrangements for such confidential conversations between the owner and those accessing services remotely, by live video and audio link (paragraphs 28A and 28B).

Distance selling pharmacies - requirements in respect of websites and health promotion zones

A pharmacy owner with a distance selling pharmacy must

- ensure that there are arrangements at the listed premises which enable a person providing pharmaceutical services there (such as a responsible pharmacist or employee) to communicate confidentially with a patient by telephone or via a live video link;[45]
- have a website for use by the public for the purpose of accessing pharmaceutical services from those premises, on which there is an interactive page, clearly promoted to any user of the website when they first access it, which provides public access to a reasonable range of up-to-date materials that promote healthy lifestyles by addressing a reasonable range of health issues.[46]

Professional standards

A pharmacy owner must provide pharmaceutical services and exercise professional judgement in conformity with the standards accepted in the pharmacy profession.[47] Effectively, this means that a pharmacy owner will need to adhere to the GPhC Standards for pharmacy professionals and pharmacy premises.

NHSmail, pharmacy profiles and Central Alerting System

A pharmacy must comply with the requirements for NHSmail (broadly, that at least two members of staff have a live link to the NHSmail for the pharmacy); that the Directory of Services and NHS website entries are comprehensive and up to date and verified quarterly; and register and keep up to date with the MHRA the NHSmail for the pharmacy. These requirements are to ensure pharmacies are notified in a timely manner of patients requiring the provision of relevant advanced services and pharmacy owner receive patient safety alerts, and, particularly for relevant advanced services, patients can find a pharmacy that is open (paragraph 29C).

Business continuity plans to deal with temporary suspensions

Pharmacies must have, at all times, an up-to-date business continuity plan for their premises, which is available at those premises, to deal with any temporary suspension

45. Paragraph 28B of Schedule 4 to the Regulations.
46. Paragraph 28C of Schedule 4 to the Regulations.
47. Paragraph 29 of Schedule 4 to the Regulations.

of pharmaceutical services owing to illness or another reason beyond the pharmacy owner's control.[48]

Inducements

A pharmacy owner must not give, promise or offer any person any gift or reward (whether by way of a share of or dividend on the profits of the business, or by way of discount, rebate or otherwise) as an inducement for any kind of prescriptions to be presented to a particular pharmacy or for receiving from the pharmacy any directed services.[49] The staff must also not give, promise or offer to any "relevant person" (e.g. a GP or a member of the GP's staff) any gift or reward (including by way of a share of, or dividend on, the profits of the pharmacy owner's business, or by way of discount or rebate) as an inducement to the person recommending to any person, that they present a prescription to the pharmacy, nominate the pharmacy for the purposes of the EPS, or request that the pharmacy provides them with any directed service (see below for details of *directed services*).

Direction of prescriptions

Closely related to inducements is the practice of direction of prescriptions. This involves the forwarding of prescriptions (which may be by a prescriber) to a pharmacy without the consent of the patient or, in some cases, inappropriate influencing of a patient to use a particular pharmacy. There may be a financial motive for this conduct. There are no regulatory provisions explicitly prohibiting this (although Principle 4 of the NHS Constitution[50] does give patients the right to be involved in all decisions about their care and treatment, and therefore decisions about where a prescription will be dispensed should be made by the patient). Community Pharmacy England and the British Medical Association published agreed guidelines on prescription direction.[51]

Fitness to practise

The pharmacist (including the superintendent pharmacist and other pharmacists who are directors of a pharmacy body corporate) must within seven days of its occurrence notify NHS England about:

- any conviction;
- police caution;
- discharge in Scottish summary proceedings;
- agreement to pay a fixed penalty to the Procurator Fiscal;
- being charged with a criminal offence;

---

48. Paragraph 29D of Schedule 4 to the Regulations.
49. Paragraph 30 of Schedule 4 to the Regulations.
50. https://www.gov.uk/government/publications/the-nhs-constitution-for-england/the-nhs-constitution-for-england (accessed 30 December 2024).
51. https://www.bma.org.uk/advice-and-support/gp-practices/prescribing/prescription-direction-to-certain-pharmacies (accessed 30 December 2024).

- becoming the subject of any investigation into their professional conduct in respect of their current or previous employment;
- becoming the subject of any investigation by the NHS Business Services Authority in relation to fraud;
- becoming the subject of any investigation by another primary care organisation that might lead to their removal from a relevant list;
- being removed, contingently removed, or suspended from, any relevant list for a reason relating to unsuitability, fraud or efficiency; or
- being notified by a regulatory or licensing body of an adverse finding.[52]

Facilitating remote access

A pharmacy owner must, to the extent reasonable, facilitate remote access to the pharmaceutical services as provided by the Regulations.

Education and training

A pharmacy owner must co-operate with NHS England in the discharge of the latter's duty as to education and training.[53]

Complaints

Patients may make a complaint about an NHS service either direct to the local Integrated Care Board or to the provider of the relevant service. Pharmacy owners are required to have in place arrangements which comply with the requirements of the Local Authority Social Services and National Health Service Complaints (England) Regulations 2009, for the handling and consideration of any complaints about the provision of pharmaceutical services (paragraph 34). The requirements for handling complaints are in **Box 3.3**.

Box 3.3 Requirements of complaints handling process

- A person must be appointed by the pharmacy owner to be responsible for ensuring the requirements of the Regulations are followed.
- A complaint may be made by the person who has received the service or is affected by it or a representative of a person who has died, a child or someone who is unable to make the complaint themselves. In the case of a child, the complaint must not be considered if the pharmacy owner is satisfied that there are reasonable grounds for the complaint being made by the representative instead of the child.
- Complaints are not required to be dealt with in accordance with the Regulations if they are made orally and are resolved to the complainant's satisfaction no later than the next working day.

---

52. Paragraph 31 of Schedule 4 to the Regulations.
53. Paragraph 33 of Schedule 4 to the Regulations.

Box 3.3: Requirements of complaints handling process (cont.)

- Complaints must normally be made within 12 months of the date on which the matter which is the subject of the complaint occurred or, if later, the date on which the matter came to the notice of the complainant.
- Complaints may be made orally, in writing or electronically.
- If a complaint is made orally, the pharmacy owner must make a written record and provide a copy of it to the complainant.
- The complainant must be acknowledged orally or in writing within three working days of receipt.
- The acknowledgment must contain an offer to discuss with the complainant at a time to be agreed, the manner in which the complaint is to be handled and the period within which the investigation of the complaint is likely to be completed and a response to the complaint is likely to be sent.
- If the offer to discuss is not accepted, the pharmacy owner must notify the complainant of the response period.
- Complaints must be investigated in a manner to resolve them speedily and efficiently; and the complainant must be kept informed of progress.
- As soon as reasonably practicable after completing the investigation, the complainant must be sent a report in writing, signed by the responsible person, which includes:
  - an explanation of how the complaint has been considered;
  - the conclusions reached, including any matters for which remedial action is considered necessary and confirmation as to whether any action needed has been taken or is proposed.
- If the response to the complaint is not sent within six months, the pharmacy owner must notify the complainant in writing and explain the reason and then send the response as soon as reasonably practicable.

Each local authority must make arrangements for independent advocacy services to provide assistance to anyone making or intending to make a complaint under a procedure operated by a health service body or independent prescriber, such as a pharmacy owner.[54] The Patient Advice and Liaison Service (known as *PALS*) fulfils this role.

Inspection and access to information

A pharmacy owner must allow persons authorised in writing by NHS England to enter and inspect the pharmacy at any reasonable time for the purpose of ensuring compliance with the terms of service and for the purposes of auditing, monitoring and analysing the provision of pharmaceutical services and the management by the pharmacy owner of the pharmaceutical services provided. Reasonable notice of the intended visit must first be given. The authority to enter the premises does not extend to entry to parts of the premises used solely for residential purposes. As an alternative to a physical inspection, a request may be made by or on behalf of NHS England for information that an official would have access to during a physical inspection. A pharmacy owner must provide such

54. Section 223A of the Local Government and Public Involvement in Health Act 2007.

information electronically. If NHS England request the completion of a questionnaire to determine whether it is necessary or expedient to inspect pharmacy premises, the pharmacy owner must submit electronically answers to the questionnaire.[55]

Emergency provision of pharmaceutical services

NHS England with the Secretary of State may prioritise the provision of pharmaceutical services where a pandemic is current or anticipated imminently, and may announce that pharmacy owners need not comply with specified terms of service. NHS England must not issue a breach or remedial notice against owners in such circumstances.[56]

Local pharmaceutical services

Local Pharmaceutical Services are dealt with in Part 13 of the Regulations. NHS England may commission any other services (LPS schemes) from pharmacies, including services not traditionally associated with pharmacy, to address local needs.[57] These pharmacies must provide dispensing services and the other services required by NHS England. Unlike the provision of services under the NHS terms of service, all LPS pharmacies must be contracted individually and there are mandatory terms specified in Schedule 7 to the 2013 Regulations that must be included in their contracts.

Directed services

In England, the Secretary of State has given Directions for advanced and enhanced services, using powers in the National Health Service Act.[58] These may be for advanced services (based on details in the Drug Tariff) which may be provided by any pharmacy owner who wishes to (on condition they meet the eligibility criteria); or for locally enhanced services (where fees are agreed between NHS England as the commissioner and the pharmacy owners, following consultation with the Local Pharmaceutical Committee), which will be provided only if NHS England and one or more pharmacy owners agree that the services will be provided.

Advanced services

The Directions set out the conditions that apply to the advanced services, including the New Medicine Service (NMS), the Appliance Use Review Service (AUR), the Stoma Appliance Customisation Service, the Seasonal Influenza Vaccination Service, the Pharmacy First service, the Hypertension Case-finding service, the Pharmacy Contraception Service (CPS), the Smoking Cessation Service (SCS), and the Lateral Flow Device (LFD) service.

---

55. Paragraph 35 of Schedule 4 to the Regulations.
56. Regulation 2(8), 11(3) and 71A.
57. Schedule 12 to the National Health Service Act 2006.
58. These include the Pharmaceutical Services (Advanced and Enhanced Services) (England) Directions 2013 published in the Drug Tariff.

Nationally enhanced services

NHS England may commission enhanced services at a national level, such as a COVID-19 Vaccination Service. There will be standard national conditions for such services.

Locally enhanced services

The 2013 Directions list services that may be the subject of arrangements for enhanced services.

The enhanced services specified in the Directions may be commissioned only by NHS England. Similar services may, however, be commissioned by a local authority or Integrated Care Board, but these are not described as enhanced services within the community pharmacy contractual framework.

The enhanced services include:

- independent prescribing services;
- monitoring and screening for patients taking anticoagulants;
- needle and syringe exchange schemes;
- screening services;
- services using PGD authorisation (**Chapter 13**);
- smoking cessation services;
- supervised administration of medicines for drug misuse;
- supplementary prescribing services; and
- supply of emergency hormonal contraception.

Disqualification

Under section 151 of the NHS Act, NHS England may remove from the pharmaceutical list a person:

- whose continued entry would be prejudicial to the efficiency of services;
- has caused, or risked causing, detriment to any health scheme by securing or trying to secure for themselves or another person any financial or other benefit that they knew they or the other person were not entitled to – a fraud case; or
- in the case of a person who is unsuitable, NHS England must remove them from the list.

If NHS England is satisfied that it is necessary to do so for the protection of members of the public or is otherwise in the public interest, it may suspend a person from the pharmaceutical list pending a decision whether to exercise its power under section 151.

Dispensing doctors

Part 8 of the Regulations deals with dispensing doctors. NHS England must prepare and publish a dispensing doctor list. GPs who are in such a list are entitled to supply medicines to patients who live in a controlled locality (see above) more than 1.6 kilometres from a pharmacy.

As Lord Justice Carnwath said in *R v North Yorkshire Family Health Services Authority, ex p. Wilson*[59] "it is implicit in the scheme of the regulations that it is

59. [1997] 33 BMLR 12.

desirable for pharmaceutical services to be provided by pharmacists and that provision by doctors is the exception". Since pharmacists are the healthcare professionals best qualified to deal with medicines, the 1.6 kilometre distance qualification is designed to ensure that medicines are supplied to patients from a pharmacy unless one of the conditions below is met.

Patients can request in writing that their doctor provides them with pharmaceutical services if one of the following conditions is met:

1. the patient satisfies NHS England that the patient would have serious difficulty in obtaining necessary drugs or appliances from a pharmacy by reason of distance or inadequacy of communication; or
2. the patient lives in a controlled locality at a distance of more than 1.6 kilometres from any pharmacy premises (other than distance selling pharmacies) and the doctor has outline consent to dispense and premises approval; or the doctor has the right to dispense based on previous Regulations; or
3. the patient lives in a reserved location within 1.6 kilometres of a pharmacy, and either the doctor has been granted outline consent to dispense or has the right to dispense based on previous Regulations. A reserved location is one in which, within 1.6 km of the application site, fewer than 2750 people are registered with a GP.

An application to NHS England by a doctor or medical practice for outline consent will be refused to the extent that any part of the geographical area specified in the application is not in a controlled locality or is within 1.6 kilometres of pharmacy premises that are not distance selling pharmacies. If the application is not refused on these grounds, it will be granted unless doing so would prejudice the proper provision of relevant NHS services. The prejudice test usually involves consideration of the financial position of any pharmacy that may cease to be viable because patients of the applicant cease to use the pharmacy and use the applicant's dispensing service instead. If an application for outline consent is refused, a new application cannot be made for five years.

If outline consent is granted, premises approval will be granted at the same time, but premises approval can also be granted separately, for example if a dispensing doctor wishes to dispense from different premises to those in respect of which outline consent has previously been granted.

General Practitioners will have contracts with NHS England for the provision of medical services, but these contracts do not govern the arrangements for the provision of pharmaceutical services by dispensing doctors: dispensing doctors have separate terms of service which can be found in Schedule 6 to the Regulations.

The NHS Constitution

The NHS Constitution establishes the principles and values of the NHS in England. It sets out patient and staff rights and responsibilities. The constitution includes a right to complain about the provision of services. There are seven key principles of the NHS Constitution (see **Box 3.4**).

Box 3.4: Key Principles of the NHS Constitution

1. The NHS provides a comprehensive service, available to all;
2. Access to NHS services is based on clinical need, not an individual's ability to pay;
3. The NHS aspires to the highest standards of excellence and professionalism;
4. The patient will be at the heart of everything the NHS does;
5. The NHS works across organisational boundaries and in partnership with other organisations in the interest of patients, local communities and the wider population;
6. The NHS is committed to providing best value for taxpayers' money and the most effective, fair and sustainable use of finite resources; and
7. The NHS is accountable to the public, communities and patients that it serves.

Under section 13C of the National Health Service Act, NHS England must, in the exercise of its functions -

a. act with a view to securing that health services are provided in a way which promotes the NHS Constitution, and
b. promote awareness of the NHS Constitution among patients, staff and members of the public.

Under section 14Z32 of the Act, each ICB must do the same.

NHS directions and policy statements

Power is also given to the Secretary of State for Health and Social Care (or equivalent ministers in Scotland and Wales) to make additional *Directions* written by senior civil servants acting under the authority of the relevant minister.

NHS Guidance

Ministers and other NHS bodies may give guidance from time to time. Since ministers and NHS bodies only have the powers given to them by an Act of Parliament or by secondary legislation, any such guidance must be consistent with their powers. Examples of cases in which guidance has been challenged include the cases of *R v Secretary of State for Health Ex p. Pfizer Ltd*[60] (involving the prescribing of Viagra) and *Gillick*[61] (also dealt with in **Chapter 24**) details of which are in **Box 3.5**.

Box 3.5: Challenges to guidance by NHS bodies

The Gillick case – guidance on family planning services

In *Gillick v West Norfolk and Wisbech Area Health Authority*, decided by the House of Lords, the Department of Health and Social Security had given guidance on family planning services. The guidance contained a section dealing with contraceptive advice and treatment for young people. Mrs Victoria Gillick argued that the guidance was unlawful because it undermined parental rights and duties. Although the guidance was held to be lawful, Lord Bridge said:

---

60. [1965] AC 512.

61. [1986] AC 112.

Box 3.5: Challenges to guidance by NHS bodies (cont.)

"We must now say that if a government department, in a field of administration in which it exercises responsibility, promulgates in a public document, albeit non-statutory in form, advice which is erroneous in law, then the court … has jurisdiction to correct the error of law by an appropriate declaration."

Lord Bridge qualified his comment by suggesting that the courts would only rarely deal with such cases and that if guidance was "interwoven with questions of social and ethical controversy", the court would only deal with questions of law: it would not express any opinion on the questions of social and ethical controversy.

This case is important in relation to the law of consent to treatment and it is discussed in more detail in **Chapter 24**.

Guidance banning the prescribing of Viagra

In *R v Secretary of State for Health Ex p. Pfizer Ltd*, Pfizer was about to obtain a marketing authorisation from the MHRA for its new drug Viagra (sildenafil) for the treatment of erectile dysfunction (ED). If the drug was available on the NHS, the cost to the NHS was expected to be considerable. The Department of Health issued a Circular to doctors with interim guidance that sildenafil should not be prescribed other than in exceptional circumstances.

Pfizer Ltd applied for judicial review of the guidance, arguing that it was unlawful. Mr Justice Collins considered the Secretary of State's duty in the National Health Service Act 1977 (the forerunner of the current National Health Service Act) to promote a comprehensive health service and effective services. The Act also imposed a duty on the Secretary of State to provide medical services "to such extent as he considers necessary to meet all reasonable requirements". The Act did not give the Secretary of State specific power to issue directions to the effect that prevented a drug from being prescribed either wholly or partly. Indeed, there was a duty which was the equivalent of the one now imposed on NHS England in section 83 of the National Health Service Act 2006 for a predecessor of NHS England to arrange with general medical practitioners (GPs) the provision of medical services.

Regulations made under the National Health Service Act required GPs to exercise professional judgement and to provide patients with all necessary and appropriate medical services. GPs were also required to order any drugs or appliances needed for the treatment of any patient by issuing a prescription form. These obligations are replicated in Part 14 of the standard General Medical Services contract for GPs.

The Secretary of State argued that the Circular was only advisory and did not have the effect of banning GPs from prescribing sildenafil. However, Mr Justice Collins held that the advice in the Circular was intended to be acted upon by GPs independently of whether in their professional judgement a patient needing treatment for ED could have sildenafil prescribed for him: the advice in the Circular was given in a manner which meant that GPs would inevitably regard it as overriding their professional judgement. The advice in the Circular was therefore held to be unlawful.

The decision in the Pfizer case may be compared with the case of *Bayer v Darlington Clinical Commissioning Group* (see **Chapter 5**, **Box 5.4**) in which the court held that it was lawful for a CCG to give guidance which *encouraged* clinicians to prescribe a lower cost drug that was unlicensed.

Health Service Commissioner

The Health Service Commissioners Act 1993 gives the Health Service Commissioner for England (the Act originally also established Commissioners for Scotland and Wales) certain powers. The Health Service Commissioner is often referred to as an Ombudsman.

Under section 2 of the Act, the Commissioner can investigate complaints concerning NHS bodies such as NHS England and Integrated Care Boards. The Commissioner's remit covers complaints by or on behalf of a person that they have sustained injustice or hardship in consequence of:

a. a failure in a service by a health service body;
b. a failure of such a body to provide a service which it was a function of the body to provide; or
c. maladministration connected with any action taken by or on behalf of such a body.

Under section 2A of the Act, the Commissioner can investigate complaints concerning persons (whether individuals or bodies) providing NHS services under a contract and specifically persons who provide pharmaceutical services, local pharmaceutical services, primary medical services or dental services under the NHS (all of whom are defined as *family health service providers*). The Commissioner can investigate complaints against family health service providers by or on behalf of a person that they have sustained injustice or hardship in consequence of action taken by the family health service provider or an employee or someone acting on behalf of the provider in connection with NHS services.

The powers of the Health Service Commissioner include investigating the exercise of clinical judgement.

The Commissioner does not have power to investigate the merits of a decision made by a health service body or a family health services provider unless there has been maladministration.

The Commissioner may not (section 4) conduct an investigation if the person aggrieved has a remedy by way of proceedings in any court of law unless the Commissioner is satisfied that it is not reasonable to expect the aggrieved person to resort to it.

Complaints must be made in writing by the person aggrieved, a member of their family or a representative (section 9). A public body may not make a complaint to the Health Services Commissioner, but a health service body may refer itself in writing to the Commissioner (section 10).

It is an offence to obstruct the Commissioner or the Commissioner's officers in the exercise of the Commissioner's functions.

The Commissioner does not have power to award compensation or impose a financial penalty, but may make recommendations, for example as to the payment of compensation or that improvements to services are made. The Commissioner must send a report to the complainant and to the health service body or the services provider in respect of whom the complaint was made.

The Commissioner's website[62] cites a February 2015 case of a patient who was prescribed medication for a sore leg. The patient was instead given antidepressant medication intended for another patient. Not knowing she had been given the wrong

62. https://www.ombudsman.org.uk/about-us/our-casework/how-our-casework-makes-difference/case-summaries/861 (accessed 30 December 2024).

medication, the patient took the antidepressant medication and became ill with dizzy spells for two weeks. The pharmacy had acknowledged its failings but had refused to pay compensation. The patient's complaint was upheld. The Commissioner was satisfied with the pharmacy's apology and service improvements but agreed with the patient that she should be paid compensation. The pharmacy owner paid the patient £250.

Health Services Safety Investigations Body

The Health and Care Act 2022 established the Health Services Safety Investigations Body (HSSIB). The HSSIB has the function of investigating incidents that occur in England during the provision of health care services and may have implications for the safety of patients. The HSSIB must publish reports on its investigations, but a report may not be produced in evidence in any criminal or civil proceedings unless the High Court orders that the report is admissible because the interests of justice served by admitting the report outweigh any adverse impact on current or future investigations by deterring persons from providing information for the purposes of investigations, or any adverse impact outweighs the improvement of the safety of health and care services.

HSSIB investigators have powers to:

- enter and inspect premises in England other than private dwellings,
- inspect and take copies of any document,
- inspect, seize, and remove any document, equipment or other item (unless that would risk the safety of any patient), and
- give a notice requiring any person to attend a place to provide information (but such a person is not required to provide any information or document if it might incriminate them).

The HSSIB must co-operate with certain other bodies, including NHS England, ICBs, the CQC and regulators such as the GPhC, and those bodies must co-operate with the HSSIB.

The HSSIB may enter into an agreement to carry out investigations into incidents in Wales.

Medicines price control

A voluntary regulatory scheme to allow the NHS to have access to good quality, proprietary medicines at reasonable prices while allowing a fair return for the pharmaceutical industry applies to the whole of the UK. It is underpinned by powers to control prices in sections 260 to 266 of the NHS Act 2006. While the bulk of the industry participates in the voluntary scheme, those that do not are subject to statutory controls. The legislation allows the NHS to control the prices it will pay to any company which chooses not to sign up to the voluntary agreement or for any (unbranded) generic medicine where there is insufficient competition in the market to maintain reasonable prices. Regulations under this Act[63] impose various duties on suppliers in the medicines

63. Health Service Products (Provision and Disclosure of Information) Regulations 2018.

supply chain and, for example, impose a duty on UK producers – defined as *a person who manufactures, distributes or supplies any UK health service products* – to record and retain for four years the following information:

a. the invoice for the purchase of the presentation,
b. if any discounts, payments, payments or benefits in kind given in connection with the purchase are not included in the invoice, a statement of those discounts, payments or payments or benefits in kind,
c. the name of the person from whom the presentation is purchased,
d. the quantity, by pack size, purchased,
e. the net purchase amount, or a reasonable estimate of the net purchase amount, paid for the purchase, and
f. the terms on which any discounts, payments, or payments or benefits in kind were given to the producer.

The producer must supply in response to a written request from the Secretary of State information about costs incurred in connection with the manufacture or distribution of health service medicines and appliances.

Local Pharmaceutical Committees

Local Pharmaceutical Committees (LPCs) are recognised by NHS England under section 167 of the NHS Act 2006 as representative of the persons providing pharmaceutical services in the area for which it is formed. LPCs will each have a constitution which governs their membership and activities.

LPCs may request NHS England to deduct from the remuneration payable to persons who provide services, sums for defraying the LPC's administrative expenses. These deductions are known as a *levy* and in part are used to finance Community Pharmacy England (see below).

Community Pharmacy England (formerly called the Pharmaceutical Services Negotiating Committee or PSNC)

Remuneration for the provision of pharmaceutical services must be determined by the Secretary of State. Section 165 of the NHS Act says that before a determination is made, the Secretary of State must consult a body appearing to him to be representative of persons to whose remuneration the determination would relate. This body is Community Pharmacy England. Community Pharmacy England is also recognised by the Secretary of State as being representative of pharmacy owners in England in relation to NHS matters generally, including terms and conditions of service.

Other NHS bodies

Other NHS bodies whose functions affect pharmacy practice include:

- *The NHS Business Services Authority* which is responsible for processing prescriptions and paying for the provision of services and, increasingly, administration functions on behalf of NHS England that relate to owners, for example, post payment verification of certain payment claims.

- *The NHS Counter Fraud Authority* which is responsible for identifying, investigating and preventing fraud and other economic crime within the NHS. Whereas the word fraud in a technical sense involves dishonesty (see **Chapter 25** for a definition of *dishonesty*) this body will, in practice, also look into cases that do not involve dishonesty. Examples of cases it investigates are set out in **Box 3.6**.

Box 3.6: The types of case investigated by the NHS Counter Fraud Authority

The types of case investigated by the NHS Counter Fraud Authority include:

- prescriptions not dispensed as claimed, such as the supply of a lower quantity or strength of medication;
- dispensing counterfeit medicines;
- improperly supplying out-of-date or split-pack medicines previously supplied to another patient or remuneration or reimbursement claims made inadvertently as well as deliberately;
- false claims made for the supply of medicines to *ghost* patients who do not exist or were deceased at the time of alleged supply;
- claims that indicate patients have not paid NHS prescription charges when patients have, in fact, done so;
- inflated claims for fees, allowances and reimbursement inconsistently with entitlement under the Drug Tariff, such as specials, claiming reimbursement for the supply of a branded product when a cheaper generic product has been supplied (see the Cardiff Crown Court example below), out of pocket expenses and No Cheaper Stock Obtainable;
- patients who dishonestly evade prescription charges; and
- patients who present forged or stolen prescriptions.

At Cardiff Crown Court on 22 October 2019, a pharmacist who was the director of a company owning four pharmacies was sentenced to 16 months' imprisonment for repeatedly submitting to the NHS Business Services Authority claims for payment that falsely stated that he had supplied a more expensive item than he had actually provided to patients. The frauds were all committed at one of the company's pharmacies and involved claiming that memantine and donepezil had been supplied in liquid form when medication had actually been supplied in tablet form at lower cost. He also altered the endorsements made by employed pharmacists to claim for the supply of liquid medication when less expensive items had been supplied. The false claims involved a fraud of £76,475.[64]

It should be noted that the NHS Counter Fraud Service does not only investigate cases where fraud is suspected. For example, it investigates what it sees as "abuse of contract" involving payment for services where the NHS terms of service have been breached; and it investigates suspected price fixing; and suspected anti-competitive conduct on the part of pharmaceutical companies who may charge unfair prices to the NHS.

64. https://cfa.nhs.uk/about-nhscfa/latest-news/director-of-pharmacy-chain-jailed-for-76K-fraud (accessed 30 December 2024).

Clinical pharmacists in general practice

Many pharmacists and pharmacy technicians work in GP practices. Each practice will usually have a primary medical services contract with NHS England.

Groups of GP practices may work together as a Primary Care Network (PCN). The Directed Enhanced Services Directions 2019 enabled certain Directed Enhanced Services (DES) to be provided by PCNs. The Network Contract DES enables PCNs to be reimbursed for the engagement of clinical pharmacists and pharmacy technicians who satisfy specified training criteria. When a PCN enters into such a contract, the primary medical services contracts of participating GPs will be varied so as to incorporate the Network Contract DES.

The training criteria and the roles are set out in Annex B of the Network Contract DES.[65]

Scotland

NHS law in Scotland

Scotland has had its own Parliament since July 1999 and it has powers to make primary legislation on healthcare. The principal Act is the National Health Service (Scotland) Act 1978 (the Act).The main regulations made under the Act are the National Health Service (Pharmaceutical Services) (Scotland) Regulations 2009 (referred to below as *the Regulations*).

Structure

NHS Scotland policy is developed and administered through the Scottish Government Health Department via 14 territorial "unified" NHS boards. Primary and secondary care are separate divisions within the unified NHS boards, with representation from each local authority to improve management of health and social care. In addition, there is oversight of the board's activities by Healthcare Improvement Scotland. This was established by the Public Services Reform (Scotland) Act 2010.

The functions of the NHS boards include the planning and provision of healthcare services and the management of pharmacy contracts. Amongst other things, Health Boards must prepare a scheme to ensure that one or more pharmacies are open at all reasonable times.[66] Any such scheme must specify the days and hours during which pharmacies are open, and the arrangements for the dispensing of medicines required urgently at other times.

The Scottish Health Council monitors the performance of the NHS boards and promotes public involvement in healthcare. Each board also supports community health partnerships, which have the same geographical areas as local authorities, and which focus on planning and provision of local health services. Each community health partnership has on its committee a place for a registered pharmacist whose name is included in, or who is fully or substantially employed by a person or body whose name is included in, a pharmaceutical list prepared by an NHS board. Most NHS boards have the

65. https://www.england.nhs.uk/wp-content/uploads/2024/03/PRN01035-ii-pcn-des-contract-specification-2024-25-pcn-requirements-and-entitlements-April-2024-version-2.pdf (accessed 30 December 2024).

66. Regulation 11 of the Regulations.

services of a pharmacist, called variously a "consultant" or "specialist" in pharmaceutical public health and who provides strategic pharmacy advice to the NHS board. The overall control of pharmaceutical services within each NHS board lies with the board's director of pharmacy. In addition, all NHS boards have an area pharmaceutical committee. These committees comprise pharmacists who work in both the hospital and community sectors and are representative of the professionals working, or living, in the area.

The Practitioner Services Division of NHS National Services Scotland manages payments for pharmacy owners. Responsibility for inspection and audit of healthcare lies with the NHS Healthcare Improvement Scotland. The Scottish Health Council represents the patient's voice in healthcare and may inspect both primary and secondary care establishments.

Under Regulation 15 of the Regulations, Health Boards are obliged to publish Pharmaceutical Care Services Plans. Boards also have to monitor their Pharmaceutical Care Services Plan annually to reflect changes in service provision or patient needs.

Area Pharmaceutical Committees

Under section 9 of the National Health Service (Scotland) Act 1978, Health Boards recognise local committees that are representative of pharmacy owners in their respective areas. These are Area Pharmaceutical Committees (APCs). Their function is to advise Health Boards (and NHS trusts, if so directed by the Secretary of State). However, it is not the function of APCs to be concerned with remuneration and conditions of service.

In exercising their functions, Health Boards and NHS Trusts must consult APCs to the extent that they are directed to do so by the Secretary of State.

Community Pharmacy Scotland

Except for locally commissioned services, remuneration for NHS services is determined by the Secretary of State. Before determining remuneration, the Secretary of State must consult a body that is representative of persons to whose remuneration the determination would relate. This body is Community Pharmacy Scotland.[67]

Scottish terms of service

The Terms of Service for pharmacists and pharmacy contractors in Scotland are contained in Schedule 1 to the Regulations.[68]

The Scottish terms of service incorporate the Patient Rights (Scotland) Act 2011. This Act requires the Scottish Ministers to publish the Charter of Patient Rights and Responsibilities.[69] In performing their functions, NHS bodies such as Health Boards and the Common Services Agency must uphold the health care principles in the Schedule

---

67. Section 28B of the Act.
68. National Health Service (Pharmaceutical Services) (Scotland) Regulations 2009.
69. https://www.gov.scot/publications/charter-patient-rights-responsibilities-revised-june-2022/pages/2/ (accessed 30 December 2024).

to the Act, and ensure that any person with whom it enters into a contract, agreement or arrangements (which would include pharmacy owners who provide services under the NHS) upholds the principles.

Features of the Charter that are relevant to pharmacy, and examples of the principles are set out in **Box 3.7**.

Box 3.7

The Charter of Patient Rights and Responsibilities
(features specifically relevant to pharmacy)

- Patients have the right to be given all the information they need about their medicines, their possible side effects, and other options which may be available in a way they can understand.
- Patients can ask for more information if they are not sure how to take any medicines.
- Patients should order repeat prescriptions in plenty of time, and only order the items they continue to need.
- Patients can speak to a healthcare professional involved in their care if they want to change or stop the treatment prescribed for them.
- Patients have the right to be involved in decisions about their treatment.

Health care principles
(Examples)

- Patients must be treated with dignity and respect.
- Healthcare is provided in a caring and compassionate manner.
- Support necessary to receive or access health care is available.
- The patient's abilities, characteristics and circumstances are considered.
- Patients participate as fully as possible in decisions relating to their health and wellbeing.
- Communication about a patient's health and wellbeing is clear, accessible and understood.

There are many similarities between the terms of service in Scotland and in England. Amongst the differences:

- When providing drugs or appliances a pharmacist must:[70]
  - use all reasonable endeavours to provide those drugs or appliances with reasonable promptness;
  - refrain from taking any action which may delay or prevent the dispensing of those drugs or appliances; and
  - contact the prescriber or dentist to discuss alternative arrangements where there is likely to be, in that pharmacist's opinion, a clinically significant delay in the dispensing of those drugs or appliances.
- Pharmacy owners may notify the Local Health Board that they wish to be excluded from the arrangements for the supply of contraceptive substances and appliances.[71]

---

70. Paragraph 4(1A).

71. Paragraph 1 of Schedule 1 to the National Health Service (Pharmaceutical Services) (Scotland) Regulations 2009.

- Pharmacies are not permitted to accept prescription forms at premises that are not a registered pharmacy, but this prohibition does not apply to collection and delivery arrangements.[72] In the *Petition of Community Pharmacy Scotland*,[73] the judge, Lord Harrower, held that the use of prescription lockers (or kiosks) from which patients collected dispensed medicines that had been prescribed for them fell within the meaning of collection and delivery services that are permitted (see **Chapter 12**), so that the use of these arrangements did not breach the terms of service.
- Pharmacies may not provide pharmaceutical services from any pharmacy or other premises which are not included in the pharmaceutical list in respect of that pharmacy contractor. However, this does not apply to collection and delivery services (see **Chapter 12**).[74]
- Although there are no prescription charges in Scotland, if an English prescription is presented, there is no obligation to supply the prescribed item unless the patient pays the prescription charge that would be applicable if the prescription had been presented in England.[75]

Core services

Core services which all pharmacies must provide comprise:

- *NHS Pharmacy First Service.* The service comprises a consultation with a pharmacist or with a trained member of staff under the direct supervision of a pharmacist and, where the pharmacist or trained member of staff under the direct supervision of a pharmacist considers it appropriate, the supply of medicines, dressings or appliances for its treatment. [76]
- *Public Health Service.* This involves community pharmacists and staff in national programmes to promote healthy lifestyles and public health interventions such as smoking cessation, chlamydia screening and supply of emergency hormonal contraception.
- *Acute Medication Service.* This involves the electronic transmission of acute prescriptions.
- *Medicines: Care and Review (includes serial prescribing).* This covers the dispensing of repeat prescriptions for patients with long-term conditions, and the management of patients' medication in conjunction with their GP. Patients who are eligible must be registered with the pharmacy that provides the service.[77] Serial prescriptions must be first presented within 24 weeks of having been signed by the prescriber, and

72. Paragraph 4(12).
73. [2023] CSOH 65.
74. Paragraph 6(4) and 6(4A)
75. Paragraph 4(1B).
76. https://www.nhsinform.scot/care-support-and-rights/nhs-services/pharmacy/nhs-pharmacy-first-scotland (accessed 30 December 2024).
77. Paragraph 4(2A).

a prescription may cover supply for up to 56 weeks. Controlled drugs are outside the scope of the service.
- Quality improvement which involves using a set of tools, techniques and ways of working to improve the quality of outcomes for people who use services.

National services

National services (which are optional) include:

- *Stoma care services.* This is provided for patients in the community.
- *Gluten Free Food Service.* Patients with coeliac disease can obtain from their local community pharmacy gluten free products from a National prescribable list without the need to obtain prescriptions from their General Practitioner.[78]
- *Unscheduled care* – care that cannot reasonably be foreseen or planned in advance. This can include Community Pharmacy Unscheduled Supply Service (CPUS). CPUS allows pharmacies to provide patients with up to one prescribing cycle of their repeat medicines and appliances when it's not possible to get a prescription, such as on weekends or holidays.

Local services

Local services that may be commissioned include:

- Advice to Residential Homes.
- Support for people with substance misuse issues.
- Needle Exchange Services.
- Compliance support solutions.
- Disposal of Patients' Unwanted Medicines.
- Out of Hours rotas.
- Collection and delivery services.

Breaches of terms of service

Arrangements for disciplinary service committees and tribunals are covered by the National Health Service (Tribunal) (Scotland) Regulations 2004 under which a tribunal can disqualify a person from providing pharmaceutical services on the grounds of efficiency or fraud.

Scottish Public Services Ombudsman

The Scottish Public Services Ombudsman, established under the Scottish Public Services Ombudsman Act 2002, has power to investigate complaints about NHS bodies and against the providers of NHS pharmaceutical services.

---

78. https://www.nhsinform.scot/care-support-and-rights/nhs-services/pharmacy/gluten-free-food-service (accessed 30 December 2024) and https://www.communitypharmacy.scot.nhs.uk/media/1512/pca2015-p-24-gf.pdf (accessed 30 December 2024).

Control of entry

Control of entry to pharmaceutical lists in Scotland (referred to in England as *market entry*) differs from that in England and in Wales. Although Pharmaceutical Care Services Plans have some similarities to Pharmaceutical Needs Assessments, applications for inclusion in a pharmaceutical list are not directly linked to them. Unlike in England, there is no provision for the inclusion in pharmaceutical lists in Scotland of distance selling pharmacies.

Applications for change of ownership will generally be granted automatically. Applications for relocation within the same neighbourhood will be granted if they are minor. A relocation will be classed as minor if there will be no significant change in the neighbourhood population in respect of which pharmaceutical services are provided by the applicant and other circumstances are such that there will be no significant effect on the pharmaceutical services provided by the applicant or any other person whose name is included in the pharmaceutical list of the Board.

All applications are considered under the terms of regulation 5(10) of the 2009 Regulations, by the NHS Board Pharmacy Practices Committee.

Other than applications for change of ownership or minor relocation, an application will be granted only if it is satisfied that the provision of pharmaceutical services at the premises named in the application is necessary or desirable in order to secure adequate provision of pharmaceutical services in the neighbourhood in which the premises are located by persons whose names are included in the pharmaceutical list. In *Lloyds Pharmacy Ltd v National Appeal Panel*,[79] Lord Drummond-Young explained:

> *"It is a two-stage test. Having identified the relevant neighbourhood, the decision maker must first consider whether the existing provision of pharmaceutical services in that neighbourhood is adequate. If it decides that such provision is adequate, that is the end of the matter and the application must fail. However, if the decision maker determines that such provision is not adequate, it must go on to consider a second question: whether the provision of a pharmaceutical services at the premises named in the application is 'necessary or desirable' in order to secure adequate provision."*

Before making an application to which the necessary or desirable test applies, the intended applicant must consult the local Health Board and undertake a joint consultation with the local Health Board to assess whether the neighbourhood already has adequate provision of pharmaceutical services, and to establish the level of support for the application from residents in the neighbourhood.[80]

If the boundaries of the neighbourhood within which an applicant intends to provide pharmaceutical services falls within any part of a controlled locality (an area that is

---

79. [2012] CSOH 22.

80. Regulation 5A.

rural in character), the Board cannot grant the application unless it is also satisfied that granting it would not prejudice the provision of NHS funded services in the controlled locality. This test refers to financial impact of granting the application on dispensing doctors and others.

The procedure for dealing with applications and for appeals is set out in Schedule 4 to the Regulations. Appeals on the decisions of the Pharmacy Practices Committee may be made to the National Appeal Panel.

Healthcare waste guidance

Guidance on the disposal of healthcare waste, including medicines, is published by the Scottish Environment Protection Agency.[81]

Wales

In Wales, the statutory powers of the NHS stem from the National Health Service (Wales) Act 2006 (the Act). Under the Act subordinate legislation has been made, such as the Pharmaceutical Services (Advanced and Enhanced Services) (Wales) Directions 2005 (which set out the advanced and enhanced services that may be provided, and the National Health Service (Pharmaceutical Services) (Wales) Regulations 2020 (the 2020 Regulations).

The Act brings together a range of provisions relating to the establishment and implementation of a Welsh health service. It defines the duty of Welsh Ministers to promote an effective, efficient and economical provision of certain administrative, professional and technical services (the shared services) as well as giving them a general power to provide these services. It allows Welsh Ministers to give directions to NHS bodies on the way in which they are established and regulated as well as how they should exercise those functions delegated to them.

The Act empowers Ministers to create Local Health Boards (LHBs) and to direct them to exercise functions in the areas of each LHB. The National Health Service (Wales) Act 2006 contains equivalent legislation to the NHS Act 2006 which applies to England. However, the NHS Act 2006 also contains some legislation that applies to both England and Wales. Key sections of this Act include section 72 which places a duty on NHS bodies to co-operate with each other in exercising their functions and section 82 which places a duty on NHS bodies and local authorities to co-operate with one another in order to secure and advance the health and welfare of the people of England and Wales. All NHS bodies in Wales are required to take cognisance of any wider, relevant legislative framework.

Responsibilities and accountability

The Welsh Government's Health and Social Services Director General has responsibility for the issuing of instructions and guidance to NHS bodies in relation to the conduct of

81. https://www.sepa.org.uk/media/woqdaa1l/guidance-for-the-storage-and-treatment-of-healthcare-waste.pdf (accessed 30 December 2024).

certain activities. Welsh Ministers have established arrangements for providing for the delivery and strategic planning of shared services as well as a governance framework. They have also made arrangements for the reporting and monitoring of performance of the shared services by the NHS Wales Shared Services Partnership Committee (the Committee). The LHBs and Trusts have now delegated responsibility and accountability for the continued development, operational management, and performance of Shared Services to the Director, NHS Wales Shared Services (*the Director of Shared Services*) who has been appointed on their behalf. The Director is accountable to the Chief Executive of the NHS in Wales.

Shared Service Provision and Pharmacy in Wales

The NHS Wales Shared Services Partnership (NWSSP) is an independent organisation, owned and directed by NHS Wales, providing support functions and services. These functions include some of those carried out in England by the NHS Business Services Authority and the NHS Counter Fraud Service. NWSSP also deals with applications for inclusion in the pharmaceutical list.

Welsh Health Boards and NHS Trusts have collaborated over the operational arrangements for the provision of the NHS Shared Services and have agreed the terms of a Co-operation Agreement for implementation of these services (the Co-operation Agreement) setting out how they will work together to ensure that the arrangements are introduced and operate effectively by collective decision making.

NWSSP Primary Care Services provide a wide range of services to and on behalf of Welsh Health Boards and the Welsh Government. These cover primary care owners, appliance contractors, reimbursements to primary care owners, post-payment verification (PPV) and patient registration services.

The Shared Service relevant to pharmacy is Primary Care Services, a division of the NHS Wales Shared Services Partnership. The partnership is responsible for reimbursement services to pharmacies, GPs and appliance contractors for the medicines and devices they provide on NHS prescriptions. Additionally, they are responsible for the provision of prescribing and dispensing information to NHS staff delivering medicines management services.

Community Pharmacy Contract in Wales

Like England and Scotland, pharmaceutical lists must be maintained, listing pharmacy owners who have undertaken to provide pharmaceutical services. Applications for inclusion in a pharmaceutical list are made to the LHB in which it is proposed to establish the pharmacy. The National Health Service (Pharmaceutical Services) (Wales) Regulations 2020 (the 2020 Regulations) contain the detailed arrangements for the provision of pharmaceutical services in Wales. In summary:

- Part 2 requires LHBs to prepare pharmaceutical needs assessments (PNAs) at least every five years. Schedule 1 to the 2020 Regulations sets out the information that must be included in PNA.
- Part 3 requires LHBs to prepare and maintain pharmaceutical lists and dispensing doctor lists.

- Part 4 deals with procedures in rural areas.
- Part 5 deals with the different types of application that may be made for inclusion in a pharmaceutical list or for relocation. They include applications:
  - for preliminary consent that, if granted, enable an application to be made on a later occasion in the knowledge that the later application will be granted;
  - for inclusion in a pharmaceutical list that will be granted if the LHB is satisfied that granting it will meet a need for pharmaceutical services or pharmaceutical services of a specified type, in the area of the LHB and which have been included in the PNA. In a controlled locality (one which is rural in character), the HB must also be satisfied that granting the application will not prejudice the proper provision of primary medical, dispensing or pharmaceutical services in any locality. There is an exception to this prejudice test if the premises are in a reserved location (which, subject to certain exceptions, is a location in respect of which the number of individuals on the lists of GPs for the area within 1.6 kilometres of the proposed premises is less than 2,750 persons);
  - for relocation within a LHB's area, which will be granted if:
    a. amongst other things, the LHB is satisfied that the relocation is to meet a need for pharmaceutical services, or pharmaceutical services of a specified type, identified in the relevant PNA and, if granted, the relocation would not result in a significant change to the arrangements that are in place for the provision of pharmaceutical services (other than those provided by dispensing doctors); or
    b. the relocation is not to meet a need for pharmaceutical services, or pharmaceutical services of a specified type, but, amongst other things, for the patients who are accustomed to accessing pharmaceutical services at the existing premises, the location of the new premises is not significantly less accessible;
  - for relocation to a neighbouring LHB area if, amongst other things, the LHB for the area to which the relocation would be made is satisfied that the change is to meet a need identified in that LHB's PNA and there would not be a significant change in the arrangements that are in place for the provision of pharmaceutical services (other than those provided by dispensing doctors);
  - for change of ownership.
- Part 6 deals with applications by doctors for inclusion in dispensing doctor lists, giving them the right to be paid by the NHS for supplying medicines to their patients.
- Part 7 deals with the fitness of applicants for inclusion in pharmaceutical lists and removal from pharmaceutical lists.
- Part 9 deals with performance related sanctions and market exit, including breaches of terms of service and remedial notices and breach notices.
- Part 10 deals with the Welsh Drug Tariff and remuneration.

The terms of service for pharmacies providing NHS services are in Schedule 5 to the 2020 Regulations. Like the terms of service in England, the terms set out, amongst other things, essential services, the hours during which services are to be provided, clinical governance and complaints. Like England, Wales has regulations that lists drugs, medicines or other substances that may not be prescribed or which may only be prescribed in certain circumstances.[82] For example, in 2024, the regulations were amended so as to restrict the circumstances in which drugs and medicines that consist of or contain gonadotrophin-releasing hormone analogues (known as puberty blockers) could be prescribed.

Waste management

Guidance on the disposal of medicines waste is included in a Welsh Technical Memorandum.[83]

Complaints and concerns

Complaints and concerns about Welsh NHS services are governed by the National Health Service (Concerns, Complaints and Redress Arrangements) (Wales) Regulations 2011. Under these regulations, obligations are placed on responsible bodies. The definition of "responsible body" includes both Local Health Boards and primary care providers such as pharmacy owners.

Each responsible body must designate a person to take overall responsibility for the effective day to day operation of the arrangements for dealing with concerns in an integrated manner. Each responsible body must also designate a senior investigations manager, to undertake responsibility for the handling and consideration of concerns. The functions of a senior investigations manager can be delegated to another person who is authorised by the responsible body.

A concern may be notified:

(a) in writing;
(b) electronically; or
(c) verbally, either by telephone or in person, to any member of the staff of the responsible body, the exercise of whose functions is the subject of the concern.

Where a concern is notified verbally, the member of staff of the responsible body to whom the concern has been notified must:

(a) make a written record of the concern; and
(b) provide a copy of the written record to the person who notified the concern.

A concern about a primary care provider may be notified either to the Local Health Board or to the provider not later than twelve months after:

(a) the date on which the matter which is the subject of the concern occurred; or

---

82. The National Health Service (General Medical Services Contracts) (Prescription of Drugs Etc.) (Wales) Regulations 2004 were amended by the National Health Service (General Medical Services Contracts) (Prescription of Drugs Etc.) (Wales) (Amendment) Regulations 2024 and the National Health Service (Prescription of Drugs Etc.) (Wales) (Amendment) (No.2) Regulations 2024.

83. https://nwssp.nhs.wales/ourservices/specialist-estates-services/specialist-estates-services-documents/whtms-library/whtm-07-01-safe-management-of-healthcare-waste-pdf/ (accessed 30 December 2024).

(b) if later, the date on which the matter which is the subject of the concern came to the notice of the person notifying the concern.

If a concern about a provider is notified to a Local Health Board, the Health Board must decide whether to consider the concern or whether it is more appropriate for the provider to consider and investigate it.

The responsible body that considers the concern must prepare a written response and take all reasonable steps to send it within 30 days to the person who notified the concern. Amongst other things, the report must:

(a) summarise the nature and substance of the matter or matters raised in the concern;
(b) describe the investigation undertaken;
(c) where appropriate, contain an apology;
(d) identify what action, if any, will be taken;
(e) contain details of the right to notify the concern to the Public Services Ombudsman for Wales;
(f) offer the person notifying the concern the opportunity to discuss the contents of the response with the responsible officer or a person acting on their behalf;
(g) be signed by the responsible officer or a person acting on their behalf.

Complaints about health service bodies and the providers of NHS services, such as pharmacies, may be made to the Public Health Service Ombudsman for Wales.[84]

Cases considered by the Ombudsman include:

- A complaint that a patient was having difficulty with his medication supply, and that he had not received a response to a formal complaint. Following contact from the Ombudsman, the pharmacy agreed to issue the patient with a written apology and a formal response to the patient's complaint within 14 days of the Ombudsman's decision letter.[85]
- A complaint that a patient had not received a response from a pharmacy to a complaint she had made regarding its prescription and home delivery service. Following contact from the Ombudsman, the complaint was resolved by the pharmacy agreeing to apologise to the patient within 20 working days for the failure to process her complaint, and to investigate and respond to her complaint in writing.[86]

Welsh language

Schedule 5 to the 2020 Regulations provides:

1. Where an NHS pharmacist provides pharmaceutical services through the medium of Welsh, the NHS pharmacist must notify the Local Health Board on whose pharmaceutical list the NHS pharmacist is included, in writing.

---

84. Established under the Public Services Ombudsman (Wales) Act 2019.

85. https://www.ombudsman.wales/findings/health-a-pharmacy-in-the-area-of-betsi-cadwaladr-university-health-board/ (accessed 30 December 2024).

86. https://www.ombudsman.wales/findings/clinical-treatment-outside-hospital-pharmacy-a-pharmacy-in-the-area-of-swansea-bay-university-health-board/ (accessed 30 December 2024).

2. An NHS pharmacist must make available a Welsh language version of any document or form for use by patients and/or members of the public, provided by the Local Health Board.
3. Where an NHS pharmacist displays a new sign or notice in connection with pharmaceutical services, the text on the sign or notice must be in English and Welsh, and an NHS pharmacist may utilise the translation service offered by the Local Health Board for this purpose.
4. An NHS pharmacist must encourage the wearing of a badge, provided by the Local Health Board, by those delivering pharmaceutical services who are Welsh speaking, to convey that they are able to speak Welsh.
5. An NHS pharmacist must encourage those delivering pharmaceutical services to utilise information and/or attend training courses and events provided by the Local Health Board, so that they can develop:
   a. an awareness of the Welsh language (including awareness of its history and its role in Welsh culture), and
   b. an understanding of how the Welsh language can be used in connection with the pharmaceutical services provided.
6. An NHS pharmacist must encourage those delivering pharmaceutical services to establish and record the Welsh or English language preference expressed by or on behalf of a patient.

The terms of service for appliance contractors are in Schedule 6 and the terms of service for dispensing doctors are in Schedule 7 to the 2020 Regulations.

Community Pharmacy Wales

Under section 88 of the Act, the Welsh Ministers have the power to determine remuneration for the provision of pharmaceutical services and the Welsh Ministers may also authorise any LHB to do so. Negotiations on remuneration and reimbursement are undertaken by Community Pharmacy Wales (CPW). The status of CPW as a negotiating body for Welsh pharmacy owners was legally established in April 2004. Wales has adopted a community pharmacy contractual framework that is similar to that in England, particularly with regard to essential, advanced and enhanced service levels. However, the detailed arrangements, especially fees and some services, diverge from those in England; for example, Wales does not charge for NHS prescriptions and has not adopted either Local Pharmaceutical Services (LPS) schemes or the exemptions to control of entry that apply in England. These differences are current at the time of writing but other differences in the provision of services will emerge and readers are advised to check the websites for CPW[87] and NHS Wales[88] for current information.

87. https://cpwales.org.uk/ (accessed 30 December 2024).
88. www.nhs.wales (accessed 30 December 2024).

SUMMARY

- The legal framework for NHS services differs between England, Scotland and Wales. There are common features, but also variations in the law and regulation of NHS pharmaceutical services.
- NHS England in England and Local Health Boards in Wales and Scotland secure the provision of primary care, including pharmaceutical services, through 'contracts' with local owners of pharmacies.
- Integrated Care Boards commission many services locally in England for the populations for whom they are responsible.
- Pharmacy premises that are included in pharmaceutical lists are often referred to as having an *NHS contract*.
- England and Wales have arrangements for inclusion of premises in pharmaceutical lists (called *market entry* in England and *control of entry* in Wales) that are mainly based on local Pharmaceutical Needs Assessments.
- Control of entry (as it is termed) in Scotland is mainly based on a necessary or desirable test.
- In each country, there are simplified procedures for pharmacy relocations and changes of ownership.
- Persons providing NHS pharmacy services must comply with conditions set out in the applicable NHS Terms of Service.
- In each country, a key service is the provision of prescribed medicines which pharmacy owners are required to supply with reasonable promptness. Other services and applicable conditions vary from country to country.
- Terms of service set out the requirements for the provision of services, and include opening hours, record keeping and clinical governance amongst other features.
- England has an NHS Constitution. Scotland has a Charter of Patient Rights and Responsibilities.
- Different requirements for complaints handling and waste disposal apply in each country.
- Specifications for the amount and conditions which apply to payments under the NHS Terms of Service are set out in the Drug Tariff for each country.
- Negotiations for payments take place nationally through Community Pharmacy, Community Pharmacy Wales or Community Pharmacy Scotland and locally through LPCs or their Welsh or Scottish equivalents.
- The public interest in the NHS is represented in a number of ways including community health councils in Wales, local health councils in Scotland and Local Healthwatch organisations in England.

FURTHER READING

- Welsh Government: *The NHS (Pharmaceutical Services) (Wales) Regulations 2020: Non-statutory Guidance for Local Health Boards* **https://www.gov.wales/sites/default/files/publications/2020-10/nhs-pharmaceutical-services-wales-regulations-2020.pdf** (accessed 30 December 2024).

CHAPTER 4

Human medicines and medical devices: scope of regulation

There is end-to-end regulation of the medicines supply chain. In other words, regulation starts with manufacturing and extends through clinical trials, brokering, marketing, wholesaling, and supply to patients. Among the regulators are the Medicines and Healthcare products Regulatory Agency (MHRA) and the General Pharmaceutical Council (GPhC).

Consolidation of medicines legislation

The Human Medicines Regulations 2012 (HMR) consolidated most UK medicines legislation. The HMR leave parts of the Medicines Act 1968 (the Act) in place, principally Part IV of the Act, which deals with the registration and conduct of pharmacies (**Chapter 2**). Most current law was introduced through the Medicines Directive 2001/83/EC (the Directive). Following the UK's departure from the EU, new powers to amend the law were created in the Medicines and Medical Devices Act 2021. The exercise of these powers is subject to the requirement that the overarching objective of making regulations must be to safeguard public health for human medicines and medical devices.

The HMR provide that medicines may be supplied to the public only from pharmacies, except those medicines which can with reasonable safety be sold without the supervision[1] of a pharmacist.[2] The Regulations also cover matters relating to the labelling of medicines, the containers in which they are supplied (see **Chapter 18**) and the manner in which their sale is promoted, whether by advertisement or oral representation (see **Chapter 19**).

Certain pieces of medicines legislation have not been consolidated, including those concerned with clinical trials, and the administration of radioactive medicinal products. Various orders made under section 62 of the Act to prohibit the sale, supply and

1. At the time of writing, there is a proposal to amend the Act and the HMR, among other things so as to allow pharmacy technicians to supervise the supply of certain medicines. If and when such amendments are made, it is likely that the reference to the supervision of a pharmacist will be amended to refer also to the supervision of a pharmacy technician.
2. This is subject to exceptions that are described elsewhere in this book.

importation of products containing particular substances also remain in force along with section 62 (see Prohibition orders within **Chapter 21**).

Sections 104 and 105 of the Act say that Ministers may make an Order to the effect that provisions of the HMR will apply to an article or substance that is not a medicinal product if that article or substance is used for a medicinal purpose.

Since the Medicines Act 1968 remains partly in force, it should be read in conjunction with the HMR. References to Parts, Regulations and Schedules in this chapter relate to the Human Medicines Regulations 2012 and references to sections to the Medicines Act 1968, unless otherwise stated.

Neither the Act nor the HMR apply to medical devices (see elsewhere in this chapter and **Chapter 22**) or veterinary medicines (**Chapter 15**).

The Human Medicines Regulations 2012

The HMR comprise 17 Parts and numerous Schedules. This book focuses on those Parts of greatest relevance to pharmacists, pharmacy technicians and other healthcare professionals who supply medicines, and to pharmacy practice. The contents of the HMR are set out below with chapter numbers where they are predominantly discussed within this book.

Part 1	General: **Chapter 4**
Part 2	Administration: **Chapter 4**
Part 3	Manufacture, brokering and distribution of medicinal products and active substances: **Chapters 5** and **6**
Part 4	Requirement for authorisation: **Chapter 4**
Part 5	Marketing authorisations: **Chapters 4** and **5**
Part 6	Certification of homoeopathic medicinal products: **Chapter 16**
Part 7	Traditional herbal registrations: **Chapter 17**
Part 8	This Part is now limited to the recognition of Article 126a authorisations: **Chapter 5**.
Part 9	Borderline products: **Chapter 5**
Part 10	Exceptions to requirement for marketing authorisation, etc.: **Chapter 5**
Part 11	Pharmacovigilance: **Chapters 4** and **5**
Part 12	Dealings with medicinal products: **Chapters 10, 11, 12** and **13**
Part 12A	Sale of medicines to the public at a distance: **Chapter 8**
Part 13	Packaging and leaflets: **Chapter 18**
Part 14	Advertising: **Chapter 19**
Part 15	British Pharmacopoeia: **Chapter 20**
Part 16	Enforcement: **Chapter 2** and **4**
Part 17	Miscellaneous and general: **Chapter 4**

In addition, **Chapters 2** and **7** cover the provisions of the Act that relate to pharmacies, chapters 21 and 26 deal with provisions in the Act for protection of the purchaser, and **Chapter 15** covers the legislation on veterinary medicines.

Part 1 General

Definitions of medicinal product and related words

Although, for convenience, the words *medicine* and *medicinal product* are used interchangeably in this book, the HMR do not use the term *medicine* but *medicinal product*, which is defined (HMR Reg.2) as:

a. any substance or combination of substances presented as having properties of preventing or treating disease in human beings; or
b. any substance or combination of substances that may be used by or administered to human beings with a view to:
   i. restoring, correcting or modifying a physiological function by exerting a pharmacological, immunological or metabolic action; or
   ii. making a medical diagnosis.

It is important to note that (a) and (b) are separate definitions which were imported from the Directive. Definition (a) relates to presentation and definition (b) relates to function. A substance will be a medicinal product if it falls within either or both definitions. The question of whether a product comes within the definition of a medicinal product was considered by the European Court of Justice in *The Upjohn Company and Upjohn NV v Farzoo and Kortmann*[3] – see **Box 4.1**.

Box 4.1: Consideration by the courts of whether a product is a medicinal product

The European Court of Justice (ECJ) considered whether a product came within the definition of *medicinal product* in the case of *The Upjohn Company and Upjohn NV v Farzoo and Kortmann*. The two applicants (referred to as *Upjohn*) manufactured and marketed *Regaine* lotion, containing minoxidil, which was intended to counteract alopecia androgenetica, or natural baldness. Farzoo was a US corporation, represented in the Netherlands by Mr Kortmann. Farzoo marketed an identical product under the name *Minoxidil*. The Farzoo product was marketed as a cosmetic product, not as a medicinal product. Upjohn complained that Farzoo was infringing Netherlands (and EU) law and was competing unfairly. Upjohn sought an order from the Netherlands court to restrain Farzoo from marketing Minoxidil and the case was referred to the ECJ. The question for the ECJ was whether the Farzoo product, which was not "for the treating or preventing of disease in human beings or animals" should nevertheless be regarded as a medicinal product if it may be administered to human beings with a view to restoring, correcting or modifying physiological functions.

The ECJ confirmed that the first definition was designed to catch not only medicinal products that have a genuine therapeutic or medical effect, but also those that do not have such an effect if their presentation might lead one to expect that the product would have such an effect. This is to protect consumers not only from harmful or toxic medicinal products but also from a variety of product they may use instead of the appropriate remedies. A broad view was to be taken of the concept of "presentation". In this case, Farzoo's Minoxidil was a medicinal product because of its presentation.

---

3. C-112/89 [1991]; [1993] 1 CMLR 657. British courts remain bound by decisions of the European Court of Justice made before 31 December 2020 (section 6 of the European Union Withdrawal Act 2018).

Box 4.1: Consideration by the courts of whether a product is a medicinal product (cont.)

With regard to the second definition of a medicinal product, the ECJ held that this is concerned with the function of products. A product that treats disease or has a physiological effect will come within the definition of a medicinal product even if it is not presented as such. Other products may fall within both definitions of a medicinal product: the ECJ gave the example of contraceptive substances. The second definition must be given a broad interpretation to cover all substances capable of having an effect on the actual functioning of the body, but this does not include cosmetics that, while having an effect on the human body, do not significantly affect the metabolism and thus do not strictly modify the way in which it functions.

Decisions whether a substance is a medicinal product should be decided on a case-by-case basis.

In the English case of *R v Chapman (Sonny)*[4] (decided before nitrous oxide became a controlled drug and therefore is now outside the scope of the Psychoactive Substances Act), four defendants had been found in possession of large numbers of canisters containing nitrous oxide gas (commonly known as laughing gas), a substance which was used as a recreational drug because it produces a psychoactive effect and, although used in medicine, was also used in the catering industry as the propellant found in aerosols for whipped cream. The defendants were convicted of an offence under the Psychoactive Substances Act 2016 of unlawful possession of a psychoactive substance with intent to supply. In their appeals, they argued that nitrous oxide did not come under the Psychoactive Substances Act 2016 because it was exempted as a medicinal product.

The appeals were unsuccessful. The Court of Appeal referred to the *Upjohn* case (above) and noted that a substance may be a medicinal product for one purpose (and thus subject to legal restrictions), but not for another purpose. While nitrous oxide may be a medicinal product in some circumstances, because it may modify the physiological functions of those who inhale it, it was not used in the Chapman case for beneficial effects to human health. In reaching its conclusion, the court noted that the canisters had been manufactured and distributed for use in catering, which in itself was a strong indicator that they were not medicinal products.

4. [2017] EWCA Crim 1743.

The external form of a product (such as a tablet or capsule) does not necessarily amount to presentation, but the form and the way it is presented may bring a product within the definition of medicinal product if the form and manner in which it is packaged render it sufficiently similar to a medicine, especially if any information given with the product create that impression, for example by referring to testimonials from medical practitioners.[5]

The European Union (Withdrawal) Act 2018 stipulates that these legal provisions derived from EU law remain in force in the UK after its exit from the European Union.

Medicinal products may include immunological products, medicinal products based on human blood or blood constituents and medicinal products based on radioisotopes (radiopharmaceuticals). However, the definition does not include whole human blood

5. *The Republic (France) v Jean-Marie Delattre* [1993] CMLR 445.

or any human blood component other than plasma prepared by a method involving an industrial process (HMR Reg.2). Homoeopathic medicinal products are dealt with separately (HMR Part 6) (and see **Chapter 16**).

The word *administer* is defined in the HMR as:

> *"to administer to a human being orally, by injection or by introduction into the body in any other way or by external application (whether or not by direct application to the body), either in its existing state or after it has been dissolved or dispersed in, or diluted or mixed with, a substance used as a vehicle."*

Blood component means red cells, white cells, platelets or plasma (HMR Reg.8).

Radiopharmaceutical means a medicinal product which, when ready for use, contains one or more radionuclides included for a medicinal purpose (HMR Reg.8).

Licensing authority and ministers

The licensing authority is responsible for the grant, renewal, variation, suspension and revocation of licences, authorisations, certificates, designations, opinions and registrations under the HMR (Reg.6). The *licensing authority* means the Secretary of State for Health and Social Care (who must enforce or secure the enforcement of the Regulations). While the minister comprises the licensing authority, these licensing functions are carried out by the Medicines and Healthcare products Regulatory Agency (MHRA) which is an executive agency of the Department of Health and Social Care. The MHRA is also the licensing authority for all other licences required under the Regulations (e.g. manufacturer's, wholesale dealer's) and is also the enforcement authority for these matters in the UK.

Manufacturer's licences

It is unlawful to manufacture or assemble a medicinal product without a manufacturer's licence. Without a manufacturer's licence, it is also unlawful to import a medicinal product except from Northern Ireland or a country on the MHRA's approved country list.[6] Without a manufacturer's licence, it is also unlawful to possess a medicinal product for manufacture, assembly or import.[7]

Exemptions from the need for a manufacturer's licence

Where medicinal products are assembled in the course of the professional practice of a doctor, dentist, nurse, midwife or herbalist for the treatment of their patients, no manufacturing licences are required (HMR Reg.3). Similarly, where medicines are prepared under the supervision of a pharmacist[8] and in accordance with exemptions

6. The list can be found at https://www.gov.uk/government/publications/list-of-approved-countries-for-authorised-human-medicines/list-of-approved-countries (accessed 31 December 2024).
7. HMR Reg.17.
8. See footnote 1.

in the retained parts of section 10 of the Act (**Chapter 5**), no licences are required (HMR Reg.4).

Marketing authorisations and other registrations

A person may not sell, supply, or offer to sell or supply a medicinal product except in accordance with a marketing authorisation, a certificate of registration, a traditional herbal registration (see **Chapter 17** in relation to the latter two), or an Article 126a authorisation (see **Chapter 5**).[9]

Classification and reclassification of medicines

Regulation 5 of the HMR provides definitions of the three classifications governing the sale or supply of medicines; these are medicines subject to general sale (see **Chapter 10**), Pharmacy medicines (see **Chapter 11**), and Prescription Only Medicines (see **Chapter 12**). Regulation 62 of the HMR provides that a UK marketing authorisation must include a term indicating which of these three classifications is applicable to the product in question. If a medicinal product has been granted a marketing authorisation, an application may be made to the MHRA to vary the classification from one category to another on the basis that the medicinal product meets the criteria for the new category. The criteria for medicinal products subject to general sale, Pharmacy medicines, and Prescription Only Medicines are set out at the beginning of **Chapters 10, 11** and **12** respectively. HMR Reg.64A provides that if a medicinal product is reclassified, and the application for reclassification was supported by the results of significant pre-clinical tests or clinical trials, the licensing authority may not, for the period of one year, refer to the results of the tests or trials when examining an application by another applicant for a change of classification of the same kind. This provision prevents a later applicant from taking advantage of the financial investment by a marketing authorisation holder who has incurred significant expense in satisfying the licensing authority that a change of classification should be granted.

Borderline products

Some products are hard to distinguish from medicines, for example products that might be medical devices, cosmetics, food supplements or biocidal products. If the manufacturer or seller is unsure whether a product is a medicinal product, or if the MHRA receives a complaint that a medicinal product has been placed on the market without a marketing authorisation, the MHRA will decide whether the product is a medicinal product. (See also **Chapter 5**.)

---

9. This refers to Article 126a of EU Directive 2001/83/EC. These authorisations were granted for certain products that did not have a marketing authorisation but allowing them to be placed on the market was justified for public health reasons. No new Article 126a authorisations will be granted for Great Britain, but some that were granted before the UK left the EU will remain in force until their expiry dates.

Advertisements relating to medicinal products

Regulation 7 of the HMR defines an advertisement as including anything to promote the prescription, supply, sale or use of a medicinal product. Advertising and sales promotion are discussed in **Chapter 19**.

Part 2 Administration

Two advisory bodies are established under the HMR, namely the Commission on Human Medicines (HMR Reg.9) and the British Pharmacopoeia Commission (BPC) (HMR Reg.11). An advisory body, or the advisory bodies acting jointly, may with the approval of the licensing authority appoint one or more subcommittees, known as expert advisory groups (see below). Each advisory body must give a report to the ministers each year (HMR Reg.12), about the performance of its functions and of those of any expert advisory group appointed by it. The Secretary of State must lay a copy of each report before parliament.

Commission on Human Medicines

The Commission on Human Medicines was established before the HMR came into force, and the HMR continue to provide for this body (HMR Reg.9).

If the Minister (or ministers) request it or the Commission considers it appropriate to give it,[10] the Commission on Human Medicines must:

a. give advice with respect to the safety, quality and efficacy of medicinal products and promote the collection and investigation of information relating to adverse reactions, for the purposes of enabling such advice to be given; and
b. advise the licensing authority if the licensing authority:
   i. is required under Schedule 11 or the Clinical Trials Regulations,[11] to consult the Commission about any matter arising under those provisions, or
   ii. consults the Commission about any matter arising under those provisions.

Recent examples of the Commission's work include:

1. considering the legal classification of medicines, for example from Prescription Only Medicine to Pharmacy medicine status; or from Pharmacy medicine status to general sale status, or from Pharmacy medicine status to a Prescription Only Medicine, such as in 2024 in the case of codeine linctus[12] (see also **Chapters 10, 11** and **12**);
2. advising that the use of antibiotic-containing lozenges to treat sore throat sepsis is not clinically appropriate;
3. advising on strengthened safety measures for isotretinoin (Roaccutane and Reticutan) because of concerns that the product has been linked to suicide ideation;
4. the risks to male patients who take valproate products.

---

10. HMR Reg.10.
11. Medicines for Human Use (Clinical Trials) Regulations 2004.
12. https://assets.publishing.service.gov.uk/media/65d33fc20f4eb1ec90a98147/PAR_-_codeine_linctus.pdf (accessed 30 December 2024).

British Pharmacopoeia Commission

The Act established the legal status of the British Pharmacopoeia Commission (BPC) and of the British Pharmacopoeia (BP) as the UK standard for medicinal products. The BPC must prepare, or cause to be prepared, editions of the BP and any other compendia (HMR Reg.317) and lists of British Approved Names (HMR Reg.318) (**Chapter 20**).

Expert advisory groups

The licensing authority may direct that either of the above advisory bodies appoint one or more sub-committees (HMR, Reg.14), known as expert advisory groups, to assist them in their work. Further provisions about advisory bodies and expert advisory groups are found in Schedule 2 to the HMR.

There is also a Devices Expert Advisory Committee which is responsible for providing MHRA with independent, external, expert clinical and scientific input and advice on a wide range of aspects relating to the introduction and safe use of medical devices.

Part 11 Pharmacovigilance

Part 11 of the HMR places general obligations on the licensing authority, with respect to pharmacovigilance, including an obligation to operate and audit a pharmacovigilance system. Further obligations are applied to the holders of UK marketing authorisations (**Chapter 5**).

Part 16 Enforcement

A failure to comply with a provision in the Act or in the HMR is usually a criminal offence. Part 16 of the HMR covers enforcement. The primary duty of enforcing the Regulations in England, Wales and Scotland rests with the Secretary of State (HMR Reg.323). There are provisions for ministers to delegate many of their functions to other authorities. In England, Wales and Scotland, arrangements can be made or directions given whereby local drugs authorities and/or the General Pharmaceutical Council (GPhC) can have certain duties or exercise certain powers concurrently with the ministers. In Scotland, these enforcement authorities cannot themselves institute proceedings. Under HMR Reg.323 (2), the Secretary of State may delegate (and has delegated) the duty of enforcement in connection with pharmacies and the retail distribution of medicines to the GPhC (**Chapters 2** and **24**). Other enforcement duties may be given to the GPhC and to drugs authorities (which are the local government authorities for the relevant area)[13] as the appropriate ministers may decide. In addition, Part IV of the Act (Pharmacies) remains in force and, under that legislation, the GPhC is responsible for the maintenance of the Register of Pharmacy Premises (**Chapter 2**) and for compliance in relation to bodies corporate and representatives of pharmacists carrying on retail pharmacy businesses (**Chapter 7**). The GPhC may enforce breaches of the law through fitness to practise proceedings (see **Chapter 25**) or it may enforce breaches of the law through prosecution and it has published a Prosecution Policy that

13. HMR Reg.323(10).

describes what factors are considered when a decision to prosecute is made.[14] The Crown Prosecution Service (in England and Wales), and the Crown Office and Procurator Fiscal Service (in Scotland) also have powers to prosecute. Some of the prosecutions for breaches of the Medicines Act that are referred to in **Chapter 26** were brought by the Crown Prosecution Service.

The GPhC, concurrently with the Minister, is also required to enforce the provisions relating to sale and supply of medicines not subject to general sale (HMR Reg.220) and sale or supply of a Prescription Only Medicine (POM; HMR Reg.214). The provisions relating to sale or supply of medicinal products subject to general sale (HMR Reg.221) and sale of medicinal products from automatic machines (HMR Reg.222) are enforced, concurrently with the Minister, by the GPhC in relation to premises that are registered pharmacies and, in each area for which there is a drugs authority, by that drugs authority in relation to premises that are not registered pharmacies. Here, *premises* includes any place and a ship, aircraft, hovercraft or vehicle (HMR Reg.323(11)).

The Secretary of State may make arrangements for either or both of the GPhC or, in respect of each area for which there is a drugs authority, the drugs authority for the area, concurrently with the Secretary of State, to enforce the following provisions:

1. compliance with standards specified in certain publications (HMR Reg.251);
2. offences relating to dealings with medicinal products: compliance with standards specified in certain publications (HMR Reg.255(1)(e));
3. packaging and leaflets (HMR Part 13); and
4. requirements relating to advertising (HMR Part 14).

Arrangements made with the GPhC in relation to HMR Part 14 (**Chapter 2**) are to be limited to the enforcement of those provisions in respect of:

1. advertisements displayed or representations made on or in any premises where medicinal products are sold by retail or supplied in circumstances corresponding to retail sale;
2. advertisements displayed on any website associated with such premises; and
3. advertisements displayed on, or in close proximity to, a vending machine in which medicinal products are offered or exposed for sale.

Under the Act, the GPhC is also required to enforce the provisions relating to:

1. prohibition of sale or supply, or importation, of medicinal products of specified description (s.62) (**Chapter 21**);
2. sale and supply and offer of sale or supply of adulterated medicinal products (s.63) (**Chapter 26**);
3. sale of medicinal products not of the nature or quality demanded (s.64) (**Chapter 26**);
4. annual return of premises to the Registrar (s.77) (**Chapter 2**);
5. restrictions on use of titles, descriptions and emblems (s.78) (**Chapter 7**);
6. regulations imposing further restrictions on titles (s.79(2)) (**Chapter 7**);
7. regulations relating to requirements for containers (s.87(2)) (**Chapter 18**); and

---

14. https://assets.pharmacyregulation.org/files/gp201489_gphc_criminal_prosecution_policy.pdf (accessed 30 December 2024).

8. regulations relating to distinctive colours, shapes and marking of medicinal products (s.88(3)) (**Chapter 18**).

Prosecutions for breaches of the HMR and the Act are dealt with in further detail in **Chapter 26**.

Medical devices

The regulation of medical devices is governed by the Medical Devices Regulations 2002. This is dealt with in **Chapter 22**.

SUMMARY

- European Directives and Regulations which were in force before the UK left the EU together with the Medicines Act 1968 and the Human Medicines Regulations 2012 regulate the manufacture, distribution and importation of medicines for human use.
- The advisory structure for ministers is principally the Commission on Human Medicines, which may delegate some of its functions to expert advisory groups.
- The definition of a medicinal product is set out in the Human Medicines Regulations 2012.
- There are obligations under the Human Medicines Regulations 2012 to operate a pharmacovigilance system.
- The enforcement of parts of the Regulations falls upon the MHRA and the GPhC; some elements are enforced by *drugs authorities*. The GPhC has a policy that dictates when it will bring a prosecution. The Crown Prosecution Service and the Crown Office and Procurator Fiscal Service may prosecute in the case of breaches of the Medicines Act 1968 or the Human Medicines Regulations 2012.
- Medical devices are regulated by the Medical Devices Regulations 2002 and are administered by the MHRA.

FURTHER READING

- Human Medicines Regulations (2012) SI 2012 No. 1916, *Explanatory memorandum*: **http://www.legislation.gov.uk/uksi/2012/1916/pdfs/uksiem_20121916_en.pdf** (accessed 30 December 2024).

CHAPTER 5

Human medicines: manufacturing, clinical trials and marketing

It is not lawful to manufacture medicinal products without a licence, clinical trials are regulated, and it is not lawful to sell or supply a medicinal product without a marketing authorisation. In each case, there are key features, conditions, and exemptions.

Introduction

Modern medicines legislation in the UK was triggered by the thalidomide tragedy. Thalidomide was a drug prescribed in the late 1950s and early 1960s to relieve morning sickness during pregnancy. Tragically, it later became apparent that the drug could cause serious birth defects, with around 10,000 cases worldwide. The realisation that drugs may come with serious risk led to the evolution of the current regulatory environment in the UK. In particular, the Medicines Act 1968 was enacted.

References to a pharmacy and to pharmacy premises are to pharmacy premises that are registered with the General Pharmaceutical Council. The definitions or meaning of some of the key terms used in this chapter are given in **Box 5.1** below.

Box 5.1: Definitions[1]

Assemble – includes the various processes of dividing up, packaging and presentation of the product or substance, and *assembly* has a corresponding meaning.

Dispense – perhaps surprisingly, there is no legal definition of the word *dispense*. It can mean different things in different contexts in a pharmacy. It is often used to refer to the handing of a medicine to a patient, for example over the counter in a pharmacy. *Dispense* may also mean the same as *assemble* in some circumstances, including hub and spoke dispensing (see below). In a tax case, *Customs and Excise Commissioners v Wellington Private Hospital Ltd*[2] the Court of Appeal said:

> *"The word 'dispense' was not a word of art. Its (relevant) dictionary definition was 'make up (medicine) according to a prescription, give out a prescribed medicine.' There was no reason to confine its meaning … to the first of those meanings …"*

The Department of Health and Social Care said in response to a consultation on amending the Human Medicines Regulations 2012 (HMR) to allow hub and spoke dispensing to be carried out on a wider basis than the law currently allows:

1. These definitions are in HMR Reg.8, except for the definition of retail, which is in section 131 of the Medicines Act.
2. [1997] STC 44.

"Dispensing covers a number of processes and includes activities such as the taking in of a prescription, the clinical and accuracy checks, the sourcing of products, the preparation, assembly and supply of medicines and providing advice to and counselling a patient, for example, to ensure that they know how and when to take the medicine."

Hospital – includes a clinic, nursing home or similar institution.

Manufacture – includes any process carried out in the course of making the product but does not include dissolving or dispensing the product in, or diluting or mixing it with, a substance for the purpose of administering it.

Medicinal product – see **Chapter 4**.

Place on the market – the expression is not defined in the HMR. UK Government guidance says:

"A product is placed on the market when it is first made available for distribution, consumption or use on the GB market as part of a commercial activity. This can be in return for payment or free of charge. This happens after a product has been fully manufactured. A product is placed on the market when an offer or agreement is made for the transfer of ownership, possession or any other property right. Placing on the market can take place before the physical transfer of a product. It does not necessarily require the physical handover of a product."[3]

(see also **Box 5.4**).

In the case of medical devices, there is a definition in the Medical Devices Regulations 2002 (see chapter 22).

Prepare – neither the Medicines Act nor the HMR define this word: it is suggested that it includes doing something that involves getting it ready to be dispensed or to be given to a patient.

Retail – means selling to a person who does not buy for the purpose of selling or supplying or for the purpose of administering it or causing it to be administered to another person. In general terms a retail sale is a sale to a patient or patient's representative. The Medicines Act also uses the expression *circumstances corresponding to retail sale* because supplies on NHS prescriptions do not involve a sale.

Supervision – see **Chapter 8** for the meaning of *supervision*.

3. https://www.gov.uk/guidance/placing-manufactured-goods-on-the-market-in-great-britain (accessed 30 December 2024).

Manufacturer's licences

Under regulation 17 of the HMR, it is not lawful to manufacture or assemble a medicinal product except in accordance with a manufacturer's licence granted by the MHRA. It is also unlawful to import a medicinal product except from Northern Ireland or an approved country for import unless the importation is in accordance with a manufacturer's licence.

No licence is required for the importation of a medicinal product by a person who imports a medicinal product for administration to themselves or to any other person who is a member of that person's household (HMR Reg.17(6)).

Patents

A patent for an invention such as a new medicinal product grants the owner of the patent the right to exclude others from using the invention for a limited period of time.

The patent owner therefore has a monopoly on the commercial use of the patented product during the lifetime of the patent. This monopoly is a reward for the invention. A patent only comes into being once it has been registered.[4] In the UK, patents are registered with the Intellectual Property Office. A number of the cases referred to in this book involved patents for medicinal products.

Active substances

An *active substance* means "any substance or mixture of substances intended to be used in the manufacture of a medicinal product and that, when used in its production, becomes an active ingredient of that product intended to exert a pharmacological, immunological or metabolic action with a view to restoring, correcting or modifying physiological functions or to make a medical diagnosis".[5]

Active substances (also referred to as *active ingredients*) are thus used to give medicinal products their therapeutic effect. Anyone based in the UK who wishes to manufacture, import or distribute active pharmaceutical ingredients must register with the Medicines and Healthcare products Regulatory Agency (MHRA).[6] The standards of Good Manufacturing Practice (see below) will apply.

The identification of active ingredients is also important if a patent holder wishes to apply for a Supplementary Protection Certificate (see below). In 2024, the UK Intellectual Property Office decided[7] (subject to appeal) that recombinant human hyaluronidase was not an active ingredient in Herceptin (trastuzumab) because its marketing authorisation describes it as an excipient.

Exemptions from the need for a manufacturer's licence

Pharmacies

The definitions of *manufacture* and *assembly* (see **Box 5.1**) are wide enough to cover extemporaneous dispensing as well as other activities that are commonly performed in a pharmacy, such as the repackaging of medicines, or putting medicines into a monitored dosage system or compliance aid. Even the labelling of a medicinal product comes within the definition of assembly. However, section 10 of the Medicines Act 1968 provides a range of exemptions from the need for a manufacturer's licence for certain activities, provided that certain conditions are met.

In the case of things done on pharmacy premises by or under the supervision of a pharmacist, a manufacturer's licence is not required for:

1. Preparing or dispensing a medicinal product in accordance with a prescription.
2. Assembling, provided that the pharmacy business on the pharmacy premises is restricted to retail sale or supply (i.e. that the business does not involve wholesaling),

---

4. Roughton, Johnson and Cooke on Patents (published by LNUK, 5th edition, 2022).
5. HMR Reg.8.
6. HMR Reg.45M.
7. https://www.ipo.gov.uk/p-challenge-decision-results/o025724.pdf (accessed 30 December 2024).

and the assembling is done with a view to sale or supply either at or from the same premises or at or from another pharmacy that forms part of the same pharmacy business.

The assembly of a medicine at one pharmacy with a view to supplying it at or from a different pharmacy is commonly referred to as *hub and spoke dispensing* where the pharmacy that receives a prescription is a spoke, and the pharmacy where the assembly is carried out is the hub. There are proposals to change the law in 2025; see **Box 5.2**.

Box 5.2: Hub and spoke dispensing

At the time of going to press, there were proposals to amend the law in 2025. This box sets out what the law will be if those proposals are brought into effect. Readers can check whether the proposals have been brought into effect by checking www.legislation.gov.uk or using a subscription service such as Westlaw for the latest version of [e.g. the Medicines Act 1968/ the Human Medicines Regulations 2012 or searching those sites for the Human Medicines (Amendments Relating to Hub and Spoke Dispensing etc.) Regulations *followed by the year].*

The words *that forms part of the same pharmacy business* mean that hub and spoke dispensing may only be carried out if the hub and the spoke have the same owner. However, these words will be deleted, so that any hub can assemble medicines on behalf of any spoke. Under the law in force at the time of going to print, a supply from a hub to a spoke which does not have the same owner would be a wholesale transaction, but if and when the law is changed, the supply will be deemed to be a retail transaction to avoid the need for a wholesale dealer's licence.

This exemption is subject to the further condition that the medicinal product has not been the subject of an advertisement.

3. Procuring the preparation or dispensing of a medicinal product in accordance with a prescription or procuring the assembly of a medicinal product.
4. Preparing or dispensing in accordance with a specification by the person to whom the product is to be sold or supplied where the product is to be administered to that person or under that person's care.
5. Preparing or dispensing for administration to a person where the pharmacist is requested by or on behalf of that person to do so in accordance with the pharmacist's own judgement as to the treatment required and that person is present in the pharmacy at the time of the request.
6. Preparing a stock of medicinal products with a view to dispensing them as mentioned in paragraphs 1, 4 or 5, provided that the preparation is done with a view to retail sale or supply on an NHS prescription from the pharmacy where the preparation takes place or another pharmacy that has the same owner.
7. Preparing a stock of medicinal products. Medicines that are prepared according to a pharmacopoeia for sale over the counter (and not in accordance with a prescription) are commonly referred to as chemist's nostrums. Nostrums fall into this exemption.

In 2016, the Department of Health and Social Care considered removing this exemption but, following a consultation, decided not to do so.[8]

8. Preparing a medicinal product with a view to retail sale or for supply on an NHS prescription.

At the time of going to press, the Department of Health and Social Care proposes to change the law to enable pharmacists to authorise pharmacy technicians to carry out supervision. These proposals are covered in more detail in **Chapter 11**.

Hospitals, care home services and health centres

Exemptions for hospitals, care home services and health centres will be found in **Chapter 9**.

Doctors and dentists

No licence is required where a medicinal product is manufactured or assembled by a doctor or dentist and is supplied to a patient in the course of their treatment. The medicinal product must not be manufactured or assembled on a large scale or by an industrial process (HMR Reg.3).

Nurses and midwives

Exemptions for nurses and midwives will be found in **Chapter 9**.

Issue, suspension and revocation of licences

Manufacturer's licences are issued by the Medicines and Healthcare products Regulatory Agency (MHRA). The MHRA may grant, refuse, review, suspend, revoke or vary them (HMR Regs.23 and 26). A licence remains in force until it is revoked by the authority or surrendered by the holder (HMR Reg.25). When an application for a licence is refused, the authority must state the reasons for refusal in a notice served on the applicant (HMR Reg.23(6)). If the holder of a licence contravenes any provision of that authorisation, a notice suspending or revoking it may be served on the holder (HMR Reg.26). Similarly, a licence may be suspended where it appears to the licensing authority that it is necessary in the interests of safety (HMR Reg.28). For example, in July 2023, the MHRA partly suspended the licence of Sciensus after an incident in which a patient died and three others were hospitalised after being administered incorrect amounts of an unlicensed version of the chemotherapy drug cabazitaxel manufactured as a special; an investigation found that the product was set up with the incorrect strength in the

8. https://www.gov.uk/government/consultations/pharmacy-dispensing-models-and-displaying-prices-on-medicines/outcome/pharmacy-dispensing-models-and-displaying-prices-on-medicines-response-to-the-2016-consultation#proposal-4-redesigning-the-pharmacists-exemption-in-section-10-of-the-medicines-act-1968 (accessed 30 December 2024).

company's IT systems.[9] The MHRA maintains an online list of licences that have been suspended or revoked.[10]

Good manufacturing practice and other licence conditions

The holder of a manufacturer's licence is required by HMR Reg.37(2) to comply with the Good Manufacturing Practice Directive (GMP).[11] GMP is the minimum standard that a medicines manufacturer must meet in their production processes.

Under GMP, products must:

- be of consistent high quality;
- be appropriate to their intended use; and
- meet the requirements of the marketing authorisation (MA) or product specification.

In addition to GMP, the holder of a manufacturer's licence must comply with certain conditions regarding manufacture, assembly and importation (HMR Regs.37-41). There are different types of licence available, which can apply to the manufacture of authorised medicinal products, or special medicinal products (named-patient medication – see below), or investigational medicinal products (for clinical trials). A licence is not required for the manufacture of chemicals and other substances used in the manufacture of ingredients of medicinal products.

The premises of licence holders will be inspected by the MHRA. Under the terms of the UK's agreement with the EU, manufacturing facilities do not need to undergo separate UK and EU inspections because each party will ordinarily recognise the inspections carried out by the other.

Qualified Person

In an application for a manufacturer's licence, the qualifications of the production manager and of a qualified person (QP) must be given, and the name and function of the person to whom they are responsible. Where relevant, the qualifications of the person in charge of animals, and of the person responsible for the culture of any living tissue, must also be given. At least one QP is required to be nominated whose responsibilities are set out in the Regulations (Articles 41, 46 and 48 of the Medicines Directive).[12] Schedule 7 to the HMR sets out the requirements to be a QP. HMR Reg.41 says that those requirements are met if the person concerned person produces evidence that he or she is a member of one of the following bodies and is regarded by that body as satisfying those requirements:

---

9. https://questions-statements.parliament.uk/written-questions/detail/2023-11-21/hl464 (accessed 30 December 2024).

10. https://www.gov.uk/government/publications/suspended-licences-for-manufacturers-and-wholesalers-of-medicines (accessed 30 December 2024). https://www.gov.uk/government/publications/suspended-licences-for-manufacturers-and-wholesalers-of-medicines (accessed 30 December 2024).

11. GMP is contained in the Good Manufacturing Practice Directive 2003/94/EC. HMR Reg.B17 gives Ministers the power to set out principles and guidance for GMP in Great Britain and to replace the Directive with a British version. Guidance can be found here https://www.gov.uk/guidance/good-manufacturing-practice-and-good-distribution-practice (accessed 30 December 2024).

12. 2001/83/EC.

a. the Royal Society of Biology;
b. the Royal Pharmaceutical Society;
c. the Pharmaceutical Society of Northern Ireland;
d. the Royal Society of Chemistry; and
e. such other body as may be specified by the licensing authority.

The QP is responsible for the quality control requirements of GMP. Schedule 7 to the Regulations also sets out details of the quality control measures the QP is obliged to carry out.

Self-regulation of the pharmaceutical industry

The Association of the British Pharmaceutical Industry (ABPI) is a membership organisation for pharmaceutical manufacturers. The ABPI has a Code of Practice that deals, for example, with claims that are made for products, advertising and the promotion of products to health professionals. The Prescription Medicines Code of Practice Authority administers the Code on behalf of the ABPI and it has a Code of Practice Panel. For example, in a 2024 case against Nordisk in 2024, the company had supplied free of charge to certain pharmacy chains sharps, bins and wallets for use with injectables. These were held to be an inducement to purchase its product, Wegovy (semaglutide). The Panel decided that this was of serious concern bearing in mind the heightened public interest in and sensitivities around weight loss medication, and the particular importance in ensuring that the arrangements withstood public scrutiny, were robust, transparent and complied with the Code. The company was found in breach of a number of parts of the Code, including bringing discredit upon, and reducing confidence in the pharmaceutical industry; and failing to maintain high standards.[13]

Clinical trials

A *clinical trial* is defined in Reg.2 of the Medicines for Human Use (Clinical Trials) Regulations 2004 (the Clinical Trials Regulations) as:

> *"any investigation in human subjects, other than a non-interventional trial, intended:*
>
> *a. to discover or verify the clinical, pharmacological or other pharmacodynamic effects of one or more medicinal products,*
> *b. to identify any adverse reactions to one or more such products, or*
> *c. to study absorption, distribution, metabolism and excretion of one or more such products,*
>
> *with the object of ascertaining the safety or efficacy of those products."*

13. https://www.pmcpa.org.uk/media/1zbpampo/3821-case-report-25-september-2024.pdf (accessed 30 December 2024).

As His Honour Judge Pelling said in *Exelogen v University of Birmingham*,[14] "It is common ground that in order to bring a pharmaceutical product to market various pre-licensing clinical trials and regulatory steps have to be completed including (a) a Phase 1 trial to demonstrate safety; (b) a Phase 2 trial, which consists of a proof of concept trial and then a clinical trial on a relatively small cohort of patients to demonstrate both efficacy and safety; (c) a Phase 3 clinical trial, which is again concerned with efficacy and safety but utilising a much larger cohort of patients and a final phase concerned with obtaining regulatory approvals. Only after completion of each of these stages can commercial exploitation of the product commence".

Authorisation

A marketing authorisation is not required for the manufacture or assembly of a medicinal product to be used only for the purpose of a clinical trial, but authorisation must be granted by the licensing authority for the purposes of clinical trials.

Details of the requirements for a clinical trial application are outlined in the Clinical Trials Regulations. Notification of the supplier's intention must be sent to the licensing authority. The notice must be accompanied by particulars of the trial and summaries of pharmaceutical data and of reports made and tests performed as specified in the Clinical Trials Regulations. There is provision for termination of the exemption in certain circumstances, usually on the grounds of safety and for appeals to a person appointed. The Clinical Trials Regulations lay down the principles and detailed guidelines for good clinical practice as regards investigational medicinal products for human use.

Investigational medicinal products

An *investigational medicinal product* means a pharmaceutical form of an active substance or placebo being tested, or to be tested, or used, or to be used, as a reference in a clinical trial, and includes a medicinal product which has a marketing authorisation but is, for the purposes of the trial:

a. used or assembled (formulated or packaged) in a way different from the form of the product authorised under the authorisation,
b. used for an indication not included in the summary of product characteristics under the authorization for that product, or
c. used to gain further information about the form of that product as authorised under the authorisation.

The manufacture of the investigational medicinal product must be carried out in accordance with GMP.

Preventing avoidable harm

Plainly, at the point when patients are the subject of a clinical trial, care is required to prevent avoidable harm. In 2006, in a private clinical research unit at Northwick Park

14. [2023] EWHC 1523 (Comm).

Hospital, six healthy male volunteers in a first-in-man trial developed multi-organ failure after the trial drug was administered.[15] Cases of this kind are likely to result in claims for damages by injured volunteers. Following a report into what happened, the Clinical Trials Regulations were simplified and streamlined.

Trials are likely to be conducted as double-blind i.e. that neither clinicians nor patients know whether the patient is being given an active substance or a placebo. However, in one recent case in which a patient died from an underlying condition, a coroner expressed concern that if a patient was taken ill and treated in a different hospital to the one in which a clinical trial was carried out, action should be taken to enable the hospital where the patient was treated to ascertain whether or not the patient was treated with an active substance.[16]

Modular manufacture

The Clinical Trials Regulations have recently been amended to allow licences to be granted for the manufacture of medicinal products from a specific site. This is known as modular manufacture (MM) and the products are referred to as MM medicinal products. These licences will each have standard provisions in addition to the standard provisions generally applicable to manufacturer's licences.

Point of care

The Clinical Trials Regulations have also been recently amended so as to:

- facilitate clinical trials in the UK, including global "multi-site" trials, through the integration of the regulatory and ethics reviews of clinical trial applications;
- provide for the manufacture and supply of medicines that are innovative and have particular characteristics such as a very short shelf life, or that are highly personalised to the recipient. These characteristics mean that the medicines have to be manufactured in small amounts very close to the place where they are administered. These sites are likely to be healthcare facilities such as pharmacies, operating theatres and clinics. This type of manufacture is known as point of care (POC) and the products are referred to in the Regulations as POC medicinal products;
- regulate POC medicinal products by way of authorisation and a master file relating to the product, instead of the normal provision that a licence requires each site to be named on a licence and inspected.

Amendments to the Clinical Trials Regulations

The Clinical Trial Regulations are due to be significantly amended in 2026. Details of the amendments are in **Box 5.3**.

---

15. https://nibsc.org/about_us/latest_news/nibsc_and_tgn1412.aspx (accessed 31 December 2024).
16. https://www.judiciary.uk/wp-content/uploads/2022/09/Roy-Draper-Prevention-of-future-deaths-report-2022-0242_Published.pdf (accessed 30 December 2024).

Reporting clinical trials

It is obviously of the utmost importance that data from clinical trials are reported honestly and accurately, because the grant of a future marketing authorisation will depend on the data showing that a product can be taken safely. For this reason, the General Pharmaceutical Council's guidance on the outcomes of fitness to practise cases identifies dishonesty in clinical drug trials as so serious that removal from the register may be the only proportionate and appropriate outcome.[17]

Box 5.3

Amendments to the Clinical Trials Regulations are expected to come into force in January 2026. This box gives an outline of the changes. Readers can check whether the proposals have been brought into effect by checking the latest versions of the Clinical Trials Regulations and the HMR, or searching those sites for and the Medicines for Human Use (Clinical Trials) (Amendment) Regulations 2025, at www.legislation.gov.uk or using a subscription service such as Westlaw.

The draft Regulations cover:

- Requirement to register a trial.
- Requirement to share trial findings with participants.
- A combined regulatory (MHRA) and ethics approval process.
- Introduction of a notification scheme for low intervention trials.
- Membership or constitution of Research Ethics Committees.
- Simplified means of seeking agreement from participants for cluster trials using established medicines (existing treatments).
- Remove the requirement for individual suspected unexpected adverse reactions (SUSARs) to be reported to all investigators.
- Remove the requirement to report SUSARs and annual safety reports to Research Ethics Committees (in addition to MHRA).
- SUSARs can be reported in an aggregate manner.
- Introduce an overarching expectation for sponsors to identify and document the risks to patient safety and the reliability of the data and conduct the trial in a risk-proportionate manner.
- ICH GCP principles (ICH GCP stands for the International Council for Harmonisation of Technical Requirements for Pharmaceuticals for Human Use Guideline for Good Clinical Practice (GCP)). GCP is a set of internationally recognised standards for the ethical and scientific quality of clinical trials that involve human subjects.
- Introducing the term *non-investigational medicinal product*.
- Where a medicine is labelled according to its marketing authorisation (and no blinding is required), that specific clinical trial labelling may not be required.
- Radiopharmaceuticals used as diagnostics in a trial may be exempted from the need to hold a Manufacturers Authorisation for IMPs.

Marketing authorisations

Under HMR Reg.46, a person may not sell or supply or offer to sell or supply a medicinal product unless that product has a UK marketing authorisation.

---

17. https://assets.pharmacyregulation.org/files/2024-04/gphc-fitness-to-practise-hearings-outcomes-guidance-march-2024.pdf (accessed 30 December 2024).

UK marketing authorisations

A marketing authorisation is the regulatory approval of a specific medicinal product, thus enabling it to be marketed. The approving authority in the UK is the Medicines and Healthcare products Regulatory Agency (MHRA).

International Recognition Procedure Marketing authorisations that were previously granted for Great Britain (GB) have automatically been converted to UK marketing authorisations. In addition, under the International Recognition Procedure (IRP), an applicant for a marketing authorisation who has received an authorisation from a Reference Regulator will be entitled to have that authorisation recognised in the UK.[18] The applicant must be established in the UK or the EU/EEA. The Reference Regulators are the MHRA's equivalent bodies in:

- Australia
- Canada
- European Union/European Economic Area
- Japan
- Singapore
- Switzerland
- United States

Homeopathic products and Traditional Herbal Registrations are not covered by the International Recognition Procedure.

There are two categories of marketing authorisation:[19]

Category 1 – This category includes products that were authorised in the EU through the centralised procedure and subsequently converted to UK or GB authorisations at the time of EU Exit. This category also includes generic, hybrid or biosimilar products.

Category 2 – this category consists of medicinal products that do not fall into category 1, including medicines that have been granted an authorisation for the UK or GB other than through conversion from a central EU authorisation. Marketing authorisations are specific and apply solely to that product; the marketing authorisation holder must comply with the terms of the authorisation. Only following approval may the product be potentially available for patient treatment.

To apply for a marketing authorisation in the UK, an applicant has to be registered with the MHRA and to appoint one or more company administrators (which may include third party consultants). Applications must be submitted with adequate evidence of safety and efficacy to enable the MHRA to conclude that the risk-benefit balance of the medicinal product is positive. It is obviously important that the data in support of an application for a marketing authorisation is accurate. In 2024, a company director received a prison sentence after he and his company were convicted of falsifying medicines quality data.[20]

18. See https://www.gov.uk/government/publications/international-recognition-procedure/international-recognition-procedure (accessed 30 December 2024).
19. HMR Reg.49.
20. https://www.gov.uk/government/news/disgraced-company-director-convicted-of-falsifying-medicine-quality-data (accessed 30 December 2024).

If a medicinal product would fulfil an unmet medical need, for example for a serious and life-threatening disease where no satisfactory treatment methods are available or where the product offers a major therapeutic advantage, the MHRA may grant a Conditional Marketing Authorisation where comprehensive clinical data are not yet complete, but it is judged that such data will become available soon. Where a condition to be treated is rare or because collection of full information is not possible or is unethical, there is a scheme for marketing authorisations to be granted under exceptional circumstances.

Exemptions from the requirement for a marketing authorisation

There are exemptions from the need for a marketing authorisation in section 10 of the Medicines Act: these exemptions are the same as the exemptions from the requirement for a manufacturer's licence in paragraphs 1, 2, 3, 5, 6, and 7 in the section on pharmacies under the heading *Exemptions from the need for a manufacturer's licence* above.

There is a further exemption in section 10 of the Medicines Act for medicinal products prepared or dispensed by or under the supervision of a pharmacist in a pharmacy for retail sale or supply, provided that the medicinal products have not been the subject of an advertisement.

Part 10 of the HMR contains other exemptions from the need for a marketing authorisation. For example, HMR Reg.168 provides an exemption for the sale or supply of medicinal products that are not Prescription Only Medicines (see **Chapter 12**), which are sold to a healthcare professional for use in the course of their business for the purposes of administering them or causing them to be administered. In such cases, the medicinal product must have been manufactured in the UK in accordance with the healthcare professional's specification for use by a patient of theirs to meet the patient's special needs. The product cannot have been advertised and must be supplied in response to an unsolicited order.

Other exemptions apply to special medicinal products and products under the Early Access to Medicines Scheme (both of which are covered below).

There are also exemptions in certain circumstances for coronavirus and flu vaccinations.

Implications of marketing authorisations and definitions

HMR Reg.50 deals with material that must accompany an application. In dealing with an application for a marketing authorisation, the licensing authority must give particular consideration to the safety, quality and efficacy of the products.

Applications must be accompanied by a summary of product characteristics (SmPC). This is a description of the medicinal product's properties and the conditions attached to its use. The MHRA may publish (a) guidance on the presentation and content of SmPC; (b) scientific guidelines relating to the quality, safety and efficacy of medicinal products; and (c) guidelines describing the active substance manufacturing process controls. These are the fundamental information for healthcare professionals in terms of therapeutic indication, posology and safety. SmPCs are also the basis for the preparation of patient information leaflets (see **Chapter 18**), and it is a requirement that they are kept updated during the lifespan of the relevant product as new efficacy or safety data emerge. SmPCs have been used to effect regulatory changes. For example, in 2024, the SmPC for valproate products was changed so as to stipulate that valproate must not be started in any patient (male or female) younger than 55 years, unless two specialists independently consider and document that there is no other effective or tolerated treatment, or there are compelling reasons that the reproductive risks (as to which, see **Chapter 12**) do not apply.[21]

In addition to the SmPC, the particulars required to be given in a full application include the kind of activity to be undertaken (e.g. selling, procuring manufacture, etc.); the pharmaceutical form of the product; its composition, physical characteristics and medicinal use; method of manufacture and assembly; quality control procedures; containers and labelling; reports of experimental and biological studies and of clinical trials and studies; any adverse reactions; and where the product is made abroad, must include documentary evidence of authorisation relating to manufacture, assembly, and so on. Special additional conditions apply for applications concerning immunological products, radiopharmaceuticals and medicinal products derived from human blood or human plasma.

Abridged applications are permitted where the relevant data have been submitted in an earlier application, or data about the kind of product in question are well documented (see below). A typical example would be for a generic product; the application does not need full pre-clinical and clinical efficacy studies, as would be the case for a new active drug. Renewal applications for licences and certificates are dealt with in HMR Reg.66.

A marketing authorisation must specify the product's legal classification, namely whether the product is to be subject to general sale, a Pharmacy medicine or a Prescription Only Medicine (see **Chapters 10, 11** and **12** respectively).

As a result of the grant of a marketing authorisation for a medicinal product the holder of the authorisation may, so long as the terms of the marketing authorisation are complied with:

a. sell, supply, offer for sale or supply, or export the product;
b. procure its sale, supply or exportation; and
c. procure its manufacture or assembly.

Exporting

Medicinal products may be exported if an appropriate marketing authorisation is held. Medicinal products must be labelled with the words "UK only" (see **Chapter 18**).[22] This means that such medicines may not be exported to an EU state. However, the inclusion of the words "UK Only" on packaging does not prevent exporting from the UK to other

21. https://www.gov.uk/government/news/new-valproate-safety-measures-apply-from-31-january (accessed 30 December 2024).

22. MHRA guidance states that medicines produced solely for export do not need to be labelled with the words "UK only"; see: https://www.gov.uk/government/publications/windsor-framework-explainer/windsor-framework-agreement-on-the-supply-of-medicines-in-northern-ireland-explained (accessed 31 December 2024).

non-EU country or territory where the import of those medicines is compliant with local legal requirements or provisions.

The MHRA requires that any exporter of medicines should be able to show proof that they have followed both UK laws and the laws of the country receiving the medicines.

Obligations of marketing authorisation holders

The HMR include obligations of marketing authorisation holders:

- to notify the MHRA within two months that a product has been placed on the market or withdrawn (HMR Reg.73);
- to take account of scientific and technical progress, including keeping under review the methods of manufacture; and, as soon as reasonably practicable after becoming aware of the need to do so, applying to vary the marketing authorisation to make any changes to those methods that are required to ensure they are generally accepted scientific methods (HMR Reg.74);
- to provide as soon as is reasonably practicable information relating to safety, including positive and negative results of clinical trials or other studies and any information that the holder considers might influence the evaluation of the benefits and risks of the product (HMR Reg.75);[23]
- to ensure that the product information relating to the product is kept up to date with current scientific knowledge (HMR Reg.76);
- to keep records, specifically, any documents or information that will facilitate the withdrawal or recall from sale or supply of any product to which the authorisation relates (HMR Reg.77); and
- to take all reasonable steps to ensure appropriate and continued supplies of the product to which the authorisation relates to pharmacies and persons authorised to supply the product so that the needs of patients in the UK are met (HMR Reg.78).

Standard conditions and obligations for marketing authorisations are to be found in Schedule 4 to the HMR. These provisions are automatically incorporated into marketing authorisations (unless a request to exclude or modify them is granted).

The MHRA expects marketing authorisation holders to monitor stocks of licensed products to minimise the effects of shortages. Under regulation 28 of the Health Service Products (Provision and Disclosure of Information) Regulations 2018, where the Secretary of State considers that there is a supply shortage of a health service medicine, the Secretary of State may by notice in writing require a manufacturer, a wholesaler or other distributor, or an importer to provide information about the quantity of stocks held and the quantity held of any therapeutically alternative product. Under regulation 29 of these Regulations, a UK marketing authorisation holder or (if a UK producer does not hold the marketing authorisation for a product), the manufacturer or importer, must provide the Secretary of State with information at least six months in advance about:

23. The time frame for publishing the summary of results is within six months of the end of trial for paediatric clinical trials or within one year of the end of trial for non-paediatric clinical trials.

- an intention to discontinue the manufacture or supply if this is likely to have a direct impact on any patient who takes or may need to take the medication; or
- where it is considered that there may be a shortage of the product, the anticipated duration of the shortage and any steps taken to address it.

Off-label prescribing

Off-label prescribing refers to the prescribing of a medicinal product to treat a patient who has a condition for which the product does not have a marketing authorisation. In some cases, a medicinal product has a marketing authorisation to treat one condition but not another condition for which it may nevertheless be effective. Supplies of medicines prescribed off-label come within the exemption from the need for a marketing authorisation for a medicinal product prepared or dispensed in accordance with a prescription (see Exemptions from the requirement for a marketing authorisation above). In its guide *Good practice in prescribing and managing medicines and devices*[24] the General Medical Council advises medical practitioners that they should "usually prescribe licensed medicines in accordance with the terms of their licence", but says practitioners may prescribe unlicensed medicines where, on the basis of an assessment of the individual patient, the practitioner concludes, for medical reasons, that it was necessary to do so to meet the specific needs of the patient.

The GMC's previous guidance came under consideration by the Court of Appeal in *Bayer PLC and Novartis Pharmaceuticals UK Ltd v NHS Darlington CCG and others.*[25] The court also considered the meaning of the expression *placing on the market*. A summary of the case is given in **Box 5.4**. Aspects of the case that relate specifically to hospitals are covered in **Chapter 9** and **Box 9.1**.

Box 5.4: *Bayer PLC and Novartis Pharmaceuticals UK Ltd v NHS Darlington CCG and others* [2020] EWCA Civ 449

Facts

Darlington Clinical Commissioning Group (CCG) and a number of other CCGs, all of which were also Defendants, had adopted a policy that the NHS Trusts from which they commissioned services should use Avastin as the preferred treatment for a form of the eye disease, wet age-related macular degeneration (WAMD).

WAMD is very common. Avastin was originally developed for the treatment of colorectal cancer and it is licensed for such treatment in the UK. It has been found to be effective in the treatment of WAMD, but no application has been made to license its use in the UK to treat WAMD. Indeed, its formal Summary of Product Characteristics says it is not formulated for intravitreal use.

---

24. https://www.gmc-uk.org/-/media/documents/prescribing-guidance-updated-english-20210405_pdf-85260533 – paragraphs 103 to 106 (accessed 30 December 2024).

25. [2020] EWCA Civ 449.

Box 5.4: *Bayer PLC and Novartis Pharmaceuticals UK Ltd v NHS Darlington CCG and others* [2020] EWCA Civ 449 (cont.)

Avastin is supplied in glass vials. For treating colorectal cancer, the contents of the vial are diluted before administration. To treat WAMD, however, Avastin is not diluted and the contents of a vial were repackaged into a large number of syringes for injection.

Use of a medicine for a purpose other than the one(s) specified in a licence is generally described as "off-label". Off-label use of a drug is not necessarily unsafe or otherwise inappropriate provided that the clinician takes full responsibility for the decision to use it.

There are two licensed products for the treatment of WAMD, Eylea for which Bayer holds the marketing authorisation and Lucentis for which Novartis holds the marketing authorisation in Europe. The evidence before the court was that Avastin was just as safe and effective as Eylea and Lucentis for the treatment of WAMD, but Eylea cost about £800 per injection and Lucentis costs about £550, whereas Avastin cost about £28.

Standard conditions require NHS Trusts to co-operate with CCGs, so they are required to take the CCG's policy into account.

Bayer and Novartis sued the twelve CCGs and alleged that implementation of the policy would breach the HMR.

There are exemptions in section 10 of the Medicines Act 1968 from the need for a marketing authorisation. These include medicinal products prepared in a pharmacy in accordance with a prescription for an individual patient; and any medicinal product prepared in a pharmacy in accordance with the prescriptions of a pharmacopoeia and is intended to be supplied by patients of the pharmacy.

Ordinarily, preparing, dividing up or changing packaging or presentation – which is done when Avastin is used for WAMD – requires a marketing authorisation.

Judgment

The Court held that:

- the process of "placing on the market" comes to an end at the point where a clinician prescribes the product for a particular patient. Once a product is under the control of a treating doctor, what happens to the product is "downstream" of the scope of the Medicines Directive. Thus, any subsequent transfer of the product is not part of placing it on the market but is essentially part of the clinical process.
- It follows that someone who divides or repackages Avastin or alters its presentation, without modifying the product, does not require a marketing authorisation so long as it is done on the basis of an individual prescription. "Modifying" means changing the substance of the medicinal product i.e. changing its biological, chemical or physical state in a way which might significantly affect its quality, efficacy or safety. A risk of contamination because of poor quality control was immaterial to the need for a licence: such processes were under the control of doctors and/or pharmacists who are subject to separate professional regulation. However, any hospital pharmacy that undertook syringe filling would have to give careful thought to how to ensure its processes are safe and accord with any professional rules.
- The person who carries out the modification does not need to have the prescription in their hands at the moment the Avastin is prepared or supplied. It is enough to be informed that the prescription exists – though the prescription must actually be in existence.
- The person who fills syringes with Avastin does not have to point to a particular syringe and identify it as allocated to a particular patient. It would be enough if 20 syringes are being prepared and they are covered from the start by 20 existing prescriptions.
- Similarly, a manufacturing authorisation is not required to divide Avastin (the term "compounding" is used in the judgment) so long as this is done in a dispensing

Box 5.4: *Bayer PLC and Novartis Pharmaceuticals UK Ltd v NHS Darlington CCG and others* [2020] EWCA Civ 449 (cont.)

pharmacy or by a person legally authorised to do the compounding and this is done solely for retail supply.

- Section 10(1) of the Medicines Act 1968 contains exemptions from the need for a manufacturer's licence for anything done in a registered pharmacy or hospital under the supervision of a pharmacist, consisting of:
  a. preparing or dispensing a medicinal product in accordance with a prescription; or
  b. assembling a medicinal product in a hospital or pharmacy under the supervision of a pharmacist.
- Novartis argued that "preparation" did not cover the bulk filling of syringes. The Court rejected this and held that section 10 was "perfectly apt" to cover preparing syringes in bulk. The Court also held that when syringes were filled in a pharmacy or hospital and supplied to a hospital for a patient to whom it had been prescribed, this was "dispensing".
- Novartis additionally argued that when Avastin syringes were prepared in one hospital and supplied to another hospital, a wholesale dealer's licence was required. The definition of "wholesale distribution" excludes supplies to the public, so supplies to a hospital for administration to a particular patient constitute retail rather than wholesale supplies, and such supplies do not require a wholesale dealer's licence.
- The word "dispensing" does not appear often in legislation and is not defined. The Court held that the term covered the preparation of syringes and supply by one hospital to another in response to individual prescriptions.
- The GMC had clarified its position on off-label prescribing, and stated that "doctors must … use resources efficiently for the benefit of patients and the public". The GMC added that "the treatment options that can be offered to patients may be affected by limits on resources". Specifically in relation to Avastin, the Chief Executive of the GMC had said that a prescribing decision would not raise fitness to practise issues so long as the broader principles of GMC guidance were followed. In view of this evidence, the Court concluded that clinicians are not prohibited from prescribing an unlicensed drug simply because there are licensed alternatives. As the Court put it:

  > *"There is nothing inherently illegitimate in prescribing decisions being influenced by cost considerations where the evidence shows no differences in efficacy or safety."*

The CCGs were held to have acted lawfully and the appeals by Bayer and Novartis were dismissed.

In addition to the issues that arose in the *Bayer* case, off-label prescribing may give rise to legal and professional conduct issues when medicines are in short supply. For example, an NHS patient safety alert in January 2024 asked prescribers not to use medicines licensed for the treatment of diabetes off-label (referring to Ozempic) for the management of obesity, and that existing stock be conserved for use in patients with diabetes. This was due to supply shortages caused by an increase in demand.[26]

26. https://www.pharmacyregulation.org/patients-and-public/standards-you-can-expect-using-pharmacy-services/weight-loss-medications-faq (added 30 December 2024).

Revocation, variation or suspension

There is provision in the Regulations for a marketing authorisation to be revoked, varied or suspended (HMR Reg.68 and Reg.69). A summary of the grounds for revocation, variation or suspension is given in **Box 5.5**.

Box 5.5: Summary of grounds for revocation, variation and suspension of UK marketing authorisation or parallel import licence

The licensing authority may revoke, vary or suspend a UK marketing authorisation or parallel import licence if any of the following conditions is met.

Condition A is that the licensing authority thinks that:

a. the product to which the authorisation relates is harmful;
b. the positive therapeutic effects of the product do not outweigh the risks of the product to the health of patients or of the public;
c. the product lacks therapeutic efficacy, in that therapeutic results cannot be obtained from the product; or
d. the product's qualitative or quantitative composition is not as described in the application for the authorisation or the material supplied with it.

Condition B is that the licensing authority thinks that the application or the material supplied with it is incorrect.

Condition C is that the licensing authority thinks that there has been a breach of:

a. a term of the authorisation or licence;
b. in the case of a UK marketing authorisation, a requirement concerning packaging and leaflets; or
c. in the case of a parallel import licence, a requirement in relation to packaging and leaflets imposed by the licensing authority.

Condition D is that the licensing authority thinks that a condition to which the UK marketing authorisation or parallel import licence is subject has not been fulfilled.

Condition E is that the licensing authority thinks that the holder of the authorisation has not complied with requirements to provide information.

Condition F is that the holder of the authorisation has ceased to be established in the United Kingdom.

Condition G is that:

a. the product to which the authorisation relates is manufactured in the United Kingdom; and
b. the licensing authority thinks that the holder of the manufacturer's licence for the product has failed to comply with the principles and guidelines for good manufacturing practice set out in the Good Manufacturing Practice Directive (see below) and other provisions of HMR Reg.37 (manufacturing and assembly), HMR Reg.38 (imports from states other than approved countries for import), HMR Reg.39 (further requirements for manufacturer's licence), HMR Reg.40 (obligation to provide information relating to control methods) or HMR Reg.41 (requirements as to qualified persons).

Condition H is that:

a. the product to which the authorisation relates is manufactured in a member State and
b. the licensing authority thinks that the licensee under the manufacturer's licence for the product has failed to comply in relation to the product with provision giving effect to Article 41 of the 2001 Directive (requirements relating to manufacturing authorisations) in that member State.

Condition I is that the licensing authority thinks that urgent action to protect public health is necessary, in which case it may suspend the authorisation or licence.

Box 5.5: Summary of grounds for revocation, variation and suspension of UK marketing authorisation or parallel import licence (cont.)

Condition J is that:

a. the holder applies to vary the authorisation licence; and
b. the licensing authority thinks that the application should be granted.

Condition K is that the manufacture of the product to which the authorisation relates is not carried out in compliance with the particulars of the manufacturing and control methods provided when the marketing authorisation was applied for.

Condition L is that the licensing authority thinks that the term of the authorisation which specifies the way in which the product is to be made available as described is incorrect.

Condition M is that, in respect of a parallel import licence, the UK marketing authorisation has been varied, suspended or revoked by the licensing authority.

Condition N is that, in respect of a parallel import licence, the licensing authority is no longer satisfied that the product is essentially similar to a product that has been granted a UK marketing authorisation.

Condition O is that the licensing authority thinks that a variation of a UK marketing authority is necessary as a result of the submission of the results of a study by the holder of that authorisation.

Conditions P, Q and R relate to steps that may be required as a result of the UK's exit from the EU.

It is possible for the marketing authorisation holder to apply for a variation of licence. Marketing authorisations are very specific, and it is quite common for a change to be sought at some point in the product lifecycle. Changes could involve the types of medicinal product in respect of which the licence was granted, an operation carried out under the licence, or an amendment to any premises, equipment or facilities in respect of which the licence was granted. Data justifying the variation may be needed, depending on the complexity. After the granting of a UK marketing authorisation, the licensing authority may impose obligations on the holder of the authorisation. Holders must operate a pharmacovigilance system and they may be required to conduct a post-authorisation safety study (if there are concerns about the risks of a medicinal product) or a post-authorisation efficacy study (if the understanding of the disease or the clinical methodology indicate that previous efficacy evaluations might have to be revised significantly) (HMR Reg.61).

Pharmacovigilance

Part 11 of the Human Medicines Regulations 2012 covers the obligations of the licensing authority (MHRA) and marketing authorisation holders with regard to pharmacovigilance.

A full account of these requirements is outside the scope of this book, but both the licensing authority and holders of manufacturing authorisations must operate a pharmacovigilance system for UK authorised products to capture and evaluate all information and take all appropriate measures to minimise and prevent risk, particularly concerning adverse drug reactions, presented by use of the medicinal product after the authorisation is granted. In brief (HMR Reg.182):

- the marketing authorisation holder must operate a pharmacovigilance system;
- the marketing authorisation holder must have permanently and continuously at its disposal an appropriately qualified person responsible for pharmacovigilance

(*QPPV*)[27]. The QPPV must reside and operate in the UK or the EU/EEA and is responsible for the establishment and maintenance of the pharmacovigilance system for UK authorised products. This individual should have access to the reports of suspected adverse reactions referred to in HMR Reg of the HMRs and the Pharmacovigilance System Master File for UK authorised products. The individual should be able to facilitate responses to pharmacovigilance queries raised by the MHRA, including via inspections;

- The QPPV must have qualifications. In the case of marketing authorisations that are specific to Great Britain, the legal requirements for these qualifications are outlined in Schedule 12A to the HMR. These mirror the requirements in relation to marketing authorisations that are not specific to Great Britain;
- The QPPV's details must be notified to the MHRA;
- if the QPPV resides and operates in the EU/EEA, there must be a national contact person for pharmacovigilance;
- the pharmacovigilance system must enable the collection of information on the risks that medicinal products present to patients' health or public health;
- the licence holder must have permanently and continuously an appropriately qualified person responsible for the establishment and maintenance of the pharmacovigilance system;
- the licence holder must maintain permanently and make immediately available when requested a pharmacovigilance system master file (PSMF) that describes the pharmacovigilance system for UK authorised products. The PSMF must be accessible electronically from the UK at the same site at which reports of suspected adverse reaction may be accessed;
- the licence holder must use its pharmacovigilance system to evaluate scientifically all information relevant to the product, consider options for minimising and preventing the risk presented by the use of the product, and take appropriate measures as soon as is reasonably practicable to investigate the potential risks of the product, communicate the risks, and implement actions for minimising and preventing the risks.

The licence holder is also required to submit to the MHRA regular Periodic Safety Update Reports (PSURs) (HMR Regs.191-195), Individual Case Safety Reports (ICSRs), Risk Management Plans (RMPs) and Post-Authorisation Safety Studies (PASS) protocols and final study reports.

HMR Reg.178 states that the licensing authority must:

a. take all appropriate measures to encourage the reporting to it of suspected adverse reactions;
b. facilitate reporting through the provision of alternative reporting formats in addition to web-based formats;

---

27. The legal requirements concerning the qualifications and responsibilities of the QPPV are outlined in paragraph 10 of Schedule 12A to the HMR and statutory guidance concerning the QPPV for UK authorised products is described in the Good Pharmacovigilance Practices (GVP) Module 1.

c. take all appropriate measures to obtain accurate and verifiable data for the scientific evaluation of suspected adverse reaction reports;
d. ensure that the public is given important information on pharmacovigilance concerns relating to the use of a medicinal product in a timely manner, through publication on the UK web portal, and through other means of publicly available information as necessary; and
e. ensure that all appropriate measures are taken to identify any biological medicinal product (including name and batch number) prescribed, dispensed or sold in the UK which is the subject of a suspected adverse reaction report through the methods for collecting data and, where necessary, the follow up of suspected adverse reaction reports.

For many years, the MHRA has operated what is known as the Yellow Card Scheme for collecting and monitoring information on suspected safety concerns or incidents involving medicines and medical devices. The Scheme relies on voluntary reporting of suspected adverse drug reactions (ADRs) by health professionals and patients. The purpose of the Scheme is to provide an early warning that the safety of a product may require further investigation. The Scheme came under scrutiny by the Independent Medicines and Medical Devices Safety Review chaired by Baroness Cumberlege (the Cumberlege Review) whose report published in 2020 was entitled *First Do No Harm.*[28] The Review concerned hormone pregnancy tests, such as Primodos, which were withdrawn from the market in the late 1970s and which are thought to be associated with birth defects and miscarriages; with sodium valproate, an anti-epileptic drug which causes physical malformations, autism and developmental delay in children when it is taken by their mothers during pregnancy; and pelvic mesh implants, the use of which has been linked to crippling, life-changing complications.

The Review concluded that the Yellow Card Scheme could not be relied upon to identify promptly significant adverse outcomes arising from a medicinal product or device because the system lacks the means to do so. It was clear that there was under-reporting and the system was "too complex and too diffuse to allow early signal detection". The Cumberlege Review recommended that the Yellow Card system should be reformed to provide a "user-friendly, accessible transparent repository of adverse event reports".

The MHRA has published guidance on pharmacovigilance.[29]

Article 126a products

Where it is considered justified for public health reasons, Article 126a of the Medicines Directive allows an EU member state to authorise the placing on the market of a medicinal product that does not have a marketing authorisation. Such authorisations will be recognised by the UK until their expiry dates, but the MHRA will not grant Article 126a authorisations for products to be placed on the market in Great Britain.

---

28. https://www.immdsreview.org.uk/downloads/IMMDSReview_Web.pdf (accessed 30 December 2024).
29. See, for example, https://www.gov.uk/guidance/guidance-on-qualified-person-responsible-for-pharmacovigilance-qppv-including-pharmacovigilance-system-master-files-psmf (accessed 30 December 2024) and https://assets.publishing.service.gov.uk/media/6772707b94d6140e8459dc84/Exceptions_and_modifications_to_the_EU_guidance_on_good_pharmacovigilance_practices_that_apply_to_UK_MAHs__1_Jan_2025_.pdf (accessed 31 December 2024).

Product licences of right

At the time the Medicines Act 1968 came into force, the equivalent of a marketing authorisation was a product licence. The owners of certain products that were already on the market at the time the Act came into force were entitled to apply for a product licence of right, so that they did not need to comply with the stringent requirements of a product licence application. Product licences of right remain in effect and do not require a marketing authorisation.[30]

Orphan drugs

Orphan drugs[31] are drugs that are used to treat conditions that occur so infrequently that the cost of developing and bringing to the market a medicinal product to diagnose, prevent or treat the condition would not be recovered by the expected sales of the medicinal product; the pharmaceutical industry would be unwilling to develop the medicinal product under normal market conditions. The provisions governing orphan drugs in HMR Reg.58D and Schedule 9A to the HMR apply to a medicinal product that is intended for the diagnosis, prevention or treatment of a life-threatening or chronically debilitating condition affecting not more than five in 10,000 persons in the UK. The MHRA is responsible for reviewing applications from companies for new orphan designations. To qualify for orphan designation:

- the product must be intended for the treatment, prevention or diagnosis of a disease that is life-threatening or chronically debilitating;
- the prevalence of the condition in the UK must not be more than 5 in 10,000, or it must be unlikely that marketing of the medicine would generate sufficient returns to justify the investment needed for its development;
- no satisfactory method of diagnosis, prevention or treatment of the condition concerned exists in the UK or, if such a method exists, the medicine must be of significant benefit to those affected by the condition.

To incentivise applications for orphan products, orphan medicinal products will benefit from up to 10 years of market exclusivity from similar products in the approved orphan indication, commencing on the date of first approval of the product by the MHRA. Orphan drugs for paediatric indications are eligible for an additional two years of market exclusivity.

All medicines that gain a Great Britain orphan marketing authorisation will be listed in the Orphan Register.

Generic products

Generic medicinal product (HMR Reg.48(2)), in relation to a reference medicinal product (RMP), means a medicinal product:

---

30. Paragraph 3 of Schedule 32 to the HMR.

31. For MHRA guidance, see https://www.gov.uk/guidance/orphan-medicinal-products-in-great-britain (accessed 30 December 2024).

a. that has the same qualitative and quantitative composition in active substances as the RMP;
b. that has the same pharmaceutical form as the RMP; and
c. whose bioequivalence with the RMP has been demonstrated by appropriate bioavailability studies.

RMPs for new generic medicines or other abridged marketing authorisations must comply with the following in order to provide evidence that the safety and efficacy profiles of the proposed product will be equivalent to that of the RMP and for which safety and efficacy has been demonstrated clinically:

- The MHRA must be satisfied that any differences between a non-UK comparator and the RMP are not therapeutically significant.
- Comparator products used in bioequivalence, pharmacokinetic and therapeutic equivalence studies supporting abridged applications should be representative of the RMP supporting the application.
- Comparator products should be sourced from the UK. If they are not sourced from the UK market, they should be authorised in and sourced from a country with similar scientific and regulatory standards as the UK. Examples include the EU/EEA, Switzerland, USA, Canada, Australia and Japan. Evidence should be provided that the comparator is representative of the RMP.

Generics, as they are commonly known, are typically cheaper than proprietary medicinal products (commonly referred to as *branded* medicines). As such, there is often pressure on prescribers from NHS bodies to prescribe generic medicines,[32] and there is frequent litigation between the owners of proprietary medicinal products against manufacturers of generics over patent rights (see also **Chapter 24**). There is also a hybrid known as a *branded generic*. Branded generics are essentially generics that have a brand name. Some Clinical Commissioning Groups, before they were replaced by Integrated Care Boards, encouraged medical practitioners in their areas to prescribe branded generics which have a lower price than non-branded generics.

Protection of branded products and abridged procedure for generics

If a product has a valid UK patent, the patent holder may apply for a Supplementary Protection Certificate (SPC) to protect the active ingredient (see the meaning of *active ingredient* above). A SPC will not extend the patent but, if granted, it can give similar protection to a patent for up to five years from when the patent expires.

Typically, the manufacturer of a branded medicinal product will have incurred the considerable cost of years of research, development and bringing their product to market, including clinical trials and the possibility that for every product that is granted a marketing authorisation, many others will not have been efficacious or passed clinical trials. A balance has to be struck between the research costs incurred by the original innovator and allowing a person applying for a marketing authorisation for a follow-on

32. See, for example, the NHS Business Services website https://www.nhsbsa.nhs.uk/epact2/dashboards-and-specifications/medicines-optimisation-generic-prescribing (accessed 30 December 2024).

product (e.g. a generic product) to omit the results of pre-clinical tests and of clinical trials. This balance is achieved[33] by allowing a follow-on competitor to rely on the data for the reference medicinal product only if a UK marketing authorisation for the reference medicinal product has been held for not less than eight years. If a marketing authorisation is granted for the generic product, it is a term of the authorisation that the generic product must not be sold or supplied, or offered for sale or supply, in the United Kingdom before the expiry of ten years beginning with the date on which the UK marketing authorisation for the reference medicinal product was granted.

If during the first eight of the ten years referred to above, the marketing authorisation holder for the reference medicinal product obtained a UK marketing authorisation for one or more new therapeutic indications, and, during the scientific evaluation prior to their authorisation, the MHRA considers the new indications bring a significant clinical benefit in comparison with existing therapies, the period of ten years referred to in paragraph is extended to eleven years.

The possibility of extending the period of protection to eleven years was considered by the High Court in *R (on the application of Napp Pharmaceuticals Ltd) v Secretary of State for Health (acting as licensing authority) and Sandoz Ltd*[34] (see **Box 5.6**).

Box 5.6: High Court consideration of the abridged procedure

In *R (on the application of Napp Pharmaceuticals Ltd) v Secretary of State for Health (acting as licensing authority) and Sandoz Ltd*, Napp had obtained a marketing authority for BuTrans, a transdermal patch containing buprenorphine, using the abridged procedure and referring to Temgesic, a sub-lingual product containing buprenorphine, which had been in use for just over 10 years. Sandoz applied for a marketing authorisation for Reletrans, also a transdermal patch containing buprenorphine, mainly relying on the data that Napp had provided, along with some new data to demonstrate that Reletrans was bio-equivalent to BuTrans. Napp challenged a decision by the MHRA to grant the Sandoz application, arguing that Sandoz should have provided its own data. Mrs Justice Whipple rejected the Napp challenge, holding that the purpose of the procedure was to ensure that medicines were safe and effective, and that upholding the Napp case would lead to "unnecessary repeat testing which is contrary to the public interest; it would also act as a disincentive to the development of generic alternatives which are in the public interest".

Advanced therapy medicinal products

An advanced therapy medicinal product (ATMP) means:

a. a gene therapy medicinal product;
b. a somatic cell therapy medicinal product; or
c. a tissue engineered product.[35]

A combination ATMP includes one or more medical device.

---

33. HMR reg.51B.
34. [2016] EWHC 1982 (Admin).
35. HMR Reg.2A.

A manufacturer's licence is required to manufacture an ATMP unless the ATMP is a special medicinal product (see below) or unless an exemption for hospital manufacture applies (see **Chapter 9**).

Before treating a patient with an ATMP, there must be a system in place for patient and product traceability. The system must contain sufficient detail to enable the linking of the product to the patient who received it and vice versa.[36]

Biological medicinal products and biosimilars

A biological medicinal product is a product, the active substance of which is a biological substance. A biological substance is a substance that is produced by or extracted from a biological source and that needs for its characterisation and the determination of its quality a combination of physico-chemical-biological testing, together with the production process and its control. Biological medicinal products are immunological medicinal products and medicinal products derived from human blood and human plasma.[37]

A *biosimilar* is a biological medicinal product that contains a version of the active substance of an already authorised original biological medicinal product (the reference product or RP). If an applicant for a marketing authorisation for a biosimilar is not able to show that it meets a condition for it being a generic version of a similar medicinal product because of differences relating to raw materials or differences in manufacturing processes of the biological medicinal product and the RP for an authorised product, the applicant may omit from the application the results of pre-clinical tests and of clinical trials relating to a reference medicinal product which is or has been authorised for not less than eight years, but must provide the results of appropriate pre-clinical tests or clinical trials relating to the differences in raw materials or manufacturing processes.[38]

Borderline products

A question may arise whether a product is a medicinal product or, for example, a food supplement or a medical device or a cosmetic product. Specifically in relation to nutritional and dermatological products, the Advisory Committee on Borderline Substances advises on their use in NHS primary care. Where the licensing authority – the MHRA – is of the opinion that a product is a medicinal product, they may serve written notice on any person who has placed the product on the market informing them that the product is a relevant medicinal product and requires a marketing authorisation. Statutory provisions provide for initial representations to be made to the licensing authority and, if necessary, for further representations to be made to the Independent Review Panel for Borderline Products. Once a final determination has been made, the licensing authority may serve notice requiring the person not to put the product on

36. HMR Reg.154.
37. HMR Reg.8.
38. HMR Reg.53B.

the market or to stop marketing it from a date specified. An example of this relates to products containing cannabidiol.[39] The MHRA has published guidance on products at the borderline between medicinal products and medical devices.[40] Detailed procedures for determining whether a substance is a medicinal product are set out in the legislation (HMR Reg.159) and in guidance published by the MHRA which includes a summary of relevant case law.[41] It is an offence to sell, supply or offer to sell or supply a product once a notice has been served (HMR Reg.166).

Immunity from liability for unauthorised medicinal products

In response to the suspected or confirmed spread of pathogenic agents, toxins, chemical agents or nuclear radiation which may cause harm to humans, the licensing authority may recommend or require the use of:

1. a medicinal product without an authorisation; or
2. a medicinal product with an authorisation, but for a therapeutic indication that is not permitted under the authorisation.

HMR Reg.345 provides that specific categories of people shall not have any civil liability for any loss or damage resulting from the use of the product in accordance with the recommendation or requirement. As amended during the COVID-19 pandemic, so as to facilitate the use of a vaccine for which there had not been time to obtain a marketing authorisation, and to give some assurance to companies willing to co-operate in a mass vaccination programme that they would not be exposed inappropriately to civil liability, the regulation gives immunity to:

1. any holder of an authorisation for the product;
2. if there is no holder of an authorisation for the product but the sale or supply of the product is authorised by the licensing authority on a temporary basis, the person responsible for placing the product on the market;
3. any manufacturer of the product;
4. any officer, servant, employee or agent of a person referred to above;
5. any health care professional;[42] or
6. any person, not being a health care professional, who administers the product in accordance with a protocol.

The immunity does not extend to any liability under the Consumer Protection Act 1987 for defective products (see **Chapter 24** regarding product liability).

---

39. MHRA statement on products containing Cannabidiol (CBD), October 2016 (https://www.gov.uk/government/news/mhra-statement-on-products-containing-cannabidiol-cbd (accessed 30 December 2024).
40. https://assets.publishing.service.gov.uk/government/uploads/system/uploads/attachment_data/file/284493/Borderlines_between_medical_devices_and_medicinal_products.pdf (accessed 30 December 2024).
41. https://assets.publishing.service.gov.uk/government/uploads/system/uploads/attachment_data/file/872742/GN8_FINAL_10_03_2020__combined_.pdf (accessed 30 December 2024).
42. As defined in HMR Reg.8 – the definition includes pharmacists, pharmacy technicians, doctors, nurses and dentists, amongst others.

Early Access to Medicines Scheme (EAMS)

The aim of the Early Access to Medicines Scheme (EAMS) is to enable patients to have access to medicines which have not yet been authorised, in cases of life-threatening or seriously debilitating conditions, and where no suitable alternative may be available. The scheme is voluntary and consists of two parts.[43] The first (promising innovative medicine) derives from early clinical data and an application approved by the MHRA could mean that the medicine is available several years ahead of a formal marketing authorisation approval. The second part of the scheme is based on scientific opinion and considers the benefit/risk profile of the medicine. The opinion supports the prescribing decision with regard to the use of a medicine before licensing approval. Applications to the MHRA can be made via the dedicated EAMS webpage.

Importing

The importation of a medicinal product which is a version of one already the subject of a UK marketing authorisation is known as parallel importing. The licence granted to a wholesale dealer in Great Britain will permit the importation of medicinal products from a country which is on an *approved country for imports list.* Initially, this list will be countries in the EU and European Economic Area. HMR Reg 18A allows importation from such countries, provided that the UK wholesale dealer has nominated and named on the wholesale dealer's licence a Responsible Person (import) (RPi) who will carry out specific functions and confirms that each batch has been certified by a Qualified Person in a listed country.

A RPi is not required if the medicine imported from a listed country is not licensed in the UK or the listed country and the medicinal product is either for use as a special medicinal product or is to be exported by the importer as an introduced medicine.

If a medicine is not licensed in the UK or a country on the approved country for imports list, importers require a Responsible Person, not an RPi, and the wholesale dealer's licence will need to cover both the product that does not have an authorisation and the wholesale distribution from an unlisted country.

If a medicine is imported from a country on the approved country for imports list with a view to exporting as an introduced medicinal product, the importer will need to hold a wholesale dealer's licence that authorises both import and export.

Different rules apply to the sourcing of medicinal products from Northern Ireland. Medicines that are authorised in Northern Ireland will be granted an authorisation in Great Britain and the sourcing of such medicines is permitted with a wholesale dealer's licence, under the supervision of an ordinary Responsible Person.

The prices of medicinal products vary from country to country. Holders of a wholesale dealer's licence have been able to take advantage of currency fluctuations so that it may be cheaper to use an imported product in the UK than to purchase the same or equivalent product in the UK. Alternatively, the price may make it advantageous to export medicines

43. HMR Reg.167C

purchased in the UK to other countries. However, branded products that are parallel imported sometimes have different brand names to the same product for which there is a marketing authorisation in the UK. If a prescription refers to a product by its brand name, only the product bearing that name may supplied (see **Chapter 12**).[44]

Legal basis for parallel imports

Parallel distributors (in the UK) involved in repackaging or relabelling must employ at least one Qualified Person and hold a Manufacturing (assembly) Licence. A Wholesale Dealer's Licence is needed to distribute the product.

A product licence (parallel import) is granted for 5 years but normally continues in force only so long as *both* the UK marketing authorisation and the EU marketing authorisation to which it relates remain in force. If either marketing authorisation is revoked, the product licence (parallel import) will automatically be revoked also. If a marketing authorisation is withdrawn, it may be possible to continue to market the product in the UK, but only if the product licence (parallel import) satisfies the strict criteria that the ECJ have set for the survival of the product licence (parallel import) in these circumstances. These criteria follow from a referral to the ECJ in 1998.[45]

The decision in *The Queen v Royal Pharmaceutical Society of Great Britain, ex parte Association of Pharmaceutical Importers and Others*[46] (**Box 5.7**) made it clear that the regulator (now the GPhC) may make additional rules concerning the use of licensed medicines on professional grounds for the protection of the public.

Box 5.7: Importation of medicines from the EU

The Queen v Royal Pharmaceutical Society of Great Britain, ex parte Association of Pharmaceutical Importers and Others

In 1989, the then professional regulator, the Royal Pharmaceutical Society of Great Britain (RPSGB) had adopted a provision in its Code of Ethics which, among other things, prohibited a pharmacist from substituting, except in an emergency, any other medicine for the medicine specifically ordered on a prescription, even if they believed that the quality and therapeutic effect were identical. In 1986, the RPSGB had published a statement to the effect that this rule applied to imported medicines as well as to medicines licensed in the UK. The Association of

44. In *The Queen v Royal Pharmaceutical Society of Great Britain, ex parte Association of Pharmaceutical Importers and Others* [1990] 1 Q.B. 534, the European Court of Justice rejected a challenge by the Association of Parallel Importers to the requirement only to supply the branded product named in a prescription, holding that a national rule of this kind may be justified under European law on the grounds of the protection of public health even where the effect of such a rule is to prevent the pharmacist from supplying a therapeutically equivalent product licensed by the national authority. The court upheld the objective of leaving in the hands of the doctor treating a patient the entire responsibility for the patient's treatment, noting that the doctor may often prescribe a particular product for psychosomatic reasons.
45. *R v Medicines Control Agency Ex p. Rhone Poulenc Rorer Ltd* (C94/98) [2000] All ER (EC) 46.
46. [1990] 1 QB 534.

Box 5.7: Importation of medicines from the EU (cont.)

Parallel Importers, which represented companies which were involved in importing medicines from the European Community, maintained that the RPSGB rule infringed the provisions of the Treaty of Rome on the basis that its effect was to impose a quantitative restriction on their importing medicines – *parallel imports* – from the Community.

The ECJ held that in the absence of any Community legislation regulating the doctor–pharmacist relationship, and in particular the doctor's freedom to prescribe any medicine they chose, it was for each EU Member State to decide, within the limits of the Treaty, the degree to which they wish to protect the health of their people and how that was to be achieved. The ECJ held that there was no evidence that the RPSGB rule went beyond what was necessary to achieve the objective, which was to leave the entire responsibility for the treatment of the patient in the hands of the doctor treating them. It followed, therefore, that the rule could also be justified under the Treaty on the grounds of the protection of public health.

Registration certificates for homoeopathic medicines for human use

The legislation relating to homoeopathic medicines is discussed more fully in **Chapter 16**.

In the case of a registrable homoeopathic medicinal product which meets the requirements laid out in HMR Reg.102 a marketing authorisation is not required provided that a certificate of registration has been granted. Applications for a certificate of registration under the simplified procedure for a registrable homoeopathic medicinal product must be made in the manner prescribed in the Regulations (HMR Reg.103). A *national homoeopathic product* means a homoeopathic medicinal product which does not satisfy the conditions of HMR Reg.102 and is indicated for the relief or treatment of minor symptoms or minor conditions in humans. Symptoms or conditions are minor "if they can ordinarily and with reasonable safety be relieved or treated without the supervision or intervention of a doctor". The application for the grant of a UK marketing authorisation for a national homoeopathic product is required to be made in accordance with Schedule 10 of the Human Medicines Regulations 2012, including safety and efficacy data. The holder of the marketing authorisation must keep the data up to date and supply any information which entails amendment to the information.

Product Licences of Right for homoeopathic (and anthroposophic) medicines for human use

A *Product Licence of Right*, means a product licence as defined in section 25(4) of the Medicines Act 1968, issued in relation to the requirements of section 7(2) of the 1968 Act and which was still in force immediately before the implementation of the HMR.

Under transitional arrangements (HMR Reg.347 – Schedule 32) these product licences, granted in the 1970s for medicinal products on the market at that time, are permitted to continue in force subject to certain specified provisions.

The majority of products granted Product Licence of Rights in the 1970s have either been removed from the market or have gained a marketing authorisation, a certificate of registration, a traditional herbal registration or other suitable authorisation. However, there are some homoeopathic medicinal products that are not eligible for these schemes which continue to be on the market under these transitional arrangements with Product Licences of Right.

Registration of traditional herbal medicinal products

The legislation relating to herbal medicines, including definitions of key terms, is discussed more fully in **Chapter 17**.

Applications for a traditional herbal registration under the simplified procedure for a traditional herbal medicinal product must be made in the manner prescribed in the Regulations (HMR Reg.127). The application must provide the material specified in Schedule 12 to the HMR and such other material that the MHRA reasonably considers necessary to deal with the application. It is possible for herbal practitioners to be exempted from a traditional herbal registration licence, provided that the herbal medicines are manufactured or assembled and supplied to patients on their premises following one-to-one consultation (HMR Reg.3).

If a herbal medicinal product can satisfy the criteria on quality, safety and efficacy as for (conventional) medicinal products, then a marketing authorisation may be applied for as outlined above (see Marketing authorisations for human medicines).

E-cigarettes

Nicotine Containing Products (NCPs) that are presented for cutting down, quitting and reducing the harms of smoking are considered to be medicinal products. The MHRA is responsible for regulating NCPs that are medicinal products, including electronic cigarettes. Electronic cigarettes for which a marketing authorisation has been granted may be available in strengths and volumes greater than those permitted under the European Tobacco Products Directive (TPD)[47] (i.e. containing more than 20 mg/mL nicotine, more than 2 mL for single use cartridge/disposable products or more than 10 mL for refill containers), as well as lower-strength, and lower volume products. This is intended to ensure products are available which meet appropriate standards of safety, quality and efficacy to help users cut down their smoking and to quit.

It is unlawful to sell nicotine-containing products to anyone under the age of 18 or someone acting on their behalf.[48]

Falsified Medicines

In order to reduce the risk of counterfeit medicines entering the supply chain, the Falsified Medicines Directive (Directive 2011/62/EU, amended the Medicines Directive 2001/83/EC), introduced a requirement for medicines to bear a 2D barcode and a tamper-evident device.[49] The Falsified Medicines Directive ceased to have legal force in Great Britain on 31 December 2020 because pharmacies in Great Britain no longer had

---

47. 2014/40/EU.
48. The Nicotine Inhaling Products (Age of Sale and Proxy Purchasing) Regulations 2015 (England and Wales) and the Health (Tobacco, Nicotine etc. and Care) (Scotland) Act 2016.
49. Implementation was through Commission Delegated Regulation (EU) 2016/161.

access to the EU central repository for verifying the genuineness of medicinal products. However, if medicinal products do bear a barcode or tamper-evident device, these elements must not be removed.[50]

Special medicinal products

An unlicensed medicinal product may be supplied in order to meet the special needs of an individual patient, provided certain conditions are met. Medicinal products of this type are commonly referred to as *specials*. HMR Reg.167 provides that specials do not require a marketing authorisation. Typical examples of such products would be for a patient who would have an allergy to a particular active ingredient or excipient, or lacks the ability to swallow medication in tablet form.

The manufacturer or assembler of *specials* must hold a Manufacturer's *Specials Licence*. A holder of such a licence may also be a registered pharmacy supplying unlicensed medicinal products prepared under the exemption provided by HMR Reg.4. Labelling requirements for specials are dealt with in **Chapter 18**. The MHRA has given guidance on *specials*.[51]

A doctor, dentist, supplementary or independent prescriber does not require a marketing authorisation in respect of *specials*, prepared by them for administration to a particular patient[52] if:

1. the medicinal product is supplied in response to an unsolicited order;
2. the medicinal product is manufactured and assembled in accordance with the specification of a doctor, dentist, nurse independent prescriber, pharmacist independent prescriber or supplementary prescriber;
3. the medicinal product is for use by a patient for whose treatment that person is directly responsible in order to fulfil the special needs of that patient; and
4. the conditions outlined in HMR Reg.167 are met.

   These conditions include, but are not limited to:

   a. the medicinal product is supplied to a doctor, dentist, nurse independent prescriber, pharmacist independent prescriber or supplementary prescriber, or for use under the supervision of a pharmacist in a registered pharmacy, a hospital or a health centre;
   b. no advertisement relating to the medicinal product is published by any person (but see **Chapter 19**);
   c. the manufacture and assembly of the medicinal product are carried out under such supervision, and such precautions are taken, as are adequate to ensure that the medicinal product meets the specification of the person who requires it; and
   d. written records of the manufacture or assembly of the medicinal product in accordance with condition 3 are maintained and are available to the licensing authority or to the enforcement authority on request.

---

50. HMR Reg.257A.
51. https://assets.publishing.service.gov.uk/government/uploads/system/uploads/attachment_data/file/964017/QA_Version_3_-_Aseptic_manip_updates.pdf (accessed 30 December 2024).
52. HMR Reg.167.

The exemption extends to the preparation of a medicinal product at the request of another practitioner for administration to one of their patients.

Mixing of medicines

HMR Reg.20 deals with the mixing of medicines. Mixing of medicines means the combining of two or more medicinal products together for the purposes of administering them to meet the needs of an individual patient.

Although HMR Reg.17 provides that, except in accordance with a manufacturer's licence, no person may manufacture, assemble or import any medicinal product other than from an approved country, this prohibition does not apply to the mixing of medicines by:

- a nurse independent prescriber,
- a pharmacist independent prescriber,
- a supplementary prescriber (if the mixing of medicines forms part of the clinical management plan for an individual patient),
- a physiotherapist independent prescriber,
- a podiatrist independent prescriber,
- a therapeutic radiographer independent prescriber, or
- a paramedic independent prescriber.

If the mixing of medicines forms part of the clinical management plan for an individual patient, the prohibition in HMR Reg.17 also does not apply to a person acting in accordance with the written directions of a:

- doctor,
- dentist,
- nurse independent prescriber,
- pharmacist independent prescriber,
- physiotherapist independent prescriber,
- podiatrist independent prescriber,
- therapeutic radiographer independent prescriber,
- paramedic independent prescriber, or
- a supplementary prescriber if the mixing of medicines forms part of the clinical management plan for an individual patient.

Hospitals

See **Chapter 9**.

SUMMARY

- Manufacturers of active pharmaceutical ingredients must be registered with the MHRA.
- The word *manufacture* has a wide definition and includes the assembly of medicinal products.
- The manufacturers of medicinal products must have a licence.

SUMMARY (CONT.)

- There are exemptions from the need for a manufacturer's licence for certain activities carried out in a pharmacy by or under the supervision of a pharmacist, provided specified conditions are met.
- There are exemptions from the need for a manufacturer's licence for certain activities in hospitals and by other healthcare professionals (see also **Chapter 9**).
- Manufacturers must meet the standards of Good Manufacturing Practice.
- Manufacturers must have a Qualified Person.
- Clinical trials are subject to regulations and registration.
- A marketing authorisation is required in order to sell or supply medicinal products.
- The MHRA may grant UK or Great Britain marketing authorisations, and has an international recognition procedure for authorisations granted in certain other countries.
- There are exemptions from the need for marketing authorisations if specified conditions are met.
- Marketing authorisation holders must comply with a range of requirements, including taking account of scientific and technical progress, maintaining the continuity of supply of their products, and record-keeping.
- Marketing authorisation holders have pharmacovigilance obligations and must have a QPPV.
- Separate regulatory regimes apply to certain other products, including homeopathic products and herbal remedies.

FURTHER READING

- Good manufacturing practice and good distribution practice – The Medicines and Healthcare products Regulatory Agency website (**https://www.gov.uk/guidance/good-manufacturing-practice-and-good-distribution-practice**) (accessed 31 December 2024) provides guidance in the following areas: Good Manufacturing Practice , Good Distribution Practice, Good Pharmacovigilance Practice, Good Clinical Practice for Clinical Trials, and Good Practice, Inspections and Enforcement.
- Human Medicines Regulations 2012, Explanatory memorandum: **http://www.legislation.gov.uk/uksi/2012/1916/pdfs/uksiem_20121916_en.pdf** (accessed 31 December 2024).
- MHRA – Notes for applicants and holders of a Manufacturer's Licence **https://assets.publishing.service.gov.uk/government/uploads/system/uploads/attachment_data/file/405883/Medicines_-_notes_for_applicants_and_holders_of_a_manufacturer_licence.pdf** (accessed 31 December 2024).
- Royal Pharmaceutical Society, Royal Society of Chemistry and Royal Society of Biology (November 2018). Code of Practice for Qualified Persons. London **https://www.rsb.org.uk/images/QP_Code_of_Practice_2018.pdf** (accessed 31 December 2024).
- Rules and Guidance for Pharmaceutical Manufacturers and Distributors [The Orange Guide] (2017). London: Pharmaceutical Press.

CHAPTER 6

Human medicines: wholesale dealing and brokering

There is end-to-end regulation of the medicines supply chain. The next link in the chain after manufacturing is wholesaling, for which a licence is required. Brokering requires registration with the MHRA.

Introduction

Regulations in Part 3 of the Human Medicines Regulations 2012 (HMR) control the distribution of medicinal products by way of wholesale dealing. This control is exercised by prohibiting the distribution of medicinal products by way of wholesale dealing or the possession or importation from an approved country for the purpose of wholesale dealing except in accordance with a wholesale dealer's licence. The restriction also applies to the supply of certain products to Northern Ireland.

The term *distributing by way of wholesale dealing* is defined in regulation 18(4) as:

1. selling or supplying, or
2. procuring or holding a product or exporting it for the purpose of sale or supply, to a person who, in the course of a business they carry on, receives it for one of the following purposes:
   - selling or supplying the product, or
   - administering it or causing it to be administered to one or more human beings.
     If HMR Reg.19 applies (see Exemptions below), the prohibition does not apply to:
     a. anything done in relation to a medicinal product by the holder of a manufacturer's licence,
     b. investigational medicinal product or radiopharmaceutical products in which the radionuclide is in the form of a sealed source.

In addition, the prohibition does not apply to imports from an EEA country of medicinal products that were released for sale, supply or distribution in the UK before 31 December 2020.

Importing

The Medicines and Healthcare products Regulatory Agency (MHRA) publishes a list of approved countries for import.[1]

1. https://www.gov.uk/government/publications/list-of-approved-countries-for-authorised-human-medicines/list-of-approved-countries (accessed 30 December 2024). At the time of going to press, these countries are EU states plus Iceland, Liechtenstein and Norway.

A wholesaler dealer in the UK may only import medicines from an approved country if certain checks are made by a Responsible Person (import) (RPi). The MHRA will maintain a register of persons eligible to act as an RPi. The RPi must demonstrate that they are eligible to act as an RPi through a combination of relevant qualifications and experience. An RPi is expected to be a member of a professional body with a published code of conduct. An RPi does not have to be an employee of the licence holder but must be continuously contactable. The RPi is responsible for ensuring that batches of authorised medicines imported from countries on an approved country list have been appropriately certified prior to being placed on the market in the UK. Initially, approved countries are those belonging to the EEA. The RPi is required to implement a system for confirming when importing into Great Britain that a Qualified Person in the approved country has certified the products.

Conditions of sales by way of wholesale dealing

Although it is usual to refer to *wholesale dealer's licences* (and the term is still used in the HMR and by the MHRA), technically they are Wholesale Distribution Authorisations and, in the case of medicines for human use, the abbreviation *WDA(H)* is used.

Having a wholesale dealer's licence is not sufficient to avoid the prohibition on distribution; the distribution must be in accordance with the wholesale dealer's licence and distribution must be carried on or the product must be held at premises in the UK. Those premises must be specified in the licence.

Standard provisions for wholesale dealer's licences are incorporated in every licence unless the applicant has successfully applied for any to be excluded or modified (HMR Reg.24). HMR Regs 42 to 45AA list the conditions applicable to all licences. The key standard provisions are set out in **Box 6.1**.

Box 6.1: Key standard provisions of wholesale dealer's licences

The standard provisions of wholesale dealer's licenses include:

- complying with the guidelines on Good Distribution Practice;
- ensuring, within the limits of the licence holder's responsibility, the continued supply of medicinal products to pharmacies, and other persons who may lawfully sell medicinal products by retail or supply them in circumstances corresponding to retail sale[2], so that the needs of patients in the UK are met;
- providing and maintaining such staff, premises, equipment and facilities for the handling, storage and distribution of medicinal products as are necessary to maintain the quality of the products; and to ensure their proper distribution;
- informing the MHRA of changes to premises;
- not selling or supplying a medicinal product (other than a special medicinal product) that does not have a UK or GB marketing authorisation, certificate of registration or certificate of registration for a traditional herbal remedy;
- sales or supplies must be in accordance with the authorisation or registration;
- distributing by wholesale dealing only to another holder of a wholesale dealer's licence or to persons who may lawfully sell by retail or lawfully administer those products (HMR Reg.44);

2. This is a term used to refer to the supply of medicines on NHS prescriptions where there is no sale (see chapter 3).

Box 6.1: Key standard provisions of wholesale dealer's licences (cont.)

- having at all times at their disposal the services of a person – a *responsible person* – who possesses in the opinion of the licensing authority (HMR Reg.45):
  a. knowledge of the activities to be carried out and of the procedures to be performed under the licence, and
  b. experience in those activities and procedures which is adequate for those purposes;
- keeping documents to facilitate the withdrawal or recall from sale of medicinal products and having an emergency plan to ensure the effective implementation of a product recall;
- keeping records in relation to the receipt and dispatch of medicinal product including dates, names of product, quantity and the name and address of the person from whom the products were received or to whom they are dispatched;
- where a licence holder obtains a medicinal product through a broker, the licence holder must check that the broker is registered with the MHRA; and
- for the purpose of enabling the MHRA to determine whether there are grounds for suspending, revoking or varying the licence, the licence holder must permit a person authorised in writing by the MHRA, on production of identification, to carry out any inspection, or to take any samples or copies.

The MHRA regularly publishes online a list of licences that have been suspended or revoked. Examples of cases in which the courts have considered the suspension of a licence are given in **Box 6.2**.

Box 6.2: Examples of cases in which the courts have considered the suspension of a licence

In *Spl (2004) Ltd v Secretary of State for Health*,[3] the MHRA had discovered during an inspection of Spl's premises that, in breach of the terms of its wholesale dealer's licence, it had been importing Prescription Only Medicines from outside the European Economic Area. The MHRA suspended Spl's licence for three months in order to conduct further investigations. Spl applied to the court to overturn the suspension. Mr Justice Singh rejected the application, holding that a decision of a public body to safeguard the public interest, in particular, the health and safety of the public, outweighed the potentially catastrophic financial effect on Spl's business.

****

In *Blackbay Ventures Ltd v Secretary of State for Health*,[4] Blackbay Ventures owned a number of pharmacies that also held wholesale dealer's licences. In breach of a requirement that a wholesale dealer could obtain supplies only from specified persons, including other holders of a wholesale dealer's licence, the MHRA discovered that Blackbay Ventures had purchased medicinal products from pharmacies that did not hold a wholesale dealer's licence, and suspended Blackbay Venture's wholesale dealer's licence for three months. Blackbay argued that they were entitled to purchase from sellers who did not have a wholesale dealer's licence because the restrictions that applied to wholesale dealers did not apply to pharmacies. Rejecting this argument, Mr Justice Supperstone said:

3. [2013] EWHC 4520 (Admin).
4. [2012] EWHC 2635 (Admin).

Box 6.2: Examples of cases in which the courts have considered the suspension of a licence (cont.)

> *"In my view it is for good reason that wholesale dealers have been made subject to a strict EU-wide regime, the purpose of which is to ensure that the entire chain of distribution of medicinal products can be controlled, and public health can be protected across the EU. ... If pharmacies holding WDLs were able to purchase from pharmacies not holding WDLs the primary purpose of the Directive provisions relating to safeguarding public health would potentially be undermined."*

Although the UK has left the EU, the purpose of the HMR and GDP remain the same, so it is likely that a court would make the same decision with equivalent reasoning if the case were heard today.

****

In *The Queen (on the application of Chemistree Homecare Ltd and Blackbay Ventures Ltd) v Medicines & Healthcare Products Agency,*[5] Chemistree and Blackbay Ventures held wholesale dealer's licences, one of the conditions of which was that they would allow the MHRA to inspect their premises. Chemistree and Blackbay Ventures had an ongoing dispute with the MHRA over the manner in which the MHRA required them to conduct their businesses. When the MHRA sought to inspect their premises, Chemistree and Blackbay Ventures refused and suggested instead that an inspection be carried out by a third-party auditor. The MHRA imposed a three-month suspension of the licences. Mr Justice Nicol dismissed an application to overturn the suspension, saying:

> *"The [MHRA] are the regulator. They act under regulations approved by parliament, which undeniably gives them the power to inspect the premises of those whom they are regulating. It is for the regulator to decide who is to carry out those inspections."*

5. [2013] EWHC 4491 (Admin).

Good distribution practice

Holders of wholesale dealer's licences must comply with MHRA guidelines on Good Distribution Practice (GDP). The MHRA has power to publish guidelines pursuant to HMR Reg.C17. The guidelines can be found in The Orange Guide. Amongst other things, good distribution practice requires that medicines are obtained from the licensed supply chain and are consistently stored, transported and handled under suitable conditions, as required by the MA or product specification.

The MHRA will issue wholesalers with a GDP certificate when its inspector accepts the wholesaler's response to a post-inspection letter.

The responsible person

GDP requires holders of wholesale dealer's licences to have a responsible person. There is no statutory requirement for the responsible person to be a pharmacist, although this is desirable. However, the responsible person should have access to pharmaceutical knowledge and advice when it is required and have personal knowledge of:[6]

1. the relevant provisions of the Human Medicines Regulations 2012 and amendments;
2. other legal requirements and guidelines for GDP;
3. the conditions attached to the wholesale dealer's licence for which they are nominated;
4. the products traded under the licence and the conditions necessary for their safe storage and distribution; and
5. the categories of persons to whom products may be distributed.

Exporting – continuity of supply

There have been numerous shortages of medicines in the UK in recent years. Some shortages may be the result of medicines being exported in order to take advantage of better prices elsewhere. The Department of Health and Social Care publishes a list of medicines in short supply which must not be exported.[7] As an example of the way in which it seeks to enforce the licence condition to maintain continuity of supplies, on 3 October 2019, it wrote to the holders of wholesale dealer's licences saying it had published a list of medicines in short supply in the UK and warning:

> *"Any sales for parallel export [of products on the list] will be considered a breach of regulation 43(2) of the Human Medicines Regulations 2012 ... A breach of regulation 43(2) may lead to regulatory action by the Medicines and Healthcare products Regulatory Agency (MHRA). This could include (i) an immediate suspension of the licence or suspension of the supply of certain products under the licence and/or (ii) a 28-day notice proposing to vary the licence to restrict or prevent export activity as necessary. Any continuation of the offending activity would constitute a criminal offence under regulation 34(1), read together with regulation 18(1), of the Human Medicines Regulations 2012."*[8]

At the time of going to press, recent additions to the list included antibiotics for the treatment of streptococcus A, and ADHD medications.

Persons to whom Pharmacy medicines and Prescription Only Medicines may be sold by wholesale

HMR Reg.249 and Schedule 22 to the HMR place restrictions on whom the holder of a wholesale dealer's licence may sell to. A person whose business consists (wholly or

---

6. MHRA Guidance Note no.6 https://assets.publishing.service.gov.uk/government/uploads/system/uploads/attachment_data/file/717500/Guidance_Note_6_-_WDA_and_Brokers_-_19th_June_2018_Update.pdf (accessed 30 December 2024).
7. https://www.gov.uk/government/publications/medicines-that-cannot-be-parallel-exported-from-the-uk (accessed 30 December 2024).
8. https://assets.publishing.service.gov.uk/media/5d95b627ed915d08f0f326a8/letter-to-wda-holders.pdf (accessed 30 December 2024).

partly) of manufacturing medicinal products or selling them by wholesale dealing may only sell Prescription Only Medicines (POMs) and Pharmacy medicines to:

1. doctors or dentists;
2. any person lawfully conducting a retail pharmacy business;
3. authorities or persons carrying on the business of an independent hospital, independent clinic, independent medical agency or a hospital or health centre which is not an independent hospital or clinic;
4. holders of wholesale dealer's licences, or persons to whom the requirements to hold a wholesale dealer's licence do not apply by virtue of an exemption conferred by the HMR;
5. Ministers of the Crown and government departments; Scottish, Welsh or Northern Irish Ministers;
6. an NHS trust or foundation trust, health authority, special health authority;
7. a local authority in the exercise of its public health functions
8. Public Health Agency, the Common Services Agency or a local authority in the exercise of public health functions (within the meaning of the National Health Service Act 2006);
9. any person other than an exempted person who carries on a business consisting (wholly or partly) of supplying medicinal products in circumstances corresponding to retail sale, or of administering such products, pursuant to an arrangement made with an NHS trust or NHS foundation trust, the Common Services Agency, an Integrated Care Board, NHS England,[9] a local authority, Public Health Agency, a health authority or a special health authority;
10. a person other than an exempted person who carries on a business consisting (wholly or partly) of the supply or administration of medicinal products for the purpose of assisting the provision of healthcare by or on behalf of, or under arrangements made by, a police force in the UK, a prison service, His Majesty's Forces or a contractor carrying out helicopter search and rescue operations on behalf of the Maritime and Coastguard Agency;
11. any person who is the subject of an exemption in HMR Schedule 17 but only in respect of the medicinal products covered by the exemption (**Chapter 13** and HMR Reg.250);
12. registered optometrists in that there are certain POMs which optometrists are entitled to supply to their patients or use in their practice (**Chapter 13**); and
13. any person selling or supplying by retail, or administering, unit preparations of POMs (other than controlled drugs) diluted to one part in a million (6×) having been requested by or on behalf of the particular person and in that person's presence to use their own judgement as to the treatment required (see also **Chapter 13**).

Exceptions for supplies to certain persons

HMR Reg.250 combined with Schedule 17 to the HMR list exceptions to the restrictions on persons to whom sales by wholesale may be made. There is not space here to list all

9. Shortly before going to press, the Prime Minister announced that NHS England would be abolished as a separate body, and its functions will be exercised by the Department of Health and Social Care.

the exceptions. They include supplies of POMs to persons who operate ships, aircraft, oilrigs, mountain rescue services, members of the His Majesty's armed forces and the Royal National Lifeboat Institution.

In some cases, the exceptions are subject to conditions, for example the provision of a signed order.

The exceptions include the sale of:

- a Pharmacy medicine which is for the purpose of being administered to human beings in the course of a business to any person carrying on such a business;
- sales to a person listed in Schedule 17 to the HMR of the Prescription Only Medicines listed in that Schedule. Amongst other things, this exemption allows the sale of:
  - Prescription Only Medicines (POMs) to universities and other higher education institutions for research;
  - POMs to a GPhC inspector;
  - certain POMs to midwives;
  - water for injection to persons lawfully conducting a pharmacy business;
  - eye drops that are POMs only by reason that they contain not more than 0.5% chloramphenicol, or are eye ointments that are POMs only by reason that they contain not more than 1% chloramphenicol, or are POMs by reason only that they contain any of cyclopentolate hydrochloride, fusidic acid or tropicamide to a person lawfully conducting a retail pharmacy business;
  - certain products to registered optometrists;
  - POMs to holders of UK marketing authorisations that refer to those products;
  - certain products to registered chiropodists or podiatrists if the relevant register is annotated to signify that they are qualified to use those medicines;
  - POMs to the Royal National Lifeboat Institution and its certified first aiders;
  - POMs to the owner or master of a ship;
  - controlled drugs to persons authorised by licence to supply those drugs;
  - ampoules of still water for injection that contain no more than 2 mL of water each to persons employed or engaged in the provision of lawful drug treatment services;
  - the operator or commander of an aircraft; and
  - inhalers containing salbutamol to a person carrying on the business of a school.

In the case of the supply of a salbutamol inhaler to a person who carries on the business of a school, the person to whom the supply is made must have been trained to administer it. This exception is not without legal difficulties because of uncertainty over the meaning of *a person carrying on the business of a school* (compare, for example, the discussion of who carries on a pharmacy business in **Chapter 7**); and in the case of a school that is owned by a body corporate, it is plainly not possible to train a company to administer an inhaler. However, it seems likely that if a court were called on to determine the scope of the exception, it would take into account the purpose of the exception which is "to allow schools to hold stocks of inhalers containing salbutamol for emergency use".[10]

---

10. The Explanatory Memorandum to the Human Medicines (Amendment) (No. 2) Regulations 2014 https://www.legislation.gov.uk/uksi/2014/1878/pdfs/uksiem_20141878_en.pdf (accessed 30 December 2024).

Wholesale dealing from a pharmacy

Until the HMR came into force, section 10(7) of the Medicines Act 1968 had permitted pharmacies to make supplies by wholesale without the need for a wholesale dealer's licence. This exemption was repealed by the HMR (although ignorance of the repeal appears to persist). However, the MHRA has issued guidance, the relevant parts of which are reproduced in **Box 6.3**[11] which indicate that the prohibition on wholesale dealing without a licence would not be enforced in certain circumstances.

Box 6.3: MHRA Guidance for pharmacists on the repeal of Section 10(7) of the Medicines Act 1968

MHRA is concerned to ensure that the repeal of the Section 10(7) exemption does not adversely impact on arrangements for supply of medicines in the UK. In determining how to address this issue, MHRA has taken careful account of the particular arrangements for delivery of healthcare in the UK which involve a wide range of individuals and in a diverse range of locations. In particular:

- Many healthcare professionals and others authorised or entitled to supply medicines to the public in the UK need to hold small quantities of medicines for local healthcare provision and look to a local community or hospital pharmacy to supply them as part of their professional practice.
- In contrast, some pharmacies engage in commercial trade in medicines, not solely as part of their professional practice within the UK healthcare system.
- Pharmacists may also occasionally need to obtain small quantities of a particular medicine or medicines from another pharmacist in order to meet the needs of individual patients.

MHRA enforcement

MHRA takes the view that the supply of medicines by community and hospital pharmacies to other healthcare professionals in the UK who need to hold small quantities of medicines for treatment of or onward supply to their patients represents an important and appropriate part of the professional practice of both community and hospital pharmacy. Also, community and hospital pharmacies may need to obtain small quantities of a medicine from other pharmacies to meet a patient's individual needs. Both these activities are considered by MHRA to fall within the definition of provision of healthcare services. In such circumstances, provided the transaction meets all of the following criteria, MHRA will not deem such transactions as commercial dealing and pharmacies will not be required to hold a WDA(H):

- it takes place on an occasional basis;
- the quantity of medicines supplied is small;
- the supply is made on a not-for-profit basis;
- the supply is not for onward wholesale distribution.

Conversely, pharmacies who wish to engage in commercial trading in medicines are entitled to do so only if they hold a WDA(H) and comply with all the relevant requirements. As the authority responsible for enforcement, MHRA will take appropriate action to enforce the requirement of the legislation and will require any commercial trade in medicines to be undertaken only by holders of a WDA(H). These restrictions do not apply to the exchange of stock between pharmacies that are part of the same legal entity, although where a legal entity holds a WDA(H) as one (or more) of its pharmacies is involved in the commercial trade of medicines, the supplying pharmacy must also be named on the WDA(H) if the stock supplied is for the purposes of wholesale.

---

11. MHRA (2014) Guidance for pharmacists on the repeal of Section 10(7) of the Medicines Act 1968 https://assets.publishing.service.gov.uk/government/uploads/system/uploads/attachment_data/file/423246/Guidance_for_pharmacist_on_repealed_exemption.pdf (accessed 30 December 2024).

If the pharmacist does not possess a wholesale dealer's licence, then the only records required to be kept are a copy of the order or invoice relating to the supply or an entry made in the Prescription Only Register by the owner of the retail pharmacy business. Orders or invoices (and all orders required as a condition in connection with any exempted sale of a POM; **Chapter 12**) must be kept for 2 years from the date of the sale or supply.

If the pharmacist does possess a wholesale dealer's licence, then all the provisions of the licence apply (see above).

At the time of going to press, the Department of Health proposed to amend the HMR in 2025 to allow pharmacies in receipt of prescriptions (spokes) to send them to a pharmacy with a different owner (a hub) to be dispensed. The proposed amendments would allow medicinal products to be supplied from a spoke to a hub or from a hub to a spoke. At the time of going to press, such supplies would be wholesale transactions requiring the supplier to have a wholesale dealer's licence. However, the proposed amendments will include a provision that such supplies will be deemed to be retail transactions, avoiding the need for a licence.

Wholesale dealing of veterinary products

See **Chapter 15**.

Exemptions

There is an exemption from the need for a wholesale dealer's licence (HMR Reg.19) if, until the sale, the medicinal product has been kept on the premises of the person who manufactured or assembled the product and those premises are authorised for manufacture or assembly by that person's manufacturer's licence (see **Chapter 5**) and:

1. the product for sale is the holder of a UK or GB marketing authorisation, certificate of registration or traditional herbal registration; or
2. the person is not the holder of an authorisation in relation to the product but manufactured or assembled the product in the United Kingdom to the order of a person who is the holder of an authorisation relating to the product.

There are also exemptions in the event of or in anticipation of pandemic disease.

Brokering

In order to ensure that there is an end-to-end verification system for medicinal products and to minimise the risk of falsified medicines entering the supply chain, regulation of the supply chain includes not only manufacturers, wholesalers and pharmacies, but also brokers who are involved in the sale or purchase of medicinal products but who do not actually sell or purchase them themselves, and who do not own or physically handle medicinal products.

HMR. Reg.8 defines *brokering* as

> *"all activities in relation to the sale or purchase of medicinal products, except for wholesale distribution, that do not include physical handling and that consist of negotiating independently and on behalf of another legal or natural person."*

Reg 45A of the HMR says that a person may not broker a medicinal product in Great Britain unless the product has a UK or GB marketing authorisation or an authorisation granted in an approved country for import, the person is validly registered with the competent authority and has a permanent address in the UK. In the UK, the competent authority is the MHRA and its functions include ensuring that brokers comply with GDP in so far as it applies to brokers.

SUMMARY

- Normally, a person who sells medicines by way of wholesale dealing requires a wholesale dealer's licence, which requires special premises, records to be kept, and the appointment of a responsible person whose function is to ensure that the conditions of the licence are being complied with and that the quality of the products is maintained in accordance with the requirements of the appropriate marketing authorisation.
- A pharmacist may supply medicines by way of wholesale dealing (e.g. to a doctor) provided the sales takes place on an occasional basis and the quantity of medicines supplied is small and intended to meet the needs of an individual patient, and the supply is made on a not-for-profit basis.
- The need for end-to-end verification of medicinal products to reduce the risk of falsified medicines entering the lawful supply chain requires not only the licensing of wholesalers, but also the registration of brokers.

FURTHER READING

- Human Medicines Regulations (2012) SI 2012 No. 1916, *Explanatory memorandum*: **http://www.legislation.gov.uk/uksi/2012/1916/pdfs/uksiem_20121916_en.pdf** (accessed 30 December 2024).
- MHRA Guidance Note 6 (2018) Notes for applicants and holders of a Wholesale Dealer's Licence (WDA(H)) or Broker Registration **https://assets.publishing.service.gov.uk/government/uploads/system/uploads/attachment_data/file/717500/Guidance_Note_6_-_WDA_and_Brokers_-_19th_June_2018_Update.pdf** (accessed 30 December 2024).
- The MHRA Orange Guide (Pharmaceutical Press).

CHAPTER 7

Lawfully conducting a retail pharmacy business

Many activities that are carried out in a pharmacy are unlawful unless they are carried out by a person (a pharmacy owner) who satisfies the requirements of lawfully conducting a retail pharmacy business. This chapter also covers ancillary issues like the protection the law gives to titles like "pharmacy", "pharmacist" and "pharmacy technician".

Introduction

Part IV of the Medicines Act 1968 (*the Act*) is one of the few areas of the Act that was not replaced by the Human Medicines Regulations 2012 (HMR). This Part of the Act is concerned with:

- Persons lawfully conducting a retail pharmacy business.
- Registration of pharmacies (see **Chapter 2**).
- Provisions as to the use of certain titles, descriptions and emblems.
- Disqualification, and removal of premises from the register (see **Chapter 25**).
- Offences for breaching the provisions of Part IV.

Pharmacies take various forms and are situated in different types of location, including shops, supermarkets, within GP premises and health centres, distance selling premises and internet pharmacies, and hospitals. Although pharmacies that operate as shops and within supermarkets and GP premises are these days normally referred to as community pharmacies (and the use of the terms *Chemist*, *Chemists* and *Chemists shop* persist),[1] these forms of pharmacy are usually referred to[2] in legislation as *retail pharmacy businesses* which are defined in regulation 8 of the HMR as:

> *"a business (other than a professional practice carried on by a doctor or dentist) which consists of or includes the retail sale of medicinal products that are not subject to general sale".*

---

1. The *Independent Review of Community Pharmacy Contractor Representation and Support* by Professor David Wright *et al.* in June 2020, says "Chemist is an outdated term which has no relevance to modern community pharmacy practice". https://pharmacyreview175657019.files.wordpress.com/2020/06/independent-review-of-community-pharmacy-contractor-representation-and-support.pdf (accessed 31 December 2024).
2. The term chemist is still used in some legislation, such as the National Health Service (Pharmaceutical and Local Pharmaceutical Services) Regulations 2013.

The word *retail* refers to a sale of something to a person who does not buy it for the purpose of re-selling it or for the purpose of administering it or causing it to be administered to one or more human beings.[3] In other words, a retail sale is a sale to the end user rather than a sale by wholesale.

The Medicines Act also refers to supplies in *circumstances corresponding to retail sale*. When a medicine is supplied on an NHS prescription, there is no sale (see **Chapter 3**). The expression *circumstances corresponding to retail sale* was therefore created in order to apply the same laws to a supply on an NHS prescription that apply to a sale of a medicine on a private prescription or a sale over the counter.

The significance of lawfully conducting a retail pharmacy business

Sections 69 to 71 of the Medicines Act create a definition of *lawfully conducting a retail pharmacy business*. This definition is fundamental to the lawfulness of key pharmacy activities. For example, HMR220 states that it is unlawful to sell or supply a medicinal product that is not subject to general sale (i.e. Pharmacy medicines and Prescription Only Medicines - see **Chapters 11** and **12**) unless certain conditions are met, one of which is that the person who sells or supplies is lawfully conducting a retail pharmacy business. Another condition is that the sale or supply is made on[4] premises that are registered with the General Pharmaceutical Council (GPhC) as a pharmacy; section 74B of the Medicines Act states that a person may only apply for the registration of premises if that person is lawfully conducting a retail pharmacy business. In addition, certain exemptions from the restrictions on selling or supplying Prescription Only Medicines only apply if the person selling or supplying is lawfully conducting a retail pharmacy business. These exemptions include:

- Emergency sales (HMR Regs.224 and 225).
- Supplies under a Patient Group Direction (HMR. Reg.229).
- Collection and delivery services (HMR Reg.248).

In addition, the holder of a marketing authorisation may only sell medicinal products to certain categories of person (HMR Reg.249). One such category is a person lawfully conducting a retail pharmacy business (Schedule 22 to the HMR).

Under section 4(1) of the Misuse of Drugs Act 1971, it is an offence to produce or to supply or offer to supply a controlled drug. Under section 5 of the Misuse of Drugs Act, it is unlawful for a person to have a controlled drug in their possession. However, section 7 of the Misuse of Drugs Act gives the Secretary of State power to make exceptions for persons lawfully conducting a retail pharmacy business. This power was used to make

---

3. Section 131 of the Medicines Act 1968.
4. At the time of going to print, the Department of Health and Social Care has proposed to amend the HMR by changing the word "on" to "at or from" (see Chapter 11).

the Misuse of Drugs Regulations 2001 which permit a person lawfully conducting a retail pharmacy business to produce, supply, offer to supply or possess controlled drugs.[5]

The definition of lawfully conducting a retail pharmacy business

The person who carries on a retail pharmacy business is not an employee or locum such as a pharmacist who works in a pharmacy, but the owner or person who employs that pharmacist. This was made clear by the Court of Appeal in *R v Lee (Elizabeth)*.[6] In this case, Mrs Lee was a locum pharmacist at a pharmacy owned by Tesco Stores Limited (Tesco). She made a dispensing error involving applying an incorrect label when supplying propranolol when prednisolone had been prescribed. In the Crown Court, Mrs Lee was convicted of a labelling offence *in the course of a business carried on by her*. The Court of Appeal considered whether Mrs Lee was the person carrying on the business. The Court posed the question "whose business was it?" and concluded that it was Tesco's business, saying: "the person who is carrying on the business ... is the employer, not the 'employee'". As a result, the conviction for the labelling offence was overturned.

Section 69 of the Medicines Act provides that:

> *"a person carrying on a retail pharmacy business shall be taken to be a person lawfully conducting such a business if:*
> - *that person (or, if the business is carried on by a partnership, each, or, in Scotland, one or more, of the partners) is a pharmacist and the conditions specified in section 70 of this Act are fulfilled in relation to the business, or*
> - *that person is a body corporate and the conditions specified in section 71 of this Act are fulfilled in relation to the business, or*
> - *that person is a representative of a pharmacist ... and the conditions specified in [section 72(2) of the Act] are fulfilled."*

Persons who may lawfully conduct a retail pharmacy business

The effect of section 69 is that the only persons who may lawfully conduct a retail pharmacy business on fulfilling the required conditions are:

- a registered pharmacist;
- a partnership in England and Wales in which all the partners are pharmacists;
- a partnership in Scotland in which at least one of the partners is a pharmacist;
- a body corporate (usually a limited company or a limited liability partnership); and
- the representatives of a deceased pharmacist, a pharmacist who has lost mental capacity or who is adjudged bankrupt or enters into a composition or scheme or deed of arrangement with the pharmacist's creditors, or, in Scotland, sequestration of the

5. Regulations 8 and 9 of the Misuse of Drugs Regulations 2001.
6. [2010] EWCA Crim 1404.

pharmacist's estate is awarded or the pharmacist makes a trust deed for the benefit of their creditors or a composition contract.

A guide to bodies corporate and partnerships is given in **Box 7.1**.

Box 7.1: A guide to bodies corporate and partnerships

A body corporate (the plural is *bodies corporate*, but *corporate bodies* may also be referred to) is a distinct legal entity which means it has legal personality. The law recognises a body corporate as having its own existence and the word *person* in legislation refers to a body corporate as well as to an individual unless the legislation indicates otherwise.

Different forms of body corporate

Commonly, businesses that trade do so as limited companies or (less often) as limited liability partnerships. Companies are mostly regulated by the Companies Act 2006 and Limited Liability Partnerships by the Limited Liability Partnerships Act 2000. A company becomes a body corporate by incorporating. It does so by filing documents at the Companies Registry (commonly referred to in England as *Companies House*). The principal documents are a Memorandum of Association which sets out the company's objects and Articles of Association which set out the rules by which the company regulates itself. The Articles of Association may include the powers of directors and other officers of the company, and the rights of shareholders. The company is then issued with a certificate of incorporation and allocated a unique company number.

The word Limited or Ltd in a company name and in the name of a limited liability partnership (commonly referred to as an LLP) signifies that the company or LLP has limited liability. Some large companies with limited liability have the letters PLC or Plc after their name, standing for public limited company. However, if the registered office is stated as being situated in Wales (a "Welsh" company), its name may instead end with "cyfyngedig" or "cyf" or, in the case of a public limited company, "Cwmni Cyfyngedig Cyhoeddu" or CCC.

Other forms of bodies corporate include:

- some co-operative societies are registered with and regulated by the Financial Conduct Authority;
- bodies created by legislation such as the Department of Health and Social Care, the General Pharmaceutical Council and Integrated Care Boards; and
- non-trading companies such as Community Pharmacy England, Community Pharmacy Scotland, Community Pharmacy Wales, and Local Pharmaceutical Committees.

When reference is made to the board of a body corporate, this is to the directors of the company.

A body corporate is distinct from the directors and officers who run the body corporate and any shareholders who own it.

Restrictions on company names

Among restrictions on company names, the following titles are protected under section 78 of the Medicines Act:

- Chemist;
- Chemist and druggist;
- Dispensing chemist;
- Dispensing druggist;
- Druggist;
- Fferyllydd
- Pharmacist; and
- Pharmacy.

Box 7.1: A guide to bodies corporate and partnerships (cont.)

The Registrar of Companies will decline to incorporate a company whose name includes one of those titles unless an email or letter from the General Pharmaceutical Council is produced, authorising the proposed name.

Distinguishing between company names and trading names

The official name of a company should be distinguished from a trading name it uses. For example, a pharmacy business may be incorporated as Dale & Appelbe Ltd. If it had wished to incorporate as Dale & Appelbe (Pharmacy) Limited, it would first be necessary to obtain authorisation from the GPhC. However, Dale & Appelbe Ltd could use *Dale & Appelbe Pharmacy* as a trading name and no such authorisation would be required.

The difference between partnerships and limited liability partnerships

A partnership is an arrangement between persons (the partners) who carry on a business with a view of profit.[7] A partnership is not a body corporate. However, a body corporate may be a partner in a partnership although, in the case of a pharmacy business, only in Scotland.

Unlike a body corporate, the partnership is not separate from the persons who are the partners. Unlike limited companies, the liability of partners in a partnership is unlimited.

Because the risk of unlimited liability may discourage enterprise, the Limited Liability Partnerships Act 2000 enabled businesses to form limited liability partnerships. Their names end with LLP so that people who trade with them know that there is limited liability and limited liability partnerships are often referred to as *LLPs*.

LLPs are incorporated at the Companies Registry. They have to observe certain formalities that do not apply to partnerships. LLPs are bodies corporate. As such, an LLP that carries on a retail pharmacy business must have a superintendent in order to fulfil the conditions of lawfully conducting a retail pharmacy business.

7. This is a paraphrase of section 1 of the Partnership Act 1890.

The conditions to be fulfilled

All pharmacies – the requirement for a responsible pharmacist

In the case of a retail pharmacy business carried on by a pharmacist or a partnership, the conditions referred to in section 69 of the Medicines Act are set out in section 70 of the Act. In the case of pharmacies owned by a body corporate, the conditions are set out in section 71 of the Act.

At all premises at or from which a pharmacy business is carried on and medicinal products, other than medicinal products on a General Sale List, are sold by retail, the conditions are that:

1. a responsible pharmacist is in charge of the business carried on at or from the premises, so far as concerns:
   a. the retail sale at or from those premises of medicinal products (whether they are on a General Sale List or not), and
   b. the supply at or from those premises of such products in circumstances corresponding to retail sale.

2. a notice is conspicuously displayed at those premises stating:
   a. the name of the responsible pharmacist for the time being,
   b. their GPhC registration number of his registration, and
   c. the fact that they are for the time being in charge of the business carried on at or from those premises.

The Medicines (Pharmacies) (Responsible Pharmacist) Regulations 2008 (the Responsible Pharmacist Regulations)[8] do not require the presence of a responsible pharmacist when no medicinal products (whether they are on a General Sale List or not) are being:

a. offered or exposed for sale by retail or supply in circumstances corresponding to retail sale at or from the premises, or
b. assembled, prepared or dispensed at or from the premises with a view to such sale or supply. (See **Box 5.1** in **Chapter 5** for the meanings of *assembly*, *prepare* and *dispense*.)

A responsible pharmacist is not required to be in charge of premises that are closed to the public if the only medicines-related activity is, for example, stacking shelves; but if the premises are closed to the public and, for example, monitored dosage trays are being filled, a responsible pharmacist must be in charge of the premises.[9]

The words "or from" mean that the responsible pharmacist is responsible for medicines that are sent from the pharmacy to be delivered to patients or to be placed into automated lockers or kiosks for collection elsewhere than on the pharmacy premises.

The meaning of General Sale List is explained in **Chapter 10**. It does not include the many medicines that are not on a General Sale List but which are subject to general sale.

Bodies corporate

In the case of a pharmacy business carried on by a body corporate, if a responsible pharmacist is not the superintendent pharmacist, the responsible pharmacist must be a pharmacist who is a manager or assistant and is subject to the directions of the superintendent.

In addition to the condition requiring a responsible pharmacist at the premises, there is a condition in section 71 of the Medicines Act that there must be a superintendent in relation to the retail pharmacy business. The superintendent must be a pharmacist[10] and is usually referred to as a *superintendent pharmacist*, or a *pharmacy superintendent*. The term *superintendent pharmacist* is used in this chapter. Further details of the role of superintendent pharmacists are given below.

Section 78 of the Medicines Act prohibits the use of the title *chemist* by a body corporate in connection with the sale of any goods (not only medicinal products) or

---

8. Regulation 3(6).
9. Section 72A(A1)(b) of the Medicines Act 1968. These activities require the supervision of a pharmacist (or a pharmacy technician if the Medicines Act is amended as proposed at the time of going to print) - see Chapter 11.
10. Section 71(6) of the Act.

the supply of any goods in circumstance corresponding to retail sale unless the body corporate is a person lawfully conducting a retail pharmacy business.

Representatives

In the case of a pharmacist who has died, in addition to the condition requiring a responsible pharmacist at the premises, a representative may carry on the business in accordance with the conditions in section 72 of the Medicines Act. The word *representative* means the deceased's executor or administrator and, for a period of three months from the date of their death if they have died leaving no executor who is entitled and willing to carry on the business, the word *representative* includes any person beneficially interested in their estate. The representative of a deceased pharmacist may carry on the business for a period of up to five years from the date of their death. Should they cease to be a representative before the expiry of five years, on completing the distribution of the deceased pharmacist's estate, their authority lawfully to carry on the pharmacy business would also come to an end.

In the case of a pharmacist who is adjudged bankrupt or, in Scotland, sequestration of their estate is awarded, the trustee in bankruptcy or in the sequestration is the pharmacist's representative. They may carry on the pharmacist's business for a period of three years from the date on which the pharmacist is adjudged bankrupt or the date of the award of sequestration, as the case may be.

Where a pharmacist enters into a composition or scheme or deed of arrangement with their creditors, or in Scotland makes a trust deed for benefit of their creditors, or a composition contract, *representative* means the trustee in bankruptcy or the trustee in the sequestration or any trustee appointed under the composition scheme, deed of arrangement, trust deed or composition contract, the trustee may carry on the business for three years from the date of their appointment.

In the case of a person in England and Wales who lacks capacity (within the meaning of the Mental Capacity Act 2005) to carry on the business and in respect of whom there is a donee of an enduring power of attorney or lasting power of attorney or for whom a deputy is appointed by the Court of Protection, or, in Scotland, a guardian or judicial factor is appointed for them on the ground that they suffer from mental disorder, the word *representative* means the donee, deputy, curator bonis, judicial factor, controller or guardian. The representative may carry on the business for three years from the date of appointment or, in the case of a donee of a power of attorney, for three years from the date on which the power of attorney was registered.

The period for carrying on the business may be extended for such longer period as the GPhC's Fitness to Practise Committee may direct, having regard to all the circumstances of the case.

The role and duty of responsible pharmacists

The responsible pharmacist must be a pharmacist. A person may not be the responsible pharmacist in respect of more than one set of premises at the same time, except in circumstances specified by the General Pharmaceutical Council in rules relating to premises, and then only if conditions in such rules are complied with.[11]

Section 72A of the Medicines Act imposes a duty on the responsible pharmacist to secure the safe and effective running of the pharmacy business carried on at or from the premises in question so far as concerns:

a. the retail sale at or from[12] those premises of medicinal products (whether they are on a General Sale List or not), and
b. the supply at or from those premises of such products in circumstances corresponding to retail sale (i.e. supplied on NHS prescriptions – see above and footnote 3).

The practical application of the responsible pharmacist's duty was illustrated by the case of *Abdul-Razzak v General Pharmaceutical Council* (see **Box 7.2**).[13]

Box 7.2: *Abdul Razzak v General Pharmaceutical Council*

Mohammed El-Hadi Abdul-Razzak was the responsible pharmacist at Safeer Pharmacy, 194 Edgware Road, London. In September 2012, the BBC was carrying out an investigation into whether certain pharmacies were unlawfully selling prescription only medicines to patients or members of the public without prescriptions. Reporters equipped with concealed filming and audio recording devices visited Safeer Pharmacy on more than one occasion and were able to buy prescription only medicines.

Mr Abdul Razzak did not make any supply himself, but it was alleged that he failed adequately to supervise the counter assistants who made supplies to a reporter of amoxicillin 500 mg on one occasion, diazepam 5 mg and Viagra 100 mg later on the same day and, eight days later, diazepam 5 mg.

Mr Abdul-Razzak was referred to the GPhC's Fitness to Practise Committee, accused of failing adequately to supervise the unlawful supplies or permitting them to be made from the pharmacy. Video evidence was shown at a fitness to practise hearing. The Fitness to Practise Committee found that Mr Abdul-Razzak was only seen on video in relation to one of the three supplies. It found that the allegations were proved and directed the removal of Mr Abdul-Razzak's name from the register.

Mr Abdul-Razzak appealed against the decision to the High Court. Reviewing the video evidence, the judge found that the evidence of the second supply showed that there were conversations between the reporter and the counter assistant with some of it conducted with the reporter at the counter and the counter assistant at the dispensary, while Mr Abdul-Razzak was seen in the dispensary close to the counter assistant. The counter assistant went to the dispensary to obtain one of the medicines requested by the reporter (almost certainly Viagra). The Fitness to Practise Committee had concluded that Mr Abdul-Razzak must have been aware that the assistant was talking to the reporter about a medicine. Mr Abdul-Razzak did not speak to the counter assistant and that he showed not the slightest interest in what the counter assistant was saying or doing; or in the medicine that he was obtaining from the dispensary for the customer.

---

11. At the time of going to press, no rules had been made.
12. For an explanation of the significance of the words "or from", see the section above entitled "All pharmacies – the requirement for a superintendent pharmacist."
13. [2016] EWHC (Admin) 1204.

Box 7.2: *Abdul Razzak v General Pharmaceutical Council* (cont.)

Dismissing the appeal, the judge (Sir Stephen Silber) referred to the requirement in the Medicines Act for a responsible pharmacist who, he said:

> *"performs a crucial function ... Thus, the responsible pharmacist must be present in the pharmacy to supervise the sale or supply of prescription only medicines and in addition, he or she must be in a position to give advice and intervene in connection with the sale or supply of prescription only medicines. In other words, the responsible pharmacist performs a very important role in ensuring that prescription only medicines do not get into the wrong hands."*

This case is best seen as an illustration of the role of a responsible pharmacist in securing the safe and effective running of the pharmacy business at the premises, rather than as a case that shows that responsible pharmacists have a legal duty to supervise the supply of medicines. For example, some pharmacies may operate with more than one pharmacist on the premises and which pharmacist may be responsible for supervision may depend on the arrangements put in place by the pharmacy owner. Supervision is dealt with in **Chapter 11**.

Section 72A of the Medicines Act gives the General Pharmaceutical Council power to make rules in relation to responsible pharmacists. For the regulated roles of pharmacists in Scotland in relation to children and protected adults, see **Chapter 2**.

The pharmacy record

The Responsible Pharmacist Regulations set out certain requirements relating to responsible pharmacists.[14] Regulation 5 of the Responsible Pharmacist Regulations states that the pharmacy record must be kept in writing or electronic form or both, and must include:

a. the responsible pharmacist's name;
b. the responsible pharmacist's registration number;
c. the date and time at which the responsible pharmacist became the responsible pharmacist;
d. the date and time at which the responsible pharmacist ceased to be the responsible pharmacist; and
e. in relation to any absence of the responsible pharmacist from the premises:
    i. the date of the absence;
    ii. the time at which the absence commenced; and
    iii. the time at which the responsible pharmacist returned to the premises.

The pharmacy record must be available at the premises for inspection by the person carrying on the pharmacy business, the superintendent (if any), the responsible pharmacist and pharmacy staff.

Section 72A requires the person carrying on the business to secure that the record of who the responsible pharmacist is at the premises is properly maintained and that it is preserved for at least five years. If the record is kept electronically, the five-year period

14. These Regulations were revoked by the Pharmacy (Responsible Pharmacists, Superintendent Pharmacists etc.) Order 2022, but remain in effect until the General Pharmaceutical Council makes rules under section 72A of the Medicines Act 1968.

will commence on the day on which it is created. If the record is a written one, the five-year period will commence on the last day to which the record relates.[15]

Absence of the responsible pharmacist

The Regulations say that:

1. The maximum period for which the responsible pharmacist may be absent from the premises is two hours during the pharmacy's business hours.
2. If there is more than one responsible pharmacist during the pharmacy's business hours, the two-hour maximum period relates to the total period of absence for all of them.
3. The responsible pharmacist must not be absent from the premises unless, where it is reasonably practicable:
   a. arrangements are in place to secure that medicinal products are ordered, stored, prepared, sold, supplied, delivered and disposed of in a safe and effective manner;
   b. there are procedures that deal with the circumstances in which a member of pharmacy staff who is not a pharmacist may give advice about medicinal products;
   c. there are procedures for identifying which members of staff are, in the view of the responsible pharmacist, competent to perform certain tasks relating to the pharmacy business;
   d. there are procedures for keeping records about the arrangements in place;
   e. the arrangements which are to apply during the responsible pharmacist's absence;
   f. the steps to be taken when there is a change of responsible pharmacist at the premises;
   g. the procedure which is to be followed if a complaint is made about the pharmacy business;
   h. the procedure which is to be followed if an incident occurs which may indicate that the pharmacy business is not running in a safe and effective manner; and
   i. the manner in which changes to the pharmacy procedures are to be notified to pharmacy staff.

The arrangements that, where reasonably practicable, must be put in place in the absence of the responsible pharmacist are:

1. The pharmacy procedures must be in writing or in electronic form, or both.
2. The pharmacy procedures must be available at the premises for inspection by the person carrying on the pharmacy business, the superintendent pharmacist, the responsible pharmacist and the pharmacy staff.
3. The pharmacy procedures must be reviewed regularly.
4. Where it is not reasonably practicable to put in place the above arrangements, arrangements must ensure that another pharmacist is both available and contactable to provide advice to other pharmacy staff.

---

15. Regulation 5 of the Medicines (Pharmacies) (Responsible Pharmacist) Regulations 2008.

5. The retail sale of medicinal products on a general sale list[16] may continue during the responsible pharmacist's absence.

It has been argued that because the National Health Service (Pharmaceutical and Local Pharmaceutical Services) Regulations 2013 require pharmacies in England to be open during the hours listed and because many NHS services require the presence of a pharmacist, for example to supervise the supply of medicines (see **Chapter 3**), a pharmacist is required to be on premises that provide NHS services at all times.[17] However, it is clear from the Explanatory Memorandum[18] published with the Responsible Pharmacist Regulations (which may be used as an aid to interpreting the Medicines Act – see **Chapter 1**) that the policy underlying the Responsible Pharmacist Regulations included enabling General Sale List medicines which could be sold from other retail outlets to be sold from pharmacies in the absence of a pharmacist.

In so far as the NHS terms of service or the contractual terms for providing advanced or enhanced services require the presence of a pharmacist, there is no requirement for any service to be provided the instant that a patient or patient's representative enters a pharmacy or that any particular service will be provided at all times throughout a pharmacy's listed opening hours. For example, the obligation in the terms of service of England, Scotland and Wales to supply prescribed medicines, which must be done by a pharmacist or under the supervision of a pharmacist (see **Chapter 3**), is to do so with reasonable promptness.[19] Even if a responsible pharmacist is present, there is no obligation to supply a prescribed medicine immediately a prescription is presented. If a prescription is presented during the responsible pharmacist's absence of up to two hours, it is reasonable to conclude that the terms of service would not be breached if the prescribed medication is not supplied until after the responsible pharmacist's return, so long as the supply is made with reasonable promptness.

Eligibility to be a responsible pharmacist

The responsible pharmacist must be a pharmacist. A pharmacy can have more than one pharmacist working at any time, but there can only be one responsible pharmacist at pharmacy premises. If there is more than one pharmacist, the record must identify which of them is the responsible pharmacist and that individual will be the one with the

16. The Responsible Pharmacist Regulations refer to "a general sale list", not to "medicinal products subject to general sale". Nevertheless, for the purpose of enforcement, it is likely that the two expressions will be treated as identical.

17. This is the effect of advice on the Community Pharmacy England website https://cpe.org.uk/quality-and-regulations/other-regulatory-and-terms-of-service-requirments/responsible-pharmacist/ (accessed 31 December 2024).

18. http://www.legislation.gov.uk/uksi/2008/2789/pdfs/uksiem_20082789_en.pdf (accessed 31 December 2024).

19. Paragraph 5(2) of Schedule 4 to the National Health Service (Pharmaceutical and Local Pharmaceutical Services Regulations 2013, paragraph 4(1) of Schedule 1 to the National Health Service (Pharmaceutical Services (Scotland) Regulations 2009 and paragraph 5(1) of Schedule 5 to the National Health Service (Pharmaceutical Services) (Wales) Regulations 2020.

legal duties of a responsible pharmacist and may not be the responsible pharmacist for any other pharmacy at the same time.

Section 72B of the Medicines Act provides that a person is not to be considered as the responsible pharmacist:

a. if they fail to comply with the requirement to be in charge of only one set of premises – in other words, if they are named as the responsible pharmacist of more than one set of premises at the same time, the law will not regard them as the responsible pharmacist for any of the premises;
b. if they fail to comply with any rules made by the GPhC; or
c. if they fail to comply with the requirements in any rules made by the GPhC regarding absence from the premises.

Superintendent pharmacists

Eligibility and role of a superintendent pharmacist

Section 71(6) of the Medicines Act provides that:

a. the superintendent must be a pharmacist;
b. a statement in writing, signed by the superintendent and the body corporate, specifying the superintendent's name must have been sent to the registrar of the GPhC;
c. The superintendent pharmacist must be a senior manager of the retail pharmacy business who has the authority to make decisions that affect the running of the retail pharmacy business so far as concerns:
   (i) the retail sale of medicinal products (whether they are on a general sale list or not), and
   (ii) the supply of such products in circumstances corresponding to retail sale.

In order to be a senior manager of a retail pharmacy business, so far as concerns the retail sale or supply of all medicines, the person must play a significant role (irrespective of whether other individuals also do so) in:

(i) the making of decisions about how the whole or a substantial part of the activities of the business are to be managed or organised, or
(ii) the actual managing or organising of the whole or a substantial part of those activities.

If a superintendent ceases to be the superintendent pharmacist, that person must notify the registrar of the GPhC of that fact within 28 days of ceasing to be the superintendent (unless the reason is that the superintendent had died).

Legal duty of a superintendent pharmacist

Section 72AA imposes a legal duty on superintendent pharmacists to secure that the retail pharmacy business is at all times carried on in ways that ensure its safe and effective running so far as concerns:

(a) the retail sale of medicinal products (whether they are on a general sale list or not), and
(b) the supply of such products in circumstances corresponding to retail sale.

Failure to fulfil the conditions of lawfully conducting a retail pharmacy business

If the conditions of lawfully conducting a retail pharmacy business are not fulfilled then, amongst other things, any supplies of medicinal products, other than those on a General Sale List, will involve the commission of a criminal offence; and the presence on the premises of controlled drugs will involve the offence of unlawful possession.

Separately, section 72B of the Medicines Act provides that a failure to comply with sections 72A or 72AA of the Medicines Act may constitute misconduct that could result in fitness to practise proceedings (see **Chapter 25**).

Comparing the legal roles of superintendent pharmacists and responsible pharmacists

A comparison of the legal roles of superintendent pharmacists and responsible pharmacists is given in **Box 7.3** below.

Box 7.3: Comparison of the legal position of superintendent pharmacists and responsible pharmacists

Superintendent pharmacist	Responsible pharmacist
Senior manager of the business	Acts at direction of superintendent pharmacist (if not the superintendent pharmacist)
Notification to the GPhC	Notice at the premises displaying name
Decision-making authority relating to medicinal products	The business at the pharmacy premises
More than one body corporate	One pharmacy
Relates to all medicines	Relates to all medicines
Safe and effective running of **the business** carried on by the body corporate	Safe and effective running of **the business at or from the premises**
The legal duty is continuous, whether any pharmacy is open or closed	The legal duty applies only when signed in at one pharmacy

Future changes to the law

The legal provisions above may be amended in 2025 as a result of changes to the law to enable hub and spoke dispensing arrangements between pharmacies that do not have the same owner. These changes are described in **Box 7.4** below.

Box 7.4: Future changes to the law

At the time of going to press, there were proposals to amend the law to allow pharmacies to send prescriptions to another pharmacy that does not have the same owner, so that the prescribed medicines can be dispensed at that other pharmacy (known as hub and spoke dispensing). This box sets out what the law will be if those proposals are brought into effect. Readers can check whether the proposals have been brought into effect by checking www.legislation.gov.uk or using a subscription service such as Westlaw for the latest version of the Medicines Act 1968 or searching those sites for the Human Medicines (Amendments Relating to Hub and Spoke dispensing etc.) Regulations *[followed by the year].*

A new regulation 222A of the HMR will require spokes to display conspicuously a notice that they have arrangements with the name and address of any hub with whom the spoke has arrangements, and a brief statement of the general effect of the arrangements.

Professional responsibilities

The legal duties and responsibilities set out above are essential to satisfy the requirements for lawfully conducting a retail pharmacy business. It is important to distinguish those legal duties and responsibilities from professional responsibilities. The GPhC has express power[20] to publish standards specifically relating only to the conduct, ethics and performance expected of responsible pharmacists and superintendent pharmacists.

The professional responsibilities of responsible pharmacists

The GPhC has not published specific guidance on the professional responsibilities of responsible pharmacists, but has previously referred to guidance published by the Department of Health when the Responsible Pharmacist Regulations were due to be introduced. This guidance[21] focusses mainly on a responsible pharmacist's legal duties and responsibilities.

The professional responsibilities of superintendent pharmacists

The GPhC has not published specific guidance on the professional responsibilities of superintendent pharmacists, but it gives some general guidance on its website[22] and the Department of Health guidance on the Responsible Pharmacist Regulations addresses the respective roles of responsible pharmacists and superintendent

20. Article 48(1A) of the Pharmacy Order 2010.
21. https://webarchive.nationalarchives.gov.uk/20130124045445/http://www.dh.gov.uk/prod_consum_dh/groups/dh_digitalassets/documents/digitalasset/dh_095569.pdf (accessed 31 December 2024).
22. https://www.pharmacyregulation.org/pharmacists/changes-registration/becoming-superintendent-pharmacist (accessed 31 December 2024).

pharmacists. Extracts from this guidance relating to superintendent pharmacists are set out in **Box 7.5**.

Box 7.5: The role of superintendent pharmacists – DHSC guidance (extracts)

The superintendent pharmacist has a wider legal role - separate but complementary to that of the responsible pharmacist. In carrying out his/her legal and professional responsibilities, the superintendent pharmacist provides the overarching operational framework for the company's pharmacies – and this should support each responsible pharmacist in complying with the legal duty to secure safe and effective running of the individual pharmacy.

- A superintendent pharmacist may also be the responsible pharmacist for a particular pharmacy. However, where a company owns a large number of pharmacies, the superintendent pharmacist is unable to meet the legal requirements relating to the responsible pharmacist - the pharmacist in charge of the day-to-day running of an individual pharmacy. For example, the superintendent pharmacist is not in a position to secure the safe and effective running of each pharmacy or to comply with requirements relating to the responsible pharmacist's absence from the pharmacy. Therefore, where not also the responsible pharmacist, the superintendent pharmacist will need to ensure that another pharmacist is responsible for each pharmacy owned by the company. As now, these pharmacists remain subject to the directions of the superintendent pharmacist.
- As the company manager of the pharmacy business where this relates to the keeping, preparing, dispensing, and sale of medicines, the superintendent pharmacist should:
  - ensure arrangements are in place to appoint the responsible pharmacist in charge of each set of registered premises owned by the company;
  - enable each responsible pharmacist to comply with the legal duty – including allowing the responsible pharmacist to exercise his/her professional judgement, as appropriate, in securing the safe and effective running of the pharmacy concerned;
  - ... and
  - ensure preservation of the pharmacy record for at least the minimum time set out in the regulations.

While superintendent pharmacists have overall responsibility for the systems in place at all pharmacies owned by a body corporate, not just in relation to medicinal products, they may delegate functions to others. This was illustrated in an unreported 1982 case, *The Queen v The Statutory Committee of the Pharmaceutical Society of Great Britain, ex parte Lewis & Jeffreys Limited, Berg and others*. An advertising feature for a Lewis & Jeffreys pharmacy appeared in a local newspaper in breach of professional restrictions on advertising that were in effect at the time. Mr Berg was the superintendent pharmacist of the company. He had been about to go on holiday and had given another pharmacist instructions regarding the advertising feature, saying it should not be published before Mr Berg had approved its contents. The feature was published before Mr Berg had approved it. Mr Berg was found guilty of misconduct and reprimanded. The High Court quashed (overturned) the finding of misconduct. Mr Justice Woolf said:

"It is true that certain duties of the superintendent pharmacist cannot be delegated. However, when you bear in mind that a company as large as Boots only has one superintendent pharmacist, it cannot be the intention [of the Medicines Act 1968] that superintendents should not use other pharmacists to perform certain of their functions ... [Mr Berg] was presumably entitled to go on holiday and could not be blamed for what happened while he was away, as long as he had arranged that no advertisement was to appear of which he had not approved."

Pharmacy owners and those with leadership and management roles

The GPhC has published guidance to support its Standards for registered pharmacies (see **Chapter 2**). The guidance to ensure a safe and effective pharmacy team[23] includes advice for pharmacy owners. The guidance addresses the roles of members of the board of bodies corporate and those with leadership and management roles. It is notable that board members (typically company directors) do not have any legal duties in pharmacy legislation, and that this guidance therefore extends professional responsibilities to individuals who would not have such responsibilities unless they were also a superintendent pharmacist. Indeed, the guidance extends to board members whether or not they are registered as pharmacists or pharmacy technicians.

Superintendent pharmacists clearly have management roles, so the guidance applies to them in any event. Whether other pharmacists and pharmacy technicians will be considered to have management roles will be a question of fact in each case.

The guidance says:

"Pharmacy owners must make sure that pharmacy professionals who work for them can meet their own professional and legal obligations and are able to exercise their professional judgement in the interests of patients and the public. Managers who have responsibility for leading and managing teams, and for co-ordinating many aspects of the day-to-day pharmacy operations, have an important role to play. Members of the board, people in leadership roles and managers have significant responsibilities, and influence over the culture, practices and environment of the pharmacy, and how the safe and effective delivery of pharmacy services is maintained."

The guidance does not define *management role*. The reference to *managers* appears to refer to roles within the body corporate, so the manager of a branch may not be considered to come within this guidance. In *Registrar of Restrictive Trading Agreements v W.H Smith & Son Ltd*,[24] the Registrar of Restrictive Trading Agreements

23. https://www.pharmacyregulation.org/pharmacies/standards-and-guidance-registered-pharmacies (accessed 31 December 2024).

24. [1969] 1 WLR 1460.

had certain powers in relation to a person who was "director, manager, secretary or other officer of [a] body corporate". Similar words are used in some provisions of the Medicines Act 1968. The Registrar took action against the manager of a branch of W.H. Smith & Son Ltd. The Court of Appeal held that the word *manager* referred to those who were concerned with the management of the affairs of a company as a whole and did not include a branch manager.

Company directors who are pharmacists but not the superintendent pharmacist have faced fitness to practise proceedings when the company has failed to comply with standards (see **Chapter 25**). In addition, if a body corporate commits an offence under the Medicines Act and the offence is proved to have been committed through the neglect, consent or connivance of a director or an officer of the body corporate (including the superintendent pharmacist), that director or officer will also be guilty of the offence.[25]

Restricted titles, descriptions and emblems

Section 78 of the Medicines Act prohibits the use of the titles chemist and druggist, druggist, dispensing chemist, and dispensing druggist, and the use the title of chemist in connection with the sale of any goods by retail or the supply of any goods in circumstances corresponding to retail sale unless certain conditions are met. The conditions are that:

1. The person using the title is lawfully conducting a retail pharmacy business;
2. The title is not used in connection with any premises at which any goods are sold by retail, or are supplied in circumstances corresponding to retail sale, unless those premises are a registered pharmacy.

The Court considered these provisions in the case of *Norris v Weeks*,[26] see **Box 7.6.**

Box 7.6: *Norris v Weeks*

The Pharmacy Act 1954 (s.19) read: "it shall not be lawful for any person, unless he is a registered pharmaceutical chemist ... to take or use, in connection with the sale of goods by retail, the title of chemist". The provision is equivalent to the words in the Medicines Act 1968.

A notice, about 1 ft high by 2.5 ft wide (30 cm by 75 cm) was displayed at Mr Weeks' drug store over goods intended for retail sale. It bore the wording on three lines, *Wyn's/Chemist/ Sundries*. The word *chemist* was in larger script than the other words and in a different colour. The magistrate dismissed a summons under section 19(1)(b) on the ground that, having regard to the articles displayed, the word *chemist* was merely descriptive of the type of goods sold.

The High Court dismissed an appeal against this decision. It held that an offence is committed only if a person asserts that they are a chemist or takes to themself the title *chemist*. It could not be said that an offence is committed whenever the word *chemist* appears.

No person may, in connection with any business, use any title, description or emblem likely to suggest that they possess any qualification with respect to the sale, manufacture

25. Section 124 of the Medicines Act 1968.
26. The Times, 6 March 1970; *Pharm J*, 14 March 1970 p. 268.

or assembly of medicinal products which they do not in fact possess, or that any person employed in the business possesses any such qualification which that person does not in fact possess (s.78 (6)).

Furthermore, the use of certain titles and descriptions is specifically restricted as follows.

1. The term *pharmacy* may only be used in respect of a registered pharmacy or the pharmaceutical department of a hospital or a health centre. It may not be used in connection with any business, other than a pharmacy, which consists of or includes the retail sale of any goods, or the supply of any goods in circumstances corresponding to retail sale (s.78(4)). Its use in connection with a business carried on at any premises shall be taken as likely to suggest that the person carrying on the business (where that person is not a body corporate) is a pharmacist, and that any other person under whose personal control the business is carried on at those premises (so far as concerns the retail sale of medicinal products or the supply of such products in circumstances corresponding to retail sale) is also a pharmacist.
2. Only a person who is registered as a pharmacist in Part 1 of the GPhC's Register may take the titles *pharmacist* and *fferyllydd* (its equivalent in the Welsh language) in connection with a business carried on (either by that person or someone else) at or from any premises which consists of or includes the retail sale or supply of any goods (not just medicines) unless those premises are a registered pharmacy or a hospital or health centre (s.78(5A)).

None of the restricted titles may be used at any premises connected with a business which includes the retail sale or supply of any goods unless those premises are a registered pharmacy (s.78(3)). Anyone wishing to form a company with a name that includes any of the restricted titles must provide the Registrar of Companies with a letter of authorisation from the GPhC.

Under the Pharmacy Order 2010 (Art 38), a person (including a pharmacy student or pre-registration trainee) commits an offence if they:

a. use the title "pharmacist" or "fferyllydd" (its equivalent in the Welsh language) without being entered as a pharmacist in Part 1 of the Register;
b. use the title "pharmacy technician" or "technegydd fferylliaeth" (its equivalent in the Welsh language) without being entered as a pharmacy technician in Part 2 of the Register; or
c. use a title in respect of a particular annotation, which is a prescribed specialist title, where that person does not have an entry in any part of the Register with that particular annotation. An example would include a reference to being an independent prescriber by a person whose entry in the Register did not have an annotation to that effect.

Between 2012 and 2021, the GPhC brought 17 criminal prosecutions for practising as a pharmacist or pharmacy technician while not on the register, each of which resulted in a conviction and fines imposed by the courts of up to £4,000.[27]

27. The information was supplied to the authors by the GPhC in response to a request under the Freedom of Information Act 2000.

SUMMARY

- Pharmacy legislation refers to *retail pharmacy businesses*.
- The Medicines Act 1968 creates a definition of lawfully conducting a retail pharmacy business.
- Only pharmacists, partnerships of pharmacists (or at least one pharmacist, in Scotland) and bodies corporate may lawfully conduct a retail pharmacy business.
- Pharmacy businesses must fulfil certain conditions in order to come within the definition of lawfully conducting a retail pharmacy business.
- If pharmacy businesses are not lawfully conducting a retail pharmacy business, they cannot lawfully sell or supply medicines other than those on a General Sale List, nor can they lawfully be in possession of controlled drugs.
- A key requirement for all pharmacies in fulfilling the conditions for lawfully conducting a retail pharmacy business is the presence of a responsible pharmacist.
- The responsible pharmacist may be absent from the premises for up to two hours a day, subject to meeting certain requirements.
- The responsible pharmacist has a legal duty to secure the safe and effective running of the pharmacy business at the premises in relation to the supply of all medicines.
- A record must be kept of the name of the responsible pharmacist on duty.
- Bodies corporate must additionally have a superintendent pharmacist in order to fulfil the conditions of lawfully conducting a retail pharmacy business.
- The superintendent pharmacist must be a senior manager of the retail pharmacy business who has the authority to make decisions that affect the running of the retail pharmacy business so far as concerns the retail sale or supply of all medicines.
- A superintendent pharmacist has a legal duty to secure that the business is carried on in ways that ensure its safe and effective running so far as concerns the retail sale or supply of all medicines.
- Superintendent pharmacists and responsible pharmacists have professional responsibilities, as do owners and others with leadership and management roles.
- There are restrictions on the use of titles such as *pharmacy*, *pharmacist* and *chemist*.
- Pharmacy premises must be registered with the GPhC.

CHAPTER 8

Online pharmacy services

This chapter concerns online pharmacy and the greater risks to patients who obtain medicines online rather than in person from a community pharmacy, and the legal and professional measures being used to manage those risks. (The risk of counterfeit medicines being purchased online is outside the scope of this chapter.)

Introduction

In this chapter, we use the term *online pharmacy*, but other terms referring to the provision of remote pharmacy services may also be used, such as *internet pharmacy*. The General Pharmaceutical Council (GPhC) guidance referred to below uses the words *providing pharmacy services at a distance including on the internet* and the scope of the guidance is wider than that of this chapter.

In principle, the regulation of online pharmacy should be the same as the regulation of the pharmacy provision of other retail pharmacy services because online pharmacy services are provided from bricks and mortar premises, and patients who are not present on pharmacy premises should not be treated differently to patients who are on the premises. However, the reality, risk and regulation of online pharmacy services are different.

The context for additional regulation

There is increasing consumer demand for online healthcare in general and many pharmacies provide a lawful and professionally run service. However, the provision of services online poses greater risks to patients in certain circumstances; and a disproportionately large number of regulatory activity and fitness to practise cases involve the provision of online pharmacy services (see also **Chapters 2** and **25**)

Some of the greater risks arise from the prescribing and sale of medicines that are liable to misuse or abuse. Patients who seek them may be vulnerable.

Typically, patients who seek medication online visit a website where they are asked to answer a questionnaire, select a product and make a payment. The questionnaire is reviewed by a prescriber who will often be a medical practitioner or a pharmacist. If the prescriber decides to write a private prescription, a pharmacy linked to the website owner supplies the prescribed medication to the patient.

Websites will not necessarily be owned by the pharmacy businesses that prescribe or make supplies but, for convenience, reference may be made in this chapter to *online pharmacies* to cover the website operators, prescribers and pharmacy.

Regulators

The provision of online pharmacy services is regulated throughout Great Britain by the General Pharmaceutical Council (GPhC), the Medicines and Healthcare products Regulatory Agency (MHRA) and, if the prescribers are not pharmacists, in England, by the Care Quality Commission (CQC). In Scotland, the equivalent functions of the Care Quality Commission are carried out by Health Improvement Scotland and, in Wales, by Health Inspectorate Wales. These regulators and the General Medical Council and Nursing and Midwifery Council co-ordinate their approach to regulation.[1] In fact, all these regulators take action in respect of online pharmacies, examples of which are given below.

Risk

The risks associated with online pharmacy include:

- the absence of the patient from the premises and the inability of a pharmacist to make a face-to-face assessment of the patient and ask pertinent questions;
- the need to check the genuineness of the patient, the patient's age and medical history;
- patients may not tell the truth about their condition or, when seeking treatment for weight loss, their weight;
- the ability of a patient to order more medication than is reasonably needed, including the ability to order from more than one online pharmacy (see **Box 8.1**);
- the ability of a patient to order medication that is not suitable for them;
- the patient's choice whether the online pharmacy should notify the patient's regular doctor of what has been prescribed and supplied online.

Box 8.1

The regulation 28[2] coroner's report[3] on Ania Sohail who ordered propranolol from a number of online pharmacies which she then used to commit suicide. Each pharmacy did not know what had been supplied by any other pharmacy. The coroner's jury concluded that:

> *"a lack of an integrated national system, which could be accessed by online pharmacies for dispensing medication ... and a lack of consent to sharing information, contributed to Miss Sohail's death."*

While the same risk might have materialised if Miss Sohail had approached a number of private doctors for prescriptions and then visited different bricks and mortar pharmacies, the availability of online pharmacies that provide prescribers make it much easier to obtain private prescriptions.

2. Regulation 28 of the Coroners (Investigations) Regulations 2013.
3. https://www.judiciary.uk/prevention-of-future-death-reports/ania-sohail-prevention-of-future-deaths-report/ (accessed 31 December 2024).

1. Letter to providers dated 24 August 2017 https://www.cqc.org.uk/sites/default/files/20170824_joint_letter_providers_online_primary_care.pdf (accessed 31 December 2024).

In England, there have been a number of coroner's reports after deaths resulting from the use of medicines obtained online, expressing concern that further deaths would occur unless actions are taken.[4] The law of manslaughter is covered in **Chapter 26**. Probably the most likely scenario for a pharmacist to be convicted of manslaughter would involve the sale or supply of a medicine online.

Advertising

The advertising of medicinal products is covered in **Chapter 19**. The word advertising is defined in regulation 7 of the Human Medicines Regulations 2012 (HMR) as including "anything designed to promote the prescription, supply, sale or use of [a medicinal product]". This definition is wide enough to cover any website that features medicinal products that prospective patients are encouraged to or able to buy.

Under regulation 284 of the HMR it is unlawful to publish an advertisement that is likely to lead to the use of a Prescription Only Medicine (POM).[5] The MHRA takes the view that any advertisement of a POM that is aimed at the public (rather than at healthcare professionals) is likely to lead to the use of that POM and therefore breaches regulation 284.

The MHRA's specific views on what is and is not permissible under regulation 284 in relation to online pharmacies are contained in the Blue Guide[6] which includes the following:

- A home page should focus on medical conditions and the services provided by the website.
- A home page should not name POMs or give prices.
- A home page should not contain links to specific POMs.
- Neither hover text nor small print should refer to specific POMs.
- A home page should make it clear that the customer is being offered a medical consultation and that this may or may not lead to the provision of a prescription.
- Indicative prices may be given on a home page, but not actual prices.
- Special offers should not appear anywhere.
- Icons that say "Buy now" or "Add to basket" should not be used anywhere on websites offering POM treatments, because they invite customers to buy POMs and are intended to promote sales.
- Specific POMs should not be promoted because they are likely to encourage the purchase of a POM.
- Website addresses should not include the name of a POM in the core URL.

---

4. Coroners' reports are explained in more detail in Chapter 1. Examples of reports may be found at https://www.judiciary.uk/wp-content/uploads/2021/02/Katie-Corrigan-2021-0045-Redacted.pdf (a case that received national press attention) and https://www.judiciary.uk/wp-content/uploads/2024/06/Nigel-Dixon-Prevention-of-future-deaths-report-2024-0312_Published.pdf (both accessed 31 December 2024).
5. Exceptions to this include approved (by Ministers) campaigns relating to the suspected or confirmed spread of pathogenic agents (Reg.291A) and approved vaccination campaigns (Reg.292).
6. https://assets.publishing.service.gov.uk/government/uploads/system/uploads/attachment_data/file/956846/BG_2020_Brexit_Final_version.pdf (accessed 31 December 2024).

NHS terms of service

The requirement for NHS distance selling pharmacies in England to have a website is covered in **Chapter 3**.

Online market places – poisons and chemicals etc.

The sales and supplies of poisons and chemicals using online market places are covered in **Chapter 21**.

Veterinary medicinal products

There are specific legal requirements governing the online sale of veterinary medicines. These requirements are set out in **Chapter 15**.

GPhC

The GPhC has published *Guidance for registered pharmacies providing pharmacy services at a distance including on the internet.*[7]

A failure to follow the new guidance may lead to enforcement action against the pharmacy, the pharmacy owner and/or, if the pharmacy is owned by a body corporate, against the superintendent pharmacist. Other pharmacy professionals may also become the subject of investigation, depending on the circumstances.

Risk assessments

Because there are different risks than when providing services face-to-face, risk assessments must be carried out to help with identifying and managing risks. These should look at the ways pharmacy services could cause harm to people who use them; and help identify what measures need to be put in place to keep the amount of risk as low as reasonably practicable.

Expectation of pharmacy control over websites and over prescribers

To the extent referred to below, the new guidance requires pharmacies to have control over websites, even websites that are not owned by the pharmacies that provide services. To the extent referred to below, the guidance also requires pharmacies that provide services to have control over prescribers, whether the prescribers are employed by the pharmacy or not. It follows that if, for example, a website does not display all the required information or if a pharmacy cannot be satisfied that all prescribers comply with their respective professional obligations, the pharmacy should not provide services.

7. https://assets.pharmacyregulation.org/files/2025-02/gphc-guidance-registered-pharmacies-providing-pharmacy-services-distance-february-2025.pdf (accessed 5 March 2025). The guidance is concerned with all pharmacy services that are provided at a distance, including, for example, hub and spoke dispensing and the use of automated collection machines. This chapter deals with the Guidance only insofar as it is relevant to the provision of online services.

Prescribers

Pharmacies must make sure that:

- each prescriber is registered with the relevant professional regulator in the country they are based in (that is, where the prescription is issued), and they can lawfully issue prescriptions online to people in the UK,
- the prescriber is working within national prescribing guidelines for the UK, and
- the prescriber carries out regular prescribing audits to assure the safety and quality of the treatments provided.

Audits

Regular audits should be carried out. These should include prescribing decisions. Among other things:

- audits should include the reasons for prescribing decisions. This should include, for example, records of decisions to:
  - make or refuse a sale, or
  - supply or refuse to supply a medicine against a prescription in line with national and good practice guidance, and
- any information about the pharmacy services on any associated website.

Websites

Systems

Systems should be able to identify and flag up:

- multiple orders to the same address,
- a person using multiple accounts to make orders,
- orders that seem to be from different people but are using the same payment details,
- inappropriate combinations of medicines, or
- requests that are too large or made too often.

Display of medicines

Pharmacy medicines may only be displayed for sale on a website, app or digital platform that is associated with the registered pharmacy. If the website is not owned by the pharmacy that supplies medicines, this could be under a service-level agreement or some other arrangement.

Information to appear prominently

Websites should prominently display:

- the pharmacy's GPhC registration number,
- the name of the owner of the registered pharmacy,
- the name of the superintendent pharmacist, if there is one,
- the name and physical address of the registered pharmacy or pharmacies that supply the medicines, with relevant phone numbers and email addresses,

- details of the registered pharmacy where medicines are prepared, assembled, dispensed, and labelled for individuals against prescriptions (if any of these things happen at a pharmacy different from that supplying the medicines),
- information about how to check the registration status of the pharmacy, the responsible pharmacist and the superintendent pharmacist, if there is one,
- details of how users of pharmacy services can give feedback and raise concerns, and
- information by way of a privacy policy which clearly sets out how information gathered will be used.

Websites should be arranged so that a person has an appropriate consultation with a prescriber before any supply of a POM is made. The website can allow people to give their preferred choice of medicine, for example a preferred brand or formulation, before the consultation. However, it should be made clear that the decisions about treatment are for both the prescriber and the person to consider together during the consultation.

If a person is prescribed medicines following an online consultation, the website should prominently display:

- the name of the prescriber, the address of the prescribing service and their contact details,
- the prescriber's registration number and the country they are registered in,
- whether the prescriber is a doctor or a non-medical independent prescriber – for example a pharmacist, nurse, or physiotherapist, and
- information about how to check the registration status of the prescriber and if the service is regulated.

Identity checks

For sales or supplies of Pharmacy medicines and POMs, pharmacy staff should check that the person receiving pharmacy services is who they claim to be by carrying out an identity check appropriate for the medicine being supplied.

Prescribers

Pharmacist independent prescribers should follow the GPhC guidance for pharmacist prescribers[8] (see **Chapter 24**) and the Royal Pharmaceutical Society's *Competency Framework for All Prescribers*.[9]

Pharmacies should make sure that non-pharmacist prescribers follow the General Medical Council's *Good practice in proposing, prescribing, providing and managing medicines and devices*.

If a patient does not have a regular prescriber such as a GP, or if the patient does not consent to share information with a regular prescriber, the online prescriber should decide whether it is safe to prescribe. They will need to think about the patient's best interests and carry out an individual risk-based assessment about whether they can prescribe safely.

---

8. https://assets.pharmacyregulation.org/files/2024-01/in-practice-guidance-for-pharmacist-prescribers-february-2020.pdf (accessed 31 December 2024).
9. https://www.rpharms.com/Portals/0/RPS%20document%20library/Open%20access/Prescribing%20Competency%20Framework/RPS%20English%20Competency%20Framework%203.pdf?ver=mctnrKo4YaJDh2nA8N5G3A%3d%3d (accessed 31 December 2024).

Prescribing of specific medicines

Some medicines are not suitable to be prescribed by a questionnaire model alone. Also, some medicines should not be supplied unless extra safeguards have been put in place to make sure they are clinically appropriate. Examples include, but are not limited to:

- antimicrobials, which must take into account antimicrobial stewardship guidelines relevant for the person and their setting,
- medicines liable to misuse, such as opioids, sedatives, laxatives, gabapentinoids, stimulants and nootropics,
- medicines which have a higher risk of fatality or serious harm if taken in overdose, for example, amitriptyline, propranolol, colchicine and carbamazepine,
- medicines and long-term conditions that require ongoing monitoring or management, for example:
  - medicines with a narrow therapeutic index such as lithium and warfarin,
  - medicines used for diabetes, asthma, epilepsy, heart conditions and mental health conditions, and
  - medicines which are part of a pregnancy prevention programme (PPP) – for example sodium valproate and oral retinoids – because they carry a high risk of causing damage to the unborn baby and developmental problems,
- medicines where there needs to be a physical examination of the person to support a safe prescribing decision, for example, non-surgical cosmetic medicinal products,
- medicines used for weight management and those known to be misused to achieve weight loss, and
- medicines labelled with a black triangle (▼ or ▼*) as they need additional monitoring and suspected drug reactions should be reported through the MHRA yellow card scheme.

When supplying medicines used for weight management, the prescriber must independently verify the person's weight, height and/or body mass index. The prescriber must not rely only on information given by the patient. This could be done through a video consultation, in person, from the patient's clinical records or by contacting another healthcare provider such as the patient's GP. Verifying information through a phone call is not considered appropriate.

Consultations

Pharmacies should decide which method of consultation is best suited to get the information needed to deliver safe and effective care. This includes deciding which method is best suited to deal with any specific requirements, or concerns. Examples include (but are not limited to):

- if the person has a potentially serious, high-risk condition where there is a need for a physical examination or other assessments,
- if there is a need for a diagnostic test before prescribing a medication, or
- whether two-way communication can be established, if needed.

Recipients of pharmacy services

Recipients of pharmacy services should:

- have the chance to ask questions about their medicines, and

- know who to contact if they have any questions or want to discuss something with the pharmacist or pharmacy staff.

GPhC logo

The GPhC has a voluntary internet pharmacy logo scheme to reassure patients and the public that they are buying medicines online from registered pharmacies who have to meet the GPhC standards. The GPhC does not allow the logo to be used by anyone other than a pharmacy that is registered with it.

Conflicts of interest and freedom of choice

Pharmacies should be able to show that arrangements with medical or non-medical prescribers are lawful, ethical and transparent, and do not:

- cause conflicts of interest, for example by giving incentives to prescribers to issue prescriptions,
- restrict a person's choice of pharmacy, or
- unduly influence or mislead people needing services, deliberately or by mistake.

Enforcement

The GPhC's enforcement powers and the steps it has taken in relation to online sales that breach its standards are covered in **Chapter 2**. If an allegation of misconduct is made, the new Guidance makes it clear that if a pharmacy is owned by a body corporate, fitness to practise proceedings may also be brought against superintendent pharmacists (see **Chapter 7** in relation to superintendent pharmacists and **Chapter 25** in relation to fitness to practise).

Examples of two fitness to practise cases are given in **Box 8.2**.

Box 8.2: Online pharmacy – examples of fitness to practise cases

In May 2022, the GPhC's Fitness to Practise Committee dealt with a case involving a pharmacist independent prescriber who worked for an online pharmacy business. Prescriptions written by overseas prescribers were referred to him and he wrote corresponding prescriptions that enabled the online pharmacy to supply the prescribed medicines. Although there was no evidence that harm was caused, the pharmacist wrote prescriptions for humans that included treatments for mental health, paediatric epilepsy, HIV, and cancer, all of which were beyond his competence to prescribe. He also wrote prescriptions for animals (dogs, cats, and a parrot). The Committee decided that a finding that the pharmacist's fitness to practise was impaired would "send a clear message to professionals and the public that misconduct of this sort when prescribing at a distance will not be tolerated by the regulator".

The Committee considered that the public interest considerations raised by the facts of the case were particularly acute because prescribing at a distance carries particular risks which the registrant failed to take into account.

The Committee said that a four-month suspension from practice would "ensure that the public can continue to have confidence in the profession, particularly as the provision of on-line pharmacy services continues to become more popular, along with upholding professional standards and maintaining the public's confidence in the Regulator itself".

****

Box 8.2: Online pharmacy – examples of fitness to practise cases (cont.)

In a 2023 case, the Fitness to Practise Committee dealt with the case of a superintendent pharmacist of a company whose online business was mainly concerned with the prescribing and dispensing of opioids, zolpidem and zopiclone.

The Committee upheld allegations of misconduct because:

- although the website owned by the company the superintendent worked for used a third party to check identification evidence provided by website users, there were no regular audits of:
  - patient verification identification,
  - how many prescriptions had been refused by the prescribers,
  - the number of people who submitted incorrect details of their regular doctor, and
  - the process for receiving responses back from people's regular doctors;
- the absence of regular audits in the context of medicines liable to misuse or abuse increased the risk that people with addiction problems go undetected by the pharmacy and supplies would continue;
- the pharmacy did not consistently keep and maintain records of clinical decisions;
- in the absence of audits and reviews, there was no evidence to demonstrate that robust systems were in place to monitor and ensure the veracity of the clinical decision making and that the medication that was supplied was clinically justified;
- the absence of prescribing monitoring/reviews and the risk to patient safety was compounded by the fact that the Pharmacy had a payment structure based on incentivised prescribing in that prescribers were paid on the basis of prescriptions approved. Cancelled requests did not result in payment. While not unlawful, this payment structure was open to abuse and required corresponding systems to ensure patient safety.

The Committee said that the failings found proved were serious, fundamental, and wide-ranging. There was no evidence of harm to patients. However, the role of a pharmacist was to "act as gatekeeper of medications which are known to be open to misuse and abuse. Without the appropriate procedures in place, there is undoubtedly a risk of harm and indeed of death ...".

The Committee decided that the superintendent pharmacist's fitness to practise was impaired and imposed a nine-month suspension from practice.

Care Quality Commission (CQC), Health Improvement Scotland (HIS) and Healthcare Inspectorate Wales (HIW)

More detailed information about the statutory basis of the CQC, its powers and obligations are given in **Chapter 2** and in **Box 3.1** in **Chapter 3**. HIS and HIW have equivalent powers.

Under section 60(1)(a) of the Health and Social Care Act 2008 Act, the CQC may for the purposes of its regulatory functions carry out inspections of the carrying on of a regulated activity. Under section 61, where such an inspection is carried out, the CQC must (i) prepare a report on the matters inspected; (ii) without delay send a copy of the report to the person who carries on the regulated activity in question; and (iii) publish the report.

Under Regulation 20A of the Health and Social Care Act 2008 (Regulated Activities) Regulations 2014, where a report gives a rating, the service provider must display that rating conspicuously and legibly in each and every place where the regulated activity is delivered, and on its website, where people will be sure to see it.

The CQC published a press release on 6 April 2017, headed *CQC continues to take action against websites selling prescription medicines.*[10] In the press release, the CQC announced it had published inspection reports on four online providers associated with pharmacies. The reports detailed "examples of people being put at risk of harm, with insufficient checks on their identity, poor recording of their medical history and clarification of their symptoms, inappropriate medicines being prescribed, and lack of communication with the patient's GP".

Even if a pharmacy owner does not agree with the contents of a CQC report, it is unlikely that the owner could prevent publication unless there are exceptional circumstances, as illustrated in the case of *R (on the application of Hexpress Healthcare Ltd) v Care Quality Commission*[11] – see **Box 8.3** below.

Box 8.3

In *R (on the application of Hexpress Healthcare Ltd v Care Quality Commission* [2022] EWHC 2943 (Admin), Hexpress Healthcare Limited (Hexpress) ran an online pharmacy business which was registered with the CQC. Its website offered treatments for conditions such as erectile dysfunction, weight loss and sexually transmitted infections. Patients seeking treatment were asked to fill in an online questionnaire which was referred to a medical practitioner who may prescribe. What was prescribed was then supplied by Hexpress.

Between 28 April 2021 and 14 August 2021, five incidents took place concerning patients who had received medication from Hexpress. One patient suffered from a non-fatal overdose of Saxenda, a weight loss injection pen. Two suffered from non-fatal overdoses, and two from fatal overdoses, of the beta-blocker propranolol. The claimant in response changed its systems before suspending propranolol prescriptions entirely. These five incidents were brought to the CQC's attention.

On 17 May 2022 an announced, fully comprehensive inspection of the Hexpress business took place. The inspection remit was the fundamental standards of care and the safety of the service of the provider. Out of 60,000 medical records available, the CQC randomly selected nine to review. However, three of those were for technical reasons unreviewable, producing no evidence. Therefore, the sample size was six, representing 0.01% of all patient records. Out of these six records, five raised concerns.

The CQC treated its findings in relation to five out of six records as representative of the whole and sent Hexpress a draft report.

Hexpress applied to the court for an interim injunction to prevent the report being published before a final hearing of judicial review proceedings. Hexpress argued that the CQC breached its obligations in the 2008 Act, by using only six medical records as its sample. The CQC's case was that this approach to the records was reasonable firstly because it only had one day to inspect and did not have easy access through the system and secondly because "while the sample was relatively small, a very worryingly high proportion of the records examined contained issues".

Without deciding whether a report based on such a small number of records was unlawful, Mr Justice Mostyn refused to grant an interim injunction to restrain publication of the CQC report prior to the final hearing of the judicial review application. He said:

---

10. https://www.cqc.org.uk/news/releases/cqc-continues-take-action-against-websites-selling-prescription-medicines (accessed 31 December 2024).
11. [2022] EWHC 2943 (Admin).

Box 8.3 (cont.)

"Where an injunction is sought to prevent a public body from publishing a report it is under a statutory duty to publish [there must be] the most compelling reasons to prohibit a public body … from publishing its decision".

Compelling reasons might exist if a public body had engaged in a vendetta against the person the subject of the adjudication or if the adjudication was prompted by a deliberate desire to inflict damage on the reputation of the person criticised. Other examples might involve fraud or corruption, or perhaps involving the intention to proceed with a report which can be shown to be manifestly untrue or riddled with error. However, there were no such compelling reasons in this case.

SUMMARY

- The prescribing, sale or supply of medicines online carries risks to patients over and above those when medicines are sold or supplied in a pharmacy (and a disproportionately high number of regulatory action and fitness to practise cases arise from the online sale or supply of medicines). Patients who seek certain medicines online may be vulnerable.
- Patients may seek online medicines that are liable to abuse or misuse.
- It is unlawful to advertise a POM in a way that is likely to lead to its use.
- The law on advertising medicines is mainly enforced by the MHRA which has specific views about what constitutes an advertisement on a website.
- The GPhC has published guidance on online pharmacy services. Amongst other things:
    - risk assessments and regular audits are required;
    - there are requirements for systems, how medicines are displayed and what information should appear prominently;
    - there are requirements relating to identity checks, consultations and prescribers; and
    - examples of medicines that require extra safeguards are listed.
- The Care Quality Commission (in England), Health Improvement Scotland and Healthcare Inspectorate Wales inspect online services such as prescribing, and publish reports of their inspections.

CHAPTER 9

Hospital pharmacy and other relevant pharmacy services

The medicinal products supplied from hospital pharmacies (and other pharmacies that are not community pharmacies) are subject to the same laws that are applicable to community pharmacies. However, there are different exemptions from the general legal requirements, and hospital pharmacies may (depending on whether they are registered with the GPhC) be subject to different regulation and enforcement.

Introduction

This chapter is concerned with the way that pharmacies in hospitals are regulated and about the manufacture and supply in hospitals of medicinal products. However, there are laws that concern the possession, administration and supply to and by midwives, who typically work from hospital settings, and ambulance services, which are closely connected to hospitals. Aspects of those laws are included in this chapter. Also, an amendment in 2022 of the Medicines Act 1968 provided *relevant pharmacy services* with a defence if they were prosecuted under the Act for making a dispensing error. The term *relevant pharmacy services* is defined in section 67F of the Medicines Act so as to refer (broadly speaking) to hospitals, care homes and prisons. It is therefore convenient to include some laws relevant to all those services in this chapter. It is also the most convenient chapter to cover the legal role of *chief pharmacist*, which was created when the Medicines Act was amended in 2022.

Definition of hospital

In the Human Medicines Regulations 2012 (HMR), the word *hospital* includes a clinic, nursing home or similar institution.[1]

In the National Health Service Act 2006, the word *hospital* means:

(a) any institution for the reception and treatment of persons suffering from illness,
(b) any maternity home, and
(c) any institution for the reception and treatment of persons during convalescence or persons requiring medical rehabilitation,

and includes clinics, dispensaries and out-patient departments maintained in connection with any such home or institution.[2]

1. HMR Reg.8.
2. Section 275.

Which of these definitions is applicable will depend on the activity that is carried out.[3]

NHS trusts and NHS foundation trusts

Chapter 3 of Part 2 of the National Health Service Act 2006 gives the Secretary of State for Health and Social Care power to establish NHS trusts in England. **Chapter 5** of Part 2 of the National Health Service Act gives the Secretary of State power to create NHS foundation trusts. Many hospitals are NHS trusts or NHS foundation trusts. NHS trusts and NHS foundation trusts have different governance arrangements that are outside the scope of this book.

Registration with the General Pharmaceutical Council

The Registrar of the General Pharmaceutical Council (GPhC) is required to maintain a register,[4] Part 3 of the register is for pharmacy premises. Premises are only eligible for registration if the premises are used for lawfully carrying on a retail pharmacy business. The meaning of lawfully carrying on a retail pharmacy business is considered in **Chapter 7**, but an essential ingredient of the term *retail pharmacy business* is that the business consists of or includes the retail sale of medicinal products that are not subject to general sale.[5]

The Medicines Act 1968 defines *retail sale* as referring to "selling a substance or article to a person who does not buy it for the purpose of selling or supplying it or administering it or causing it to be administered to one or more human beings in the course of a business carried on by the buyer".[6]

Historically, many NHS hospitals appear to have taken the view that they are not required to register their pharmacies with the GPhC because they do not sell medicines to patients. The GPhC does not require hospitals to register because the requirement in the HMR to sell or supply medicines that are not subject to general sale only from registered pharmacy premises[7] does not apply to a sale or supply in the course of the business of a hospital.[8] These exemptions are referred to in more detail below.

The GPhC adds on its website:

> *"Trusts/Health Boards may include several different hospitals on different sites but all the hospitals within a Trust/Health Board are viewed as being part of a single*

---

3. The Department of Health and Social Care observed in its consultation on introducing a statutory defence for prosecutions for dispensing errors: "There is no generally recognised definition of what constitutes a 'hospital'". It therefore opted to use the definition of "hospital" from the HMR when amending the Medicines Act.
4. Article 19 of the Pharmacy Order 2010.
5. HMR Reg.8.
6. Section 131 of the Medicines Act 1968. For completeness, the section gives the expression "circumstances corresponding to retail sale" a similar meaning.
7. HMR Reg.220.
8. https://www.pharmacyregulation.org/pharmacies/registration-and-renewal/pharmacy-owners-and-employers-faqs (accessed 31 December 2024).

legal entity. The supply of medicines from one hospital to a patient in another hospital of the same Trust/Health Board is a supply within the same legal entity and would therefore be regarded as a supply in the course of the business of that hospital. As such the supplying hospital pharmacy would not be required to be registered ..."

The GPhC would require a hospital to register with it if the hospital wished to supply Pharmacy medicines or Prescription Only Medicines (POMs) to patients in a hospital belonging to a different trust or Health Board. It would also require a hospital to register with it if the hospital wished to supply POMs or Pharmacy medicines to private patients of another legal entity based in the same hospital. Hospitals would also be required to register with the GPhC if they wished to supply a community pharmacy service to staff or to the public.

Regulation by the GPhC

If a hospital pharmacy is registered with the GPhC, it will be subject to inspection and regulation by the GPhC (see **Chapter 2**).

Regulation by the Care Quality Commission, Health Improvement Scotland and Healthcare Inspectorate Wales

If a hospital pharmacy is not registered with the GPhC, it will be subject to inspection and regulation by the Care Quality Commission (CQC) in England, Health Improvement Scotland or Healthcare Inspectorate Wales (see **Chapter 2** and **Box 3.1** in **Chapter 3**).

A person who is registered with the CQC will owe a statutory duty of candour (see **Chapter 2**). This does not apply to services provided from hospitals that are registered with the GPhC.

Manufacturing medicinal products

It is not unusual for hospitals to engage in manufacturing medicinal products. Ordinarily, manufacturing is not lawful unless the manufacturer holds a manufacturer's licence that has been granted by the Medicines and Healthcare products Regulatory Agency (MHRA).[9]

However, there are exemptions for hospitals from the need for a manufacturer's licence if certain conditions are satisfied. These are dealt with below.

Exemptions for hospitals, care home services and health centres[10]

If a hospital pharmacy is registered with the GPhC, it will be able to rely on exemptions for pharmacies in section 10 of the Medicines Act 1968. These exemptions, which are described in more detail in **Chapter 5**, were considered by the Court of Appeal in *Bayer PLC and Novartis Pharmaceuticals UK Ltd v NHS Darlington CCG and others*[11] – see **Box 9.1**.

---

9. HMR Reg.17.
10. Section 10 of the Medicines Act 1968.
11. [2020] EWCA Civ 449.

Box 9.1

Darlington Clinical Commissioning Group (CCG) and some other CCGs (before Clinical Commissioning Groups were replaced by Integrated Care Boards) had adopted a policy that the NHS Trusts from which they commissioned services should use Avastin as the preferred treatment for a form of the eye disease, wet age-related macular degeneration (WAMD). Avastin had a marketing authorisation for treating colorectal cancer, but did not have a marketing authorisation for the treatment of WAMD.

Avastin is supplied in glass vials. For treating colorectal cancer, the contents of the vial are diluted before administration. To treat WAMD, however, Avastin is not diluted and the contents of a vial were put repackaged into a large number of syringes for injection.

Ordinarily, preparing, dividing up or changing packaging or presentation – which is done when Avastin is used for WAMD – requires a marketing authorisation unless it was done on a prescription for an individual patient.

Bayer, who held the patent for a product that did have a marketing authorisation for the treatment of WAMD, challenged the CCGs' policy.

- Amongst other things, Bayer argued that putting the contents of vials into syringes gave rise to a risk of contamination and/or would affect its quality, safety or efficacy. However, the court held that any risk of contamination because of poor quality control was immaterial to the need for a licence: such processes were under the control of doctors and/or pharmacists who are subject to separate professional regulation. However, any hospital pharmacy that undertook syringe filling would have to give careful thought to how to ensure its processes are safe and accord with any professional rules.
- The syringes were filled in bulk. Unless there was a prescription for each syringe, a marketing authorisation would be needed. The person who filled syringes with Avastin did not have to point to a particular syringe and identify it as allocated to a particular patient. It would be enough if 20 syringes were being prepared and they were covered from the start by 20 existing prescriptions.
- Similarly, a manufacturing authorisation is not required to divide Avastin (the term "compounding" is used in the judgment) so long as this is done in a dispensing pharmacy or by a person legally authorised to do the compounding and this is done solely for retail supply.
- Section 10 of the Medicines Act was "perfectly apt" to cover preparing syringes in bulk. When syringes were filled in a pharmacy or hospital and supplied to a hospital for a patient to whom it had been prescribed, this was "dispensing".
- The word "dispensing" does not appear often in legislation, and is not defined. The Court held that the term covered the preparation of syringes and supply by one hospital to another in response to individual prescriptions.

In the case of a hospital pharmacy that is not registered with the GPhC, then in the case of things done there by or under the supervision of a pharmacist, a manufacturer's licence is not required for:

1. Preparing or dispensing a medicinal product in accordance with a prescription.
2. Assembling, provided that the pharmacy business on the pharmacy premises is restricted to retail sale or supply (i.e. that the business does not involve wholesaling), and the assembling is done with a view to sale or supply either at or from the same premises or at or from another pharmacy that forms part of the same pharmacy business. See **Chapter 5** for the meaning of *assembly*.

This exemption is subject to the further condition that the medicinal product has not been the subject of an advertisement.

3. Procuring the preparation or dispensing of a medicinal product in accordance with a prescription or procuring the assembly of a medicinal product.

These exemptions also apply to things done by or under the supervision of a pharmacist in a care home service or a health centre. (*Care home service* has the meaning given in schedule 12 to the Public Services Reform (Scotland) Act 2010 and a *health centre* means a health centre maintained under NHS legislation.)[12]

A manufacturer's licence is not required for preparing a stock of medicinal products in a hospital or health centre by or under the supervision of a pharmacist, with a view to dispensing in accordance with a prescription. (This exemption does not apply if the intention is to dispense in accordance with a direction.)

It will be noted that most of these exemptions are subject to the existence or anticipated existence of a prescription. Such exemptions will not be available if the supply is not to be made in accordance with a prescription but instead is to be made in accordance with directions.

For the meaning of *supervision* and proposals to change the law, see **Chapters 11** and **12**.

Exemption for nurses and midwives

A manufacturer's licence is not required where a medicinal product is assembled by a registered nurse or a registered midwife if the nurse or midwife is acting in the course of their profession and the medicinal product is supplied to a patient in the course of the treatment of that patient. The medicinal product must not be assembled on a large scale or by an industrial process (HMR Reg.3).

Aseptic facilities

At the time of going to press, the Department of Health and Social Care had undertaken a consultation on a proposal to insert a new regulation 4A into the HMR.[13] If this proposal was brought into force, it would allow the preparation, assembly and dispensing of medicines in hospital aseptic facilities without the need for a manufacturer's licence, if these activities are supervised by a pharmacy technician instead of a pharmacist. To benefit from this provision, the pharmacy service would have to be overseen by a chief pharmacist (or someone fulfilling the statutory functions of a chief pharmacist) – see below.

---

12. Through a combination of section 132 of the Medicines Act 1968 and regulation 8 of the Human Medicines Regulations 2012, the legislation referred to is the National Health Service Act 2006, the National Health Service (Scotland) Act 1978, and the National Health Service (Wales) Act 2006.

13. https://www.gov.uk/government/consultations/pharmacy-supervision/pharmacy-supervision#summary-of-proposals (accessed 31 December 2024).

Wholesaling, and hub & spoke dispensing

The assembly of a medicine at one pharmacy with a view to supplying it at or from a pharmacy that has a different owner or is part of a different trust requires a wholesale dealer's licence. However, a supply on prescription to another hospital for administration to a specific patient would not be a wholesale transaction and a wholesale dealer's licence is not required.[14]

At the time of going to press, the Department of Health and Social Care had announced plans to change the law so that a wholesale dealer's licence would not be required if a hospital pharmacy which is a registered pharmacy provides hub services for spokes in the community (see **Chapters 5** and **12** for more details of the hub and spoke proposals).

Prescriptions

Prescriptions are dealt with in more detail in **Chapter 12** and, in the case of controlled drugs, in **Chapter 14**.

Other than prescriptions for controlled drugs in Schedule 4 or 5 to the Misuse of Drugs Regulations, where hospital patients are provided with prescriptions for controlled drugs, NHS prescriptions must be on forms provided by NHS England,[15] NHS Scotland or NHS Wales (or a Local Health Board or Health Board), or must be electronic.[16]

It is not necessary for the prescriber to specify the patient's name and address when prescribing a controlled drug if the order is written on the patient's bed card or case sheet.

Private prescriptions for controlled drugs may be on a form provided by NHS England, NHS Scotland or NHS Wales (or a Local Health Board or Health Board), or must be electronic. However, if a controlled drug other than one in Schedule 4 or 5 to the Regulations is to be supplied by a pharmacist in a hospital, a prescriber is not required to use a form provided by NHS England or an equivalent body and a pharmacist is permitted to supply a controlled drug that is not prescribed on such a form and which does not specify the prescriber's identification number.[17]

Electronic prescriptions may be used for any medicinal product (except for an NHS prescription for a substance in Schedule 1 to the Misuse of Drugs Regulations) if the electronic prescription has an advanced electronic signature (see **Chapter 12**).

Patient Group Directions (PGDs)

Exemptions from the requirements of the HMR when a supply is made under a PGD are covered in **Chapter 13**.

---

14. *Bayer PLC and Novartis Pharmaceuticals UK Ltd v NHS Darlington CCG and others* [2020] EWCA Civ 449.
15. Shortly before going to press, the Prime Minister announced that NHS England would be abolished as a separate body, and its functions will be exercised by the Department of Health and Social Care.
16. Regulation 15 of the Misuse of Drugs Regulations 2001.
17. Regulation 16 of the Misuse of Drugs Regulations 2001.

Exemption from the requirement to supply Prescription Only Medicines in accordance with a prescription

Ordinarily, it is not lawful to supply a Prescription Only Medicine (POM) except in accordance with a prescription.[18] HMR Reg.227 provides an exemption from this requirement if the sale or supply is made in the course of the business of a hospital and it is for the purpose of administering the medicine (at the hospital or elsewhere) to a particular person (i.e. a specific patient), in accordance with directions given by an appropriate practitioner. Appropriate practitioners include:

- a doctor,
- a dentist,
- a supplementary prescriber,
- a nurse independent prescriber, or
- a pharmacist independent prescriber.

Other healthcare professionals are appropriate practitioners for specific medicines (see **Chapter 12**).

In the case of supplementary prescribers, they may not give directions for parenteral administration except in accordance with a clinical management plan unless they are acting in accordance with another person who is an appropriate practitioner (other than a supplementary prescriber or an approved country health professional).[19]

Exemptions for NHS trusts and foundation trusts from other HMR requirements

HMR Reg.229 provides that the restrictions imposed by the HMR on the supply of:

(a) medicines subject to general sale (HMR Reg.121 – see **Chapter 10**);
(b) Pharmacy medicines (HMR Reg.120 – see **Chapter 11**); or
(c) POMs (HMR reg.214 – see **Chapter 12**),

do not apply to a supply of a medicinal product by an NHS trust or an NHS foundation trust if the product is supplied for the purpose of being administered to a person in accordance with the written directions of:

- a doctor,
- dentist,
- nurse independent prescriber,
- optometrist independent prescriber
- physiotherapist independent prescriber,
- podiatrist independent prescriber,
- therapeutic radiographer independent prescriber,
- paramedic independent prescriber, or
- pharmacist independent prescriber.

---

18. HMR Reg.214(1).
19. HMR Reg.216.

Sale or supply of medicines subject to general sale and Pharmacy medicines – exemptions

The legal restrictions on the sale or supply of medicines subject to general sale (see **Chapter 10**) or Pharmacy medicines (see **Chapter 11**) do not apply where the product is sold, offered for sale or supplied in the course of the business of a hospital or health centre for the purpose of being administered to a person in accordance with directions relating to that person and those directions are given by:

- a doctor,
- dentist,
- supplementary prescriber,
- pharmacist independent prescriber,
- optometrist independent prescriber,
- nurse independent prescriber,
- community practitioner nurse prescriber,
- podiatrist independent prescriber,
- physiotherapist independent prescriber,
- therapeutic radiographer independent prescriber, or
- paramedic independent prescriber.[20]

The restrictions in HMR Regs.220 and 221 do not apply[21] to medicines subject to general sale or to Pharmacy medicines if they are sold or supplied by a registered midwife in the course of their professional practice or if the product is delivered or administered by a registered midwife on being supplied with it under arrangements made by the Secretary of State. This exemption also applies[22] to POMs containing:

(a) diclofenac,
(b) hydrocortisone acetate,
(c) miconazole,
(d) nystatin, and
(e) phytomenadione.

Administration

On being supplied with one of the five POMs listed immediately above under arrangements made by the Secretary of State, a registered midwife or a student midwife may deliver or administer that product otherwise than in accordance with a prescription given by a doctor or dentist.[23]

Student or registered midwives may also parenterally administer, in the course of their professional practice, POMs containing any of the following substances (HMR Sch. 17 Part 3(2)):

---

20. HMR Reg.223.
21. HMR Reg.223.
22. HMR Reg.235 and Schedule 17 to the HMR.
23. HMR Reg.223.

- adrenaline,
- anti-D immunoglobulin,
- carboprost,
- cyclizine lactate,
- diamorphine,
- ergometrine maleate,
- gelofusine,
- Hartmann's solution,
- hepatitis B vaccine,
- hepatitis immunoglobulin,
- lidocaine hydrochloride (only to be administered while attending on a woman in childbirth),
- morphine,
- naloxone hydrochloride,
- oxytocins, natural and synthetic,
- pethidine hydrochloride,
- phytomenadione,
- prochlorperazine, or
- sodium chloride 0.9%.

Where administration is by a registered midwife, the medicinal product must be administered in the course of their professional practice.

Where administration is by a student midwife it must be administered under the direct supervision of a registered midwife and not include diamorphine, morphine or pethidine hydrochloride. For the meaning of *direct supervision*, see **Chapter 11**.

Midwives may also supply or administer POMs, Pharmacy medicines and GSL products under PGDs (see **Chapter 13**).

Directions

It is common in hospitals for medicines for patients to be ordered in written directions. The exemptions in HMR Reg.227 and Reg.229 make it clear that the requirements for writing prescriptions (see **Chapter 12**) do not apply to directions.

There is no definition of *directions*, but they must be in writing. Directions may take the form of drug charts, bed cards, case sheets, or discharge summary forms that patients receive when they leave hospital (sometimes referred to as a *TTO*, which is an abbreviation of "to take out").

There is no requirement for directions to be on paper, so directions given by electronic means are valid. Unlike prescriptions, there is no requirement for directions to be signed. However, it should be apparent to the person who makes the supply of medicinal products that the person giving a direction falls within a class of healthcare professional who may give a direction.

Adulterated medicinal products

Whether or not a hospital holds a manufacturing licence, the medicinal products that are manufactured must not be adulterated, or an offence will be committed contrary to section 63 of the Medicines Act 1968. This includes, for example, manufacturing in hospital aseptic units. Even though it is an offence to sell or supply an adulterated medicinal product, a hospital that buys in an adulterated product from a licensed manufacturer to whom manufacture was outsourced would have a defence if the hospital has exercised all due diligence and the offence was due to the act or default of another person.[24] For example, total parenteral nutrition for babies that was manufactured by ITH Pharma for St Thomas' Hospital in 2014 was found to have been contaminated by a strain of *Bacillus cereus* and risked serious harm or death to premature babies. ITH Pharma was convicted of offences under section 64 (see below) and fined £1.25m. No prosecution was brought against the hospital.

Medicines not of the nature or quality demanded

As described in **Chapter 26**, it is an offence contrary to section 64 of the Medicines Act 1968 to supply to the prejudice of a patient a medicinal product that is not of the nature or quality specified.

According to the wording of the section, the offence can only be committed if the medicinal product is (a) sold or (b) supplied in pursuance of a prescription. It follows that the offence cannot be committed if the medicinal product was supplied in an NHS hospital in accordance with directions, because the product will have been neither sold nor will there have been a prescription. It should, however, be noted that the defence in section 67C of the Medicines Act (see below) refers to a product that "has been sold or supplied in pursuance of a prescription or directions", and it is possible that section 67C was drafted by someone who overlooked that section 64 does not include the word "directions".

If a patient is harmed by a medicinal product sold by a private hospital and/or supplied by any hospital on prescription, for example because the medicinal product is defective or because of a dispensing error, then an offence is committed. Heavy financial penalties have been imposed on hospitals that have been convicted of an offence contrary to section 64 (see **Chapter 26**).

When the medicinal product has been supplied by a relevant pharmacy service, section 67C of the Medicines Act provides a defence to a prosecution if certain conditions are met (see **Chapter 26**). One of the conditions is that the relevant pharmacy service has a chief pharmacist (see below).

Relevant pharmacy service

Section 67F of the Medicines Act defines a *relevant pharmacy service* as:

(a) A service provided in England where the service is provided by a person in the course of carrying out a regulated activity in respect of which the person is registered for the provision of health and social care under the Health and Social

24. Section 121 of the Medicines Act 1968.

Care Act 2008, including hospitals, care homes and places where people are lawfully detained, such as prisons.

(b) A service provided in Scotland in the course of the business of a hospital, in a prison, in a removal centre, short-term holding facility or pre-departure accommodation for immigrants to be deported, a person providing a registered independent health care service and a person carrying on a registered care service.

(c) A service provided in Wales in the course of the business of a hospital, in a prison or youth detention accommodation, in a removal centre, short-term holding facility or pre-departure accommodation for immigrants to be deported, a person carrying on or managing a registered care home or a person providing a regulated service

It should be noted that the section applies to a service, and is not limited to specific premises.

Chief pharmacists

Legal status

Section 67F of the Medicines Act 1968 says a chief pharmacist is a pharmacist who:

(a) plays a significant role (irrespective of whether other individuals also do so) in -
   i. the making of decisions about how the whole or a substantial part of the activities of the pharmacy service are to be managed or organised, or
   ii. the actual managing or organising of the whole or a substantial part of those activities,

(b) has the authority to make decisions that affect the running of the pharmacy service so far as concerns the sale or supply of medicinal products, and

(c) is responsible for securing that the pharmacy service is carried on safely and effectively.

A pharmacy service is carried on safely and effectively if it is carried on in ways that ensure its safe and effective running so far as concerns the sale or supply of medicinal products.

The person who holds the chief pharmacist position need not have this title, but must have the relevant responsibilities. Conversely, giving a person the title Chief Pharmacist will not enable the statutory defences to be relied on if that person does not also have the responsibilities in paragraphs (a), (b) and (c) above. The position of chief pharmacist is seen as a key element of the governance underpinning the defence. The Explanatory Memorandum accompanying the statutory instrument that introduced the defence for such institutions said the policy was "to create a powerful incentive for chief pharmacists ... to remain on top of what is happening in their pharmacy service ... If any appropriate person knows of the error but does nothing about it, the new defence is lost to all the potential defendants".[25]

25. Footnote 2 of the Explanatory Memorandum https://www.legislation.gov.uk/uksi/2022/851/pdfs/uksiem_20220851_en.pdf (accessed 31 December 2024).

If the role falls vacant

The chief pharmacist role is viewed as an important one for a pharmacy service. When the Department of Health and Social Care announced that the Medicines Act would be amended to include section 67F, it expressed the view that "if the chief pharmacist post becomes vacant, it would be expected that arrangements would be made to cover the role, albeit on a temporary or acting basis until a permanent replacement is in place, such that the statutory functions, which are a condition of the dispensing error defence, would be met".[26]

Professional regulation

Although the role of *chief pharmacist* only has legal status in the context of the statutory defence to a prosecution for breaching section 64 of the Medicines Act 1968, the GPhC has published standards for chief pharmacists.[27]

The standards are:

1. Provide strategic and professional leadership.
2. Develop a workforce with the right skills, knowledge, and experience.
3. Delegate responsibly and make sure there are clear lines of accountability.
4. Maintain and strengthen governance to ensure safe and effective delivery of pharmacy services.

Breach of the standards may be considered to be misconduct, giving rise to fitness to practise proceedings (see **Chapter 25**).

Controlled drugs

Under section 4 of the Misuse of Drugs Act 1971, it is an offence to produce or supply to another person a controlled drug.

At the time of going to press, the Department of Health and Social Care proposes to change the law relating to pharmacist supervision (see **Chapter 11**). If and when this change is made, it is expected that regulations 8 and 9 of the Misuse of Drugs Regulations, which are referred to in the following paragraphs, will also be amended so that the references to a pharmacist are to a pharmacist or pharmacy technician.

Manufacturing or compounding Schedules 2 to 5 controlled drugs

Regulation 8 (in relation to drugs in Schedules 2 and 5) and Regulation 9 (in relation to drugs in Schedules 3 and 4) of the Misuse of Drugs Regulations permit the following:

(a) a pharmacist or a practitioner may manufacture or compound a drug. This provision will apply to a hospital pharmacist at a pharmacy that is not registered with the GPhC;
(b) a person lawfully conducting a retail pharmacy business may manufacture or compound a drug at registered pharmacy premises. This provision will apply to a pharmacy that is registered with the GPhC.

26. https://www.gov.uk/government/consultations/pharmacy-legislation-on-dispensing-errors-and-organisational-governance/outcome/rebalancing-medicines-legislation-and-pharmacy-regulation-programme-consultation-outcome (accessed 31 December 2024).

27. https://assets.pharmacyregulation.org/files/2024-01/consultation-on-draft-standards-for-chief-pharmacists-january-2024.pdf (accessed 31 December 2024).

(c) a nurse independent prescriber or a supplementary prescriber may compound a drug for the purpose of administration to a patient;
(d) any person acting in accordance with the written directions of:
- a doctor,
- dentist,
- nurse independent prescriber,
- pharmacist independent prescriber,
- paramedic independent prescriber,
- therapeutic radiographer independent prescriber, or
- a supplementary prescriber,

may compound any drug for the purposes of administration to a patient.

Supply of Schedule 2 and 5 controlled drugs

Regulation 8 also permits the supply of controlled drugs in Schedule 2 or 5 to a patient by the following persons, amongst others:
(a) a practitioner;
(b) a pharmacist;
(c) a person lawfully conducting a retail pharmacy business;
(d) the person in charge or acting person in charge of a hospital or care home which is wholly or mainly maintained by a public authority out of public funds or by a charity or by voluntary subscriptions, provided that there is no pharmacist responsible for the dispensing and supply of medicines;
(e) the person in charge or acting person in charge of an organisation providing ambulance services, provided (i) that there is no pharmacist responsible for the dispensing and supply of medicines, and (ii) that any supply is made directly to employees of the organisation for the immediate treatment of sick or injured persons;
(f) the senior registered nurse, acting senior registered nurse, or registered midwife, for the time being in charge of a ward, theatre or other department in the hospital, care home or prison, in the case of a drug supplied to them by a person responsible for the dispensing and supply of medicines at that hospital, care home or prison;
(g) an operating department practitioner in the case of a drug supplied to them by a person responsible for the dispensing and supply of medicines in that hospital.

In the case of (f) and (g), the permission to supply is subject to the condition that the supply must be for administration to a patient in that ward, theatre or department in accordance with the directions of a doctor, dentist, supplementary prescriber, nurse independent prescriber or pharmacist independent prescriber.

In the case of directions by a nurse independent prescriber or a pharmacist independent prescriber, the directions may relate only to controlled drugs that they are entitled to prescribe under the Regulations.

Supply of Schedule 3 and 4 controlled drugs

Regulation 9 of the Misuse of Drugs Regulations permits the supply to a patient of any drug in Schedule 3 or 4 to the Regulations by, amongst others:
(a) a practitioner;

(b) a pharmacist;
(c) a person lawfully conducting a retail pharmacy business;
(d) the person in charge or acting person in charge of a hospital, organisation providing ambulance services or care home if they do not have a pharmacist there responsible for the dispensing and supply of medicines;
(e) the senior registered nurse, acting senior registered nurse or registered midwife, for the time being in charge of a ward, theatre or other department in the hospital, care home or prison in the case of a drug supplied to them by a person responsible for the dispensing and supply of medicines at that hospital, care home or prison;
(f) a hospital operating department practitioner in the case of a drug supplied to them by a person responsible for the dispensing and supply of medicines in that hospital.

In the case of (e) and (f), the permission to supply is subject to the condition that the supply must be for administration to a patient in that ward, theatre or department in accordance with the directions of a doctor, dentist, supplementary prescriber, nurse independent prescriber or pharmacist independent prescriber.

In the case of directions by a nurse independent prescriber or a pharmacist independent prescriber, the directions may relate only to controlled drugs that they are entitled to prescribe under the Regulations.

Requisitions for controlled drugs

Regulation 14 of the Misuse of Drugs Regulations provides that where the person responsible for the dispensing and supply of medicines at any hospital, care home or prison supplies a controlled drug to an operating department practitioner, senior registered nurse, acting senior registered nurse, or registered midwife, for the time being in charge of any ward, theatre or department in that hospital, care home or prison, the person who makes the supply shall:
(a) obtain a requisition in writing, signed by the recipient, which specifies the total quantity of the drug to be supplied; and
(b) mark the requisition in such manner as to show that it has been complied with, and any requisition obtained shall be retained in the dispensary at which the drug was supplied and a copy of the requisition or a note of it shall be retained or kept by the recipient.

This provision prevents, for example, nurses on a ward requisitioning controlled drugs electronically because no provision is made in the Regulations for electronic signatures.

Midwives

Regulation 11 of the Misuse of Drugs Regulations permits registered midwives to possess or supply, so far as necessary to their professional practice, any controlled drug which they may lawfully administer.[28]

---

28. The Misuse of Drugs Regulations purport to require midwives to take certain steps, such as notifying a local supervising authority. However, this layer of regulation was removed by the Nursing and Midwifery Amendment Order 2017, which amended the Nursing and Midwifery Order 2001. When the amendments were made, it appears that the need for consequential amendments to the Misuse of Drugs Regulations 2001 were overlooked.

Administration of controlled drugs

A doctor or dentist is permitted to administer to a patient any drug in Schedule 2, 3 or 4 to the Misuse of Drugs Regulations 2001, and a person who is not a doctor or dentist may administer any such drug to a patient in accordance with the directions of a doctor or dentist.[29]

Nurse independent prescribers and pharmacist independent prescribers may administer without the directions of a doctor or dentist any drug that they are entitled to prescribe; and if a nurse independent prescriber or pharmacist independent prescriber gives specific directions for the administration to a patient of a controlled drug that the nurse independent prescriber or pharmacist independent prescriber is entitled to prescribe, any person may administer the drug in accordance with such directions.

Supplementary prescribers may administer any drug in Schedules 2, 3 or 4 to the Misuse of Drugs Regulations without the directions of a doctor or dentist; and any person may administer such a drug to a patient in accordance with the directions of a supplementary prescriber.

Physiotherapist independent prescribers, chiropodist independent prescribers, paramedic independent prescribers and therapeutic radiographer independent prescribers may administer controlled drugs that they are entitled to prescribe, as are persons acting in accordance with their specific directions.

Any person may administer to another person any drug in Schedule 5 to the Misuse of Drugs Regulations.

For further details of the law on controlled drugs, see **Chapter 14**.

Supplementary prescribers

Unless otherwise mentioned, when supplementary prescribers are permitted to take an act or give directions, the supplementary prescriber must be acting under and in accordance with the terms of a written clinical management plan for a specific patient. The plan must be one that is used by a doctor or dentist who is party to the plan.[30]

Restrictions on the labelling of aspirin, paracetamol and elemental iron

The exemption for hospitals from the requirements for labelling aspirin, paracetamol and elemental iron is covered in **Chapter 18**.

Chloroform

See **Chapter 21**.

---

29. Regulation 7 of the Misuse of Drugs Regulations 2001.

30. HMR Reg.215.

SUMMARY

- The word hospital is defined in different terms in different statutory provisions.
- If a hospital pharmacy is registered with the GPhC, it will be subject to regulation and enforcement by the GPhC.
- If a hospital pharmacy is not registered with the GPhC, it will be subject to regulation by the CQC, Health Improvement Scotland or Healthcare Inspectorate Wales.
- There are exemptions for hospitals from the need for a manufacturer's licence when medicinal products are manufactured or assembled if certain conditions are met.
- There are exemptions for nurses and midwives from the need for a manufacturer's licence if certain conditions are met.
- Prescription Only Medicines may be supplied in accordance with a prescription or in accordance with directions. Directions must be in writing but do not need to contain all the details that are required for prescriptions.
- There are exemptions for hospitals from the legal restrictions on the sale or supply of medicinal products.
- There is a defence for hospitals and relevant pharmacy services (and their staff) if they are prosecuted for supplying an adulterated medicinal product or a product that is not of the nature or quality demanded. The defence is only available if conditions are met, including the appointment of a chief pharmacist.
- There are requirements in relation to the production, supply and possession of controlled drugs that are specific to hospitals.

FURTHER READING

- Royal Pharmaceutical Society: *Professional Standards for Hospital Pharmacy Services: Standards Handbook* **https://www.rpharms.com/recognition/setting-professional-standards/hospital-pharmacy-professional-standards/hospital-pharmacy-standards-handbook** (accessed 31 December 2024).

CHAPTER 10

Human Medicines: General sale medicines

The availability of medicines varies by their legal classification. Those medicines with the least control are termed general sale medicines, *or more colloquially* GSL *(or General Sale List) medicines. This chapter outlines the controls on these medicines, including specific restrictions on aloxiprin, aspirin, paracetamol and ibuprofen.*

Introduction

It has often been said that medicines are not ordinary articles of commerce. Medicinal products may ordinarily be sold or supplied only from a registered pharmacy. There is an exception for medicinal products that are subject to general sale. Regulation 62 of the Human Medicines Regulations 2012 (HMR) requires a UK marketing authorisation to include a term whether the product is to be available (a) only on prescription, (b) only from a pharmacy, or (c) on general sale. HMR Reg.62 goes on to say that a marketing authorisation may include a term that the product to which the authorisation relates is to be available on general sale only if the licensing authority (the Medicines and Healthcare products Regulatory Agency – MHRA) considers that the product can with reasonable safety be sold or supplied otherwise than by, or under the supervision of, a pharmacist. For the meaning of supervision, see **Chapter 11**. At the time of going to press, the Department of Health and Social Care proposes to amend the HMR concerning supervision. See **Box 10.1** for further details.

Box 10.1

At the time of going to press, there were proposals to amend the law. This box sets out what the law will be if those proposals are brought into effect. Readers can check whether the proposals have been brought into effect by checking www.legislation.gov.uk or using a subscription service such as Westlaw for the latest version of the *Human Medicines Regulations 2012 or searching those sites for the* Human Medicines (Authorisation by Pharmacists Supervision by Pharmacy Technicians Order) *[followed by the year].*

If and when the HMR are amended, it is likely that HMR Reg.62 will refer to products that can with reasonable safety be sold or supplied otherwise than by or under the supervision of a pharmacist or a pharmacy technician who has been authorised by a pharmacist to supervise.

Before the HMR came into force, section 51 of the Medicines Act 1968 had empowered Ministers to specify descriptions or classes of medicinal products which in their opinion could with reasonable safety be sold or supplied otherwise than by or under the supervision of a pharmacist. Such medicinal products were listed in what was known as a General Sale List and the products on the list were known as *General Sale List* medicines or *GSL* medicines.

The Regulations[1] creating the General Sale List are still in force. The list was updated from time to time, but no products have been added to the list since 2001. It is still common to refer to *General Sale List* or *GSL* medicines, but the relevant sections of the Medicines Act 1968 were repealed by the HMR. Instead of using a General Sale List, HMR Reg.8 refers to *medicinal products that are subject to general sale.* This leads to an anomaly in the duties of superintendent pharmacists and responsible pharmacists which are set out in the Medicines Act. Their respective duties (see **Chapter 7**) are expressed so as to include medicines on a General Sale List, but are not expressed so as to include medicines that are subject to general sale.

It is anticipated that when the HMR are amended to allow hub and spoke dispensing (see **Chapter 12**), the HMR will be amended to say that references to a general sale list are to medicines subject to general sale. This should remove the anomaly. Section 132 of the Medicines Act 1968 says that expressions that are defined in the HMR will have the same meaning in the Medicines Act 1968.

Definition of medicinal products subject to general sale

HMR Reg.5 defines *a medicinal product subject to general sale* as a product that is not a Prescription Only Medicine (see **Chapter 12**) or a Pharmacy medicine (see **Chapter 11**) but is a product that is covered by an authorisation of which it is a term that the product is to be available on general sale. Until the HMR are amended as above, this definition is not wide enough to include products that are on a General Sale List (see below).

It is thus the marketing authorisation of a product that determines its classification as a product which is subject to general sale and the marketing authorisation that specifies any conditions which govern the sale or supply of the product.

General Sale List Order

In parallel with the marketing authorisation of a medicinal product, the GSL Order (see footnote 1) remains in force in relation to the medicinal products it lists. The listed products which in the opinion of Ministers can reasonably be sold or supplied otherwise than by or under the supervision of a pharmacist, included medicinal products for which a traditional herbal registration had been granted. The GSL Order also refers to *product licences of right* which are licences issued for historic reasons at the time the Medicines Act became law and which were still in force when the HMR became law. HMR Reg.347 (with Schedule 32) preserves product licences of right.

Schedule 1 to the GSL Order lists products which may be classified as being GSL, and Schedule 2 to the GSL Order lists products which are subject to a product licence of right which may be classified as being GSL.[2] Products listed within Schedules 1 and 2 may be subject to a specified maximum dose, maximum daily dose, use, pharmaceutical form or

1. Medicines (Products Other Than Veterinary Drugs) (General Sale List) Order 1984 *(the GSL Order)*.
2. Product licences of right are explained in Chapter 5.

route of administration, maximum strength or maximum amount released. Schedule 3 to the GSL Order lists those classes of medicinal products which are not to be on general sale.

Sale at or from pharmacies

Medicinal products subject to general sale (along with Pharmacy medicines) are often termed *over-the-counter* or *OTC* medicines, because of their ability to be sold to patients without the need for a prescription. As outlined in **Chapter 7**, the role and duties of responsible pharmacists, and of superintendent pharmacists, extend to the retail sale of all medicines, including those medicinal products subject to general sale. The sale of medicinal products subject to general sale does not require supervision by a pharmacist. Therefore, although the sale of such medicines at or from a pharmacy requires a responsible pharmacist to be in charge of the pharmacy at the time of the sale, the sale of medicinal products subject to general sale may be undertaken even if the responsible pharmacist is absent from the premises (see **Chapter 7** for the arrangements to be put in place in the absence of a responsible pharmacist).[3]

Conditions applicable to medicinal products subject to general sale

Regulation 221 of the HMR sets out that a person may sell or supply, or offer for sale or supply, a medicinal product that is subject to general sale at a place elsewhere than at a registered pharmacy only if the following conditions are met:

1. the place at which the medicinal product is sold, supplied, or offered for sale or supply, consists of premises of which that person is the occupier and which they are able to close so as to exclude the public;
2. the medicinal product was made up for sale in its immediate and outer packaging elsewhere than at the place at which it is sold, supplied or offered for sale or supply and the immediate and outer packaging has not been opened since the product was made up for sale in it; and
3. the medicinal product is of a kind specified in Schedule 15 to the HMR (see below) and is presented for sale in accordance with the requirements specified in that Schedule for a product of that kind.

Schedule 15 to the HMR relates to the retail pack sizes of certain products (see below).

The above does not apply to the supply of a medicinal product in the event or anticipation of pandemic disease (see **Chapter 12**).

Sales on aircraft and trains

Schedule 17 to the HMR permits the sale of GSL medicines from aircraft and trains, subject to certain conditions. The sale may be made by the operator or commander of an aircraft or the operator of a train providing that the medicinal product:

a. has been made up for sale or supply in a container elsewhere than at the place at which it is sold or supplied; and

3. Article 5 of the Pharmacy (Responsible Pharmacists, Superintendent Pharmacists etc.) Order 2022.

b. is stored in a part of the aircraft or train which the operator is able to close so as to exclude the public.

This does not mean that the sale must be made in person by the operator or commander, and may be sold by another person on their behalf.[4]

Automatic machines

Medicinal products which are subject to general sale may be sold or offered for sale from automatic machines (HMR Reg.222). Such machines must be located in premises which the occupier is able to close so as to exclude the public.

Retail pack sizes of certain products

Limits are imposed on the pack sizes of certain GSL products when they are sold or supplied by retail from businesses other than pharmacies because of the risk of accidental overdose or deliberate overdose (for example if paracetamol is used in a suicide attempt, because the effect of overdose may be irreversible if the person attempting suicide changes their mind). If sold outside the limits laid down, the medicinal products concerned are classed as Pharmacy medicines or POMs. The limits for general sale are as follows.

Aloxiprin, aspirin and paracetamol

A medicinal product that contains aloxiprin, aspirin or paracetamol (or, where appropriate, any combination of those substances) and that is in the form specified in **Table 10.1** must be presented for sale in a separate and individual package containing not more than the amount of the product specified in the corresponding entry.

The limits imposed by the HMR are set out in **Table 10.1** below and are contained within Schedule 15 to the HMR.

Table 10.1: *Retail pack sizes of aloxiprin, aspirin and paracetamol (Sch.15 to HMR)*

Form of product	Maximum amount
Effervescent tablets: a. that do not contain aspirin, or b. that do not contain more than 325 milligrams of aspirin per tablet	30 tablets
Effervescent tablets: a. that contain more than 325 milligrams of aspirin per tablet, but b. do not contain more than 500 milligrams of aspirin per tablet	20 tablets
Non-effervescent tablets: a. that are enteric-coated, b. that contain aspirin only, and c. that do not contain more than 75 milligrams of aspirin per tablet	28 tablets

4. *R v Family Health Services Appeal Authority, ex parte Elmfield Drugs Limited* (1999) 46 B.M.L.R. 191.

Table 10.1: *Retail pack sizes of aloxiprin, aspirin and paracetamol (Sch.15 to HMR)* (cont.)

Form of product	Maximum amount
Other non-effervescent tablets or capsules	16 tablets or capsules
Powder or granules	10 sachets
Liquid preparations of paracetamol intended for persons aged 12 years and over	160 mL
Liquid preparations of paracetamol intended for persons younger than 12 years	Individual unit doses of not more than 5 mL each, to a maximum of 20 unit doses

Effervescent, in relation to a tablet or capsule, means containing not less than 75%, by weight of the tablet or capsule, of ingredients included wholly or mainly for the purpose of releasing carbon dioxide when the tablet or capsule is dissolved or dispersed in water (HMR Reg.8).

Paracetamol

The MHRA has expressed concern at times that retailers have been selling multiple packs of paracetamol[5] and in 2012 published *Best practice guidance on the sale of medicines for pain relief*[6] to the effect that "sales of medicines for pain relief should be restricted to a maximum of two packs in any one transaction".

Ibuprofen

A medicinal product that contains ibuprofen and that is in the form specified in **Table 10.2** must be presented for sale in a separate and individual package containing not more than the amount of the product specified in the corresponding entry.

Table 10.2: *Retail pack sizes of ibuprofen (Sch. 15 to HMR)*

Form of product	Maximum amount
Tablets or capsules	16 tablets or capsules
Powder or granules	12 sachets
Liquid preparations of ibuprofen	Individual unit doses of not more than 5 mL each, to a maximum of 20 unit doses

The limits imposed by the HMR are set out in table 10.2 above and are contained within Schedule 15 to the HMR.

5. See, for example, Discount shops defy MHRA over paracetamol sales, *The Pharmaceutical Journal*, Oct 2007, Vol 279, p431.
6. Appendix 4 to its publication *The Blue Guide* https://assets.publishing.service.gov.uk/government/uploads/system/uploads/attachment_data/file/824548/Appendix_4_-_Blue_Guide.pdf (accessed 31 December 2024).

Pseudoephedrine

The HMR also restrict the sale of medicines containing pseudoephedrine (Reg. 237; see **Chapter 12**).

Pack size limitations on other products

Pack size limitations, other than for paracetamol, aspirin, aloxiprin, ibuprofen and pseudoephedrine, are now covered by the relevant marketing authorisations

Sale of stimulant laxatives

For restrictions to the GSL sale of stimulant laxatives (bisacodyl, senna and sennosides, sodium picosulfate), see **Chapter 11**.

Homoeopathic medicines for which general sale is permitted

Regulation 242 also contains an exemption from the restrictions on sale or supply of Pharmacy medicines (HMR Reg.220; see **Chapter 11**) subject to a number of conditions:

1. the medicinal product is neither for parenteral administration nor a product subject to special medical prescription (for example, a controlled drug);
2. the conditions regarding medicines subject to general sale (HMR Reg.221) are met; and
3. the medicinal product is one that consists solely of one or more unit preparations of:
   a. any substance where the unit preparation has been diluted to at least one part in a million million (6c or 12×),
   b. any substance that is listed in HMR Part 2 of Schedule 21 where the unit preparation has been diluted to at least one part in a million (6×), or
   c. any substance that:
      i. is the active substance of a medicine that is subject to general sale,
      ii. is listed in HMR Part 3 of Schedule 21, diluted to at least one part in ten (1×), or
      iii. in the case of a medicinal product for external use only, is listed in HMR Part 4 of Schedule 21, where the unit preparation has been diluted to at least one part in ten (1×).

This enables homoeopathic medicines at specified levels of dilution to be sold in accordance with the requirements of general sale, but without the restrictions that normally apply to Pharmacy medicines.

Appendix 2 lists these products.

Products not to be on general sale

The Human Medicines Regulations 2012 (Sch.1) specify certain classes of medicinal product which are to be available only from a pharmacy: that is, which are not to be on general sale. They are:

a. a product comprising eye ointment;
b. a product that contains vitamin A, vitamin A acetate or vitamin A palmitate, in each case with a maximum daily dose equivalent to more than 7500 international units of vitamin A or 2250 micrograms of retinol; and

c. a product that contains vitamin D with a maximum daily dose of more than 400 units of antirachitic activity.

The following medicinal products shall be available only from a pharmacy unless they are the subject of a marketing authorisation or traditional herbal registration that classifies them as medicinal products subject to general sale:

a. a product that is for use as an anthelmintic;
b. a product that is for parenteral administration;
c. a product that is for use as an enema;
d. a product that is for use wholly or mainly for irrigation of wounds, or the bladder, vagina or rectum;
e. a product that is for administration wholly or mainly to children being a preparation of aloxiprin or aspirin; or
f. if it is a medicinal product of a kind specified in Schedule 15 (see above) but is not presented for sale in accordance with the requirements specified in that Schedule for a product of that kind to be subject to general sale.

In addition, Schedule 3 to the GSL Order lists those classes of medicinal products which are not to be on general sale.

SUMMARY

- Medicines which in the opinion of the Ministers can, with reasonable safety, be sold other than by, or under, the supervision of a pharmacist are classified as medicinal products subject to general sale. They may only be sold from closable premises and in their original packs. The reference to supervision is likely to be extended to pharmacy technicians in addition to pharmacists when proposals to amend the HMR are implemented by the Department of Health and Social Care.
- Certain medicines may be sold other than, by or under, the supervision of a pharmacist subject to certain pack sizes. These include aspirin, aloxiprin, ibuprofen and paracetamol.
- Certain medicines cannot be on general sale. These include eye ointments, most anthelmintics, parenterals, those medicines promoted as enemas or for use as irrigations, and aspirin for children.

FURTHER READING

- Human Medicines Regulations (2012) SI 2012 No. 1916, *Explanatory memorandum*: **http://www.legislation.gov.uk/uksi/2012/1916/pdfs/uksiem_20121916_en.pdf** (accessed 31 December 2024).

CHAPTER 11

Human medicines: Pharmacy medicines

Pharmacy medicines can be sold over the counter. The key differences between Pharmacy medicines and general sale medicines are that Pharmacy medicines may only be sold on registered pharmacy premises, and if the supply is not made personally by a pharmacist, the supply must be made under the supervision of a pharmacist. Proposals to change the law are discussed below.

Pharmacy medicines defined

A Pharmacy medicine is defined in Human Medicines Regulations 2012 (Reg.5(5)) as a medicinal product which is not a Prescription Only Medicine (POM) (see **Chapter 12**) or a medicinal product subject to general sale (see **Chapter 10**) but is:

(a) covered by a marketing authorisation of which it is a term that the product is to be available only from a pharmacy;
(b) available only from a pharmacy by virtue of Part 2 of Schedule 1 to the HMR (see below); or
(c) the result of:
(d) the assembly, or
    i. the reformulation (including the combining with other substances),
    ii. of a medicinal product that is a Pharmacy medicine by virtue of paragraph (a) above.

The products which are Pharmacy medicines by virtue of Part 2 of Schedule 1 to the HMR are:

(a) a product comprising eye ointment;
(b) a product that contains Vitamin A, Vitamin A acetate or Vitamin A palmitate, in each case with a maximum daily dose equivalent to more than 7500 international units of Vitamin A or 2250 micrograms of retinol;
(c) a product that contains Vitamin D with a maximum daily dose of more than 400 units of antirachitic activity;
(d) a product which is authorised by the MHRA on a temporary basis under regulation 174 of the HMR (in response to the temporary or confirmed spread of pathogenic agents, toxins, chemical agents or nuclear radiation); and
(e) an Early Access to Medicines Scheme product (see **Chapter 5**) in circumstances where the MHRA has attached a condition to the scientific opinion on which it is based that it is only to be available from a pharmacy.

All medicines made in a pharmacy for retail sale under the exemptions from licensing granted to pharmacists under section 10 of the Medicines Act 1968 (see **Chapter 5**) are Pharmacy medicines, unless for some reason the product must be classified as a POM (see **Chapter 12**). Schedule 1 of the HMR also specifies certain classes of medicinal product which are to be available only from a pharmacy, that is, are not to be on general sale (**Chapter 10**). Some medicines that would otherwise be subject to general sale, when presented in packs exceeding specified quantities, may only be sold or supplied from pharmacies (see retail pack sizes of certain products, **Chapter 10**). Some POMs when presented in packs not exceeding specified quantities may only be sold or supplied from pharmacies (see Exemptions from prescription only control, **Chapter 13**).

Marketing authorisations for Pharmacy medicines

Regulation 62 of the Human Medicines Regulations 2012 (HMR) provides that a UK marketing authorisation must include a term that the product to which the authorisation relates is to be available (a) only on prescription; (b) only from a pharmacy; or (c) on general sale. Unless the licensing authority (the Medicines and Healthcare products Regulatory Agency – MHRA) is satisfied that a medicinal product can with reasonable safety be sold or supplied otherwise than by, or under the supervision of, a pharmacist, its marketing authorisation will include a term that the product is to be available only from a pharmacy or only on prescription.

If proposals to change the law on supervision are implemented, it is likely that HMR Reg.62 will be amended. See **Box 11.7** for further information.

Product licences of right

Instead of a marketing authorisation, some medicinal products may have a historic product licence of right which determines their status as a Pharmacy medicine (see **Chapter 5**).

Restrictions on sale or supply

Regulation 220 of the Human Medicines Regulations (HMR) provides that medicinal products which are not subject to general sale (see **Chapter 10**), may not be sold or supplied, or offered for sale or supply by a person unless:

1. that person is a person lawfully conducting a retail pharmacy business (see **Chapter 7**);
2. the product is sold, supplied or offered or offered for sale or supply on premises which are a registered pharmacy (see **Chapter 2**); and
3. that person is a pharmacist, or, if the transaction is carried out on their behalf by another person, then that other person is, or acts under the supervision of a pharmacist (defined in HMR Reg.8 as a person registered with the General Pharmaceutical Council (GPhC)) (see below).

These conditions do not apply to the supply of a medicinal product in the event or anticipation of pandemic disease; see pandemic exemption, **Chapter 12**.

Sale or supply

In *R v Family Health Services Appeal Authority, ex parte Elmfield Drugs Limited*[1] (the *Elmfield Drugs* case) the Court of Appeal, held that *supply* means nothing more than handing over a medicinal product, describing it as a *mechanical act* (see **Box 11.1**).

> **Box 11.1: *R v Family Health Services Appeal Authority, ex parte Elmfield Drugs Limited***
>
> The Medicines Act (in a provision now in HMR Reg.223) allowed doctors by way of exemption to supply Prescription Only Medicines to their patients (see **Chapter 12**).
>
> General practitioners in Westerham in Kent applied under NHS Regulations (see **Chapter 3**) for permission to become dispensing doctors so that they could supply prescribed medicines to their own patients. Elmfield Drugs Limited owned a pharmacy in Westerham and were concerned that granting the application would result in patients having their prescribed medicines dispensed by their GPs instead of taking their prescriptions to the Elmfield Drugs pharmacy.
>
> Elmfield Drugs argued that the application to become dispensing doctors should not be granted because it would result in unlawful supplies because the GPs did not intend to supply medicines personally to their patients; the GPs intended to arrange for receptionists or other unqualified members of staff to make supplies.
>
> The Court of Appeal held that *supply* was the mechanical act of handing over a medicinal product; and that an employee of the GPs could lawfully act as the agent of a doctor in handing medicines to patients. When doing so, it was the same in law as if the GP had made the supply.

Transaction

If the sale or supply is not made by a pharmacist, the transaction must be supervised by a pharmacist. The word *transaction* is not defined in the HMR and has not been considered in any of the cases mentioned in this chapter. While it is arguable that the word *transaction* refers to a sale or supply, it is equally arguable that *transaction* has a wider meaning that encompasses arrangements or dealings.

Giving the word *transaction* a wider meaning than *sale or supply* would be consistent with the decision of the Court of Appeal in *Summers v Congreve Horner & Co* (see below).

Supervision

A requirement for supervision was introduced into the law by the Pharmacy and Poisons Act 1933. Neither that Act (which is no longer in force) nor subsequent legislation that has replaced it has contained a definition of *supervision*. There has been much debate within pharmacy over the years over what *supervision* involves. Issues have included whether supervision requires a pharmacist to carry out a final check of a

---

1. [1999] 46 BMLR 191. (It should be noted that in the context of where a product is supplied from for the purpose of the provision of pharmaceutical services under the NHS, the Court of Appeal expressed the position differently in *Central Liverpool Primary Care Trust v Charles S Bullen Stomacare Limited* [2005] EWCA Civ 1514 (see Box 3.2 in Chapter 3).)

prescription before it is handed to a patient; whether supervision requires a pharmacist to carry out a clinical check on what is prescribed; whether a pharmacist is required to carry out an accuracy check of what is being sold or supplied; and whether a pharmacist must be physically present to supervise or whether remote supervision is or should be permitted.

In a case decided under the 1933 Act, *Roberts v Littlewoods Mail Order Stores* (see **Box 11.2**), the court decided that a pharmacist who does not personally make a sale must know what is being sold or supplied and be in a position to supervise the person who makes the sale. However, as discussed below, the case should be read in the context of its era and the wording of the legislation in force at the time.

Box 11.2: *Roberts v Littlewoods Mail Order Stores Ltd* (1943)

The Pharmacy and Poisons Act 1933 (s.18) provided: "... it shall not be lawful for a person to sell any poison in Part I of the Poisons List unless ... the sale is effected by, or under the supervision of, a registered pharmacist". A Part I poison was equivalent to a Pharmacy medicine in the HMR. Similar wording is now included in HMR Reg.220.

A sale of a Part I poison was made at a Littlewoods pharmacy to one of the Pharmaceutical Society's inspectors while the sole pharmacist was in a stockroom upstairs and unaware that the sale was being made by an unqualified assistant. The magistrates found that the sale, though not effected by the pharmacist, was effected sufficiently under his supervision. His actual presence was not reasonably required.

The decision of the magistrates was reversed in the High Court, where it was held that the sale had not been supervised. The Lord Chief Justice, Viscount Caldecote, said:

> *"... the man who was upstairs might have been a person who was exercising personal control of a business, but I do not think that, while he was upstairs and therefore absent, he could be a person who was supervising a particular sale. It has been suggested that a man can supervise a sale without being bodily present. I do not accept that contention ... each individual sale must be, not necessarily effected by the qualified person, but something which is shown by the evidence to be under his supervision in the sense that he must be aware of what is going on at the counter, and in a position to supervise or superintend the activities of the young woman by whom each individual sale is effected."*

A later case, *Pharmaceutical Society of Great Britain v Boots Cash Chemists (Southern) Ltd*, also decided under the 1933 Act, is described in **Box 11.3**. The case was decided in 1953 when self-service in shops was a recent development. The court held that supervision of a sale requires a pharmacist to be able to intervene to prevent the sale from being made if the sale would be inappropriate.

Box 11.3: *Pharmaceutical Society of Great Britain* v *Boots Cash Chemists (Southern) Ltd*

This was a case arising under the requirement for supervision in what was then the Pharmacy and Poisons Act 1933.

A Boots pharmacy was arranged on a self-service system. A customer could select goods, including Part I poisons (roughly equivalent today to Pharmacy medicines), from the shelves,

Box 11.3: *Pharmaceutical Society of Great Britain* v *Boots Cash Chemists (Southern) Ltd* (cont.)

place them in a wire basket and take them to the cash desk. Before the cashier accepted payment, a pharmacist at the cash desk could, if they thought fit, prevent a sale. It was argued by the Pharmaceutical Society that a purchase was completed when a customer took an article and put it in the basket so that the pharmacist could not later intervene. That suggestion was rejected in the High Court by Lord Goddard, the Chief Justice, who had said that self-service was no different to other transactions in a shop. He continued:

> *"by using the words 'The sale is effected by, or under the supervision of, a registered pharmacist' the Act envisages that the sale may be effected by someone who is not a pharmacist. I think, too, that the sale is effected under his supervision if he is in a position to say 'You must not have that; that contains poison ...'"*

The case is an important one in the law of contract and the Pharmaceutical Society appealed to the Court of Appeal mainly on the question of whether a contract was formed when a customer picked up a medicine in the shop. In dismissing the appeal, Lord Justice Birkett and Lord Justice Romer expressly agreed with what Lord Goddard had said about supervision.

Social changes and changes in pharmacy practice since 1933

In 1933, the role of pharmacists would generally have been limited to manufacturing medicines, dispensing and supplying them in a pharmacy. Home deliveries would have been rare. There was no National Health Service; and there were no clinical services of the kind that pharmacists provide today; and it would have been rare for pharmacists to see patients in a consultation area.

Both society and pharmacy practice have continually developed since 1933. For example, home deliveries are now a common feature of pharmacy practice. If the *Littlewoods* and *Boots* cases continue to represent the law, then unless the delivery is made by a pharmacist in person, the supply is not supervised. Other features of modern pharmacy practice that differ from the circumstances of 1933 include dispensing into monitored dosage systems, and the use of dispensing robots. These features mean that what is supervised is not limited to the physical handing over of a medicinal product; and supervision may instead relate to the arrangements in place at a pharmacy to ensure that medicines are supplied in a way that is safe and effective. This approach is supported by the decision of the Court of Appeal in *Summers v Congreve Horner & Co* (see below).[2]

In view of the significant changes in society and in pharmacy practice since the Pharmacy and Poisons Act 1933 was passed, it is open to doubt whether the *Littlewoods* and *Boots* cases which were decided under that Act reflect what is meant by *supervision* in the HMR.[3]

---

2. [1992] 7 WLUK 105.
3. See Bennion, Bailey and Norbury on Statutory Interpretation, paragraph 14.1 (8th edition, 2020) published by LNUK.

Modern cases

In a non-pharmacy context, a definition of supervision was given in the Court of Appeal in *Summers v Congreve Horner & Co* (see **Box 11.4**), treating it as "a matter of degree".

This case was concerned with supervision in a surveyor's practice. Although this is a very different context to a pharmacy, the decision was referred to in 2005 guidance by the Royal Pharmaceutical Society of Great Britain when it was the regulator of the pharmacy profession, and it was referred to by the GPhC in guidance on supervision that it published in 2010.

Box 11.4: *Summers v Congreve Horner & Co*

In its 2010 *Guidance for Responsible Pharmacists*, The General Pharmaceutical Council cited the case of *Summers v Congreve Horner & Co*[4] in considering the meaning of supervision, as applied to the assembly of medicines. The case sets out that *supervision* can exist, even in the absence of physical presence.

D, a firm of surveyors, sent T, a graduate with three and a half years' practical experience, to carry out a structural survey of the house in question. T was provided with a checklist by H, a partner, and his subsequent draft report was then submitted to, discussed with and eventually approved by H, who did not, however, visit the property. When P, the purchasers, subsequently brought proceedings claiming that the report was negligent, D sought to rely upon their professional indemnity policy. The policy was expressed not to cover any claim arising from the survey, inspection or valuation of real property unless the work had been carried out (a) by a fellow or associate of one of a number of professional bodies or (b) by anyone who had not less than five years' experience of such work or such other person nominated by the assured to carry out such work subject always to the supervision of such work by a person qualified in accordance with (a) above. In the Court of Appeal, Lord Justice Staughton said:

> *"One then has to ask what is meant by supervision. It cannot, in my judgment, mean watching somebody for every moment of the day while he is doing his work. If that were the case there would be virtually no point in employing staff at all, and there would be no point in a clause allowing an unqualified person to do anything. 'Supervision' in common parlance means keeping an eye on somebody, watching over them, but it cannot in this case mean keeping a constant eye or a constant watch."*

Lord Justice Staughton did not accept that the requirement for supervision inevitably meant that a qualified surveyor had to attend the site in order to supervise an unqualified person. He went on to say:

> *"It seems to me that supervision is a matter of degree ... it is enough if the unqualified person receives that degree of supervision which good practice requires in the profession of surveying for a person of his training and experience."*

NB Although the GPhC Guidance document has been withdrawn, the GPhC has not replaced it and has not repudiated the view it previously took regarding the significance of this case.

4. [1992] 7 WLUK 105.

The case may be seen as authority for the proposition that supervision can consist of instructions to a person competent to follow them and communication with the person being supervised.[5] Although *Summers v Congreve Horner* was not concerned with pharmacy practice, it is consistent with other cases in which supervision was considered in a healthcare context (see **Box 11.5**).

Box 11.5

The provision of health services performed by or directly supervised by an appropriately qualified and registered health professional is exempt from Value Added Tax.[6]

The meaning of supervision has been considered in a number of VAT cases by specialist tribunals. The decisions of these tribunals do not create binding precedents (see **Chapter 1**), but they are persuasive.

In *Elder Home Care Ltd v Customs and Excise Commissioners*,[7] the tribunal had to decide whether carers who had to administer medicines were directly supervised by enrolled or registered nurses. The tribunal said:

> *"It seems to us that supervision does not necessarily involve standing over an employee at all times but simply checking on the employee as often as is necessary in the circumstances and having a system to enable the employee to contact the supervisor as required ..."*

In *Allergycare (Testing) Ltd v Commissioners of Customs and Excise*,[8] Allergycare Testing Limited arranged for allergy testing to be carried out in pharmacies, clinics, and health food shops. The tribunal said:

> *"In our judgment, supervision involves some degree of oversight of another person's work, and implies that the supervisor has some kind of authority to ensure that the work is being carried out properly at all times ..."*

In *E Moss Ltd v HMRC*,[9] a case about whether registered chiropodists employed by a company ultimately owned by the pharmacy chain E Moss Ltd had directly supervised others, the Tribunal said:

> *"'supervision' means the appropriate level of supervision depending on the circumstances of the case; the proper extent of supervision is a question of degree and relates to the level of risk."*

In *Vision Dispensing Limited v Revenue and Customs Commissioners*,[10] a case concerning the online sale of contact lenses, the tribunal reviewed the preceding cases and said:

> *"We consider that supervision in this context is made up of three elements. Firstly, appropriate training of the non-qualified individuals, so that they can competently carry out the functions delegated to them. Secondly, access to an appropriately qualified person at all relevant times to help unqualified individuals with any questions of difficulty. Finally, there must be an element of proactive (supervisor-initiated) oversight of the unqualified individuals."*

6. Group 7 of Schedule 9 to the Value Added Tax Act 1994 and see VAT Notice 701/57 https://www.gov.uk/guidance/health-professionals-pharmaceutical-products-and-vat-notice-70157 (accessed 31 December 2024).
7. (1993) VAT Decision 11185.
8. [2002] Lexis Citation 980.
9. (2006) VAT Decision 19510.
10. [2023] UKFTT 991 (TC).

5. This proposition is acknowledged by the Department of Health and Social Care in its 2023 consultation on supervision https://www.gov.uk/government/consultations/pharmacy-supervision/pharmacy-supervision (accessed 31 December 2024).

The case of *Abdul-Razzak v General Pharmaceutical Council*[11] (**Box 11.6**) is the most recent case in which the issue of supervision by a pharmacist has been considered by the High Court. The meaning of supervision was not the subject of legal argument and cases like *Summers v Congreve Horner & Co* do not appear to have been cited. However, the *Abdul Razzak* case was relied on by the GPhC's Fitness to Practise Committee in 2024, although, again, there does not seem to have been any legal argument about the meaning of supervision.

Box 11.6: *Abdul-Razzak v General Pharmaceutical Council*

In September and October 2012, the BBC was carrying out an investigation into whether certain London pharmacies were unlawfully selling Prescription Only Medicines to patients or the public without prescriptions. Mohammed Abdul-Razzak was the responsible pharmacist at a pharmacy in the Edgware Road area when, on two occasions on 27 September 2012 and again on 5 October 2012, a counter assistant sold Prescription Only Medicines to an undercover BBC reporter without a prescription. It was alleged that Mr Abdul-Razzak had failed to supervise the counter assistant.

Mr Abdul-Razzak was seen on video only when one of the sales was made. That video showed that Mr Abdul Razzak was in the vicinity of the dispensary close to the counter assistant. It was apparent that the counter assistant went to the dispensary to obtain one of the medicines requested by the reporter "almost certainly Viagra". The Committee concluded that Mr Abdul Razzak must have been aware that the same assistant was talking to the reporter about a medicine. In respect of this supply, the Fitness to Practise Committee found first that it was apparent that Mr Abdul-Razzak spoke not a word to the counter assistant, and second that he "showed not the slightest interest in what the counter assistant was saying or doing; or in the medicine that he was obtaining from the dispensary for the customer". It proceeded to find that, "in our view tellingly, the assistant displayed no concern at the proximity of Mr Abdul-Razzak and no endeavour to obscure and conceal from him what he was doing". The Committee noted that the assistant "conversed quite openly with the customer (reporter) in the presence and hearing of Mr Abdul-Razzak".

The GPhC's Fitness to Practise Committee upheld the allegations and directed the removal of Mr Abdul-Razzak's name from the register.

Mr Abdul-Razzak appealed to the High Court. In dismissing Mr Abdul-Razzak's appeal, the judge said:

> *"A basic and essential duty of [Mr Abdul-Razzak], as a responsible pharmacist, was to adequately supervise the counter assistants so as not to permit or cause an unlawful supply of prescription-only medicines without a prescription. This was an essential and vital policing duty, but as explained by the Committee, the Appellant failed to comply with this duty."*

It appears from this quotation that the judge conflated the separate duty of a responsible pharmacist to secure the safe and effective running of the pharmacy business (see **Chapter 7**) and the requirement for sales or supplies of certain medicines to be made by or under the supervision of a pharmacist.

---

11. [2016] EWHC 1204 (Admin).

Must a pharmacist be on the pharmacy premises in order to supervise?

In so far as the law requires a pharmacist to be on pharmacy premises, this does not arise from the law requiring supervision, but from the Medicines (Pharmacies) (Responsible Pharmacist) Regulations 2008 which require retail pharmacies to have a responsible pharmacist – see **Chapter 7**. (These regulations may in future be replaced by rules made by the GPhC.)

Regulation 3(6) of the Responsible Pharmacist Regulations expressly permits the sale of general sale list medicines in the absence of the responsible pharmacist. It follows that a responsible pharmacist must be on the pharmacy premises when Pharmacy medicines (and POMs) are sold or supplied. However, it is important to distinguish between the requirement for a responsible pharmacist to be present and the requirement for supervision. The law does not specify who should supervise; for example, the responsible pharmacist may not be the only pharmacist on the premises.[12]

Even though a responsible pharmacist must be physically present for the sale or supply of Pharmacy medicines (and POMs), HMR Reg.220 does not expressly forbid supervision by remote means such as a video link and as far back as 1943 in *Roberts v Littlewoods Mail Order Stores*, the Lord Chief Justice said:

> *"It is conceivable, with the mechanical assistance of a telephone or something of that sort, that a person might be supervising something although he was not on the spot."*

The HMR reg.220 may usefully be compared to paragraph 23(1) of the Veterinary Medicines Regulations 2013 which provides that:

> *"No person may use sheep dip which contains a veterinary medicinal product unless they hold, or they are acting under the supervision and in the presence of a person who holds [a specified qualification]"*

Presence and *supervision* plainly involve different things; and if *supervision* in the Veterinary Medicines Regulations requires the holder of a specified qualification to be physically present, then the words "in the presence of" would be redundant.[13]

The *Congreve Horner* case referred to above (**Box 11.4**) and the VAT cases (**Box 11.5**) support the view that a pharmacist need not be physically present on

---

12. Although there is no statutory requirement for a responsible pharmacist to supervise the sale or supply of Pharmacy medicines, this may be a requirement of the responsible pharmacist's contract with the pharmacy owner.

13. According to Bennion, Bailey and Norbury on Statutory Interpretation, "There is a presumption that every word in an enactment is to be given meaning ... Given the presumption that the legislature does nothing in vain, the court must endeavour to give significance to every word of an enactment. It is presumed that if a word or phrase appears, it was put there for a purpose and must not be disregarded." (8th edition, 2020, published by LNUK).

pharmacy premises in order to exercise supervision. However, the idea of remote supervision is controversial, and in 2024, the GPhC brought fitness to practise proceedings against a pharmacist who used an electronic messaging system (WhatsApp) to check medication and/or give instructions about the sale or supply of medicines when he was not on the premises. Allegations that the pharmacist was guilty of misconduct because he had failed to supervise adequately were upheld by the Fitness to Practise Committee.

Supervision – summary of key points

It is suggested that the following points can be derived from the wording of the HMR and the decided cases:

- A sale or supply of a Pharmacy medicine by someone who is not a pharmacist is permitted.
- If a sale or supply is made by someone who is not a pharmacist, the transaction must be supervised by a pharmacist.
- Since supervision by a pharmacist of another person is an alternative to a pharmacist making a sale or supply in person, whatever form supervision takes, it should secure the safe and effective provision of the product in a way that is no less safe and effective than if the pharmacist had provided the product in person.
- A pharmacist who is physically present on the pharmacy premises, who (1) is aware of what is being sold or supplied by someone else, and (2) is in a position to intervene to prevent a sale or supply that would be inappropriate, will be found to have adequately supervised.
- A responsible pharmacist must be on the pharmacy premises when Pharmacy medicines (and POMs) are sold or supplied, but the law does not require the responsible pharmacist to be the pharmacist who supervises.
- Whether a pharmacist who is absent from the premises but who has put arrangements in place for the safe and effective supply of medicines can be said to have supervised (depending on the specific facts of a particular case), is not something the courts have considered.
- There is no current guidance from the GPhC on:
  - whether a pharmacist's involvement in a transaction in other ways amounts to supervision, or
  - the meaning of *transaction*.
- Whether supervision can be undertaken by remote means is controversial.

Future changes to supervision

In 2023, the Department of Health and Social Care published a consultation paper[14] which did not propose to amend the law in relation to the meaning of supervision, but

14. https://www.gov.uk/government/consultations/pharmacy-supervision (accessed 31 December 2024).

made a number of proposals to amend the law. These proposals are summarised in **Box 11.7**. The proposals, if implemented, will retain supervision by pharmacists, but provide alternative means of selling or supplying Pharmacy medicines (and POMs).

Box 11.7

At the time of going to press, there were proposals to amend the law. This box sets out what the law will be if those proposals are brought into effect. Readers can check whether the proposals have been brought into effect by checking www.legislation.gov.uk or using a subscription service such as Westlaw for the latest version of the Medicines Act 1968/ the Human Medicines Regulations 2012 or searching those sites for the Human Medicines (Authorisation by Pharmacists and Supervision by Pharmacy Technicians) Order *[followed by the year].*

- Instead of selling or supplying only on pharmacy premises, sales or supplies must be made at or from pharmacy premises.
- A pharmacist may:
  - authorise a pharmacy technician to sell or supply Pharmacy medicines and Prescription Only Medicines;
  - authorise a pharmacy technician to supervise another person who sells.
- If a pharmacist is absent from the pharmacy and a medicine that has been dispensed under a pharmacist's supervision is ready for sale or supply, the pharmacist may authorise another person (who need not be a pharmacy technician) to sell or supply in the pharmacist's absence. For the meaning of *dispense*, see **Chapter 5**.
- The pharmacist will be treated as absent from the premises if they are at the pharmacy but not available to intervene in, or not in a position to intervene in, the transaction in question.
- Authorisations may be general or specific.
- Authorisations may be written or oral.
- In giving an authorisation, a pharmacist "must have due regard to patient safety". Failure to do this will not invalidate the authorisation, but may be regarded as misconduct.

Self-selection or open display

The General Pharmaceutical Council's (GPhC) view[15] is that Pharmacy medicines should not be available for self-selection by customers unless "key safeguards" are in place. As an example of key safeguards, the GPhC says:

> *"This could include technological solutions to prevent inappropriate sales being completed, or safeguards relating to staff roles, responsibilities and training as well as ongoing team learning. For example, the tills may be programmed to recognise P-Medicines and prevent sales being made either by unqualified staff or in an unregistered part of the premises."*

---

15. https://www.pharmacyregulation.org/pharmacies/standards-and-guidance-registered-pharmacies/faq-self-selection-and-open-display-pharmacy-medicines (accessed 31 December 2024).

In 2024, the GPhC found that a pharmacy had not met all standards because Pharmacy medicines, including medicines liable to misuse, were available for sale in the retail area and sold by staff who were not healthcare trained. The pharmacy was unable to demonstrate that it had sufficiently managed the risks of doing this.[16]

Sale of stimulant laxatives

In August 2020, following concerns over many years relating to abuse and misuse by people with eating disorders, the Medicines and Healthcare products Regulatory Agency introduced pack size restrictions, changed recommendations on ages for use, and added new safety warnings for the sale of stimulant laxatives (bisacodyl, senna and sennosides, sodium picosulfate) for both oral and rectal use. Changes include:[17]

- large packs of stimulant laxatives will no longer be available from general sale outlets, such as newsagents and supermarkets; smaller packs will continue to be available in these outlets for short-term, occasional constipation in adults; and
- pharmacies will continue to be able to sell larger packs of up to 100 tablets for use in adults and children aged 12 years or older, under the supervision of a pharmacist.

SUMMARY

- Pharmacy medicines comprise all medicinal products which are not classified as being subject to general sale or POM status or are exempt in some way from the latter.
- The legislation requires that retail sales or supplies of Pharmacy medicines have to be made by a person conducting a retail pharmacy business, at a registered pharmacy and by, or under the supervision of, a pharmacist.
- A sale or supply of a Pharmacy medicine by someone who is not a pharmacist is permitted if the transaction is supervised by a pharmacist.
- The word *supervision* is not defined. There are different ways to interpret the requirement for supervision which may or may not involve the physical presence of a pharmacist who is observing the transaction. A pharmacist who is physically present on the pharmacy premises, who (1) is aware of what is being sold or supplied by someone else, and (2) is in a position to intervene to prevent a sale or supply that would be inappropriate, will be found to have adequately supervised. Supervision may also be adequate if a pharmacist has oversight of the selling or supplying and the ability to check that work is being carried out properly.

16. https://inspections.pharmacyregulation.org/pharmacy/detail/john-bell-&-croyden-1041345 (accessed 31 December 2024).
17. See: https://www.gov.uk/drug-safety-update/stimulant-laxatives-bisacodyl-senna-and-sennosides-sodium-picosulfate-available-over-the-counter-new-measures-to-support-safe-use (accessed 31 December 2024).

SUMMARY (CONT.)

- The Department of Health and Social Care proposes to amend the law to enable pharmacists to authorise pharmacy technicians to sell or supply Pharmacy medicines and to authorise pharmacy technicians to supervise sales or supplies by others.
- The General Pharmaceutical Council's view is that Pharmacy medicines may not be available for self-selection by customers unless "key safeguards" are in place.

FURTHER READING

- Human Medicines Regulations (2012) SI 2012 No. 1916, Explanatory memorandum: **http://www.legislation.gov.uk/uksi/2012/1916/pdfs/uksiem_20121916_en.pdf** (accessed 31 December 2024).

CHAPTER 12

Human medicines: Prescription Only Medicines

Prescription Only Medicines (POMs) are only available for sale or supply to patients in accordance with a prescription given by an appropriate practitioner unless specific exemptions apply (for example, the supply of POMs via Patient Group Direction). As with Pharmacy medicines, if the supply is not made personally by a pharmacist, the transaction must be under the supervision of a pharmacist. Proposals to change the law are discussed below.

Prescription Only Medicines defined

A *Prescription Only Medicine* (POM) is defined in regulation 5 of the Human Medicines Regulations 2012 (HMR) as a medicinal product that is:

a. covered by a UK marketing authorisation of which it is a term that the product is to be available only on prescription;
b. a POM by virtue of Part 1 of Schedule 1 of the HMR (see below); or
c. the result of the assembly, or the reformulation (including the combining with other substances), of a medicinal product that is a POM by virtue of (a) or (b), above.

Part 1 of Schedule 1 to the HMR describes the classes of medicinal product which are always to be available only on prescription. They are products that are:

1. for parenteral administration;
2. a controlled drug, unless it is covered by a marketing authorisation in which the product is classified as a Pharmacy medicine (see **Chapter 11**) or as a medicinal product subject to general sale;
3. cyanogenic substances,[1] other than preparations for external use;
4. medicinal substances that on administration emit radiation, or contain or generate any substance which emits radiation, in order that radiation may be used;
5. covered by a marketing authorisation in which the product is classified as a Pharmacy medicine or as a medicinal product subject to general sale, and consists of or contains

1. The HMR (Part 1 of Schedule 1) defines cyanogenic substances as preparations which: (a) are presented for sale or supply under the name of, or as containing, amygdalin, laetrile or vitamin B17; or (b) contain more than 0.1 per cent by weight of any substance having the formula either: (i) alpha-Cyanobenzyl -6-O-Beta-d-glucopyranosyl -Beta-d-glucopyranoside, or (ii) alpha-Cyanobenzyl-Beta-d-glucopyranosiduronic acid.

aloxiprin, aspirin or paracetamol in the form of non-effervescent tablets or capsules (see below for exemptions);
6. covered by a marketing authorisation in which the product is classified as a Pharmacy medicine or as a medicinal product subject to general sale, and consists of or contains (in any pharmaceutical form) pseudoephedrine salts or ephedrine base or salts (see below for exemptions);[2] or
7. not covered by a marketing authorisation, and is a POM by virtue of Articles 5 and 10 of, and Schedules 1 and 2 to, the POM Order.[3]

In addition, Ministers have power to specify descriptions or classes of medicinal products as POMs. They must exercise these powers:

(a) in the case of any product that is likely to present a direct or indirect danger to human health, even when used correctly, if used without the supervision of a doctor or dentist; or
(b) is frequently and to a very wide extent used incorrectly, and as a result is likely to present a direct or indirect danger to human health; or
(c) contains substances or preparations of substances of which the activity requires, or the side-effects require, further investigation; or
(d) is normally prescribed by a doctor or dentist for parenteral administration.

Marketing authorisations for Prescription Only Medicines

Regulation 62 of the Human Medicines Regulations 2012 (HMR) provides that a marketing authorisation must include a term that the medicinal product to which the authorisation relates is to be available only on prescription, only from a pharmacy, or on general sale. In making a determination as to whether a product should be available only on prescription, the licensing authority, the Medicines and Healthcare products Regulatory Agency (MHRA) must have regard to the following in relation to the product:[4]

- the maximum single dose;
- the maximum daily dose;
- the strength of the product;
- its pharmaceutical form;
- its packaging; and
- such other circumstances relating to its use as the licensing authority considers relevant.

There is power to reclassify POMs as Pharmacy medicines and the reverse is also the case. For example, in 2023, the MHRA considered but decided not to reclassify

2. It seems an anomaly that a product may have a marketing authorisation that classifies it as a Pharmacy medicine, yet the HMR designates it as a POM.
3. The Prescription Only Medicines (Human Use) Order 1997. The HMR (Schedule 35) repealed the whole of the POM Order except articles 1(1) to (5), 5 and 10, and Schedules 1 and 2.
4. HMR Reg.62(2).

Aquiette 2.5 mg tablets (which contain the active ingredient oxybutynin) as a Pharmacy medicine.[5]

Conversely, the MHRA decided in 2024 to change the classification of codeine linctus from Pharmacy medicine to POM owing to the risk of dependence, addiction and overdose.[6]

Product licences of right

Instead of a marketing authorisation, some medicinal products may have a historic product licence of right which determines their status as a Prescription Only Medicine (see **Chapter 5**).

Sale or supply of Prescription Only Medicines

HMR Reg.214 states:

> *"A person may not sell or supply a Prescription Only Medicine except in accordance with a prescription given by an appropriate practitioner."*

Selling or supplying in accordance with a prescription

A prescription may be on an NHS form or it may be a non-NHS prescription, usually referred to as a *private prescription*. The legal requirements for NHS and private prescriptions are the same and are set out below. NHS prescriptions are supplied in accordance with NHS terms of service. There is no sale in the case of an NHS prescription because a patient does not pay for the medicine (any prescription charge paid is in the nature of a tax collected by the pharmacy owner). Medicines supplied on private prescriptions are sold, because there is a contract between the pharmacy owner and the patient who pays for the medicine.[7] In order to satisfy the requirement to sell or supply in accordance with a prescription:

- The prescription must be genuine and satisfy certain conditions (see below).
- The prescription must be in existence at the time of sale or supply (unless there is an exemption for an emergency supply – see **Chapter 13**) but if the prescription is not an electronic one, the person who makes the sale or supply, need not be in physical possession of the prescription at the time of sale or supply (see the *Bayer* case described in **Box 5.4** in **Chapter 5**).

---

5. https://www.gov.uk/government/news/mhra-maintains-prescription-only-status-of-aquiette-25mg-tablets-for-symptoms-of-overactive-bladder (accessed 31 December 2024).
6. https://www.gov.uk/drug-safety-update/codeine-linctus-codeine-oral-solutions-reclassification-to-prescription-only-medicine (accessed 31 December 2024).
7. *Pfizer Corporation v Ministry of Health* [1965] AC 512.

- The quantity supplied must be the same as the quantity prescribed, except in relation to certain supplies in original packs[8] – see the sections below on Supplies in original packs and on Valproate products.
- If a medicinal product is prescribed by reference to its brand name, only the product bearing that brand name may be supplied; a therapeutically equivalent generic product may not be supplied instead.[9]
- A supply of a valproate product will normally be treated as not having been made in accordance with a prescription unless the product is supplied in a manufacturer's original pack – see the section on Valproate products below.
- Section 64 of the Medicines Act 1968 prohibits the sale or supply to the prejudice of a patient a medicinal product that that is not of the nature or quality specified in a prescription. (This section is discussed further below and in **Chapter 26**.)

Since POMs are not subject to general sale, HMR Reg.220 applies to any sale or supply or offer for sale or supply of a POM. A POM may not be sold or supplied unless:

1. the person who sells or supplies the POM is a person lawfully conducting a retail pharmacy business (see **Chapter 7**);
2. the product is sold or supplied, or offered for sale or supply, on premises that are a registered pharmacy; and
3. the transaction is carried out by a pharmacist or a person who acts under the supervision of a pharmacist.

These requirements are dealt with in more detail in **Chapter 11**.

Supplies in original packs

The quantity of a medicinal product in a manufacturer's original pack may be different to the quantity of that product on a prescription. The supply of a Prescription Only Medicine in a manufacturer's original pack is generally considered desirable (and, in the case of valproate products – see below – mandatory). The use of original packs makes it more likely that a patient information leaflet will be included (see **Chapter 18**). The supply in an original pack also enables the use of dispensing robots that can read barcodes. The use of robots is considered to be more accurate than manual dispensing because it eliminates the risk that an incorrect product will be selected from a dispensary shelf.[10]

HMR Reg.217B treats the supply of a Prescription Only Medicine in a different quantity to the quantity on the prescription as being in accordance with that prescription if it is in a manufacturer's original pack, subject to the following limitations:

---

8. HMR Reg.217B and Reg.217C.
9. A challenge to this requirement on the basis that it infringed European law was rejected by the European Court of Justice in *The Queen v Royal Pharmaceutical Society of Great Britain, ex parte Association of Pharmaceutical Importers and Others* [1990] 1 QB 534. However, the rationale of that decision may no longer be applicable following the UK's exit from the EU.
10. Takase T *et al*. Evaluating the safety and efficiency of robotic dispensing systems. *Journal of Pharmaceutical Health Care and Sciences*. 2022 Oct 1;8(1):24.

(a) the quantity supplied must not be more than 10% greater or 10% less than the quantity specified on the prescription;
(b) the supply of a different quantity to that on the prescription is not permissible if, in the exercise of the pharmacist's professional skill and judgement, the supply of a different quantity may mean that the patient does not, or is not able to, follow the medication regimen as intended by the prescriber;
(c) The 10% limitation in (a) above does not apply to:
  (i) a medicine in a form that makes it not practicable to dispense in the exact quantity on the prescription (for example, medication delivered via an inhaler);
  (ii) a medicine in a container that has an integral means of application or from which it is not practicable to dispense an exact quantity (for example, a medication where the container includes a roll-on applicator);
  (iii) a medicine that cannot be dispensed in the quantity on the prescription without adversely affecting the medicine (for example, a medication where the container cannot be split because it contains a desiccant).

Valproate products

The valproate products to which this section relates are sodium valproate, valproic acid and valproate semisodium.

It has been known for many years that if valproate products are taken in pregnancy, four in ten babies are at risk of developmental disorders and one in nine are at risk of birth defects.[11]

Manufacturers' original packs of valproate products contain patient information leaflets with warnings to females able to have a baby, and display a graphic warning on the outer packaging. However, there have been continued instances of women and girls giving birth to babies with developmental disorders and/or birth defects because they took a valproate product while unaware of the risks as a result of the product having been repackaged before supply and the new packaging did not bear the graphic warning and/or the new packaging did not contain a patient information leaflet.

HMR Reg 217C says that the supply of a valproate product will not be in accordance with a prescription unless:
(a) it is sold or supplied in its manufacturer's original outer packaging; and
(b) if the sale or supply is of a different quantity to the quantity on the prescription, it is sold or supplied in a quantity which is as close as possible to the quantity on the prescription.

This requirement to supply in a manufacturer's original pack does not apply where:
(a) the sale or supply is by or under the supervision of a pharmacist (see **Chapter 11** as to the meaning of supervision); and
(b) the pharmacist is satisfied that;

11. See: https://www.gov.uk/guidance/valproate-use-by-women-and-girls (accessed 31 December 2024) and see the report of the Independent Medicines and Medical Devices Safety Review chaired by Baroness Cumberlege https://www.immdsreview.org.uk/Report.html (accessed 31 December 2024).

(i) a risk assessment is in place that refers to the need for the patient to be sold or supplied the product in different packaging to the manufacturer's original pack (for example in a monitored dosage system); and
(ii) unless the product is unauthorised (other than because it has ceased to be unauthorised because it has been repackaged), processes are in place to ensure the supply to or for the patient of a patient information leaflet.

In addition, following a change to the Summary of Product Characteristics which is part of the marketing authorisation for valproate:

- no new male children or men under the age of 55 years should be initiated on valproate unless two specialists independently consider and document that there is no other effective or tolerated treatment or the risk of infertility or potential risk of testicular toxicity are not applicable
- there is a special warning in the case of female children, women of childbearing potential aged under 55 years and pregnant women that valproate must only be initiated by two specialists who independently consider and document that there is no other effective or tolerated treatment.
- the special warning in the Summary of Product Characteristics adds that pharmacists must ensure that:
    - the Patient Card is provided with every valproate pack dispensation and that patients understand its content,
    - patients are advised not to stop valproate medication and to immediately contact their GP to be referred to a specialist in case of planned or suspected pregnancy.

In addition to the risks of harm in the event of non-compliance, there is a risk of legal consequences for prescribers and suppliers if these requirements are not complied with. A baby who is born with, for example, a neurodevelopmental disorder as a result of its mother or father having taken valproate may be entitled to claim very high damages (see **Chapter 26**).[12]

Finasteride

The GPhC has published advice for pharmacists relating to actions they should take when supplying certain drugs on prescription. While these actions may not be a legal requirement, there may be consequences from a legal perspective in not following the advice should any adverse effects materialise. One such example is the drug finasteride.

Finasteride is licensed for benign prostatic hyperplasia and androgenic alopecia in men and has been reported to be associated with depressed mood, depression, suicidal thoughts and sexual dysfunction. Because of a perceived lack of awareness of these potential side effects, the GPhC is advising that pharmacists should:[13]

---

12. https://resolution.nhs.uk/sodium-valproate/ (accessed 31 December 2024).
13. https://www.pharmacyregulation.org/about-us/news-and-updates/regulate/update-provision-finasteride (accessed 31 December 2024).

- include a patient alert card in all packs of finasteride to raise awareness of the risk of psychiatric and sexual side-effects, including the potential for sexual dysfunction (decreased libido and erectile dysfunction) which can continue after stopping treatment;
- ask patients if they have a history of depression or suicidal ideation before providing finasteride; and
- monitor patients for psychiatric and sexual side-effects from the start of their treatment.

Puberty blockers

The Medicines (Gonadotrophin-Releasing Hormone Analogues (Restrictions on Private Sales and Supplies) Order 2024 prohibits the sale or supply of puberty blockers on private prescriptions for the treatment of gender dysphoria and gender incongruence. Further details of the prohibition are in **Chapter 21**.

Appropriate practitioners

A POM may not be sold or supplied except in accordance with a prescription given by an appropriate practitioner (HMR Reg.214).

In the HMR doctors, dentists, supplementary prescribers, nurse independent prescribers and pharmacist independent prescribers are designated as appropriate practitioners in relation to any POM. The word *doctor* means a medical practitioner registered with the General Medical Council; and *dentist* means a person registered with the General Dental Council.[14]

A *nurse independent prescriber* means a registered nurse or registered midwife noted in the professional register as qualified to order drugs, medicines and appliances as a nurse independent prescriber or a nurse independent/supplementary prescriber (HMR Reg.8).

A pharmacist independent prescriber means a pharmacist who is noted in the relevant register as qualified to order drugs, medicines and appliances as a pharmacist independent prescriber (HMR Reg.8).

A *supplementary prescriber* means a pharmacist, a registered nurse or midwife, a chiropodist, podiatrist, physiotherapist, paramedic, radiographer, a registered optometrist or a registered dietitian who is noted in the relevant register as qualified to order drugs, medicines and appliances as a supplementary prescriber (or, in the case of a registered nurse or registered midwife, as a nurse independent/supplementary prescriber) (HMR Reg.8).

The specified conditions for supplementary prescribers do not apply in relation to the prescribing and administration of medicines in accordance with the directions of another person who is an appropriate practitioner (other than a supplementary prescriber or an approved country health professional) in relation to the POM in

14. HMR Reg.8.

question (HMR Reg.216). The words *in accordance with* allow for the possibility that a POM may lawfully be supplied even though the pharmacist responsible for dispensing the prescription does not have the prescription. This may arise, for example, if a photo of the prescription has been emailed to a pharmacy but the original prescription has not yet reached the pharmacy; or if a prescriber telephones details of a prescription that requires to be dispensed before the prescriber can get the prescription to the pharmacy. So far as the law is concerned, the prescription must exist, and the pharmacist will need to know sufficient details of the prescription in order to dispense in accordance with it.[15] However, the pharmacist will need to exercise professional judgement and weigh any risk involved when making a supply of a POM without possession of the prescription.

Community practitioner nurse prescribers are appropriate practitioners in relation to POMs specified in Schedule 13 to the HMR (see below). A *community practitioner nurse prescriber* means a registered nurse or a registered midwife against whose name is recorded in the professional register an annotation signifying that the person is qualified to order drugs, medicines and appliances from the *Nurse Prescribers' Formulary for Community Practitioners* in the current edition of the *British National Formulary* (HMR Reg.8).

HMR Reg 214 states that the following are appropriate practitioners:

- optometrist independent prescribers in relation to any POM other than medicinal products that are subject to special medical prescription,[16] or for parenteral administration. An *optometrist independent prescriber* means a registered optometrist against whose name is recorded in the relevant register an annotation signifying that the person is qualified to order drugs, medicines and appliances as an optometrist independent prescriber (HMR Reg.8);
- podiatrist independent prescribers in relation to any POM unless it contains a product subject to special medical prescription other than dihydrocodeine or temazepam. A *podiatrist independent prescriber* means a registered podiatrist against whose name is recorded in the relevant register an annotation signifying that the person is qualified to order drugs, medicines and appliances as a podiatrist independent prescriber;
- physiotherapist independent prescribers in relation to any POM unless it contains a product subject to special medical prescription other than dihydrocodeine, fentanyl, morphine, oxycodone or temazepam. A *physiotherapist independent prescriber* means a registered physiotherapist against whose name is recorded in the relevant register an annotation signifying that the person is qualified to order drugs, medicines and appliances as a physiotherapist independent prescriber;

15. *Bayer PLC and Novartis Pharmaceuticals UK Ltd v NHS Darlington CCG and others* [2020] EWCA Civ 449 – see Box 5.4 in Chapter 5.
16. HMR Reg.213 defines a *product subject to special medical prescription* as any substance or product specified in Schedule 1, 2 or 3 to the Misuse of Drugs Regulations 2001.

- therapeutic radiographer independent prescribers in relation to any POM unless it contains a product subject to special medical prescription other than codeine, fentanyl, midazolam, morphine, oxycodone, temazepam or tramadol. (In relation to controlled drugs that therapeutic radiographer independent prescribers may prescribe, see **Chapter 14**.). A *therapeutic radiographer independent prescriber* means a registered radiographer, against whose name is recorded in the relevant register an entitlement to use the title "therapeutic radiographer" and an annotation signifying that the person is qualified to order drugs, medicines and appliances as a therapeutic radiographer independent prescriber;
- paramedic independent prescribers in relation to any POM unless that POM contains a product subject to special medical prescription other than codeine, fentanyl, midazolam, or morphine; and
- approved country health professionals in relation to any POM other than a product subject to special medical prescription.

An *approved country health professional* is defined in HMR Reg 213 as a person who is practising in a profession included in the list published under regulation 214(6A) in a country that is included in that list in relation to that profession. The listed professions are:

- doctors;
- dentists;
- pharmacists;
- nurses;
- physiotherapists;
- chiropodists or podiatrists;
- community nurses;
- optometrists;
- therapeutic radiographers; and
- paramedics.

At the time of writing, the approved countries list comprises EEA countries plus Switzerland.[17] The lists will be reviewed at least every three years.

For a prescription to be valid, the prescriber must be a person of equivalent professional status to a healthcare professional within the meaning of regulation 8 of the HMR. Essentially this means that the healthcare professionals in question must be entitled to prescribe in their own countries. An approved country health professional is an appropriate practitioner in relation to any POM other than a controlled drug specified in Schedule 1, 2 or 3 to the Misuse of Drugs Regulations 2001 or any POM which is not the subject of a marketing authorisation.

---

17. https://www.gov.uk/guidance/prescriptions-issued-in-the-eea-and-switzerland-guidance-for-pharmacists#eel-decline (accessed 31 December 2024).

Pharmacist independent prescribers

In order to be annotated as a pharmacist independent prescriber in the GPhC's register, a pharmacist must have completed a GPhC-accredited course. The GPhC has published Standards for the education and training of pharmacist independent prescribers.[18] A pharmacist independent prescriber may prescribe autonomously for any condition within their clinical competence, except for certain controlled drugs for the treatment of addiction (cocaine, diamorphine and dipipanone).

If a supply can be made under an exemption, for example in accordance with a Patient Group Direction (see **Chapter 13**), instead of prescribing, the pharmacist independent prescriber may choose to make a supply in reliance on the exemption from the need for a prescription. Furthermore, a pharmacist independent prescriber is not required to prescribe because, for example, the pharmacist independent prescriber may consider that prescribing would be outside their clinical competence.

Supervision

Since POMs are not subject to general sale, a POM may not be sold or supplied or offered for sale or supply unless (1) the person who sells or supplies the POM is a person lawfully conducting a retail pharmacy business (see **Chapter 7**); (2) the product is sold or supplied, or offered for sale or supply, on premises that are a registered pharmacy; and (3) the transaction is carried out by a pharmacist or a person who acts under the supervision of a pharmacist. These requirements and the meaning of *supply, transaction* and *supervision*, together with expected changes in the law, are dealt with in more detail in **Chapter 11**.

It should be noted that dispensing and supplying medicinal products are done in different ways, including placing medicines in monitored dosage units, the use of automation and delivery services. The way in which a transaction is supervised may vary depending on, for example, whether the prescribed item is an acute medicine or a repeat; whether it is a controlled drug or product liable to abuse or misuse; whether the selection and labelling has been done by robot; and whether the patient or patient's representative is present in the pharmacy or whether the prescribed item is to be delivered to the patient's home or a collection point.

It is common for dispensed medicines to be put on a pharmacy shelf for collection by the patient or patient's representative. It is unclear whether HMR Reg.220 requires a pharmacist to supervise the handing out of the medicine when it is collected, but it is arguable that because the HMR refer to supervision of the *transaction* (see **Chapter 11**), not to the *supply*, the requirements of the HMR are satisfied by supervision of the dispensing process rather than requiring the handing out to be supervised. At the time of writing, the Department of Health and Social Care has proposed to make changes to

18. https://assets.pharmacyregulation.org/files/document/standards-for-the-education-and-training-of-pharmacist-independent-prescribers-october-2022.pdf (accessed 31 December 2024).

the law. If, and when, the changes in the law are made, the position will be as set out in **Box 12.1**.

Box 12.1

At the time of going to press, there were proposals to amend the law. This box sets out what the law will be if those proposals are brought into effect. Readers can check whether the proposals have been brought into effect by checking www.legislation.gov.uk or using a subscription service such as Westlaw for the latest version of the Medicines Act 1968/ the Human Medicines Regulations 2012 or searching those sites for the Human Medicines (Authorisation by Pharmacists and Supervision by Pharmacy Technicians) Order *[followed by the year].*

- If a pharmacist is absent from the pharmacy and a medicine that has been dispensed under a pharmacist's supervision is ready for sale or supply, the pharmacist may authorise another person (who need not be a pharmacy technician) to sell or supply in the pharmacist's absence. For the meaning of *dispense*, see **Chapter 5**.
- The pharmacist will be treated as absent from the premises if they are at the pharmacy but not available to intervene in, or not in a position to intervene in, the transaction in question.
- Authorisations may be general or specific.
- Authorisations may be written or oral.
- In giving an authorisation, a pharmacist "must have due regard to patient safety". Failure to do this will not invalidate the authorisation, but may be regarded as misconduct.

Direct supervision and direct personal supervision

The requirement for supervision may be compared to the requirements elsewhere in legislation governing aspects of pharmacy practice for *direct supervision* and for *direct personal supervision*.

The NHS terms of service in England and Scotland[19] require prescribed medicines and appliances to be supplied by a pharmacist or under the *direct supervision* of a pharmacist. When a supply is made under a Serious Shortage Protocol (see below), reference is also made to *direct supervision*. The term *direct supervision* is also used in the HMR in other contexts, and legislation governing aspects of pharmacy practice refers to other types of supervision. For example, a student midwife may administer lidocaine hydrochloride to a woman in childbirth, but only under the direct supervision of a registered midwife.[20]

It is not clear what *direct supervision* means in a pharmacy context. In a midwifery context, the Nursing and Midwifery Council's Standards for preregistration midwifery education[21] for preregistration midwifery education say:

---

19. In England, in paragraph 8 of Schedule 4 to the National Health Service (Pharmaceutical and Local Pharmaceutical Services) Regulations 2013 and in Scotland in paragraph 7 of the National Health Service (Pharmaceutical Services) (Scotland) Regulations 2009; and see Chapter 3.
20. Schedule 17 to the HMR.
21. https://www.nmc.org.uk/globalassets/sitedocuments/standards/nmc-standards-for-preregistration-midwifery-education.pdf (accessed 31 December 2024).

> *"Direct supervision is where the practising midwife would normally be in close proximity to the student, either by working directly with them or close enough to directly monitor their activities."*

The concept of *direct supervision* implies closer involvement of a pharmacist than the concept of *supervision* though not necessarily closer physical proximity of the pharmacist to the person who sells or supplies. While it seems natural to expect that a registered midwife would have to be in physical proximity to a student midwife who is injecting a woman in childbirth, there is no obvious need for the same kind of physical proximity of a pharmacist to a registered pharmacy technician who hands out a POM. This view is supported by a series of VAT cases in which the supply of services would be exempt from VAT if the supply was made under the direct supervision of a health professional. In those cases, tribunals have held that *direct* means not through a third party.[22]

The requirement for direct supervision may be compared with the regulations requiring *direct personal supervision* in the safe custody of controlled drugs[23] (see **Chapter 14**). These regulations require controlled drugs in a pharmacy to be kept in a locked safe, cabinet or room except when a controlled drug is under the *direct personal supervision* of a pharmacist. One may envisage that to achieve the objective of these regulations by minimising the risk of misappropriation of a controlled drug, direct personal supervision involves a pharmacist not only being present on the premises, but able to see the controlled drug.

The use of the terms *direct supervision* and *direct personal supervision* help to shed light on the meaning of *supervision* in the HMR. It is suggested that there is a hierarchy in which:

- *Supervision* is the least restrictive – it does not require the same degree of physical proximity of a pharmacist to be to the person making a sale or supply as direct supervision.
- *Direct supervision* is more restrictive than *supervision*. It requires the closer involvement of a pharmacist in a sale or supply carried out by a non-pharmacist than *supervision*, and possibly greater physical proximity.
- *Direct personal supervision* is more restrictive than *direct supervision*. It requires physical proximity and an ability to see the medicinal products that are subject to the requirement.

Hub and spoke dispensing

Hub and spoke dispensing involves a pharmacy (a spoke) that is presented with a patient's prescription sending the prescription to another pharmacy (a hub) to be

---

22. *E Moss Ltd v HMRC (2006) VAT Decision 19510*; *Elder Home Care Ltd v Customs and Excise Commissioners* (1993) VAT Decision 11185; *Land v Customs and Excise Commissioners* (1998) VAT Decision 15547.
23. Misuse of Drugs (Safe Custody) Regulations 1973.

dispensed. At the time of going to print, this is only lawful if the hub pharmacy and the spoke pharmacy have the same owner. If a hub and spoke arrangement is used, supervision will be required at both the hub and the spoke. What is done at the hub will fall within the meaning of *assembly* in HMR Reg.8, and HMR Reg.17 would therefore require a manufacturer's licence, but there is an exemption from the need for such a licence for assembling at a pharmacy under the supervision of a pharmacist (see **Chapter 5**). HMR Reg.220 will also require the transaction at the spoke to be supervised if the dispensed medicine is handed out at the spoke by a person who is not a pharmacist. At the time of going to print, the Department of Health and Social Care proposes to amend the HMR in 2025 to allow all pharmacies to use hub and spoke dispensing arrangements.[24] If and when the law is amended, the position will be as set out in **Box 12.2**. The supervision requirement is the subject of other proposals to amend the HMR, details of which are given in **Chapter 11**.

Box 12.2

At the time of going to press, there were proposals to amend the law to allow pharmacies to send prescriptions to another pharmacy that does not have the same owner, so that the prescribed medicines can be dispensed at that other pharmacy (known as hub and spoke dispensing). This box sets out what the law will be if those proposals are brought into effect. Readers can check whether the proposals have been brought into effect by checking www.legislation.gov.uk or using a subscription service such as Westlaw for the latest version of the Medicines Act 1968 or searching those sites for the Human Medicines (Amendments Relating to Hub and Spoke dispensing etc.) Regulations *[followed by the year].*

- All pharmacies and dispensing doctor practices that are spokes will be able to send prescriptions to a pharmacy that is a hub to be assembled.
- The spoke may carry out some of the dispensing actions, such as the clinical check.
- The hub and the spoke must enter into written arrangements with each other.
- The spoke must conspicuously display the name and address of any hub pharmacies with whom they have entered into arrangements with a brief statement of the general effect of the arrangements. The statement must be on the premises if the spoke supplies medicinal products who are on the premises; and the statement must be on the spoke's website if the spoke supplies medicinal products via the internet.
- The hub is not required to hold the prescription.
- Where both the hub and the spoke are pharmacies and a pharmacist is permitted to vary the quantity to be supplied so as to supply in a manufacturer's original pack or under a Serious Shortage Protocol, the final decision about the quantity lies with a pharmacist at the spoke.
- A sale or supply of a medicinal product by a hub to a spoke will be treated as a retail transaction, not a wholesale transaction.

24. https://www.gov.uk/government/consultations/hub-and-spoke-dispensing/outcome/government-response-to-the-consultation-on-hub-and-spoke-dispensing (accessed 31 December 2024).

Agency

The *Elmfield Drugs* case (see **Box 11.1**) demonstrates the importance of the doctrine of agency – that one person may properly act as the agent of another and do things on behalf of that other person. When a supply is made from a pharmacy, HMR Reg.220 expressly contemplates that a supply may be made by an agent, namely a pharmacist if the pharmacist is not the owner of the business or someone acting under the supervision of a pharmacist.

Equally as importantly, a medicinal product may be sold or supplied to someone who is an agent of the patient or customer. It is generally taken for granted that a representative of a patient is entitled to receive medication on behalf of the patient, but the supply to a patient's representative is only lawful because the patient's representative is an agent of the patient.

The doctrine of agency extends further still. The home delivery of medicines was rare at the time the Medicines Act 1968 was passed. Indeed, an exception to the Medicines Act had to be made[25] to allow pharmacies to deliver dispensed medicines to a location from which patients or their representatives could collect them (see Exemption for collection and delivery arrangements below). It was expected at the time that this exemption would be used in rural areas where patients might find it difficult to get to a pharmacy that was relatively remote from them. In 2005, pharmacy owners were expressly permitted to apply for the inclusion of a pharmacy in the pharmaceutical list if they provided NHS services only to patients or their representatives who were not on the pharmacy premises.[26] Home deliveries are only lawful if the person who delivers a medicinal product does so as the agent of the patient and a pharmacist has supervised the handing over of the medicinal product(s) to the person who makes the delivery, or if the requirement to supervise the *transaction* in HMR Reg.220 has a wider meaning than supervising the *supply* of medicinal products (see Supervision in **Chapter 11**). The doctrine of agency also features in arrangements for what are known as dispensing kiosks. These kiosks often have the appearance of a vending machine. Following dispensing by or under the supervision of a pharmacist, a member of the pharmacy staff, acting as the patient's agent, may load the dispensed medicinal product into the kiosk for later collection by the patient or the patient's representative.

Reliance on the doctrine of agency will become superfluous, if and when the Department of Health and Social Care's proposals to amend the law relating to supervision are brought into effect.

Exemption for collection and delivery arrangements

When a collection and delivery arrangement is used by a person lawfully conducting a retail pharmacy business, HMR Reg.220 (requiring the supply to be made on registered

---

25. Medicines (Collection and Delivery Arrangements - Exemption) Order 1978 - now in HMR Reg.248
26. The equivalent provision is now in regulation 25 of the National Health Service (Pharmaceutical and Local Pharmaceutical Services) Regulations 2013.

pharmacy premises and for the transaction to be supervised by a pharmacist if the sale or supply is not made by a pharmacist) does not apply provided that the medicinal product has been prepared or dispensed at a registered pharmacy by or under the supervision of a pharmacist (HMR Reg.248).

The reference to a *collection and delivery arrangement* means an arrangement whereby a person may take or send a prescription given by an appropriate prescriber[27] to premises other than a registered pharmacy and which are capable of being closed by the occupier to exclude the public, and collect or have collected on their behalf from such premises a medicinal product prepared or dispensed in accordance with such a prescription at a registered pharmacy by or under the supervision of a pharmacist.

The use of the word *dispense* is not used often in pharmacy law and it is noteworthy here as having a meaning that is distinct from the meaning of *supply*. In the context of HMR Reg.248, the meaning is similar to *prepare*. In other contexts, the word *dispense* refers to the entire process from presentation of a prescription to the point at which the medicinal product is handed to a patient or the patient's representative. (The meaning of "dispense" is also discussed in **Box 5.1** in **Chapter 5**.)

As explained above, collection and delivery arrangements were originally intended to meet patients' needs in rural areas. However, the High Court made clear in *R v Statutory Committee of the Royal Pharmaceutical Society of Great Britain, ex parte Boots the Chemists Limited*[28] that such arrangements can be used anywhere (see **Box 12.3**), and have been used to enable patients to collect prescribed medicines from automated kiosks.

Box 12.3

When the Royal Pharmaceutical Society of Great Britain (RPSGB) was the pharmacy regulator, it issued a statement to the effect that collection and delivery arrangements should only be used in rural areas where there were no existing pharmacies. Boots the Chemists Limited (Boots) operated collection and delivery services in two rural villages where there were pharmacies owned by other businesses. Boots collected prescriptions from local surgeries, dispensed the prescribed medicines in local branches, and delivered the medicines to the surgeries for patients to collect from there. The existing pharmacies were bypassed by the collection and delivery arrangement. Boots knew that the use of the surgery as a collection point was in breach of the RPSGB statement. Fitness to practise proceedings were brought against Boots and its superintendent pharmacist. The High Court quashed a finding of misconduct. The case illustrates the potentially wide application of collection and delivery services. For example, some pharmacies now use automated dispensing kiosks as a collection point at premises that are not registered as a pharmacy.

---

27. For the purposes of Reg.248, an appropriate prescriber is a doctor, dentist, nurse independent prescriber, pharmacist independent prescriber, physiotherapist independent prescriber, podiatrist independent prescriber, therapeutic radiographer independent prescriber, paramedic independent prescriber, or optometrist independent prescriber.
28. [1997] Lexis Citation 2670.

If, and when, the HMR is amended (particularly HMR Reg.220) to allow POMs (as well as Pharmacy medicines) to be supplied "at or from" a pharmacy, it seems that the need for the collection and delivery exemption will become redundant, or at least will decline in use because there will no longer be a requirement to supply them only on pharmacy premises.

Prescriptions

To make a lawful sale or supply of a POM, certain conditions must be satisfied, which are slightly different for approved country health professionals (HMR Reg.218) and other appropriate practitioners (HMR Reg.217). The conditions are that the prescription:

1. is signed in ink by the appropriate practitioner or the approved country health professional giving it;
2. is written in ink or otherwise so as to be indelible or (in the case of a health prescription which is not for a controlled drug) is written in ink or otherwise so as to be indelible or by means of carbon paper or similar material [N.B. approved country health professionals cannot issue health prescriptions];
3. is not dispensed after the end of the period of six months beginning with the appropriate date; or, in the case of a repeatable prescription, is not dispensed for the first time after the end of that period, and is dispensed in accordance with the directions contained in the prescription;
4. in the case of a repeatable prescription that does not specify the number of times it may be dispensed,
    a. it is not dispensed on more than two occasions, or
    b. in the case of a prescription for an oral contraceptive, it is not dispensed on more than six occasions or after the end of the period of six months beginning with the appropriate date;
5. for an appropriate prescriber who is an approved country health professional, the prescription is issued in an approved country and the prescribing approved country health professional is legally entitled to issue a prescription of that kind in the country in which the prescription is issued; pharmacists may not dispense controlled drugs specified in Schedule 1, 2 or 3 of the Misuse of Drugs Regulations 2001, or any POM which is not the subject of a marketing authorisation, on prescriptions written by EEA or Swiss healthcare professionals;[29]
6. contains the particulars set out in **Table 12.1**.

29. The Medicines (Gonadotrophin-Releasing Hormone Analogues) (Emergency Prohibition) (England, Wales and Scotland) Order 2024 prohibited the prescribing of puberty blockers by non-UK prescribers (see also chapter 21).

Table 12.1: *Particulars which must be included on a prescription for a POM*

Description (the information in this column does not form part of the HMR but is included to improve clarity)	Particulars to be included for prescriptions issued by a non-approved country appropriate practitioner (i.e. by a UK registered prescriber)	Particulars to be included for prescriptions issued by an approved country health professional for dispensing in the UK, or by a non-approved country appropriate practitioner for dispensing in an approved country
Date	The appropriate date	The issue date of the prescription
Patient details	The patient's name and address, and the patient's age if they are under 12 years	The patient's surname, first names written out in full and the patient's date of birth (whatever the age of the patient)
Prescriber details	The prescriber's address and an indication of the kind of appropriate practitioner issuing the prescription	The prescriber's: ● first names written out in full; ● surname; ● professional qualifications; and ● direct contact details including email address, telephone or fax number with the appropriate international prefix, work address, and name of the relevant member State in which that approved country health professional works or confirmation that the prescriber works as a health professional in the UK
Details about the prescribed medicine	The HMR do not specify that any particular information relating to the prescribed medicine is required by law	Details about the prescribed product, including where applicable: ● the common name of the product; ● brand name (if the prescribed product is a biological medicinal product, or the prescriber deems it medically necessary for that product to be dispensed) and the prescriber's reasons justifying the use of the branded product;[30] ● pharmaceutical formulation (tablet, solution, etc.); ● quantity and strength of the medicinal product; and ● dosage regimen

An appropriate practitioner[31] (other than an approved country health professional) may issue a prescription to be dispensed in an EEA State other than the UK (i.e., a GB prescriber for dispensing within the EEA).

If the prescription is not a health prescription for a Schedule 1 controlled drug or, in the case of approved country prescriptions, for a Schedule 2 or 3 controlled drug, it may be issued as an electronic prescription (HMR Reg.219 and 219A). In this case, as

30. See Chapter 5 in relation to imports which are branded products.

31. In this context, "appropriate practitioner" refers to a doctor, dentist, supplementary prescriber, nurse independent prescriber, pharmacist independent prescriber, community practitioner nurse prescriber, optometrist independent prescriber, podiatrist independent prescriber or physiotherapist independent prescriber; HMR Reg.217A.

an alternative to fulfilling conditions 1 and 2 specified above (for both non-approved country and approved country health professionals) the conditions are set out below, followed by an explanation of the terms that are used. The conditions are that the prescription is:

a. created in an electronic form;
b. signed with an advanced electronic signature;
c. sent to the person by whom it is dispensed as an electronic communication (whether or not through one or more intermediaries); and
d. sent via the Electronic Prescription Service if it is for a Schedule 2 or 3 controlled drug. (HMR Reg 219)

Note that a health prescription for a Schedule 2 or 3 controlled drug may be issued via the Electronic Prescription Service by a UK prescriber who is entitled to prescribe that drug.

Advanced electronic signature[32] means an electronic signature that is:

a. uniquely linked to the person giving the prescription (the signatory);
b. capable of identifying the signatory;
c. created using means that the signatory can maintain under their sole control; and
d. linked to the data to which it relates in such a manner that any subsequent change of the data is detectable.

Note that a photograph of a prescription that is emailed or sent by a messaging service such as WhatsApp would not satisfy the requirement for an advanced electronic signature and could not be treated as a valid prescription.

Electronic Prescription Service means the service of that name which is managed by NHS England[33] established under section 1H of the National Health Service Act 2006.

Electronic communication (HMR Reg.8) means a communication transmitted (whether from one person to another, from one device to another or from a person to a device or vice versa):

a. by means of an electronic communications network within the meaning of section 32(1) of the Communications Act 2003; or
b. by other means but while in an electronic form.

Repeatable prescription (HMR Reg.213) means a prescription which contains a direction that it may be dispensed more than once.

Health prescription (HMR Reg.213) means a prescription issued by a doctor, dentist, supplementary prescriber, nurse independent prescriber, optometrist independent prescriber, pharmacist independent prescriber, physiotherapist independent prescriber, podiatrist independent prescriber, therapeutic radiographer independent prescriber, paramedic independent prescriber or community practitioner nurse prescriber under:

a. in England, the National Health Service Act 2006;
b. in Scotland, the National Health Service (Scotland) Act 1978; or

---

32. HMR Reg.219.
33. Shortly before going to press, the Prime Minister announced that NHS England would be abolished as a separate body, and its functions will be exercised by the Department of Health and Social Care.

c. in Wales, the National Health Service (Wales) Act 2006.

The *appropriate date* (HMR Reg.217) is the date on which the prescription was signed by the appropriate practitioner giving it, or, in the case of a health prescription only, the date indicated by the appropriate practitioner as being the date before which it should not be dispensed. Where a health prescription bears both dates, the later of those dates is the appropriate one. Approved country health professionals cannot issue health prescriptions, so for an approved country prescription, the "appropriate date" will always be the date on which it is signed by the approved country health professional.

Prescribing and administration by supplementary prescribers

A supplementary prescriber may give a prescription for a POM, parenterally administer a POM or give directions for the parenteral administration of a POM providing they are acting in accordance with the terms of a clinical management plan that relates to the patient to whom the product is prescribed/administered, has effect when the prescription is given or when the product is administered or the direction to administer is given (HMR Reg.215) and includes the particulars specified in Schedule 14 to the HMR (see **Box 12.4**). In addition, the supplementary prescriber must have access to the health

Box 12.4: Supplementary prescribing: clinical management plan

Meaning of clinical management plan (HMR Reg.8)

A clinical management plan means a written plan (which may be amended from time to time) relating to the treatment of an individual patient, agreed by the patient to whom the plan relates, the doctor or dentist who is a party to the plan and any supplementary prescriber who is to prescribe, give directions for administration or administer under the plan.

Particulars to be included in a clinical management plan (HMR Sch.14)

A clinical management plan must contain the following particulars:

a. the name of the patient to whom the plan relates;
b. the illnesses or conditions which may be treated by the supplementary prescriber;
c. the date on which the plan is to take effect and when it is to be reviewed by the doctor or dentist who is a party to the plan;
d. reference to the class or description of medicinal product which may be prescribed or administered under the plan;
e. any restrictions or limitations as to the strength or dose of any product which may be prescribed or administered under the plan, and any period of administration or use of any medicinal product which may be prescribed or administered under the plan;
f. relevant warnings about the known sensitivities of the patient to, or known difficulties of the patient with, particular medicinal products;
g. the arrangements for notification of
    i. suspected or known adverse reactions to any medicinal product which may be prescribed or administered under the plan, and
    ii. suspected or known adverse reactions to any other medicinal product taken at the same time as any medicinal product prescribed or administered under the plan; and
h. the circumstances in which the supplementary prescriber should refer to, or seek the advice of, the doctor or dentist who is a party to the plan.

records of the patient to whom the plan relates and are used by any doctor or dentist who is a party to the plan. The above does not apply if the supplementary prescriber is a community practitioner nurse prescriber and the POM prescribed or administered, or in respect of which they gave directions for administration, is specified in Schedule 13 to the Regulations.

Forgeries, prescription defects and due diligence

HMR Reg.255 makes it an offence if a POM is sold or supplied otherwise than in accordance with a prescription. A *prescription* means a genuine prescription. In 1984, at a pharmacy owned by Storkwain Limited (*the company*), two private prescriptions for Ritalin tablets, Physeptone ampoules and Valium tablets were presented and the items were supplied. It was later discovered that the prescriptions were forgeries. The Pharmaceutical Society, which was then the pharmacy regulator, prosecuted the company for breach of the equivalent provision in HMR Reg.255 (then in the Medicines Act 1968). The company argued that it could not be convicted unless the prosecution proved that whoever supplied the POMs knew or was reckless as to whether the prescriptions were not genuine (sometimes referred to by the Latin term *mens rea* or a guilty mind). The issue was finally determined by the House of Lords,[34] which ruled that an offence was committed even if the person who made the supply did not know and could not reasonably have known that the prescriptions were forgeries. Following the conviction of Storkwain Ltd, pressure was brought to bear by pharmacists who objected to the Pharmaceutical Society prosecuting its own members in the circumstances of this case. This pressure led to the introduction of a due diligence defence which now appears in the HMR and is described below.[35]

The sale or supply by a pharmacist is not rendered unlawful if made against a forged prescription provided the pharmacist has exercised all due diligence and believes on reasonable grounds that the prescription is genuine (HMR Reg.245)

Where a prescription given by an appropriate practitioner does not fulfil a required condition, the sale or supply is not rendered unlawful if the person making the sale or supply, having exercised all due diligence, believes on reasonable grounds that that condition has been met (HMR Reg.246).

There is an exemption from the general prohibition from supplying POMs except in accordance with a prescription in the case of the sale or supply by a pharmacist in accordance with a prescription given by someone who is not an appropriate practitioner if the pharmacist, having exercised all due diligence, believes on reasonable grounds that the person who wrote the prescription is: (HMR Reg.228):

a. another pharmacist;
b. a registered nurse or a registered midwife;

34. *Pharmaceutical Society of Great Britain v Storkwain Ltd* [1986] 1 WLR 903.

35. It should be noted that certain of the items supplied in the *Storkwain* case are controlled drugs and there are separate provisions that relate to forged prescriptions in the Misuse of Drugs Regulations 2001 – see chapter 14.

c. a person whose name is entered in the part of the Health and Care Professions Council Register relating to chiropodists and podiatrists, physiotherapists, radiographers (diagnostic or therapeutic), or paramedics; or
d. a registered optometrist.

The exemption in HMR Reg.228 also applies to the sale or supply of a POM by a pharmacist where the sale or supply is in accordance with a prescription given by a supplementary prescriber and the pharmacist, having exercised all due diligence, believes on reasonable grounds that the supplementary prescriber has complied with the requirements for prescribing by supplementary prescribers.

The requirement for a prescription in HMR Reg.214 does not apply to the sale or supply of a POM if the seller or supplier, having exercised all due diligence, believes on reasonable grounds that the product is not a POM (HMR Reg.244).

Administration of Prescription Only Medicines

HMR Reg.214 states that no person shall parenterally administer a POM, otherwise than to themselves, unless the person is an appropriate practitioner or is acting in accordance with the directions of such an appropriate practitioner. (In the case of parenteral administration, an approved country practitioner is not within the definition of *appropriate practitioner*.) However, this Regulation does not apply to the administration of:

1. certain medicines by way of parenteral injection for the purpose of saving life in an emergency (as listed in **Box 12.5**);
2. smallpox vaccine, administered for the purpose of providing protection against smallpox virus:

Box 12.5: Medicinal products for parenteral administration in an emergency (HMR Sch.19)

- Adrenaline (epinephrine) 1:1000 up to 1 mg for intramuscular use in anaphylaxis.
- Atropine sulphate injection.
- Atropine sulphate and obidoxime chloride injection.
- Atropine sulphate and pralidoxime chloride injection.
- Atropine sulphate, pralidoxime mesilate and avizafone injection.
- Chlorphenamine injection.
- Dicobalt edetate injection.
- Glucagon injection.
- Glucose injection.
- Hydrocortisone injection.
- Naloxone hydrochloride.
- Pralidoxime chloride injection.
- Pralidoxime mesilate injection.
- Promethazine hydrochloride injection.
- Snake venom antiserum.
- Sodium nitrite injection.
- Sodium thiosulphate injection.
- Sterile pralidoxime.

a. in the event of a suspected or confirmed case of smallpox in the UK where the vaccine has been supplied by, on behalf of, or under arrangements made by the Secretary of State, the Scottish ministers, the Welsh ministers, the Department of Health, Social Services and Public Safety, or an NHS body,
b. to members of HM Forces or other persons employed or engaged by them where the vaccine has been supplied by, on behalf of, or under arrangements made by, HM Forces;

3. (a) a radioactive medicinal product, administration of which results in a medical exposure; or (b) any other POM if it is being administered in connection with a medical exposure. In either case, certain conditions must be met (see also below).

Radioactive substance is defined in Reg.2 of the Ionising Radiation (Medical Exposure) Regulations 2017 as any substance that contains one or more radionuclides the activity or activity concentration of which cannot be disregarded from a radiation protection point of view.

Medical exposure means an exposure of ionising radiation:

a. to patients as part of their own medical diagnosis or treatment;
b. to individuals as part of health screening programmes;
c. to patients or other persons voluntarily participating in medical or biomedical, diagnostic or therapeutic, research programmes;
d. to carers and comforters;
e. to asymptomatic individuals; and
f. to individuals undergoing non-medical imaging using medical radiological equipment.

The restriction in HMR Reg.214 on parenteral administration of a POM is disapplied[36] in relation to radioactive medicinal products if:

a. the POM is administered by an operator acting in accordance with the procedures and protocols in the Ionising Radiation (Medical Exposure) Regulations 2017 which apply to the exposure;
b. the medical exposure has been authorised by an ionising radiation medical exposure (IRME) practitioner, or, where it is not practical for an IRME practitioner to authorise the exposure, by an operator acting in accordance with written guidelines issued by an IRME practitioner;
c. the IRME practitioner is be the holder of an appropriate licence[37] granted by the ministers (an IRME is a registered health care professional who is entitled in accordance with the employer's procedures to take responsibility for an individual exposure);
d. the POM is not a product subject to special medical prescription;
e. in the case of a POM that is not a radioactive substance, it is specified in the protocols referred to in (a) above.

---

36. HMR Reg.240.
37. In accordance with regulation 5 of the Ionising Radiation (Medical Exposure) Regulations 2017.

Use of POMs in cosmetic procedures

Botox

Under the Botulinum Toxin and Cosmetic Fillers (Children) Act 2021, it is an offence:

(a) to administer to a person under the age of 18 botulinum toxin or subcutaneous, submucous or intradermal injection of a filler for a cosmetic purpose: or

(b) if a business owner administers these products to a person under 18 in the course of a business.

In the case of an offence by a body corporate, a director or secretary or manager of the body will also be guilty of the offence if they consent, connive at the offence or the offence is attributable to their neglect.

In the case of these offences, it is a defence if a pharmacist, nurse or dentist administers the products in accordance with the directions of a medical practitioner. There are also due diligence defences in the Act.

It is also an offence under the Act to *make arrangements* (such as book an appointment) for the treatments to be given to anyone under the age of 18 in England. Parents cannot give valid consent for children to receive treatment.

The government has given guidance for businesses[38] and the GPhC has given guidance.[39]

POMs in cosmetic procedures generally

There has been concern about the unregulated nature of non-surgical cosmetic procedures, including the injection of substances. In relation to England, a consultation has been conducted on a proposal that 'any procedure which requires a prescription-only medicine (POM) must, at the very least, be overseen by a qualified and regulated healthcare professional. This includes any procedure that uses a POM directly, for example, injectable toxins; and/or any adjunctive procedure that uses a POM alongside the primary procedure to assist or complement it, for example, lidocaine for anaesthetic purposes, or hyaluronidase for managing complications of medical devices such as dermal fillers. This recognises the risks associated with certain procedures and the need for practitioners to have access to - and support from - experienced clinicians who are able to deal with medical emergency situations and complications and have independent prescribing rights'.[40]

In relation to non-surgical cosmetic procedures that do not involve POMs, see **Chapter 2**.

---

38. https://www.gov.uk/government/publications/botulinum-toxin-and-cosmetic-fillers-for-under-18s-guidance-for-businesses/botulinum-toxin-and-cosmetic-fillers-for-under-18s-guidance-for-businesses (accessed 31 December 2024).
39. https://www.pharmacyregulation.org/about-us/news-and-updates/regulate/botulinum-toxin-and-cosmetic-fillers-children-act-what-you-need-know (accessed 31 December 2024).
40. https://www.gov.uk/government/consultations/licensing-of-non-surgical-cosmetic-procedures/the-licensing-of-non-surgical-cosmetic-procedures-in-england (accessed 31 December 2024).

Products exempt from Prescription Only control

Medicinal products exempt due to conditions specified in Schedule 1 of the POM Order

A medicinal product that is not the subject of a marketing authorisation is a POM for the purposes of the Human Medicines Regulations 2012 if it, or a substance in it, is listed in column 1 of Schedule 1 of the POM Order, unless there is:

a. an entry in Columns 2, 3, 4 or 5 of that Schedule which contains a condition and that condition is satisfied; or
b. more than one such condition which applies where that substance is used in that product and each of those conditions are satisfied.

The conditions mentioned above differ for different products but may pertain to the maximum strength, a route of administration, use for a specified purpose or in a specified class of persons, a particular pharmaceutical form or a maximum quantity that may be sold or supplied.

All these exempted medicinal products will be Pharmacy medicines (see **Chapter 11**).

Preparations of aloxiprin, aspirin or paracetamol in the form of non-effervescent tablets or capsules exempt due to maximum strength or quantity sold or supplied

Products consisting of or containing aloxiprin, aspirin or paracetamol are exempt from POM control if the quantity of the product sold or supplied to a person at any one time does not exceed 100 tablets or capsules (HMR Reg.236).

In addition, these preparations may be exempt from POM control, if the strength of the preparation does not exceed stated maxima.[41] These are as follows:

- *Aspirin.* If the pack size for non-effervescent tablets or capsules does not exceed 32 and the maximum strength 500 mg then the product is a Pharmacy medicine. The total quantity sold to a person at any one time must not exceed 100.
- *Aspirin.* If the pack size for non-effervescent tablets or capsules does not exceed 100 and the maximum strength 75 mg then the product is a Pharmacy medicine (see **Chapter 11**).
- *Paracetamol.* If the pack size for non-effervescent tablets or capsules does not exceed 32 and the maximum strength 250 mg (wholly or mainly for children under 12) or maximum strength 500 mg (for adults or children over 12), then the product is a Pharmacy medicine. The total quantity sold to a person at any one time must not exceed 100.

Aspirin and paracetamol in preparations other than non-effervescent tablets and capsules are also Pharmacy medicines.

Maximum strength is defined in the POM Order as either:

a. the maximum quantity of a substance by weight or volume contained in a dosage unit of a medicinal product; or
b. the maximum percentage of a substance contained in a medicinal product calculated in terms of weight in weight (w/w), weight in volume (w/v), volume in weight (v/w)

41. The Prescription Only Medicines (Human Use) Order 1997.

or volume in volume (v/v) and if the maximum percentage calculated in those ways differ, the higher or highest percentage.

Maximum dose (MD) in relation to a product for internal use means the maximum quantity of the substance contained in the amount of the product that it is recommended should be taken or administered at any one time (HMR Reg.213).

Maximum daily dose (MDD) in relation to a product for internal use means the maximum quantity of the substance contained in the amount of the product that it is recommended should be taken or administered in any period of 24 hours (HMR Reg.213).

Preparations of pseudoephedrine salts or ephedrine base or salts exempt due to conditions

Restrictions are placed on pseudoephedrine and ephedrine sales because of concerns that medicines (such as nasal decongestants) containing these active substances could be used in the illicit manufacture of the controlled drug methylamphetamine.[42] Products consisting of or containing pseudoephedrine salts or ephedrine base or salts that are POMs by virtue of Schedule 1 to the Regulation, are exempt from POM control, if the following conditions are met (HMR Reg.237):

1. a product that contains pseudoephedrine salts is not sold or supplied at the same time as another medicinal product that consists of or contains ephedrine base or salts;
2. the medicinal products sold or supplied to a person at any one time do not in total contain more than:
   a. in the case of pseudoephedrine salts, 720 mg pseudoephedrine salts; or
   b. in the case of ephedrine base or salts, 180 mg ephedrine base or salts.

High dilution products

See **Chapter 13**.

Drugs to procure abortion

It is an offence for a pregnant woman to administer to herself any drug with the intention of causing a miscarriage.[43]

It is an offence to supply unlawfully or to procure a drug, knowing that it is intended to be unlawfully used with the intent to procure a miscarriage.[44]

These offences are not committed if a pregnancy is terminated in accordance with the Abortion Act 1967 when, amongst other conditions, two registered medical practitioners are of the opinion that the conditions for termination of pregnancy are satisfied. The Act provides that the termination must be carried out in an NHS hospital, but section 1(3A)

---

42. https://www.gov.uk/drug-safety-update/pseudoephedrine-and-ephedrine-regular-review-of-minimising-risk-of-misuse-in-the-uk (accessed 27 July 202031 December 2024).
43. Section 58 of the Offences Against the Person Act 1861. Miscarriage has the same meaning as 'abortion'.
44. Section 59 of the Offences Against the Person Act 1861.

of the Act gives the Secretary of State power to approve a different place if the treatment consists primarily of the use of medicines.

If (a) the treatment consists of the prescription and administration of medicine and (b) the registered medical practitioner terminating the pregnancy is of the opinion, formed in good faith, that, if the medicine is administered in accordance with their instructions, the pregnancy will not exceed ten weeks at the time when the medicine is administered (or in the case of a course of medicine, when the first medicine in the course is administered), then:

- if the usual place of residence of the medical practitioner terminating the pregnancy is in England and Wales, the medical practitioner may prescribe from that place; and
- if the pregnant woman's usual place of residence is in England or Wales and she has had a consultation (in person, by telephone or by electronic means) with a registered medical practitioner, registered nurse or registered midwife about the termination of the pregnancy, the medicine may be self-administered by the pregnant woman at that place.

Drugs and devices for contraception

The supply and use of drugs (including emergency hormonal contraception) and devices for contraception do not breach the Offences Against the Person Act 1861 (see above), when they are for use as contraceptives, because they are used before pregnancy occurs.[45]

Pharmacy records

A person lawfully conducting a retail pharmacy business must, in respect of every sale or supply of a POM, make or cause to be made an entry in a written or computerised record kept for that purpose (HMR Reg.253), unless:

1. it is a sale or supply in pursuance of a health prescription or a prescription for oral contraceptives;
2. a separate record of the sale or supply is made in accordance with controlled drugs legislation (**Chapter 14**);
3. the sale is by way of wholesale dealing and the order or invoice relating to the sale (or a copy of it) is retained by the person lawfully conducting the retail pharmacy business who makes the sale;
4. in Scotland, the sale or supply is to a doctor of medicines and appliances for immediate treatment or personal administration which, under the NHS, the doctor is entitled or required to supply.[46]

---

45. *R (on the application of Smeaton) v Secretary of State for Health* [2002] EWHC 610 (Admin), in which the court held that pregnancy occurred not at the time of conception, but when a fertilised egg became implanted in the womb.

46. National Health Service (General Medical Services Contracts) (Scotland) Regulations 2004 (provision of drugs, medicines and appliances for immediate treatment or personal administration) – note that this provision has been repealed and replaced by paragraph 45 of Schedule 6 to the National Health Service (General Medical Services Contracts) (Scotland) Regulations 2018, but the HMR still refer to the 2004 Regulations.

An entry must be a written or computerised record kept for the purpose in respect of each sale or supply. The entry must be made on the day the sale or supply takes place or, if that is not reasonably practicable, on the following day. In retail pharmacies, the records are made in what is usually referred to as a *prescription register*.

Chapter 6 deals with the requirement for record-keeping in relation to wholesale transactions involving POMs.

Particulars of prescriptions to be recorded

The particulars to be recorded in the case of a sale or supply of a POM in pursuance of a prescription given by an appropriate practitioner are:

a. the date on which the POM was sold or supplied;
b. the name, quantity and, except where it is apparent from the name, the pharmaceutical form and strength of the POM sold or supplied;
c. the name and address of the person giving the prescription;
d. the name and address of the person for whom the POM was prescribed;
e. the date on the prescription; and
f. in relation to an emergency sale or supply under HMR Reg.224 (see below), the date on which the prescription relating to that sale or supply is received.

For second and subsequent supplies made on a repeat prescription it is sufficient to record the date of supply and a reference to the entry in the register relating to the first supply.

Additional particulars must be recorded in the case of emergency supplies to patients (see below).

Preservation of pharmacy records, CD prescriptions and private prescriptions

The POM record must be preserved by the person lawfully conducting the retail pharmacy business for a period of two years from the date of the last entry in the record. Unless it is a health prescription or a prescription for a Schedule 1, 2 or 3 controlled drug, a prescription must be retained for two years from the date on which the POM was sold or supplied, or, for a repeat prescription, the date on which the medicine was supplied for the last time. Where a sale of a POM is by way of wholesale dealing, the order or invoice relating to the sale (or a copy of it) must be retained by the person lawfully conducting the retail pharmacy business who makes the sale for two years from the date on which the POM was sold or supplied.

Even if a photograph of a private prescription on a patient's mobile phone would otherwise be valid (see above) it cannot be dispensed because the prescription is not in a form that can be retained.

Labelling of dispensed medicines

See **Chapter 18**.

Exemptions from the need for a prescription

Exemption for supplies by doctors, dentists or other healthcare professionals to their patients

The restrictions on retail sale of medicinal products do not apply (HMR Reg.223) to the:

1. sale or supply of a Prescription Only Medicine by a doctor or dentist to their patient;
2. sale, offer for sale, or supply of medicines subject to general sale and Pharmacy medicines, to a patient or a person under whose care such a patient is;
3. sale, offer for sale, or supply of medicines subject to general sale and Pharmacy medicines in the course of the business of a hospital or health centre, in the circumstances described in **Chapter 9**.

The meaning of *by a doctor or dentist to a patient of his* under the Medicines Act 1968 was tested in the unreported case of *Pharmaceutical Society v Wright* in 1981 (see **Box 12.6**).

Box 12.6: The meaning of "to a patient of [that doctor or dentist]"

Pharmaceutical Society v Wright (1981)

The Medicines Act said that no person could sell a POM product except in accordance with a prescription given by an appropriate practitioner. However, this provision did not apply to the sale or supply of a medicinal product to a patient of theirs by a doctor or dentist who is an appropriate practitioner. The equivalent exemption is now in HMR Reg.223 which says that HMR Reg.214 does not apply to the sale or supply of a POM by a doctor or dentist to a patient of that doctor or dentist.

Once a week, Dr Wright ran a slimming clinic and those attending were given a medicinal product which was on the POM list. Many of the persons attending the clinic were patients of other doctors in the town and only attended the clinic, which was supervised by a nurse, for slimming purposes. The issue turned upon whether or not there was a doctor-patient relationship between the attendees and Dr Wright.

Lord Justice Donaldson referred described the concept of a doctor/patient relationship as "... elastic, not to say woolly". In dismissing the appeal brought by the Pharmaceutical Society (which only became 'Royal' in 1988), Lord Donaldson, who sat with Mr Justice Bingham, said that it was for the Society to prove there was no doctor/patient relationship not for Dr Wright to prove there was one.

Mr Justice Bingham, agreed with Lord Justice Donaldson and added:

"... if a doctor acting as such, treats or gives advice to a person and assumes responsibility for that treatment or advice, that person may very well be his patient ... in determining whether the relationship does exist it is not ... of primary importance whether the person is a patient of another doctor as well nor whether the treatment or advice is given by the doctor's staff under his supervision rather than the doctor himself. Nor ... whether the relationship is a short-lived or long-lived. Nor ... need it be of primary importance whether the doctor takes less care in giving the advice or treatment than he should."

The exemption does not require the supply to be made personally by a doctor, dentist or other healthcare professional; instead, the supply may be made by someone, such as an employee, acting on behalf of the doctor, dentist or other healthcare professional.[47] The meaning of supply is considered further in **Chapters 3** and **11**.

Exemptions for hospitals, clinics and similar settings

The exemption for hospitals, clinics and similar settings can be found in **Chapters 9** and **13**.

Exemptions for persons conducting retail pharmacy businesses

The meaning of *lawfully conducting a retail pharmacy business* is explained in **Chapter 7**. In Part 12 of the HMR, there are specific exemptions for persons lawfully conducting retail pharmacy businesses from the conditions or restrictions on the retail sale and supply of POMs. Exemptions from control for other persons are to be found in **Chapter 13**.

In an emergency, a person lawfully conducting a retail pharmacy business may sell or supply a POM if and so long as certain conditions are satisfied. There are two kinds of emergency supply (those made at the request of a prescriber, and those made at the request of a patient) and different conditions apply to each of them.

Exemption for emergency supply at the request of a prescriber

HMR Reg.224 describes the conditions for an emergency sale at the request of a relevant prescriber, a *relevant prescriber* is defined in HMR Reg.213 as any of the following:

- a doctor;
- a dentist;
- a supplementary prescriber;
- a nurse independent prescriber;
- a pharmacist independent prescriber;
- a community practitioner nurse prescriber;
- a physiotherapist independent prescriber;
- a podiatrist independent prescriber;
- a therapeutic radiographer independent prescriber;
- a paramedic independent prescriber;
- an optometrist independent prescriber;
- an approved country health professional.

The conditions that apply for emergency supply made at the request of a relevant prescriber are that:

1. the pharmacist by or under whose supervision the POM is to be sold or supplied is satisfied that the sale or supply has been requested by a relevant prescriber (see above) who by reason of an emergency is unable to provide a prescription immediately;

47. *R v Family Health Services Appeal Authority, ex parte Elmfield Drugs Limited* [1999] 46 B.M.L.R. 191.

2. the relevant prescriber has undertaken to provide the person lawfully conducting the retail pharmacy business with a prescription within the period of 72 hours beginning with the sale or supply;
3. the POM is sold or supplied in accordance with the directions of the relevant prescriber;
4. the POM is not a controlled drug specified in Schedule 1, 2 or 3 of the relevant Regulations other than a POM that consists of or contains phenobarbital or phenobarbital sodium, and is sold or supplied for use in the treatment of epilepsy (note that, in the case of an approved country health professional, no Schedule 1, 2 or 3 controlled drugs may be ordered, so such prescribers may not order phenobarbital or its salts);
5. an entry is made in the prescription register (see above) on the day of the sale or supply, or, if that is not reasonably practicable, on the day following that day, stating,
6. the date on which the POM was sold or supplied,
7. the name, quantity and, except where it is apparent from the name, the pharmaceutical form and strength of the POM sold or supplied,
8. the name and address of the person giving the prescription,
9. the name and address of the person for whom the POM was prescribed,
10. the date on the prescription (this may be entered on the day that the prescription is received), and
11. the date on which the prescription relating to that sale or supply is received (this may be entered on the day that the prescription is received).

Exemption for emergency supply at the request of a patient

The conditions that apply for an emergency supply made at the request of a patient set out in HMR Reg.225 are:

1. that the pharmacist by or under whose supervision the POM is to be sold or supplied has interviewed the person requesting it and is satisfied,
    a. that there is an immediate need for the POM to be sold or supplied and that it is impracticable in the circumstances to obtain a prescription without undue delay,
    b. that treatment with the POM has on a previous occasion been prescribed by a relevant prescriber for the person requesting it, and
    c. as to the dose which in the circumstances it would be appropriate for that person to take;
2. that the quantity of the product sold or supplied, for a POM shown in column A of table 12.2, does not exceed that shown in column B of the table for that POM;
3. that the POM,
    a. does not consist of or contain a substance specified in **Box 12.7**,
    b. is not a controlled drug specified in Schedule 1, 2 or 3 of the relevant Regulations other than a POM that consists of or contains phenobarbital or phenobarbital sodium, and is sold or supplied for use in the treatment of epilepsy [N.B. in the case of the patient of an EEA prescriber, no Schedule 1, 2 or 3 controlled drugs

may be ordered, so the patients of such prescribers may not order phenobarbital or its salts];

4. that an entry is made in the prescription register (see above) on the day of the sale or supply, or, if that is not reasonably practicable, on the day following that day, stating:
    a. the date on which the POM was sold or supplied,
    b. the name, quantity and, except where it is apparent from the name, the pharmaceutical form and strength of the POM sold or supplied,
    c. the name and address of the person requiring the POM, and
    d. the nature of the emergency;
5. that the inner or outer packaging of the POM is labelled to show:
    a. the date on which the POM is sold or supplied,
    b. the name, quantity and (unless apparent from the name) the pharmaceutical strength of the POM,
    c. the name of the person requesting the POM,
    d. the name and address of the registered pharmacy from which the POM is sold or supplied, and
    e. the words "Emergency Supply".

Table 12.2: *Maximum quantities that may be sold or supplied for emergency supply at the request of a patient*

Column A: description	Column B: maximum quantity
A POM that: (a) is a preparation of insulin, an aerosol (a product that is dispersed from its container by a propellant gas or liquid) for the relief of asthma, an ointment or cream, and (b) has been made up for sale in a package elsewhere than at the place of sale or supply	The smallest pack that the pharmacist has available for sale or supply
An oral contraceptive	A quantity sufficient for a full treatment cycle
An antibiotic for oral administration in liquid form	The smallest quantity that will provide a full course of treatment
A controlled drug within the meaning of Schedule 4 or 5 of the Misuse of Drugs Regulations 2001 or phenobarbital for the treatment of epilepsy	A quantity for five days of treatment
Any other POM	A quantity for 30 days of treatment

Box 12.7 lists the substances that may not be sold or supplied by a pharmacist without a prescription in response to a request for an emergency supply from a patient.

Box 12.7: Substances that may not be sold or supplied by a pharmacist without a prescription in response to a request for an emergency supply from a patient

- Ammonium bromide.
- Calcium bromide.
- Calcium bromidolactobionate.
- Embutramide.
- Fencamfamin hydrochloride.
- Fluanisone.
- Hexobarbitone [hexobarbital].
- Hexobarbitone sodium [hexobarbital sodium].
- Hydrobromic acid.
- Meclofenoxate hydrochloride.
- Methohexital sodium.
- Pemoline.
- Piracetam.
- Potassium bromide.
- Prolintane hydrochloride.
- Sodium bromide.
- Strychnine hydrochloride.
- Tacrine hydrochloride.
- Thiopental sodium.

Urgent supplies without prescription under NHS terms of service

In England, the NHS terms of service[48] permit a pharmacy to provide a drug or appliance (other than a scheduled drug or controlled drug other than one in Schedule 4 or 5 to the Misuse of Drugs Regulations 2001) before a prescription form is received, if the pharmacy is requested to do so by a prescriber in a case of urgency. The prescriber must undertake to give a prescription form or transmit an electronic prescription within 72 hours of the request. The Scottish NHS terms of service[49] permit a supply in a case of urgency where a prescriber, personally known to a pharmacist, requests that pharmacist to dispense a drug or appliance. The drug or appliance is subject to the same exclusions as in England and the same undertaking to provide a prescription within 72 hours. The Welsh NHS terms of service contain a very similar provision to the Scottish terms of service except that the prescriber does not have to be personally known to the pharmacist.[50]

---

48. Paragraph 6 of Schedule 4 to the National Health Service (Pharmaceutical and Local Pharmaceutical Services) Regulations 2013.
49. Paragraph 23 of Schedule 1 to the National Health Service (Pharmaceutical Services) (Scotland) Regulations 2009.
50. Paragraph 7 of Schedule 5 to the National Health Service (Pharmaceutical Services) (Wales) Regulations 2020.

Emergency supply by a pharmacist: pandemic diseases

The restrictions on the sale or supply of a POM do not apply in certain circumstances related to pandemic diseases (HMR Reg.226). The conditions are that the sale or supply of the POM is made by a person lawfully conducting a retail pharmacy business and:

1. the supply is made while a disease is, or in anticipation of a disease being imminently, pandemic and a serious risk, or potentially a serious risk, to human health;
2. the pharmacist by or under whose supervision the POM is to be sold or supplied is satisfied:
   a. that treatment with the POM has on a previous occasion been prescribed by a relevant prescriber for the person to be treated with it, and
   b. as to the dose which in the circumstances it would be appropriate for that person to take.

Exemption for supply in the event or anticipation of pandemic disease

The restrictions on the sale or supply of a POM (or a Pharmacy medicine or a medicine subject to general sale, **Chapters 11** and **10**) do not apply in certain circumstances related to pandemic diseases (HMR Reg.247). The conditions are that the supply:

1. is made while a disease is, or in anticipation of a disease being imminently, pandemic and a serious risk, or potentially a serious risk, to human health;
2. is in accordance with a protocol that:
   a. is approved by the ministers or an NHS body,
   b. specifies how the medicinal product is to be used for the prevention of or as a treatment for the disease, and
   c. contains requirements as to the recording of the name of the person who supplies the product to the person to be treated (*the patient*) or to a person acting on the patient's behalf, and evidence that the product was supplied to the patient or to a person acting on the patient's behalf.

Exemptions from requirements for Prescription Only Medicines for certain persons, including persons who supply under Patient Group Directions

These exemptions are covered in **Chapter 13**.

Serious shortage protocols

The requirement that POMs may be sold or supplied from registered pharmacy premises only in accordance with a prescription does not apply where a sale or supply has been made in accordance with a serious shortage protocol (SSP) issued by a Minister after forming the opinion that the United Kingdom or any part of it is experiencing or may experience a serious shortage of a POM or POMs of a specified description, provided that the following conditions are met (regulation 226A of the HMR).

SSPs permit the sale or supply by or under the supervision of a pharmacist:

i. of a different strength, quantity or pharmaceutical form of the POM to the strength, quantity or form prescribed; or
ii. of a different POM to the one prescribed.

If a different POM is to be sold or supplied, this may include the supply of a generic version of the POM prescribed or a different generic medicine; or a similar biological medicinal product may be sold or supplied to one that has been prescribed; or a POM may be sold or supplied that has a similar therapeutic effect to the one prescribed.

The SSP exemption is subject to the following conditions:

- the requirements of the SSP must be followed;
- the sale or supply is by or under the supervision of a pharmacist who is of the opinion, in the exercise of his or her professional skill and judgement that the substitution was reasonable and appropriate. The proposal to amend the HMR to enable a pharmacist to authorise a pharmacy technician to carry out supervision of certain sales or supplies (see **Chapter 11**) does not extend to the supervision of a sale or supply under an SSP.

If an SSP has been issued, a pharmacist is not obliged to sell or supply pursuant to it. If a pharmacist purports to supply in accordance with it but fails to meet a condition, then the pharmacist may commit an offence.

The amendment to the HMR to enable the issue of SSPs was challenged in *The Queen (on the application of The Good Law Project) v Secretary of State for Health and Social Care*.[51] The Good Law Project argued that the Secretary of State had no legal power to make the amendment permitting supplies under SSPs; and that supplying a different medicinal product to the one prescribed would be unlawful because section 64 of the Medicines Act 1968 prohibits supplying a medicinal product that is not of the nature or quality demanded (see **Chapter 24**). The Court of Appeal rejected the challenge and refused permission to apply for judicial review. Amongst other things, the Court rejected the argument that supplying in accordance with a SSP would breach the prohibition on supplying a POM otherwise than in accordance with a prescription: the Court held that although a prescription must exist in order for a supply to be made in accordance with a SSP, a supply of an alternative product will be made in accordance with the SSP (provided the applicable conditions are satisfied) and not in pursuance of a prescription that would involve a breach of section 64 of the Medicines Act.

51. [2019] EWCA (Civ) 1211. The ruling is not a binding precedent because the hearing was an application for permission to apply for judicial review, not a full hearing.

SUMMARY

- Certain medicines are POMs by description or class, including controlled drugs (unless exempted by virtue of a marketing authorisation), parenteral products and cyanogenic substances.
- Subject to exemptions, a POM may not be sold or supplied except in accordance with a prescription.
- Products consisting of or containing aloxiprin, aspirin or paracetamol are exempt from POM control if the strength, quantity per pack, and quantity of the product sold or supplied to a person at any one time, does not exceed stated limits.
- Products consisting of or containing pseudoephedrine salts or ephedrine base or salts that are POM are exempt from POM control, if certain conditions are met.
- The supply of a POM in a manufacturer's original pack is generally considered desirable (and, in the case of valproate products, mandatory) and the HMR treats the supply of a POM in a different quantity to the quantity on the prescription as being in accordance with that prescription, subject to certain limitations.
- Doctors, dentists and other healthcare professionals may supply POMs to their patients.
- In the HMR doctors, dentists, supplementary prescribers, nurse independent prescribers and pharmacist independent prescribers are designated as appropriate practitioners in relation to any POM. Community practitioner nurse prescribers, optometrist independent prescribers, physiotherapist independent prescribers, podiatrist independent prescribers, therapeutic radiographer independent prescribers, paramedic independent prescribers and approved country health professionals are appropriate practitioners in relation to a slightly more restricted range of POMs.
- The requirement for supervision is varied when a collection and delivery arrangement is in place, or where a pandemic situation exists.
- If a POM is sold or supplied by a person other than a pharmacist, the transaction must be supervised by a pharmacist. The NHS terms of service require medicines to be supplied under the direct supervision of a pharmacist, but the meaning of *direct supervision* is uncertain.
- Certain POMs may be administered parenterally for the purpose of saving life in an emergency, for example adrenaline (epinephrine) injection.
- Detailed prescription requirements are laid down and these differ for prescriptions written by a UK and approved country health professional. There are other provisions for prescriptions written by UK practitioners for dispensing in an approved country.
- Detailed record keeping requirements are imposed for POMs, although there are some exemptions (e.g. for those on a health prescription or oral contraceptives).
- The HMR allow for an emergency supply of a POM to be made at the request of a doctor, dentist, supplementary prescriber, nurse independent prescriber, pharmacist independent prescriber, community practitioner nurse prescriber, optometrist independent prescriber, physiotherapist independent prescriber, podiatrist independent prescriber, therapeutic radiographer independent prescriber, paramedic independent prescriber or an approved country health professional. The HMR describe the conditions for such a supply to be made, for example including the exclusion of many controlled drugs from these arrangements.
- The HMR allow for an emergency supply of a POM to be made at the request of a patient. The HMR describe the conditions for such a supply to be made, for example including the exclusion of many controlled drugs from these arrangements and the removal of certain

SUMMARY (cont.)

conditions in the case of a declared pandemic. Detailed quantity, labelling and record conditions apply.

- NHS terms of service permit certain supplies to be made without a prescription in cases of urgency if conditions are met.
- The restrictions on the sale or supply of a POM (or Pharmacy medicine or GSL, **Chapters 11** and **10**) do not apply in certain circumstances related to pandemic diseases.
- Under certain conditions, POMs may be supplied under Patient Group Directions (see **Chapter 13**).
- The Regulations allow for the mixing of medicines in certain circumstances.

FURTHER READING

- Human Medicines Regulations (2012) SI 2012 No. 1916, *Explanatory memorandum*: **http://www.legislation.gov.uk/uksi/2012/1916/pdfs/uksiem_20121916_en.pdf** (accessed 31 December 2024).
- Royal Pharmaceutical Society (member access only; lists legal classifications of medicines and further practice guidance): **http://www.rpharms.com**.
- Royal Pharmaceutical Society (published annually). *Medicines, Ethics and Practice*. London: Royal Pharmaceutical Society (includes practice guidance on many of the topics in this chapter; free to members).

CHAPTER 13

Human medicines: exemptions from controls

It will be apparent to readers that the manufacture, sale and supply of medicines, whether they are subject to general sale, Pharmacy medicines or Prescription Only Medicines, are subject to a range of regulatory restrictions. Many of the restrictions are subject to exemptions that are brought together in this chapter, but the number and type of exemptions is so wide that it is not practicable to include every exemption here; some exemptions are covered in the relevant chapters.

Introduction

The Human Medicines Regulations 2012 (HMR) specify exemptions for certain classes of person from the conditions or restrictions on retail sale and/or supply which apply to medicines subject to general sale (HMR Reg.221), Pharmacy medicines (HMR Reg.220) and Prescription Only Medicines (POMs) (HMR Reg.214). Exemption from the restriction on the administration of POMs for parenteral use is also conferred on certain persons (HMR Reg.214). There are also some continuing exemptions that are defined in earlier legislation.[1] The classes of person and the body exempted, the medicinal products to which the exemptions apply and the conditions (if any) which attach to the retail sale, supply or administration by these exempted persons are described in this chapter.

Exemption for supplies by doctors, dentists or other healthcare professionals to their patients

See **Chapter 12**.

Exemptions for midwives

Exemptions for midwives are set out below and see also **Chapter 12**.

Patient Group Directions

A Patient Group Direction (PGD) is a written direction which allows the sale or supply or administration of a description or class of medicines to patients without having to meet the usual requirements for the sale or supply of medicinal products subject to

1. Medicines (Pharmacy and General Sale – Exemption) Order 1980.

general sale, of Pharmacy medicines or of POMs (as applicable) (HMR Reg.213). MHRA guidance[2] states that they take a significant amount of time and resource to develop and implement and should be used only where there is an advantage for the patient without compromising patient safety. The MHRA further advises that PGDs should be constructed by a multidisciplinary group including a doctor, a pharmacist and a representative of any professional group expected to supply the medicines under the PGD.

PGDs have been used effectively within the NHS in a number of clinical areas including immunisation by vaccination such as the administration of the seasonal influenza vaccination from community pharmacies, and in relation to emergency preparedness, resilience and response[3] (for example, to enable the initial supply of ciprofloxacin to individuals with known or suspected exposure to anthrax). Current examples of where PGDs are used for the private (i.e. non-NHS) supply of medication include vaccines for shingles, oral cholera and rabies, and other uses such as the supply of oral contraception, treatment of fungal skin infections and the supply of fusidic acid for impetigo. PGDs have also been used within private healthcare for the supply of medication not available via the NHS. For example, in 2007 before Viagra was available on the NHS, the supply of sildenafil without prescription for erectile dysfunction was made possible via a PGD.[4]

There are different provisions for the supply under a PGD, according to who authorises the supply; these appear in HMR Regs.229 to 234 together with Schedule 16 to the Regulations.

Box 13.1 shows the provisions that apply for all PGDs and the classes of individuals by whom supplies may be made. Note that different types of PGDs allow for sale, supply or administration, and the details in **Box 13.1** reflect these different arrangements.

Box 13.1: Provisions that must be in place for all PGDs and classes of individuals by whom supplies may be made

The following provisions must be in place for all PGDs:

- The PGD must be in effect at the time at which the medicinal product is sold, supplied or administered (as the case may be for that particular PGD).
- The PGD must contain the particulars specified in Part 1 of Schedule 16 (see Appendix 3).
- The product must be sold or supplied (as the case may be for that particular PGD) for the purpose of being supplied or administered (as the case may be) to a person in accordance with a PGD.
- The individual who sells or supplies or (as the case may be) administers the product is one of the classes of individual permitted to do so (as specified in Part 4 of Schedule 16 – see Appendix 3).

---

2. MHRA Guidance. Patient group directions: who can use them: https://www.gov.uk/government/publications/patient-group-directions-pgds/patient-group-directions-who-can-use-them (accessed 31 December 2024).
3. For further details see: https://www.england.nhs.uk/ourwork/eprr/hm/ (accessed 31 December 2024).
4. Boots launches private PGD service to supply Viagra, *The Pharmaceutical Journal*, Feb 2007, Vol 278, p197.

Box 13.1: Provisions that must be in place for all PGDs and classes of individuals by whom supplies may be made (cont.)

- When the product is supplied or (as the case may be) administered, a UK marketing authorisation, certificate of registration or traditional herbal registration is in force in relation to it.

The following groups may make supplies under a PGD (HMR Schedule 16, Part 4):

- pharmacists;
- registered chiropodists and podiatrists;
- registered dental hygienists;
- registered dental therapists;
- registered dietitians;
- registered midwives;
- registered nurses;
- registered occupational therapists;
- registered optometrists;
- registered orthoptists;
- registered orthotists and prosthetists;
- registered paramedics;
- registered pharmacy technicians;
- registered physiotherapists;
- registered radiographers;
- registered speech and language therapists.

Supply under a Patient Group Direction by NHS bodies and local authorities

The usual restrictions on sale or supply of medicines subject to general sale, Pharmacy medicines and POMs do not apply (HMR Reg.229) to the supply of any such medicine by any of the organisations listed in **Box 13.2**, if the product is supplied for the purpose of being administered to a person in accordance with the written directions of a doctor, dentist, nurse independent prescriber, optometrist independent prescriber, physiotherapist independent prescriber, podiatrist independent prescriber, therapeutic radiographer independent prescriber, paramedic independent prescriber or pharmacist independent prescriber relating to that person, regardless of whether the directions comply with HMR Reg.217 (requirements for prescriptions).

Also, the usual restrictions on sale or supply of medicines subject to general sale, Pharmacy medicines and POMs do not apply to the supply of any such medicine, by any of the organisations listed in **Box 13.2**, subject to the following conditions:

1. the requirements set out in **Box 13.1** are met;
2. the PGD relates to the supply of a description or class of medicinal product by the person by whom the medicinal product is supplied and has effect at the time at which it is supplied;
3. the PGD is signed on behalf of the relevant body named above (the HMR specify the classes of person who may act as signatory – see Appendix 3 for details), and with whom an arrangement is made;

the individual who supplies the product is designated in writing, on behalf of the authorising person, for the purpose of the supply or administration of products under the PGD.

Box 13.2: Persons permitted to supply medicines under a PGD, in accordance with HMR Reg.229

These include:

1. the Common Services Agency;
2. a health authority or special health authority;
3. an NHS trust;
4. an NHS foundation trust;
5. a local authority in the exercise of public health functions (within the meaning of the National Health Service Act 2006);
6. the United Kingdom Health Security Agency;
7. a person who is not a doctor, a dentist or a person lawfully conducting a retail pharmacy business where the person supplies a product pursuant to an arrangement with an integrated care board, NHS England or one of the persons specified in paragraphs 1-6.[5]

5. Shortly before going to press, the Prime Minister announced that NHS England would be abolished as a separate body, and its functions will be exercised by the Department of Health and Social Care.

Supply under a Patient Group Direction to assist doctors or dentists

The restrictions on the sale, supply or administration of medicines subject to general sale, Pharmacy medicines and POMs do not apply where an individual, acting in accordance with a PGD, supplies or administers the product to assist a doctor in the provision of NHS primary medical services or a dentist in the provision of NHS primary dental services, subject to certain conditions (HMR Reg.230):

1. the requirements set out in **Box 13.1** are met;
2. the PGD relates to the supply or (as the case may be) administration of a description or class of medicinal product in order to assist the doctor or dentist in providing the services (whether or not it relates to such supply in order to assist any other doctor or dentist);
3. the PGD is signed by the doctor or dentist, or where it also relates to supply or administration to assist one or more other doctors or dentists, by one of those doctors or dentists;
4. that the PGD is signed:
   a. in the case of NHS primary medical services, or NHS primary dental services in England or Wales, on behalf of the health authority, local authority or NHS England with which a contract or agreement for the provision of those services has been made or which provides those services,
   b. in the case of dental services in Scotland under the National Health Service (Scotland) Act 1978, on behalf of the health authority with which an arrangement for the provision of those services has been made, and
   c. in the case of personal dental services provided under a pilot scheme in Scotland, on behalf of the health authority which is a party to the pilot scheme;
5. the individual supplying the product is designated in writing for the purpose of the supply or administration of medicinal products under the PGD by the doctor or dentist, or where it also relates to supply, to assist one or more other doctors or dentists by one of those doctors or dentists.

Supply under a Patient Group Direction by independent hospitals etc.

HMR Reg.231 relates to an independent hospital, an independent clinic or an independent medical agency. It removes the restrictions on the sale, supply or administration of medicinal products, in accordance with the following conditions:

1. if in England, the registered provider at the hospital, clinic or agency is registered with the Care Quality Commission in compliance with section 10 of the Health and Social Care Act 2008 in respect of one or more of the following regulated activities (as set out in section 8 of that Act):
   a. treatment of disease, disorder or injury by or under the supervision of a health care proessional, or a team which includes a health care professional, or a social worker, or a team which includes a social worker, where the treatment is for a mental disorder. For the purpose of such PGDs, the definition of *health care professional* includes medical practitioners, dental practitioners, nurses, paramedics and certain others,[6] but the definition excludes pharmacy professionals,
   b. assessment or medical treatment of persons detained under the Mental Health Act 1983,
   c. surgical procedures,
   d. diagnostic and screening procedures,
   e. maternity and midwifery services, and
   f. family planning,

   (this requirement does not apply to independent hospitals, clinics or medical agencies in Scotland or Wales);
2. the requirements set out in **Box 13.1** are met;
3. that the PGD relates to the sale or supply or (as the case may be) administration of a description or class of medicinal product by the person by whom the medicinal product is sold or supplied or administered;
4. that the PGD is signed by or on behalf of the registered provider, and, if there is a relevant manager for the independent hospital, clinic or medical agency, or nursing home, by that manager;
5. that the individual who sells or supplies or (as the case may be) administers the product is designated in writing for the purpose of the sale or supply or (as the case may be) administration of products under the PGD by or on behalf of the registered provider, or, if there is a relevant manager for the independent hospital, clinic or medical agency, or nursing home, by that manager.

---

6. The full list of *health care professionals* in paragraph 4(4) of Schedule 1 to the Health and Social Care Act 2008 (Regulated Activities) Regulations 2014 is: medical practitioners, dental practitioners, dental hygienists, dental therapists, dental nurses, dental technicians, orthodontic therapists, nurses, midwives, biomedical scientists, clinical scientists, operating department practitioners, paramedics, and radiographers and associates. "Associate" means a person registered under the Anaesthesia Associates and Physician Associates Order 2024.

Supply under a Patient Group Direction by dental practices and clinics: England and Wales

HMR Reg.232 provides that the restrictions on the sale or supply, or administration, of a medicinal product do not apply in a dental practice or dental clinic:

1. in England, in respect of which the registered provider is registered with the Care Quality Commission in compliance with section 10 of the Health and Social Care Act 2008 in respect of the treatment of disease, disorder or injury, and/or diagnostic and screening procedures;
2. in Wales, in which dental services are provided by private dentists and those dentists are registered with Healthcare Inspectorate Wales in accordance with the Regulations,[7] in relation to the services provided by those dentists.

The following conditions must be met:

1. the requirements set out in **Box 13.1** are met;
2. the PGD relates to the sale or supply or (as the case may be) administration of a description or class of medicinal product by the person by whom the medicinal product is sold or supplied or administered;
3. that the PGD is signed:
   a. in England by or on behalf of the registered provider, and, if there is a relevant manager for the practice or clinic, by that manager;
   b. in Wales by the private dentist who is treating the person, and, if there is a manager for the practice or clinic, by that manager;
4. the individual who sells or supplies or (as the case may be) administers the product is designated in writing for the purpose of the sale or supply or (as the case may be) administration of products under the PGD:
   a. in England, by or on behalf of the registered provider or, if there is a relevant manager for the practice or clinic, by that manager, or
   b. in Wales, by the private dentist who is treating the person.

In relation to Wales, in this Regulation *manager* means the person who carries on the dental practice or dental clinic, or, if there is no such person, a person who manages the practice or clinic.

Supply under a Patient Group Direction by a person conducting a retail pharmacy business

Under HMR Reg 233, the restrictions on retail sale, supply or administration of POMs do not apply to the sale, supply or administration of any such medicine by a person lawfully conducting a retail pharmacy business where the person sells, supplies or (as the case may be) administers the POM in accordance with a PGD pursuant to an arrangement for the supply or administration of POMs with one of the following bodies (the relevant body):

---

7. Registration of Private Dentistry (Wales) Regulations 2017.

1. the Common Services Agency, a health authority or special health authority, an NHS trust, an NHS foundation trust, an integrated care board, NHS England, a local authority in the exercise of public health functions (within the meaning of the National Health Service Act 2006) or the UK Health Security Agency; a police force or a prison service;
2. His Majesty's forces; or
3. an authority or person carrying on the business of an independent hospital, an independent clinic or an independent medical agency. HMR Reg.213 defines "independent medical agency" in relation to England as "an undertaking (not being an independent hospital) which consists of or includes the provision of services by medical practitioners". As stated above, the independent medical agency must be registered with the Care Quality Commission.

The PGD must:

1. meet the requirements set out in **Box 13.1**;
2. relate to the sale or supply or (as the case may be) administration of a description or class of medicinal product by the person lawfully conducting a retail pharmacy business who sells or supplies or (as the case may be) administers the POM;
3. be signed on behalf of the body with which the arrangement is made (the HMR specify the classes of person who may act as signatory – see Appendix 3 for details):
   a. in relation to a police force, in addition to the individual specified in Schedule 16 (Part 3), the PGD also needs to be signed by a doctor who is not employed or engaged by, and does not provide services under arrangements made with, any police force,
   b. in relation to an authority or person carrying on the business of an independent hospital, an independent clinic or an independent medical agency, in addition to a signature from the relevant provider, if there is a relevant manager for the establishment or agency in question, the PGD must be signed by that manager;
4. where the POM is administered by the person lawfully conducting a retail pharmacy business, that person is designated in writing for the purpose of the administration of medicinal products under the PGD on behalf of the body with which an arrangement has been made.

N.B. As far as pharmacies are concerned, there is no provision in the HMR that allows PGDs to be used for the supply or administration of Pharmacy medicines and medicines subject to general sale; however, such supplies are permitted in order to assist a doctor or dentist with the provision of NHS services (HMR Reg.230).

Supply under a Patient Group Direction to assist the police, etc.

HMR Reg.234 provides that the restrictions on the supply, or administration of a medicinal product, do not apply if the following conditions are met:

1. the individual supplies or (as the case may be) administers the product to assist the provision of healthcare by, on behalf of, or under arrangements made by, one of the following bodies (*the relevant body*)
   a. a police force,

   b. a prison service,
   c. His Majesty's Forces, or
   d. a contractor carrying out helicopter search and rescue operations on behalf of the Maritime and Coastguard Agency;
2. the requirements set out in **Box 13.1** are met;
3. the PGD relates to the supply or (as the case may be) the administration of a description or class of medicinal product to assist the provision of healthcare by, on behalf of, or under arrangements made by, the relevant body;
4. the PGD is signed on behalf of the relevant body (the HMR specify the classes of person who may act as signatory – see Appendix 3 for details), and with whom an arrangement is made;
5. Part 3 of Schedule 16 to the HMR designates the person by whom, or on whose behalf, the PGD must be signed. Typically, this is the Chief Constable. In addition, the PGD needs to be signed by a doctor who is not employed or engaged by, and does not provide services under arrangements made with, any police force;
6. the individual who supplies the product is designated in writing by or on behalf of the relevant body for the purpose of the supply or (as the case may be) the administration of medicinal products under the PGD.

Other exemptions for sale, supply or administration by certain persons

Schedule 17 is divided into five parts, which cover many exemptions from restrictions:

- *Part 1*: sale and supply of POMs;
- *Part 2*: supply of POMs;
- *Part 3*: administration of POMs;
- *Part 4*: for certain persons who sell, supply or offer for sale or supply certain P or medicinal products on a general sale list (GSL);
- *Part 5*: for certain persons who supply certain P or GSL medicinal products.

Note: Medicinal products that are subject to general sale by virtue of their marketing authorisations will not usually be on a general sale list (GSL) but when the HMR are amended to widen the scope of hub and spoke dispensing, there will probably be no practical difference between GSL medicines and medicines subject to general sale (see **Chapter 10**).

Only some of these exemptions are discussed below. Where reference is made to restrictions on sale or supply, these are the restrictions that require medicines not subject to general sale to be sold or supplied by a pharmacist or under the supervision of a pharmacist and only from pharmacy premises. In the case of POMs, the restrictions also include the prohibition on supplying except in accordance with a prescription. These restrictions are in HMR Regs.214 and 220 in particular and are covered in more detail in **Chapters 11** and **12**.

Registered nurses

Community practitioner nurse prescribers may prescribe, but not sell or supply, a limited list of POMs (HMR Sch. 13).

Registered nurses may also supply or administer POMs, Pharmacy medicines and GSL products under PGDs (HMR Sch. 16).

Registered dental therapists and registered dental hygienists

Dental therapists or *dental hygienists* means a person who is registered under that title in the dental care professionals register.[8]

The restrictions on retail supply or sale do not apply to the sale or supply (or offer for sale or supply) of certain medicinal products by registered dental therapists and registered dental hygienists who are qualified to use the medicines specified, of all GSL and Pharmacy medicines, along with certain POMs which are not for parenteral administration, provided they are only in the course of their professional practice (HMR Sch. 17, Part 2(13) and Part 4(14)).

The POMs to which this exemption applies are:

- lidocaine 15%, cetrimide 0.15% oromucosal spray;
- lidocaine 2.5% and prilocaine 2.5% periodontal gel;
- minocycline 2% periodontal gel;
- nystatin oral suspension;
- sodium fluoride 0.619% (2800 ppm fluoride) dental paste;
- sodium fluoride 1.1% (5000 ppm) dental paste;
- sodium fluoride varnish, 50 mg/mL (2.26%) dental suspension (containing 22600 ppm fluoride).

Registered dental therapists and registered dental hygienists may administer the following POMs for parenteral administration only in the course of their professional practice (HMR Sch. 17 Part 3(12)):

- articaine hydrochloride 4% with 1:100,000 adrenaline;
- articaine hydrochloride 4% with 1:200,000 adrenaline;
- lidocaine 2% with 1:80,000 adrenaline;
- mepivacaine hydrochloride 3%;
- prilocaine 3% with felypressin 0.54 microgram/mL.

Registered optometrists

Registered optometrist means a person whose name is entered in the Register of Optometrists.[9]

The requirement in HMR Reg.214 to supply POMs in accordance with a prescription does not apply to the sale or supply (or offer for sale or supply) of the following POMs which are not for parenteral administration:[10]

a. eye drops which are POMs by reason only that they contain not more 0.5% chloramphenicol, or
b. eye ointments and are POMs by reason only that they contain not more than 1% chloramphenicol, or

8. The *dental care professionals register* means the register established and maintained under section 36B of the Dentists Act 1984.
9. Maintained under the Opticians Act 1989.
10. HMR Reg.235(1) and Part 1 of Schedule 17.

c. items which are POMs by reason only that they contain cyclopentolate hydrochloride, fusidic acid or tropicamide.

The restriction in HMR Reg.220 on selling or supplying medicines that are not subject to general sale only on registered pharmacy premises with pharmacist supervision does not apply to the sale or supply by a registered optometrist of Pharmacy medicines and to the products listed in a., b. and c. above, provided that the sale or supply is in the course of the optometrist's professional practice and in an emergency.[11] In addition to the items in a., b. and c. the exemption applies to eye drops and eye ointments that are prescription only medicines by reason only that they contain not more than 30% sulphacetamide sodium, However, in the case of sulphacetamide sodium, the supply must be in accordance with a prescription.[12]

Pharmacists may sell or supply to patients the products in a., b. and c. (not for parenteral administration) following the production of an order signed by a registered optometrist.

It is lawful to sell to a registered optometrist by wholesale the POMs listed in Part 1(6) of HMR Schedule 17 – see above (HMR Reg.250(5)) – and a product that is a prescription only medicine by reason only that it contains one or more of the following substances (HMR Reg.250(6)):

- amethocaine hydrochloride;
- lidocaine hydrochloride;
- oxybuprocaine hydrochloride;
- proxymetacaine hydrochloride.

(See **Chapter 6** regarding wholesale dealing.)

Registered optometrists may also supply or administer POMs, Pharmacy medicines and GSL products under PGDs (see above).

An *optometrist independent prescriber* is a registered optometrist whose name is annotated in the relevant register as qualified to order drugs, medicines and appliances as an optometrist independent prescriber.[13]

Additional supply optometrist means a person who is registered as an optometrist and against whose name particulars of the additional supply specialty has been entered in the register.[14] They may sell or supply the following POMs, not in a form for parenteral administration, in the course of their professional practice and in an emergency (HMR Sch. 17, Part 1(9)):

- acetylcysteine;
- atropine sulphate;
- azelastine hydrochloride;

---

11. HMR Reg.235(4) and Part 4 of Schedule 17.
12. This is because the sulphacetamide products are in Part 4 of Schedule 17 to the HMR, which does not provide exemption from HMR Reg.214.
13. Defined in HMR Reg.8.
14. Defined in HMR Reg.250(10).

- diclofenac sodium;
- emedastine;
- homatropine hydrobromide;
- ketotifen;
- levocabastine;
- lodoxamide;
- nedocromil sodium;
- olopatadine;
- pilocarpine hydrochloride;
- pilocarpine nitrate;
- polymyxin B/bacitracin;
- polymyxin B/trimethoprim;
- sodium cromoglicate.

Persons lawfully conducting a retail pharmacy may sell these items on the presentation of a signed order from an additional supply optometrist (HMR Sch. 17, Part 1(8)).

Additional supply optometrists may also *purchase* for use in their practice (but not for sale or supply) a medicine which is a POM by reason only that it contains thymoxamine hydrochloride (HMR Reg.250).

Registered dispensing opticians may *purchase* for themselves, or a doctor attending their practice, to use in their practice (but not for sale or supply) medicines which are POMs that contain any one or more of the following substances (HMR Reg.250):

- amethocaine hydrochloride;
- chloramphenicol;
- cyclopentolate hydrochloride;
- fusidic acid;
- lidocaine hydrochloride;
- oxybuprocaine hydrochloride;
- proxymetacaine hydrochloride;
- tropicamide.

Registered dispensing opticians may *purchase,* for use in their practice as a contact lens specialist, medicines which are POMs that contain lidocaine hydrochloride, oxybuprocaine hydrochloride or proxymetacaine hydrochloride (HMR Reg.250).

Registered chiropodists and podiatrists

Sale or supply (HMR Sch. 17 Part 4(1))

The restrictions on retail sale or supply of certain medicinal products by registered chiropodists and podiatrists do not apply to:

1. medicinal products for external human use that are on a GSL; and
2. any of the following Pharmacy medicines for external use only:
   a. potassium permanganate crystals or solution,
   b. ointment of heparinoid and hyaluronidase,

c. products containing, as their only active ingredients, any of the following substances, at a strength, in the case of each substance, not exceeding that specified in relation to that substance:
   - 9.0% borotannic complex;
   - 10.0% buclosamide;
   - 3.0% chlorquinaldol;
   - 1.0% clotrimazole;
   - 10.0% crotamiton;
   - 5.0% diamthazole hydrochloride;
   - 1.0% econazole nitrate;
   - 1.0% fenticlor;
   - 10.0% glutaraldehyde;
   - 1.0% griseofulvin;
   - 0.4% hydrargaphen;
   - 2.0% mepyramine maleate;
   - 2.0% miconazole nitrate;
   - 2.0% phenoxypropan-2-ol;
   - 20.0% podophyllum resin;
   - 10.0% polynoxylin;
   - 70.0% pyrogallol;
   - 70.0% salicylic acid;
   - 1.0% terbinafine;
   - 0.1% thiomersal.

A registered chiropodist or podiatrist against whose name is recorded in the relevant register an annotation signifying that they are qualified to use the following medicines may sell or supply any of them in the course of their professional practice, as long as the product has been made up for sale or supply in a container elsewhere than at the place at which it is sold or supplied (HMR Sch. 17 Part 1(11) and Part 4(2)):

- Ibuprofen, other than preparations of ibuprofen which are Prescription Only Medicines.
- The following Prescription Only Medicines:
  - amorolfine hydrochloride cream: the maximum strength of amorolfine not to exceed 0.25% w/w;
  - amorolfine hydrochloride lacquer: the maximum strength of amorolfine not to exceed 5% w/v;
  - amoxicillin;
  - co-codamol;
  - co-dydramol 10/500 tablets;
  - codeine phosphate;
  - erythromycin;
  - flucloxacillin;
  - silver sulfadiazine;
  - tioconazole 28%;
  - topical hydrocortisone not exceeding 1% w/v.

Administration (HMR Sch. 17 Part 3(1))

Registered chiropodists or podiatrists against whose names are recorded in the relevant register annotations signifying that they are qualified to use the following medicines may administer them in the course of their professional practice. Where the medicine includes a combination of substances, those substances shall not have been combined by the chiropodist or podiatrist. The medicinal products to which this exemption applies are parenteral formulations of:

- adrenaline;
- bupivacaine hydrochloride;
- bupivacaine hydrochloride with adrenaline where the maximum strength of adrenaline does not exceed 1 mg in 200 mL bupivacaine hydrochloride;
- levobupivacaine hydrochloride;
- lidocaine hydrochloride;
- lidocaine hydrochloride with adrenaline where the maximum strength of adrenaline does not exceed 1 mg in 200 mL lidocaine hydrochloride;
- mepivacaine hydrochloride;
- methylprednisolone;
- prilocaine hydrochloride;
- ropivicaine hydrochoride.

Registered chiropodists may also supply or administer POMs, Pharmacy medicines and GSL products under PGDs (see above).

Registered orthoptists

Registered orthoptist means a person who is registered in Part 7 of the Health and Care Professions Council register.

The restrictions on retail supply or sale do not apply to the sale or supply (or offer for sale or supply) by registered orthoptists, of all GSL and Pharmacy medicines, along with certain POMs provided they are only in the course of their professional practice (HMR Sch. 17, Part 1(13) and Part 4(13)).

The POMs to which this exemption applies are:

- atropine;
- chloramphenicol;
- cyclopentolate;
- fusidic acid;
- lidocaine with fluorescein;
- oxybuprocaine;
- proxymetacaine;
- tetracaine;
- tropicamide.

Registered paramedics

Registered paramedic means a person who is registered in Part 8 of the Health and Care Professions Council's Register.

Registered paramedics may administer the following POMs for parenteral administration only for the immediate necessary treatment of sick or injured persons (HMR Sch. 17 Part 3(8)):

- diazepam 5 mg/mL emulsion for injection;
- succinylated modified fluid gelatin 4% intravenous infusion;
- medicines containing ergometrine maleate 500 mcg/mL with oxytocin 5 IU/mL but no other active ingredient;
- POMs containing one or more of the following substances, but no other active ingredient:
  - adrenaline acid tartrate;
  - adrenaline hydrochloride;
  - amiodarone;
  - anhydrous glucose;
  - benzylpenicillin;
  - compound sodium lactate intravenous infusion (Hartmann's solution);
  - ergometrine maleate;
  - furosemide;
  - glucose;
  - heparin sodium (only for the purpose of cannula flushing);
  - lidocaine hydrochloride;
  - metoclopramide;
  - morphine sulfate.
  - nalbuphine hydrochloride;
  - naloxone hydrochloride;
  - ondansetron;
  - paracetamol;
  - reteplase;
  - sodium chloride;
  - streptokinase;
  - tenecteplase.

Individuals who are state registered paramedics may also supply or administer POMs, Pharmacy medicines and GSL products under PGDs (see above).

Public analysts, sampling officers and other such persons

The restrictions on retail sale or supply do not apply to persons who sell or supply any medicinal product (HMR Sch. 17 Part 1(2) and Part 4(8)) to any of the following:

a. a public analyst appointed under section 27 of the Food Safety Act 1990;
b. an authorised officer within the meaning of section 5(6) of the Food Safety Act 1990;
c. an inspector acting under Regulations 325 to 328 of the HMR;
d. a sampling officer within the meaning of HMR Schedule 31.

The sale or supply must be only in connection with the statutory functions performed by these persons and is subject to the presentation of an order signed by or on behalf of the analyst, authorised officer, sampling officer or enforcement officer, as the case may be. It must state the status of the person signing it and the amount of the medicine required.

National Health Service drug testing

The restrictions on retail sale or supply of POMs do not apply to persons who sell or supply such medicinal products to any person employed or engaged in connection with the scheme for testing the quality and amount of the drugs and appliances supplied under the National Health Service Act 2006, the National Health Service (Scotland) Act 1978 and the National Health Service (Wales) Act 2006 or any subordinate legislation made under those Acts or that Order (HMR Sch. 17 Part 1(3)).

The sale or supply must be for the purpose of the relevant scheme and is subject to the presentation of an order signed on behalf of the person so employed or engaged stating the status of the person signing it, and the amount of the medicinal product required.

Owners and masters of ships

The restrictions on supply (but not sale) of any medicinal product do not apply when the supply is made by the owner or the master of a ship which does not carry a doctor on board as part of her complement (HMR Sch. 17 Part 2(2) and Part 5(9)). An owner or master may also, in these circumstances, administer POMs that are for parenteral administration (HMR Sch. 17 Part 3(4)). The supply or administration shall be only so far as is necessary for the treatment of persons on the ship.

Offshore installations

Persons employed as qualified first-aid personnel on offshore installations may, only so far as is necessary for the treatment of persons on the installation (HMR Sch. 17 Part 2(8), Part 3(7) and Part 5(14)):

1. supply any medicinal product; and
2. administer all parenteral POMs.

Statutory requirements for medical treatment of employees

The restrictions on supply (but not sale) of medicinal products do not apply to supplies made by persons requiring medicinal products for the purpose of enabling them, in the course of any business carried on by them, to comply with any requirements made by or in pursuance of any enactment with respect to the medical treatment of employees (HMR reg.235 and Sch. 17 Part 2(5) and Part 5(8)). For example, the Health and Safety (First-Aid) Regulations 1981 place a duty on employers to provide, or make available, such equipment and facilities as are adequate and appropriate for enabling first-aid to be rendered to employees if they are injured or become ill at work. The Health and Safety Executive gives advice on the contents of first aid kits[15] (and many pharmacies sell first aid kits).

The exemption extends to the POMs and the Pharmacy medicines specified in the relevant enactment and to GSL products.

15. https://www.hse.gov.uk/simple-health-safety/firstaid/index.htm (accessed 31 December 2024).

The supply shall be:

1. for the purpose of enabling them to comply with any requirements made by or in pursuance of any such enactment; and
2. subject to such conditions and in such circumstances as may be specified in the relevant enactments.

Persons employed or engaged in the provision of lawful drug treatment services

Persons employed or engaged in the lawful provision of drug treatment services may, in the course of providing those services, supply ampoules of sterile water for injection containing not more than 2 mL each (HMR Sch.17 Part 2(4)). As an exemption from the restrictions on the sale or supply of medicinal products subject to general sale (see **Chapter 10**) and Pharmacy medicines (see **Chapter 11**), persons employed or engaged in the provision of lawful drug treatment services may supply ampoules of sterile water for injection that contain no more than 5 mL each (HMR Sch. 17 Part 5(7)); however, in practice this latter exemption is limited to 2 mL owing to product range availability and concerns over the increased risk of infection transmission between individuals which may occur with the sharing of larger vial volumes.

Supply of naloxone

Amendments to the HMR[16] extended the range of individuals who can supply naloxone hydrochloride without being an authorised prescriber, from those working for drug treatment services, to include individuals working for the police, prison services, probation services and youth justice services, as well as a list of registered health care professionals provided those individuals have undergone appropriate training. Regulation 237A allows the following to supply naloxone for an *appropriate purpose* (see below):

(a) a person employed or engaged in the provision of drug treatment services provided by or on behalf of, or under arrangements with, one of the following:
  (i) an NHS body,
  (ii) a local authority,
  (iii) the Secretary of State;

(b) a person employed or engaged in the provision of services as part of the medical services of His Majesty's forces;

(c) a person employed or engaged by, or by an entity commissioned to provide drug treatment services by or on behalf of, one of the bodies listed below, if the listed body is satisfied that the person has undergone appropriate training in the storage and supply of naloxone products:
  (i) a police force,
  (ii) a prison service,

16. Amendments introduced by the Human Medicines (Amendments Relating to Naloxone and Transfers of Functions) Regulations 2024.

(iii) a provider of probation services, or
(iv) a provider of youth justice services;

(d) a person who is one of the following:
(i) a pharmacist,
(ii) a registered pharmacy technician,
(iii) a registered nurse,
(iv) a registered midwife, or
(v) a registered paramedic,

if that person has undergone appropriate training in the storage and supply of naloxone products; and

(e) a person employed or engaged by a local naloxone provider, if that local naloxone provider is satisfied that the person has undergone appropriate training in the storage and supply of naloxone products.

The following are *appropriate purposes* for the purposes of this regulation:

(a) the naloxone product is needed by the person to whom or for whom it is supplied for the purpose of saving life in an emergency;

(b) in the reasonable expectation of the appropriate supplier of naloxone, the supply of the naloxone product is to enable it to be kept at a place where a person resides or which they frequent, in circumstances where that person may need, at that place:
(i) to administer it to themselves in an emergency for the purposes of saving their own life, or
(ii) to administer it to another person, or to have it administered to them, in accordance with regulation 238;[17] or

(c) in the reasonable expectation of the appropriate supplier of naloxone, the supply of the naloxone product is to enable it to be carried about by the person to or for whom it is supplied, that person being a person who may need it:
(i) to administer it to themselves in an emergency for the purposes of saving their own life, or
(ii) to administer it to another person, or to have it administered to them, in accordance with regulation 238.

Temporary arrangements relating to coronavirus and influenza vaccinations and immunisations

The Secretary of State may make protocols for vaccination and immunisation relating to coronavirus and immunisation. For example, at the time of writing (and until 1 April 2026), HMR Reg.3A(1) permits the preparation and assembly of coronavirus vaccine when carried out under the supervision of a doctor, nurse or pharmacist at any location, without the need for a manufacturer's licence or marketing authorisation, on condition that these acts are done under NHS arrangements (or the medical services of HM Forces). Under HMR Reg.247A, Ministers may make protocols that, amongst other

---

17. Regulation 238 allows the administration of a prescription only medicine specified in Schedule 19 to the HMR (see Box 12.4) where this is for the purpose of saving life in an emergency.

things, would allow supply or administration without a prescription and without the supervision of a pharmacy professional.

Holders of controlled drugs authorities

The restrictions on the supply of POMs and some Pharmacy medicines do not apply to persons authorised by licences granted under Regulation 5 of the Misuse of Drugs Regulations[18] to supply the controlled drugs specified in the licence (HMR Sch. 17 Part 2(3) and 5(6)).

The supply shall be subject to such conditions and in such circumstances and to such an extent as may be specified in the licence. Similarly, the restrictions on the administration of POMs do not apply to persons who are authorised as members of a group by a group authority granted under Regulations 8(3) or 9(3) of the Misuse of Drugs Regulations (HMR Sch. 17 Part 3(3)). The exemption is limited to the administration of controlled drugs that are specified in the group authority and is subject to such conditions and in such circumstances and to such an extent as may be specified in the group authority.

Royal National Lifeboat Institution

The restrictions on the supply of any medicinal product do not apply to supply by the Royal National Lifeboat Institution or certificated first aiders of the Institution (HMR Sch. 17 Part 2(1) and Part 5(1)). The supply of any medicine shall be only so far as it is necessary for the treatment of sick or injured persons in the exercise of the functions of the Institution.

British Red Cross Society and other such organisations

The restrictions on the supply of Pharmacy and GSL medicines (but *not* POMs) do not apply to supply by the bodies specified below and their certificated first-aid and certificated nursing members (HMR Sch. 17 Part 5(2)-(5)). In all cases the supply shall be only so far as it is necessary for the treatment of sick or injured persons. The bodies concerned are:

- British Red Cross Society.
- St John Ambulance Association and Brigade.
- St Andrew's Ambulance Association.
- Order of Malta Ambulance Corps.

School and pre-school dental schemes

Pharmacy medicines that are for use in the prevention of dental caries and consist of or contain sodium fluoride may be supplied in the course of "school dental schemes", by persons carrying on the business of a school providing full-time education and in the course of "pre-school dental schemes", by health authorities or primary health trusts (HMR Sch. 17 Part 5(11) and (12)).

---

18. Misuse of Drugs Regulations 2001.

A *school dental scheme*[19] means a scheme supervised by a doctor or dentist in which medicinal products are supplied at a school to pupils of that school for the purpose of preventing dental caries. A supply, under such a scheme, may be made to a child under 16 years of age only with the consent of the parent or guardian of that child.

A *pre-school dental scheme* means a scheme supervised by a doctor or dentist in which medicinal products are supplied to parents or guardians of children under five years of age for use by such children for the purpose of preventing dental caries. The supplies made under such a scheme must be made by a registered nurse

Any medicinal products containing sodium fluoride which are POMs may not be sold, supplied or administered under this exemption.

Sale of salbutamol inhalers to schools

Salbutamol inhalers may be sold or supplied to a school for the purpose of supplying the medicinal product to pupils at the school in an emergency, subject to the presentation of an order signed by the principal or head teacher at the school concerned (HMR Sch. 17 Part 1(12)), stating:

i. the name of the school for which the medicinal product is required;
ii. the purpose for which that product is required; and
iii. the total quantity required.

A person, in the course of carrying on the business of a school who is trained to administer the relevant medicine may supply a salbutamol inhaler to a pupil of that school who is known to suffer from asthma, where the pupil requires the medicinal product in an emergency (HMR Sch. 17 Part 2(11)). In 2015, the Department of Health published guidance on the use of emergency salbutamol inhalers in schools.[20]

Administration of adrenaline auto-injectors in schools

A person carrying on the business of a school who is trained to administer the relevant medicine may administer an adrenaline auto-injector where the administration is to a pupil at that school who is known to be at risk of anaphylaxis and the pupil requires the medicinal product in an emergency (HMR, Sch. 17, Part 3(11).

Mountain rescue teams

Pharmacy medicines and medicines on a general sale list, along with POMs which are sold or supplied in response to an order in writing signed by a doctor, may be sold or supplied to persons who hold a certificate in first aid from the Mountain Rescue Council of England and Wales or from the Northern Ireland Mountain Rescue Co-ordinating Committee. These persons may then supply these medicinal products as far as is necessary for the treatment of sick or injured persons in the course of mountain rescue services (HMR Sch. 17 Part 2(9) and Part 5(16)).

---

19. Defined in the Medicines (Pharmacy and General Sale – Exemption) Order 1980.
20. https://assets.publishing.service.gov.uk/government/uploads/system/uploads/attachment_data/file/416468/emergency_inhalers_in_schools.pdf (accessed 31 December 2024).

Occupational health schemes

Pharmacy medicines, medicines on a GSL and POMs may be supplied by a person operating an *occupational health scheme*,[21] that is, a scheme in which persons, in the course of a business carried on by them, provide facilities for their employees for the treatment or prevention of disease.

The supply/administration must be made in the course of the scheme. For Pharmacy medicines and medicines on a GSL, the medicinal products may be supplied to the person operating the scheme, and for POMs, in response to a written order signed by a doctor or a registered nurse (HMR Sch. 17 Part 5(10)).

The individual supplying or administering the medicines in the course of the scheme, if not a doctor, must be:

1. a registered nurse; and
2. where the medicinal product in question is a POM, acting in accordance with the written instructions of a doctor as to the circumstances in which POMs of the description in question are to be used in the course of the occupational health scheme.

Operators or commanders of aircraft

The commander or operator of an aircraft may supply all Pharmacy medicines, medicines on a GSL, and such POMs which are not for parenteral administration and which have been sold or supplied to the operator or commander of an aircraft in response to an order in writing signed by a doctor (HMR Sch. 17 Part 2(7) and Part 5(13)). The *operator* means the person for the time being having the management of the aircraft. The supply shall be only so far as is necessary for the immediate treatment of sick or injured persons on the aircraft and, in the case of a POM, shall be in accordance with the written instructions of a doctor as to the circumstances in which the POMs of the description in question are to be used on the aircraft.
The commander or operator of an aircraft may also administer POMs for parenteral use which have been sold or supplied to them in response to an order in writing signed by a doctor. The administration shall be only so far as is necessary for the immediate treatment of sick or injured persons on the aircraft and shall be in accordance with the written instructions of a doctor as to the circumstances in which POMs of the description in question are to be used on the aircraft (HMR Sch.17 Part 3(6)).

In addition, an operator or commander of an aircraft may also sell, supply or offer for sale or supply any medicine on a general sale list that has been made up for sale or supply in a container elsewhere than at the place at which it is sold or supplied. The GSL medicine must be stored in a part of the aircraft which the operator is able to close so as to exclude the public (HMR Sch. 17 Part 4(11)).

---

21. Defined in the Medicines (Pharmacy and General Sale – Exemption) Order 1980.

Operator of a train

An operator of a train may sell, supply or offer for sale or supply any medicinal product on a general sale list that has been made up for sale or supply in a container elsewhere than at the place at which it is sold or supplied. The GSL product must be stored in a part of the train which the operator is able to close so as to exclude the public (HMR, Sch. 17 Part 4(12)).

Universities, higher education institutions or institutions concerned with research

The restrictions on retail sale or supply of medicinal products do not apply to persons selling or supplying such products to a university, an institution concerned with higher education or an institution concerned with research but only for the purposes of the education or research with which the institution is concerned (HMR Sch. 17 Part 1(1)). The sale or supply is subject to the presentation of an order signed by the principal of the institution for education or research or the appropriate head of department in charge of a specified course of research. The order must state:

1. the name of the institution for which the medicinal product is required;
2. the purpose for which it is required; and
3. the total quantity required.

Supplies by holders of UK marketing authorisations

The restrictions on sale or supply do not apply to holders of UK marketing authorisations and holders of manufacturer's licences who sell or supply medicinal products referred to in the licences to pharmacists so as to enable them to prepare an entry relating to the medicinal product in question in a tablet or capsule identification guide or similar publication. No greater quantity than is reasonably necessary for that purpose may be supplied (HMR Sch. 17 Part 1(10)).

High dilution products

HMR Reg.242 contains an exemption from the restrictions which apply to both the sale or supply of Pharmacy medicines (HMR Reg.220; see **Chapter 11**) and medicines subject to general sale (HMR Reg.221; see **Chapter 10**) subject to a number of conditions:

1. the medicinal product is neither for parenteral administration nor a product subject to special medical prescription (for example, a controlled drug);[22]
2. the person selling or supplying the product has been requested to do so by or on behalf of a particular person, and in that person's presence, and the seller has used their own judgement as to the treatment required; and
3. the medicinal product consists solely of one or more unit preparations of:
   a. any substance where the unit preparation has been diluted to at least one part in a million (6×);

22. HMR Reg.213 classifies a "product subject to special medical prescription" as any substance or product for the time being specified in Schedule 1, 2 or 3 to the Misuse of Drugs Regulations 2001.

b. any substance that is listed in HMR Part 1 of Schedule 21 where the unit preparation has been diluted to at least one part in a thousand (3×); or
c. any substance that:
   i. is the active substance of a medicine that is subject to general sale,
   ii. is listed in HMR Part 3 of Schedule 21, or
   iii. in the case of a medicinal product for external use only, is listed in HMR Part 4 of Schedule 21,

   where the unit preparation has been diluted to at least one part in ten (1×).

This enables homoeopathic medicines at specified levels of dilution to be sold if the seller is requested by a customer to use the seller's own judgement as to the treatment required, without the restrictions that normally apply to general sale or Pharmacy medicines.

Serious shortage protocols

Serious shortage protocols are covered in **Chapter 12.**

SUMMARY

- Doctors and dentists may sell or supply all medicines to their own patients.
- Certain organisations and health professionals can supply medicines under PGDs. These are listed in Appendix 3.
- For the purposes of their professional practice, midwives have a list of medicines which can be sold or supplied by them and another list of medicines which they may administer.
- Community practitioner nurse prescribers may prescribe, but not sell or supply, a limited list of POMs.
- Optometrists have a list of medicines which they may sell or supply to their patients in the course of their professional practice (for POMs, this is permitted only in an emergency). They may also purchase a limited list of POMs for use in their practice, but not for sale or supply.
- Chiropodists and podiatrists may sell or supply to their patients, in the course of their professional practice, any medicinal product subject to general sale for external use and a limited list of Pharmacy medicines. Chiropodists and podiatrists holding a certificate of competence in the use of certain medicines may administer, in their practice, those medicines (many of these are local anaesthetics).
- Registered orthoptists may sell or supply to their patients, in the course of their professional practice, medicinal products subject to general sale and Pharmacy medicines, along with a limited list of POMs.
- Registered ambulance paramedics may parenterally administer certain medicines for the immediate, necessary treatment of the sick or injured.
- Schools may supply salbutamol inhalers, and administer adrenaline auto-injectors, to pupils at the school in an emergency, subject to certain conditions.
- Other categories of activities also have limited lists of medicines which they may sell or supply. These include dental and occupational health schemes, owners and masters of ships,

SUMMARY (CONT.)

offshore installations, the Royal National Lifeboat Institution, public analysts, aircraft commanders, train operators, universities, mountain rescue teams and the British Red Cross.

- Many exemptions whose details are set out in Schedule 17 to the HMR refer to medicines "on a general sale list". This term does not include many medicines that are subject to general sale by virtue of their marketing authorisation but which are not on a general sale list (see also **Chapter 10**).

CHAPTER 14

Controlled drugs and psychotropic and psychoactive substances

The manufacture, possession and all dealings with controlled drugs are unlawful. However, the Misuse of Drugs Regulations 2001 provide exemptions for medical practitioners, pharmacists, nurses and other healthcare professionals. The Regulations spell out the circumstances in which the exemptions apply and, amongst other things, the exemptions vary according to the different types of healthcare professional, and the Schedule in which specific drugs are listed. There are also provisions relating to record-keeping and safe custody.

Introduction

The aim of the Misuse of Drugs Act 1971 is to control *dangerous or otherwise harmful drugs.*[1] This control is exercised by rendering unlawful all activities associated with the drugs controlled under it, other than some limited provisions for licences for importation and exportation (s.3). Apart from these provisions, *any* other activity associated with controlled drugs is rendered unlawful by the Act, except as permitted in Regulations made under the Act. The extent to which these Regulations lift the restrictions is dealt with in this chapter and, in relation to veterinary medicines, in **Chapter 15**.

The laws governing controlled drugs have evolved over many years, dictated by patterns of abuse or misuse, risk of dependency, and social and policy factors.[2] Between 1974 and 1998, Britain's most prolific serial killer, Dr Harold Shipman, an English general practitioner, murdered at least 215 of his patients by injecting them with diamorphine which he obtained lawfully through pharmacies.[3] A public inquiry chaired by Dame Janet Smith produced a number of reports whose recommendations resulted in changes to the law on the controls of the use of Schedule 2, 3 and 4 controlled drugs that are reflected in this chapter, including:

- the limit on the duration of validity of a prescription for a Schedule 2, 3 and 4 controlled drugs to be reduced from 13 weeks to 28 days (see *Prescription requirements for Schedule 2 and 3 controlled drugs* below);

---

1. Preamble to the Misuse of Drugs Act 1971.
2. For example, the Chair of the Advisory Council on the Misuse of Drugs was dismissed by the Home Secretary in 2009 because of the views publicly expressed by the former http://news.bbc.co.uk/1/hi/8334774.stm (accessed 31 December 2024).
3. Baker, R. Implications of Harold Shipman for general practice. Postgrad Med J 2004;80:303–306.

- the requirement for private prescriptions for Schedule 2 or 3 controlled drugs to be written on specific forms (see *Prescription requirements for Schedule 2 and 3 controlled drugs* below);
- the requirement for prescriptions other than a health or veterinary prescription to be sent to the relevant NHS service agency for monitoring purposes (see *Endorsing the prescription*) below; and
- a requirement for designated bodies to appoint an Accountable Officer and oversight of the management of controlled drugs by the Care Quality Commission (CQC) (see *Accountable Officers* below).

The reports also recommended that prescriptions for Schedule 2, 3 or 4 controlled drugs are limited to a maximum of 28 days' supply. However, this recommendation has not been made a legal requirement, instead the recommendation of a limit of 30 days' supply as a good practice requirement was implemented for human prescriptions (see *Prescription requirements for Schedule 2 and 3 controlled drugs* below). Additionally, the reports recommended the inclusion of running balances within controlled drug registers, but this recommendation has not been made a legal requirement, although maintaining running balances to facilitate the identification of theft or loss is now regarded as good practice (see *Running balances* below).[4]

In the case of prescriptions for the treatment of animals, the Royal College of Veterinary Surgeons recommends that for acute conditions, the maximum quantity prescribed should not exceed 30 days' worth; exceptionally, to cover a justifiable clinical need and after consideration of any risk, a prescription can be issued for a longer period, but the reasons for the decision should be recorded in the animal's clinical notes; and that if more than 30 days' worth of treatment is prescribed, the prescribing veterinary surgeon must be sure that the owner is competent to use the medicine safely.[5]

In this chapter, references to *the Act* and to sections, are to the Misuse of Drugs Act 1971 and those to *the Regulations* are to the Misuse of Drugs Regulations 2001, unless otherwise stated. References to the Secretary of State are to the Home Secretary. For some (but not all) parts of the Act, references to *the ministers* are to the Scottish Ministers if in Scotland, and the Welsh Ministers if in Wales, concerned with health or education.

Advisory Council on the Misuse of Drugs

The Act requires that there is an Advisory Council (s.1), called The Advisory Council on the Misuse of Drugs (ACMD), which advises the ministers.

The ACMD is required to keep under review the situation in the UK with respect to drugs which are being, or appear to them likely to be, misused and which are having or

---

4. See also the Coroner's matters of concern from the case of Michael Lobban in Box 1.6 in Chapter 1.
5. https://www.rcvs.org.uk/setting-standards/advice-and-guidance/controlled-drugs-guidance-a-to-z/ (accessed 31 December 2024).

could cause harmful effects, which might constitute a social problem. It has a duty to advise the ministers on the action to be taken. In particular, it must advise on measures:

1. to restrict the availability of such drugs or to supervise the arrangements for their supply;
2. to enable persons affected by the misuse of such drugs to obtain proper advice, and to secure the provision of proper facilities and services for the treatment, rehabilitation and aftercare of such persons;
3. to promote co-operation between the various professional and community services which, in the opinion of the ACMD, have a part to play in dealing with social problems connected with the misuse of such drugs;
4. to educate the public (particularly the young) in the dangers of abusing such drugs, and to give publicity to those dangers; and
5. to promote research into, or otherwise to obtain information about, any matter which in the opinion of the ACMD is of relevance for the purpose of preventing the misuse of such drugs or dealing with any social problem connected with their misuse. The Secretary of State has authority to conduct or assist in conducting such research (s.32).

The ACMD also has a duty to consider, and advise on, any matter relating to drug dependence or misuse of drugs which any of the ministers may refer to it. In particular, the ACMD is required to advise the Home Secretary on communications relating to the control of any dangerous or otherwise harmful drug received from any authority established under a treaty, convention or other agreement to which HM Government is a party. The Home Secretary and other ministers are obliged to consult the ACMD before laying orders before Parliament or before making regulations (or any changes to the same) under the Act. Recent examples of issues on which the ACMD has advised Ministers include the medicinal use of cannabis-based products and whether nitrous oxide should be a controlled drug (see below).[6]

Class A, B and C drugs

The drugs subject to control are listed in Schedule 2 to the Act and the term *controlled drug* means any substance or product either listed in Schedule 2 or in a temporary class drug order as a drug subject to temporary control (ss.2A and 2B).[7] The Schedule is divided into three parts or classes largely on the basis of decreasing order of harmfulness: Part I (class A), Part II (class B) and Part III (class C). This division into three classes is solely for the purpose of determining penalties for offences under the Act (s.25); the relevant penalties are set out in Schedule 4 to the Act. Some examples of drugs in each class are given in **Box 14.1**. A full list is not given here but is available on the Home Office website or by reference to the legislation.

---

6. https://www.gov.uk/government/publications/response-to-consultation-on-cannabis-based-medicinal-products (accessed 31 December 2024); and https://www.gov.uk/government/publications/nitrous-oxide-updated-harms-assessment/nitrous-oxide-updated-harms-assessment-accessible (accessed 31 December 2024) – the ACMD did not recommend specifying nitrous oxide as a controlled drug but the Home Secretary did not accept this advice.
7. Added by s.151 of the Police Reform and Social Responsibility Act 2011.

Box 14.1: Some commonly encountered controlled drugs, according to their classification under the Act

Class A	Class B	Class C
Cocaine Diamorphine Lysergic acid diethylamide (LSD) Methadone Methylamphetamine 3,4-Methylenedioxymethamphetamine (MDMA)	Amphetamine Cannabis and cannabis resin Codeine Dihydrocodeine Ketamine Methylphenidate	Anabolic steroids Benzodiazepines, including diazepam, midazolam and temazepam (amongst others) Buprenorphine Khat Tramadol Zopiclone

Changes may be made to the list of controlled drugs subject to consultation with the ACMD. Amendment is made by an Order in Council[8] which must be approved by an affirmative resolution of each House of Parliament (s.2). For example, in March 2024 changes were made[9] to the list of drugs classified under the Act. A total of fifteen synthetic opioids, including fourteen nitazenes, were brought under control as class A drugs, cumyl-PeGaClone, diphenidine, ephenidine, and methoxyphenidine under control as class B drugs, and remimazolam under control as a class C drug under the Act.

In January 2025, new drugs were added to Schedule 1 to the Regulations, and xylazine (see also **Chapter 15**) was added to Part 1 of Schedule 4 to the Regulations.[10]

It should be noted that the classification of controlled drugs for purposes of control when these drugs are used for lawful purposes appears in the Schedules to the Misuse of Drugs Regulations 2001, rather than in Schedules to the Act. This classification is of importance to practitioners and pharmacists in their daily work (see section on Regimes of control, below).

Restrictions and exemptions

The importation or exportation of controlled drugs is prohibited, except in accordance with a licence issued by the Secretary of State (s.7) or when permitted by Regulations (s.3). Certain activities are specifically declared to be unlawful, unless permitted by regulations:

1. producing a controlled drug (s.4);
2. supplying or offering to supply a controlled drug to another person (s.4);

8. As discussed in Chapter 1, an Order in Council is made by the Privy Council (which is usually composed of ministers).
9. Changes were made via the Misuse of Drugs Act 1971 (Amendment) Order 2024.
10. The Misuse of Drugs and Misuse of Drugs (Designation) (England and Wales and Scotland) (Amendment) (No. 2) Regulations 2024.

3. possessing a controlled drug (s.5); and
4. cultivating any plant of the genus *Cannabis* (s.6).

Producing a controlled drug means producing it by manufacture, cultivation or any other method, and supplying includes distribution (s.37). For the purposes of the Act, the things which a person has in their possession are taken to include anything subject to their control which is in the custody of another (s.37).

Exemptions from these controls may be authorised by the Secretary of State, who may (s.7):

1. by regulations, exempt any specified controlled drug from any of the restrictions on import, export, production, supply or possession;
2. by regulations, make it lawful for persons to produce, supply or possess controlled drugs to the extent which the Secretary of State thinks fit; and
3. permit, by licence or other authority, any of the activities in 2 and prescribe any conditions to be complied with.

The Home Secretary must exercise powers to make regulations which make it lawful for practitioners, pharmacists and persons lawfully conducting retail pharmacy businesses – see **Chapter 7** for the meaning of *lawfully conducting a retail pharmacy business* – (when acting in their professional capacity) to possess, supply, manufacture or compound controlled drugs, and for practitioners (when acting in their professional capacity) to prescribe and administer such drugs (s.7). The term *practitioner* (except in the specific expression *veterinary practitioner*) means a doctor, dentist, veterinary practitioner or veterinary surgeon (s.37).

If the Home Secretary considers that it is in the public interest for a drug to be used only for the purposes of research or other special purposes, the Home Secretary may make an order to that effect. It is then unlawful for a practitioner, pharmacist or a person lawfully conducting a retail pharmacy business to possess or do anything in relation to that drug except under licence. When making an order of this kind, the Home Secretary must act on the recommendation of the ACMD or after consulting it (s.7).

The Regulations define "exempt" products (Reg.2), which are products that are not subject to control under the Act or Regulations. An exempt product is a preparation or other product consisting of one or more component parts, any of which contains a controlled drug, where:

1. the preparation or other product is not designed for administration of the controlled drug to a human being or animal;
2. the controlled drug in any component part is packaged in such a form or in combination with other active or inert substances in such a manner that it cannot be recovered by readily applicable means or in a yield which constitutes a risk to health; and
3. no one component part of the product or combination contains more than 1 mg of the controlled drug or 1 microgram in the case of lysergide or any other *N*-alkyl derivative of lysergamide.

Other exemptions apply, for example to *in vitro* diagnostic devices or kits used by laboratories for the detection of drugs of misuse or for clinical diagnosis or other products containing very small quantities of controlled drugs (e.g. radioactive research compounds). The provisions of the Act apply to the possession of a stock of controlled drugs for the purpose of producing kits and other exempted products. The Misuse of Drugs (Safe Custody) Regulations 1973 also apply to any stock of Schedule 1 and 2 controlled drugs (except some liquid preparations of Schedule 2 controlled drugs and quinalbarbitone (secobarbital)) and stocks of Schedule 3 controlled drugs (unless exempted). Schedule 3 controlled drugs currently requiring safe custody include buprenorphine, diethylpropion, flunitrazepam and temazepam (see Safe custody of controlled drugs below).

Prohibitions on possession, prescribing and supply

Directions following convictions

Where a pharmacist or practitioner has been guilty of any offence under the Act or of any offence under the Customs and Excise Act 1952 or the Customs and Excise Management Act 1979 relating to the unlawful importation or exportation of controlled drugs, or of an offence under section 12 or 13 of the Criminal Justice (International Co-operation) Act 1990, which is concerned with substances useful for the manufacture of controlled drugs, the Secretary of State may make a direction in respect of them. If they are a practitioner, the direction will prohibit them from having in their possession, prescribing, administering, manufacturing, compounding[11] and supplying, and from authorising the administration and supply of the controlled drugs specified in the direction. If they are a pharmacist, the direction will prohibit them from having in their possession, manufacturing, compounding and supplying and from supervising and controlling the manufacture, compounding and supply of the controlled drugs specified in the direction (s.12).

A direction takes effect when a copy has been served on the person concerned and it is then an offence for him/her to contravene it. The Secretary of State may cancel or suspend any direction or bring a suspended direction into force again by cancelling its suspension (s.12).

Prohibitions affecting practitioners

If the Secretary of State is of the opinion that a practitioner has been prescribing, administering, supplying, or authorising the administration or supply of any controlled drugs in contravention to regulations made under the Act, the Secretary of State may give a direction in respect of the practitioner, prohibiting them from the prescribing, administering, supplying or authorising the administration and supply of the controlled drugs specified in the direction. Furthermore, if the Secretary of State is of the opinion

---

11. *Compounding* is the mixing of drugs prior to administration to a patient and in relation to controlled drugs, has been described as "the 'mixing' of two or more drugs which include a controlled drug(s), for instance for palliative care". See: https://www.gov.uk/government/publications/nurse-and-pharmacist-independent-prescribing-mixing-of-medicines-possession-authorities-under-patient-group-directions-and-personal-exemption-provisions-for-schedule-4-part-ii-drugs/circular-0092012-nurse-and-provisions-pharmacist-independent-prescribing-for-schedule-4-part-ii-drugs (accessed 31 December 2024).

that a practitioner is or has been prescribing, administering or supplying or authorising the administration or supply of any controlled drugs in an irresponsible manner, the Secretary of State may make a direction prohibiting a practitioner from prescribing, administering or supplying, or authorising the administration or supply of, the controlled drugs specified in the direction. The practitioner commits an offence if they contravene a direction (s.13).

Tribunals, advisory bodies and professional panels

The Act sets out that if the Secretary of State considers that there are grounds for giving a direction, prohibiting a doctor or other practitioner from prescribing, administering or supplying controlled drugs, the Secretary of State must follow the procedure set out in the Act (ss.14, 15 and 16).

In a case of irresponsible prescribing, if the Secretary of State considers circumstances require that a direction be given with the minimum of delay, the Secretary of State may refer the matter to a *professional panel* consisting of three members of the practitioner's profession appointed by the Secretary of State (one of whom who will be appointed as the chairman). If the panel considers there are reasonable grounds for thinking that there has been irresponsible prescribing, the Secretary of State may give a direction at once which is effective for a period of six weeks. The Secretary of State must also refer the case at once to a tribunal, in accordance with the procedures outlined above. After the tribunal, or the advisory body as appropriate, has considered the case, the Secretary of State may, if they think fit, make a permanent direction, if that is the advice received. If no such direction is given, the temporary prohibition will cease (s.15).

Although the legal underpinning for such tribunals is still in place, in practice the Misuse of Drugs Tribunal is now in abeyance and the Home Office has no oversight of this process. Instead, fitness to practise cases involving medical practitioners (including interim order applications that may involve suspension – see **Chapter 2** and **Chapter 25**) are run by the Medical Practitioners Tribunal Service.

Scheduled substances: substances used in the manufacture of narcotic drugs or psychotropic substances

Drug precursor chemicals (DPCs) are chemicals which may be used for the illicit manufacture of narcotic drugs or psychotropic substances. Article 12 of the United Nations Convention against Illicit Traffic in Narcotic Drugs and Psychotropic Substances (to which the UK is a signatory) establishes controls to prevent the illicit manufacturing of DPCs while also allowing for legitimate trade, delivered through a requirement for licensing and, additionally in some cases, for "pre-export notifications" to the receiving country and export checks. Regulations[12] allow for a competitive internal market for legitimate trade in drug precursors (which can be used in the manufacture of other substances, such as

12. Controlled Drugs (Drug Precursors) (Intra-Community Trade Regulations 2008 and the Controlled Drugs (Drug Precursors) (Community External Trade) Regulations 2008.

perfumes or flavourings) whilst preventing their diversion for illicit manufacture. There is a licensing system for UK-based operators who trade in these chemicals.

Powers of the Secretary of State

The Act empowers the Secretary of State to make Regulations (ss.7, 10, 22 and 31). Regulations may make different provisions for different cases and circumstances and for different controlled drugs and different classes of person. The opinion, consent or approval of a prescribed authority or of any person may also be made material to a regulation. For example, a chief officer of police may certify for use a safe, cabinet or room for the keeping of controlled drugs as an alternative to a controlled drugs cabinet that meets the technical requirements for safekeeping that are specified in Regulations.[13] Any licence or other authority issued by the Secretary of State for the purposes of the Act may be made subject to such conditions as the Secretary of State thinks proper and may be modified or revoked at any time (s.30).

The application of any provision of the Act which creates an offence and those provisions of the Customs and Excise Management Act 1979 that apply to the importation and exportation of controlled drugs may, in prescribed cases, be excluded by regulation. Similarly, any provision of the Act or any regulation or order made under it may, by regulation, be made applicable to servants and agents of the Crown (s.22).

Most of the Regulations are designed to render lawful various activities in connection with controlled drugs which would otherwise be unlawful under the Act. For example, they are necessary to enable doctors, pharmacists and others to prescribe, administer, manufacture, compound or supply controlled drugs as appropriate to their particular capacities. They also govern such matters as the safekeeping of controlled drugs and their destruction and the supply of controlled drugs to addicts.

Regimes of control

The drugs controlled under the Act are classified in the Misuse of Drugs Regulations 2001 into five schedules in descending order of control, the most stringent controls applying to drugs in Schedule 1. As the detail can change from time to time, full lists of the drugs included in each schedule are not included here. For information regarding classification under the Regulations, reference may be made to information on the Home Office website or by reference to the legislation.

Schedule 1

Schedule 1 lists controlled drugs which may not be used for medicinal purposes, their production and possession being limited, in the public interest, to purposes of research or other special purposes. Certain limited classes of person have a general authority to possess these drugs in the course of their duties, for example constables or carriers

---

13. Reg.4 of the Misuse of Drugs (Safe Custody) Regulations 1973 (made under s.31 of the Misuse of Drugs Act 1971).

(Reg.6). Other persons may only produce, supply or possess the drugs within the authority of a licence issued by the Secretary of State. The requirements of the Misuse of Drugs Regulations relating to documentation, the keeping and preservation of records, supply on prescription, marking of containers and procedure for destruction, apply in full to these drugs in Schedule 1.

Examples of drugs in Schedule 1 include cannabis (except for certain products licensed by the MHRA; cannabis-based products for medicinal use in humans are in Schedule 2), cannabis resin, khat, LSD (lysergic acid diethylamide) and MDMA (3,4-methylenedioxymethamphetamine).

As with drugs classified under the Misuse of Drugs Act, changes to the classification under the Regulations also take place. For example, in 2021 changes were made[14] which added three benzodiazepines (flualprazolam, flunitrazolam and norfludiazepam) to Schedule 1 to the Regulations.

Cannabis

Cannabis (except in the expression cannabis resin) means any plant of the genus Cannabis or any part of any such plant (by whatever name designated) except that it does not include cannabis resin or any of the following products after separation from the rest of the plant, namely:

- mature stalk of any such plant;
- fibre produced from mature stalk of any such plant; and
- seed of any such plant.

There has been considerable public debate about both the legalisation of cannabis for "recreational use" and for medicinal use. Successive governments have been firmly opposed to the decriminalisation of recreational cannabis, but a number of cases involving children[15] led to a change in the law[16] to enable the prescribing of certain medicinal cannabis products:[17]

- unlicensed cannabidiol (CBD) food supplements which must not contain any tetrahydrocannabinol (THC);
- licensed cannabis-based products and synthetic products such as:
    - Sativex (Schedule 4) – a cannabis extract oromucosal spray containing THC and CDB,

---

14. Changes were made via the Misuse of Drugs and Misuse of Drugs (Designation) (Amendment) (England, Wales and Scotland) Regulations 2021.
15. For example, the case of Billy Caldwell which appeared in many news reports including https://news.sky.com/story/billy-caldwell-in-life-threatening-condition-after-cannabis-treatment-refusal-family-11405999 (accessed31 December 2024).
16. Regulation 16A of the Regulations. Reg.16A is unusual in its wording because the structure of the Misuse of Drugs Act makes things unlawful except as permitted in regulations. However, Reg.16A does not expressly permit anything; it says that ordering (prescribing) is not permitted unless certain conditions are met.
17. See also this Hansard report of proceedings in the House of Lords https://hansard.parliament.uk/Lords/2018-06-19/debates/9D48AFBA-2C20-43B2-A50C-94405D7E7B69/DrugsLicensing (accessed 31 December 2024).

  - Nabilone (Schedule 2) – a synthetic cannabinoid,
  - Epidyolex (Schedule 5) – a product containing pure CBD, and
  - Dronabinol (Schedule 2) – synthetic version of THC without a UK marketing authorisation;
- cannabis-based products for medicinal use (CBPMs) – unlicensed Schedule 2 products. Prescribing of these products requires the doctor to be listed on the Specialist Register of the General Medical Council.[18]

Prior to the reclassification of certain licenced cannabis products from Schedule 1 in 2018, a case from 2005 clarified that consideration of whether an individual needed to use cannabis for medical reasons is not incompatible with the Act and Regulations (see **Box 14.2**).[19]

Box 14.2: *R v Quayle; Ditchfield; Lee; Taylor; Kenny; Wales*

This case concerned an appeal against convictions for the cultivation, production and possession of cannabis and cannabis resin. Owing to their individual illnesses, three of the appellants (Q, K and W) were all in severe pain and grew cannabis at their homes for personal use. The other two appellants (L and T) supplied cannabis to individuals with similar illnesses from a holistic centre. In the original trial of Q, K, L and T the judge did not allow a defence of necessity to be put to the jury; the defence was left to the jury in the case of W, who was convicted.

The appeal involved the claim that the cultivation and use of cannabis was permissible in law as it was required to alleviate the suffering caused by severe pain. They claimed that failing to meet the common law defence of necessity was a contravention of their human rights. Furthermore, L and T claimed that the defence of necessity should have been available to them as they genuinely believed that providing cannabis was necessary to prevent pain.

Dismissing the appeal, the judge stated that juries could not be expected to balance whether an individual's need outweighed any legislative control as, if this was the case, juries are effectively being asked to legislate. Furthermore, it was held that this legislative position was not in conflict with the European Convention on Human Rights (see **Chapter 1**).

Consumer cannabidiol (CBD) products such as CBD oil are derived primarily from the plant Cannabis. Like other cannabis products, CBD contains tetrahydrocannabinol (THC) which is a psychoactive component. As a matter of policy, the Home Office issues licences for cultivation of plants from approved seed types with a THC content not exceeding 0.2%. It treats CBD with a THC content not exceeding 0.2% as exempt from the Regulations (see above) because the cannabis cannot be recovered by readily applicable means or in a yield which constitutes a risk to health. CBD is marketed as a dietary supplement. The Food Standards Agency has announced plans to regulate the CBD market. The Government has accepted advice from the ACMD on consumer cannabidiol products that, amongst other things, the total dose of THC will not be allowed to exceed 50 micrograms per unit of consumption. What amounts to a unit of consumption was stated in the advice as "... being defined as the typical quantity of a CBD product consumed on one occasion" and will be the subject of further consideration.[20]

20. See: https://www.gov.uk/government/publications/acmd-advice-on-consumer-cannabidiol-cbd-products (accessed 31 December 2024).

---

18. For further details of the Specialist Register of the General Medical Council, see: https://www.gmc-uk.org/registration-and-licensing/the-medical-register/a-guide-to-the-medical-register/specialist-registration (accessed 31 December 2024).
19. *R v Quayle; Ditchfield; Lee; Taylor; Kenny; Wales* [2005] EWCA Crim 1415.

Schedule 2

Schedule 2 includes the opioids (such as diamorphine, fentanyl, methadone, morphine and oxycodone), medicinal cannabis, and the major stimulants (such as the amphetamines). A licence is needed to import or export drugs in this schedule.

They may be manufactured or compounded, when acting in a professional capacity, by a practitioner, a pharmacist, or a person lawfully conducting a retail pharmacy business. If and when the Human Medicines Regulations are amended to enable pharmacists to authorise pharmacy technicians to carry out supervision (see **Chapter 11**), it is expected that the Misuse of Drugs Regulations will be amended to add pharmacy technicians to the list of persons who may manufacture or compound controlled drugs in Schedule 2. They may be compounded (but not manufactured) by a nurse independent prescriber, or a supplementary prescriber (acting under and in accordance with the terms of a clinical management plan).

Compounding (but not manufacturing) may be carried out by person acting in accordance with the written directions of any of a doctor, dentist, nurse independent prescriber, pharmacist independent prescriber, paramedic independent prescriber or therapeutic radiographer independent prescriber. Except in the case of a pharmacist or person lawfully conducting a retail pharmacy business, the compounding must be for the purposes of administration (Reg.8).[21]

A pharmacist may supply a Schedule 2 drug to a patient (or the owner of an animal) only on the authority of a prescription in the required form issued by an appropriate practitioner (Regs.15 and 16). See section on Prescription requirements for Schedule 2 and 3 controlled drugs, below. For avoidance of doubt, the word *patient* in this chapter refers to human beings; in the case of veterinary supply of controlled drugs, see **Chapter 15**.

The drugs may only be administered to a patient by (Reg.7):

- a doctor or dentist or by any person acting in accordance with the directions of a doctor or dentist (including via a patient group direction);
- a nurse or pharmacist independent prescriber or by any person acting in accordance with the directions of a nurse or pharmacist independent prescriber;
- a supplementary prescriber acting under and in accordance with the terms of a clinical management plan, or any person acting in accordance with the directions of a supplementary prescriber, acting under such a plan;
- a registered physiotherapist[22] or registered chiropodist[23] independent prescriber or by any person acting in accordance with the directions of a registered physiotherapist or registered chiropodist independent prescriber (for those drugs, and in such

---

21. It seems anomalous, but the Regulations do not permit a paramedic independent prescriber or a therapeutic radiographer independent prescriber to compound Schedule 2 controlled drugs, but the Regulations do permit a person acting in accordance with the written directions of a paramedic independent prescriber or therapeutic radiographer independent prescriber to do so.

22. A registered physiotherapist independent prescriber may prescribe diazepam, dihydrocodeine, lorazepam, oxycodone and temazepam by oral administration, fentanyl by transdermal administration, and morphine by oral administration or by injection (Reg.6C(1)).

23. A registered chiropodist independent prescriber may prescribe diazepam, dihydrocodeine, lorazepam and temazepam by oral administration (Reg.6C(2)).

circumstances that such independent prescribers may prescribe – see footnotes as to the drugs they are authorised to prescribe); and

- a paramedic[24] independent prescriber or a therapeutic radiographer[25] independent prescriber or by any person acting on the specific instructions of a paramedic independent prescriber or a therapeutic radiographer independent prescriber (for those drugs, and in such circumstances that such independent prescribers may prescribe; see footnotes as to the drugs they are authorised to prescribe).

At the time of writing, none of the controlled drugs registered podiatrists or chiropodist independent prescribers may prescribe are listed within Schedule 2. However, an October 2020 consultation proposed adding four additional controlled drugs to the list, one of which, morphine, is listed within Schedule 2.[26] Although already permitted to prescribe certain Schedule 2 controlled drugs, a similar consultation was launched at the same time in relation to physiotherapist independent prescribers.[27]

Requirements as to safe custody in pharmacies and control over destruction apply to these drugs, and the provisions relating to the marking of containers and the keeping of records, must also be complied with (Regs.18 and 19).

Schedule 3

Schedule 3 includes the barbiturates (except quinalbarbitone (secobarbital), which is a Schedule 2 controlled drug), buprenorphine, diethylpropion, meprobamate, pentazocine and tramadol, as well as three benzodiazepines (flunitrazepam, midazolam and temazepam), and the gabapentinoids.

These drugs are considered to be less harmful, when misused, than the drugs in Schedule 2.

The controls which apply to Schedule 2 also apply to drugs in Schedule 3, except that:

1. they may also be manufactured by persons authorised in writing by the Secretary of State;
2. there is a difference in the classes of person who may possess and supply them; and
3. entries in a controlled drugs register need not be made in respect of these drugs but invoices or like records must be kept for a period of two years (see below).

---

24. A paramedic independent prescriber may prescribe codeine phosphate by oral administration, diazepam and morphine sulphate by oral administration or by injection, lorazepam by injection, and midazolam by oromucosal administration or by injection (Reg.6D(2)).
25. A therapeutic radiographer independent prescriber may prescribe codeine, diazepam, lorazepam, oxycodone and tramadol by oral administration, and morphine by oral administration or by injection (Reg.6D(1)).
26. The other controlled drugs being gabapentin, pregabalin and tramadol (all listed within Schedule 3); see: https://www.england.nhs.uk/wp-content/uploads/2020/10/podiatrist-consultation-summary.pdf (accessed 31 December 2024).
27. The consultation includes codeine (listed within Schedules 2 and 5), and gabapentin, pregabalin and tramadol (all listed within Schedule 3); see: https://www.england.nhs.uk/wp-content/uploads/2020/10/physiotherapy-full-consultation.pdf (accessed 31 December 2024).

Schedule 4, Part I

Part I of Schedule 4 contains many of the benzodiazepines and zaleplon, zolpidem and zopiclone (sometimes referred to as *Z drugs*). The restrictions applicable to Schedule 3 drugs apply to these drugs with the relaxations 2 to 4 which apply to Schedule 4 Part II drugs below.

Schedule 4, Part II

Part II of Schedule 4 contains the anabolic and androgenic steroids and derivatives, together with an andrenoceptor stimulant and polypeptide hormones. The restrictions applicable to Schedule 3 drugs apply to them with the following relaxations:

1. there is no restriction on the possession of any Schedule 4 Part II drug when contained in a medicinal product;
2. prescription requirements under the Misuse of Drugs Regulations do not apply,[28] but the usual labelling requirements do apply (see **Chapter 18**);
3. records need not be kept by retailers;
4. there are no safe custody requirements;
5. destruction requirements apply only to importers, exporters and manufacturers; and
6. there is no restriction on imports or exports provided they are imported or exported by a person for self-administration.

Schedule 5

Schedule 5 specifies those preparations of certain controlled drugs for which there is only negligible risk of abuse. There is no restriction on the import, export, possession or administration of these preparations, and safe custody requirements do not apply to them. A practitioner or pharmacist, acting in their capacity as such, may manufacture or compound any of them.

No record in the register of controlled drugs need be made in respect of Schedule 3, 4 or 5 drugs obtained by a retail dealer, but for controlled drugs within Schedules 3 and 5, the invoice, or a copy of it, must be kept for two years (Reg.24(3) & (4)). Producers and wholesale dealers must retain invoices of quantities of Schedule 3 and 5 controlled drugs obtained and supplied (Reg.24(1)). No authority is required to destroy these drugs, and there are no special labelling requirements, although the usual labelling requirements apply (see **Chapter 18**).

A *retail dealer* is defined as a person lawfully conducting a retail pharmacy business[29] or a pharmacist engaged in supplying drugs to the public at an NHS health centre. The Department of Health and Social Care has conducted a consultation on amending the law to enable pharmacists to authorise pharmacy technicians to supervise the supply of medicines (see **Chapter 11**). If the law is amended as proposed, a further amendment is likely to extend the definition of retail dealer to include pharmacy technicians.

---

28. Note that whilst the prescription requirements do not apply, a prescription for a Schedule 4 controlled drug may not be supplied later than 28 days after the date specified on the prescription.
29. See Chapter 7 for the definition of lawfully conducting a retail pharmacy business.

Nitrous oxide

Nitrous oxide (sometimes known as *laughing gas*) is in Schedule 5 mainly because of reports by police in England that it was linked to anti-social behaviour – intimidating gatherings on high streets and in children's parks, where it was said to be the third most used drug among 16 to 24-year-olds, and because of the nuisance caused by empty canisters strewn across public spaces.[30]

Nitrous oxide has legitimate uses in medical, dental and veterinary settings. It is also legitimately used as a fuel additive, a food additive and food extraction solvent (for example, as a propellant in whipped cream dispensers); and it is widely used in industrial processes. In view of its legitimate uses, nitrous oxide is exempt from the restrictions that apply to other drugs in Schedule 5, as follows:[31]

- Importation and exportation are not unlawful unless the intention of the importer or exporter is to wrongfully inhale it or the importer or exporter knows or is reckless as to whether it is likely to be wrongfully inhaled by some other person.
- The supply of nitrous oxide, including by way of administration, is not unlawful unless the supply is made by a person who intends to wrongfully inhale it or intends to supply it to another person for wrongful inhalation by another person.
- Possession of nitrous oxide is not unlawful unless the person in possession intends to wrongfully inhale it or intends to supply it to another person for its wrongful inhalation by any person.

References to *wrongful inhalation* mean any inhalation other than for medical or dental purposes or of nitrous oxide which has been released into the atmosphere. The term *medical purposes* is defined as *the purposes of preventative medicine, medical diagnosis, medical research or the provision of medical care and treatment.*

Poppy-straw

Poppy-straw (which means all parts of the opium poppy, except the seeds, after mowing), and concentrate of poppy-straw (which means the material produced when poppy-straw has entered into a process for the concentration of its alkaloids) are listed as class A controlled drugs under the Act. Poppy straw is not included in any of the schedules to the regulations.

Although a licence is required to import or export poppy-straw, its production, possession and supply are free from control (Reg.4). Concentrate of poppy-straw is designated as a Schedule 1 controlled drug under the Regulations, and so all of the stringent controls, described above, for this Schedule apply to this substance.

Import and export

Controlled drugs may only be imported or exported in accordance with the terms and conditions of a licence issued by the Secretary of State (s.3 of the Act) but drugs in

---

30. https://www.gov.uk/government/news/nitrous-oxide-to-be-illegal-by-end-of-the-year (accessed 31 December 2024).

31. Reg.4C of the Misuse of Drugs Regulations 2001.

Schedule 5 (except nitrous oxide) are exempted from this requirement (Reg.4). Drugs in Schedule 4 Part II are also exempted, in the case of importation or exportation which is carried out in person for administration to that person. Unlawful import or export is an offence under the Customs and Excise Management Act 1979 (see below).

Possession and supply

It is unlawful for any person to be in possession of a controlled drug.[32] Regulation 6 of the Misuse of Drugs Regulations 2001 gives general authority to possess controlled drugs to:

(a) a constable when acting in the course of their duty;
(b) a person engaged in the business of a carrier in the course of that business;
(c) a person engaged in the business of a postal operator when acting in the course of that business;
(d) an officer of customs and excise when acting in the course of their duty;
(e) a person engaged in the work of any laboratory to which the drug has been sent for forensic examination; and
(f) a person engaged in conveying the drug to a person who may lawfully have that drug in his possession.

In addition, regulation 10 provides that the following may possess controlled drugs that are in Schedules 2, 3 and 4 to the Regulations:

(a) a practitioner;
(b) a pharmacist;
(c) a person lawfully conducting a retail pharmacy business (see **Chapter 7** for the meaning of this expression);
(d) the person in charge or acting person in charge of a hospital or care home which (for Schedule 2 drugs) is wholly or mainly maintained by a public authority out of public funds or by a charity or by voluntary subscriptions;
(e) the person in charge of an organisation providing ambulance services;
(f) in the case of such a drug supplied to them by a person responsible for the dispensing[33] and supply of medicines at a hospital, care home or prison, the senior registered nurse, acting senior registered nurse, or registered midwife, for the time being in charge of a ward, theatre or other department in the hospital, care home or prison;
(g) in the case of such a drug supplied to him by a person responsible for the dispensing and supply of medicines at a hospital, an operating department practitioner practising in that hospital;
(h) a person who is in charge of a laboratory the recognised activities of which consist in, or include, the conduct of scientific education or research and which (for Schedule 2 controlled drugs) is attached to a university, university college or such a hospital as aforesaid or to any other institution approved for the purpose under this sub-paragraph by the Secretary of State;

32. Section 5 of the Misuse of Drugs Act 1971.
33. For the meaning of "dispensing", see Box 5.1 in Chapter 5.

(i) a public analyst appointed under section 27 of the Food Safety Act 1990;
(j) a sampling officer within the meaning of Schedule 3 to the Medicines Act 1968;
(k) a person employed or engaged in connection with a scheme for testing the quality or amount of the drugs, preparations and appliances supplied under the National Health Service Act 1977 or the National Health Service (Scotland) Act 1978 and the regulations made thereunder;
(l) a General Pharmaceutical Council inspector (see **Chapter 2**); and
(m) a supplementary prescriber acting under and in accordance with the terms of a clinical management plan.

If and when the Human Medicines Regulations are amended to enable pharmacists to authorise pharmacy technicians to carry out supervision (see **Chapter 11**), it is expected that the Misuse of Drugs Regulations will be amended to add pharmacy technicians to the list of persons who may possess controlled drugs in Schedules 2, 3 and 4.

A person may possess a controlled drug that has been prescribed for them by a person authorised to prescribe it (see Prescribing permissions below).

Table 14.1 shows those classes of persons who may possess and supply specified controlled drugs. In each case where the Regulations permit certain activities in relation to a person because they are a member of a class of people, they may only lawfully undertake those activities, whilst acting in their capacity as a member of that class. In addition, those authorised to supply specified controlled drugs may only supply them to those who are authorised to possess such drugs. Where a person, for example a supplementary prescriber, or registered physiotherapist or registered chiropodist independent prescriber, is permitted to make a supply, the supply must be made in accordance with the applicable conditions (i.e. under a clinical management plan, in the case of supplementary prescribing, or of those drugs and for those purposes permitted for registered physiotherapist or registered chiropodist independent prescribing).

Table 14.1: *Administration, production, supply and possession of controlled drugs (Regs.4, 6, 6B, 6C, 6D, 7-10 and Sch. 8)*

	Class of person	Permitted activities
1	A practitioner (doctor or dentist)[34]	May possess, manufacture, compound, administer, supply or offer to supply any Schedule 2, 3, 4 or 5 drug
2	A pharmacist	May possess, manufacture, compound, supply or offer to supply any Schedule 2, 3, 4 or 5 drug
	Class of person	**Permitted activities**
3	A person lawfully conducting a retail pharmacy business	May possess, manufacture, compound, supply or offer to supply any Schedule 2, 3, 4 or 5 drug The manufacture or compounding of the drug must take place at the registered pharmacy at which that person carries on that business

34. The Misuse of Drugs Act defines a practitioner (s.37) as "a doctor, dentist, veterinary practitioner or veterinary surgeon". For the law relating to controlled drugs and veterinary practice, see Chapter 15.

Table 14.1: *Administration, production, supply and possession of controlled drugs (Regs.4, 6, 6B, 6C, 6D, 7-10 and Sch. 8)* (cont.)

	Class of person	Permitted activities
4	A nurse independent prescriber or pharmacist independent prescriber	May compound any Schedule 2, 3, 4 or 5 drug for the purposes of administration, and may possess, administer, supply or offer to supply any Schedule 2, 3, 4 or 5 drug
5	A registered physiotherapist independent prescriber, registered chiropodist independent prescriber, therapeutic radiographer independent prescriber, or paramedic independent prescriber	May possess and administer, supply or offer to supply any Schedule 2, 3, 4 or 5 drug (for those drugs, and in such circumstances that such independent prescribers may prescribe)
6	A supplementary prescriber acting under and in accordance with the terms of a clinical management plan	May compound any Schedule 2, 3, 4 or 5 drug for the purposes of administration, and may possess, administer, supply or offer to supply any Schedule 2, 3, 4 or 5 drug
7	Any person acting in accordance with the directions of a doctor, a dentist, a nurse independent prescriber, pharmacist independent prescriber, or a supplementary prescriber acting under and in accordance with the terms of a clinical management plan	May compound any Schedule 2, 3, 4 or 5 drug for the purposes of administration, and may possess and administer, any Schedule 2, 3, 4 or 5 drug (in relation to compounding, the directions must be in writing)
8	Any person acting in accordance with the directions of a registered physiotherapist independent prescriber or chiropodist independent prescriber	May possess and administer any Schedule 2, 3, 4 or 5 drug (for those drugs, and in such circumstances that such independent prescribers may prescribe)
9	Any person acting in accordance with the directions of a therapeutic radiographer independent prescriber, or paramedic independent prescriber	May possess, compound and administer any Schedule 2, 3, 4 or 5 drug (for those drugs, and in such circumstances that such independent prescribers may prescribe) (in relation to compounding, the directions need to be in writing)
10	A registered midwife	See the section on *Midwives and controlled drugs*
11	A registered nurse or a pharmacist	May possess, supply or offer to supply, under and in accordance with the terms of a Patient Group Direction (PGD), diamorphine or morphine where administration of such drugs is required for the immediate, necessary treatment of sick or injured persons
12	Any of the following: • a registered nurse • a person holding a certificate of proficiency in ambulance paramedic skills issued by, or with the approval of, the Secretary of State • a registered paramedic • a registered midwife • a registered optometrist • a registered chiropodist • a registered orthoptist; • a registered physiotherapist • a registered radiographer • a registered occupational therapist • a registered orthotist and prosthetist • a pharmacist	May possess, supply or offer to supply, under and in accordance with the terms of a PGD: • any drug specified in Schedule 4 or 5 • ketamine • midazolam The following may not be supplied: • anabolic steroid drugs specified in Part II of Schedule 4 • any drug or preparation which is designed for administration by injection and which is to be used for the purpose of treating a person who is addicted to a drug

Table 14.1: *Administration, production, supply and possession of controlled drugs (Regs.4, 6, 6B, 6C, 6D, 7-10 and Sch. 8)* (cont.)

	Class of person	Permitted activities
13	A person who is authorised as a member of a group, under and in accordance with the terms of their group authority and in compliance with any attached conditions	May possess any Schedule 2, 3, 4 or 5 drug, or nitrous oxide, supply or offer to supply any Schedule 2, 3, 4 or 5 drug
14	The senior or acting senior registered nurse, or registered midwife, for the time being in charge of a ward, theatre or other department in the hospital, care home or prison, where the drug was supplied to them by a person responsible for the dispensing and supply of medicines at a hospital, care home or prison	May possess, supply or offer to supply any Schedule 2, 3, 4 or 5 drug. The supply must be for administration to a patient in that ward, theatre or department in accordance with the directions of a doctor, dentist or a supplementary prescriber or nurse or a pharmacist independent prescriber lawfully prescribing that drug
15	The person in charge or acting person in charge of a hospital or care home which is wholly or mainly maintained by a public authority out of public funds or by a charity or by voluntary subscriptions	May possess, supply or offer to supply any Schedule 2, 3, 4 or 5 drug, but not if there is a pharmacist responsible for the dispensing and supply of medicines
16	The person in charge or acting person in charge of a hospital or care home	May possess, supply or offer to supply any drug specified in Schedule 3, 4 or 5, but not if there is a pharmacist responsible for the dispensing and supply of medicines
17	The person in charge or acting person in charge of an organisation providing ambulance services	May possess, supply or offer to supply any Schedule 2, 3, 4 or 5 drug, but not if there is a pharmacist responsible for the dispensing and supply of medicines. Such supplies may only be made directly to employees of the organisation for the immediate treatment of sick or injured persons
18	An operating department practitioner practising in a hospital, where the drug was supplied to them by a person responsible for the dispensing and supply of medicines at that hospital	May possess, supply or offer to supply any Schedule 2, 3, 4 or 5 drug The supply must be for administration to a patient in that ward, theatre or department in accordance with the directions of a doctor, dentist or a supplementary prescriber or nurse or a pharmacist independent prescriber lawfully prescribing that drug
19	The installation manager of an offshore installation or the owner of a ship, or the master of a ship which does not carry a doctor among the seamen employed in it	May possess, supply or offer to supply any Schedule 2, 3, 4 or 5 drug to any person on that installation or ship in order to comply with provisions as a result of: (a) the Mineral Workings (Offshore Installations) Act 1971; (b) the Health and Safety at Work etc. Act 1974; or (c) the Merchant Shipping Act 1995. They may also supply or offer to supply any Schedule 2, 3, 4 or 5 drug to any person who may lawfully supply that drug to them or (for Schedule 2 or 5 drugs) to any constable for the purpose of the destruction of that drug
20	The master of a foreign ship which is in a port in Great Britain	May possess any Schedule 2, 3, 4 or 5 drug, so far as necessary for the equipment of the ship (as authorised by the proper officer of the port health authority, or equivalent)

Table 14.1: *Administration, production, supply and possession of controlled drugs (Regs.4, 6, 6B, 6C, 6D, 7-10 and Sch. 8)* (cont.)

	Class of person	Permitted activities
21	A person engaged in conveying the drug to a person who may lawfully have that drug in their possession	May possess any controlled drug or supply any controlled drug to any person who may lawfully have that drug in their possession
22	A person who is in charge of a laboratory, the recognised activities of which consist in, or include, the conduct of scientific education or research and which is attached to a university, university college or such a hospital as aforesaid or to any other institution approved for the purpose under this sub-paragraph by the Secretary of State	May possess any Schedule 2 drug or nitrous oxide, and supply or offer to supply any Schedule 2 or 5 drug to any person who may lawfully have that drug in their possession[35]
23	A person in charge of a laboratory, the recognised activities of which consist in, or include, the conduct of scientific education or research	May possess, supply or offer to supply any drug specified in Schedule 3, 4 or 5 to any person who may lawfully have that drug in their possession
24	A person in charge of a laboratory	May possess, supply or offer to supply any drug specified in Schedule 3 which is required for use as a buffering agent in chemical analysis to any person who may lawfully have that drug in their possession
25	A public analyst appointed under section 27 of the Food Safety Act 1990	May possess, supply or offer to supply any Schedule 2, 3, 4 or 5 drug
26	A sampling officer within the meaning of Schedule 3 to the Medicines Act 1968	May possess, supply or offer to supply any Schedule 2, 3, 4 or 5 drug
27	A person employed or engaged in connection with a scheme for testing the quality or amount of the drugs, preparations and appliances supplied under the National Health Service Act 1977 or the National Health Service (Scotland) Act 1978 and the regulations made thereunder	May possess, supply or offer to supply any Schedule 2, 3, 4 or 5 drug
28	A person authorised by the General Pharmaceutical Council for the purposes of section 108 or 109 of the Medicines Act 1968	May possess, supply or offer to supply any Schedule 2, 3, 4 or 5 drug
29	A constable when acting in the course of their duty as such	May possess any controlled drug, or supply or offer to supply any controlled drug to any person who may lawfully have that drug in their possession
30	A person engaged in the business of a carrier when acting in the course of that business	May possess any controlled drug, or supply or offer to supply any controlled drug to any person who may lawfully have that drug in their possession
31	A person engaged in the business of a postal operator (within the meaning of Part 3 of the Postal Services Act 2011) when acting in the course of that business	May possess any controlled drug, or supply or offer to supply any controlled drug to any person who may lawfully have that drug in their possession

35. These individuals may also possess, supply or offer to supply any drug specified in Schedules 3 or 4 to any person who may lawfully have that drug in their possession as per entry in the following row.

Table 14.1: *Administration, production, supply and possession of controlled drugs (Regs.4, 6, 6B, 6C, 6D, 7-10 and Sch. 8)* (cont.)

	Class of person	Permitted activities
32	An officer of customs and excise when acting in the course of their duty as such	May possess any controlled drug, or supply or offer to supply any controlled drug to any person who may lawfully have that drug in their possession
33	A person engaged in the work of any laboratory to which the drug has been sent for forensic examination when acting in the course of their duty as a person so engaged	May possess any controlled drug, or supply or offer to supply any controlled drug to any person who may lawfully have that drug in their possession
34	Any person licensed under the Wildlife and Countryside Act 1981	May supply, offer to supply or have in their possession any drug specified in Schedule 2 or 3 for the purposes for which that licence was granted
35	A person with an appropriate licence from the Home Office, at the premises specified in that authority and in compliance with any specified conditions	May possess any drug specified in Schedule 3, 4 or 5, or nitrous oxide, produce, supply or offer to supply any drug specified in Schedule 3, 4 or 5

In addition,[36] registered chiropodists or registered podiatrists[37] may, if they are qualified to do so, supply or offer to supply the following controlled drugs:

- co-codamol 8/500, 15/500 and 30/500;
- co-dydramol 10/500; and
- codeine phosphate.

Possession of ketamine by healthcare professionals acting under Patient Group Directions (see **Chapter 13**) is lawful.

Other general authorities to possess and supply include:

1. any person who is lawfully in possession of a controlled drug may supply that drug to the person from whom they obtained it (for example, for the purpose of disposal if the drug is no longer required); (Reg.6(1))
2. any person who is in possession of a Schedule 2, 3, 4 or 5 drug which has been supplied for them by, or on the prescription of, somebody authorised to prescribe that item, or under a Patient Group Direction (PGD), may supply that drug to any doctor, dentist or pharmacist for the purpose of destruction; (Reg.6(2),[38] (6)(2A))
3. any person who is in lawful possession of a Schedule 2, 3, 4 or 5 drug which has been supplied by, or on the prescription of, a veterinary surgeon or veterinary practitioner for the treatment of animals may supply that drug to any veterinary surgeon, veterinary practitioner or pharmacist for the purpose of destruction; (Reg.6(3))

36. Regulation 8(8)(c).
37. There is no professional difference between a chiropodist and a podiatrist. The regulator is the Health and Care Professions Council which maintains a single register for those who are called chiropodists and podiatrists. The legislation uses both terms (see, for example, regulation 8(8A), and both terms are used in this chapter.
38. If and when the Human Medicines Regulations are amended to allow pharmacists to authorise pharmacy technicians to supervise, the Reg.6(2) is expected to be amended so as to allow drugs in Schedules 2, 3, 4 and 5 to be supplied also to a pharmacy technician for the purpose of destruction.

4. any person may possess a Schedule 2, 3, 4 or 5 drug for administration for medical, dental or veterinary purposes in accordance with the directions of a practitioner, a supplementary prescriber (acting under and in accordance with a clinical management plan), a nurse, pharmacist, physiotherapist, podiatrist, paramedic or therapeutic radiographer independent prescriber. Such possession will not be lawful if the person for whom the drug was prescribed (or to whom that drug was supplied under a PGD):
   a. was then being supplied with any controlled drug by or on the prescription of another prescriber, or under a PGD, and failed to disclose that fact to the person prescribing or making the supply (primarily to avoid misusers from obtaining controlled drugs from more than one source), or
   b. made a declaration or statement, or had such a statement made on their behalf, which was false in any particular, for the purpose of obtaining the supply or prescription. (Reg.10(2)).[39]

Prescriptions for controlled drugs

Prescribing permissions

Doctors may prescribe any controlled drug specified in Schedules 2-5 (although a licence from the Home Office is required to prescribe cocaine, diamorphine or dipipanone for the treatment of addiction).[40]

Dentists, nurse and pharmacist independent prescribers, and supplementary prescribers (under the terms of a clinical management plan) may prescribe any controlled drug specified in Schedules 2-5, except cocaine, diamorphine or dipipanone for the treatment of addiction.

Approved country health professionals (see **Chapter 12**) may not prescribe drugs specified in Schedule 2 or 3, but may prescribe those in Schedules 4 or 5.[41]

A registered physiotherapist independent prescriber may prescribe any of the following controlled drugs for the treatment of organic disease or injury, provided that the drug is prescribed to be administered by the specified method:

- diazepam by oral administration;
- dihydrocodeine by oral administration;
- fentanyl by transdermal administration;
- lorazepam by oral administration;
- morphine by oral administration or by injection;
- oxycodone by oral administration; and
- temazepam by oral administration.

A therapeutic radiographer independent prescriber may prescribe any of the following controlled drugs for the treatment of organic disease or injury:

- codeine by oral administration;

---

39. Reg 10(2).
40. Misuse of Drugs (Supply to Addicts) Regulations 1997.
41. Reg.214(6) of the Human Medicines Regulations 2012.

- diazepam by oral administration;
- lorazepam by oral administration;
- morphine by oral administration or by injection;
- oxycodone by oral administration; and
- tramadol by oral administration.

A paramedic independent prescriber may prescribe any of the following controlled drugs for the treatment of organic disease or injury:

- codeine phosphate by oral administration;
- diazepam by oral administration or by injection;
- lorazepam by injection;
- midazolam by oromucosal administration or by injection; and
- morphine sulphate by oral administration or by injection.

A registered chiropodist independent prescriber may prescribe diazepam, dihydrocodeine, lorazepam and temazepam, for oral administration, for the treatment of organic disease or injury.[42]

Schedule 1 controlled drugs

Since Schedule 1 drugs will rarely (if ever) be prescribed, they are not mentioned in this section. However, should a Schedule 1 drug ever be prescribed, it should be noted that all of the requirements in this section that apply to Schedule 2 controlled drugs apply equally to Schedule 1 drugs.

Prescription requirements for Schedule 2 and 3 controlled drugs

A prescription for a Schedule 2 or 3 controlled drug for human use (veterinary prescriptions are considered in **Chapter 15**) must not be issued unless it complies with the following requirements (Reg.15(1)):

1. it must be written so as to be indelible, be dated and be signed by the person issuing it with their usual signature or be prescribed on an electronic prescription form (it is unlikely that a carbon copy, even one bearing an original signature would be sufficient to satisfy the indelibility requirement);[43]
2. except in the case of a health prescription,[44] or unless prescribed on an electronic prescription form, it must be written on a prescription form provided by NHS England,[45] by NHS Scotland or NHS Wales for the purposes of private prescribing (this is the "standardised private controlled drug prescription form": FP10PCD in England, PPCD(1) in Scotland and WP10PCD in Wales);
3. except in the case of a health prescription, specify the prescriber identification number and address of the person issuing it;
4. if issued by a dentist, have the words "for dental treatment only" written on it;

42. Regulation 6C.
43. Misuse of Drugs and the Misuse of Drugs (Supply to Addicts) (Amendment) Regulations 2005.
44. A *health prescription* is an NHS prescription – see Chapter 12.
45. Shortly before going to press, the Prime Minister announced that NHS England would be abolished as a separate body, and its functions will be exercised by the Department of Health and Social Care.

5. it must specify the name and address of the person for whose treatment it is issued;
6. it must specify the dose to be taken;
7. in the case of a prescription containing a controlled drug which is a preparation, it must specify the form and, where appropriate, the strength of the preparation, and either the total quantity (in both words and figures) of the preparation or the number (in both words and figures) of dosage units, as appropriate, to be supplied; in any other case, it must specify the total quantity (in both words and figures) of the controlled drug to be supplied;
8. in the case of a prescription for a total quantity intended to be dispensed by instalments, it must contain a direction specifying the amount of the instalments of the total amount which must be dispensed and the intervals to be observed when dispensing.

Unless there is a good reason to do otherwise, it is recommended that the maximum quantity of Schedule 2, 3 or 4 controlled drugs prescribed is no more than 30 days.[46]

A Schedule 2 or 3 controlled drug must not be supplied by any person on a prescription (Reg.16):

- unless the prescription complies with the prescription requirements set out above;
- unless the prescriber's address on the prescription is within the UK;
- unless the supplier is either acquainted with the prescriber's signature, and has no reason to suppose that it is not genuine, or has taken reasonably sufficient steps to satisfy him/herself that it is genuine;[47]
- before the date on which the prescription was signed (which will normally be the date on the prescription); and
- later than 28 days after the date on which it was signed by the prescriber (which will be presumed to be the date on the prescription unless it is an instalment prescription – see below). In calculating the period of 28 days, the date of the prescription is excluded. In other words, controlled drugs in Schedules 2, 3 or 4 on a prescription dated 1 March may be supplied up to midnight on 29 March of the same year. However, if the prescriber has indicated on the prescription form that a supply should not be made before a specified date, the period of 28 days will run from the day after the specified date.[48]

No prescription requirements are laid down for any controlled drug in Schedules 4 or 5 to the Regulations.

Note that whilst the above requirements do not apply to prescriptions for Schedule 4 and 5 drugs, a prescription for a Schedule 4 controlled drug may not be supplied later than 28 days after the date specified on the prescription.

---

46. NICE (2016) Controlled drugs: safe use and management; NICE guideline [NG46].
47. NHS England has produced the following guide to spotting a forged or fraudulent prescription: https://www.england.nhs.uk/south/wp-content/uploads/sites/6/2021/08/2021-22-forged-prescriptions-guidance.pdf accessed 31 December 2024).
48. As to the calculation of periods of time where the word "after" is used, see *Zoan v Rouamba* [2000] 1 W.L.R 1509 CA.

Endorsing the prescription

A person supplying a Schedule 2 or 3 controlled drug on prescription shall, at the time of the supply, mark on the prescription the date on which the drug was supplied. Every prescription, other than a health[49] or veterinary prescription, must be sent to the relevant NHS service agency for monitoring purposes.

Instalment prescriptions

Prescriptions for Schedule 2 or 3 controlled drugs, which contain a direction that specified instalments of the total amount may be supplied at stated intervals must not be supplied otherwise than in accordance with the directions (Regs.16(4)), and:

1. the first instalment must be supplied not later than 28 days after the date specified on the prescription;
2. the prescription must be marked with the date when each instalment is supplied;
3. the prescription (other than a health prescription, although see *Endorsing the prescription* above in relation to reimbursement) must be sent to the relevant NHS service agency; and
4. repeat prescriptions as such are not provided for, in that the total quantity of drug prescribed must be stated on the prescription.

Technical errors on prescriptions

A pharmacist[50] may supply a Schedule 2 or 3 controlled drug if the prescription contains minor typographical errors or spelling mistakes or if it specifies the total quantity of the preparation, or of the controlled drug, or the number of dosage units (as the case may be) in either words or figures but not both, provided that (Reg.16):

1. having exercised all due diligence, they are satisfied on reasonable grounds that the prescription is genuine;[51]
2. having exercised all due diligence, they are satisfied on reasonable grounds that the supply of the drug is in accordance with the intention of the person issuing the prescription;
3. they amend the prescription in ink or otherwise indelibly to correct the minor errors or mistakes or to add either the total quantity in word or figures, as necessary; and
4. they mark the prescription so that the amendment they have made is attributable to them.

---

49. Although not a requirement under Reg.23 of the Misuse of Drugs Regulations, all health prescriptions for Schedule 2 or 3 controlled drugs will be sent to the relevant NHS service agency for reimbursement purposes.
50. If and when the Human Medicines Regulations are amended to enable pharmacists to authorise pharmacy technicians to carry out supervision (see **Chapter 11**), it is expected that the Misuse of Drugs Regulations will be amended to enable pharmacy technicians to deal with prescriptions that have typographical errors in the same way as pharmacists.
51. See also the requirements for non-controlled drug prescriptions and the case of *Storkwain* (Chapter 12).

Procedures for when the drug is collected

A person who is asked to supply a Schedule 2 controlled drug must first ascertain whether the person collecting the drug is the patient, the patient's representative or a healthcare professional acting in their professional capacity on behalf of the patient, and (Reg.16(6)):

1. where the person is the patient or the patient's representative, they may request evidence of identity, and refuse to supply the drug if they are not satisfied as to the identity of that person;
2. where the person is a healthcare professional acting in their professional capacity on behalf of the patient, they must obtain that person's name and address and must, unless they are acquainted with that person, request evidence of the identity of the person but may supply the drug even if not satisfied as to the identity of that person.

Prescribing in hospitals, etc.

A pharmacist may supply a Schedule 2 or 3 controlled drug other than on a health prescription in a hospital if it does not comply with the usual requirements for private prescriptions for such drugs, i.e. to be written on the standardised private prescription form and to specify the prescriber identification number of the person issuing it.

A prescription issued for the treatment of a patient in a hospital, care home or prison and written on the patient's bed card or case sheet need not specify the name and address of the patient (Reg.15(3)). When a drug is administered from stock held in the ward, the prescription requirements do not apply.

See also **Chapter 9**.

Exemption for certain prescriptions and other provisions

Nothing in the Regulations relating to prescriptions (Regs.15 and 16) has effect in relation to prescriptions issued for the purposes of a scheme for testing the quality and amount of the drugs, preparations and appliances supplied under the NHS or to any prescriptions issued for the purposes of the Medicines Act 1968 to sampling officers within the meaning of that Act (Reg.17).

Emergency supplies

It is not lawful to make an emergency supply (**Chapter 12**) at the request of a patient or prescriber of any Schedule 2 or 3 controlled drug, with the exception of medicines containing phenobarbital or phenobarbital sodium, for use in the treatment of epilepsy. Emergency supplies of Schedule 4 and 5 drugs are permitted. In all cases, supplies must be made in accordance with the HMR. When the supply is made at the request of a patient, for phenobarbital (for epilepsy), or a Schedule 4 or 5 drug, a maximum of five days' supply may be given.[52]

52. Note that although the Misuse of Drugs Regulations permit the supply without prescription of phenobarbital or phenobarbital sodium for the treatment of epilepsy, the omission of phenobarbital and phenobarbital sodium from the NHS terms of service suggests that these products cannot be supplied in an emergency under the NHS. Such a supply would be lawful, but the pharmacy owner would not be entitled to be paid by the NHS.

Marking of containers

The container in which a controlled drug, other than a preparation, is supplied must be plainly marked with the amount of drug contained in it. If the drug is a preparation made up into tablets, capsules or other dosage units, the container must be marked with the amount of controlled drug(s) in each dosage unit and the number of dosage units in the package. For any other kind of preparation, the container must be marked with the total amount of the preparation in it and the percentage of controlled drug(s) in the preparation (Reg.18(1)). These requirements do not apply to:

- any exempt product;
- poppy-straw;
- Schedule 4 or 5 controlled drugs;
- any Schedule 3 drug contained in or comprising a preparation used as a buffering agent in chemical analysis, which has present in it both a substance in that Schedule and a salt of that substance or is pre-mixed in a kit;
- Controlled drugs supplied on the prescription of a practitioner, a supplementary prescriber, a nurse independent prescriber, a registered chiropodist or registered podiatrist independent prescriber, a paramedic independent prescriber, a therapeutic radiographer independent prescriber, or a pharmacist independent prescriber; or
- the supply of a controlled drug for administration in a clinical trial or a medicinal test on animals (Reg.18(2)).

Registers and records

Register means either a bound book, which does not include any form of loose-leaf register or card index (Reg.2), or a computerised system which is in accordance with best practice guidelines endorsed by the Secretary of State for Health.

There is no statutory format for the register provided the minimum information specified below is recorded. An entry in a controlled drugs register must be made in respect of every quantity of any drug in Schedule 1 or 2 which is obtained or supplied (whether by way of administration or otherwise), except for (Reg.19(3)):

- drugs returned to a practitioner or a pharmacist[53] for the purposes of destruction;
- the supply of a drug by a person who holds a Home Office licence, within the terms of that licence, if the licence does not require a register to be kept;
- the receipt or supply of a drug by the senior or acting senior registered nurse or registered midwife, for the time being in charge of a ward, theatre or other department in a hospital, care home or prison.

Note that there are different provisions for drugs obtained and supplied by midwives – see section on Midwives and controlled drugs, below.

---

53. If and when the Human Medicines Regulations are amended to enable pharmacists to authorise pharmacy technicians to carry out supervision (see **Chapter 11**), it is expected that the Misuse of Drugs Regulations will be amended to provide that, like pharmacists, pharmacy technicians are not required to enter in a controlled drugs register Schedule 1 or 2 controlled drugs that have been returned to them for the purposes of destruction.

General provisions relating to the keeping of records in the controlled drugs register

The class of drug recorded, together with its strength and form, must be specified at the head of each page of the register. Entries in the register must be made in chronological sequence. A separate register or separate part of the register must be used in respect of each class of drugs and a separate page should be used in respect of each strength and form of that drug (Reg.20).

Entries must be made on the day of the transaction or, if that is not reasonably practicable, on the following day. No cancellation, obliteration or alteration of any entry may be made, and corrections must be by way of marginal notes or footnotes, which must be dated. Every entry and every correction of such an entry must be in ink or be otherwise indelible or shall be in a computerised form in which every entry is attributable and capable of being audited, and which is in accordance with best practice guidelines endorsed by the Secretary of State.

A separate register must be kept in respect of each set of premises of the business. There may only be one such register for each premises unless the Secretary of State has approved the keeping of separate registers in different departments. The register must be kept at the premises to which it relates, and where the register is in a computerised form, it must be accessible from those premises. This means a pharmacist cannot, for example, take home a register that is kept on paper to write up entries overnight and bring back to the pharmacy in the morning.

Nothing prevents the use of the register to record additional information to that required or allowed under these provisions, but the register must not be used for any purpose other than for purposes related to these regulations.

Minimum information to be recorded regarding controlled drugs obtained

The headings in respect of entries made for drugs obtained are (Reg.19(d)):

1. date supply received;
2. name and address from whom received;
3. quantity received.

Minimum information to be recorded regarding controlled drugs supplied

The following information must be recorded, in respect of drugs supplied (Reg.19(e)):

- date supplied;
- name and address of person or firm supplied;
- details of authority to possess – prescriber or licence holder's details;
- quantity of drug supplied;
- person collecting Schedule 2 drug (i.e. patient/patient's representative/healthcare professional and, if a healthcare professional, their name and address – see section above on *Procedures for when the drug is collected*);
- was proof of identity requested of patient/patient's representative (Yes/No); and
- was proof of identity of person collecting provided (Yes/No).

Where a supply of a Schedule 2 drug is made to a member of the crew of a ship or a person on an offshore installation, an entry, specifying the drug, in the official log book or installation log book is a sufficient record. In the case of a ship which is not required to carry an official log book, a report signed by the master of the ship is sufficient if it is delivered as soon as may be to the superintendent of a mercantile marine office (Reg.21).

Return of controlled drugs from patients

A pharmacist or practitioner is not required to record any prescribed drug returned to them for destruction, but NICE recommends[54] that the destruction and disposal of such drugs is recorded in a separate book, kept for this purpose, with the record including the dates of receipt and destruction and the signatures of any witness and of the person destroying the controlled drugs. It would seem sensible to also record the quantity, strength and name of the controlled drug returned.

Note that standard operating procedures set out under Welsh legislation are required to detail arrangements for the disposal and destruction of controlled drugs, and standard operating procedures set out by Accountable Officers in England and Scotland may include specific details as to such arrangements.

Running balances

At present there is no legal requirement to keep running balances. However, it is recommended by NICE[55] that they be kept in accordance with a standard operating procedure.

Furnishing of information with respect to controlled drugs

The persons listed below must, in response to a request made by the Secretary of State or by a person authorised in writing by them, provide any particulars requested in respect of producing, obtaining, supplying or the stocking of any controlled drug. The register, the stocks of drugs and other relevant books and documents must also be produced if requested. If records are held in a computerised form, a copy of the computerised form must be supplied if requested.

Those required to furnish information are (Reg.26(2)):

- practitioners;
- wholesale dealers;
- retail dealers;
- persons or acting persons in charge of hospitals, organisation providing ambulance services or care homes;
- persons in charge of a laboratory;
- persons authorised under the Act or regulations to produce, import or export any controlled drug;
- persons authorised under Regulation 9(4)(a) to supply drugs in Schedules 3 and 4;
- supplementary prescribers;
- nurse independent prescribers;
- registered chiropodist or registered podiatrist independent prescribers;

54. NICE (2016) Controlled drugs: safe use and management; NICE guideline [NG46].

55. NICE (2016) Controlled drugs: safe use and management; NICE guideline [NG46].

- paramedic independent prescribers; and
- therapeutic radiographer independent prescribers.

Professional personal records relating to the physical or mental health of an individual are exempt.

Preservation of records

All registers and midwives' record books must be preserved for two years from the date on which the last entry is made therein (Reg.23).

For controlled drugs in Schedules 3 and 5 to the Regulations, it is sufficient if every invoice is preserved for two years from the date on which it is issued. Producers and wholesalers must keep invoices in respect of Schedule 3 and 5 drugs obtained or supplied by them, and retail dealers must keep invoices in respect of the drugs they obtain. Copies of invoices (e.g. in a computerised form) may be retained in place of the original document (Reg.24).

Record-keeping requirements for Schedule 3 and 4 drugs

There are specific record-keeping requirements for those licensed to produce Schedule 3 or 4 drugs, those authorised to import or export Schedule 3 or 4 drugs and for specified persons (not, for example, patients, constables or carriers) who are authorised to possess or destroy, or cause to be destroyed, specified Schedule 4 cannabis containing products, which possess a marketing authorisation issued by the MHRA (Reg.22).

Destruction of controlled drugs

Persons who are required to keep records in respect of controlled drugs in Schedules 1, 2, 3 or 4 may only destroy them in the presence of an authorised person. An *authorised person* is either an individual or a member of a class who has been authorised by the Secretary of State or an Accountable Officer. Authorised persons include police constables and GPhC inspectors and anyone appointed by an Accountable Officer (see below). An Accountable Officer cannot be an authorised person.

Particulars of the date of destruction and the quantity destroyed must be entered in the register of controlled drugs and signed by the authorised person in whose presence the drug was destroyed. The authorised person may, for the purposes of analysis, take a sample of the drug which is to be destroyed, and destruction must be carried out according to their directions.

A pharmacist or practitioner may destroy prescribed drugs returned by a patient or the patient's representative without legally being required to make any record and without the presence of an authorised person (but see *Registers and records* above). However, it is suggested[56] that a second member of staff (preferably a registered health professional) should witness the destruction and disposal of these drugs.

Controlled drugs, whether stock or returned by patients, are subject to the same considerations as for other returned medicines, so disposal via the sewage system would

56. NICE (2016) Controlled drugs: safe use and management; NICE guideline [NG46].

not generally be permitted. As part of the disposal process, controlled drugs should be denatured in such a way as to render the drug irretrievable. There are a number of specially designed controlled drug denaturing kits which enable pharmacists to denature controlled drugs as part of the disposal process.

The denaturing of controlled drugs would be classified as "treatment" of waste, which would require a permit, but pharmacies can register an exemption with the Environment Agency to store, sort and denature controlled drugs at the place they become waste.[57] In relation to the storage, sorting and denaturing of controlled drugs, the Environment Agency has produced a regulatory position statement (RPS).[58] If the RPS is complied with, the Environment Agency will permit an authorised person to store, sort and denature waste controlled drugs:

- returned by patients or healthcare workers to a pharmacy or medical practice;
- brought together at collection points or denaturing sessions; and
- in patients' homes.

The permission granted by the RPS is subject to satisfying certain conditions. These including limiting the applicability of the RPS to medicines:

- from diagnosis, treatment or prevention of disease in humans;
- from research, diagnosis, treatment or prevention of disease involving animals; or
- separately collected as household waste.

In addition, the RPS imposes a maximum storage volume of one cubic metre at any one time, and a limit of six months on the storage of waste controlled drugs.

The master of a ship or installation manager of an offshore installation may not destroy any surplus drugs but may dispose of them to a constable or to a person who is lawfully entitled to supply them (i.e. to any pharmacist or licensed dealer who could have supplied them to them) (Reg.27). If and when the Human Medicines Regulations are amended to enable pharmacists to authorise pharmacy technicians to carry out supervision (see **Chapter 11**), it is expected that regulation 27 of the Misuse of Drugs Regulations will be amended to refer to pharmacy technicians as well as pharmacists.

Midwives and controlled drugs

A registered midwife who has, in accordance with the Nursing and Midwifery Order 2001, notified to the local supervising authority[59] their intention to practise may, as far as is necessary for their professional practice, possess and administer or supply any controlled drug which the law permits them to administer. Supplies may only be made to them, or possessed by them, on the authority of a Midwife's Supply Order (MSO), that is, an order in writing specifying:

---

57. For further details, see: https://www.gov.uk/guidance/waste-exemption-t28-sort-and-denature-controlled-drugs-for-disposal#t28-sort-and-denature-controlled-drugs-for-disposal (accessed 31 December 2024).

58. https://www.gov.uk/government/publications/denaturing-controlled-drugs-that-have-become-waste-rps-4/denaturing-controlled-drugs-that-have-become-waste-rps-4 (accessed 31 December 2024).

59. In fact, local supervising authorities were abolished by the Nursing and Midwifery (Amendment) Order 2017, but the reference to them remains in the Misuse of Drugs Regulations.

- the name and occupation of the midwife obtaining the controlled drug;
- the name of the person to whom it is to be administered or supplied; and
- the purpose for which it is required and the total quantity to be obtained (Reg.11).

Regulation 11 says that an MSO must be signed by the appropriate medical officer, which means:

1. a doctor who is for the time being authorised in writing for the purposes of regulation 11 by the local supervising authority for the region or area in which the controlled drug was, or is to be, obtained; or
2. a person appointed under, and in accordance with, the Nursing and Midwifery Order 2001 by that authority to exercise supervision over registered midwives within their area.

The requirements for MSOs in the Regulations have not been amended since the abolition of local supervising authorities (see above footnote). However, the Explanatory Memorandum to the Misuse of Drugs (Amendment) (No. 2) (England, Wales and Scotland) Regulations 2015[60] states (paragraph 7.8) that an MSO can be signed by "a doctor or head of midwives". Explanatory Memoranda do not have legal force, but it seems likely that an MSO signed by a doctor or head of midwives will be taken by enforcement agencies to satisfy the requirements of the exemption.

A midwife may surrender any stocks of controlled drugs in their possession which are no longer required by them to the appropriate medical officer (Reg.11) or to the person from whom they obtained them (Reg.6). (See above as to *appropriate medical officer.*)

The midwife must, on each occasion on which they obtain a supply of a Schedule 2 controlled drug, enter in a book kept by them solely for this purpose, the date, the name and address of the person from whom the drug was obtained, the name of the person to whom it is to be administered or supplied, the amount obtained and the form in which it was obtained. When administering or supplying such a drug to a patient, they must enter in the same book as soon as practicable the name and address of the patient, the name of the person to whom it was administered or supplied, the amount administered and the form in which it was administered (Reg.21). An MSO must be retained for two years by the pharmacist who supplies the controlled drug (not submitted to the relevant NHS service agency) and they must make an appropriate entry in their register of controlled drugs (Reg.19).

See also **Chapter 9**.

Requisitions

When a person (the supplier) other than a practitioner supplies a Schedule 1, 2 or 3 controlled drug otherwise than on a prescription or by way of administration, to a person authorised to possess that drug, they may do so only on receipt of a requisition in writing in an approved form. The requisition must be signed by the recipient, stating their name, address and profession or occupation, and must specify the total quantity of the drug to be supplied and the purpose for which it is required. The supplier must be reasonably satisfied that the signature is that of the person purporting to have signed the requisition and that they are engaged in the profession or occupation stated

60. https://www.legislation.gov.uk/uksi/2015/891/pdfs/uksiem_20150891_en.pdf (accessed 31 December 2024).

(Reg.14(2)). The following persons are authorised to requisition a controlled drug via this mechanism:

- a practitioner;
- the person in charge or acting person in charge of a hospital, organisation providing ambulance services or care home;
- a person who is in charge of a laboratory;
- the owner of a ship or the master of a ship which does not carry a doctor among the seamen employed in it;
- the master of a foreign ship in a port in Great Britain;
- the installation manager of an offshore installation;
- a supplementary prescriber;
- a nurse independent prescriber;
- a pharmacist independent prescriber; and
- a person who holds a certificate of proficiency in ambulance paramedic skills issued by, or with the approval of, the Secretary of State, or a person who is a registered paramedic.

Approved requisition forms are produced by the NHS. Since 2015, practitioners who wish to obtain a stock of a Schedule 2 or 3 controlled drug from a community pharmacy should use a standard Controlled Drug Requisition Form (FP10CDF in England, GP10A for NHS supplies and CDRF for private supplies in Scotland, and WP10CDF in Wales) (Reg.14). Supply to hospices and prisons are exempt from the need to use the form (Reg.14(7)).

Some transactions are exempt from the requirement to use an approved requisition form, including where supplies are made to a hospital ward from a dispensary within the same hospital. Some hospital wards source their controlled drugs from other Trusts or wards which do not form part of the same legal entity. In these cases, the approved form is required, although the Home Office has issued guidance[61] on the use of a "bulk" or "global" requisition.

A requisition is not required for the supply of:

- Schedule 4 or 5 drugs or poppy-straw;
- Schedule 3 drugs contained in or comprising a preparation which is required for use as a buffering agent in chemical analysis, has present in it both a substance specified in paragraph 1 or 2 of that Schedule and a salt of that substance and which is pre-mixed in a kit;
- any exempt product;
- any drug which is required for use in a prison or hospice;
- any drug, when supplied by a wholesale dealer to a registered pharmacy.

Other than in the case of a veterinary requisition, the supplier must mark the requisition (in ink or otherwise indelibly) with their name and address and send the original document to the relevant NHS agency. The Royal Pharmaceutical Society

61. The Home Office (2015) Additional Guidance issued by the Home Office on the use of the mandatory requisition form for Schedule 2 and 3 controlled drugs https://www.nhsbsa.nhs.uk/sites/default/files/2017-03/Mandatory_Requisition_Forms_-_Additional_Guidance.pdf (accessed 31 December 2024).

advises that it is good practice for pharmacies to retain a copy of the requisition for two years from the date of supply.[62] These requirements as to marking the requisition and sending it to the relevant NHS agency do not apply where the supplier is a wholesale dealer or a person responsible for the dispensing and supply of medicines at a hospital, organisation providing ambulance services, care home or prison.

Note that an MSO (see *Midwives and controlled drugs* above) should be treated differently to a requisition for the purposes of these Regulations, as unlike requisitions for controlled drugs, they should be retained for two years following supply.

Where a recipient is a practitioner who represents that they urgently require a controlled drug for the purpose of their profession, the supplier, if they are reasonably satisfied that the practitioner requires the drug and is by reason of some emergency unable to furnish a written requisition, may deliver the drug on an undertaking by the practitioner to furnish a written requisition within the next 24 hours. Failure to provide the requisition within that time is an offence on the part of the practitioner (Reg.14(2)).

A requisition furnished by the person in charge or acting person in charge of a hospital, organisation providing ambulance services or care home must be signed by a doctor or a dentist employed or engaged in that hospital, organisation or care home (Reg.14(5)).

A requisition furnished by the master of a foreign ship must contain a statement that the quantity of drug to be supplied is the quantity necessary for the equipment of the ship (Reg.14(5)) signed by the proper officer of the port health authority or, in Scotland, a health board competent person designated under section 3 of the Public Health etc. (Scotland) Act 2008 by the health board within whose jurisdiction the ship is.

An operating department practitioner, senior or acting senior registered nurse or registered midwife for the time being in charge of any ward, theatre or other department of a hospital, care home or prison who obtains a supply of a controlled drug from the person responsible for dispensing and supplying medicines at that hospital, care home or prison must furnish a requisition in writing signed by them which specifies the total quantity of the drug required. They must retain a copy or note of the requisition. The person responsible for the dispensing and supply of medicines must mark the requisition in such a manner as to show that it has been complied with and must retain the requisition in the dispensary (Reg.14(6)).

On occasion, a third party who is not, themselves, authorised to possess the drug will be sent by the recipient (i.e. the person who is lawfully permitted to order the drug via a requisition) to collect the drug on their behalf. This third party is sometimes called a "messenger", although this term is not found in the Regulations. Where such a messenger purports to have been sent on behalf of the recipient, then the drug may not be supplied to them until they furnish, to the supplier, a statement in writing signed by the recipient to the effect that the messenger is empowered by the recipient to receive

62. Royal Pharmaceutical Society. Medicines Ethics and Practice (47th Edition) London: Royal Pharmaceutical Society, July 2024.

that drug on behalf of the recipient. The supplier must be reasonably satisfied that the document is genuine.

Accountable Officers

Regulations applicable in England and Scotland[63] and in Wales[64] provide for the appointment of Accountable Officers. The regulations across all three nations are broadly similar. The arrangements for accountable officers are overseen by the CQC in England, by Health Improvement Scotland (HIS), and by Healthcare Inspectorate Wales (HIW).

The Regulations provide that designated bodies (typically NHS England, NHS Trusts, Health Boards and Local Health Boards, independent hospitals and ambulance boards or trusts) must nominate or appoint an Accountable Officer who is a fit, proper and suitable experienced person, to ensure the safe, appropriate and effective management and use of controlled drugs within organisations subject to their oversight. The Accountable Officer must not routinely supply or handle controlled drugs themselves as part of their duties within their organisation.

The Regulations set out how Accountable Officers should be appointed, together with their responsibilities. The Accountable Officer must establish and operate appropriate arrangements for securing the safe management and use of controlled drugs, and review those arrangements as appropriate. Their role extends either to their employing organisation or to those contracted to provide services on behalf of that organisation (e.g. community pharmacies contracted to provide services by a commissioning body) and includes duties to secure:

- the safe and effective use and management of controlled drugs within their own organisations and by any body or person providing services to their organisation;
- systems for assessing, investigating and recording concerns (including complaints) relating to the safe management or use of controlled drugs, and take action on well-founded concerns;
- incident reporting systems for untoward incidents relating to the safe management or use of controlled drugs;
- the implementation of up-to-date standard operating procedures in relation to the management and use of controlled drugs (see section on Standard operating procedures, below);
- that appropriate information, education or training is delivered to relevant individuals within their organisation, in relation to the required standard operating procedures;
- appropriate arrangements for monitoring and auditing the designated/provider body's management and use of controlled drugs;
- appropriate arrangements for the safe destruction and disposal of controlled drugs by their designated body;

63. Controlled Drugs (Supervision of Management and Use) Regulations 2013.

64. Controlled Drugs (Supervision of Management and Use) (Wales) Regulations 2008.

- appropriate arrangements for ensuring the proper sharing of information, with relevant persons/bodies.

Accountable Officers have the right of access, to carry out periodic inspections of premises, to investigate concerns and to take action if there are well-founded concerns. Accountable Officers must always act to protect the safety of patients and the general public and are immune from civil action when sharing information if disclosure is made in good faith.

Under the Controlled Drugs (Supervision of Management and Use) Regulations 2013 and the Controlled Drugs (Supervision of Management and Use) (Wales) Regulations 2008, the CQC, HIS and HIW must compile, maintain and publish a list of accountable officers.

Standard operating procedures

One role of the Accountable Officer is to ensure that up-to-date standard operating procedures are in place in relation to the management and use of controlled drugs. In Wales,[65] these must cover the following matters:

- who has access to the controlled drugs;
- where the controlled drugs are stored;
- security in relation to the storage and transportation of controlled drugs as required by the misuse of drugs legislation;
- disposal and destruction of controlled drugs;
- who is to be alerted if complications arise;
- maintaining relevant controlled drugs registers under the misuse of drugs legislation;
- maintaining a record of Schedule 2 controlled drugs that have been returned by patients.

In England and Scotland[66] the Regulations state only that the standard operating procedures must cover (among other matters) best practice relating to:

- the prescribing, supply and administration of controlled drugs; and
- clinical monitoring of patients who have been prescribed controlled drugs.

Substance misusers

A person is regarded as being addicted to a drug "if, and only if, they have, as a result of repeated administration, become so dependent upon that drug that they have an overpowering desire for the administration of it to be continued".[67] The expression *drug* in this context means those specified in the Misuse of Drugs (Supply to Addicts) Regulations 1997, namely:

65. Controlled Drugs (Supervision of Management and Use) (Wales) Regulations 2008.
66. Controlled Drugs (Supervision of Management and Use) Regulations 2013.
67. Misuse of Drugs (Supply to Addicts) Regulations 1997.

1. cocaine, dextromoramide, diamorphine, dipipanone, hydrocodone, hydromorphone, levorphanol, methadone, morphine, opium, oxycodone, pethidine, phenazocine and piritramide;
2. any stereoisomeric form of a substance specified in item 1 above, except dextrorphan;
3. any ester or ether of a substance specified in items 1 or 2 above not being a substance for the time being specified in Part II of Schedule 2 to the Misuse of Drugs Act 1971;
4. any salt of a substance specified in any of items 1 to 3 above; and
5. any preparation or other product containing a substance or product specified in any of items 1 to 4 above.

Provisions for preventing misuse

The Secretary of State may make such regulations as appear necessary or expedient for preventing the misuse of controlled drugs (s.10). In particular, they may make provisions that:

- require precautions to be taken for the safe custody of controlled drugs;
- impose requirements as to the documentation of transactions involving controlled drugs, and require copies of documents relating to such transactions to be furnished to the prescribed authority;
- require the keeping of records and the furnishing of information with respect to controlled drugs and in such circumstances and in such manner as may be prescribed;
- provide for the inspection of any precautions taken or records kept in pursuance of regulations under this section;
- relate to the packaging and labelling of controlled drugs;
- regulate the transport of controlled drugs and the methods used for destroying or otherwise disposing of such drugs when no longer required;
- regulate the issue of prescriptions containing controlled drugs and the supply of controlled drugs on prescriptions, and require persons issuing or dispensing prescriptions containing such drugs to furnish to the prescribed authority such information relating to those prescriptions as may be prescribed;
- require any doctor who attends a person who they consider, or has reasonable grounds to suspect, is addicted (within the meaning of the Regulations) to controlled drugs of any description to furnish to the prescribed authority such particulars with respect to that person as may be prescribed; and
- prohibit any doctor from administering, supplying and authorising the administration and supply to persons so addicted, and from prescribing for such persons, such controlled drugs as may be prescribed, except and in accordance with the terms of a licence issued by the appropriate authority in pursuance of the Regulations.

In addition to making regulations about safe custody, the Secretary of State may also, by notice in writing, require the occupier of any premises where controlled drugs are kept to take further precautions as specified in a written notice (s.11).

Warnings of tolerance, dependence and addiction are added to patient information leaflets for opioids (see **Chapter 18**).[68]

Information concerning misuse

Doctors, pharmacists and persons lawfully conducting retail pharmacy businesses in any area may be called upon to give particulars of the quantities of any dangerous or otherwise harmful drugs (not necessarily controlled under the Act) which have been prescribed, administered or supplied over a particular period of time. The Home Secretary may call for this information if it appears that a social problem, caused by such drugs, exists in that area.

A notice in writing may be served on the persons concerned specifying the period and requiring particulars of the drug to be furnished in such a manner and within such time as set out in the notice. Pharmacists may be required to give the names and addresses of the prescribing doctors but may not be required to identify the patients concerned. It is an offence to fail, without reasonable excuse, to give the information required or to give false information (s.17).

Prescribing for addicted persons

When prescribing for an addicted person, anyone who may prescribe Schedule 2 controlled drugs may administer or authorise the supply of cocaine, diamorphine or dipipanone, or the salts of any of these, for the purpose of treating organic disease or injury. However, only doctors may prescribe these drugs to treat addiction and only if licensed to do so by the Secretary of State.[69]

There is provision for addicted persons to receive instalment prescriptions. Instalment prescriptions are useful in helping patients manage their medication as smaller portions of the prescribed medication can be supplied, via the patient's pharmacy, daily or via some other pattern of instalments. In addition, some patients will be required to consume their medication in front of the pharmacist as part of the collection arrangements. Therefore, dispensing in instalments means there is less risk of overdosing than if the entire prescribed quantity was supplied at the same time, and leads to increased adherence. Furthermore, the supply of smaller quantities, and supervised consumption arrangements, decrease inappropriate use of the medication (for example, selling on the street) and the risk theft from the patient.

In England, instalments can be dispensed on form FP10MDA. Schedule 2 drugs, buprenorphine, buprenorphine/naloxone (Suboxone) and diazepam may be ordered on this form.[70] In Wales, instalments of any Schedule 2, 3, 4 or 5 controlled drug may be ordered on form WP10MDA. Both FP10MDA and WP10MDA forms are limited to a maximum period of treatment of 14 days. The above are administrative arrangements

68. https://www.gov.uk/government/news/uk-regulator-strengthens-opioid-warnings (accessed 31 December 2024).

69. Misuse of Drugs (Supply to Addicts) Regulations 1997.

70. Along with any diluents or water for injection.

made under the NHS and do not form part of the Misuse of Drugs Regulations. The prescriber must specify the instalment amount and the interval between each instalment.

In Scotland, there is no specific form for instalments; they can be written on any prescription type. GPs can order instalments on the standard GP10 form, whilst hospital-based prescribers prescribing for substance misuse patients use form HBP(A). When using these forms to order instalments, prescribers indicate that such instalments are required by including instructions to that effect in the prescribing instructions. There are no legal limitations on the number of days' treatment that may be ordered (although as outlined above, unless there is a good reason to do otherwise, it is recommended that no more than 30 days should be supplied) and no limitations on the drugs that may be ordered, other than restrictions related to the prescribing of drugs as determined by the Scottish Drug Tariff.

Supply of articles for administering or preparing controlled drugs

In general, it is unlawful for a person to supply, or offer to supply, any article which may be used or adapted to be used in the unlawful preparation or administration of a controlled drug (s.9A). It is not an offence to supply or offer to supply a hypodermic syringe, or any part of one (so as to encourage addicted persons to use clean needles).

Certain persons may, when acting in a professional capacity, supply or offer to supply the specified articles for administering or preparing controlled drugs (Reg.6A). Those persons are:

- a practitioner;
- a pharmacist;
- a person employed or engaged in the lawful provision of drug treatment services;
- a supplementary prescriber acting under and in accordance with the terms of a clinical management plan; and
- a nurse independent prescriber.

The articles that may be supplied or offered to supply are:

- a swab;
- utensils for the preparation of a controlled drug;
- citric acid or ascorbic acid;
- a filter; and
- ampoules of water for injection, only when supplied, or offered for supply, in accordance with the Medicines Act and its Regulations.

If and when the Human Medicines Regulations are amended to enable pharmacists to authorise pharmacy technicians to carry out supervision (see **Chapter 11**), it is expected that the Misuse of Drugs Regulations will be amended to add pharmacy technicians to the list of persons who may supply the specified articles.

In addition, a person employed or engaged in the lawful provision of drug treatment services may, when acting in that capacity, supply or offer to supply aluminium foil in the context of structured steps to engage a patient in a drug treatment plan, or which form part of a patient's drug treatment plan. Here, a *drug treatment plan* means a written plan, relating to the treatment of an individual patient, and agreed by the patient and the person employed in the lawful provision of drug treatment services (Reg.6A).

Safe custody of controlled drugs

The Misuse of Drugs (Safe Custody) Regulations 1973 relates to the safe custody of all controlled drugs, except :

1. any drug in Schedule 4 or 5;
2. any liquid preparations, apart from injections, which contain any of the following:
    a. amphetamine,
    b. benzphetamine,
    c. chlorphentermine,
    d. fenethylline,
    e. mephentermine,
    f. methaqualone,
    g. methylamphetamine,
    h. methylphenidate,
    i. phendimetrazine,
    j. phenmetrazine,
    k. pipradrol,
    l. any stereoisomeric form of a substance specified in any of paragraphs (a) to (k) above,
    m. any salt of a substance specified in any of paragraphs (a) to (l) above.
3. any of the following:
    a. any 5,5-disubstituted barbituric acid,
    b. cathine,
    c. ethchlorvynol,
    d. ethinamate,
    e. gabapentin,
    f. mazindol,
    g. meprobamate,
    h. methylphenobarbitone (methylphenobarbital),
    i. methyprylone,
    j. midazolam,
    k. pentazocine,
    l. phentermine,
    m. pregabalin,
    n. tramadol,
    o. any ester of gabapentin or pregabalin,
    p. any stereoisomeric form of a substance specified in (a) to (o) above,
    q. any salt of a substance specified in (a) to (p) above,
    r. any preparation or other product containing a substance or product specified in (a) to (q) above.

The premises to which the safe custody requirements apply are:

1. any premises occupied by a retail dealer for the purposes of their business; and
2. any care home within the meaning of the relevant legislation.

The definition of *retail dealer* is given above in the section headed Schedule 5.

The occupier and every person concerned in the management of any of these premises must ensure that all controlled drugs (except those exempted, as mentioned above) are, so far as circumstances permit, kept in a locked safe, cabinet or room which is so constructed and maintained as to prevent unauthorised access to the drugs. This requirement does not apply in respect of any controlled drug which is for the time being constantly under the direct personal supervision of:

1. a pharmacist in the premises of a retail dealer (e.g. when dispensing prescriptions; see Direct supervision and direct personal supervision in **Chapter 12**); or
2. in the case of a care home, the person in charge of the premises, or any member of their staff designated by them for the purpose.

It is suggested that *direct personal supervision* means that the pharmacist must be able to see the drugs and be physically able to move them out of the reach of anyone who should not have access to them (see also the discussion of supervision in **Chapters 11** and **12**).

Schedule 2 to the Regulations sets out detailed requirements as to the specifications (such as materials, construction, fixing etc.) which apply to safes, cabinets and rooms in which controlled drugs are kept. The owner of a pharmacy may, as an alternative, elect to apply to the police for a certificate that their safes, cabinets or rooms provide an adequate degree of security. After inspection by the police, and if the degree of security is found to be adequate, a certificate, renewable annually, may be issued. The certificate may specify conditions to be observed and may be cancelled if there is a breach of any condition, if the occupier has refused entry to a police officer or if there has been any change of circumstances lowering the degree of security.

Apart from these special requirements, which affect only certain classes of premises, a person having possession of any controlled drug to which the safe custody regulations apply must ensure that, as far as circumstances permit, it is kept in a locked receptacle which can be opened only by them or by a person authorised by them. This requirement does not apply to a carrier in the course of their business or to a person engaged in the business of a postal operator when acting in the course of that business, or to a person to whom the drug has been supplied on the prescription of a practitioner for their own treatment or that of another person or an animal.

Offences, penalties and enforcement

Schedule 4 to the Act is a tabulated summary of offences under the Act and the penalties applicable to them according to the class (A, B or C) into which the drug falls.

The occupier or manager of any premises commits an offence (s.8) if they knowingly permit or suffers any of the following to take place on the premises:

- producing or supplying, or attempting to produce or supply, or offering to supply any controlled drug in contravention of the Act;
- preparing opium for smoking; and
- smoking cannabis, cannabis resin or prepared opium.

It is an offence (s.9) for any person to:

1. smoke or otherwise use prepared opium; or
2. frequent a place used for the purpose of opium smoking; or

3. have in their possession
   a. any pipes or other utensils made or adapted for use in connection with the smoking of opium, being pipes or utensils which have been used by them or with their knowledge and permission in that connection or which they intend to use or permit others to use in that connection; or
   b. any utensils which have been used by them or with their knowledge and permission in connection with the preparation of opium for smoking.

Other offences are described in some detail in Schedule 4. Those relating to contravention of the Regulations or of conditions of any licence, or of directions relating to safe custody of controlled drugs, are of particular relevance to pharmacy professionals (ss.11 and 18). A person commits an offence if, in the UK, they assist in or induce the commission in any place outside the UK of an offence punishable under the provisions of a corresponding law in force in that place (s.20). Inciting another to commit any offence under the Act is also an offence (s.19).[71]

Where any offence under the Act or the Criminal Justice (International Co-operation) Act 1990 committed by a body corporate is proved to have been committed with the consent or connivance of, or to be attributable to any neglect on the part of, any director, manager, secretary or other similar officer of the body corporate, or any person purporting to act in any such capacity, they, as well as the body corporate, are guilty of the offence and are liable to be proceeded against accordingly (s.21).

For some offences, the accused may be acquitted if they can prove that they did not believe, suspect or have reason to suspect that the substance or product in question was a controlled drug. The offences in question are producing, supplying, offering to supply or possessing controlled drugs, cultivating cannabis, smoking or using prepared opium, frequenting a place used for the purpose of opium smoking or possessing opium pipes and utensils. When it is necessary, in connection with any offence, to prove that a substance or product is a controlled drug, the accused may prove that they believed it to be a different controlled drug. This, in itself, will not constitute a defence unless there could have been no offence had the drug been of that description (s.28).

It is also a defence for a person accused of unlawful possession of a controlled drug to prove that they took possession of it to prevent another person committing an offence, and that they took steps to destroy it as soon as possible, or that they took possession of the drug to hand it over to some authorised person as soon as possible (s.5).

A constable or an authorised person may, for the purpose of securing the safe, appropriate and effective management and use of controlled drugs:

a. enter any relevant premises;
b. inspect any precautions taken on the premises for the safe custody of controlled drugs;
c. inspect any stocks of controlled drugs kept on the premises; and

---

71. In Scotland it is also an offence to attempt to commit an offence under any provision of the Act or attempt to incite another to commit such an offence, under Section 19 of the Act. In England and Wales, attempt is an offence under the Criminal Attempts Act 1981.

d. require any relevant records kept on the premises to be produced for inspection.[72]

In addition, GPhC inspectors have similar powers to enforce the GPhC's Standards (see **Chapter 2**).

A constable may also, on the authority of a warrant, enter any premises named in the warrant, by force if necessary, and search them and any person found therein, seizing any controlled drug or any document relevant to the transaction if they have reasonable grounds to consider that an offence under the Act has been committed (s.23). They may detain for the purposes of search any person whom they have reasonable grounds to suspect is in unlawful possession of a controlled drug. They may also stop and search any vehicle or vessel for the same reason and may seize anything which appears to be evidence of an offence under the Act (s.23).

It is an offence intentionally to obstruct a person exercising their powers of examination or search. Failure to produce any book, documents, stocks or drugs without reasonable excuse is also an offence, and proof of the reasonableness of the excuse rests with the person offering it as a defence (s.23).

Upon a conviction, anything relating to the offence may be forfeited and destroyed or otherwise dealt with by order of the court, subject to any person claiming to be the owner showing cause why the order should not be made (s.27). The Proceeds of Crime Act 2002 provides for the confiscation of the proceeds of drug trafficking received by convicted persons.

Psychoactive substances

The Psychoactive Substances Act 2016 creates a blanket ban on the production, distribution, sale and supply of psychoactive substances in the UK. Essentially, this Act makes substances which were formerly often referred to as "legal highs" illegal.[73] Under the Act, a *psychoactive substance* means any substance which is capable of producing a psychoactive effect in a person who consumes it, and is not an exempted substance. Exempted substances include controlled drugs, medicinal products, alcohol or alcoholic products, nicotine, tobacco products, caffeine or caffeine products and any substance which is ordinarily consumed as food or drink, and which does not contain a prohibited ingredient. In *R v Rochester (Kirk)*[74] the defendant, who had been accused of being in possession of a psychoactive substance, argued that a substance only fell within the definition of "psychoactive substance" if it directly stimulated or depressed the central nervous system. The Court of Appeal rejected this argument, holding that, in passing the 2016 Act, Parliament was not concerned to distinguish between direct and indirect production of the effect in question.

72. Section 20 of the Health Act 2006.

73. As an illustration of a prosecution under this Act, see the case of *R v Chapman (Sonny)* in Box 4.1 in Chapter 4. This case concerned nitrous oxide, which has become a controlled drug since the case was decided, and the product would therefore no longer come within the Psychoactive Substances Act (see also https://www.gov.uk/government/news/nitrous-oxide-to-be-illegal-by-end-of-the-year (accessed 31 December 2024)).

74. [2018] EWCA (Crim) 1936.

SUMMARY

Table 14.2 summarises controlled drugs legislation.

Table 14.2: *Summary of the Misuse of Drugs Regulations*

	Schedule 1	Schedule 2	Schedule 3	Schedule 4, Part I	Schedule 4, Part II	Schedule 5
Administration	By licence only	To a patient by a doctor, dentist, nurse independent prescriber, pharmacist independent prescriber, physiotherapist independent prescriber, chiropodist independent prescriber, paramedic independent prescriber, therapeutic radiographer independent prescriber, supplementary prescriber (acting in accordance with a clinical management plan) or by any person acting in accordance with the directions of a person who is entitled to prescribe controlled drugs				No restriction
Import and export	By licence only	By licence only	By licence only	By licence only	By licence only, except if imported or exported by a person for self-administration	No restriction (except nitrous oxide)
Possession	By licence only	See section on Possession and supply			No restriction	No restriction
Supply	By licence only	See section on Possession and supply				
Emergency supply	No	No	No, except phenobarbital for epilepsy	Yes	Yes	Yes
Production	By licence only	Licence holders, pharmacists, practitioners and persons lawfully conducting a retail pharmacy business,				
Prescription requirements	Yes – by licensed persons only	Yes	Yes	Do not apply	Do not apply	Do not apply
Register	Yes	Yes	No register, but some classes of persons are required to keep records or invoices.			
Marking of containers	Yes	Yes	Yes (with the exception of some pre-mixed kits used for chemical analysis)	No	No	No
Destruction – requirement for an authorised witness and an entry in the controlled drugs register when destroyed in the pharmacy	Yes	Yes, but do not apply to drugs returned by patients	No, except if the pharmacy is engaged in manufacturing, compounding, importing or exporting such drugs			No
Safe custody requirements	Yes	Yes (except certain liquids, quinalbarbital [secobarbital]) (see section on Safe custody)	No (except buprenorphine, diethylpropion, flunitrazepam and temazepam) (see section on Safe custody)	No	No	No
Requisition requirements	Yes	Yes	Yes	No	No	No

FURTHER READING

- Department of Health (2013). *Controlled drugs (Supervision of management and use) Regulations 2013. Information about the Regulations.*[75]
- NICE (2016). *Controlled drugs: safe use and management*; NICE guideline [NG46].[76]
- The Home Office (2015) *Additional Guidance issued by the Home Office on the use of the mandatory requisition form for Schedule 2 and 3 controlled drugs.*[77]

75. https://assets.publishing.service.gov.uk/media/5a7cc5e540f0b65b3de0b14d/15-02-2013-controlled-drugs-regulation-information.pdf (accessed 31 December 2024).
76. https://www.nice.org.uk/guidance/ng46 (accessed 31 December 2024).
77. https://www.nhsbsa.nhs.uk/sites/default/files/2017-03/Mandatory_Requisition_Forms_-_Additional_Guidance.pdf (accessed 31 December 2024).

CHAPTER 15

Veterinary medicines

Although there are similarities between the laws applicable to human medicines and the laws applicable to veterinary medicines, there are many differences. Amongst the differences are the classifications of medicines, the persons who can prescribe, different restrictions depending on the type of animal being treated, and the legal requirements in relation to antibiotics. Whereas Prescription Only Medicines may only be supplied to humans in accordance with a written prescription, some veterinary medicines may be supplied on the basis of a verbal prescription.

Introduction

The Veterinary Medicines Regulations 2013 (VMR) set out the legal controls on the production, distribution, possession, dispensing and administration of veterinary medicines in the UK, and although established under and relating to EU legislation,[1] they remain in force notwithstanding the UK's exit from the European Union[2] subject to certain amendments that are discussed below.

The Veterinary Medicines Directorate (VMD), an executive agency of the Department for Environment, Food & Rural Affairs (DEFRA), licenses veterinary medicines and inspects many of those involved in the veterinary medicines supply chain, including manufacturers and wholesale dealers, in accordance with the VMR, and updates and enforces the regulations. The VMR usually refer to the Secretary of State. For the purposes of this chapter, references to the VMD and the Secretary of State are interchangeable.

A Veterinary Products Committee (VPC) provides scientific advice on any aspect of veterinary medicines requested by the VMD, as it carries out functions specified in the VMR.[3] The Committee's main role is to provide independent scientific advice on applications for marketing authorisations (MAs) and animal test certificates (for clinical trials of veterinary medicines), to consider reports of suspected adverse events relating to veterinary medicines and to provide advice to the VMD.

Substantial changes were made to the VMR in 2024. Amongst other things, the VMR now includes measures to help tackle antimicrobial resistance by increasing restrictions

1. Directive 2001/82/EC.
2. Veterinary Medicines and Animals and Animal Products (Examination of Residues and Maximum Residues Limits) (Amendment etc.) (EU Exit) Regulations 2019 made under the European Union (Withdrawal) Act 2018 (there is related legislation on medicine residues in animals and animal products).
3. VMR Reg.28(3).
4. See the Explanatory Memorandum to the Veterinary Medicines (Amendment Etc) Regulations 2024 https://www.legislation.gov.uk/ukdsi/2024/9780348258523/pdfs/ukdsiem_9780348258523_en_001.pdf (accessed 31 December 2024).

on the use of antibiotics and antibiotics administered via feed, and support a culture change which embeds sustainable reduction in antibiotic use in animals.[4]

The word *antibiotic* is defined in the VMR[5] as "any substance with a direct action on bacteria that is used for the treatment of infections or infectious diseases", and the word *antimicrobial* is defined as "any substance with a direct action on micro-organisms that is used for treatment or prevention of infections or infectious diseases and includes antibiotics, antivirals, antifungals and antiprotozoals".

Veterinary medicines and authorisations

Veterinary medicines

The scope of the VMR is broad, applying to virtually all products (or substances) considered to be veterinary medicines (the regulations refer to *veterinary medicinal products,* but the terms *veterinary medicinal products* and *veterinary medicines* are used interchangeably in this chapter).

Veterinary medicinal products are defined as:

- any substance or combination of substances presented as having properties for treating or preventing disease in animals;
- any substance or combination of substances that may be used in, or administered to, animals with a view either to restoring, correcting or modifying physiological functions by exerting a pharmacological, immunological or metabolic action, or to making a medical diagnosis; or
- any substance or combination of substances that may be used for the purpose of euthanising an animal.[6]

VMD guidance says that a product is medicinal by *presentation* if it gives the averagely well-informed person the impression that the product treats or prevents disease, or they gain that impression[7] or if it claims to treat, prevent or control a disease, or uses words normally associated with authorised medicines, subject to the overall presentation of the product. The classification of a product as medicinal by presentation is illustrated by the Northern Ireland case of *Norbrook Laboratories Ltd v Veterinary Medicines Directorate*. See **Box 15.1.**[8]

Box 15.1: Norbrook Laboratories Limited v Veterinary Medicines Directorate (VMD)

In some cases when a dairy cow reaches the end of its milk production, the teat duct does not readily seal and can allow the ingress of bacteria through the external teat orifice into the teat canal. This can lead to a significant risk of developing mastitis.

---

5. VMR Reg.2.
6. VMR Reg.2.
7. VMD Guidance: Legal requirements for placing a veterinary medicine on the market https://www.gov.uk/guidance/legal-requirements-for-placing-a-veterinary-medicine-on-the-market (accessed 31 December 2024).
8. [2010] NICA 21.

Box 15.1: Norbrook Laboratories Limited v Veterinary Medicines Directorate (VMD) (cont.)

Norbrook Laboratories, a pharmaceutical company, developed a new product named "Noroseal" It was a thick paste that, by means of an internal applicator, was introduced into the distal teat canal. The label for Noroseal stated, amongst other things:

> *"Udder Care from Norbrook Laboratories Limited ... provides a barrier in heifers and cows to promote and maintain healthy teats by forming a seal at the orifice of the teat."*

The VMD decided that the product was not medicinal by function but, after a competitor of Noroseal had complained to the VMD, the VMD decided that it was a veterinary medicinal product by presentation, because its purpose was to prevent disease. It therefore required a marketing authorisation.

Norbrook applied for judicial review of the VMD decision. The Northern Ireland Court of Appeal rejected the application, holding that the presentation gave the impression that it should have properties that prevent mastitis, and, applying an objective test, the average well-informed consumer must be taken to know how Noroseal would apply to the animal.

A product is medicinal by *function* if it *may be used in, or administered to, animals with a view to restoring, correcting or modifying physiological functions by exerting a pharmacological, immunological or metabolic action or by making a medical diagnosis.*[9] The VMR interpret *animals* as meaning *all animals, other than human, and includes birds, reptiles, fish, molluscs, crustacea and bees.*[10]

The VMD's guidance deals with whether specific types of products may be veterinary medicines, including nutraceuticals, biocides, insecticides and repellents, shampoos, cosmetic products, teat and udder products, disinfectants, herbal products, testing kits, and colostrum.[11]

Marketing authorisations

A veterinary medicine by presentation or function must, subject to certain exemptions for small pet animals[12], have a marketing authorisation (MA) in accordance with UK regulations.[13] EU marketing authorisations that were valid when the UK left the EU were converted to GB marketing authorisations. Unless an exemption applies, it is an offence to supply[14] or to be in possession of an unauthorised veterinary medicine with the intention to supply it.[15]

---

9. VMR Reg.2.
10. VMR Reg.2.
11. As for footnote 7.
12. The details of exemptions are in Schedule 6 to the VMR.
13. VMR Reg.4.
14. VMR Reg.27.
15. VMR Reg.26.

The marketing authorisation holder (or holder of a veterinary homeopathic registration – see below) may be located either in the United Kingdom or in a country which the Secretary of State considers to have demonstrated equivalent standards to those in the United Kingdom.[16]

The VMR specify grounds for refusing applications for marketing authorisations, for example that the benefit-risk balance of the product is unfavourable; that the way that the product will be used will have an unnecessarily undesirable effect on the environment; that the product contains an antimicrobial which is presented for use in order to promote the growth of treated animals or to increase yields from treated animals; or that the risk for public health in case of development of antimicrobial resistance or antiparasitic resistance outweighs the benefits of the product to animal health.[17]

It is an offence to supply for administration to an animal a medicinal product with a marketing authorisation for human use (other than a product supplied by a veterinary surgeon or in accordance with a written prescription from a veterinary surgeon that contains all the information specified in the VMR).[18] Unless the cascade applies (see below) it would also be an offence under the Human Medicines Regulations 2012 to supply a medicine that has a marketing authorisation for human use for veterinary treatment, because it would not be in accordance with the marketing authorisation and, in the case of a medicine for human use that is a Prescription Only Medicine, a veterinary surgeon is not an appropriate practitioner for the purpose of regulation 214 of the Human Medicines Regulations.

The VMD grants MAs for veterinary medicines as appropriate, following application and any advice by the VPC. They are classed as pharmaceutical or biological. Biological veterinary products are those containing a biological substance *produced or extracted from a biological source which needs, for its characterisation and determination of quality, a combination of physiochemical-biological testing together with the production process and its control.*[19] These include immunological veterinary medicines,[20] veterinary medicines derived from blood or plasma and other products specified in European legislation.[21]

If the veterinary medicinal product contains an antimicrobial, the Secretary of State may require the holder of the marketing authorisation to conduct post-authorisation studies in order to ensure that the benefit-risk balance remains positive in relation to the development of antimicrobial resistance.[22]

---

16. Paragraph 18 of Schedule 1 to the VMR.
17. Paragraph 24 of Schedule 1 to the VMR.
18. VMR Reg.7.
19. VMD Guidance: Marketing authorisations for veterinary medicines.
20. For more information see VMD Guidance: Marketing authorisations for veterinary medicines.
21. Part A of the Annex to European Regulation (EEC) 2309/93.
22. Paragraph 22(4) of Schedule 1 to the VMR.

The VMD grants various types of MA, including generics (for products that are bioequivalent to the reference product), bibliographic (for products with well-established use), informed consent (copycats which must have consent of the MA holder) and biosimilars (similar to the reference biological product). Each MA product is labelled with the "Vm" symbol and its authorisation number, as well as a distribution category, relating to its retail supply, for example, POM-V, and MAs must be renewed after five years following initial authorisation.

There are separate market authorisation or other requirements for veterinary homeopathic[23] remedies, small pet animal veterinary medicines and veterinary medicines for animal feed, (for these see later), as well as veterinary field trials, autogenous vaccines, blood banks and equine stem cell centres. An Animal Test Certificate (ATC) is required for many veterinary clinical trials of medicines. An Autogenous Vaccine Authorisation (AVA) is required for the manufacturing premises and method of production of inactivated autogenous vaccine for administration to animals at the request of a veterinary surgeon. An autogenous vaccine may only be administered to animals in exceptional circumstances where no suitable immunological veterinary medicinal product has been authorised in relation to the target species and indication. Where a vaccine is used, it must be administered in accordance with a prescription under the cascade.[24]

A Non-Food Animal Blood Bank Authorisation (NFABBA) is required for the collection, storage and supply of blood for use in non-food producing animals (small scale blood donation carried out by veterinary surgeons is *recognised veterinary practice* and does not need to be authorised[25]). A Non-Food Animal Stem Cell Centre Authorisation (ASCCA) is required for the use of equine stem cells as an autologous treatment in non-food producing animals.[26]

The VMR do not apply to inactivated immunological veterinary medicinal products that are manufactured from pathogens or antigens obtained from an animal and used for the treatment of that animal, or veterinary medicines based on radioactive isotopes and have limited application to products intended for administration in the course of licensed scientific procedures.[27]

Where urgent action is necessary for protecting human or animal health or the environment, the Secretary of State may, on a temporary basis, restrict the supply or use of a veterinary medicine or suspend its marketing authorisation.[28]

---

23. The VMR use the spelling *homeopathic* (unlike the Human Medicines Regulations 2012) and we have used in this chapter the spelling used in the VMR.
24. Paragraph 6A of Schedule 4 to the VMR.
25. RCVS supporting guidance 25 recognised veterinary practice https://www.rcvs.org.uk/setting-standards/advice-and-guidance/code-of-professional-conduct-for-veterinary-surgeons/supporting-guidance/ (accessed 31 December 2024).
26. See https://www.gov.uk/guidance/apply-for-autogenous-vaccine-non-food-animal-blood-bank-equine-stem-cell-centre-authorisation#non-food-animal-stem-cell-centre-authorisation-ascca. (accessed 31 December 2024).
27. VMR Regs.3 and 15.
28. Paragraph 41A of Schedule 1 to the VMR.

The VMR contain powers for the Secretary of State to revoke a marketing authorisation, or to prohibit the supply of a veterinary medicine or require its recall, for example if the benefit-risk balance of the product is not positive.[29]

Homeopathic veterinary remedies

A homeopathic remedy is a veterinary medicinal product (which may contain a number of principles) prepared from homeopathic stocks in accordance with a homeopathic manufacturing procedure described in the European Pharmacopoeia or, if it is not described there, in a pharmacopoeia published by the British Pharmacopoeia Commission (see **Chapter 20**).[30]

Homeopathic veterinary remedies (described as “remedies”, not “medicines”), may be placed on the market without a marketing authorisation if they are instead placed on the market in accordance with a registration by the VMD and the holder of the registration is established in the UK or in a country which the Secretary of State considers to have demonstrated equivalent standards to those in the UK. Registration is a simpler process than applying for a marketing authorisation. Homeopathic remedies may be registered if:

- They are not immunological products;
- They are not biological products (other than homeopathic products derived from plants);
- The route of administration is either topical or oral and is as described in the European Pharmacopoeia; and
- There is a sufficient degree of dilution to guarantee the safety of the product, and in any event, it must not contain more than one part in 10,000 of the mother tincture.

All other provisions that relate to marketing authorisations apply in the same way to homeopathic remedies.

A homeopathic remedy that was on the market before 1 January 1994 may be placed on the market without being registered (and without requiring a marketing authorisation).[31]

Except for homeopathic remedies that meet the above criteria or which were on the market before 1 January 1994, a marketing authorisation is required. The VMR also provide that a homeopathic remedy may be prepared extemporaneously and supplied directly to the end user by a pharmacist in a registered pharmacy, provided that it is prepared in accordance with these criteria and supplied directly to the end user.[32]

Although homeopathic veterinary remedies are recognised in the VMR, their acceptance by the veterinary profession is qualified. The Royal College of Veterinary

---

29. For example, paragraph 41 of Schedule 1 to the VMR.
30. Paragraph 62 of Schedule 1 to the VMR.
31. Paragraph 66 of Schedule 1 to the VMR.
32. VMR Sch.1, 3 and 4.

Surgeons (RCVS) has issued a statement[33] highlighting its "commitment to promoting the advancement of veterinary medicine upon sound scientific principles":

> *"treatments offered by veterinary surgeons are underpinned by a recognised evidence base or sound scientific principles ... [and] ... Homeopathy exists without a recognised body of evidence for its use."*

The statement describes the practice of veterinary homeopathic medicine as:

> *"... complementary rather than alternative to treatments for which there is a recognised evidence base or which are based in sound scientific principles."*

Small pet animal veterinary medicines

An MA is not required for veterinary medicines for the following species - aquarium animals (including fish kept in closed water systems), cage birds, ferrets, homing pigeons, rabbits, small rodents and terrarium animals (reptiles, amphibians and arthropods kept in tanks and cages – including animals free-living in domestic gardens) – that are kept exclusively as pets. This is provided that certain conditions are met, including that:

- the person placing the product on the market must be registered with the Secretary of State;
- the active substance (it may not be an antibiotic, narcotic or psychotropic drug) is one approved by VMD;
- the pack size is limited (usually only a single course of treatment);
- the method of administration is oral or topical, or in the case of fish by addition to the water;
- labelling is as specified in the VMR; and
- the pack indicates that it is marketed in accordance with schedule 6 – exemptions for small pet animals.

The VMD advise that chickens, ducks and turkeys are food-producing animals and so are not covered by this exemption.[34]

Veterinary medicines for animal feed

The use of veterinary medicines and specified feed additives (products used in animal nutrition for the purposes of improving the quality of the feed, the quality of food from animal origin or to improve the animals' performance and health) in medicated feed or

---

33. RCVS statement on complementary medicines https://www.rcvs.org.uk/news-and-views/news/college-publishes-complementary-medicines-statement/(accessed 31 December 2024).

34. VMR Sch. 6; there is additional advice in the VMD Guidance: Exemption from authorisation for medicines for pet animals.

feedingstuffs is subject to controls in the VMR[35] and associated EU legislation, which include provisions on their manufacture, marketing and supply.

The VMR define *premixture* as “a mixture of a veterinary medicinal product or a specified feed additive with feedingstuffs materials, intended for further mixing with feedingstuffs before being fed to animals”.[36]

The VMR[37] define a *medicinal premix* as “a veterinary medicinal product authorised for incorporation into feedingstuffs”.

It is not permissible to incorporate a medicinal premix into a feedingstuff or intermediate feedingstuff, or to act as a distributor of such feedingstuffs containing a medicinal premix, without an authorisation from the VMD. The manufacturer or an authorised distributor may only supply it to an authorised distributor or an animal keeper.[38] However:[39]

(a) a veterinary surgeon, a pharmacist or a suitably qualified person (SQP) may be supplied with and may supply an intermediate feedingstuff containing a medicinal premix, or feedingstuffs containing a medicinal premix, to such a producer; and
(b) an authorisation is not required in the case of a person who incorporates a veterinary medicine into feedingstuffs in domestic premises for feeding on those premises non-food-producing animals or food-producing animals that are not sold or supplied commercially.

There are different approvals for feed business operators depending on the activity covered and approvals of designated persons responsible for aspects of the production process. Certain exemptions apply. The details are set out in the VMR and associated VMD guidance.[40] Residue surveillance of veterinary medicines and prohibited substances in food-producing animals provides further control and assurance of their use.[41]

A medicated feedingstuff prescription containing a medicinal premix must include, in addition to the general requirements for prescriptions for veterinary medicines (see below):[42]

(a) the name of the manufacturer or distributor whichever is the supplier to the end user;
(b) if the validity exceeds one month, a statement that not more than 31 days’ supply may be provided at any time;

---

35. VMR schedule 5.
36. Paragraph 1 of Schedule 5 to the VMR.
37. VMR Reg.2.
38. Paragraph 7 of Schedule 5 to the VMR.
39. Paragraph 30 of Schedule 5 to the VMR.
40. VMR schedule 5 and VMD Guidance: Manufacture and supply of medicated feedingstuffs https://www.gov.uk/guidance/manufacturing-and-supplying-veterinary-medicines-for-animal-feed (accessed 31 December 2024).
41. Guidance: Residues Surveillance https://www.gov.uk/guidance/residues-surveillance (accessed 31 December 2024).
42. Paragraph 19 of Schedule 5 to the VMR.

(c) the name, type and quantity to be used;
(d) the diagnosed disease to be treated or prevented;
(e) the name, active substance, amount of the product prescribed and inclusion rate of the medicinal premix and resulting inclusion rate of the active substance; and
(f) a statement that the prescription may not be re-used.

The prescription is valid for three months or such shorter period as may be specified in the prescription.

In the case of a prescription that relates to an antibiotic, the time between a prescription being issued and the course of treatment being started must not be more than five working days. A prescription that includes an antibiotic may not be issued for prophylactic purposes except as set out below.

In relation to food-producing animals, a medicated feedingstuffs prescription may not be used for more than one course of treatment.

The prescriber must give a copy of the prescription to the person incorporating the medicinal premix into the feedingstuff or to the distributor of the feedingstuffs, give one copy to the animal keeper, and keep a copy.

Pharmacovigilance

The word *pharmacovigilance* is defined in the VMR as "the science and activities relating to the detection, assessment, understanding and prevention of suspected adverse events or any other problem related to a medicinal product".[43]

Marketing authorisation holders are responsible for pharmacovigilance and must continually evaluate the benefit-risk balance of their authorised products and, if necessary, take appropriate measures to address any risks presented by a product. Amongst other things, marketing authorisation holders must comply with best practice in good veterinary pharmacovigilance practice; and they must establish and maintain a system for collecting, collating and evaluating information in relation to suspected adverse events.

Maximum residue limits

The European Commission adopted Commission Regulation (EC) 470/2009 in order to protect public health. The Regulation, as amended,[44] establishes maximum residue limits for any pharmacologically active substance intended for use in Great Britain. In addition, the Regulation classifies substances for which it is not necessary to establish a maximum residue limit, and a list of substances for which there could be no safe maximum.

43. VMR Reg.2.

44. In particular, by the Veterinary Medicines and Animals and Animal Products (Examination of Residues and Maximum Residue Limits) (Amendment etc.) (EU Exit) Regulations 2019 and by the Food and Drink, Veterinary Medicines and Residues (Amendment etc.) (EU Exit) Regulations 2019.

The Secretary of State must maintain a publicly available register of substances with an MLR.[45]

Signal management process[46]

A marketing authorisation holder must carry out a signal management process. This is a process for performing active surveillance of pharmacovigilance data for veterinary medicines in order to assess the data and determine whether there is any change to the benefit-risk balance of those products with a view to detecting risks to animal or public health or protection of the environment.

Qualified person responsible for pharmacovigilance (QPPV)

The marketing authorisation holder must designate a qualified responsible person (only one such person) responsible for pharmacovigilance. This person is referred to as a QPPV.[47]

The QPPV's services must be available permanently and continuously. The QPPV must, amongst other things:[48]

- establish and maintain a system that ensures that all suspected adverse events which are brought to the attention of the marketing authorisation holder are collected and recorded;
- monitor the performance of each product;
- monitor the pharmacovigilance system and ensure that, if required, an appropriate preventative or corrective action plan is prepared and implemented on behalf of the marketing authorisation holder through the use of audits and routine monitoring;
- provide to the Secretary of State any information relevant to detecting a change to the benefit-risk balance of a product including the results of any study or clinical trial;
- apply the signal management process and ensure that any of its relevant requirements are carried out;
- ensure that any person employed by the marketing authorisation holder who is engaged in pharmacovigilance receives ongoing training which is relevant to that person's duties.

In relation to a marketing authorisation issued via a UK national procedure only that is valid in Great Britain and Northern Ireland, the QPPV is not required to be located in the UK and can be located anywhere.

Adverse events[49]

An *adverse event* means "any observation in animals that occurs after any use of a veterinary medicinal product, whether or not considered to be product-related, that is unfavourable and unintended".

45. Article 14A of the Regulation.
46. Paragraphs 56A and 56C of Schedule 1 to the VMR.
47. Paragraph 56 of Schedule 1 to the VMR.
48. Paragraph 56B of Schedule 1 to the VMR.
49. Paragraph 57 of Schedule 1 to the VMR.

An *adverse environmental event* means "an event where a non-target organism, population or ecosystem is adversely affected as a result of exposure to a veterinary medicinal product, its active substance or its metabolites present in soil, water or animal remains".[50]

The VMR impose requirements in relation to the reporting of adverse events in respect of:

- animals;
- humans;
- unintended transmission of an infectious agent through a veterinary medicinal product;
- occurrence of an adverse environmental event; or
- lack of efficacy.

The marketing authorisation holder must record serious adverse events and report them to the VMD without delay and in any event within 30 days (electronically, if practicable).

Withdrawal periods

The recording and reporting requirement also applies to products of animal origin which, after the end of the withdrawal period, are found to include a pharmacologically active substance or marker residue exceeding the maximum residue limit (see above). The term *withdrawal period* means "the minimum period under normal conditions of use between the last administration of a veterinary medicinal product to an animal and the production of foodstuffs from that animal which is necessary to ensure that such foodstuffs do not contain residues in quantities harmful to public health".[51]

Inspection and additional reporting requirements

In order to verify the compliance of marketing authorisation holders with pharmacovigilance requirements, the Secretary of State must inspect the pharmacovigilance systems of marketing authorisation holders from time to time.[52]

There are also reporting requirements in relation to food safety, residues of veterinary medicines and veterinary medicines affecting other animals in the environment. Animal Test Certificate holders (with authorisation to administer veterinary medicines off-label as part of a veterinary field trial), manufacturers or distributers of specials, and manufacturers, importers and wholesalers of small pet animal veterinary medicines also have reporting responsibilities. The VMD manages the reporting of adverse events relating to animals, humans or the environment associated with the use or misuse of products, as well as incidents following the implant of a microchip in an animal.[53]

---

50. The definitions are in VMR Reg.2.
51. VMR Reg.2.
52. Paragraph 60A of Schedule 1 to the VMR.
53. VMR Sch. 1 part 8; and VMD Guidance: Veterinary pharmacovigilance: your responsibilities.

The VMD has published *Veterinary Pharmacovigilance responsibilities for authorisation holders*.[54]

Classification, prescription and supply of veterinary medicines

Categories of veterinary medicine

There are four main categories of veterinary medicine, two of which are Prescription Only Medicines (POMs). The abbreviations help to indicate who may prescribe and supply them, as follows:

1. **POM-V**: Prescription Only Medicines prescribed by a veterinary surgeon,
   - products may be supplied by a veterinary surgeon or a pharmacist and must be supplied in accordance with a prescription from a veterinary surgeon;
2. **POM-VPS**: Prescription Only Medicines prescribed by a veterinary surgeon, pharmacist or suitably qualified person (SQP – further details about SQPs are given below),
   - products may be supplied by a veterinary surgeon, pharmacist or SQP and must be in accordance with a prescription from one of these persons;
3. **NFA-VPS**: Non-Food Animal medicine (e.g. for pets) are not prescribed,
   - products may be supplied by a veterinary surgeon, pharmacist or SQP;
4. **AVM-GSL**: Authorised Veterinary Medicines on the General Sale List, are not prescribed,
   - the retail sale of these products is not subject to any control under the VMR.

The VMR specify the persons who may make retail supplies, the premises from which they may be made and the conditions of supply. *Retail supply* means any supply other than to or from the holder of a wholesale dealer's authorisation, whether or not for payment and regardless of who owns it.[55] Those who may make retail supplies are veterinary surgeons, pharmacists and SQPs, collectively referred to by the VMD as Registered Qualified Persons (RQPs).

Authorisation of Prescription Only Medicines

There are two types of Prescription Only Medicine and, briefly, the classification rules are: [56]

1. Products must be classified as **POM-V**:
   a. if containing narcotic or psychotropic substances;
   b. for administration following a diagnosis or clinical assessment by a veterinary surgeon;
   c. products containing an antimicrobial;
   d. products for the purpose of euthanasia;

---

54. https://www.gov.uk/guidance/veterinary-pharmacovigilance-your-responsibilities (accessed 31 December 2024).
55. VMR Sch. 3, paras 1 and 3.
56. VMR Schedule 3 para 1.

   e. products with a hormonal or thyrostatic function;
   f. products containing beta-agonists.
2. Products must be classified as **POM-V or POM-VPS**:
   a. for food-producing animals, subject to certain exceptions, for example where there is no risk to human or animal health as regards residues or the development of resistance to antibiotic or anthelmintic substances even when the products are used incorrectly;
   b. to avoid unnecessary risk for the target species, the person administering the product, or the environment;
   c. if the product may impede or interfere with subsequent diagnosis or therapeutic measures;
   d. if the product contains a new active substance that has not been included in an authorised veterinary medicine for five years;
   e. immunological veterinary medicinal products.

A list of authorised veterinary medicines is available on the VMD website. The details of the classification and supply of veterinary medicines, wholesale dealers and sheep dip are set out in Schedule 3 of the VMR.

POM-V medicines

A veterinary surgeon who prescribes a veterinary medicine classified as POM-V or under the cascade (as to which, see below), must first carry out a *clinical assessment* of the animal, and the animal must be *under that veterinary surgeon's care*.[57] This seeks to ensure a degree of proximity between the prescribing veterinary surgeon and the animal treated. This does not apply in relation to the administration of a medicine to a wild animal where the administration is authorised by the Secretary of State.[58]

The VMR do not define either term but the RCVS has given guidance that *clinical assessment* "is any assessment which provides the veterinary surgeon with enough information to diagnose and prescribe safely and effectively. A clinical assessment may include a physical examination; however, this may not be necessary in every case". The RCVS has given guidance that an animal is *under the care of a veterinary surgeon* when "the veterinary surgeon is given, and accepts, responsibility for the health of an animal (or a herd, flock or group of animals) whether generally, or by undertaking a specific procedure or test, or by prescribing a course of treatment".[59]

POM-VPS medicines

A veterinary surgeon, pharmacist or SQP prescribing POM-VPS medicines does not have to carry out a clinical assessment first, or have the animals under their care, and the

57. VMR Sch. 3, para 4(1).

58. VMR Sch. 3, para 4(2).

59. https://www.rcvs.org.uk/setting-standards/advice-and-guidance/under-care-new-guidance/ (accessed 31 December 2024).

prescribing process is more akin to a responsible supply function. The VMD indicates that *the prescriber must have sufficient information about the animal and the condition to be treated to enable them to prescribe and supply the most appropriate product.*[60] This is likely to be necessary to fulfil the prescriber's professional responsibilities.

In many cases POM-VPS medicines will be prescribed by veterinary surgeons following a clinical assessment of an animal under that veterinary surgeon's care, even though this is not required by the VMR.

Prescriptions

POM-V or POM-VPS veterinary medicines must be prescribed, which VMD describes as a process of deciding, instructing and recording the animal or herd's treatment.[61] Prescriptions may be *written* or *verbal.* They may be verbal if the prescriber is also the supplier, where the prescription is, in effect, the prescriber's clinical decision. They must be *written* if the prescriber is not the supplier.[62]

a. A *written prescription* must include:[63]
   - (a) the full name, address and contact details of the person prescribing the product, including that person's professional registration number (if available);
   - (b) the full name, address and contact details of the animal owner or keeper;
   - (c) the identification (including the species) of the animal or group of animals to be treated;
   - (d) the premises at which the animals are kept if this is different from the address of the owner or keeper;
   - (e) the issue date;
   - (f) the signature or electronic signature of the prescriber;
   - (g) the name and amount of the product prescribed;
   - (h) the pharmaceutical form and strength of the product;
   - (i) as regards veterinary medicinal products that are antibiotics which are prescribed for prophylactic purposes or metaphylactic purposes (as the case may be), a statement to that effect;
   - (j) the dosage regimen;
   - (k) any warnings necessary to ensure the proper use, including, where relevant, to ensure prudent use of antimicrobials;
   - (l) the words "It is an offence under the Veterinary Medicines Regulations 2013 for a person to alter a written prescription unless authorised to do so by the person who signed it";
   - (m) for food-producing animal species, the withdrawal period or a statement that the withdrawal period is equal to zero days; and

60. VMD Guidance: retail of veterinary medicines.

61. VMD Guidance: retail of veterinary medicines.

62. VMR Schedule 3 para 5(1).

63. VMR Sch. 3, para. 6.

(n) if the prescription relates to a product prescribed under the cascade, a statement to that effect.

If a prescription is not repeatable, it may not be submitted to a retailer more than once.

A standardised prescription form is not required for (private) veterinary prescriptions although the British Veterinary Association provide a standard form that many veterinary surgeons use. The VMR do not require written prescriptions to be written in ink, though this is obviously good practice. In the case of controlled drugs, prescriptions must be written so as to be indelible, and be dated and signed by the prescriber using their usual signature or be prescribed on an electronic prescription form.[64]

In the case of a verbal prescription, the prescriber must make a written record of the reason for prescribing. This record must be kept by the prescriber for a period of five years from the date on which the product was prescribed.

Unless a prescription is for a controlled drug in Schedules 2, 3 or 4 of the Misuse of Drugs Regulations 2001 (see below), a prescription for a POM-V or POM-VPS is valid for six months or such shorter period as may be specified in the prescription. If the prescription is repeatable, it must specify the number of times the product may be supplied[65] and (unlike repeatable prescriptions for human medicines) enforcement is on the basis that all repeats must be dispensed within the six-month period of validity.

Prescribing antibiotics and antimicrobials

Under the RCVS Code of Professional Conduct,[66] veterinary surgeons must make animal health and welfare their first consideration when attending to animals. If they are in practice, they must take steps to provide 24-hour emergency first aid and pain relief to animals according to their skills and the specific situation. If they prescribe, supply and administer medicines, they have a duty to do so responsibly.

Subject to their professional obligations to ensure the health and welfare of animals under their care, veterinary surgeons may only prescribe an antibiotic if they are satisfied that the product is not:

(a) used routinely;
(b) used to compensate for poor hygiene, inadequate husbandry, or poor farm management practices; or
(c) used to promote growth or increase yield.[67]

A veterinary surgeon may not prescribe an antibiotic for prophylactic purposes.[68] However, there is an exception in exceptional circumstances where the risk of an infection or of an infectious disease is very high and where the consequences of not

64. Regulation 15 of the Misuse of Drugs Regulations 2001 and see Chapter 14.
65. VMR Schedule 3, para. 6(3) and (4).
66. https://www.rcvs.org.uk/setting-standards/advice-and-guidance/code-of-professional-conduct-for-veterinary-surgeons/#animals (accessed 31 December 2024).
67. Paragraph 6(1A) and (1B) of Schedule 3 to the VMR.
68. Paragraph 7A of Schedule 3 to the VMR.

prescribing the product are likely to be severe. It should be noted that this exception is a limited one: it does not apply to every occasion where there is a risk of infection. The circumstances must be exceptional, the risk must be very high (not merely high), and the potential consequences of infection must be severe.

If a veterinary surgeon seeks to rely on the exception that allows the prescribing of an antibiotic for administration to a group of animals, the veterinary surgeon may only do so if:

(a) the rationale for prescribing the product to the group is clearly recorded by the prescriber; and
(b) a management review is carried out by a veterinary surgeon at, or as soon as reasonably practicable after, administration of the antibiotic in order to identify factors and implement measures for the purpose of eliminating the need for any future such administration.

A veterinary surgeon who prescribes an antibiotic medicine for prophylactic purposes must make a written record that shows how the conditions that allow it to be prescribed have been met. The record must be kept for at least five years.

A person who prescribes antimicrobials must ensure that the product is prescribed for the most limited period that is consistent with the risk to be addressed.[69]

Although the VMR aim to avoid the unnecessary prescribing of antibiotics, the negligent failure to prescribe antibiotics may give rise to a liability for damages, as the case in **Box 15.2** illustrates.

Box 15.2

In *J & J Franks Limited v Shotter and others* [2023] EWHC 1080 (KB), the Claimant was the owner of a three-year-old thoroughbred racehorse called Sand Diego. Sand Diego had made his debut as a two-year old racehorse in July 2019 and by February 2020 he had completed four races and had won his last race at Sandown in September 2019 before being rested for the winter.

Between 21 and 26 February 2020, Sand Diego was suffering from a bacterial infection in his right hind leg known as focal peritarsal infection. The horse was seen by a veterinary surgeon employed by the Defendant. The infection was not initially diagnosed, and the vet advised bandaging the affected leg. Antibiotic treatment for this infection was eventually commenced at 11pm on Sunday 23 February 2020. However, Sand Diego did not recover from the infection and was euthanised in Liphook Veterinary Hospital on 28 February 2020.

The Claimant alleged that the Defendant was vicariously liable for the negligence of the vet and claimed damages of £325,000.

By the time of the trial, the Defendant admitted that the veterinary surgeon had failed to arrive at the appropriate diagnosis of infection and admitted that antibiotic treatment should have been commenced when the vet was first consulted.

Despite finding that the vet was negligent in failing to diagnose an infection and failing to prescribe antibiotics from the start of treatment, the judge, Clare Padley (sitting as a Deputy

69. Paragraph 7 of Schedule 3 to the VMR.

Box 15.2 (cont.)

High Court Judge), dismissed the claim because causation had not been proved. The judge was not satisfied on the balance of probabilities that if Sand Diego had been treated with antibiotics on the morning of Saturday 22 February, he would have survived.

Civil liability (including vicarious liability) is explained in more detail in **Chapters 1** and **26**.

Controlled drugs

A prescription for a controlled drug of schedule 2, 3 or 4 of the Misuse of Drugs Regulations 2001 is valid for only 28 days.[70]

The RCVS has issued guidance on controlled drugs. Orders from veterinary surgeons for stock of schedule 2 or 3 controlled drugs must be on a requisition form (FP10CDF or equivalent; see **Chapter 14**), available within the guidance on the RCVS website.[71] Requisitions are not submitted to the NHSBSA and must be retained for five years (as for all written veterinary prescriptions). Veterinary prescriptions and requisitions for controlled drugs are subject to the Misuse of Drugs legislation generally,[72] as well as those aspects specifically listed above.

The RCVS gives specific advice regarding the storage and use of buprenorphine, fentanyl, ketamine and tramadol. Fentanyl and ketamine are Schedule 2 controlled drugs; and buprenorphine is a Schedule 3 controlled drug: as such, they are all subject to safe custody requirements in Regulations[73] (see **Chapter 14**). Although the same legal safe custody requirements do not apply to tramadol, the RCVS guidance states that "... it is an RCVS requirement that it is securely locked away". This may be in a controlled drugs cabinet that meets the regulatory requirements or, for example, in a lockable drawer.

In January 2025, xylazine (which is used in veterinary medicine as a sedative with some analgesic and muscle relaxant properties in cattle, horses, dogs and cats) was classified as a Part 1 Schedule 4 controlled drug because it has increasingly been misused (by humans) in combination with opioids such as heroin as a cheap means of stretching out each dose.[74]

The person supplying a veterinary medicine must take all reasonable steps to be satisfied that the prescription is from the prescriber and that the medicine is supplied to the person named on the prescription.[75]

---

70. Paragraph 6 of Schedule 3 to the VMR.
71. https://www.rcvs.org.uk/setting-standards/advice-and-guidance/controlled-drugs-guidance-a-to-z (accessed 31 December 2024).
72. Primarily the Misuse of Drugs Regulations 2001 and see Chapter 14.
73. The Misuse of Drugs (Safe Custody) Regulations 1973 and see Chapter 14.
74. The Misuse of Drugs and Misuse of Drugs (Designation) (England and Wales and Scotland) (Amendment) (No. 2) Regulations 2024.
75. VMR Schedule 3, para. 5(2) and (3) (additional controls apply to certain controlled drugs).

Additional prescribing responsibilities

Any person who prescribes a veterinary medicine under the cascade or a POM-V or POM-VPS (or supplies an NFA-VPS) product must:

a. before doing so, be satisfied that the person who will use the product is competent to do so safely, and intends to use it for a purpose for which it is authorised;
b. when doing so, advise on its safe administration and any warnings or contra-indications on the label or package leaflet; and
c. not prescribe (or in the case of an NFA-VPS product, supply) more than the minimum amount required for the treatment (unless the medicines are manufactured in a larger pack size and the supplier is not permitted to split the packs).[76]

In 2022, a pharmacist independent prescriber was suspended from practice by the General Pharmaceutical Council's Fitness to Practise Committee because he had prescribed POM-V medicines and prescribed for animals medicines that were only licensed for humans (see the cascade below), though he was not a veterinary surgeon. He had also prescribed other veterinary medicines for cats, dogs and a parrot despite such prescribing being outside the scope of his of competence.[77]

The cascade

Generally, the VMR (Reg.8) provide that only authorised veterinary medicines may be prescribed and administered to animals. Thus, the first step is for a prescriber to prescribe a veterinary medicine that has a valid GB or UK marketing authorisation for the indicated species and condition.

If a veterinary medicine that fulfils the first step is not available, then a prescriber may prescribe a veterinary medicine with a marketing authorisation that is valid in Northern Ireland for the indicated species and condition, in accordance with a Special Import Licence granted by the VMD.

However, if an authorised veterinary medicinal product is not available in the UK, Schedule 4 to the VMR enables a veterinary surgeon who is responsible for an animal, to treat an animal, in particular in order to avoid unnecessary suffering, with an alternative product according to what is known as *the cascade*. Only veterinary surgeons may prescribe medicines under the cascade. An SQP may supply an authorised medicine that falls within the scope of the registration they hold, against a prescription from a veterinary surgeon for use under the cascade. A pharmacist may dispense authorised veterinary and human medicines, and extemporaneous preparations they have prepared, against a prescription from a veterinary surgeon for use under the cascade. The prescriber may either administer personally a veterinary medicinal product under the cascade or may direct another person to do so under the responsibility of the prescriber. This requirement for the prescriber to administer personally or direct another person to

---

76. VMR schedule 3, para. 7.
77. https://www.pharmacymagazine.co.uk/news/gphc-suspends-pharmacist-who-prescribed-irrationally-and-unsafely (accessed 31 December 2024).

administer does not appear to apply to human medicinal products that are prescribed under the cascade. In the case of medicinal products prescribed under the cascade, there is an exemption from the prohibition on possessing an unauthorised veterinary medicinal product.[78]

The cascade is in Schedule 4 to the VMR and is the subject of guidance given by the VMD,[79] setting out the order in which medicines may be used, as follows:

1. a veterinary medicine authorised in the United Kingdom for use with another animal species, or for another condition in the same species; or
2. if no such product is available, either:
   (a) human medicinal product authorised in the United Kingdom; or
   (b) a veterinary medicine not authorised in the United Kingdom but authorised in another country for use with any animal species (in the case of a food-producing animal, it must be a food-producing species); or
   (c) if there is no such product that is suitable, a veterinary medicinal product prepared extemporaneously by a pharmacist, a veterinary surgeon or a person holding a manufacturing authorisation that authorises the manufacture of that type of product.

In the case of a veterinary medicinal product imported from another country, the veterinary surgeon must have obtained a certificate permitting importation before administration.

All substances included in a medicinal product administered to a food-producing animal under the cascade must be substances for which a maximum residue limit has been established (see above), unless it has been determined that no maximum residue limit is needed. Any such limit must be complied with.

If there is no authorised veterinary medicinal product for a food-producing horse and treatment under the cascade is unsuitable, substances listed in the Annex to European Regulation (EU) 122/2013 may be administered in accordance with the Annex.

A veterinary medicine that is administered outside its MA or has no MA (other than exempt small pet veterinary medicines) must be prescribed by a veterinary surgeon under the cascade.[80] The prescribing veterinary surgeon is personally responsible for the choice of product and, as part of the RCVS' Code of Professional Conduct for Veterinary Surgeons, must obtain the owner's consent for their animal to be treated under the cascade. They must also maintain accurate records.

A veterinary surgeon prescribing or administering a veterinary medicinal product to a food-producing animal under the cascade must specify an appropriate withdrawal period. The withdrawal period must not exceed the residue limits in Regulation (EC) 470/2009. The VMR specify minimum withdrawal periods for:

---

78. VMR Reg.26.

79. https://www.gov.uk/guidance/the-cascade-prescribing-unauthorised-medicines#about-the-cascade (accessed 31 December 2024).

80. VMR Reg.8.

- eggs;
- milk;
- meat and offal from food-producing mammals, poultry and farmed game-birds; and
- aquatic species producing meat for human consumption.

Unless the prescribing veterinary surgeon administers the veterinary medicine to the animal, the person supplying it, for example, a pharmacist, must label the product with the following information:[81]

1. the name and address of the pharmacy or veterinary practice premises or authorised premises supplying the product;
2. the name of the veterinary surgeon who prescribed it;
3. the name and address of the animal owner;
4. the identification (including the species) of the animal or group of animals;
5. the date of supply;
6. the expiry date of the product, if applicable;
7. the name or description of the product, which should include at least the name and quantity of the active ingredients;
8. the dosage and administration instructions;
9. any special storage precautions;
10. any necessary warnings for the user, target species, administration or disposal of the product;
11. the withdrawal period, if relevant (a food-producing animal); and
12. the words "Keep out of reach of children" and "For animal treatment only".

Supply by veterinary surgeons, pharmacists and suitably qualified persons

RQPs must supply veterinary medicines (in accordance with the provisions outlined already) from registered premises as follows:

- A *veterinary surgeon* must supply veterinary medicines from *veterinary practice premises* registered with the RCVS under the VMR,[82] although the premises may be more of a base, with supplies made on domiciliary visits or from mobile units. Veterinary surgeons may supply veterinary medicines they have prescribed or, against a written prescription, POM-V and POM-VPS medicines prescribed by another veterinary surgeon.
- A *pharmacist* may only supply POM-V, POM-VPS or NFA-VPS medicines, or medicines prescribed under the cascade, from premises registered as a pharmacy with the GPhC, a veterinary practice or an SQP retailer premises. Pharmacists

81. VMR, Schedule 3 para 13.
82. VMR schedule 3, para 8 (an interpretation of veterinary practice premises is provided by the RCVS, supporting guidance: veterinary medicines https://www.rcvs.org.uk/setting-standards/advice-and-guidance/code-of-professional-conduct-for-veterinary-surgeons/supporting-guidance/) (accessed 31 December 2024).

may supply POM-V medicines prescribed by veterinary surgeons, and POM-VPS medicines the pharmacist has prescribed or another RQP has prescribed.

- An *SQP* may supply a POM-VPS or NFA-VPS medicine from premises authorised as an SQP retailers' premises listed by VMD, a pharmacy or a veterinary practice premises (and only those products for which they are qualified and registered). The SQP must be present when the medicine is handed over unless the SQP:
  (a) authorises each transaction individually before the product is supplied; and
  (b) is satisfied that the person handing it over is competent to do so.
- SQPs may supply POM-VPS medicines they have prescribed or another RQP has prescribed (if the SQP is suitably qualified and registered).

A veterinary surgeon or pharmacist supplying veterinary products (other than AVM-GSL where retail supply is not subject to control under the VMR) must be present when the medicine is handed over, unless they authorise each transaction individually before the product is supplied and they are satisfied that the person handing the medicine over is competent to do so.[83]

A pharmacist may also:[84]

a. supply veterinary products prepared extemporaneously in a pharmacy in accordance with the prescription of a veterinary surgeon (and subject to relevant pharmacopoeia requirements);
b. supply certain homeopathic remedies prepared extemporaneously in a pharmacy provided they are supplied to the end-user; and
c. break open any package containing a veterinary medicine other than the immediate packaging of an injectable product.

The VMD runs a voluntary Accredited Internet Retailer Scheme (AIRS) to facilitate self-regulation of UK-based Internet retailers selling veterinary medicines. The aim of the scheme is to ensure that animal owners buying veterinary medicines over the Internet have appropriate advice from a veterinary surgeon, pharmacist or SQP and buy medicines authorised for use in the UK. Those registered with the VMD may display the AIRS logo. Details of the scheme are available on the VMD website.

It is not permitted to supply a veterinary medicine for promotional purposes. However, except for products containing an antimicrobial substance, it is permitted to supply samples of product labelled in such a way that clearly identifies them as such to:

(a) sales representatives; or
(b) those entitled to supply the product during sponsored events.[85]

83. VMR schedule 3.
84. VMR schedule 3, para 10.
85. Paragraph 3A of Schedule 3 to the VMR.

Internet sales[86]

It is not permitted to supply or offer to supply a POM-V, POM-VPS or NFA-VPS on the internet to anyone in Great Britain unless the supplier: .

(a) is established in Great Britain;
(b) has an address in Great Britain; and
(c) appears in the online register of online suppliers that is maintained by the Secretary of State.

On every part of a website where a product is offered, the supplier must include:

(a) the statement "registered internet retailer of veterinary medicines";
(b) the contact details of the Secretary of State; and
(c) a link to the published register.

Retail storage of veterinary medicines

A retailer of veterinary medicines must store veterinary medicines in accordance with the terms of any specific instructions on the label of the product and in accordance with the product's summary of product characteristics. This storage requirement applies not only to premises but also during transport.[87]

Suitably qualified persons

An SQP is a person who is trained and registered to be able to sell a limited range of veterinary medicines (for farm, equine or companion animals or a combination of these) and often works from a pet shop, saddler or agricultural merchant's premises, which must be registered with the VMD. SQPs may break open any package (other than an immediate packaging) containing a veterinary product.

VMD recognise bodies that are suitable to maintain a register[88] (currently the Animal Medicines Training Regulatory Authority (AMTRA), VetSkill Limited and Vetpol Limited), if satisfied that they have in place a system for ensuring that the person applying for registration has had adequate training to act as an SQP, has adequate standards in deciding whether to register an SQP, maintains a programme of continuing professional development (CPD) for persons registered with them; and operate an adequate appeal system if they intend to refuse to register anyone with appropriate qualifications, or to remove anyone from the register.

The VMD issues a Code of Practice for SQPs,[89] and recognised bodies take appropriate action against their registered SQPs if they do not comply with it.

---

86. Paragraphs 3B and 3D of Schedule 3 to the VMR.
87. Paragraph 3E of Schedule 3 to the VMR.
88. VMR schedule 3, para 14.
89. https://assets.publishing.service.gov.uk/media/664611c0993111924d9d3694/1999847_SQP_Code_of_Practice_-_Review_2020.pdf (accessed 31 December 2024).

Labelling requirements for authorised veterinary medicines

There are detailed labelling requirements for manufacturers of authorised veterinary medicines[90] and when a veterinary medicine is supplied by retail, the information on the manufacturer's packaging should be clearly visible. This does not apply when a veterinary surgeon, or a pharmacist, in accordance with a prescription, amends the label or adds a dispensing label, provided that the relevant (unamended) information on the manufacturer's label remains visible. If the medicine is supplied under cascade, a dispensing label is required by the VMR (see above).

If the medicine is supplied in a container other than that specified in the marketing authorisation, the container must be suitably labelled by the veterinary surgeon or pharmacist, who must also supply sufficient written information (which may include a copy of the summary of product characteristics or the package leaflet) to enable the product to be used safely.[91]

Records

Marketing authorisation holders must keep the following records of any medicines they supply:[92]

(a) the name of the veterinary medicinal product and marketing authorisation number;
(b) the pharmaceutical form and strength;
(c) the quantity supplied;
(d) the batch number and expiry date;
(e) the date of the transaction;
(f) the company name, permanent address or registered place of business of the recipient.

These records must be kept for at least five years from the date the product was placed on the market, or for one year after the date of expiry of the batch, whichever is the longer.

An authorised wholesaler must keep specified records of all incoming and outgoing sales including disposal for five years.[93]

A veterinary surgeon who administers a veterinary medicine to a food producing animal must as soon as possible either enter the following information personally in the keeper's records or give it to the keeper in writing (in which case, the keeper must enter the following into those records):[94]

(a) the name of the veterinary surgeon;
(b) the name of the product and the batch number;
(c) the date of administration of the product;

---

90. VMR schedule 1 part 7.
91. VMR schedule 3 para 12.
92. VMR Reg.21.
93. VMR Reg.22.
94. VMR Reg.18.

(d) the amount of product administered;
(e) the identification of the animals treated; and
(f) the withdrawal period.

RQPs supplying POM-V or POM-VPS medicines or who prescribe under the cascade, must keep all documents relating to the transaction that show:[95]

1. the date of receipt or supply;
2. the name of the product;
3. the pharmaceutical form and strength;
4. the batch number (except that, in the case of a product for a non-food-producing animal, this need only be recorded on the date they receive the batch or the date on which a product from the batch is first supplied);
5. the quantity;
6. the company name and permanent or registered place of business of, in the case of a purchase, the supplier and, in the case of a sale, the recipient;
7. if there is a written prescription, the name and contact details of the prescriber;
8. the expiry date.

If the documents do not include this information, the RQP must make a record of the missing information as soon as reasonably practicable following the transaction. The records must be kept for at least five years.

There are additional record-keeping provisions in the VMR, particularly in relation to antibiotics and antimicrobials (see above), and food-producing animals, including horses that could enter the food chain.[96]

Reporting of sales and usage data in relation to antibiotics

The Secretary of State (through the VMD) may serve a notice requiring the holder of an authorisation or a keeper of food-producing animals, or a feedingstuffs manufacturer or a veterinary surgeon, to provide information relating to the sales and usage of antibiotics.[97]

Annual audit

At least once a year, RQPs must carry out a detailed medicines audit, and compare the incoming and outgoing products with products currently held, and make a record of the audit. A record must be made of any discrepancies found. The records must be kept for a period of five years from the date of the audit. The Secretary of State may require production of the records within that period.[98]

95. VMR Reg.23.
96. See VMR Regs 18, 19 and 20.
97. VMR Reg.24A.
98. VMR schedule 3, para 15.

Horse passports

Horses in the UK must have a passport and, in the passport, horses can be declared as intended for human consumption (food producing), or not intended for human consumption (non-food producing). There is an exception for some semi-wild ponies.

If a veterinary surgeon is not able to prescribe a suitable authorised veterinary medicine, the cascade may be used but a food-producing horse may only be treated with:

a. a veterinary medicine that contains an active substance in the legally permitted essential substances list for such horses (European Regulation (EU) 122/2013 which is assimilated law in Great Britain);
b. a veterinary medicine in the list published by the Secretary of State, containing an active substance with a maximum residue limit (see above) or for which it has been determined that no maximum is required. This includes a medicine used under the cascade.

If a food-producing horse is treated with a veterinary medicine that is not on one of these lists, the horse must be permanently excluded from the food chain and the relevant declaration signed in the passport. VMD guidance on horse medicines and record-keeping requirements provides further information.[99]

Advertising of veterinary medicines and other substances[100]

The word advertising is defined in the VMR as:

> *"the making of a representation in any form in connection with those products in order to promote their supply, distribution, sale, prescription or use and includes any action taken for this purpose by way of the supply of samples or by means of sponsorship ..."*

It is not permitted to issue an advertisement for a relevant substance unless certain conditions are met. A relevant substance means:

(a) a veterinary medicinal product;
(b) a medicinal premix;
(c) an intermediate feedingstuff; or
(d) a compound feed.

Coccidiostats and histomonostats are not relevant substances.

The conditions are that the advertisement:

(a) must be set out in such a way that it is clear that the message is an advertisement for the purpose of promoting the supply, sale, prescription, distribution or use of the substance;
(b) encourages responsible use of the substance while presenting its characteristics in an objective manner;

99. VMD Guidance: Horse medicines and record keeping requirements https://www.gov.uk/guidance/horse-medicines-and-recording-keeping-requirements (accessed 31 December 2024).

100. VMR Regs.10 and 11.

(c) contains no information which:
  (i) is misleading,
  (ii) is incompatible with the summary of product characteristics in relation to the substance,
  (iii) might encourage improper use of the substance, or
  (iv) where the relevant substance is a veterinary medicinal product, might suggest that the substance is a feedingstuff or a biocide.

It is not permitted to advertise a veterinary medicinal product unless it has a marketing authorisation, but this prohibition does not relate to medicines that have been placed on the market in accordance with Schedule 6 to the VMR which relates to medicines for small pet animals.

It is not permitted to advertise an authorised human medicinal product for administration to animals (including sending a price list to a veterinary surgeon or veterinary practice). However, the holder of a wholesale dealer's authorisation may supply a list of authorised medicinal products, together with prices, to a veterinary surgeon for use under the cascade (see above), provided that the veterinary surgeon has requested the list and the list states clearly that the product does not have a marketing authorisation as a veterinary medicinal product, and may only be prescribed and administered under the cascade.

Advertising prescription products and products containing psychotropic drugs or narcotics

It is not permitted to advertise a veterinary medicine that is available on veterinary prescription only, or which contains psychotropic drugs or narcotics, but:

(a) there is an exception for advertisements aimed at veterinary surgeons or pharmacists. There is also an exception for the advertisement of POM-V medicines in the case of price lists and in the case of advertisements aimed at:
  (i) veterinary surgeons,
  (ii) veterinary nurses, or
  (iii) pharmacists or professional keepers of animals; and
(b) there is an exception in the case of POM-VPS medicines for price lists or advertisements aimed at:
  (i) veterinary surgeons,
  (ii) pharmacists,
  (iii) suitably qualified persons – SQPs (these are persons accredited by bodies recognised by the Secretary of State, for example, nurses on the RCVS register who have added to their qualifications),
  (iv) other veterinary health care professionals, or
  (v) professional keepers of animals.

It is not permitted to advertise antimicrobials to professional keepers of animals.

In cases where advertising is permitted, the advertiser must ensure that all factual statements concerning the characteristics of the product are consistent with the summary of product characteristics that form part of the marketing authorisation, and the advertisement must include the statement "prescription decisions are for the person issuing the prescription alone".

Advertising offences and defence

If a person does something that is not permitted, it will be an offence, but anyone prosecuted for breaching the VMR will have a defence if they prove:

(a) that their business is to publish or arrange for the publication of advertisements (for example, a magazine or trade journal); and
(b) the advertisement was received in the ordinary course of business and the person charged did not know and had no reason to suspect that its publication would amount to an offence under the VMR.

Inducements and hospitality[101]

The choice of medicines should be based on what is most suitable for the animal, not because the prescriber has received an inducement or hospitality from the manufacturer. Therefore, where veterinary medicines are being promoted to persons qualified to prescribe them, no one may offer or promise any gift, pecuniary advantage or benefit in kind unless it is inexpensive and relevant to the practice of veterinary medicine or pharmacy.

The prohibition on inducements and hospitality does not prevent the offer of hospitality (including the payment of travelling or accommodation expenses) at events for purely professional or scientific purposes to persons qualified to prescribe or supply veterinary medicines, provided that:

(a) it is subordinate to the main scientific objective of the event; and
(b) is offered only to animal health professionals.

Measures or trade practices relating to price, margins or discounts that were already in use on 17 May 2024[102] are not covered by the prohibitions above.

A person who is qualified to prescribe or supply veterinary medicines may not solicit or accept any gift, pecuniary advantage, benefit in kind, hospitality or sponsorship that is prohibited.

Sheep dips[103]

A person may not use a sheep dip that contains a veterinary medicinal product unless they hold, or they are acting under the supervision and in the presence of a person who holds, either:

- a Certificate of Competence in the Safe Use of Sheep Dips showing that Parts 1 and 2 or units 1 and 2 of the assessment referred to in the certificate have been satisfactorily completed; or
- National Proficiency Tests Council Level 2 Award in the Safe Use of Sheep Dip by a specified body.

---

101. VMR Reg.10A.
102. This is the date when the VMR were amended to include restrictions on inducements and hospitality.
103. Part 3 of Schedule 3 to the VMR.

The supply must be to a person who is qualified to use it, or to a person acting on their behalf. The supplier must keep a record of that person's certificate number as soon as is reasonably practicable and retain it for three years from the date of the supply.

If the active ingredient is an organophosphorus compound, the supplier must give to the buyer:

- a double-sided laminated notice meeting the specification set out in the regulations as to advice on sheep dipping (unless the notice has been provided to the buyer within the previous 12 months and the supplier knows or has reasonable cause to believe the buyer still has it available for use); and
- two pairs of gloves, either as described in the notice (non-lined, PVC or nitrile, heavy duty gauntlet style; 0.5 mm thick and at least 300 mm long) or providing demonstrably superior protection to the user against exposure to the dip than such gloves.

The notice must be at least A4 size with laminated cover and must tell the reader:

1. to read and act in accordance with instructions, including instructions on measuring and diluting concentrate;
2. that sheep dip is absorbed through the skin;
3. always to wear the recommended protective clothing including gloves and have a spare set of clothing;
4. always to wash protective clothing before taking it off; and
5. to direct any questions to the supplier or manufacturer.

The notice must also contain a diagram showing recommended protective clothing.

Cytotoxic drugs

Veterinary surgeons may administer or prescribe cytotoxic drugs and careful consideration should be given to their supply and use. Cytotoxic drugs are hazardous substances, as defined by the Control of Substances Hazardous to Health Regulations 2002 (COSHH) and suppliers must undertake a risk assessment and, for example, identify the hazards, evaluate the risks and record the findings, to protect the health of those involved including the animal owners to whom supplies may be made. Guidance is available from the Health and Safety Executive[104] but in many cases, pharmacies may decide to refer such prescriptions to a specialist pharmacy.

Antimicrobial and anthelmintic resistance

The World Health Organization states that antimicrobial resistance occurs naturally over time but the misuse of antimicrobials in humans and animals is accelerating this process.[105] The veterinary sector has been keen to ensure that antimicrobials and anthelmintics are used responsibly and advises that veterinary surgeons must prescribe and supply these products responsibly. There is species-specific advice from veterinary and

104. https://www.hse.gov.uk/healthservices/safe-use-cytotoxic-drugs.htm (accessed 31 December 2024).

105. https://www.who.int/news-room/fact-sheets/detail/antimicrobial-resistance (accessed 31 December 2024).

other organisations, and pharmacists supplying such veterinary medicines are advised to be aware of the relevant guidance.[106]

Fair trading

In 2005, an Order governing fair trading in the supply and prescribing of veterinary medicines was made.[107] For three years between 2005 and 2008, this Order prohibited a veterinary surgeon from charging a client a fee for a prescription. While this prohibition is no longer in force, the Order continues to provide that a veterinary surgeon may not discriminate between a client to whom they provide a prescription and a client to whom they do not, as concerns (i) the price charged for any relevant veterinary medicine (broadly veterinary medicines classified as POM-V) and (ii) the fees charged for supplying services other than giving a prescription (including, for example, consultation and medicine determination fees). An advisory note on the Order is provided by the Competition and Markets Authority.[108] In addition, the RCVS advises veterinary surgeons to provide information on medicine prices to their clients.[109]

Wholesale dealing

It is not permitted to carry out any wholesale dealing in veterinary medicinal products except in accordance with a wholesale dealer's authorisation (WDA).[110] The Secretary of State must maintain and publish on a website a register of authorised wholesale dealers and their sites.[111]

Wholesale supplies are all supplies that are not retail and may be carried out by those with a WDA as well as MA holders and those with the relevant manufacturing authorisation. In addition, one retailer supplying another by wholesale, for example, a pharmacy supplying a veterinary practice, is permitted if for the purpose of alleviating a temporary supply shortage that could be detrimental to animal welfare. Supply by wholesale must be to a person who is entitled to supply the medicine by retail or wholesale and in the case of an SQP, must be made to the listed SQP retailer premises.

106. https://www.ruma.org.uk/responsible-use-of-antimicrobials-in-veterinary-practice-the-7-point-plan/ (accessed 31 December 2024).
107. Supply of Relevant Veterinary Medicinal Products Order 2005.
108. CMA Advisory Note on Rights and obligations created by the Supply of Relevant Veterinary Medicinal Products Order 2005 and the Royal College of Veterinary Surgeons' code of conduct (2016) https://assets.publishing.service.gov.uk/government/uploads/system/uploads/attachment_data/file/514379/Vets-rights_and_obligations_-_CMA_advisory_note.pdf (accessed 31 December 2024).
109. https://www.rcvs.org.uk/setting-standards/advice-and-guidance/code-of-professional-conduct-for-veterinary-surgeons/supporting-guidance/practice-information-and-fees/ (accessed 31 December 2024).
110. Paragraph 16 of Schedule 3 to the VMR.
111. Paragraph 21A of Schedule 3 to the VMR.

An authorised wholesaler must keep specified records of all incoming and outgoing transactions. An authorised site must be weatherproof, secure and lockable, and clean and free from contaminants. The wholesaler must also have the services of technically competent staff and an effective recall plan. Records must be kept of product recalls or the discovery of any counterfeit products.[112]

The holder of a WDA must (amongst other things):

(a) store veterinary medicinal products in accordance with the terms of the MA for each product;
(b) comply with good distribution practice;
(c) notify the Secretary of State where it has reason to suspect:
  (i) a threat to the continued supply of a veterinary medicinal product;
  (ii) that it has been offered veterinary medicinal products which are counterfeit (in which case, it must also notify the MA holder).[113]

Good distribution practice means "that part of quality assurance which ensures that products are consistently stored, supplied and controlled in accordance with the quality standards appropriate for their intended use and as required by the applicable marketing authorisation or product specifications".[114]

Further requirements apply. [115]

If wholesale supplies are to a veterinary surgeon, a pharmacist or an SQP, they must be made to that person's registered or authorised premises.[116]

Wholesale supplies must be accompanied by documentation specifying:

(a) the name of the veterinary medicinal product;
(b) the strength and pharmaceutical form;
(c) the date on which the veterinary medicinal product was supplied;
(d) the quantity of product supplied;
(e) the batch number;
(f) the expiry date;
(g) the name and address of the wholesale dealer supplying the product;
(h) the means by which the product was transported and the required conditions of storage;
(i) the name of the person to whom the product was supplied and the address to which it is to be delivered.[117]

---

112. Paragraph 21C of Schedule 3 to the Regulations.

113. Paragraph 21 of Schedule 3 to the VMR.

114. Regulation 2.

115. VMR Reg.22 and schedule 3, part 2, and VMD Guidance: Veterinary medicine wholesale dealer's authorisation https://www.gov.uk/guidance/apply-for-a-veterinary-medicine-wholesale-dealers-authorisation-wda# (accessed 31 August 2024).

116. Paragraph 2 of Schedule 3 to the VMR.

117. Paragraph 21B of Schedule 3 to the VMR.

Wholesalers must carry out a detailed audit of stock at least once a year. Any discrepancy must be investigated. Records of the discrepancy and investigation must be kept for at least five years. The Secretary of State may require the production of the records within that period.[118]

Holders of WDAs must have a self-inspection programme which ensures that every aspect of its business is inspected at least once a year in order to ensure that it is complying with good distribution practice. Any non-compliance must be investigated and records of both must be maintained for at least five years.[119]

Importation of veterinary medicines

Authorised veterinary medicines may be imported into the UK only by the MA holder, the holder of a relevant manufacturing authorisation, an authorised wholesale dealer (if the MA holder has been notified in advance), a veterinary surgeon or pharmacist; and, for the medicines they may supply, a registered SQP. Unauthorised veterinary medicines are likely to be seized if they are imported.[120] There are no restrictions on the importation of AVM-GSL products.[121]

A veterinary surgeon may import an unauthorised veterinary medicine that is authorised in another country if it is for the purpose of administration by that veterinary surgeon or under their responsibility under the cascade or in exceptional circumstances. The veterinary surgeon may import personally or by using a wholesale dealer or pharmacist.[122]

A wholesale dealer or a pharmacist may import an unauthorised veterinary medicine for the purpose of storing it pending administration by a veterinary surgeon under the cascade or administration in exceptional circumstances, if: (amongst other things):

(a) the product is authorised in another country;
(b) the Secretary of State has issued a certificate that the product is needed urgently; and
(c) there is no suitable authorised medicine in Great Britain.

A pharmacist may supply to a veterinary surgeon a product that satisfies these conditions.[123]

Additional controls may apply to the importation of controlled drugs.[124]

---

118. Paragraph 21D of Schedule 3 to the VMR.

119. Paragraph 21F of Schedule 3 to the VMR.

120. https://www.gov.uk/government/collections/illegal-animal-medicines-seizure-and-improvement-notices (accessed 31 December 2024).

121. VMR Reg.9.

122. VMR Reg.25(5).

123. VMR Reg 25(6A).

124. RCVS has published guidance on controlled drugs. https://www.rcvs.org.uk/setting-standards/advice-and-guidance/controlled-drugs-guidance-a-to-z/ (accessed 31 December 2024) and see Chapter 14.

Inspection and offences

There are powers of inspection and enforcement in the VMR for authorised inspectors. As well as VMD's own inspectors, GPhC inspectors have powers under the regulations to enforce relevant provisions of the VMR relating to a pharmacy.[125]

Offences under the VMR include those relating to the manufacture, authorisation, marketing, prescription, retail supply and administration of veterinary medicines, as well those relating to the advertising and use of authorised human medicines. The offences are set out at the end of the regulations[126] and the end of each schedule.

Offences include:

1. to place a veterinary medicine on the market unless that product has a marketing authorisation (subject to exceptions);[127]
2. to administer a veterinary medicine to an animal unless:
   a. the medicine has a marketing authorisation for administration of the product in the UK, or
   b. it is administered in accordance with Schedule 4 (cascade) or Schedule 6 (exemptions for small pet animals);[128]
3. to supply a veterinary medicine (including a veterinary medicinal product that has been incorporated into a medicated feedingstuff) that has passed its expiry date;[129]
4. to supply a medicinal product authorised for human use for administration to an animal other than in accordance with a prescription given by a veterinary surgeon for administration under the cascade;[130]
5. to possess a veterinary medicine not supplied in accordance with schedule 3 of the VMR[131], and to possess an unauthorised medicine or possess it with the intention of supplying it to others (subject to various exemptions including medicines supplied as part of the cascade);[132] and
6. to advertise an authorised human medicine for administration to animals;[133] however, there is a limited exemption for wholesale dealers (see advertising of veterinary products).

There is provision in the VMR for improvement notices and seizure notices, which must usually be made public. Prosecutions are reported in the VMD's Marketing

---

125. Memorandum of Understanding between the Veterinary Medicines Directorate and the General Pharmaceutical Council, https://assets.pharmacyregulation.org/files/document/gphc-vmd-mou.pdf (accessed 31 December 2024).
126. VMR Reg.43.
127. VMR Regs.43(a) and 4.
128. VMR Regs.43(d) and 8.
129. VMR Regs.43(c) and 7(2).
130. VMR Regs.43(c) and 7(4).
131. VMR Regs.43(c) and 7(5).
132. VMR Regs.43(r) and 26.
133. VMR Regs.43(f) and 10(2).

Authorisations Veterinary Information Service (MAVIS), which is available on the VMD's website.[134]

SUMMARY

- Dealings with veterinary medicinal products are governed by the Veterinary Medicines Regulations 2013 (VMR).
- The definition of a veterinary medicinal product is broad, including products that are medicinal because of their function and those that are presented as medicinal products.
- Wholesalers must have a wholesale dealer's authorisation.
- Although veterinary medicines require Market Authorisations, there are significant exceptions including certain medicines for small pet animals.
- Marketing authorisation holders have pharmacovigilance obligations.
- Homeopathic medicinal products do not require a marketing authorisation, if they meet certain conditions, but must be registered.
- If a veterinary medicinal product does not have a marketing authorisation it is an offence to possess it with intent to supply, or to supply it (subject to exemptions).
- Veterinary surgeons may administer or supply by retail any veterinary medicine.
- There are four classes of veterinary medicines, two of which are prescription only.
- The VMR place restrictions on the prescribing and use of antibiotics to address the risk of antimicrobial resistance.
- There are detailed rules governing supply, administration and advertising of authorised veterinary medicines.
- Generally, an animal must be treated with a veterinary medicine authorised for the species and condition, but if one is not available, the cascade system provides for the prescription, administration and supply of medicines (including human medicines if necessary) which are not authorised for that species or condition.
- RQPs must be registered with the appropriate authority or organisation, and premises from which supplies are made must be registered or listed with the appropriate authority.
- Food-producing animals, horses and certain types of veterinary medicines are subject to additional controls and considerations.
- Specific requirements apply to medicated feedstuffs.
- Internet sales of veterinary medicines are not permitted unless the supplier meets certain criteria.
- Fair trading rules exist to allow pharmacists to compete with veterinary surgeons for the retail supply of POM-V medicines prescribed by veterinary surgeons.

FURTHER READING

- Animal Medicines Training and Regulatory Authority: **http://www.amtra.org.uk**.
- Department for Environment, Food and Rural Affairs: **https://www.gov.uk/government/organisations/department-for-environment-food-rural-affairs**.

---

134. https://www.gov.uk/government/collections/illegal-animal-medicines-seizure-and-improvement-notices (accessed 31 December 2024).

- Explanatory Memorandum to the Veterinary Medicines (Amendment etc.) Regulations 2024 **https://www.legislation.gov.uk/ukdsi/2024/9780348258523/pdfs/ukdsiem_9780348258523_en_001.pdf** (accessed 31 December 2024).
- Osborne Clarke: "Vet-ting" medicinal claims in Great Britain: top tips on advertising pet products with health benefits **https://www.lexology.com/library/detail.aspx?g=0a308381-6c60-47d1-b197-0075e5ecc33c** (accessed 31 December 2024).
- Prescribing POM-Vs – guidance from the RCVS and VMD **https://www.rcvs.org.uk/news-and-views/features/prescribing-pom-vs-joint-guidance-from-the-rcvs-and-vmd/?type=rfst&set=true#cookie-widget** (accessed 31 December 2024).
- RCVS – Veterinary medicines **https://www.rcvs.org.uk/setting-standards/advice-and-guidance/code-of-professional-conduct-for-veterinary-surgeons/supporting-guidance/veterinary-medicines/** (accessed 31 December 2024).
- Royal College of Veterinary Surgeons: **http://www.rcvs.org.uk**.
- Veterinary Medicines Directorate (VMD) **https://www.gov.uk/government/organisations/veterinary-medicines-directorate**.
- Veterinary Medicines Directorate: *Sell veterinary medicines online* **https://www.gov.uk/guidance/sell-veterinary-medicines-on-the-internet** (accessed 31 December 2024).
- Veterinary Medicines Directorate: *Veterinary medicines guidance*: **https://www.gov.uk/government/collections/veterinary-medicines-guidance-notes-vmgns** (accessed 31 December 2024).
- VMD and DEFRA review of the VMR that preceded amendments to the VMR in 2024 **https://consult.defra.gov.uk/vmd/review-of-the-veterinary-medicines-regulations-201/supporting_documents/VMR_2023_Consultation_document_for_VMR_amendments%20version%201.1.pdf** (accessed 31 December 2024).
- VMD Guideline Pharmacovigilance systems **https://www.gov.uk/government/publications/pharmacovigilance-of-veterinary-medicines-in-great-britain/pharmacovigilance-systems-including-risk-management** (accessed 31 December 2024).

CHAPTER 16

Human medicines: homoeopathic[1] medicines

For historic reasons, there are three regimes for regulating homoeopathic medicines. Firstly, those products with a product licence of right, secondly those registered under the Simplified Homeopathic Registration Scheme, and thirdly those registered under the National Homoeopathic Rules Scheme.

Introduction

It should not be assumed that because homoeopathic medicines are often prepared at high dilution, these medicines are harmless. As explained below, not all homoeopathic medicines have been placed on the market after safety data has become available and, as is apparent from the minutes and reports of the Advisory Board on the Registration of Homeopathic Products, a small number of suspected adverse reactions to homoeopathic medicines is reported in most years.[2] There are restrictions on advertising, but practitioners are not subject to statutory regulation unless they also happen to be registered health professionals such as pharmacists or doctors.

Definition of *homoeopathic medicinal products*

Regulation 8 of the Human Medicines Regulations 2012 (HMR) defines a *homoeopathic medicinal product* as:

> *"a medicinal product prepared from homoeopathic stocks in accordance with a homoeopathic manufacturing procedure described by:*
> *(a) the European Pharmacopoeia; or*

1. The spelling *homeopathic* is more widely used today than *homoeopathic*. However, the HMR use the spelling *homoeopathic* and the spelling in the Regulations has therefore been used in this chapter when referring to the provisions of the HMR. It has not been possible to use that spelling consistently throughout the chapter because other official documents, for example those published by the MHRA and the Advertising Standards Authority, use the spelling *homeopathic*, as does the Society of Homeopaths in its name.
2. The Advisory Board is an Expert Committee of the Medicines and Healthcare products Regulatory Agency. See, for example, the Advisory Board's annual report for 2021 https://assets.publishing.service.gov.uk/media/659d5a2baa18b1000da199f4/ABRHP_HMAC_Annual_Report_2021.pdf (accessed 31 December 2024).

(b) in the absence of such a description in the European Pharmacopoeia,

(i) in relation to a certificate of registration or marketing authorisation for a national homoeopathic product in force in Great Britain only, the British Pharmacopoeia, or in any pharmacopoeia used officially in a country that is included in a list published by the licensing authority for this purpose;

(ii) in relation to a certificate of registration or marketing authorisation for a national homoeopathic product in force in the whole United Kingdom or in Northern Ireland only, in the British Pharmacopoeia or in any pharmacopoeia used officially in an EEA State."

Because of the philosophy of homoeopathy and the nature of the products, it is difficult to demonstrate the efficacy of homoeopathic products by way of clinical trials and there are therefore no homoeopathic products which have marketing authorisations in the UK. Homoeopathic products are excluded from the International Recognition Procedure for marketing authorisations (see **Chapter 5**). In place of marketing authorisations, the Medicines and Healthcare products Regulatory Agency (MHRA) oversees three regimes: those products with a product licence of right, those registered under the Simplified Homeopathic Registration Scheme, and those registered under the National Homoeopathic Rules Scheme.

Product Licences of Right

Homoeopathic (and anthroposophic) products that were already on the market up to 1971 had Product Licences of Right. These licences were granted as of right; scientific data would not necessarily be available (in the nature of homoeopathic products) and evidence of safety was not required.

Products with a Product Licence of Right may give indications and may have a wider range of dosage forms and dilutions than other homoeopathic products.

Since 2006, holders of Product Licences of Right have been able to register their products under the National Homoeopathic Rules Scheme (see below); upon registration, the Product Licence of Right lapses. The remaining number of Product Licences of Right may be small. They remain in force under transitional arrangements in HMR Reg.347 and Schedule 32 to the HMR.

The Simplified Homoeopathic Registration Scheme

The Simplified Homoeopathic Registration Scheme is a scheme for products that are administered orally or externally for which no specific therapeutic indication appears on the labelling or in any information supplied with the product. Such a product is eligible to be registered under this scheme if:

- the product contains no more than one part per 10,000 of the mother tincture; and

- in a case where the product's active substance is a relevant allopathic (i.e. not homoeopathic substance), the product contains no more than 1/100th of the smallest concentration of that substance used in allopathy.[3]

Applicants for products under the simplified scheme are required to provide only minimal data on safety, and no data on efficacy.

National Homoeopathic Rules Scheme[4]

The National Homoeopathic Rules Scheme was established because of anomalies in the regimes for products that have a Product Licence of Right or are registered under the Simplified Homoeopathic Registration Scheme.

The national scheme is for products that are not registrable under the simplified scheme and are for the treatment of minor symptoms or minor conditions. They are minor if they can ordinarily and with reasonable safety be treated without the intervention of a doctor.

An applicant for registration under the national scheme need not comply with requirements relating to the submission of the results of preclinical tests and clinical trials, provided that they comply with the requirements relating to submission of safety and efficacy data.

The safety data provided must include information about the following aspects of the safety of the product:

- pharmacology;
- pharmacokinetics; and
- toxicity.

The applicant may seek to establish safety by way of "scientific data" (study reports or published scientific literature) or in some circumstances by non-scientific data. In some cases (where the product is derived from a homoeopathic substance present in food, or is derived from a substance from which a licensed product is derived, or which is sufficiently dilute), and provided certain other specified conditions are met, safety can be guaranteed and the applicant is not required to provide safety data. Under the new rules, the applicant can establish efficacy by study reports, published scientific literature, or by reference to special investigations called "homoeopathic provings".[5]

Exemptions for medicinal products at high dilution

See Chapter 13.

---

3. HMR Reg.102.
4. Schedule 10 to the HMR.
5. https://www.legislation.gov.uk/uksi/2006/1952/pdfs/uksiem_20061952_en.pdf (accessed 31 December 2024).

Exemption for registered products

Regulation 220 of the HMR imposes restrictions on the sale of Pharmacy medicines (**Chapter 11**), for example that sales must be made at or from registered pharmacy premises by or under the supervision of a pharmacist. Regulation 221 of the HMR imposes restrictions on the sale of medicines subject to general sale (**Chapter 10**), for example that they must be sold from premises that are capable of being closed to the public. These restrictions do not apply to homoeopathic medicines[6] where:

- a certificate of registration is in force in relation to the product;
- the product is not an *excluded product* (see below); and
- the person selling or supplying the product has been requested to do so by or on behalf of a particular person and in that person's presence and the seller has used their own judgement as to the treatment required.

In addition, the restrictions on sale or supply of Pharmacy medicines do not apply where:

- a certificate of registration is in force in relation to the product;
- the conditions for medicines subject to general sale are met; and
- the product is not an *excluded product* (see below).

An *excluded product* means a product that is promoted, recommended or marketed: for use as an anthelmintic; for parenteral administration; for use as eye drops; for use as an eye ointment; for use as an enema; for use wholly or mainly for irrigation of wounds or of the bladder, vagina or rectum; or for administration wholly or mainly to children being a preparation of aloxiprin or aspirin.

Advertising

There are restrictions on the advertising of homeopathic products. The MHRA has published the Blue Guide, which contains guidance on advertising[7] and is responsible for enforcing any breach of the HMR. For example, a complaint was made in 2011 that Boots advertised a number of homeopathic products with indications for use, even though the products in question were not licensed for the use that was advertised. The complaint was upheld and the products were withdrawn from sale.[8] Separately, the Advertising Standards Authority (ASA), which applies codes written by the Committee of Advertising Practice (CAP), has published advice[9] to homeopaths that covers:

- not making claims to treat medical conditions unless medically qualified and/or without robust evidence of efficacy;
- using broad claims about homeopathy;

6. HMR Reg.243.
7. https://assets.publishing.service.gov.uk/government/uploads/system/uploads/attachment_data/file/824550/Appendix_2_-_Blue_Guide.pdf (accessed 31 December 2024).
8. https://www.chemistanddruggist.co.uk/CD014701/Boots-removes-homeopathic-remedy-advertising-after-MHRA-upholds-complaint/ (accessed 31 December 2024).
9. https://www.asa.org.uk/advice-online/health-homeopathy.html (accessed 31 December 2024).

- avoiding claims that are misleading; and
- avoiding direct or implied efficacy claims in testimonials.

The CAP's advice is set out in **Box 16.1**.

In 2021, the ASA upheld a complaint about a website for Homeopathy UK that featured a page entitled "Conditions Directory" with text that stated, "Please find below a list of conditions where homeopathy can help ...", followed by a list of medical conditions that included depression, diabetes, infertility, psoriasis and asthma". It ruled that the advert must not appear again in the form complained about, and told Homeopathy UK to ensure that their future communications did not refer to conditions for which advice should be sought from suitably qualified health professionals.[10]

See also **Chapter 19**.

Box 16.1: CAP position on Homeopathy (extracts)

CAP understands that this discipline works on the principle of treating like with like, with the active ingredient often diluted heavily in water. The ASA and CAP have yet to be provided with robust evidence to show that remedies lacking in pharmacologically active molecules can produce clinical effects.

Do not make claims to treat medical conditions unless medically qualified and/or without robust evidence of efficacy

Some homeopaths may be medically qualified and therefore regulated by the General Medical Council. Those who are medically qualified may make claims about treating conditions but would need to make clear that efficacy is due only to conventional treatments unless they hold robust clinical evidence to support claims of efficacy for individual homeopathic treatments.

Those practitioners who are not medically qualified should not refer to serious medical conditions.

In July 2007 the General Media Panel concluded that complementary and alternative therapy practitioners offering significant or invasive treatments should encourage consumers to take independent medical advice before committing themselves to the treatment.

Use broad claims about homeopathy

Claims describing a therapy session such as "Homeopathy is a holistic approach" and "practitioners work closely with their clients" are likely to be acceptable, as are more general statements that some clients consider homeopathy to be comforting, calming or soothing. Claims describing the popularity of homeopathy are also likely to be acceptable so long as they can be supported by evidence.

Avoid direct or implied efficacy claims in testimonials

If a testimonial includes direct or indirect efficacy claims, then this will be subject to the same rules as any other claim. In other words, where efficacy has not been established, a testimonial should not be used to imply that it has. Patient testimonials alone are unlikely to substantiate objective claims about the efficacy of a product or therapy.

---

10. https://www.asa.org.uk/rulings/homeopathy-uk-a20-1078950-homeopathy-uk.html (accessed 31 December 2024),

Homeopathic practitioners

Unlike pharmacists and pharmacy technicians, homeopathic practitioners are not subject to a mandatory registration system. The Professional Standards Authority for Health and Social Care (PSA – see **Chapters 2** and **25**) has accredited in the past a voluntary register maintained by the Society of Homeopaths. Accreditation was based on the Society setting and maintaining standards of practice and conduct; handling complaints and concerns and issuing sanctions where appropriate; and assuring the quality of education and training. Homeopathic practitioners on the register were entitled to display a quality mark to signify that they meet the PSA's standards. The Society has withdrawn from the accreditation scheme and the Society and its registrants are not permitted to use the PSA's quality mark.

Controversy

The sale and supply of homeopathic products from pharmacies is controversial. The Royal Pharmaceutical Society[11] does not endorse homeopathy as a form of treatment because there is no scientific basis for homeopathy nor any evidence to support the clinical efficacy of homeopathic products beyond a placebo effect. Among other things, it considers that pharmacists must advise patients considering a homeopathic product about their lack of efficacy beyond that of a placebo. The MHRA warns that the Health Protection Agency Advisory Committee on Malaria Prevention does not recommend relying on any homeopathic remedies for the prevention of malaria.[12] It says that "There is no scientific proof that homeopathic remedies are effective in either preventing or treating malaria". In 2011, the General Pharmaceutical Council dropped fitness to practise cases against pharmacies alleged to have advised people to take homeopathic remedies to protect themselves against malaria, but said the original complaint may be taken into account in the event of any future complaint.[13] In *Watt v Lothian Health Board*,[14] a patient challenged a decision of the Health Board to cease provision of a NHS homeopathy service. The challenge – described in more detail in **Box 16.2** – was unsuccessful. In 2017, NHS England recommended that GPs and other prescribers should stop providing homeopathy because it found "no clear or robust evidence to support the use of homeopathy on the NHS".[15] The British Homeopathic Association was unsuccessful in an attempt to have the recommendation declared unlawful.[16]

---

11. https://www.rpharms.com/resources/quick-reference-guides/homeopathy (accessed 31 December 2024).
12. https://assets.publishing.service.gov.uk/media/67596f7851df3604e0a292c0/guidelines-for-malaria-prevention-in-travellers-from-the-UK-2024.pdf (accessed 31 December 2024).
13. https://www.bbc.co.uk/news/health-12153074 (accessed 31 December 2024).
14. [2015] CSOH 117 and see also Scottish Legal News https://www.scottishlegal.com/article/woman-fails-in-legal-challenge-over-health-boards-unlawful-withdrawal-of-homeopathic-services (accessed 31 December 2024).
15. https://www.nhs.uk/conditions/homeopathy/ (accessed 31 December 2024).
16. *R (on the application of British Homeopathic Association) v National Health Service Commissioning Board* [2018] EWHC 1359 (Admin).

Box 16.2: *Watt v Lothian Health Board*

On 26 June 2013, Lothian Health Board (the Board) decided to cease provision of an NHS homeopathy service in Lothian and look to re-invest the funding into other NHS healthcare of clinical value such as pain and chronic pain. The lawfulness of the decision was challenged by Mrs Honor Watt. Mrs Watt was disabled by arthritis and took a homeopathic medicine called "Bovista" for it, having found that conventional treatments for her condition were ineffective and produced undesirable side effects. The Court of Session was told that Mrs Watt experienced "great relief" of her symptoms from the homeopathic medicines, but she was informed that she was no longer entitled to the treatment during a final appointment with the service in January 2014.

Mrs Watt argued that the decision was unlawful because it was taken without due regard to the public sector equality duty (see **Chapter 1**) to eliminate discrimination and the need to advance equality of opportunity between persons who shared relevant protected characteristics and those who did not share them.

The judge, Lord Uist, sitting in the Outer House of the Court of session referred to the controversy surrounding homeopathy, somewhat unusually citing a Wikipedia entry. The judge noted that the Mrs Watt and others, including the British Homeopathic Association, consider there is "a growing body of evidence to show that homeopathy has a positive effect". The judge did not have to adjudicate between the competing views on the merits or otherwise of homeopathy: his role was to consider whether the Health Board's decision had been made lawfully.

The judge held that it was not necessary for the Health Board to have carried out a full census or survey of all patients using the homeopathic service and that it had obtained sufficient information to discharge its public sector equality duty.

He went on to say:

> *"It is plain that the Board, as it was entitled to do, accepted the view that there was no scientific evidence for the efficacy of homeopathy and that funding for it was a waste of the limited funds at its disposal. In these circumstances the countervailing factor in this case was so powerful, indeed overwhelming, that no decision other than the one taken by the Board was conceivable. A different decision, namely, to continue spending money on a service whose efficacy was not established, would have been unreasonable."*

SUMMARY

- Homoeopathic medicines with Certificates of Registration can be sold under similar circumstances. However, there are certain excluded categories.
- It is difficult to demonstrate the safety and efficacy of homoeopathic medicines through clinical trials, so marketing authorisations cannot be granted.
- Homoeopathic medicines on the market up to 1971 may have Product Licences of Right.
- There is a Simplified Registration Scheme for homoeopathic products. This is available for products at or below a specified dilution if the product is not labelled with a therapeutic indication.

SUMMARY (cont.)

- There are exemptions for registered homoeopathic medicines from the restrictions that apply to other medicines.
- There is a National Homoeopathic Rules Scheme for products that are not eligible for the Simplified Registration Scheme. Applications for inclusion in the scheme must be accompanied by information about safety.
- There are advertising restrictions which are enforced by the Advertising Standards Authority.
- Treatment (or recommending treatment) with homoeopathic medicines instead of medicines that have a marketing authorisation is controversial and may lead to fitness to practise proceedings.

FURTHER READING

- Human Medicines Regulations (2012) SI 2012 No. 1916, *Explanatory memorandum*: **http://www.legislation.gov.uk/uksi/2012/1916/pdfs/uksiem_20121916_en.pdf** (accessed 31 December 2024).
- MHRA - Homeopathic Medicines: Guidance on advertising **https://assets.publishing.service.gov.uk/government/uploads/system/uploads/attachment_data/file/824550/Appendix_2_-_Blue_Guide.pdf** (accessed 31 December 2024).

CHAPTER 17

Human medicines: herbal medicinal products

Herbal medicines may be potent or harmful. Unless an exemption applies, they must have a marketing authorisation or traditional herbal registration. Ministers have exercised powers to prohibit certain herbal medicines, and trading in endangered herbal species is banned by international treaty.

Introduction

Herbal remedies have been used for many centuries to treat disease, and it is recognised that they can contain a complex mixture of phytochemicals that in studies have proven to have pharmacological activity. Some modern medicines are derived from constituents of herbal products, such as digoxin.

Any product which makes a medicinal claim requires appropriate authorisation as a medicinal product. The Human Medicines Regulations 2012 (HMR) Part 4 establishes that products must not be sold, supplied, or offered for sale or supply unless authorised by the United Kingdom licensing authority under the HMR. References to Parts, Regulations and Schedules in this chapter relate to the HMR and to sections to the Medicines Act 1968, unless otherwise stated.

Medicinal products with herbal active ingredient(s) may be authorised either with a marketing authorisation, or with a traditional herbal registration (also known as a "THR"). Details of the requirements for marketing authorisations to be granted are specified in the HMR (see **Chapter 5**). Medicinal products that have a THR are excluded from the International Recognition Procedure for marketing authorisations (see **Chapter 5**).

The licensing authority is the Medicines and Healthcare products Regulatory Agency (MHRA), and it is responsible for the grant, renewal, variation, suspension and revocation of licences, authorisations, certificates and registrations under these Regulations. Written applications for either a marketing authorisation or a traditional herbal registration must be made in the manner prescribed, which are then assessed (see **Chapter 5**).

An MHRA expert committee known as the Herbal Medicines Advisory Committee,[1] advises on the safety, quality and efficacy in relation to human use of:

---

1. Established by the Herbal Medicines Advisory Committee Order 2005.

(a) herbal medicinal products eligible for registration as a THR;
(b) unlicensed herbal medicinal products (unless a product is subject to an application for a marketing authorisation, product licence[2] or a homeopathic certificate of registration).

If Ministers or the MHRA request advice or information, the Committee may also advise on the safety, quality and efficacy in relation to human use, of herbal medicinal products which have a marketing authorisation, product licence or homeopathic certificate of registration, or which are the subject of an application for one of these.

Definitions

The HMR Reg.8 has the following definitions:

Herbal medicinal product means a medicinal product whose only active ingredients are herbal substances or herbal preparations (or both).[3]

Herbal preparation means a preparation obtained by subjecting herbal substances to processes such as extraction, distillation, expression, fractionation, purification, concentration or fermentation, and includes a comminuted or powdered herbal substance, a tincture, an extract, an essential oil, an expressed juice or a processed exudate.

Herbal substance means a plant or part of a plant, alga, fungus or lichen, or an unprocessed exudate of a plant, defined by the plant part used and the botanical name of the plant, either fresh or dried, but otherwise unprocessed.

Traditional herbal registration means a registration granted by the licensing authority for a traditional herbal medicinal product under the HMR.

Herbal medicines with marketing authorisations

Some herbal medicines will be classified as medicinal products and, as such, will require marketing authorisations (see **Chapter 5**).

Labelling for herbal medicinal products holding a marketing authorisation

Herbal medicinal products which hold a marketing authorisation have been fully assessed by the relevant Licensing Authority for safety, quality, and efficacy. The efficacy is based on clinical evidence. The standard requirements for the labelling of containers and packages of medicinal products are set out in HMR Reg.257 and Schedule 24 (see **Chapter 18**).

---

2. Product licences have been superseded by marketing authorisations, but the MHRA's literature and that of the Committee still refers to product licences.

3. *Herbal remedy* had been defined in the Medicines Act 1968, but there is no definition of a herbal remedy in the HMR.

Registration of a traditional herbal medicinal product

In practice, it has not always been realistic or practicable to obtain a marketing authorisation for herbal medicinal products, mainly because of the difficulty in satisfying the requirement to demonstrate their efficacy. To address this situation, Part 7 of the HMR and Schedule 29 provide a scheme for the registration of traditional herbal medicines.

Traditional herbal medicines are generally registered for use in minor self-limiting conditions that are suitable for self-management and do not require the intervention of a medical practitioner.

Under the traditional herbal registration scheme, the requirement to demonstrate efficacy is replaced by evidence of traditional use. Pharmacological effects or efficacy of the medicinal product must be plausible on the basis of long-standing use and experience. Although it is not required to demonstrate efficacy as for a marketing authorisation, quality and safety must be demonstrated before a traditional herbal registration is granted. With regard to the manufacturing and quality of traditional herbal medicinal products, applications for registration of these products have to fulfil the equivalent requirements as applications for a marketing authorisation.

Under HMR Reg.125, the conditions for registration are that:

(a) by virtue of its composition and indications the product is appropriate for use without the need for a medical practitioner to:
   a. diagnose the condition to be treated by the product,
   b. prescribe the product, or
   c. monitor the product's use;

(b) the product is intended to be administered at a particular strength and in accordance with a particular posology;

(c) the product is intended to be administered externally, orally or by inhalation;

(d) the product:
   a. has been in medicinal use for a continuous period of at least 30 years, and
   b. in relation to-
      (i) a UK registration has been in medicinal use in the European Union for a continuous period of at least 15 years,
      (ii) a GB registration the product has been in medicinal use in the United Kingdom or a country included in a list published by the MHRA[4] for a continuous period of at least 15 years. The countries listed will be regarded by the MHRA as having a level of pharmacovigilance equivalent to that of the UK to ensure that any safety issues have been properly identified to support the traditional use of the product.

---

4. Under powers in HMR Reg.125A.

It is immaterial for the purposes of condition (d) whether or not during a period mentioned in that condition, the sale or supply of the product has been based on a specific authorisation, or the number or quantity of the ingredients (or any of them) has been reduced;

(e) there is sufficient information about the use of the product as mentioned in condition (d) (referred to in this Part as its "traditional use"), so that (in particular):
   a. it has been established that the traditional use of the product is not harmful, and
   b. the pharmacological effects or efficacy of the product are plausible on the basis of long-standing use and experience.

In the case of a GB registration, there is a procedure for seeking authorisation if condition (d) (15 years' use) is not met but the other conditions are satisfied (HMR Reg.130A).

HMR Reg.126A empowers the MHRA to establish and publish a list of herbal substances, preparations and combinations thereof for use in traditional herbal products. Such a list must contain with regard to each herbal substance:

(a) the indication;
(b) the specified strength and posology;
(c) the route of administration; and
(d) any other information necessary for the safe use of the herbal substance as a traditional medicinal product.

Applications for a traditional herbal medicinal product registration must be made in the manner prescribed in the Regulations (HMR Reg.127).

The registration of a medicinal product with a THR must include a term that the product is available (a) only from a pharmacy or (b) on general sale. The registration may include a term that the product may be available for general sale only if the licensing authority considers that with reasonable safety it can be sold or supplied otherwise than by or under the supervision of a pharmacist. If the HMR are amended as proposed (see **Chapter 11**), HMR Reg.131 will be amended so as to refer to supervision "by a pharmacist or a pharmacy technician who is authorised by a pharmacist to sell or supply".

If the HMR are amended as proposed (see **Chapter 11**), HMR Reg.131 will be amended so as to refer to supervision" by a pharmacist or a pharmacy technician who is authorised by a pharmacist to sell or supply".

Part 7 of the HMR includes provisions for the use, sale or supply of a traditional herbal medicine to be suspended for example if the MHRA thinks the product is harmful or the pharmacological effects or efficacy of the product are no longer plausible.

Like the holders of marketing authorisations (see **Chapter 5**), the holder of a traditional herbal registration must take all reasonable steps to ensure appropriate and continued supplies of the product to which the registration relates to pharmacies and persons authorised to supply the product so that the needs of patients in the United Kingdom are met (HMR Reg 148).

Labelling for traditional herbal medicinal products

HMR Reg.265(1) and (2), and Schedule 29 set out additional requirements for labelling of traditional herbal medicinal products, as compared to those listed above for medicinal products holding a marketing authorisation. These include the following requirements in Schedule 29 Part 1:

(a) a statement to the effect that the product is a traditional herbal medicinal product, for use for specific purposes by reason of long-standing use; and
(b) a statement that the user should consult a doctor or other health care practitioner if symptoms persist during use of the medicinal product, or if adverse effects not mentioned on the package or package leaflet occur.

HMR Reg.265(2) specifies that no information need appear on:

- a package containing a traditional herbal medicinal product where part of the package is transparent or open, provided the information required by the HMR is clearly visible through the transparent or open part of the package; or
- a paper bag or similar wrapping, in which a package that contains a traditional herbal medicinal product and bears information required by the HMR and Schedule 29 is placed at the time of sale or supply;
- a package enclosing a package of a traditional herbal medicinal product for export;
- an ampoule or other container of not more than 10 mL, which is enclosed in a package on which information appears in accordance with the requirements of the HMR and Schedule 29; or
- a blister pack or similar packaging, enclosed in a package labelled in accordance with the requirements of the HMR and Schedule 29.

Subject to the above, HMR Schedule 29 Part 2 stipulates that if the traditional herbal medicinal product is a Pharmacy medicine (see **Chapter 11**), the outer and immediate packaging must be labelled to show the capital letter 'P' within a rectangle, within which there is no other matter of any kind.

The licensing authority owns the rights to an additional visible symbol, a THR Certification Mark (see **Figure 17.1**), which can be located on the packaging of registered traditional herbal medicinal products. The MHRA can give permission to companies to use the mark on products registered under the THR scheme. The Certification Mark indicates that the herbal medicine has been registered with the MHRA under the THR scheme; and meets the required standards relating to its quality, safety, evidence of traditional use and other criteria as set out under HMR. These products can also be identified by a nine-digit authorisation number starting with the letters 'THR' on the product container or packaging.

Figure 17.1 *THR Certification Mark.*

Sale or supply by a licence holder

HMR Reg.43(5) states that the holder of a manufacturer's licence must not sell or supply a medicinal product, or offer it for sale or supply, unless:

- there is a marketing authorisation or traditional herbal registration (an "authorisation") in force in relation to the product; and
- the sale or supply, or offer for sale or supply, is in accordance with the authorisation.

It is also the responsibility of manufacturers, wholesale dealers, importers and anyone placing medicinal products on the market to ensure that they comply with the relevant legislation. (See also **Chapter 5**.)

Exemptions

Manufacturer's licences and marketing authorisations

The requirements for a manufacturer's licence and for a marketing authorisation (see **Chapter 5**) do not apply[5] where a medicinal product is manufactured or assembled by a doctor or dentist and the conditions in paragraphs (A) and (B) are met.

(A) the medicinal product is supplied to a patient in the course of the treatment of that patient or to a patient of another doctor or dentist who is a member of the same medical or dental practice; and

(B) the medicinal product is not manufactured or, as the case may be, assembled on a large scale or by an industrial process.

Neither a manufacturer's licence nor a marketing authorisation is required where:

- the manufacture or assembly takes place on premises occupied by the manufacturer (A) and A can exclude the public;
- the product is for administration to a person (B) and A has been requested by or on behalf of B, and in B's presence, to use A's judgment as to the treatment required;
- the product does not contain a substance specified in Part 1 of Schedule 20;
- the product does not contain a substance in Part 2 of Schedule 20 unless the product is sold or supplied:
    - i. in or from containers or packages labelled to show a dose not exceeding the maximum dose or maximum daily dose specified in column 2 of Part 2 of Schedule 20, or
    - ii. in the case of a product for external use only, with a percentage of the substance in the product that does not exceed the percentage specified in column 3 of Part 2 of Schedule 20; and
- the product is not manufactured or assembled on a large scale or by an industrial process.

---

5. HMR Reg.3(2).

Premises, pharmacist supervision and specified substances

HMR Part 12 (dealings with medicinal products) governs the circumstances in which medicinal products may be sold, supplied and administered. HMR Regs.220 and 221 stipulate that medicinal products classified as Pharmacy medicines, may be sold or supplied by retail only from registered pharmacies (see **Chapter 11**), unless they are products subject to general sale (see **Chapter 10**) or subject to some other exemption under the HMR.

Ordinarily, medicinal products medicines that are subject to general sale may only be sold or supplied in manufacturer's original packs (HMR Reg.221), and medicinal products that are not subject to general sale may only be sold by or under the supervision of a pharmacist on registered pharmacy premises (HMR Reg.220). However, HMR Reg.241 provides an exemption for herbal medicinal products from the requirements of these regulations. The exemption is in two parts and applies if:

1. the herbal medicinal product does not contain a substance that is listed in Part 1 of Schedule 20 to the HMR. If a herbal medicinal product is listed in Part 1 of Schedule 20, then it must be sold or supplied by or under the supervision of a pharmacist on registered pharmacy premises[6] unless its classification under its THR or marketing authorisation allows it to be on general sale;
2. the herbal medicinal product (a) does not contain a substance listed in column 1 of Part 2 of Schedule 20 or (b) does contain a substance that is listed in column 1 of Part 2 and the sale or supply is on premises that are being capable of being closed to the public, subject to the following conditions:
   (i) if the substance is listed in column 1 of Part 2, and there is a corresponding entry in column 2 of Part with a maximum dose or maximum daily dose, the product is sold or supplied in a container or package that is labelled to show a dose not exceeding the maximum daily dose, and
   (ii) also in the case of a substance listed in column 1 of Part 2, if there is a corresponding entry in column 3 of Part 2 of Schedule 20 that shows a percentage, the percentage of the substance sold or supplied must not exceed the percentage specified in column 3,

   and the patient or patient's representative has asked the seller/supplier ("the practitioner") on the practitioner's premises and in the patient's presence to use the practitioner's judgement as to the treatment required.

   References to *a substance* are to a substance that is obtained from any botanical source listed in either Part 1 or Part 2 of Schedule 20.

Banned or restricted herbal ingredients in medicines

Under the Convention on International Trade in Endangered Species of Wild Fauna and Flora (CITES), there is a ban on moving or trading without a licence[7] in species of plants

6. If the HMR are amended as proposed (see Chapter 11), HMR Reg.131 will be amended so as to refer to supervision "by a pharmacist or a pharmacy technician who is authorised by a pharmacist to sell or supply".
7. From the Department of Environment, Food and Rural Affairs.

that are endangered. In 2021, a traditional Chinese medicine company was fined £1,000 for selling illegal herbal remedies containing endangered plants.[8]

Section 62 of the Medicines Act 1968 gives Ministers power to prohibit the sale or supply or importation of medicinal products Some plant species have been made the subject of a prohibition order (see below and **Chapter 21**).

In addition to Part 1 and 2 of Schedule 20 to the HMR, and HMR Reg.241 as discussed above, the following legislation is in force:

- The Medicines (Aristolochia and Mu Tong etc.) (Prohibition) Order 2001:
  - It is not permissible to manufacture, import, sell or supply any unlicensed medicine in the UK which contains the listed herbal ingredients.
- The Medicines for Human Use (Kava-kava) (Prohibition) Order 2002:
  - Prohibits the sale, supply or importation of any medicine for human use which consists of or contains a plant (or part of a plant) belonging to the species *Piper methysticum* or an extract from such a plant, except those for external use only.
- The Medicines for Human Use (Prohibition) (Senecio and Miscellaneous Amendments) Order 2008:
  - Prohibits the sale, supply or importation of any medicine for human use which consists of or contains a plant, or part of a plant, belonging to the species *Senecio* or an extract from such a plant.

The MHRA publishes a list of banned and restricted herbal ingredients.[9]

Herbal products as food

Some herbal products may be legally sold under food legislation and are commonly known as food supplements.[10] No medicinal claims can be made for any food product.

The MHRA can determine whether any claims that are made or if the active substance(s) present would mean that a product is regarded to be a medicinal product. More information on the determination on whether a product is classified by the MHRA as medicinal can be found in **Chapter 5**.

Malaria

The MHRA warns that the Health Protection Agency Advisory Committee on Malaria Prevention "strongly advises against relying on any herbal remedies for the prevention of malaria. Herbal remedies have not been tested for their ability to prevent or treat malaria".[11]

---

8. https://www.kilburntimes.co.uk/news/22035969.chinese-medicine-company-fined-21-000-selling-remedies-containing-endangered-plants/ (accessed 31 December 2024).
9. https://www.gov.uk/government/publications/list-of-banned-or-restricted-herbal-ingredients-for-medicinal-use/banned-and-restricted-herbal-ingredients (accessed 31 December 2024).
10. Food Supplements (England) Regulations 2003; Food Supplements (Scotland) Regulations 2003; Food Supplements (Wales) Regulations 2003.
11. https://assets.publishing.service.gov.uk/media/65a16fc674ae66000d738a64/guidelines-for-malaria-prevention-in-travellers-from-the-UK-2023.pdf (accessed 31 December 2024).

Concerns over illegal herbal products

Herbal products can be legally sold under other legislation, for example as cosmetics, foods, medical devices or biocides, but are required to be compliant with the relevant legislation. Either the Inspection and Enforcement Division of the MHRA or the local Trading Standards Office can be contacted directly with any concerns over potentially illegal herbal products.

There is no distinction in the legislation for a traditional medicinal product concerning the proof of the traditional use required due to the nature of the tradition, for example Chinese or western herbal medicine. To date there have been very few traditional Chinese herbal medicinal products registered in the UK.

There exists the potential for illegal herbal products to be supplied to the market that could cause harm to the public. Typically, such products may be supplied with the addition of conventional pharmaceutical actives, with other toxic contaminants such as heavy metals, or be supplied with illegal claims. The MHRA publishes alerts about such cases, and it is advisable to inform the MHRA of any potential cases of concern. An example is discussed in **Box 17.1**.

Box 17.1: Herbal skin cream found to contain steroids – MHRA Press Release[12]

"The MHRA has been working to prevent the further sale of Zudaifu cream and advises anyone who has bought it online to stop using it immediately.

Zudaifu cream is not a licensed medicine and has been marketed in the UK as a 'natural' Chinese herbal remedy for the treatment of a range of skin conditions, most commonly eczema, psoriasis and rosacea.

Our analysis of the product found the presence of the steroid clobetasol propionate. This is the active ingredient in Prescription Only Medicines used for the treatment of a range skin conditions such as psoriasis and eczema.

Creams containing steroids should be used sparingly and as directed by the prescriber. They should not be used on children under 1 year of age.

Dr Chris Jones, Manager of the Medicines Borderline Section at MHRA said:

'We have again identified a potentially harmful cream described as a natural Chinese herbal medicine on the market.

Selling creams directly to the public that contain strong steroids is illegal and they are potentially dangerous if they are used without medical supervision.

Steroids must only be prescribed by healthcare professionals who follow strict criteria when prescribing them and can monitor patients using them. They can suppress the skin's response to infection and can also cause long-term thinning of the skin. If steroids are applied long term, particularly on children, they can lead to other medical problems.

Our advice to anyone who has bought it previously or is currently using Zudaifu cream – particularly on young children and babies – is to stop using it immediately. If you have any questions, please contact your healthcare professional.'"

12. https://www.gov.uk/government/news/herbal-skin-cream-found-to-contain-steroids (accessed 31 December 2024).

Advertising

HMR Regulation 279 states that medicinal products which do not have a valid marketing authorisation or traditional herbal registration may not be advertised for medicinal purposes.

The MHRA has published guidance on advertising traditional herbal medicines to consumers.[13]

The Advertising Standards Authority (ASA) acts as the UK's independent regulator of advertising. It has a code which it enforces. The ASA says:

> *"The variable quality of some products, especially some traditional Chinese 'medicines', has resulted in concerns about their safety. The ASA has upheld complaints against claims that Chinese herbal medicine would not interfere with the effects of western medicine (Dr & Herbs, 24 August 2004). In general, such claims are unlikely to be supported by objective substantiation and could be dangerous. Claims that western medicine has damaging side effects that Chinese medical treatment avoids are equally likely to be unacceptable (Everwell Ltd, 04 January 2006)."*[14]

See also **Chapter 19**.

Herbal practitioners

There is no definition in legislation of *herbal practitioner*. However, care should be taken by practitioners to avoid misleading patients or customers as to the practitioner's qualifications. For example, in 2013 the ASA upheld a complaint about a traditional Chinese medicine practitioner who used the prefix "Dr" throughout his website. The ASA noted that the advertiser had been awarded a bachelor's degree in medicine and had been awarded further qualifications from the Ministry of Health of the People's Republic of China which allowed him to practise. Regardless, they considered that the repeated use of "Dr" throughout the website implied that Mr Jin was a medical doctor who was currently registered with the GMC and practising allopathic medicine. Because that was not the case they concluded the advert breached its Code.[15]

For the exemption from restrictions on the sale or supply of herbal medicinal products when they are sold or supplied on a practitioner's premises following a one-to-one consultation, see the section above entitled Exemptions, particularly in relation to HMR Reg.241.

---

13. https://www.gov.uk/government/news/herbal-skin-cream-found-to-contain-steroids (accessed 31 December 2024).
14. https://assets.publishing.service.gov.uk/media/6012d82c8fa8f56545ea3d76/Appendix_1.pdf (accessed 31 December 2024).
15. https://www.asa.org.uk/advice-online/health-chinese-herbal-medicine-or-traditional-chinese-medicine.html (accessed 31 December 2024).

SUMMARY

- Herbal medicinal products are authorised either by holding a marketing authorisation or a traditional herbal registration (THR).
- Medicinal products with a traditional herbal registration are required to meet the equivalent strict quality and safety standards as all medicinal products that have a marketing authorisation.
- Herbal medicinal products with a THR and herbal medicinal products whose marketing authorisation provides that they are subject to general sale may sold over the counter in any retail outlet.
- Registered pharmacies are permitted, additionally, to sell authorised herbal medicinal products whose marketing authorisation means that they are Pharmacy medicines.
- The restrictions in the HMR that normally apply to medicines subject to general sale and to Pharmacy medicines do not apply to the sale or supply of herbal medicinal products if, amongst other things, they do not contain a substance listed in Part 1 of HMR Schedule 20 or, in some cases, Part 2 of HMR Schedule 20.
- The licensing authority provides a current list of restricted or banned herbal ingredients.
- A herbal medicinal product that does not have a marketing authorisation or a traditional herbal registration is not permitted to make any medicinal claim.
- Herbal practitioners are permitted to sell authorised traditional herbal medicinal products subject to general sale, and also those herbal ingredients subject to the requirements of Part 2 of Schedule 20 of the HMR.

FURTHER READING

- Regulation of Herbal Medicines – UK Parliamentary Library **https://researchbriefings.files.parliament.uk/documents/SN06002/SN06002.pdf** (accessed 31 December 2024).

CHAPTER 18

Human medicines: labelling, packaging and package leaflets

Labelling is required to ensure patients know when and how to take their medicines. Labelling is also essential to convey to patients any warnings of which they should be aware. Patient information leaflets serve a similar purpose. Particular requirements apply to certain medicinal products such as radionuclides, paracetamol, valproate and medicines for children.

Introduction

The packaging and presentation (including labelling) of a product both come within the definition of assembly in regulation 8 of the Human Medicines Regulations 2012 (HMR). They may therefore only be carried out in accordance with a manufacturer's licence or when an exemption applies (for example on retail pharmacy premises, by or under the supervision of a pharmacist)[1] – see **Chapter 5**.

Provisions covering packaging and leaflets for medicinal products are largely found in Part 13 (Regs.257–276) and Schedules 24 to 29 of the Human Medicines Regulations 2012 (HMR), although there are still some residual sections of the Medicines Act 1968 that are relevant to this chapter, namely:

- Section 87, which allows for regulations to be made to specify the strength, materials, shapes, or patterns of containers in order to preserve the quality of medicinal products, or to secure that medicinal products are correctly described, readily identifiable, contain appropriate and accurate warnings or information, and promote safety in relation to medicinal products; and
- Section 88 of the Act, which relates to the colours, shapes or marking of particular medicinal products.

In this chapter, references to the *licensing authority* are to the Medicines and Healthcare products Regulatory Agency (MHRA), and references to *marketing authorisations* are to United Kingdom (UK) or Great Britain (GB) marketing authorisations unless otherwise stated.

Regulation 257D of the Human Medicines Regulations 2012 (HMR) provides that the MHRA, as the licensing authority, may publish guidance on packaging and packaging

1. See Chapter 11 regarding proposals to enable pharmacists to authorise pharmacy technicians to authorise sales or supplies.

leaflets applicable to products for sale or supply. Such guidance may, in particular, include:

(a) the wording of certain special warnings for certain categories of medicinal products;
(b) the particular information needs relating to products that are a pharmacy medicine;
(c) the legibility of particulars on the labelling and package leaflet;
(d) the methods of identification and authentication of medicinal products;
(e) the list of excipients which must feature on the labelling of medicinal products and the way in which these excipients must be indicated.

Offences and enforcement

It is an offence (HMR Reg.268) for the holder of a marketing authorisation, certificate of registration, or traditional herbal registration to sell or supply, offer to sell or supply, or possess for the purpose of sale or supply a medicinal product with a package or leaflet that does not comply with the requirements of the HMR, or if a product is not accompanied by a package leaflet when the HMR require one.

If the holder of a marketing authorisation, certificate of registration, or traditional herbal registration fails to comply with any requirement in Part 13 of the HMR, the MHRA may give them notice requiring compliance. Failure to comply with a notice is an offence and may also result in suspension of the authorisation or registration until the holder complies (HMR Reg.270).

It is an offence (HMR Reg.269) for a person, other than the holder of a marketing authorisation, certificate of registration or traditional herbal registration for a medicinal product in the course of a business carried on by that person, to sell, supply, offer to sell or supply, or have in their possession to sell or supply a product knowing or having reasonable cause to believe:

1. that a package or package leaflet supplied does not comply with Part 13 of the HMR or requirements of the MHRA in relation to paediatric investigation plans (HMR Reg.50C(4), HMR Reg.50D(8), or Reg.58A(2)(b); or
2. that the product is not accompanied by a package leaflet when one is required.

Any person contravening the labelling regulations (see below) is liable on summary conviction to an unlimited fine[2] and, on conviction on indictment, to a fine or to imprisonment for a term not exceeding two years or to both (HMR Reg.271).

In the case of dispensing labels – see below under *Prescription Only Medicines – dispensing labels* – a previous version of this offence has been used in the prosecution of pharmacists who have made a dispensing error, for example by transposing the dispensing labels when supplying two prescribed medicines; or when supplying the wrong prescribed medicinal product but applying a label for the medicinal product that was actually prescribed. This is illustrated by the case of Mrs Elizabeth Lee[3] described in **Box 18.1** below.

---

2. Legal Aid, Sentencing and Punishment of Offenders Act 2012.
3. *R v Lee (Elizabeth)* [2010] EWCA Crim 1404 – the case was concerned with the equivalent provision in the Medicines Act 1968.

Box 18.1: *R v Lee (Elizabeth)*

Mrs Elizabeth Lee had been engaged as a locum pharmacist to work in a pharmacy owned by Tesco Stores Limited in one of its stores in Windsor.

August 30, 2007 was a fairly busy day in the pharmacy. About 300 items had been dispensed. Mrs Lee had worked from 9am to 7pm without a break, except for the time taken to eat lunch in the corner of the dispensary between dealing with prescriptions. In the early afternoon, a prescription was presented for Mrs Carmel Sheller. Mrs Sheller was suffering from wheezing, inflammation and infection in one lung. Her GP had prescribed amoxicillin and prednisolone. It was not known which assistant prepared the labels for the two items or who assembled them. The amoxicillin was dispensed accurately. The label for the prednisolone was properly produced. However, in error, this label was applied to a box of propranolol tablets which was supplied to Mrs Sheller. Mrs Lee did not spot the error.

As a result of taking propranolol tablets, Mrs Sheller collapsed and had to be admitted to hospital. She recovered from the effects of taking the propranolol tablets in error. However, she later died in hospital from an underlying condition.

Mrs Lee was prosecuted for an offence under section 85(5) of the Medicines Act 1968 of supplying a medicinal product in the course of a business carried on by her that was labelled in such a way that the container or package falsely described the product or was likely to mislead as to the nature or quality of the product or as to the uses or effects of the products of that description. In the Crown Court, Mrs Lee pleaded guilty to the labelling offence and a suspended prison sentence was imposed.

The conviction was overturned on appeal because the supply of propranolol was not made in the course of a business carried on by her. However, even though section 85 of the Medicines Act is no longer in force, a pharmacist who supplies a medicinal product to which an incorrect dispensing label is applied may still be guilty of an offence under HMR Reg.269 if the pharmacist owns the business and knew or had reasonable cause to believe that the package did not comply with the requirements of Part 13 of the Regulations because the label was incorrect. For example, it might be argued that a pharmacist who owned the pharmacy where the supply was made and who had made or supervised the supply had reasonable cause to believe that the label was incorrect because the pharmacist would have been aware of the wording on the dispensing label if the pharmacist had supervised the supply. (See **Chapter 11** in relation to *supervision*.)

Definitions

The terms defined here are those used in the HMR in connection with labelling which are not explained elsewhere in the text (HMR Reg.8 unless otherwise stated).

Common name in relation to a medicinal product, active substance or excipient means:

a. its International Non-proprietary Name recommended by the World Health Organization; or
b. if such a name does not exist, its usual common name.

Immediate packaging in relation to a medicinal product means the container or other form of packaging immediately in contact with the medicinal product.

A *package*, in relation to any medicinal products, means a container, any box, packet or other article in which one or more containers of the products are to be enclosed, and where any such box, package or other article is, or is to be itself, enclosed in one or more other boxes, packets or other articles, it includes each of the boxes, packets or other articles in question.

In effect, the inner receptacle which actually contains the medicinal products is a container; every outer receptacle is a package.

A *package leaflet* in relation to a medicinal product, means a leaflet that accompanies the product and contains information for the user of the product.

Labelling, in relation to a container or package of medicinal products, means affixing to or otherwise displaying on it a notice describing or otherwise relating to the contents.

Specified publication means the *European Pharmacopoeia*, *British Pharmacopoeia* (or other official compendia or list of names which may in the future be produced under the HMR), the Cumulative List of Recommended International Nonproprietary Names or a list of names published by the British Pharmacopeia Commission (HMR Reg.321).

Summary of Product Characteristics means the summary of the product characteristics as approved by the licensing authority (UK or EU) in granting or varying the authorisation or registration for a medicinal product (see **Chapter 5**).

Labelling and packaging

The regulations apply at all stages of distribution, except where otherwise stated.

General labelling provisions for medicinal products

All labelling of containers and packages must be:

1. legible, comprehensible and indelible (HMR Reg.257(6)); and
2. given in English, except in the case of a medicinal product that has been designated as an orphan medicinal product[4] where any information specified is given in a language other than English and the licensing authority accedes to a reasoned request that the information need not be given in English (HMR Reg.266).

Where the holder of a marketing authorisation, certificate of registration or traditional herbal registration for a medicinal product wishes to make changes to the packaging or the package leaflet (other than a change connected with the Summary of Product Characteristics), the proposed change must be submitted to the licensing authority and, unless the licensing authority has notified them that it does not approve the alterations, they may, after a period of 90 days from the date of notification by them, supply the product with the altered labelling (HMR Reg.267).

Except as set out below, the law does not spell out specific warnings that must be included in the labelling of medicinal products. The MHRA has given guidance on warnings to be included.[5]

Standard labelling particulars for medicinal products

The standard requirements for the labelling of containers and packages of medicinal products are set out in HMR Reg.257 and Schedule 24. There are modifications for

4. Regulation (EC) 141/2000 of the European Parliament and of the Council of 16 December 1999 on orphan medicinal products and see Chapter 5.
5. https://assets.publishing.service.gov.uk/government/uploads/system/uploads/attachment_data/file/835489/Warning_Statements.pdf (accessed 31 December 2024).

small containers and blister packs (see below) and for advanced therapy medicinal products.

The standard labelling particulars are as follows (Sch. 24, Part 1):

1. the name of the medicinal product;
2. the strength and pharmaceutical form of the product;
3. where appropriate, whether the product is intended for babies, children or adults;
4. where the product contains up to three active substances, the common name of each active substance;
5. the product's expiry date (month and year), in clear terms;
6. the manufacturer's batch number;
7. the method of administration of the product and if necessary, the route of administration;
8. a statement of the active substances in the product, expressed qualitatively and quantitatively per dosage unit or according to the form of administration for a given volume or weight, using their common names;
9. the pharmaceutical form and the contents by weight, by volume or by number of doses of the product;
10. a list of:
    a. all excipients when the product is injectable or is a topical or eye preparation, or
    b. in any other case, those excipients known to have a recognised action or effect and included in the guidance published under regulation 257D of the HMR;
11. where appropriate, space for the prescribed dose to be indicated;
12. a warning that the product must be stored out of the reach and sight of children;
13. any special warning applicable to the product;
14. any special storage precautions relating to the product;
15. any special precautions relating to the disposal of an unused product or part of a product, or waste derived from the product, and reference to any appropriate collection system in place;
16. the name and address of the holder of the UK marketing authorisation, Article 126a authorisation, or traditional herbal registration relating to the product and, where applicable, the name of the holder's representative;
17. the number of the marketing authorisation, Article 126a authorisation or traditional herbal registration for placing the medicinal product on the market; and
18. in the case of a product that is not a Prescription Only Medicine (POM), instructions for use;
19. The words "UK only".[6]

---

6. MHRA guidance says that the words must be in at least 7-point font and printed directly onto the product packaging, see: https://www.gov.uk/government/publications/labelling-and-packaging-of-medicinal-products-for-human-use-following-agreement-of-the-windsor-framework/labelling-and-packaging-of-medicinal-products-for-human-use-following-agreement-of-the-windsor-framework (accessed 31 December 2024). Further MHRA guidance states that medicines produced solely for export do not need to be labelled with the words "UK only"; see: https://www.gov.uk/government/publications/windsor-framework-explainer/windsor-framework-agreement-on-the-supply-of-medicines-in-northern-ireland-explained (accessed 31 December 2024).

These requirements do not apply to registrable homoeopathic medicinal products or advanced therapy medicinal products.

The MHRA may publish guidance on packaging.[7]

The outer packaging may be labelled to show symbols, diagrams or pictures designed to clarify certain information mentioned in 1 to 19 above and other information compatible with the Summary of Product Characteristics which is useful to the patient. Such symbols, diagrams, pictures or additional information must not include any element of a promotional nature (HMR Reg.261 – which does not apply to registrable homoeopathic products).

The name of the medicinal product must also be expressed in Braille format on the outer packaging of the product. A holder of a marketing authorisation or traditional herbal registration must ensure the package leaflet is available on request in formats suitable for blind and partially-sighted persons (HMR Reg.259).

In addition, the UK requires additional labelling showing the classification, such as *POM* or *P* in a rectangle for Prescription Only Medicines or Pharmacy medicines respectively, and other specific information for certain products such as paracetamol (see below).

The words "UK only" preclude onward movement of these medicines into any part of the European Union (EU), although they can be exported to non-EU country or territory where the import of those medicines is compliant with local legal requirements or provisions.

On medicines that are not POMs, the "UK only" label may be covered over as long as the label is permanently attached to the outer carton or bottle and cannot be removed. Over-labelling must be carried out on a site that holds an appropriate manufacturer's licence.

Blister packs for medicinal products

Where the container of a relevant medicinal product is a blister pack and is enclosed within a package which complies with the standard labelling (see above), the container must be labelled with (HMR Reg.257 and Sch. 24 Part 2):

1. the information contained in points 1-6 of the standard labelling particulars, as shown above; and
2. the name of the holder of the marketing authorisation or traditional herbal registration relating to the product.

Small containers for medicinal products

Where the container of a medicinal product is *not* a blister pack but is too small to include all the standard particulars for medicinal products it must be labelled with (HMR Reg.257 and Sch. 24 Part 3):

7. Guidance can be found at https://www.gov.uk/guidance/medicines-packaging-labelling-and-patient-information-leaflets (accessed 31 December 2024).

1. the information contained in points 1-6 of the standard labelling particulars, as shown above;
2. the method of administration of the product and, if necessary, the route of administration; and
3. the contents of the packaging by weight, by volume or by unit.

Standard labelling requirements for containers and packages for radionuclides (HMR Reg.262)

Containers and packages for radionuclides must be labelled with the standard particulars for relevant medicinal products together with the following additional particulars:

1. the carton and container must be labelled in accordance with regulations for the safe transport of radioactive materials laid down by the International Atomic Energy Agency and the labelling on the shielding and the vial must comply with the rest of the provisions of this legislation;
2. the label on the shielding must:
    a. include the information specified in Part 1 of Schedule 24,
    b. explain in full the codings used on the vial,
    c. indicate, where necessary, for a given time and date, the amount of radioactivity per dose or per vial, and
    d. indicate the number of capsules or, for liquids, the number of millilitres per container;
3. the label on the vial must include:
    a. the name or code of the medicinal product, including the name or chemical symbol of the radionuclide,
    b. the batch identification and expiry date of the product,
    c. the international symbol for radioactivity,
    d. the name and address of the manufacturer, and
    e. the amount of radioactivity; as mentioned in paragraph 2(c).

Dispensing labels

The packaging of medicines dispensed on prescription must be labelled to show the following particulars (HMR Reg.258 and Sch. 25 Part 1):

1. where the product is to be administered to a particular individual, the name of that individual;
2. the name and address of the person who sells or supplies the product;
3. the date on which the product is sold or supplied;
4. unless the pharmacist, in the exercise of professional skill and judgement, is of the opinion that the inclusion of one or more of the following particulars is inappropriate, such of the following particulars as the appropriate practitioner who prescribed the product may specify:
    a. the name of the product or its common name,

b. directions for use of the product (for example, "Take ONE tablet THREE times a day"), and
c. precautions relating to the use of the product (For example, "For External Use Only" on the label for a cream or ointment).

A container need not be labelled if it is enclosed in a package which is labelled with the required particulars.

In addition to the legal requirements listed here, the British National Formulary gives guidance on advisory and cautionary labels that pharmacists may choose to add.[8]

At the time of going to print, the Department of Health proposed to amend the HMR in 2025 to allow one pharmacy (a hub) to dispense a medicine on behalf of another pharmacy (a spoke), even though the hub and the spoke did not have the same owner. In the event that such an amendment is made, the legal position is addressed in **Box 18.2**.

Box 18.2: Hub and spoke dispensing

At the time of going to press, there were proposals to amend the law to allow one pharmacy (a hub) to dispense medicines on behalf of another pharmacy (a spoke), even if the hub and spoke do not have the same owner. This box sets out what the law will be if those proposals are brought into effect. Readers can check whether the proposals have been brought into effect by checking www.legislation.gov.uk or using a subscription service such as Westlaw for the latest version of [e.g. the Medicines Act 1968/the Human Medicines Regulations 2012 or searching those sites for the Human Medicines (Amendments relating to Hub and Spoke Dispensing etc.) Regulations *[followed by the year].*

The hub pharmacy and the spoke pharmacy must agree arrangements for the hub to provide services for the spoke. The address on the label must be that of the hub, and the date on the label must be the date on which the dispensed item is ready for sale or supply to or for the patient, which will normally be the date on which the hub supplied the dispensed item to the spoke.

Exemptions and additional requirements for unlicensed medicines

There are different labelling requirements for unlicensed medicines, which are summarised below:

a. If a medicinal product is unlicensed because it has been manufactured in a pharmacy under an exemption in section 10 of the Medicines Act 1968 (see **Chapter 5**), for example by extemporaneously dispensing the product, then the labelling requirements applicable to manufacturers will not apply (HMR Reg.4(3)). Instead, the outer packaging (or, if there is no outer packaging the immediate packaging) must be labelled[9] so as to show:
   1. where the product is to be administered to a particular individual, the name of the individual;

8. https://bnf.nice.org.uk/about/guidance-for-cautionary-and-advisory-labels.html (accessed 31 December 2024).
9. HMR Reg.4(5) and Schedule 26.

2. the name and address of the person who sells or supplies the product;
3. the date on which the product is sold or supplied;
4. any particulars specified by a prescriber as to the name of the product or its common name, directions for use and precautions relating to use of the product – unless a pharmacist in the exercise of professional skill and judgement is of the opinion that the inclusion of any of these details is inappropriate. In such a case, the pharmacist may include such particulars as the pharmacist thinks appropriate.

b. If, under a hub and spoke arrangement, a product that has a marketing authorisation is assembled at a hub pharmacy under an exemption in section 10 of the Medicines Act, resulting in a change in presentation (such as repackaging and/or applying a dispensing label), the labelling requirements applicable to manufacturers will not apply (HMR Reg.4(4)). In such a case, the labelling requirements are those set out in (a) above. At the time of writing,[10] a hub and spoke arrangement is only lawful if the hub and the spoke have the same owner; if the hub and spoke have the same owner and the hub also has a specials licence, see (d) below.
c. If the manufacture of a medicinal product has been outsourced to the holder of a specials licence and that holder is a registered pharmacy, then the labelling requirements applicable to manufacturers will not apply but the label must include the manufacturer's specials licence or number.
d. If the owner of a registered pharmacy holds a specials licence and a supply is made from that pharmacy to another pharmacy owned by the same person, the manufacture will be extemporaneous dispensing, not the supply of a special under the specials licence, because one cannot make a supply to oneself. As a result, the label should not show the specials licence or number and for the purpose of NHS remuneration, the supply will be treated as extemporaneous dispensing.
e. If a medicinal product is prepared in line with a British Pharmacopoeia formula or monograph (see **Chapter 20**), the British Pharmacopoeia or monograph may stipulate additional labelling requirements.

Serious shortage protocols (SSPs)

The HMR do not impose labelling requirements when a medicine is supplied pursuant to a SSP (see **Chapter 12**).

However, in Scotland, the NHS terms of service[11] impose requirements that the pharmacist must include in the dispensing label on the packaging, for the patient's benefit, information to the effect that the item is being supplied in accordance with a SSP, identifying the particular SSP.

10. For proposals to extend the scope of hub and spoke arrangements, see Box 12.2 in Chapter 12.
11. Paragraph 4 of Schedule 1 to the National Health Service (Pharmaceutical Services) (Scotland) Regulations 2009.

Proposed changes to labelling provisions for medicinal products

HMR Reg 257E gives Ministers the power to make regulations to require medicinal products to be labelled in a way that makes it possible to ascertain:

(a) the price of the product;
(b) any reimbursement conditions of the National Health Service;
(c) the legal status for supply to the patient;
(d) authenticity and identification of the product for the purposes of reimbursement or pharmacovigilance through the product's unique identifier.

Packaging for transport, delivery and storage (HMR Reg.258 and Sch. 25 Part 2)

An outer package, which contains a number of packages of medicinal products of the same description, must be labelled in accordance with the requirements of Part 2 of Schedule 25, for the purpose of transport, delivery or storage. The required particulars are:

1. any special requirements for the storage and handling of the product;
2. the expiry date of the product; and
3. the manufacturer's batch number.

These requirements do not apply to "specials" (see **Chapter 5**) or to any packing case, crate or other covering used solely for the purposes of transport or delivery of packages of medicinal products, so long as each of those individual packages is labelled in accordance with the Regulations.

Packaging of Pharmacy and Prescription Only Medicinal products

All Pharmacy medicines and Prescription Only Medicines when sold or supplied by retail, or held for such sale or distributed by wholesale, must bear the capital letters *P* or *POM* (as applicable) within a rectangle containing no other matter on the packaging (HMR Reg.258 and Sch. 25 Part 3).

Packaging requirements for medicines containing paracetamol (HMR Sch. 25 Part 4)

The following must appear on the package if the product contains paracetamol:

1. except where the name of the product includes the word *paracetamol* and appears on the container or package, the words "Contains paracetamol";
2. the words "Do not take more medicine than the label tells you to. If you do not get better, talk to your doctor" (these words must appear adjacent to either the directions for use or the recommended dosage);
3. unless it is wholly or mainly intended for children who are 12 years old or younger, the words "Do not take anything else containing paracetamol while taking this medicine", and
    a. if a package leaflet accompanying the product includes the words "Talk to a doctor at once if you take too much of this medicine even if you feel well. This is because too much paracetamol can cause delayed, serious liver damage", and the package must contain the words "Talk to a doctor at once if you take too much of this medicine, even if you feel well", or

b. if no package leaflet accompanies the product or the package leaflet does not include those words, the words "Talk to a doctor at once if you take too much of this medicine, even if you feel well. This is because too much paracetamol can cause delayed, serious liver damage";

4. and is wholly or mainly intended for children who are 12 years old or younger, the words "Do not give anything else containing paracetamol while giving this medicine", and
   a. if a package leaflet accompanying the product includes the words "Talk to a doctor at once if your child takes too much of this medicine even if they seem well. This is because too much paracetamol can cause delayed, serious liver damage", and the package must contain the words "Talk to a doctor at once if your child takes too much of this medicine, even if they seem well"; or
   b. if no package leaflet accompanies the product or the package leaflet does not include those words, the words "Talk to a doctor at once if your child takes too much of this medicine, even if they seem well. This is because too much paracetamol can cause delayed, serious liver damage".

Those phrases must be in a prominent position.

Valproate products

The valproate products to which this section relates are sodium valproate, valproic acid and valproate semisodium.

It has been known for many years that if valproate products are taken in pregnancy, four in ten babies are at risk of developmental disorders and one in nine are at risk of birth defects.[12]

Manufacturers' original packs of valproate products contain patient information leaflets with warnings to women and girls, and display a graphic warning on the outer packaging. However, there have been continued instances of women and girls giving birth to babies with developmental disorders and/or birth defects because they took a valproate product while unaware of the risks as a result of the product having been repackaged before supply and the new packaging did not bear the graphic warning and/or the new packaging did not contain a patient information leaflet.

Valproate products must be supplied in its manufacturer's original outer packaging (HMR Reg 217C and see **Chapter 12**). There is an exception to this requirement if:

(a) the sale of supply is by or under the supervision of a pharmacist (see **Chapter 11** as to the meaning of supervision); and

(b) the pharmacist is satisfied that;

  (i) a risk assessment is in place that refers to the need for the patient to be sold or supplied the product in different packaging to the manufacturer's original pack (for example in a monitored dosage system); and

12. See, for example, the Cumberlege Report *First Do No Harm* https://www.immdsreview.org.uk/downloads/IMMDSReview_Web.pdf (accessed 31 December 2024) and https://www.gov.uk/guidance/valproate-use-by-women-and-girls (accessed 31 December 2024).

(ii) unless the product is unauthorised (other than because it has ceased to be unauthorised because it has been repackaged), processes are in place to ensure the supply to or for the patient of a patient information leaflet.

Medicines manufactured by pharmacies under section 10 of the Medicines Act 1968

Pharmacies are permitted to manufacture medicines without the need for marketing authorisations or licences subject to conditions under section 10 of the Medicines Act 1968 (**Chapter 5**). In these circumstances the medicines must bear packaging details as set out below (HMR Reg.4 and Sch. 26 Part 2):

1. where the product is to be administered to a particular individual, the name of that individual;
2. the name and address of the person who sells or supplies the product;
3. the date on which the product is sold or supplied;
4. where the product is prescribed by an appropriate practitioner, such of the following particulars as the appropriate practitioner who prescribed the product may specify, unless paragraph 5 applies:
   a. the name of the product or its common name,
   b. directions for use of the product, and
   c. precautions relating to the use of the product;
5. this paragraph applies if a pharmacist, in the exercise of professional skill and judgement, is of the opinion that the inclusion of one or more of the particulars specified in paragraph 4, by the appropriate practitioner who prescribed the product, is inappropriate;
6. where paragraph 5 applies, the pharmacist may include such particulars, of the same kind as those mentioned in paragraph 4, as the pharmacist thinks appropriate; and
7. where the product is not prescribed by an appropriate practitioner, directions for use of the product. These may be omitted when a medicinal product is prepared or dispensed in a registered pharmacy, by or under the supervision of a pharmacist, in accordance with a specification furnished by the person to whom the product is or is to be sold or supplied, where the product is for administration to that person or to a person under their care.

Standard labelling requirements for containers and packages, and package leaflets, of homoeopathic medicinal products

The outer packaging and immediate packaging and, where a package leaflet (see next section) is included, the package leaflet of a homoeopathic medicinal product must clearly include the words "homoeopathic medicinal product". In addition, they must carry the following particulars and no others (HMR Reg.264 and Sch. 28):

1. the scientific name of the stock or stocks and the degree of dilution, making use of the symbols of the *European Pharmacopoeia* or, in the absence of an entry in the *European Pharmacopoeia*, of the *British Pharmacopoeia*;

2. the name and address of the holder of the certificate of registration and, where different, the name and address of the manufacturer;
3. the method and, if necessary, route of administration;
4. the expiry date of the product in clear terms, stating the month and year;
5. the pharmaceutical form;
6. the contents of the presentation, specified by weight, volume or number of doses;
7. any special storage precautions;
8. any special warning necessary for the product concerned;
9. the manufacturer's batch number;
10. the registration number allocated by the licensing authority;
11. the words "Homoeopathic medicinal product without approved therapeutic indications"; and
12. a warning advising the user to consult a doctor if the symptoms persist during the use of the product.

There are variations on these rules for blister packs and packaging that is too small to display the information required.

Package leaflets

General requirements

HMR Reg.260 says that a package leaflet must be included in the packaging of a medicinal product unless all the required information is conveyed on the outer packaging or the immediate packaging of the product. Registrable homoeopathic medicinal products are exempt from this requirement.

HMR Reg.268 makes it an offence for the marketing authorisation holder, Article 126a authorisation or the holder of a certificate of registration or traditional herbal registration to omit a package leaflet when one is required. HMR Reg.269 makes it an offence to sell or supply a medicinal product without a package leaflet when one is required.

The requirement to include a package leaflet does not apply if the medicinal product is the result of a process of manufacture in a pharmacy or assembly.[13] The definition of *assembly* includes the various processes of dividing up, packaging and presentation of the product.[14] Thus, if medicines are taken out of a manufacturer's original pack and repackaged, this is "assembly" (see above) and a package leaflet is not required by law. For example, medicines added to monitored dosage systems (MDS)[15] are not required to have a package leaflet.[16]

---

13. HMR Reg.4.
14. HMR Reg.8.
15. Sometimes called multi-compartment compliance aids (MCAs).
16. The National Institute for Health and Care Excellence (NICE) states at paragraph 1.1.10 of its guidance note NG67 that a patient information leaflet is legally required when supplying medicines in an MDS https://www.nice.org.uk/guidance/NG67/chapter/Recommendations#supporting-people-to-take-their-medicines (accessed 31 December 2024). This view is repeated elsewhere. However, it appears to overlook that the requirement in HMR Reg.260 does not apply when medicines are assembled.

Even if there is no legal requirement to include a package leaflet, the inclusion of such a leaflet may nevertheless be good practice in some cases. For example, before it became a legal requirement to supply valproate products in a manufacturer's original pack, thus prohibiting repackaging in most cases (see the section on Valproate products above), the inclusion of a patient leaflet was considered to be a professional requirement.[17]

Package leaflets are sometimes referred to as *patient information leaflets* or *PILs*. In practice, difficulty may be encountered when a split pack has been supplied, because the PIL included in the manufacturer's original pack will usually have been included with the first part of the pack that has been supplied to a patient, so the PIL provided by the manufacturer is not available to include with the remainder of the split pack. A PIL will not be required for the remainder in the split pack because of the exemption for medicines that have been assembled (except in the case of valproate), but it may be good practice to obtain additional PILs from manufacturers or marketing authorisation holders, or to download additional PILs unless pharmacies are able to avoid splitting a pack by supplying in a manufacturer's original pack where the supply of a different quantity to that prescribed is permissible (see **Chapter 12**).

The MHRA, as the licensing authority, must make every package leaflet publicly available.

Package leaflets are excluded from the definition of *advertisement* in the HMR, so they are not subject to the restrictions on advertising.[18]

A marketing authorisation holder must ensure that the package leaflet is made available on request in formats suitable for blind and partially-sighted people.[19]

All leaflets included in the package or container of any medicinal product must comply with HMR Reg.260 and Schedule 27.

A package leaflet for a medicinal product must:

1. be drawn up in accordance with the Summary of Product Characteristics; and
2. contain all the information specified and in the order specified in Schedule 27.

The leaflet must be legible, clear and easy to use, and the applicant for, or holder of, a marketing authorisation or traditional herbal registration relating to the product must ensure that target patient groups are consulted in order to achieve this.

The particulars which must be in a package leaflet include:

1. the name of the medicinal product;
2. the strength and pharmaceutical form of the product;
3. where appropriate, whether the product is intended for babies, children or adults;
4. where the product contains up to three active substances, the common name of each active substance;

---

17. https://www.pharmacyregulation.org/about-us/news-and-updates/regulate/supplying-valproate-safely-women-and-girls (accessed 31 December 2024).
18. HMR Reg.7.
19. HMR Reg.259.

5. the pharmaco-therapeutic group or type of activity of the product, in terms easily comprehensible for the patient;
6. the product's therapeutic indications;
7. a list of:
   a. contra-indications,
   b. appropriate precautions for use,
   c. interactions with other medicinal products which may affect the action of the product,
   d. interactions with other substances, including alcohol, tobacco and foodstuffs, which may affect the action of the product, and
   e. special warnings, if any, relating to the product;
8. the list mentioned in paragraph 7 must:
   a. take into account the special requirements of particular categories of users (including, in particular, children, pregnant or breastfeeding women, the elderly and persons with specific pathological conditions),
   b. mention, if appropriate, possible effects on the ability to drive vehicles or to operate machinery, and
   c. list any excipients,
      i. if knowledge of the excipients is important for the safe and effective use of the product, and
      ii. the excipients are included in the guidance published by the MHRA;
9. instructions for proper use of the product including, in particular:
   a. the dosage,
   b. the method and, if necessary, route of administration,
   c. the frequency of administration (including, if necessary, specifying times at which the product may or must be administered),
   d. the duration of treatment if this is to be limited,
   e. symptoms of an overdose and the action, if any, to be taken in case of an overdose,
   f. what to do if one or more doses have not been taken,
   g. an indication, if necessary, of the risk of withdrawal effects, and
   h. a specific recommendation to consult a doctor or pharmacist, as appropriate, for further explanation of the use of the product;
10. a description of the adverse reactions which may occur in normal use of the medicinal product and, if necessary, the action to be taken in such a case;
11. a reference to the expiry date printed on the packaging of the product with:
   a. a warning against using the product after that date,
   b. if appropriate, details of special storage precautions to be taken,
   c. if necessary, a warning concerning visible signs of deterioration,
   d. the full qualitative composition (in active substances and excipients), and the quantitative composition in active substances, using common names, of each presentation of the medicinal product,

e. for each presentation of the product, the pharmaceutical form and content in weight, volume or units of dosage,
f. the name and address of the holder of the UK marketing authorisation, Article 126a authorisation or traditional herbal registration relating to the product and, if applicable, the name of the holder's appointed representative, and
g. the name and address of the manufacturer of the product;

12. under HMR Reg 202A, the MHRA may establish a list of medicinal products that are subject to additional monitoring. The package leaflets for these medicines must include an inverted black triangle symbol and the statement: "▼ This medicinal product is subject to additional monitoring";
13. a standardised text relating to adverse event reporting; and
14. the date on which the package leaflet was last revised.

The outer packaging and the package leaflet of a medicinal product may include (HMR Reg.261) symbols, diagrams or pictures designed to clarify information mentioned on the outer and immediate packaging or on the leaflet, and other information, compatible with the Summary of Product Characteristics, which is useful to the patient. Such symbols, diagrams, pictures or additional information included in accordance with this regulation must not include any element of a promotional nature.

The MHRA may publish guidance on package leaflets which may, in particular, include:

a. the wording of certain special warnings for certain categories of medicinal products;
b. the particular information needs relating to products that are a Pharmacy medicine (see **Chapter 11**);
c. the legibility of particulars on the labelling and package leaflet; and
d. the methods of identification and authentication of medicinal products and the way in which these excipients must be indicated.

Leaflets for over-the-counter medicines containing opioids

The patient information leaflets for over-the-counter medicines containing opioids for non-cancer pain should contain warnings about the risk of dependence and addiction; and that there can be withdrawal symptoms if patients stop taking these medicines suddenly.

Leaflets for medicines containing paracetamol (HMR Sch. 27 Part 2)

If a medicinal product contains paracetamol, unless the product is wholly or mainly intended for children 12 years old or younger, the words "Talk to a doctor at once if you take too much of this medicine even if you feel well. This is because too much paracetamol can cause delayed, serious liver damage" must be used.

If a medicinal product contains paracetamol and is wholly or mainly intended for children 12 years old or younger, the words "Talk to a doctor at once if your child takes too much of this medicine even if they seem well. This is because too much paracetamol can cause delayed, serious liver damage" must be used.

Leaflets relating to radionuclides (HMR Reg.263)

A leaflet enclosed with a radiopharmaceutical or radionuclide generator, kit or precursor must, in addition to the general requirements (see above) include:

1. details of any precautions to be taken by the user and the patient during the preparation and administration of the product; and
2. special precautions for the disposal of the packaging and its unused contents.

Requirements relating to child safety

Regulated medicinal products means (HMR Reg.272) medicinal products containing, aspirin, paracetamol or more than 24 mg of elemental iron, which are in the form of tablets, capsules, pills, lozenges, pastilles, suppositories or oral liquids, except for:

1. effervescent tablets containing not more than 25% of aspirin or paracetamol by weight;
2. medicinal products in sachets or other sealed containers which hold only one unit of dose;
3. medicinal products that are not intended for retail sale or for supply in circumstances corresponding to retail sale; or
4. for export.

Regulated medicinal products may only be sold or supplied in containers which are opaque or dark-tinted and child resistant (HMR Reg.273), except where the sale or supply of such products is carried out (HMR Reg.274):

a. by or under the supervision of a pharmacist,[20] on premises which are a registered pharmacy and either:
    i. in accordance with a prescription given by an appropriate practitioner where it is not reasonably practicable to provide the regulated medicinal products in containers that are both opaque or dark-tinted and child resistant, or
    ii. at the request of a person who is aged 16 years or over and specifically requests that the regulated medicinal products not be contained in a child-resistant container;
b. by a doctor or dentist to a patient, or the patient's carer, for the patient's use;
c. by a doctor or dentist to a person who is an appropriate practitioner, at the request of that person, for administration to a patient of that person; or
d. in the course of the business of a hospital or health centre, where the sale or supply is for the purposes of administration, whether in the hospital or health centre or elsewhere, in accordance with the directions of an appropriate practitioner.

The term "child resistant" is defined in the Regulations in terms of the relevant British Standard or equivalent technical specification recognised for use in the EEA.

The sale or supply of a medicinal product containing aspirin or paracetamol of any colour other than white is prohibited if it is a product for children aged 12 years or under, and, in the case of paracetamol, it is in a solid form (including tablets, capsules, pills, lozenges, pastilles or suppositories) (HMR Reg.275).

---

20. If the HMR are amended as proposed in relation to supervision (see Chapter 11), regulation 274 will be amended so as to refer to the supervision of a pharmacist or a pharmacy technician pursuant to an authorisation given by a pharmacist.

SUMMARY

- Failure to comply with labelling and packaging requirements and the provision of patient information leaflets may be criminal offences.
- There are detailed requirements for the labelling of packaging.
- Medicines must bear the words *UK only*.
- There are specific packaging requirements for medicinal products that are in small containers, radionuclides, valproate products, paracetamol, and medicines for children.
- There are specific labelling provisions for medicines supplied on a prescription, but some of these may be amended by the dispensing pharmacist if, in their professional opinion, it is appropriate to do so.
- There are separate labelling requirements for medicines produced extemporaneously by pharmacists (under s.10 of the Medicines Act) and for investigational medicinal products for use in clinical trials.
- There are packaging requirements for the transport, delivery or storage of medicinal products.
- Special leaflets provisions exist for homoeopathic medicinal products.
- Special requirements apply to the sale of medicinal products which contain aspirin or paracetamol. These products must (with certain exceptions) be packed in containers which are opaque or dark-tinted and child resistant.
- Valproate products must normally be supplied in a manufacturer's original pack.
- Package leaflets (patient information leaflets – PILs) must be supplied unless the medicinal product has been assembled (such as being placed in a monitored dosage system).
- There are specific requirements as to the contents of PILs.

FURTHER READING

- Human Medicines Regulations (2012) SI 2012 No. 1916, *Explanatory memorandum*: **http://www.legislation.gov.uk/uksi/2012/1916/pdfs/uksiem_20121916_en.pdf** (accessed 31 December 2024).
- MHRA Guidance – *Medicines: packaging, labelling and patient information leaflets* **https://www.gov.uk/guidance/medicines-packaging-labelling-and-patient-information-leaflets** (accessed 31 December 2024).
- The British National Formulary gives guidance on cautionary and advisory labels **https://bnf.nice.org.uk/about/guidance-for-cautionary-and-advisory-labels.html** (accessed 31 December 2024).

CHAPTER 19

Human medicines: advertising

Laws restricting the advertising of medicinal products exist to ensure (1) that when information is given to prescribers, it is accurate and enables them to make appropriate decisions on prescribing and treatment; and (2) that the public, are protected both in terms of the claims made and by not being encouraged to seek Prescription Only Medicines.

Introduction

Control of medicines advertising in the UK is based on a system of self-regulation underpinned by statutory powers. The advertising and promotion of medicines is tightly regulated to ensure that patient safety is not compromised. Whether it be the consumer self-selecting an over-the-counter medicine or the promotion of medicines to a healthcare professional qualified to prescribe or supply medicines, control of the highest standard is imperative. Advertising of prescription only medicines to the public is prohibited.

The Human Medicines Regulations 2012 (HMR) Part 14 ensures that a relevant medicinal product is only promoted in accordance with its marketing authorisation. Unless otherwise stated, a reference to a marketing authorisation is to UK or GB marketing authorisations (for the United Kingdom or Great Britain).

Definitions

An *advertisement* relating to medicinal products is defined as (HMR Reg.7) anything designed to promote the prescription, supply, sale or use of that product. Such activities include:

- door-to-door canvassing;
- visits by medical sales representatives to persons qualified to prescribe or supply medicinal products;
- the supply of samples;
- the provision of inducements to prescribe or supply medicinal products by the gift, offer or promise of any benefit or bonus, whether in money or in kind, except where the intrinsic value of such inducements is minimal;
- the sponsorship of promotional meetings attended by persons qualified to prescribe or supply medicinal products; and
- the sponsorship of scientific congresses attended by persons qualified to prescribe or supply medicinal products, including the payment of their travelling and accommodation expenses in that connection.

It does not include:

- a medicinal product's package or package leaflet;
- reference material and announcements of a factual and informative nature, including:
  - i. material relating to changes to a medicinal product's package or package leaflet,
  - ii. adverse reaction warnings,
  - iii. trade catalogues, and
  - iv. price lists, provided that no product claim is made; and
- correspondence, which may be accompanied by material of a non-promotional nature, answering a specific question about a medicinal product.

In this Regulation, *a person qualified to prescribe or supply medicinal products* includes persons who, in the course of their profession or in the course of a business, may lawfully prescribe medicinal products, or sell them by retail, or supply medicinal products in circumstances corresponding to retail sale, and the employees of such persons.

Publication in relation to an advertisement is defined in HMR Reg.277 as the dissemination or issue of that advertisement either orally, in writing or by means of an electronic communication network or in any other way and includes causing or procuring that publication by or on behalf of another person.

Requirements related to advertising

General principles

A person may not publish an advertisement for a medicinal product unless one of the following is in force for the product:

- a marketing authorisation, a certificate of registration or a traditional herbal registration (HMR Reg.279);
- a temporary authorisation has been issued by the MHRA in response to the suspected or confirmed spread of pathogenic agents; toxins, chemical agents, or nuclear radiation, if any of them may cause harm to human beings.

Any advertisement for a product with a marketing authorisation must be for an authorised use. For example, in 2024, the MHRA required named pharmacies to change their advertisements for weight loss products because the advertisements contained images of products that were not licensed for the treatment of weight loss.[1]

See below for advertising in relation to registered homoeopathic medicinal products.

The general requirements (HMR Reg.280) are that a person may not publish an advertisement for a medicinal product:

- with a marketing authorisation, Article 126a authorisation, or a traditional herbal registration unless it complies with the particulars listed in the Summary of Product Characteristics (see **Chapter 5**);
- unless that advertisement encourages the rational use of that product by presenting it objectively and without exaggerating its properties;

1. https://www.gov.uk/government/news/herbal-skin-cream-found-to-contain-steroids (accessed 31 December 2024).

- which is misleading;
- unless, in the case of a product with a temporary authorisation, it is published as part of a campaign that has been approved by the relevant Ministers.

The Blue Guide

The Blue Guide[2] is published by the MHRA and provides guidance on the Advertising and Promotion of Medicines in the UK. It should be read alongside the HMR and provides guidance and clarification on the general legislation and regulatory procedures which govern the advertising of medicines, including advice on traditional herbal medicines, medical treatment services and homeopathic[3] medicines.

Duties of holders of marketing authorisations (HMR Reg.281)

Any person who holds a marketing authorisation, a certificate of registration, an Article 126a authorisation, or a traditional herbal registration for a medicinal product must:

- establish a scientific service to compile and collate all information relating to that product, whether received from medical sales representatives employed by them or from any other source;
- ensure that any medical sales representative who promotes the product is given sufficient training, and has sufficient scientific knowledge, to enable the representative to provide information about the product that is as precise and complete as possible;
- retain a sample of any advertisement for which they are responsible relating to that product, together with a statement indicating the persons to whom the advertisement is addressed, the method of publication and the date when it was first published; and
- provide, if required and within the period specified in a notice served by the Ministers on them, a copy of the sample and statement mentioned above, and any other information and assistance requested by them in order to carry out their functions under Part 14 of the HMR.

Advertisements directed to the public (HMR Regs.282–292)

The Regulations dealing with advertisements that are directed to the public impose a range of prohibitions, restrictions and requirements.

No advertisement may be published which is likely to lead to the use of a medicinal product:

- for the purpose of inducing an abortion in women (Reg.283);
- that is likely to lead to the use of a POM (Reg.284) (HMR Reg.292) (subject to exemptions referred to below);

---

2. *The Blue Guide: Advertising and Promotion of Medicines in the UK* https://assets.publishing.service.gov.uk/government/uploads/system/uploads/attachment_data/file/824778/Blue_Guide.pdfhttps://assets.publishing.service.gov.uk/government/uploads/system/uploads/attachment_data/file/824778/Blue_Guide.pdf (accessed 31 December 2024).
3. The HMR use the spelling *homoeopathic*, but the MHRA uses the more widely used spelling *homeopathic*.

- that contains a substance which is listed in any of Schedules I, II or IV to the Narcotic Drugs Convention[4] (where the product is not a preparation listed in Schedule III to that Convention) (typically, the Narcotic Drugs Convention covers drugs classified in the UK as controlled drugs – see **Chapter 14**) or is listed in specified Schedules to the Psychotropic Substances Convention[5] (HMR Reg.285);
- that states or implies that a medical consultation or surgical intervention is unnecessary, that offers to provide a diagnosis or suggest a treatment by post or by means of an electronic communications network or might, by a description or detailed representation of a case history, lead to an erroneous self-diagnosis (Reg.286);
- that suggests a guaranteed effect or no adverse reactions, or that the effects of taking the medicinal product are better than or equivalent to those of another identifiable treatment or medicinal product (Reg.287);
- that uses misleading or potentially alarming terms or pictures of changes in the human body caused by disease or injury or the action of the medicinal product on the human body (Reg.287);
- that refers to claims of recovery in terms that are misleading or likely to cause alarm (HMR Reg.287);
- that suggests that the health of a person not suffering from any disease or illness could be enhanced by taking the medicinal product, or that (with the exception of approved campaigns relating to the suspected or confirmed spread of pathogenic agents, chemical agents, toxins, or nuclear radiation, and to vaccination), the health of a person could be affected by not taking the medicinal product (HMR Reg.287);
- that wrongly implies that the product is a foodstuff, cosmetic or other consumer product that is not a medicinal product or that its safety or efficacy is due to the fact that it is natural (Reg.288);
- that the product is recommended by scientists, health professionals or persons who, because of their celebrity, could encourage use of the medicinal product (HMR Reg.289); or
- that contains any material that is directed principally at children (HMR Reg.290).

As an example of how a promotion might breach the prohibition on advertising POMs to the public, the General Pharmaceutical Council was reported in 2024 to have expressed the view that offering discount codes for the purchases of Wegovy and other POMs breached HMR Reg.284.[6]

4. Defined in HMR Reg.8 as the Single Convention on Narcotic Drugs signed by the United Kingdom on 30th March 1961 as amended by the Protocol Amending the Single Convention on Narcotic Drugs signed by the United Kingdom on 25th March 1972.
5. Defined in HMR Reg.8 as the Convention on Psychotropic Substances signed by the UK on 21 February 1971.
6. https://www.chemistanddruggist.co.uk/CD138389/Wegovy-GPhC-cracks-down-on-POM-discount-codes-after-CD-expos (accessed 31 December 2024).

Vaccination campaigns

Certain parts of the Regulations do not apply to an advertisement as part of vaccination campaigns that relate to the suspected or confirmed spread of pathogenic agents, chemical agents, toxins, or nuclear radiation and to a medicinal product that is a vaccine or serum and which has been approved by the Ministers (Reg.292). In essence, for the purpose of a vaccination campaign, this allows for the advertising of a medicinal product that is a POM, or contains a narcotic or psychotropic substance, and also allows for claims that the health of a person who is not suffering from any disease or injury could be enhanced by taking the medicinal product or that the health of a person could be affected by not taking the medicinal product.

Form and content of advertisements

HMR Reg.291 prohibits the publication of an advertisement relating to a medicinal product unless that advertisement is presented so that it is clear that it is an advertisement and so that the product is clearly identified as a medicinal product; and includes:

a. the name of the medicinal product,
b. the common name of the active ingredient when only one active ingredient is contained in the product,
c. the information necessary for the correct use of the product, and
d. an express and clear invitation to read carefully the instructions on the package or on the package leaflet.

These provisions do not apply if the advertisement is intended solely as a reminder of a product (which states its name, international non-proprietary name or trademark) or relates to a registered homoeopathic medicinal product.

Prohibition of supply to the public for promotional purposes

No person who is the holder of a marketing authorisation, certificate of registration or traditional herbal registration, or who carries on a medicines business, may sell or supply a medicinal product for a promotional purpose to a person who is not qualified to prescribe medicinal products (HMR Reg.293).

Advertising to persons qualified to prescribe or supply

No person may issue an advertisement relating to a medicinal product and aimed at persons qualified to prescribe or supply (PQPS) unless the advertisement contains the particulars set out in paragraphs 1 to 8 of Schedule 30 to the HMR (HMR Reg.294), as summarised below:

1. the number of the marketing authorisation, certificate of registration, Article 126a authorisation, or traditional herbal registration for the medicinal product (but this paragraph does not apply in the case of an authorisation granted on a temporary basis, in response, for example, to the suspected or confirmed spread of pathogenic agents);

2. the name and address of the holder of the temporary authorisation, or the marketing authorisation, certificate of registration, Article 126a authorisation, or traditional herbal registration for the medicinal product or the business name and address of the part of the business responsible for its sale or supply;
3. In relation to an advertisement in Great Britain where the medicinal product has a UK (GB) marketing authorisation, a statement that the product is authorised under a UK (GB) marketing authorisation;
4. the classification of the product, i.e. POM, Pharmacy, or subject to general sale;
5. the name of the medicinal product;
6. a list of the active ingredients of the medicinal product using their common names and placed immediately adjacent to the most prominent display of the name of the product;
7. one or more of the indications for the medicinal product consistent with the terms of the marketing authorisation, certificate of registration, Article 126a authorisation, or traditional herbal registration for the product or, in the case of a product which has a temporary authorisation, the indications for the medicinal product consistent with the recommendation or requirement of the MHRA as to the use of that product;
8. the entries or a succinct statement of the entries in the Summary of Product Characteristics or in any equivalent summary published by the holder of a temporary authorisation relating to:
   a. adverse reactions, precautions and relevant contra-indications,
   b. dosage and method of use relevant to the indications shown in the advertisement, and
   c. where this is not obvious, method of administration so far as relevant to those indications;
9. the cost, excluding value added tax (VAT), of either a specified package of the product or a specified quantity or recommended daily dose, calculated by reference to any specified package of the product, except that the cost may be omitted in the case of an advertisement inserted in a publication which is printed in the UK but with a circulation outside the UK of more than 15% of its total circulation; and
10. the particulars in paragraph 8 above must be printed in a clear and legible manner and be placed in such a position in the advertisement that their relationship to the claims and indications for the product can readily be appreciated by the reader.

If the advertisement relates to a medicine subject to general sale (see **Chapter 10**) or a Pharmacy medicine (see **Chapter 11**), then only the particulars set out in paragraphs 2 to 7, above, must be included, together with the statement "Information about this product, including adverse reactions, precautions, contra-indications and a method of use can be found at:" accompanied by a website address that corresponds to that statement. The website must make available the particulars set out in paragraph 1 to 9, above (i.e. those found in Schedule 30) or a copy of the Summary of Product Characteristics.

Abbreviated advertisements

Abbreviated advertisement means an advertisement, other than a loose insert, which does not exceed in size an area of 420 cm^2 in a publication sent or delivered wholly or mainly to persons qualified to prescribe or supply medicinal products (HMR Reg.295). No person may issue such an advertisement unless it:

a. contains the particulars set out in paragraphs 2 to 6 of Schedule 30 to the HMR (as set out in 2-7 of the preceding section of this chapter) for advertising to persons qualified to prescribe or supply; and
b. the statement "Information about this product, including adverse reactions, precautions, contra-indications, and method of use can be found at:", accompanied by a website address which corresponds to that statement; and
c. the name and address of the holder of the marketing authorisation, certificate of registration or traditional herbal registration for the medicinal product, or the business name and address of the part of the holder's business that is responsible for its sale or supply.

The website as mentioned here, must make available the particulars set out in Schedule 30 or a copy of the Summary of Product Characteristics.

Written material accompanying promotions

No person may send or deliver any written material to a person qualified to prescribe or supply medicinal products as part of a promotion (HMR Reg.297) unless it:

a. contains essential information compatible with Schedule 30 of the HMR; and
b. states the date on which it was drawn up or last revised.

Any such written material shall be accurate, up-to-date, verifiable and sufficiently complete to enable the recipient to form an opinion of the therapeutic value of the product to which it relates and not include any quotation, table or other illustrative matter taken from a medical journal or other scientific work unless it is accurately reproduced and the precise source is indicated.

Medical sales representatives

All medical sales representatives promoting medicinal products to persons qualified to prescribe or supply such products must give to or have available for all persons they visit, for promotional purposes, a copy of the Summary of Product Characteristics for each product promoted. Such representatives must report all information which they receive from persons visited for promotional purposes, with particular reference to any adverse drug reactions, to the scientific service established under the Regulations (HMR Reg.299).

Advertisements for registered homoeopathic products

An advertisement relating to homoeopathic medicinal products may not mention any specific therapeutic indications (HMR Reg.301) and may only contain the details specified in Schedule 28 to the Regulations (which details the labelling requirements for a registerable homoeopathic medicinal product). Nothing in Reg.291(2) (form and contents of advertisement), Reg.294 (general requirements) or Reg.295 (abbreviated advertisements) requires an advertisement relating to a homoeopathic medicinal product to which a certificate of registration relates to contain any detail not specified in Schedule 28. (See also **Chapter 16**.)

Advertisements for traditional herbal medicinal products

No person may issue an advertisement for products that are marketed in the UK under a traditional herbal registration unless it contains the words: "Traditional herbal medicinal product for use in", followed by a statement of one or more therapeutic indications for the product consistent with the terms of the traditional herbal registration for that product, followed by "exclusively based on long standing use" (HMR Reg.302). (See also **Chapter 17**).

Holders of "specials manufacturer's licences"

Specials manufacturers may not publish any advertisement, catalogue or circular relating to a special medicinal product or make any representations in respect of that product (HMR Reg.279). However, price lists may be sent at reasonable intervals or in response to an enquiry to healthcare professionals to whom the price of specials may be relevant. A *price list* would typically include the active ingredient, strength, dosage form, pack size and price for each product listed and is excluded by HMR Reg.7 from the definition of advertisement provided it makes no product claims.

Free samples for persons qualified to prescribe or supply medicinal products

A person may supply a sample of a medicinal product to another person only if the following conditions (a-f) are met (HMR Reg.298).

a. The recipient is qualified to prescribe medicinal products and receives the sample for the purpose of acquiring experience in dealing with the product in question.
b. The sample is supplied to the recipient on an exceptional basis, and in response to a request from, and signed and dated by, the recipient.
c. Taking the year in which the sample is supplied as a whole, only a limited number of samples of the product in question are supplied to the recipient in that year.
d. The sample is no larger than the smallest presentation of the product that is available for sale in the UK, is marked "free medical sample – not for resale" or bears a similar description, and is accompanied by a copy of the Summary of Product Characteristics.
e. The sample does not contain:
    i. a substance which is listed in any of Schedules I, II or IV to the Narcotic Drugs Convention (where the product is not a preparation listed in Schedule III to that Convention); or
    ii. a substance which is listed in any of Schedules I to IV to the Psychotropic Substances Convention (where the product is not a preparation which may be exempted from measures of control in accordance with paragraphs 2 and 3 of Article 3 of that Convention).

f. The supplier maintains an adequate system of control and accountability in relation to the supply of free samples.

Note that supplying samples of medicinal products to the public is unlawful.

Inducements and hospitality

Hospitality includes sponsorship of a person's attendance at a meeting or event and the payment of travelling or accommodation expenses (HMR Reg.300). When products are being promoted to persons qualified to prescribe or supply them, no person may supply, offer or promise any gift, pecuniary advantage or benefit in kind unless it is inexpensive and relevant to the practice of medicine or pharmacy.

Hospitality may be offered at events for purely professional or scientific purposes to persons qualified to prescribe or supply relevant medicinal products provided that:

- such hospitality is strictly limited to the main scientific objective of the event; and
- it is offered only to health professionals.

It is an offence for a person qualified to prescribe or supply medicinal products to solicit or accept any gift, pecuniary advantage, benefit in kind, hospitality or sponsorship prohibited by the Regulations. Examples of cases in which this issue arose, and how they were resolved are given in **Box 19.1**.

Box 19.1 Overseas Conferences Organised by UK Wholesalers

A series of overseas conferences organised by UK wholesalers, including Sigma Pharmaceuticals, Numark Limited and AAH Pharmaceuticals Limited, were reviewed by the MHRA with respect to the financial support extended by the organisers under HMR Reg.300(2).

Each conference included both scientific or professional meetings relating to pharmacy for one or two days, alongside a social programme. Attendees at the conference included healthcare professionals, guests and family members, some of whom were not healthcare professionals. Attendees paid for their own travel, accommodation and meals.

Financial support was offered by the wholesaler organising the event and other sponsors, including companies involved in the manufacture, supply or sale of medicines. The MHRA considered whether this financial support breached HMR Reg.300(2) that a person may not provide hospitality at a meeting or event held for the purpose of the promotion of a medicinal product, as this hospitality had not been limited to healthcare professionals. In addition, they considered whether the sponsorship of a conference by a pharmaceutical company, which included Persons Qualified to Prescribe or Supply (PQPS) constituted promotional activity under Regulation 7 of the HMR. The wholesalers concerned did not accept the MHRA's view that the sponsorship of a conference for PQPS by a pharmaceutical company constituted a promotional activity and maintained that the conferences were not held for the purpose of the promotion of medicines.

Resulting MHRA advice

In order to reach agreement that the review could be concluded with no further action by the MHRA, Sigma, Numark and AAH provided assurances that any similar conferences would meet the requirements of HMR Reg.300 with respect to inducement and hospitality and in particular that the sponsored hospitality would be strictly limited to that necessary to support the business programme and to healthcare professionals only.[7]

7. MHRA Decision. Overseas Conferences Organised by UK Wholesalers in 2017. 22nd February 2018. https://www.gov.uk/government/publications/advertising-investigations-december-2017/december-2017-overseas-conferences-organised-by-uk-wholesalers-in-2017 (accessed 31 December 2024).

Enforcement

Enforcement by Ministers

The MHRA acts on behalf of Health Ministers to ensure that the law is upheld, so that the promotion of the safe use of medicines can take place. The MHRA works closely with other statutory regulators and self-regulatory bodies to ensure that a consistent approach to the advertising and promotion of medicines is taken. References below to "approved" campaigns are to campaigns that have been approved by Ministers.

Under HMR Reg.304, Ministers may give a notice in writing to any person appearing to them to be concerned or likely to be concerned with the publication of advertisements relating to medicinal products. The notice may require the person to whom it is given not to publish, or further publish, during a specified period any advertisement. HMR Reg.307 empowers Ministers to require the publication of a corrective statement concerning an advertisement. The MHRA's approach is illustrated by the cases described in **Box 19.2**.

Box 19.2

Promotion of Nurofen Plus (ibuprofen & codeine) by Reckitt Benckiser

The general principles relating to the advertisement of a medicinal product include encouraging the rational use of the product by presenting it in an objective way, without exaggerating its properties. (HMR Reg.280)

The MHRA were contacted about promotional, "shelf-edge" material provided to pharmacies for the product Nurofen® Plus, which contains ibuprofen and codeine. The shelf-edge material included the statement "When you Need More from your Pain Killer". The words "Need More" and "Painkiller" were presented more prominently than the other words in the material.

The MHRA were concerned that the promotional material did not promote the "rational use of the medicine" and, based on this advice, Reckitt Benckiser agreed to withdraw the promotional material concerned and ensure future material did not use the design layout in question.[8]

Botox and other botulinum toxin injections

Following advertisements on social media, botulinum toxin, commonly referred to as Botox (but also marketed under other names), has been the subject of an Enforcement Notice applying to all promotion of botulinum toxin injections to UK consumers on social media platforms. It includes paid-for ads, non-paid-for marketing posts on suppliers' or others' pages and influencer marketing.[9] In fact, the MHRA refers the majority of complaints about botulinum toxin to the Advertising Standards Authority.

---

8. MHRA decision. Promotion of Nurofen Plus (ibuprofen & codeine) by Reckitt Benckiser. 19th December 2019 https://www.gov.uk/government/publications/advertising-investigations-december-2018/19-december-2018-promotion-of-nurofen-plus-ibuprofen-codeine-by-reckitt-benckiser (accessed 31 December 2024).
9. https://www.asa.org.uk/static/a8fa05da-b3ee-4528-82095e7bba2a3e5c/Enforcement-Notice-Advertising-Botox-and-other-botulinum-toxin-injecti.pdf (accessed 31 December 2024).

Box 19.2 (cont.)

Promotion of Viagra by PharmacyOnline.co.uk

A member of the public complained to the MHRA about branding for PharmacyOnline.co.uk that showed a car displaying the number plate VI4GRA. The MHRA decided that the combination of the number plate, the source of supply and the product claims was likely to be seen as promotion of a POM to the general public.[10]

Promotion of "vitamin B12 injection" by Vibralife Wellness Ltd (trading as VL Aesthetics)

The MHRA received two complaints about the promotion of vitamin B12 injections on social media platforms and on the website of VL Aesthetics. It was alleged that the injection was being promoted and offered free of charge to clients by the company, with the claim it would boost the immune system during the coronavirus pandemic, an indication which was outside of the product licence.

The following breaches of the advertising regulations under part 14 of the HMR were considered:

- **Regulation 280** of the Regulations states an advertisement must: comply with the particulars listed in the Summary of Product Characteristics (SmPC); encourage the rational use of the product; and not be misleading;
- **Regulation 284** which prohibits the issue to the general public of an advertisement for a POM which is likely to lead to its use;
- **Regulation 293** of the Human Medicines Regulations prohibits the sale or supply of samples of medicinal products to any member of the public by a marketing authorisation holder or any third parties. Offers to potential consumers to enable them to obtain the pack for free or for an unreasonably low sum so as to be almost free is considered to fall within this prohibition.

The complaint was upheld by the MHRA[11] who found that Vibralife Wellness Ltd had promoted a POM to the general public and for use outside of its licenced indication(s) as listed in the SmPC. The promotion was removed by the company so as to comply with Regulation 293 and they were required to review their social media platforms to ensure that it complied with MHRA guidance for providers that offer medicinal treatment service, in line with Appendix 6 of the MHRA Blue Guide.

10. https://www.gov.uk/government/publications/advertising-investigations-december-2021/december-2021-summary-report-of-viagra-by-pharmacyonlinecouk (accessed 31 December 2024).
11. https://www.gov.uk/government/publications/advertising-investigations-april-2020 (accessed 31 December 2024).

Voluntary enforcement

There are controls under existing Codes of Advertising Practice administered by the Association of the British Pharmaceutical Industry (see **Chapter 5**) and by the Proprietary Association of Great Britain (for over-the-counter medicines).[12]

Advertising Standards Authority

The Advertising Standards Authority (ASA) acts as the UK's independent regulator of advertising, and it responds to complaints made about advertising in any medium, as

12. https://www.pagb.co.uk/content/uploads/2023/08/PAGB-Code-supplement-Jan-2019.pdf (accessed 31 December 2024).

well as proactively checking the media to act against misleading, harmful or offensive advertisements.

An example of a case in which the ASA served an enforcement notice after the advertisement of a POM is given in **Box 19.3**.

Box 19.3: *Actegy Limited v The Advertising Standards Authority Limited*

Background

Actegy Ltd placed a newspaper advertisement for a medical device that applied neuromuscular electrical stimulation to the soles of the feet via footpads. The advert included claims for the efficacy of the device.

The advertisement for the *Revitive Circulation Booster* made claims that it offered fast relief from legs and swollen feet, whilst also improving circulation.

The Advertising Standards Authority (ASA) received a complaint from a member of the public that the claims were misleading and challenged whether they could be substantiated. The complaint focussed on claims:

1. "... for fast relief from aching legs & swollen feet!";
2. "... may help to reduce the swelling and, therefore, the pain and discomfort of aching legs, feet and ankles"; and
3. "... to boost the circulation in your lower limbs".

A second complaint was received in relation to the discount being offered by the seller.

4. The complainant challenged whether the claim "£50 OFF REVITIVE", when the product was being sold at £149.99, represented a genuine saving against the usual selling price of the product and could be substantiated.

Actegy Ltd supplied the ASA with a Clinical Evaluation Report (CER) and user studies which they believed provided product-specific evidence for the medical device, Revitive.

Breaches of the Committee of Advertising Practice (CAP) Code[13]

The ASA investigated the complaint and reviewed the scientific evidence provided by the company and found that there was not sufficient evidence to support claims for the efficacy of the medical device and that the advertisement had therefore breached the Committee of Advertising Practice (CAP) code. The following breaches of the code were upheld for complaints 1, 2 and 3:

- 3.1 (Misleading advertising) – advertisements must not materially mislead or be likely to do so;
- 3.7 (Substantiation) – advertisements must not mislead by exaggerating the capability or performance of a product or service; and
- 12.1 (Medicines, medical devices, health-related products and beauty products) – objective claims must be backed by evidence, if relevant, consisting of trials conducted on people. Substantiation will be assessed on the basis of the available scientific knowledge.

The following breaches of the code were upheld for complaint 4:

- 3.1 (Misleading advertising) – advertisements must not materially mislead or be likely to do so; and

13. ASA Ruling on Actegy Ltd. 11th April 2018 https://www.asa.org.uk/rulings/actegy-ltd-a17-384508.html (Accessed 31 December 2024).

Box 19.3: *Actegy Limited v The Advertising Standards Authority Limited* (cont.)

- 3.17 (Prices) – Price statements must not mislead by omission, undue emphasis or distortion. They must relate to the product featured in the marketing communication.

Legal challenge from Actegy Ltd[14]

A judicial review claim was brought by Actegy Ltd against the ASA decision. As a result of the initial ASA ruling, the company had to pull its advertising campaign, which they claimed caused them serious commercial harm. The price complaint played no part in the judicial review.

Judgment

The court dismissed the application for judicial review, holding that:

- The ASA had been entitled to uphold complaints against the newspaper advertisement placed by a health technology company about the efficacy of a medical advice;
- The ASA had assessed all the evidence, its decision was rational, and there was no unfairness in the way it had reached its decision.

14. *R (on the application of Actegy Ltd) v Advertising Standards Authority Ltd Authority* [2019] EWHC 2374 (Admin).

An example of how the ASA dealt with a complaint about a Facebook advert for menopause treatment is given in **Box 19.4**.

Box 19.4: Facebook claims for menopause treatment

A paid-for Facebook advert by Aida Wellbeing featured the text:

> *"Revealing I relieved my meno-bloat in 48 hours … 3 steps for the same results with the VolcanicX bundle: 1. Add 2-3 drops of peppermint essential oil to your VolcanicX bracelet. 2. Adjust the VolcanicX bracelet to fit you snug. 3. Wear it 24/7 for fast bloating relief & appetite control",*
>
> followed by
>
> *"This bundle includes your VolcanicX Bracelet & Peppermint Premium Scented Oil".*

Medicinal or medical claims would bring the bracelet within the definition of a medical device, but it was not registered as a medical device with the MHRA (see **Chapter 22**), and the peppermint oil would come within the definition of a medicinal product (see **Chapter 5**). If it was a medicinal product, it was unlicensed, and it is not permissible to make health claims for unlicensed products.

The ASA considered that consumers would interpret the claims "relieving meno-bloat in 48 hours" and "fast bloating relief and appetite control" to mean that the VolcanicX bracelet and the peppermint oil supplied with it could in combination treat those symptoms of the menopause. Whilst the menopause itself was not a medical condition, claims regarding the treatment and management of the adverse symptoms of menopause were medicinal or medical claims.[15] The advertiser was told that the advert must not appear again in the form complained of.

15. https://www.asa.org.uk/rulings/gkonlineco-pty-ltd-a24-1229857-gkonlineco-pty-ltd.html (accessed 31 December 2024).

SUMMARY

- The Human Medicines Regulations prohibit the advertising to the public of POMs and, in general, controlled drugs.
- It is not permitted to advertise unlicensed medicinal products.
- Requirements as to the information on medicinal products which has to be given to persons qualified to prescribe or supply medicines include essential information compatible with the Summary of Product Characteristics. This may be given by way of written information accompanying promotions or by promotion by medical representatives.
- A limited number only of free samples may be supplied to a person qualified to prescribe relevant medicinal products. The samples may only be supplied in response to a written request and suppliers must maintain an adequate system of control.
- No person who is the holder of a marketing authorisation or who carries on a business which consists of the manufacturing, selling or supplying of medicinal products shall, for promotional purposes, sell or supply medicinal products to any member of the public.
- Hospitality given to persons qualified to prescribe or supply medicines must be reasonable in level and subordinate to the main objective of meetings held solely for scientific or professional purposes. No person may supply or promise any gift, pecuniary advantage or benefit in kind unless it is inexpensive and relevant to the practice of medicine or pharmacy.
- Conditions are set out for the advertising of homoeopathic medicinal products and for traditional herbal medicinal products.
- Enforcement of the law is undertaken by the MHRA on behalf of Ministers as well as by the Advertising Standards Authority and by industry bodies.

FURTHER READING

- ABPI Code of Practice **https://www.pmcpa.org.uk/media/3406/2021-abpi-code-of-practice.pdf** (accessed 31 December 2024).
- PAGB consumer code **https://www.pagb.co.uk/otc-medicines/advertising-consumer-code-for-medicines/** (accessed 31 December 2024).

CHAPTER 20

Pharmacopoeias and compendia

Part 15 of the Human Medicines Regulations (HMR)[1] *covers pharmacopoeias and compendia which contain the standards for "official" (British or European) medicinal products and pharmaceutical substances.*

British Pharmacopoeia and compendia

The British Pharmacopoeia Commission (BPC), established under Regulation 11 of the HMR, prepares new editions of the *British Pharmacopoeia* (BP) and any amendments to such editions. A new edition comes into force on 1 January each year. The BPC must prepare editions of the BP containing such relevant information relating to substances, combinations of substances and articles as detailed below (HMR Reg.317(1) and (2)):

1. substances, combinations of substances and articles (whether medicinal products or not) which are or may be used in the practice of medicine or surgery (other than veterinary medicine or veterinary surgery), dentistry and midwifery; and
2. substances, combinations of substances and articles used in the manufacture of substances and articles listed under 1 above.

The BPC may also publish a compendium other than the BP if it thinks this appropriate (HMR Reg.317(3)). Information relating to substances and articles used in veterinary medicine and surgery (whether veterinary drugs or not) is published in a separate compendium, the *British Pharmacopoeia (Veterinary).*

Lists of names

The BPC is authorised to prepare lists of suitable names for substances and articles for placing at the head of monographs in the BP or in the compendia (HMR Reg.318). The publication of any such lists supersedes any previously published list.

Publication

Ministers must arrange the publication of the BP and any compendium prepared by the BPC (HMR Reg.317(4)). Every copy must specify the date from which it is to take effect, and notice must be given in the *London* and *Edinburgh Gazettes* not less than 21 days before that date (HMR Reg.320(1) and (2)). In addition to the BP and other compendia, the BPC must prepare such other documents as it considers appropriate, and ministers may publish them (HMR Reg.319).

---

1. Human Medicines Regulations 2012.

European Pharmacopoeia

The *European Pharmacopoeia* is defined in HMR Reg.8 as having been published by the European Directorate for the Quality of Medicines. It is published under the direction of the Council of Europe (Partial Agreement)[2] in accordance with the Convention on the Elaboration of a European Pharmacopoeia held in 1964. The standards in the *European Pharmacopoeia*, together with any amendments or alterations published in the *Gazette*, take precedence over the standards in other publications.[3] The Health Ministers may publish amendments to the BP when necessary to give effect to the Convention but, should a difference exist at any time between the two pharmacopoeias, the standard of the *European Pharmacopoeia* would prevail.[4] Although the UK has left the European Union, as the *European Pharmacopeia* is published by the Council of Europe, of which the UK retains membership, the *European Pharmacopoeia* retains its status as an official standard (see below) within the UK.[5]

Compliance with official standards

It is unlawful for any person, in the course of a business carried on by them:

a. to sell a medicinal product which has been demanded by the purchaser by, or by express reference to, a particular name; or
b. to sell or supply a medicinal product in pursuance of a prescription given by a practitioner in which the product required is described by, or by express reference, to a particular name; or
c. to sell or supply a medicinal product which, in the course of the business, has been offered or exposed for sale by, or by express reference to, a particular name;

if, in any of the above, that name is at the head of the *relevant monograph* in a specified publication, or is an approved synonym for such a name, and the product does not comply with the standard specified in that monograph (HMR Regs.251 and 255).

A product is treated as complying with the specified standard if it complies with the standard in a relevant marketing authorisation even if the standard specified in that marketing authorisation does not comply with the standard in the relevant monograph.

It is also an offence if the name in question is the name of an active ingredient of the product and, in so far as the product consists of that ingredient, it does not comply with the standard specified (HMR Reg.251(4)).

For the purpose of complying with official standards, the *relevant monograph* is ascertained as follows (HMR Reg.252).

---

2. Partial Agreements allow member States of the Council of Europe to abstain from participating in a certain activity advocated by other member States (see: https://www.thegazette.co.uk/notice/L-58904-680537 (accessed 31 December 2024).

3. Several legal texts make the *European Pharmacopoeia* mandatory; for further details, see: https://www.edqm.eu/en/European-Pharmacopoeia-Background-Mission (accessed 31 December 2024).

4. Commission Directive 2003/63/EC (amending Directive 2001/83/EC of the European Parliament and of the Council on the Community code relating to medicinal products for human use).

5. https://www.edqm.eu/en/the-european-pharmacopoeia-commission (accessed 31 December 2024).

1. If a particular edition of a particular publication is specified together with the name of the medicinal product, then the relevant monograph is (a) the monograph (if any) headed by that name in that edition of the publication or (b) if there is no such monograph in that edition, the appropriate current monograph (if any) headed by that name.
2. If a particular publication, but not a particular edition, is specified, together with the name of the medicinal product, then the relevant monograph is (a) the monograph (if any) headed by that name in the current edition of the specified publication or (b) if there is no such monograph in the current edition of the publication, the appropriate current monograph headed by that name, or (c) if there is no appropriate current monograph, then the monograph headed by that name in the latest edition of the specified publication which contained a monograph so headed.
3. If no publication is specified together with the name of the medicinal product, the relevant monograph is the appropriate current monograph, if any.

Appropriate current monograph, in relation to a particular name, means the monograph (if any) headed by that name, or by a name for which it is an approved synonym, in the current edition of the BP, or a compendium published under Part 15 of the HMR.

Current means current at the time when the medicinal product in question is demanded, described in a prescription, or offered or exposed for sale; and the current edition of a publication is the one in force at that time, together with any amendments, alterations or deletions. Any monograph shall be construed in accordance with any general monograph, notice, appendix, note or other explanatory material applicable to the monograph which is contained in the relevant edition of the publication (HMRs Reg.252(5)-(7)).

References to official standards, including pharmacopoeias, are made within the NHS Terms of service. For example, in England, paragraph 8(5) of Schedule 4 to the Regulations[6] states:

> *"If the order is for, or a product to be provided in accordance with a SSP is, a drug or appliance included in the Drug Tariff, the British National Formulary (including any Appendix published as part of that Formulary), the Dental Practitioner's Formulary, the European Pharmacopoeia or the British Pharmaceutical Codex, the drug or appliance provided must comply with any relevant standard or formula specified therein."*

Specified publications

When reference is made in a marketing authorisation, manufacturer's or wholesale dealer's licence, a certificate of registration or a traditional herbal registration (**Chapters 5**, **16** and **17**) to a specified publication, but no particular edition is mentioned, then it is to be construed as the edition of the specific publication in force at

---

6. National Health Service (Pharmaceutical and Local Pharmaceutical Services) Regulations 2013.

that time, unless the authorisation expressly provides otherwise. The HMR use the term *specified publication* to mean (HMR Reg.321):

a. *European Pharmacopoeia*;
b. *British Pharmacopoeia*;
c. the Cumulative List of Recommended International Nonproprietary Names; or
d. any other compendium or list prepared under HMR Regs.317 or 318.

The *British National Formulary* and other formularies under the *British National Formulary* are published jointly by the British Medical Association and the Pharmaceutical Press and are not "official" publications under the HMR.

SUMMARY

- The *British Pharmacopoeia* (BP) comprises information consisting of descriptions and standards for substances and articles which may be used in medicines, other than veterinary medicines, together with substances and articles used in the manufacture of medicinal products.
- The *European Pharmacopoeia*, where appropriate, takes precedence over the standards in other publications.
- It is an offence to sell, supply or dispense a medicinal product of a particular name if that name is at the head of a monograph in a pharmacopoeia, and the product does not comply with the standard specified in that monograph.
- It is also an offence if the name in question is the name of an active ingredient of the product and, in so far as the product consists of that ingredient, it does not comply with the standard specified.

FURTHER READING

- Human Medicines Regulations 2012, *Explanatory memorandum*: **http://www.legislation.gov.uk/uksi/2012/1916/pdfs/uksiem_20121916_en.pdf** (accessed 31 December 2024).
- Royal Pharmaceutical Society (published annually). *Medicines, Ethics and Practice*. London: Royal Pharmaceutical Society (includes practice guidance on many of the topics in this chapter; free to members).

CHAPTER 21

Poisons, denatured alcohols, chemicals and prohibition orders

Laws referred to in this chapter have often been made to address public concerns at the time the laws were brought into force. The very first legislation regulating aspects of pharmacy practice was the Arsenic Act 1851, passed by Parliament when there had been public alarm over trials of poisoners reported in the press. The Pharmacy and Poisons Act 1933 made pharmacy the most highly regulated of all healthcare professions through the creation of an inspectorate to enforce the law. It was passed during the Golden Age of Crime Fiction when detective stories raised public fears of deliberate and accidental poisoning. The regulation of chemical sales was tightened after terrorist bombings in London in 2005, and again after the Manchester Arena bombing in 2017. The most recent Prohibition Order was made in 2024, following the publication of the Cass Review and concern about the treatment of children and young people with puberty blockers.

Non-medicinal poisons: legal framework

Until the Medicines Act 1968 came into force, what we now call medicines were called poisons, and the supply of poisons has long been regulated by the law, much longer than medicines have been the subject of legal regulation. The first national piece of legislation to regulate the sale of medicines was the Arsenic Act 1851 following fears that arsenic was easily available and was used to commit murders.

The Poisons Act 1972 (the Act) is the most recent Act of Parliament which consolidates laws made over the years in relation to poisons. The Act continues to be amended to meet concerns and fears of the day. For example, it was substantially amended by the Deregulation Act 2015, the relevant parts of which were brought into force by the Deregulation Act 2015 (Poisons and Explosives Precursors) (Consequential Amendments, Revocations and Transitional Provisions) Order 2015. The background to this change was partly in relation to the Government's response to terrorism within the UK and the manufacture of home-made explosives. For example, the terrorist bombings in London on 7 and 21 July 2005 were undertaken with bombs which were made using hydrogen peroxide. Therefore, this legislative change was part of a strategy to deny terrorist access to hazardous materials.[1] This means that rather than being concerned

---

1. Explanatory memorandum to the Deregulation Act 2015 (Poisons and Explosives Precursors) (Consequential Amendments, Revocations and Transitional Provisions) Order 2015.

solely with Poisons, the Act is now concerned with the sale of "regulated" and "reportable" substances.

Further amendments to the legislation were made by the Control of Explosives Precursors and Poisons Regulations 2023, with the Explanatory Memorandum to these Regulations citing the outcome from the Operational Improvement Review following the Manchester Arena attack in 2017 as the driver for change.[2]

Regulated and reportable substances

A *regulated substance* means a regulated explosives precursor or a regulated poison, and a *reportable substance* means a reportable explosives precursor or a reportable poison.

Schedule 1A to the Act (see Appendix 4) lists the regulated and reportable substances, which are defined as follows.

- A *regulated poison* is a substance listed in Part 2 of Schedule 1A in a concentration higher than the limit (if any) set out for that substance in that Part.
- A *reportable poison* is a substance listed in Part 4 of Schedule 1A in a concentration higher than the limit (if any) set out for that substance in that Part.
- A *regulated explosives precursor* is a substance listed in Part 1 of Schedule 1A in a concentration higher than the limit set out for that substance in that Part.
- A *reportable explosives precursor* is a substance listed in Part 3 of Schedule 1A.

Each of the above definitions includes a mixture, or another substance in which a substance listed in the relevant Part is present in a concentration higher than the relevant limit (if such a limit is specified).

Exemptions from control under the Poisons Act

Some substances or mixtures are excluded from the above definitions; namely if they are:

a. a medicinal product as defined by regulation 2 of the Human Medicines Regulations 2012 (HMR) - see **Chapter 5**;
b. an investigational medicinal product as defined by regulation 2 of the Medicines for Human Use (Clinical Trials) Regulations 2004;
c. articles or substances which in the opinion of the Ministers are not medicinal products but are:
    i. manufactured, sold, supplied, imported or exported for use wholly or partly for a medicinal purpose,
    ii. are used as ingredients in the manufacture of medicinal products, or
    iii. if used without proper safeguards, are capable of causing danger to the health of the community,

    and to which Part 12 of the HMR (Dealings with medicinal products) or Part 6 of the Medicines for Human Use (Clinical Trials) Regulations 2004 (Manufacture and importation of investigational medicinal products) applies;[3]

---

2. Explanatory memorandum to the Control of Explosives Precursors and Poisons Regulations 2023.
3. Sections 104 and 105 of the Medicines Act 1968.

d. a veterinary medicinal product as defined by regulation 2 of the Veterinary Medicines Regulations 2013;
e. contained in a *specific object*, which means:
   i. an object that, during production, is given a special shape, surface or design that determines its function to a greater degree than does its chemical composition, or
   ii. an article that contains explosive substances or an explosive mixture of substances designed to produce heat, light, sound, gas or smoke or a combination of such effects through self-sustained exothermic chemical reactions, including pyrotechnic equipment falling within the scope of Council Directive 96/98/EC on marine equipment, and percussion caps intended specifically for toys falling within the scope of Council Directive 88/378/EEC concerning the safety of toys;
f. listed as being exempt in the Schedule to the Control of Poisons and Explosives Precursors Regulations 2015. This includes substances or articles subject to general exemptions (such as adhesives, builders' materials or cosmetic products) and those subject to special exemptions (such as barium chloride when contained in a fire extinguisher). See **Tables 21.1** and **21.2** for a full list.

Table 21.1: *Items exempt from control under the Poisons Act: general exemptions*

Adhesives; anti-fouling compositions; builders' materials; ceramics; cosmetic products; distempers; electrical valves; enamels; explosives; fillers; fireworks; fluorescent lamps; flux in any form for use in soldering; glazes; glue; inks; lacquer solvents; loading materials; matches; medicated animal feeding stuffs; motor fuels and lubricants; paints; photographic paper; pigments; plastics; propellants; rubber; varnishes; vascular plants and their seeds.

Table 21.2: *Items exempt from control under the Poisons Act 1972: specific exemptions for poisons contained in specified substances or articles*

Poison	Substance or article in which exempted
Ammonia	Substances not being solutions of ammonia or preparations containing solutions of ammonia; substances containing less than 10%, weight in weight, of ammonia; refrigerators.
Arsenic; its compounds	Pyrites ores or sulfuric acid containing arsenic or compounds of arsenic as natural impurities; in reagent kits or reagent devices, supplied for medical or veterinary purposes, substances containing less than 0.1%, weight in weight, of arsanilic acid.
Barium, salts of	Witherite other than finely ground witherite; barium carbonate bonded to charcoal for case hardening; fire extinguishers containing barium chloride; sealed smoke generators containing not more than 25%, weight in weight, of barium carbonate.
Bromomethane	Fire extinguishers.
Formaldehyde	Substances containing less than 5%, weight in weight, of formaldehyde; photographic glazing or hardening solutions.
Formic acid	Substances containing less than 25%, weight in weight, of formic acid.
Hydrochloric acid	Substances containing less than 10%, weight in weight, of hydrochloric acid.
Hydrogen cyanide	Preparations of wild cherry; in reagent kits supplied for medical or veterinary purposes, substances containing less than the equivalent of 0.1%, weight in weight, of hydrogen cyanide.

Table 21.2: *Items exempt from control under the Poisons Act 1972: specific exemptions for poisons contained in specified substances or articles* (cont.)

Poison	Substance or article in which exempted
Methomyl	Solid substances containing not more than 1%, weight in weight, of methomyl.
Nicotine; its salts; its quaternary compounds	Tobacco; in cigarettes, the paper of a cigarette (excluding any part of that paper forming part of or surrounding a filter), where that paper in each cigarette does not have more than the equivalent of 10 milligrams of nicotine; preparations in aerosol dispensers containing not more than 0.2% of nicotine, weight in weight; other liquid preparations, and solid preparations with a soap base, containing not more than 7.5% of nicotine, weight in weight.
Oxamyl	Granular preparations.
Oxydemeton-methyl	Aerosol dispensers containing not more than 0.25%, weight in weight, of oxydemeton-methyl.
Phenols	Liquid disinfectants and antiseptics containing less than 0.5% phenol and containing less than 5% of other phenols; Motor fuel treatments not containing phenol and containing less than 2.5% of other phenols; in reagent kits supplied for medical or veterinary purposes; Solid substances containing less than 60% of phenols; in tar oil distillation fractions containing not more than 5% of phenols.
Phosphoric acid	Substances containing phosphoric acid, not being descaling preparations containing more than 50%, weight in weight, of ortho-phosphoric acid.
Potassium hydroxide	Substances containing the equivalent of less than 17% of total caustic alkalinity expressed as potassium hydroxide; accumulators; batteries.
Sodium fluoride	Substances containing less than 3% of sodium fluoride as a preservative.
Sodium hydroxide	Substances containing the equivalent of less than 12% of total caustic alkalinity expressed as sodium hydroxide.
Sodium silicofluoride	Substances containing less than 3% of sodium silicofluoride as a preservative.

The Act follows the definition of the Medicines Act for *persons lawfully conducting a retail pharmacy business* and the definition of the HMR for *retail pharmacy business* (**Chapter** 7).

Powers of the Secretary of State

The Secretary of State has powers to make regulations to amend parts of the Poisons Act. For example, 2,4 dinitrophenol (commonly known as DNP), was added to the list of regulated poisons in 2023 because of its use as a "diet pill" for weight loss, when its toxicity had led to a number of deaths.[4] It is intended that, in determining the distribution of substances between the various Parts of Schedule 1A, substances should be allocated to Parts 3 and 4 (and so be "reportable" rather than "regulated") if they are in common use, or are likely to come into common use, for purposes other than the treatment of human ailments, and it is reasonably necessary to include them in one of those Parts if members of the general public are to have adequate facilities for obtaining them (Section 2A).

4. See: https://pharmaceutical-journal.com/article/news/government-to-change-law-to-reclassify-so-called-diet-drug-as-a-poison (accessed 31 December 2024) and https://www.judiciary.uk/wp-content/uploads/2022/12/Jack-Knapman-Prevention-of-future-deaths-report-2022-0405_Published-1.pdf (accessed 31 December 2024).

The Secretary of State is, further, empowered to make regulations to disapply some or all of the requirements of the Act or to apply exclusions in specified circumstances (Section 9B).

Inspection and enforcement

It is the duty of the GPhC to secure compliance with the provisions of the Act by registered pharmacists and persons carrying on a retail pharmacy business (Section 9). This is achieved by the GPhC inspectorate (**Chapter 2**).

An inspector appointed by the GPhC may at all reasonable times:

a. enter any registered pharmacy to ascertain whether an offence relating to the Act has been committed by a pharmacist or a person carrying on a retail pharmacy business;
b. enter any premises in which the inspector has reasonable cause to suspect that a breach of the law has been committed in respect of any regulated poison; whether in a retail pharmacy business or any other premises, an inspector has power to make such examination and inquiry and to do such other things (including the taking, on payment, of samples) as may be necessary to ascertain that the Act is being complied with.

It is an offence for any person wilfully to delay or obstruct an inspector, to refuse to allow a sample to be taken, or to fail, without reasonable excuse, to give any information which the Act requires them to give to an inspector. It is specifically provided that nothing in the Act authorises an inspector to enter or inspect the premises of a doctor, a dentist, a veterinary surgeon or a veterinary practitioner unless those premises are a shop.

The police also have powers under the Police and Criminal Evidence Act 1984 to enter and search premises in relation to certain offences under the Act (section 9A).

Penalties and legal proceedings

Section 8 of the Act sets out the various penalties that apply in the case of a breach of the Act. These include terms of imprisonment and/or fines. In the case of proceedings in connection with the supply of a regulated or reportable substance, where the act in question was done by an employee, it is not a defence that the employee acted without the authority of the employer; and any material fact known to the employee is deemed to have been known to the employer.

For certain offences under the Act it is a defence for the accused to prove that they did not know, did not suspect or had no reason to suspect the existence of some fact (alleged by the prosecution) that the prosecution relies on to prove that they committed the offence. This defence operates where the accused proves (on a balance of probabilities) that they lacked the necessary knowledge (Section 7A).

Sale and supply of regulated substances

Requirement for a licence

Certain chemicals can be used in the illicit manufacture of explosives or to cause harm. Under Section 3A of the Act, members of the public who want to acquire, import, possess or use these chemicals (i.e. regulated substances which are included in Part 1 or Part 2) must have a valid explosives precursors and poisons (EPP) licence, or a recognised non-GB licence (referred to hereafter as "licences"), and an associated photographic identity document. "Use" in this context includes processing, formulating, storing, treating or mixing a regulated substance or including one in the production of an article (Section 3). The licence may permit, and will specify, which of these activities is or are permitted with respect to one or more of the regulated substances.

A *member of the general public* means an individual who is acting (alone or with others) for purposes not connected with his or her trade, business or profession or the performance by him or her of a public function (Section 3). Business-to-business transactions are exempt from the requirement to hold a licence.

Licences issued in Great Britain are granted by the Secretary of State and each licence is valid for a maximum of three years, although individuals may apply to renew their licence and the Secretary of State has powers to vary, suspend or revoke the licence before it expires (Section 4A). In deciding whether to grant or amend a licence with respect to a substance, the Secretary of State must have regard to all the circumstances of the case, including in particular:

a. the use intended to be made of the substance;
b. the availability of alternative substances that would achieve the same purpose;
c. the proposed arrangements to ensure that the substance is kept securely;
d. any danger to public safety or public order that may be caused by possession of the substance; and
e. whether the applicant is a fit and proper person to possess the substance.

If there are reasonable grounds for doubting the legitimacy of the use intended to be made of the substance or the intentions of the user to use the substance for a legitimate purpose, the Secretary of State must in any event refuse the application so far as it relates to that substance.

A licence may be granted or amended subject to such terms and conditions as may be specified in the licence. Such terms and conditions may relate to the storage, use, maximum quantities or maximum levels of concentration that may be purchased and the reporting of disappearances or thefts (Section 4A).

As well as the licences described, above, there may also be recognised non-GB licences. These are licences issued in a member State[5] which is "recognised" for these purposes in accordance with Article 7(6) of the Precursors Regulation.[6] The Secretary of State must publish a list from time to time of recognised member States (if there are any) (Section 4B).

5. The Explanatory Note to the Deregulation Act 2015 states that Section 4B allows for the recognition of equivalent licences granted by the authorities in other EU Member States or in Northern Ireland (the wording "other" pre-dates the UK's exit from the European Union).

6. Regulation (EU) 98/2013.

Supply of regulated substances to business customers[7]

A person must not supply a regulated substance or a reportable substance to a business customer unless the supplier first notifies the business customer in writing that the substance is a regulated substance or a reportable substance for the purposes of the Act.

A person must not supply a regulated explosives precursor to a business customer unless the suppler first complies with the following requirements:

(a) The supplier must obtain the following from the business customer:
   1. the business customer's name and address;
   2. if the business customer is not an individual, the name of an individual who is authorised on behalf of the business customer to acquire the regulated explosives precursor;
   3. a form of photographic identification of the business customer or, if the business customer is not an individual, of the individual referred to in 2 above;
   4. a statement of the nature of the business customer's trade, business or profession, or of the public function that the business customer performs; and
   5. the business customer's VAT registration number, if the business customer has such a number.

(b) The supplier must be reasonably satisfied that the acquisition of the regulated explosives precursor by the business customer is reasonably consistent with the nature of the business customer's trade, business or profession, or of the public function that the business customer performs.

(c) The supplier must make a record of the information, document and statement obtained from the business customer in accordance with (a) above.

(d) The supplier must preserve the record referred to in (c) above for a period of 18 months beginning with the date on which the record is made.

A supplier is not required to comply with (a) to (d) above if the supplier has made a previous supply to the same business customer and made the record referred to in (c) above within the preceding 18 months.

Supply of regulated substances to members of the public

It is an offence to supply a regulated substance (i.e. a regulated explosives precursor or regulated poison) to a member of the general public without first verifying that the member of the general public has a licence (section 3A). Such a licence is also required by a member of the public for them to possess and use such a substance (Section 3).

The Home Office[8] advise that, when a member of the public requests to purchase a regulated substance, the seller should:

1. ask to see their Explosives Precursors and Poisons (EPP) Licence and associated photographic ID;
2. compare the photograph to the customer;

---

7. See the Control of Explosives Precursors and Poisons Regulations 2023.
8. The Home Office. Supplying explosives precursors and poisons, April 2018, see: https://www.gov.uk/government/publications/supplying-explosives-precursors/supplying-explosives-precursors-and-poison (accessed 31 December 2024).

3. verify the photographic ID reference against the ID reference on the front page of the licence;
4. check the product being purchased is allowed as part of the licence conditions: substance, concentration, volume;
5. record the transaction details in the table on the back of the licence; and
6. if it is a regulated poison and the seller is not a registered pharmacist or operating under the supervision of a registered pharmacist, refuse the sale. If it is a regulated poison and the seller is a registered pharmacist, or operating under the supervision of a registered pharmacist, enter the transaction details into the poisons register.

If the seller considers the transaction is suspicious or unusual in any way, the Home Office advises sellers to refuse the sale, report it and phone the police.

Provision of information to workers

A person who carries on a trade, business or profession involving the supply of regulated substances or reportable substances, and who engages a worker in connection with making such supplies must ensure that the worker is not involved in the making of supplies of regulated substances or reportable substances unless first provided with such information on the following matters as is relevant to the worker's role and responsibilities:[9]

(a) the requirements that are imposed by the Act, the Control of Poisons and Explosive Precursors Regulations 2015 and the Control of Explosives Precursors and Poisons Regulations 2023;
(b) the offences that apply if the requirements in (a) are not complied with; and
(c) the regulated substances or reportable substances that are supplied.

Online marketplaces

Under regulation 5 of the Control of Explosives Precursors and Poisons Regulations 2023, any person (an *operator*) who controls access to, and the contents of, an online market place (which includes a website) must take all reasonably practicable measures to provide information to any supplier who uses the marketplace about the requirements of the Act and the Control of Explosives Precursors Regulations and the offences that apply if there is a failure to comply with the requirements of the Act and the Regulations.[10]

An operator of an online marketplace must take all reasonably practicable measures to identify any relevant transaction that a supplier makes or proposes to make that would give the operator reasonable grounds for believing the transaction to be suspicious. The operator must report any such transaction.

Reporting suspicious transactions

Where suspicious transactions have to be reported, this must be done within 24 hours, beginning with the time when the person required to make a report forms the belief that

9. Regulation 4 of the Control of Explosives Precursors and Poisons Regulations 2023.
10. Regulation 5 of the Control of Explosives Precursors and Poisons Regulations 2023.

the transaction is suspicious; or in the case of a disappearance or theft, the time when the person required to report discovers the disappearance or theft.[11]

Reports must be made electronically or by telephone, using the details provided by the Home Office.[12]

See, also, *Reporting of suspicious transactions, disappearances and thefts* below.

Supply of regulated poisons

A regulated poison may only be supplied to a member of the general public if (Section 3B):

a. the person making the supply is lawfully conducting a retail pharmacy business;
b. the supply is made on premises that are a registered pharmacy; and
c. the supply is made by or under the supervision of a pharmacist.

The person making the supply must make (or cause to be made) a record of the supply, which must be signed by the member of the general public purchasing the item. The record must state:

a. the date of the supply;
b. the name and address of the member of the general public;
c. the name and quantity of the regulated poison supplied; and
d. the purposes for which it is stated by the member of the general public to be required.

These record-keeping requirements are in addition to those required for all regulated substances (i.e. that the details of the transaction are entered on to the licence) before the regulated substance is supplied to a member of the general public.

Storage of poisons in retail premises

A regulated poison or reportable poison may be stored in a retail shop, or in premises used in connection with a retail shop, only if:[13]

a. it is stored in a cupboard or drawer reserved solely for the storage of poisons;
b. it is stored in a part of the premises that is partitioned off, or is otherwise separated from, the remainder of the premises and to which customers are not permitted to have access; or
c. it is stored on a shelf reserved solely for the storage of poisons and no food or drink is kept directly under the shelf.

In the case of a poison to be used in agriculture, horticulture or forestry, the poison may be stored in a cupboard or drawer only if that is reserved solely for the storage of poisons to be used in agriculture, horticulture or forestry. Such a poison may not be stored in any part of premises in which food or drink is kept or on any shelf.

---

11. Regulation 6 of the Control of Explosives Precursors and Poisons Regulations 2023.
12. The reporting arrangements are given here https://www.gov.uk/government/publications/supplying-explosives-precursors/supplying-explosives-precursors-and-poison (accessed 31 December 2024).
13. Control of Poisons and Explosives Precursors Regulations 2015.

Labelling and packaging of regulated and reportable substances

Regulated and reportable substances are subject to the GB Classification, Labelling and Packaging of chemicals (GB CLP) Regulations (see section on Labelling of chemicals, below). Regulated substances must bear the warning label, "acquisition, possession or use by the general public is restricted", before such substances are supplied to a member of the general public. This phrase should be placed in the section for supplemental information within the GB CLP label on products that fall within the scope of GB CLP.

Reporting of suspicious transactions, disappearances and thefts

A supplier must report any transaction involving the supply, or proposed supply, of a regulated or reportable substance to a customer if the supplier has reasonable grounds for believing the transaction to be suspicious (Section 3C). This applies to all such supplies, or proposed supplies, whether they be to an end user or a customer higher up the supply chain and whether to a business or to a private customer.

A transaction involving one of these substances is "suspicious" if there are reasonable grounds for suspecting that the substance in question is intended for:

a. the illicit manufacture of explosives (in the case of a regulated or reportable explosives precursor); or
b. any illicit use (in the case of a regulated or reportable poison).

In deciding whether there are reasonable grounds for suspicion, in these transactions, regard must be had to all the circumstances of the case including, in particular, where the prospective customer:

a. appears unclear about the intended use of the substance;
b. appears unfamiliar with the intended use of the substance or cannot explain it plausibly;
c. intends to buy substances in quantities, combinations or concentrations uncommon for private use;
d. is unwilling to provide proof of identity or place of residence; or
e. insists on using unusual methods of payment, including large amounts of cash.

A person carrying on a trade, business or profession that involves regulated or reportable substances must report the disappearance or theft of any such substances if the disappearance or theft is significant and is from stocks in the person's possession, custody or control in Great Britain. In deciding whether a disappearance or theft is significant, regard must be had to whether the amount involved is unusual in all the circumstances of the case.

A duty under this section to "report" something is a duty to give notice of it to the Secretary of State in accordance with such requirements as may be specified by the Secretary of State by regulations (for the requirements, see the section above on Reporting suspicious transactions).

Denatured alcohols

Denatured alcohol is alcohol which has been made unsuitable for drinking by the addition of denaturants. The Denatured Alcohol Regulations 2005 describe three classes of denatured alcohol (see below) and the Schedule to the Denatured Alcohol Regulations 2005 outlines the formula for each. The law relating to alcohol and denatured alcohol is contained mainly in the Customs and Excise Management Act 1979, the Denatured Alcohol Regulations 2005 and the Finance (No.2) Act 2023 (the 2023 Act).

Alcohol (defined in regulation 2 of the Denatured Alcohol Regulations 2005 by reference to section 44 of the 2023 Act) means spirits, beer, cider, wine, and any other fermented product.

Retail sales of "intoxicating liquor" and alcohol duty

Businesses, organisations and individuals who want to sell or supply alcohol must have a licence or other authorisation from a licensing authority; this is usually a local council. The licensing system relates both to premises and personal licences. Legislation also governs such things as permitted opening hours. In addition, an excise duty (*alcohol duty*) is charged on alcoholic products that are produced in, or imported into, the United Kingdom. Alcohol duty is not charged on denatured alcohol.[14]

HM Revenue and Customs grants relief from excise duty on spirits used for medical or scientific purposes.[15] No spirits may remain in the final product unless it is an ethyl ester or ether (and less than 1.2% ABV) or a medicinal product.[16] Since pharmacists will rarely be involved in the sale or supply of "intoxicating liquors", this chapter will not consider these matters further but will focus, instead, on the production, sale and supply of denatured alcohols.

Classes of denatured alcohols

Regulation 4 of the Regulations stipulates three classes of denatured alcohol:

a. completely denatured alcohol (CDA);
b. industrial denatured alcohol (IDA); and
c. trade specific denatured alcohol (TSDA).

Pharmacists are generally concerned only with the first two classes – completely denatured alcohol and industrial denatured alcohol.

The Regulations set out the particulars for the supply, receipt, sale, storage, and so on of all types of denatured alcohol, although the provisions for licensing and inspection are to be found in the Act itself.

---

14. Section 90 of the Finance (No.2) Act 2023.
15. The power to grant relief is in section 78(3) of the Finance (No.2) Act 2023 and may be subject to certain conditions.
16. https://www.gov.uk/government/publications/excise-notice-47-duty-free-spirits-use-in-manufacture-or-for-medical-or-scientific-purposes/excise-notice-47-duty-free-spirits-use-in-manufacture-or-for-medical-or-scientific-purposes (accessed 31 December 2024).

Production and distribution of denatured alcohol

A licence or authorisation, issued by HM Revenue and Customs (HMRC), is required before any person may denature alcohol. In addition, unless the premises at which the denatured alcohol is made are approved as an excise warehouse, the producer must "make entry" of each set of premises with HMRC; this essentially means to register the premises with them.[17] Producers of denatured alcohols are responsible for the security of the alcohol and HMRC will check to make sure that any security systems are sufficient.

A licence issued by HMRC is also required by persons who wish to distribute denatured alcohol. Distributors who hold stocks of denatured alcohol must also "make entry" of their premises with HMRC, before beginning to hold any stocks of denatured alcohol.

Supply of denatured alcohol by producers or distributors

A producer or distributor can supply CDA to anyone, including the general public, and can supply IDA to authorised persons on receipt of a copy of their authorisation.

Wholesale quantities of industrial denatured alcohol and trade specific denatured alcohol may only be supplied by licensed or authorised producers and distributors. Wholesale quantities are those greater than 20 litres.

HMRC sets out rules and procedures for the receipt or supply of denatured alcohols outside of the UK.

Completely Denatured Alcohol (CDA)

As the name suggests, this is the most heavily denatured alcohol. When produced in the UK, the standard formulation is for every 100 parts by volume of alcohol to mix 3 parts by volume of isopropyl alcohol, 3 parts by volume of methyl ethyl ketone and one gram of denatonium benzoate. Prior to 1 July 2013 the formulation also included methyl violet dye, although such inclusion is no longer mandatory. Some formulations still include the purple dye; this is permitted, and the resultant mixture is still treated as CDA.

CDA can be used for heating, lighting, cleaning, and general domestic use and can be obtained, by members of the public from a variety of retailers, including DIY shops. CDA must not be purified, re-distilled or made drinkable. No licence or authorisation is required for a member of the public to purchase or use CDA, there are no restrictions on the amount that may be purchased and there are no conditions on its use.

A person who deals wholesale in CDA does not require an excise licence.[18]

Industrial Denatured Alcohol (IDA)

This class of denatured alcohol is designed for industrial use. It usually consists of 95 parts by volume of alcohol and 5 parts by volume of wood naphtha, or a substitute for wood naphtha. IDA can be used for a wide range of industrial, scientific and external

17. Regulation 8(7) of the Denatured Alcohol Regulations 2005.
18. Regulation 15 of the Alcoholic Products (Excise Duty) Regulations 2023.

medical applications. It must not be used for heating, lighting or for the preparation of beverages, nor may it be purified, recovered or re-distilled without the written agreement of HMRC.

IDA can be used in the manufacture of hand gel and hand sanitisers. During the 2020 COVID-19 pandemic, HMRC prioritised applications to use IDA (and TSDA) in hand sanitising products,[19] and temporary changes were made to the use and supply of denatured alcohol and duty-free spirits.[20]

Authorisation to receive and use IDA

Any person, including persons lawfully conducting a retail pharmacy business, wishing to receive IDA must be authorised by HMRC to do so. The authorisation sets out the conditions of use of the IDA, and these must be adhered to.

Those who wish to hold stocks of denatured alcohol must also “make entry” of their premises with HMRC, before beginning to hold any stocks of denatured alcohol.

All stocks of IDA (and TSDA) must be kept under lock and key, and under the control of the authorised person or that of a responsible person appointed by them.

Supply of IDA by a pharmacist

A pharmacist, who is an authorised user of IDA may supply IDA:

- in quantities of less than 20 litres at any one time to another authorised user; the pharmacist must hold a copy of that user’s authorisation to receive IDA;
- for medical use in response to the prescription or order of a medical or veterinary practitioner. There is no limit on the amount of IDA which can be supplied on an order.

An order is not defined in the regulations but is a request to be supplied with a specific quantity of IDA. There is no set format for an order, but it should include the quantity and class of denatured alcohol required.

Medical use means any medical, veterinary, surgical or dental purpose other than administration internally and *medical or veterinary practitioner* means any person entitled by law to provide medical or veterinary services in the UK. HMRC have confirmed that this includes dentists, nurses and chiropodists.

Under the Regulations, schools, colleges or universities wishing to use up to 5 litres of IDA per annum do not need to be authorised and so a copy of an authorisation to receive and use denatured alcohol is not needed in the case of such sales.

Records

Producers and distributors must keep records which show:

- purchases of materials used in the production of denatured alcohol;
- imports of denatured alcohol, including details of the country of origin;

---

19. See: https://www.gov.uk/government/news/hmrc-prioritise-applications-to-use-denatured-alcohol-in-hand-sanitising-products (accessed 31 December 2024).

20. See: https://www.gov.uk/guidance/producing-hand-sanitiser-and-gel-for-coronavirus-covid-19 (accessed 31 December 2024).

- the class of denatured alcohol held in containers, that is whether it is CDA, IDA or TSDA;
- quantities of alcohols, denaturants, markers, dyes and denatured alcohol held and used on their premises;
- the results of stocktakes and action taken to investigate deficiencies and surpluses identified by those stocktakes;
- exports and sales of denatured alcohol;
- copy authorisations received in support of orders for denatured alcohols.

Users (this will include pharmacists) must keep records which show:

- purchases of IDA or TSDA;
- imports of IDA or TSDA, including details of the country of origin;
- the class of denatured alcohol held in containers, that is whether it is IDA or TSDA;
- quantities of IDA or TSDA held and used on their premises;
- the results of stocktakes and action taken to investigate deficiencies and surpluses identified by those stocktakes;
- sales of IDA or TSDA to other authorised users;
- copy authorisations received in support of supplies of IDA or TSDA.

HMRC will, from time to time, visit those who use, produce or distribute denatured alcohols in order to inspect their records and premises and to examine any denatured alcohol held on the premises. If HMRC uncover any errors then they may require the user, producer or distributor to pay the duty on any alcohol lost as the results of those errors. Errors can include:

- unexplained losses of undenatured or denatured alcohol;
- as a producer, a failure to carry out denaturing to the required standards;
- as a producer or distributor, the making of supplies to persons who are not authorised users or without receiving copy authorisations, or
- as a user, using the denatured alcohol for an unauthorised use.

Further penalties may also be applied and HMRC may withdraw the person's authorisation.

Chemicals

Great Britain Classification, labelling and packaging (GB CLP)

The classification of chemicals placed on the market in Great Britain is regulated by the GB Classification, Labelling and Packaging Regulation, known as GB CLP. GP CLP is an amended form of European Regulation (EC) 1272/2008 on classification, labelling and packaging of substances and mixtures, which came into force on 20 January 2009 in all EU Member States, including the UK. The European Regulation is assimilated law in the UK in an amended form, and references below to Articles are to Articles in this Regulation, known now as GB CLP.[21] The GB CLP adopted the United Nations Globally Harmonized System of the classification and labelling of chemicals (UN GHS)

21. https://www.hse.gov.uk/chemical-classification/legal/clp-regulation.htm (accessed 31 December 2024).

in a similar way to EU CLP. Those CLP functions formerly carried out by the European Chemicals Agency and the European Commission are now carried out in Great Britain by HSE.

The purpose of the GB CLP Regulation is to "ensure a high level of protection of human health and the environment". This is achieved by providing an obligation for (Art.1):

a. manufacturers, importers and downstream users to classify substances and mixtures placed on the market;
b. suppliers to label and package substances and mixtures placed on the market;
c. manufacturers, producers of articles and importers to classify those substances not placed on the market that are subject to registration or notification under Regulation (EC) 1907/2006.

Retailers (including pharmacists) who store and sell chemicals to consumers without altering them in any way, can rely on the classification and labelling information that has been provided to them by those further up the supply chain (e.g. from the manufacturer). If they alter the chemical in any way (e.g. by reformulating it) before placing it on the market, they then adopt the role of a downstream user and become responsible for classifying, labelling and packaging that chemical.

Definitions

The following definitions are included in GB CLP (Art.2):

- *Distributor* means any natural or legal person established within the United Kingdom, including a retailer, who only stores and places on the market a substance, on its own or in a mixture, for third parties.
- *Downstream user* means any natural or legal person established within the UK, other than the manufacturer or the importer, who uses a substance, either on its own or in a mixture, in the course of his industrial or professional activities. A distributor or a consumer is not a downstream user.
- *Importer* means any natural or legal person established within the UK who is responsible for import.
- *Manufacturer* means any natural or legal person established within the United Kingdom who manufactures a substance within the UK.
- *Mixture* means a mixture or solution composed of two or more substances.
- *Substance* means a chemical element and its compounds in the natural state or obtained by any manufacturing process, including any additive necessary to preserve its stability and any impurity deriving from the process used, but excluding any solvent which may be separated without affecting the stability of the substance or changing its composition.
- *Supplier* means any manufacturer, importer, downstream user or distributor placing on the market a substance, on its own or in a mixture, or a mixture.

Downstream users include those who formulate mixtures, transfer substances or mixtures from one container or packaging into another or who re-import chemicals. Hence, pharmacists who stock and sell chemicals to consumers in their original packaging, are defined as distributors under GB CLP.

The Globally Harmonized System of Classification and Labelling of Chemicals (the GHS)

GB CLP sets out that, in order to facilitate worldwide trade in chemicals, whilst also protecting human health and the environment, it is necessary for there to be an internationally agreed system of chemicals classification and labelling. Such a system has been developed within the United Nations (UN) structure, resulting in the Globally Harmonized System of Classification and Labelling of Chemicals (or GHS).

The UN GHS is not a formal treaty, but is, instead, a non-legally binding international agreement. This means that countries (or trading blocs) must create local or national legislation to implement the GHS.

Application of the Regulations and exceptions

The GB CLP Regulation applies to the classification, packaging and labelling of any substance or mixture which has been classified as hazardous. It also applies where a mixture, which has not been classified as hazardous, contains any substance which has been classified as hazardous.

GB CLP does not apply to the following chemicals:

a. radioactive substances and mixtures;
b. substances and mixtures which are subject to customs supervision (with certain provisos);
c. non-isolated intermediates;
d. substances and mixtures for scientific research and development, which are not placed on the market, provided they are used under controlled conditions in accordance with community workplace and environmental legislation;
e. waste.

It also does not apply to substances and mixtures in the following forms, which are in the finished state, intended for the final user:

a. medicinal products;
b. veterinary medicinal products;
c. cosmetic products;
d. medical devices;
e. food or feeding stuffs, including when they are used as a food additive, a flavouring, an additive in feeding stuffs or in animal nutrition.

Except where Article 33 applies (specific rules for labelling of outer packaging, inner packaging and single packaging), GB CLP does not apply to the transport of dangerous goods by air, sea, road, rail or inland waterways.

Classification

Classification is the process by which the hazards which chemicals may pose are identified. GB CLP places an obligation on manufacturers, importers and downstream users to classify substances or mixtures, in accordance with the Regulation, before placing them on the market. When classifying a chemical, there are criteria for:

a. physical hazards (e.g. being corrosive);

b. health hazards (e.g. carcinogenicity, skin irritation etc.); and
c. environmental hazards (e.g. harmful to the aquatic environment, etc.).

Labelling of chemicals

A substance or mixture classified as hazardous and contained in packaging must bear a label including the following elements:

a. the name, address and telephone number of the supplier(s);
b. the nominal quantity of the substance or mixture in the package made available to the general public, unless this quantity is specified elsewhere on the package;
c. product identifiers as specified in Article 18;
d. where applicable, hazard pictograms in accordance with Article 19;
e. where applicable, signal words in accordance with Article 20;
f. where applicable, hazard statements in accordance with Article 21;
g. where applicable, the appropriate precautionary statements in accordance with Article 22;
h. where applicable, a section for supplemental information in accordance with Article 25.

Product identifiers

For a substance, these are usually the substance name and an identification number, as included in Annex VI of GB CLP, or the *CAS number*. Product identifiers for a mixture are usually the trade name or the designation of the mixture and the identity of all substances in the mixture that contribute to the classification of the mixture as regards acute toxicity, skin corrosion or serious eye damage, germ cell mutagenicity, carcinogenicity, reproductive toxicity, respiratory or skin sensitisation, specific target organ toxicity or aspiration hazard.

Hazard pictograms

These are intended to alert users to the presence of a hazardous chemical. They consist of a black symbol on a white background with a red frame (and must always adhere to this colour scheme); they must be sufficiently wide to be clearly visible (and not smaller than 1 cm^2). The hazard pictograms are shown in **Figure 21.1**. The colour and presentation of any label must be such that the hazard pictogram stands out clearly.

The GB CLP hazard pictograms are very similar to those used in the old labelling system (which were black on an orange background). A package may bear one or more pictograms.

Signal words

A signal word, either "Danger" or "Warning" (but not both) is assigned to hazardous chemicals, in accordance with their classification. This signal word must appear on the label. For those with less severe hazards, the signal word is "Warning" and for those with a more severe hazard, the signal word is "Danger". The signal word relevant for each specific classification is set out in Annex I of the GB CLP Regulation.

Figure 21.1: *GB CLP Hazard pictograms*

Gas under pressure Symbol: Gas cylinder	Explosive Symbol: Exploding bomb	Oxidising Symbol: Flame over circle

Flammable Symbol: Flame	Corrosive Symbol: Corrosion	Health hazard/hazardous to the ozone layer Symbol: Exclamation mark

Acute toxicity Symbol: Skulls and crossbones	Serious health hazard Symbol: Health hazard	Hazardous to the environment Symbol: Dead tree and fish

Hazard statements

These are statements that describe the nature of the hazard associated with the substance or mixture. The hazard statements to be applied are determined by the classification of the chemical and are set out in Parts 2 to 5 of Annex I of the GB CLP Regulation. Examples include statements such as:

- Extremely flammable gas;
- May be corrosive to metals;
- Toxic if swallowed.

Precautionary statements

These are statements that set out the precautions that should be taken to minimise or prevent the potential hazards that might arise when using or disposing of hazardous chemicals. The precautionary statements to be applied are set out in Parts 2 to 5 of

Annex I of the GB CLP Regulation, taking into account the hazard statements and the intended or identified use or uses of the substance or the mixture. Examples include statements such as:

- If medical advice is needed, have product container or label at hand;
- Keep container tightly closed;
- Do not eat, drink or smoke when using this product.

Supplemental information

Supplementary information may be obligatory or non-obligatory. Obligatory information is required where a hazardous chemical has particular physical or health properties and includes phrases such as:

- Reacts violently with water (this is a physical property);
- Repeated exposure may cause skin dryness or cracking (this is a health property).

Other obligatory information includes (but is not limited to) required labelling elements arising from other legislation, such as UK REACH.[22]

Non-obligatory supplemental information includes elements that are not required by legislation, but which are necessary for the safe handling and use of the product, such as usage instructions.

Statements such as "non-toxic", "non-harmful", "non-polluting", "ecological" or any other statements indicating that the substance or mixture is not hazardous or any other statements that are inconsistent with the classification of that substance or mixture must not appear on the label or packaging of any substance or mixture.

Substances restricted to professional users

UK REACH specifies that certain substances must be marked legibly and indelibly with the phrase "Restricted to professional users or For professional users only". These include:

- *Restricted to professional users*:
  - 2-naphthylamine and its salts;
  - benzidine and its salts;
  - 4-nitrobiphenyl;
  - 4-aminobiphenyl and its salts.
- *For professional users only*:
  - substances classified as flammable gases category 1 or 2, flammable liquids categories 1, 2 or 3, flammable solids category 1 or 2, substances and mixtures which, in contact with water, emit flammable gases, category 1, 2 or 3, pyrophoric liquids category 1 or pyrophoric solids category 1, regardless of whether they appear in the GB mandatory classification and labelling list or not.

General rules for labels

The label on the package must be written in English. Suppliers may use more languages on their labels than English, provided that the same details appear in all languages used.

22. The UK version of the regulation concerning the Registration, Evaluation, Authorisation and Restriction of Chemicals (REACH) (EC) 1907/2006.

Table 21.3: *Label dimensions for supply*

Capacity of package	Dimensions of label (in mm)
3 litres or less.	If possible, at least 52 × 74.
Exceeding 3 litres but not exceeding 50 litres.	At least 74 × 105.
Exceeding 50 litres but not exceeding 500 litres.	At least 105 × 148.
Exceeding 500 litres.	At least 148 × 210.

Labels must be firmly affixed to one or more surfaces of the packaging immediately containing the substance or mixture and must be able to be read horizontally when the package is set down normally. The label elements must be clearly and indelibly marked and must stand out clearly from the background and be of such size and spacing as to be easily read.

The hazard pictograms, signal word, hazard statements and precautionary statements must be located together on the label, although the supplier may decide the order of the hazard statements and precautionary statements on the label. Groups of hazard statements and groups of precautionary statements should be located together on the label by language, where more than one language is used. Supplemental information, including that arising from other legislation, should be placed in the supplemental information section of the label.

In addition to its use in hazard pictograms, colour may be used on other areas of the label to implement special labelling requirements. The dimensions of the label must be as shown in **Table 21.3**.

Derogations from labelling requirements

The following special cases have derogations from the labelling requirements:

a. transportable gas cylinders;
b. gas containers intended for propane, butane or liquefied petroleum gas;
c. aerosols and containers fitted with a sealed spray attachment and containing substances or mixtures classified as presenting an aspiration hazard;
d. metals in massive form, alloys, mixtures containing polymers, mixtures containing elastomers;
e. explosives, as referred to in section 2.1 of Annex I, placed on the market with a view to obtaining an explosive or pyrotechnic effect;
f. substances or mixtures classified as corrosive to metals but not classified as skin corrosion or as serious eye damage (Category 1).

In addition, if the size, shape or form of the packaging means that the full labelling requirements cannot be applied, GB CLP allows for the use of fold-out labels, tie-on tags or for the outer packaging to be used to include all of the necessary label elements. If it is impossible to meet the labelling requirements (because of the small size, shape or form of the package) and the full label information cannot be provided in fold-out labels, on tie-on tags or on an outer packaging, GB CLP allows for the use of reduced label information, subject to conditions specified in Annex I to the Regulation.

Packaging of chemicals

GB CLP requires that packaging containing hazardous substances or mixtures must satisfy the following requirements:

a. the packaging must be designed and constructed so that its contents cannot escape, except in cases where other more specific safety devices are prescribed;
b. the materials constituting the packaging and fastenings must not be susceptible to damage by the contents, or liable to form hazardous compounds with the contents;
c. the packaging and fastenings must be strong and solid throughout to ensure that they will not loosen and will safely meet the normal stresses and strains of handling;
d. packaging fitted with replaceable fastening devices must be designed so that it can be refastened repeatedly without the contents escaping;
e. if the product is supplied to the general public, the packaging must not have either a shape or design likely to attract or arouse the active curiosity of children or to mislead consumers, or have a similar presentation or a design used for foodstuff or animal feeding stuff or medicinal or cosmetic products, which would mislead consumers.

Child resistant fastenings and tactile warning devices

GB CLP requires that some substances or mixtures must, when supplied to the general public, be packaged with a child-resistant fastening and/or a tactile warning device. A tactile warning device is a raised triangle that can be felt by touch; it is designed to be understood by those with impaired vision.

The requirements to include a child-resistant fastening and/or a tactile warning device as part of packaging is determined either by the classification of the substance or mixture under a certain hazard class or category or because the substance meets a specified concentration. Annex II of GB CLP sets out the details of this.

Examples of classifications that would require the substance or mixture to be packaged with a child-resistant fastening include those classified for acute toxicity (categories 1-3), specific target organ toxicity (single exposure category 1 or repeated exposure category 1) and skin corrosion (category 1).

Examples of classifications that would require the substance or mixture to be packaged with a tactile warning include those classified for acute toxicity, skin corrosion, germ cell mutagenicity (category 2), carcinogenicity (category 2), reproductive toxicity (category 2), respiratory sensitisation, or specific target organ toxicity (categories 1 and 2), aspiration hazard, or flammable gases, liquids (categories 1 and 2) and solids.

UK REACH and Safety Data Sheets

Distributors (as defined under GB CLP), such as pharmacies, have duties under UK REACH (Registration, Evaluation, Authorisation and Restriction of Chemicals) Regulations[23] to pass information to their customers. UK REACH also imposes further

---

23. The UK version of the EU Regulation concerning the Registration, Evaluation, Authorisation and Restriction of Chemicals (REACH) (EC) 1907/2006 and the REACH Enforcement Regulations 2008.

duties on manufacturers, importers and downstream users. The UK Government introduced equivalent legislation to the EU requirements that previously applied in the UK and anyone making, selling or distributing chemicals within the UK must comply with UK REACH. The Health and Safety Executive has provided guidance on this transition.[24]

One important element of UK REACH is the duty to provide purchasers of chemicals with a Safety Data Sheet (SDS) pertaining to that chemical.

An SDS must be provided when a substance or mixture, which is subject to UK REACH (this will include all chemicals controlled under GB CLP), is supplied for the first time in connection with work, for example a supply to a doctor for use in their practice, to a health centre or to factories. This is to ensure that the recipient can take any necessary precautions relating to the protection of health and safety at work and relating to the protection of the environment. The SDS should be provided to the recipient free-of-charge, on paper or electronically. The supplier does not need to re-supply the SDS, for subsequent orders from the same recipient, unless the sheet's contents have changed. If there are any updates to the SDS the new version of the SDS must be supplied to all customers (who received an SDS in connection with the receipt of the substance/mixture in question) from the preceding 12 months.

SDSs do not have to be given when supplies are made to the general public for private use, so long as the supplier provides sufficient information to enable users to take the necessary measures as regards safety and the protection of human health and the environment.

Control of substances hazardous to health

The COSHH Regulations[25] impose duties on employers to protect employees and other persons who may be exposed to substances hazardous to health and impose certain duties on employees concerning their own protection in the workplace. The Regulations apply to any place of work including hospital or community pharmacies, pharmaceutical laboratories or administrative offices. They cover virtually any substance (except those subject to specific legislation such as lead, asbestos and radioactive substances) but, in a pharmacy context, are particularly relevant to chemicals and harmful microorganisms.

The COSHH Regulations require that a risk assessment is made of substances used and procedures operated in the workplace.

Risk, in relation to the exposure of an employee to a substance hazardous to health, means the likelihood that the potential for harm to the health of a person will be attained under the conditions of use and exposure, and also the extent of that harm.

Every employer must ensure that the exposure of their employees to substances hazardous to health is either prevented or, where this is not reasonably practicable, is adequately controlled.

Substances hazardous to health (which includes mixtures) means:

---

24. See: https://www.hse.gov.uk/reach/about.htm (accessed 31 December 2024).
25. Control of Substances Hazardous to Health Regulations 2002.

a. any which meets the criteria for classification as hazardous within any health hazard class laid down in the GB CLP Regulation;
b. for which the Health and Safety Executive has approved a workplace exposure limit;
c. which is a biological agent;
d. which is dust (with some exceptions);
e. which, because of its chemical or toxicological properties and the way it is used or is present at the workplace, creates a risk to health.

An employer must not carry out work which is liable to expose their employees to any hazardous substance unless they have made a suitable and sufficient assessment of the risks created by that work and the steps needed to avoid risk as set out in the Regulations. Where employees are exposed to risk, the employer must ensure that they are under suitable health surveillance. Manufacturers of substances which may be hazardous to health must provide full details (e.g. labels, leaflets, data sheets, instruction manuals) of the precautions to be taken when handling the substance. Employers must take measures to train and inform staff of the dangers associated with substances hazardous to health, to prevent or minimise exposure where possible and, if necessary, to monitor exposure and implement a health surveillance programme for all those exposed. Risk can be reduced by avoiding the substance altogether, using a safer substance or the same substance in a safer form, by enclosing the process and extracting the by-products, by improving ventilation or hygiene facilities, by instituting safer handling procedures or by introducing personal protective equipment such as gloves, masks and respirators. In cases of difficulty, advice should be sought from the local area office of the Health and Safety Executive or from the local authority environmental health officer.

Regulation of drug precursors

Regulations[26] exist to prevent the unauthorised possession or trade of a number of identified drug precursors. The aims of the Regulations are to control chemicals used in the manufacture of narcotic drugs and psychotropic substances, and to reduce drug trafficking. Drug precursors are divided into three categories:

- category 1 covers the most sensitive substances (the "main" drug precursors), for example piperonal which, in addition to legitimate use as a flavouring and in the production of perfumes, can be used in the illicit production of methamphetamine;
- category 2 covers less sensitive substances and pre-precursors, for example acetic anhydride which, in addition to its legitimate use in the photographic inductor, can be used in the illicit production of heroin; and
- category 3 covers bulk chemicals that can have different types of uses in the manufacturing process (for example, as feedstock, solvents or impurities removers).

Licensing and registration requirements vary by category. Further information from the Home Office can be found on the Government website.[27]

---

26. Controlled Drugs (Drug Precursors) (Intra-Community Trade) Regulations 2008 and Controlled Drugs (Drug Precursors) (Community External Trade) Regulations 2008.
27. See: https://www.gov.uk/guidance/precursor-chemical-licensing (accessed 31 December 2024).

Prohibition orders

The Medicines Act 1968[28] (the Act) provides power (s.62) for ministers to make a prohibition, either total or limited in some way, on the sale, supply or importation of specified classes of medicinal product or of particular medicinal products if it appears to them necessary to do so in the interest of safety. Prohibition orders are relatively rare. In *The King (on the application of (1) Transactual CIC and (2) YY) v Secretary of State for Health and Social Care and another,*[29] Mrs Justice Laing considered that this was because "the processes for obtaining a marketing authorisation (see **Chapters 4** and **5**) create a high level of assurance that the product is safe and clinically effective for the specified uses".

Before making such an Order, the ministers are required to consult the appropriate committee. These requirements may be waived if, in the opinion of the ministers, it is essential to make the Order with immediate effect to avoid serious danger to health. An Order made without consultation is effective for 3 months only but may be renewed. In 2024, following the Cass review[30] of the prescribing puberty blockers for children and young people, an emergency Prohibition Order was made without consultation and renewed on successive occasions before a final order was made (see below). Any person who, otherwise than for performing or exercising a statutory duty or power, is in possession of such a medicinal product, knowing or having reasonable cause to suspect that it was sold, supplied or imported in contravention of the Order, is guilty of an offence (s.67).

Section 62 Orders

Bal Jivan Chamcho

The sale, supply or importation of Bal Jivan Chamcho is prohibited. This is a baby tonic in the form of a dark brown aromatic solid substance affixed to a spoon-shaped metal appliance. The prohibition[31] does not apply if the importation is from an "approved country for import"[32] and is being, or is to be, exported to a country other than the UK. The prohibition also does not apply to the sale or supply to a public analyst, an authorised officer of a drugs authority, a sampling officer, a person duly authorised by an enforcement authority under the Act or a GPhC inspector.[33]

---

28. Most provisions of the Act have been repealed and incorporated into the Human Medicines Regulations 2012. Section 62 of the Act has not been repealed. Other Regulations referred to in this chapter are still in force but refer to provisions in the Medicines Act that have been repealed. The status of such provisions is unclear.
29. [2024] EWHC 1936 (Admin).
30. https://cass.independent-review.uk/home/publications/final-report/ (accessed 31 December 2024).
31. Medicines (Bal Jivan Chamcho Prohibition) (No. 2) Order 1977.
32. The term "approved country for import" has the meaning given in regulation 8(1) of the HMR.
33. Medicines (Bal Jivan Chamcho Prohibition) (No. 2) Amendment Order 1997.

Herbal products

Four other section 62 banning orders have been made in relation to herbal medicines, namely for *Aristolochia*, Mu Tong or Fangji,[34] Kava-kava[35] and Senecio[36] (see also **Chapter 17**).

Puberty blockers

The Medicines (Gonadotrophin-Releasing Hormone Analogues) (Restrictions on Private Sales and Supplies) Order 2024 prohibits sales or supplies of GnRH analogues – referred to here as *puberty blockers* (subject to review by October 2027 and at least every 4 years after that). The prohibition does not apply to supplies on NHS prescriptions because the position is covered by NHS Regulations (see **Chapter 3**). There are three exemptions for non-NHS prescriptions. These are described below.

The Prohibition Order creates the concept of a *standard private prescription* and distinguishes between a *private prescription*, which may be a prescription or a direction given in a hospital as an alternative to a prescription, and a *standard private prescription* which is defined in such a way as to exclude a direction.

The exceptions for private prescriptions and standard private prescriptions are:

1. The patient was aged over 18 on the day the prescription was issued and:
   (a) if the prescription is a standard private prescription written by an approved UK prescriber, the prescription includes the patient's age and is annotated by the prescriber with "SLS"; or
   (b) the person to whom the puberty blocker is to be sold or supplied produces to the seller/supplier a birth certificate or national identity document that verifies to the reasonable satisfaction of the seller/suppler the age and identity of the patient.
   In the case of a non-UK prescriber, the seller/supplier must obtain the evidence in 1(b).
2. In the case of a private prescription, the patient was aged under 18 at the date the prescription was issued and the prescription was issued for a purpose other than treatment for puberty suppression in respect of gender dysphoria or gender incongruence. If the prescription is a standard private prescription, the same evidence of age and identity must be provided as in 1(a) or 1(b).
3. In the case of a standard private prescription, the patient was aged under 18 and the prescription is for the purposes of puberty suppression in respect of gender dysphoria or gender incongruence and the patient had started a course of treatment with a GnRH analogue before 3 June 2024. Puberty blockers can be sold or supplied on prescriptions written after 3 June 2024 by approved UK prescribers if the patient has already started a course of treatment in the six-month period before 3 June 2024. The provisions in 1(a) and (b) for providing evidence of age identity apply to this exemption.

---

34. Medicines (Aristolochia and Mu Tong etc.) (Prohibition) Order 2001.
35. Medicines for Human Use (Kava-kava) (Prohibition) Order 2002.
36. Medicines for Human Use (Prohibition) (Senecio and Miscellaneous Amendments) Order 2008.

Chloroform

The sale or supply of medicinal products for human use which consist of or contain chloroform is prohibited[37] subject to the following exceptions. A sale or supply made:

1. by a doctor or dentist to their patient, where the medicinal product has been specially prepared by that doctor or dentist for administration to that particular patient;
2. by a doctor or dentist who has specially prepared the medicinal product at the request of another doctor or dentist for administration to a particular patient of that other doctor or dentist;
3. from a registered pharmacy or hospital or by a doctor or dentist where the medicinal product has been specially prepared in accordance with a prescription given by a doctor or dentist for a particular patient;
4. to a hospital, a doctor or a dentist for use as an anaesthetic;
5. to a person who buys it for the purpose of reselling it to a hospital, a doctor or a dentist for use as an anaesthetic;
6. where the medicinal product contains chloroform in a proportion of not more than 0.5 % w/w or v/v;
7. where the medicinal product is solely for use in dental surgery;
8. where the medicinal product is solely for use by being applied to the external surface of the body which for the purpose of this Order does not include any part of the mouth, teeth or mucous membranes;
9. where the medicinal product is for export; or
10. where the medicinal product is sold for use as an ingredient in the preparation of a substance or article in a registered pharmacy, a hospital or by a doctor or dentist.

The effect of the Prohibition Order is that only products falling within items 6 and 8 above may be sold by retail to the public.

Section 104 and Section 105 Orders

Orders made under section 104(1) of the 1968 Act can extend the application of specified provisions of the HMR or Clinical Trials Regulations[38] to articles and substances, which are not medicinal products as defined in the HMR, but which are manufactured, sold, supplied, imported or exported for use wholly or partly for a medical purpose. The Medicines (Cyanogenetic Substances) Order 1984 regulates dealings with cyanogenetic products (including sale, supply or importation), the packaging and promotion of products and miscellaneous and supplementary provisions. Licensing requirements are not applied.

Orders made under section 105(1)(a) of the Act extend the application of specified provisions of the HMR or Clinical Trials Regulations to certain substances, which are not medicinal products, but which are used in the manufacture of medicinal products.

Orders made under section 105(1)(b) and 105(2) of the Act extend the application of specified provisions of the Act to substances which, if used without proper safeguards,

37. Medicines (Chloroform Prohibition) Order 1979.
38. Medicines for Human Use (Clinical Trials) Regulations 2004.

are capable of causing damage to the health of the community, or of causing danger to the health of animals generally or of one or more species of animals. One Order has been made under this section, but has subsequently been repealed by the HMR.

SUMMARY

- The Poisons Act 1972 applies to "regulated" and "reportable" substances.
- Schedule 1A to the Act (see Appendix 4) lists the regulated and reportable substances.
- The Act includes provisions as to the possession of a licence by members of the general public who wish to import, acquire, possess or use a regulated substance; the seller must enter details of the sale on to the licence.
- There are provisions relating to the application of a warning label to the packaging of a regulated substance before it is supplied to a member of the general public.
- Regulated poisons may only be supplied to a member of the general public from a registered pharmacy, by or under the supervision of a pharmacist and records of the sale must be made.
- Sellers of regulated or reportable substances have a legal duty to report suspicious transactions, disappearances and thefts of these substances.
- There are three types of denatured alcohol, but the pharmacist is generally concerned with two types: completely denatured alcohol (CDA) and industrial denatured alcohol (IDA). There are specific Regulations governing the supply, receipt, sale, storage, and so on, of all types of denatured alcohol.
- The GB CLP Regulation applies to the Classification, Labelling and Packaging of chemicals.
- GB CLP places an obligation on manufacturers, importers and downstream users to classify substances or mixtures, in accordance with the Regulation, before placing them on the market.
- There are detailed labelling and packaging requirements for substances or mixtures controlled under GB CLP.
- The UK REACH Regulations include a duty to provide purchasers of chemicals with a Safety Data Sheet pertaining to that chemical.
- The COSHH Regulations impose duties on employers to protect employees and other persons who may be exposed to substances hazardous to health and impose certain duties on employees concerning their own protection in the workplace.
- Employers must take measures to train and inform staff of the dangers, to prevent or minimise exposure where possible and, if necessary, to monitor exposure and implement a health surveillance programme for all those exposed.
- The sale or supply of some medicinal products is either prohibited (e.g. Bal Jivan Chamcho) or prohibited subject to exceptions (e.g. chloroform).

FURTHER READING

- Control of Substances Hazardous to Health Regulations 2002.
- European Chemicals Agency (20202021) Guidance on labelling and packaging in accordance with Regulation (EC) No 1272/2008 Version 4.12.
- European Chemicals Agency: **https://echa.europa.eu/** (accessed 31 December 2024)..
- European Regulation (EC) 1272/2008 on classification, labelling and packaging of substances and mixtures.
- European Regulation (EC) 1907/2006 concerning the Registration, Evaluation, Authorisation and Restriction of Chemicals (REACH).
- Health and Safety Executive: **http://www.hse.gov.uk/chemical-classification/index.htm**; **http://www.hse.gov.uk/reach/index.htm**; **http://www.hse.gov.uk/coshh/index.htm** (accessed 31 December 2024).
- HM Revenue and Customs: **http://www.hmrc.gov.uk** (accessed 31 December 2024).
- Home Office (2014) Guidance: Refusing a sale (accessible at: **https://www.gov.uk/government/publications/refusing-a-sale/refusing-a-sale**) (accessed 31 December 2024).
- Home Office (2015) Guidance for pharmacies selling non-medicinal poisons to the general public (accessible at: **https://www.gov.uk/government/publications/guidance-for-pharmacies-selling-non-medicinal-poisons-to-the-general-public**) (accessed 31 December 2024).
- Home Office (2018) Guidance: Licensing for home users of poisons and explosive precursors (accessible at: **https://www.gov.uk/government/publications/licensing-for-home-users-of-explosives-precursors/licensing-for-home-users-of-poisons-and-explosive-precursors**) (accessed 31 December 2020)
- Home Office (2018) Guidance: Supplying explosives precursors and poisons (accessible at: **https://www.gov.uk/government/publications/supplying-explosives-precursors/supplying-explosives-precursors-and-poison**) (accessed 31 December 2024).
- Home Office: **https://www.gov.uk/government/organisations/home-office** (accessed 31 December 2024).
- Legislation (can be searched on year and SI number or title): **http://www.legislation.gov.uk** (accessed 31 December 2024).
- Production, distribution and use of denatured alcohol (Excise Notice 473) (Updated 10 September 2020) (accessible at **https://www.gov.uk/government/publications/excise-notice-473-production-distribution-and-use-of-denatured-alcohol/excise-notice-473-production-distribution-and-use-of-denatured-alcohol#recordshttps://www.gov.uk/government/publications/excise-notice-473-production-distribution-and-use-of-denatured-alcohol/excise-notice-473-production-distribution-and-use-of-denatured-alcohol**) (accessed 31December 2024).
- Regulation (EC) No 1907/2006 of the European Parliament and of the Council on the Registration, Evaluation, Authorisation and Restriction of Chemicals (REACH) (accessible at **https://echa.europa.eu/web/guest/regulations/reach/legislation**) (Accessed 31 December 2024).
- Royal Pharmaceutical Society: **www.rpharms.com** (accessed 31 December 2024).
- RPS (2018) Quick Reference Pharmacy Guides: Poisons and chemicals from pharmacy.

CHAPTER 22

Medical devices

Medical devices vary in form and can include inhalers, condoms and apps. Concerns about post-market surveillance, especially against the backdrop of the Cumberlege review have led to further changes in the law.

Introduction

The law governing medical devices in Great Britain is primarily found in the Medical Devices Regulations 2002 ("the Medical Devices Regulations"). These Regulations have been amended from time to time. The current power to make amendments is in the Medicines and Medical Devices Act 2021. The law has been influenced by the Independent Medicines and Medical Devices Safety Review chaired by Baroness Cumberlege and the Medical Devices Regulations are likely to be amended soon, as outlined below.

Definition

A medical device is defined in the Medical Devices Regulations[1] as:

> *"any instrument, apparatus, appliance, software, material or other article, whether used alone or in combination, together with any accessories, including the software intended by its manufacturer to be used specifically for diagnosis or therapeutic purposes or both and necessary for its proper application, which:*
>
> *a. is intended by the manufacturer to be used for human beings for the purpose of:*
> - *diagnosis, prevention, monitoring, treatment or alleviation of disease,*
> - *diagnosis, monitoring, treatment, alleviation of or compensation for an injury or handicap,*
> - *investigation, replacement or modification of the anatomy or of a physiological process, or*
> - *control of conception; and*
>
> *b. does not achieve its principal intended action in or on the human body by pharmacological, immunological or metabolic means, even if it is assisted in its function by such means,*
>
> *and includes devices intended to administer a medicinal product or which incorporate as an integral part a substance which, if used separately, would be a*

1. Regulation 2.

medicinal product and which is liable to act upon the body with action ancillary to that of the device."

Medical devices that may typically be sold or supplied in pharmacies include:[2]

- blood pressure monitors,
- condoms,
- dressings,
- glucose meters and test strips,
- inhalers,
- needles,
- screening tests, such as pregnancy, hepatitis B, COVID-19 or HIV,
- stoma care products,
- syringes, and
- thermometers.

There are occasions when consideration has to be given to whether a product is a medicinal product or a medical device (see below and **Chapter 5**).

In 2020, during the COVID-19 pandemic, the MHRA issued guidance[3] for members of the public and professional users about when an app is likely to be a medical device and offered practical examples:

- you enter certain information about yourself and that information is used to calculate medicine doses for you to take/inject;
- it tells you that you have a medical condition or disease or gives you an individual percentage risk score of having one; and
- it helps you manage or monitor your symptoms.

If there is a borderline between whether a product is a medical device or a medicinal product, the MHRA will determine its status.[4]

The Cumberlege review

Following the crippling, life-changing, complications suffered by women who had pelvic mesh implants inserted, the Independent Medicines and Medical Devices Safety Review was set up under Baroness Cumberlege. The review published its report *First Do No Harm*[5] in July 2020. Amongst other things, the review found that the current yellow card system for reporting adverse reactions (see **Chapter 5**) could not be relied upon

2. https://www.rpharms.com/resources/pharmacy-guides/medical-devices (accessed 31 December 2024).
3. https://www.gov.uk/government/publications/regulatory-status-of-software-including-apps-used-in-the-diagnosis-treatment-and-management-of-patients-with-coronavirus-covid-19/advice-for-members-of-the-public-and-professional-users-software-and-apps-used-in-covid-19-pandemic (accessed 31 December 2024.
4. https://assets.publishing.service.gov.uk/government/uploads/system/uploads/attachment_data/file/948871/Borderlines_between_medical_devices_and_medicinal_products.pdf (accessed 31 December 2024).
5. https://www.immdsreview.org.uk/downloads/IMMDSReview_Web.pdf (accessed 31 December 2024).

to identify promptly significant adverse outcomes arising from a device, and the system was not safe enough for those being treated using new devices and techniques, exposing them to risk of harm when they did not need to be. Among other things, the review recommended:

- more robust, publicly accessible post-marketing surveillance of devices;
- a statutory requirement for adverse event reporting;
- a register of devices to make it possible to know which devices are (or were) on the UK market at any given time. Entry on the register should be a condition for selling in the UK, with the MHRA being able to de-register devices and remove them from sale, if necessary; and
- the MHRA's role would be more akin to a licensing authority than in the past, including involvement in the pre-market phase of medical device development and a greater emphasis on vigilance.

Post-market surveillance

Part 4A of the MDR applies to medical devices put into service by the manufacturer or placed on the market on or after 16 June 2025.

The provisions of Part 4A include:

- Regulation 44ZE requires manufacturers to have a post-market surveillance system. Regulation 44ZF specifies the contents of a post-market surveillance plan.
- Regulations 44ZG, 44ZJ and 44ZK set requirements in relation to preventive actions, corrective actions, and field safety corrective actions.
- Regulations 44ZH and 44ZI, and 44ZL to 44ZP impose investigation and reporting requirements on manufacturers in relation to serious incidents, trends in incidents and the post-market surveillance of their devices generally.
- Regulation 44ZQ provides for the retention of the documentation produced by manufacturers.

Registration and the MHRA

Under regulation 7A of the Medical Devices Regulations, a person may not place a medical device on the market unless that person is established in Great Britain. A person who places a device on the market must first:

(a) if they are a manufacturer based in Great Britain, have informed the MHRA of their registered place of business;
(b) if they are a manufacturer based outside Great Britain, have appointed a sole UK responsible person who has provided evidence of the manufacturer's written authority to act as their responsible person;
(c) if that person is not the manufacturer, provide the MHRA with the address of their registered place of business in Great Britain.

A description of every medical device must have been supplied by the person who places it on the market.

The expression *placing on the market* means the first making available in return for payment or free of charge of a new or fully refurbished device, other than a device intended for clinical investigation, with a view to distribution, use, or both, on the Great Britain market.[6]

The MHRA's functions include:

- the registration of manufacturers;
- the registration of devices;
- designating and monitoring UK Conformity Assessment Bodies;
- performing market surveillance of medical devices; and
- investigating as a result of adverse incident reports or intelligence indicating a potential problem.

The MHRA has power to enter premises for the purpose of carrying out inspections, to require the production of documents and to seize records or goods as evidence in proceedings for an offence in respect of a contravention.

Responsible Person for overseas manufacturers

In order to be registered with the MHRA, a manufacturer who is not already established in the UK must, in most cases, designate a Responsible Person to register and act on its behalf.[7] The Responsible Person will assume the responsibilities of the manufacturer in terms of registering the device with the MHRA and will carry out specified tasks in relation to the manufacturer's obligations.

In summary, the UK Responsible Person must:

- ensure that the declaration of conformity and technical documentation have been drawn up and, where applicable, that an appropriate conformity assessment procedure has been carried out by the manufacturer;
- keep available a copy of the technical documentation, a copy of the declaration of conformity and, if applicable, a copy of the relevant certificate, including any amendments and supplements for inspection by the MHRA;
- in response to a request from the MHRA, provide the MHRA with all the information and documentation necessary to demonstrate the conformity of a device;
- forward to the manufacturer any request by the MHRA for samples, or access to a device, and ensure that the MHRA receives the samples or has been given access to the device;
- co-operate with the MHRA on any preventive or corrective action taken to eliminate or, if that is not possible, mitigate the risks posed by devices;
- immediately inform the manufacturer about complaints and reports from healthcare professionals, patients and users about suspected incidents related to a device for which they have been designated; and
- terminate the legal relationship with the manufacturer if the manufacturer acts contrary to its obligations under these Regulations and inform the MHRA and, if applicable, the relevant notified body or UK Approved Body of that termination.

6. Regulation 2 of the Medical Devices Regulations 2002.
7. Regulation 7A.

CE marking

Before the UK's exit from the European Union, the Medical Devices Regulations prohibited the placing on the market or putting into service a medical device unless that device, or its sterile pack, bore a CE[8] marking. Conformity was assessed in the case of each device by a notified body. Medical devices with CE marking may still be placed on the market in Great Britain (see below) according to the following timelines:

- general medical devices compliant with the EU medical devices directive (EU MDD) or EU active implantable medical devices directive (EU AIMDD) with a valid declaration – until the sooner of expiry of certificate or 30 June 2028;
- in vitro diagnostic medical devices (IVDs) compliant with the EU in vitro diagnostic medical devices directive (EU IVDD) until the sooner of expiry of certificate or 30 June 2030; and
- general medical devices, including custom-made devices, compliant with the EU medical devices regulation (EU MDR) and IVDs compliant with the EU in vitro diagnostic medical devices regulation (EU IVDR) until the 30 June 2030.

UKCA marking

From 1 January 2021, following the UK's exit from the EU, a *UKCA* mark was introduced in Great Britain[9] (alongside the continued validity of CE marking); see **Figure 22.1**. The initials UKCA stand for "United Kingdom Conformity Assessment".

Figure 22.1: *The United Kingdom Conformity Assessment (UKCA) mark.*

A medical device may not be placed on the market in Great Britain unless it bears a UK marking or a valid CE marking (see above).[10] The MHRA is responsible for the designation and monitoring of UK Conformity Assessment Bodies.

In most cases, the UKCA marking must be applied to the product itself or to the packaging. Only the manufacturer or the manufacturer's authorised representative may place the UKCA marking on a product. The manufacturer must not attach other markings on the product that would affect the visibility, legibility or meaning of the UKCA marking.

8. The letters are an abbreviation of Conformité Europèene.
9. https://www.gov.uk/guidance/using-the-ukca-mark-from-1-january-2021#future-use-of-markings-in-the-uk (accessed 31 December 2024).
10. Regulation 10 of the Medical Devices Regulations.

By attaching the UKCA marking, the MHRA will treat the manufacturer as taking full responsibility for its product's conformity with the requirements of the relevant UK legislation. The UKCA marking may not be used to show conformity with any other legislation.

A CE marked device with a valid declaration of conformity will be viewed as meeting the UKCA mark requirements while the CE mark continues to be recognised in Great Britain. Therefore, any enforcement or market surveillance powers available in respect of the UKCA mark will apply to CE marked devices.

Approved Bodies

The MHRA designates Approved Bodies, of which it maintains a register. It is the function of Approved Bodies to assess conformity with the standards of safety and performance appropriate to the device before the device can be placed on the market. This involves full quality assurance, examination of design and assessment of full technical examination and unannounced audits of manufacturers.

The Court of Appeal considered the issue of continued compliance and the manufacturer's duty to satisfy the Approved Body of a product's safety in *R (on the application of RRR Manufacturing Pty Ltd) v British Standards Institution and MHRA*.[11] The case is outlined in **Box 22.1**.

Box 22.1

In *R (on the application of RRR Manufacturing Pty Ltd) v British Standards Institution and MHRA*, RRR Manufacturing Pty Ltd (RRR) was the manufacturer of a small, portable defibrillator. It was a medical device. It had previously been granted a certificate by the British Standards Institution (BSI) which was an Approved Body.

BSI wrote to RRR to say it had received concerns that there was a "lack of available clinical data to confirm safe and effective use" of the defibrillator. RRR applied to the court for an order requiring BSI to renew its certificate when the certificate expired. RRR argued that there was no evidence that the defibrillator was not safe.

The court (on appeal) held that an order should not be made. Lady Justice Elizabeth Laing said:

> *"BSI does not have to satisfy the court that the device is unsafe; RRR, rather, has to satisfy BSI that the device is safe … The underlying principles which apply to the facts of this case are, first, that great weight must be given to the protection of public health, and, second, in this regulatory framework, that the manufacturer must satisfy the approved body that a device is safe and effective …"*[12]

12. [2024] EWCA Civ 530.

11. [2024] EWCA Civ 530.

Manufacturers must keep documentation to demonstrate that their products conform to the regulatory requirements. These documents must be retained for up to 10 years after the product was placed on the market.

Enforcement

Regulation 61 of the Medical Devices Regulations places a duty on each weights and measures authority (operated by local authorities) to enforce the Regulations. Section 12 of the Consumer Protection Act 1987 creates various offences that would apply if UKCA and CE marking requirements are not complied with. It follows that if a medical device has marking that is not genuine, a person who sold it would be committing an offence even if that person did not know and could not reasonably have discovered that the marking was not genuine. The absence of a central registry against which to check the genuineness of markings has been a serious deficiency.

Where the MHRA, as the enforcement authority, has reasonable grounds to suspect that a person involved in marketing or supplying a medical device is not complying with a medical devices provision, it may serve a compliance notice,[13] requiring specified measures to be taken to comply with that provision. Alternatively, a suspension notice may be served,[14] prohibiting the person on whom it is served from supplying a medical device, offering to supply it, agreeing to supply it, exposing it for supply or possessing it for supply. Alternatively, a safety notice may be served,[15] imposing prohibitions or requirements that are considered necessary to restrict the availability of a medical device in order to protect health or safety. For the purpose of deciding whether to serve or revoke a compliance notice, a suspension notice or a safety notice, an information notice may be served.[16] Breach of any of these notices is an offence.[17] However, it is a defence for a person charged with an offence to show that they took all reasonable steps and exercised all due diligence to avoid commission of the offence (section 29 of the Act). If an offence is committed by a body corporate or a Scottish partnership and is proved to have been committed with the consent or connivance of, or to be attributable to any neglect on the part of an officer, that officer as well as the body corporate or partnership commits an offence.

As an alternative to criminal sanctions, if the Secretary of State is satisfied beyond reasonable doubt that a person has committed an offence in breaching an enforcement notice or certain other provisions of the Regulations, a financial penalty may be imposed.[18] This would be a civil sanction, not a criminal one, so no criminal record would be involved.

---

13. Section 21 of the Medicines and Medical Devices Act.
14. Section 18 of the Medicines and Medical Devices Act.
15. Section 19 of the Medicines and Medical Devices Act.
16. Section 22 of the Medicines and Medical Devices Act.
17. Section 28 of the Medicines and Medical Devices Act.
18. Schedule 2 to the Medicines and Medical Devices Act.

Section 35 of the Act empowers the enforcement authority to organise a recall of a device if this is necessary in order to protect health or safety if the device has already been supplied or made available to members of the public.

Future changes

At the time of writing, the MHRA has conducted a consultation on an international reliance scheme which would involve reliance on authorisations granted in the EU, Australia, Canada and the USA.

SUMMARY

- Medical devices are regulated by the Medical Devices Regulations 2002.
- UKCA marking has effect alongside CE marking .
- Overseas manufacturers without a place of business in the UK must have a Responsible Person in the UK.
- The MHRA is responsible for regulation and enforcement except that some enforcement powers, as specified in this chapter, rest with the local weights and measures authority.

FURTHER READING

- MHRA – An introductory guide to the Medical Device Regulation **https://assets.publishing.service.gov.uk/government/uploads/system/uploads/attachment_data/file/640404/MDR_IVDR_guidance_Print_13.pdf** (accessed 31 December 2024).
- MHRA – Regulating medical devices in the UK **https://www.gov.uk/guidance/regulating-medical-devices-in-the-uk** (accessed 5 August 2024 (accessed 31 December 2024).
- Royal Pharmaceutical Society – Medical devices **https://www.rpharms.com/resources/pharmacy-guides/medical-devices** (accessed 31 December 2024).

CHAPTER 23

Confidentiality and data protection

The common law has always protected patient information. The Data Protection Act 2018 and UK General Data Protection Regulation (GDPR) add extra layers of protection. Breach of the duty of confidentiality and the misuse of private information may give rise to claims for damages. Data protection breaches may result in criminal prosecution or the imposition of heavy financial penalties that are civil, not criminal. Unauthorised access to patient information may result in fitness to practise proceedings.

Confidentiality

Information that is confidential

The common law protects information that is, by its nature, provided or received in confidence. Information provided by a patient to a healthcare professional is a classic example of such confidential information, and the healthcare professional has a legal duty to keep the confidence. The duty is not to disclose confidential information – negligently failing to protect computerised information from being hacked would not give rise to liability.[1] Whether an employer is vicariously liable for a breach of confidentiality by an employee or others is considered in **Chapter 26**.

A patient who has mental capacity may consent to the disclosure of confidential information and consent may be oral or in writing. However, in the absence of consent, a person who breaches a duty to maintain confidence, for example by obtaining information without a patient's consent or by the unauthorised use of confidential information, may face fitness to practise proceedings and/or may be sued for compensation by the person whose confidentiality has been breached.

Confidentiality does not normally cease on the death of a patient. However, it may be necessary to obtain the authorisation of a court to override confidentiality, for example on the basis of the public interest – see the case of *Lewis v Secretary of State for Health*[2] in **Box 23.1**].

1. *Warren v DSG Retail Ltd* [2021] EWHC 2168 (QB).
2. [2008] EWHC 2196 (QB).

Box 23.1: *Lewis v Secretary of State for Health*

In early 2007, it emerged that some individuals who had worked in the nuclear industry at Sellafield in Cumbria and who had died between November 1962 and August 1991 had had tissues removed for analysis. The analysis was to determine the presence, if any, of radionuclides within the organs. It was uncertain whether the next-of-kin knew or had been asked for consent. As a result, the Secretary of State for Trade and Industry set up the Redfern Inquiry. The remit of the Inquiry was widened when it became apparent that similar practices may have been used in respect of people who had worked at the Atomic Weapons Establishment at Aldermaston.

Dr Nicholas Lewis was a medical practitioner who specialised in occupational health involved in the company that provided occupational health services to those working at AWE Aldermaston; he was the custodian of occupational health records of about 30,000 former employees at AWE Aldermaston, many of whom were dead. Dr Lewis was asked to disclose records to the Inquiry. He was concerned that the records remained confidential and should not be disclosed.

Mr Justice Foskett held that a patient's confidentiality was capable of continuing after a patient's death.

He said:

> *"I would not regard … the passage of time generally in a matter of this nature, as eradicating or diminishing significantly the strength of the obligation of confidentiality."*

The judge went on to hold that confidentiality is not absolute in the sense that it could be overridden and this was an appropriate case in which to hold that the public interest in disclosure of the material sought outweighed the public interest in maintaining the confidentiality of medical records and information, provided proper safeguards were put in place to ensure that no inappropriate information became public. The judge pointed out that there was a difference between something that was in the public interest and something that interested the public. He therefore authorised the disclosure subject to a number of conditions to provide necessary safeguards.

The General Pharmaceutical Council's *Standards for registered pharmacies*[3] include at Principle 1.7:

> *"Information is managed to protect the privacy, dignity and confidentiality of patients and the public who receive pharmacy services."*

A Performance Monitoring Report included in General Pharmaceutical Council (GPhC) papers in December 2017 referred to breach of Principle 1.7 as having entered the "top five standards not met" for the preceding quarter. The report listed typical issues found on inspections as:

- prescription forms being left on the medicines counter; and
- cases where the consultation room was being used for additional dispensing space but without appropriate precautions being taken to protect patient data.

3. https://assets.pharmacyregulation.org/files/document/standards_for_registered_pharmacies_june_2018_0.pdf (accessed 31 December 2024).

The GPhC has also published *In practice: Guidance on confidentiality.*[4] The Guidance refers to the trust that people have that their confidentiality and privacy will be maintained by pharmacy professionals, whether in a healthcare setting or online. It describes maintaining confidentiality as a vital part of the relationship between a pharmacy professional and a person under their care. The Guidance points out that a person may be reluctant to ask for advice, or give a pharmacy professional the information they need to provide proper care if they believe that the pharmacy professional may not keep the information confidential. As the Guidance points out, confidential information includes:

- electronic and hard copy data,
- personal details,
- information about a person's medication (prescribed and non-prescribed),
- other information about a person's medical history, treatment or care that could identify them, and
- information that people share that is not strictly medical in nature, but that the person disclosing it would expect to keep confidential.

In 2024, the GPhC's Fitness to Practise Committee (the Committee) dealt with the case of a pharmacist who had accessed without authority the medical records of three patients on more than 30 occasions. Details of the case are set out in **Box 23.2**.

Box 23.2

The Fitness to Practise Committee decided that the pharmacist had breached the GPhC's Standard 6 by not behaving in a professional manner and by not maintaining and respecting the confidentiality and privacy of the three people, and by abusing his position and not demonstrating leadership.

The Fitness to Practise Committee described the unauthorised access as:

> *"a course of conduct of such seriousness that it must be marked by a finding of current impairment as the public would rightly expect a public declaration that this behaviour is unacceptable and that a sanction be considered."*

The Fitness to Practise Committee also described the pharmacist's conduct as a breach of trust because he had abused his privileged access, as a pharmacist, to NHS medical records. The Fitness to Practise Committee said:

> *"Patients increasingly rely on healthcare professionals having ready access to their medical records online and on these records being accessible by the various specialist services, including pharmacy. The public needs to be able to trust that healthcare professionals will only access such records when clinically required and with consent. It is therefore especially important that misconduct comprising unauthorised access to such records is marked in public and that the Standards are declared and upheld."*

The sanction imposed by the Fitness to Practise Committee was a warning.
The Committee said:

---

4. https://assets.pharmacyregulation.org/files/2024-01/in_practice_guidance_on_confidentiality_june_2018.pdf (accessed 31 December 2024).

Box 23.2 (cont.)

"The purpose of this warning is to mark the seriousness of the misconduct and to remind the profession of the importance of only accessing any person's medical records when clinically necessary and with the person's consent. As health care professionals rely on having access to and sharing medical records, it is imperative that the public can trust that their confidential medical records are safe and that all healthcare professionals with privileged access to such data respect their privacy and access records in accordance with the high standards of professionalism expected of them."

Even though information is confidential, there may be some cases in which it can be disclosed because the patient does not have a reasonable expectation that the information will be withheld from disclosure. The case of *W, X, Y and Z v the Secretary of State for Health and the Secretary of State for the Home Department*[5] (see **Box 23.3**) is an example of such a case.

Box 23.3: *W, X, Y and Z v the Secretary of State for Health and the Secretary of State for the Home Department*

Immigration Rules had been introduced that enabled sanctions to be imposed on individuals who were not resident in the UK and who had unpaid NHS debts of at least £1,000. The applicants challenged the lawfulness of guidance that proposed that NHS Trusts should pass patient information to the Department of Health for transmission to the Home Office to take action to recover the debts.

The Court of Appeal held that the information to be transmitted was not confidential for the purpose of the guidance. The Court also addressed the concerns of doctors expressed through the British Medical Association which had made submissions in the case. Lord Dyson, the Master of the Rolls, said:

"We accept ... that the Information is inherently private information, particularly because it reveals information of substance about the health of the data subjects, namely that they were unwell to the extent that they had to seek medical care at a particular point in time from one or more NHS bodies. In our view ... there would be a reasonable expectation of privacy in respect of such information on the part of the patient. The fact that the data also includes charging information, which in itself reveals whether the treatment was relatively fleeting or extensive, only reinforces the conclusion that the Information is inherently private in nature.

A patient liable to charges will reasonably expect that, in the event of default, steps will be taken to enforce payment, which may include informing others of the fact, duration and cost of his stay at the hospital concerned; and that to this extent their stay at the hospital will not necessarily be kept confidential ... the question whether there is a reasonable expectation of privacy is a broad one which takes account of all the circumstances of the case. We do not see how overseas visitors who, before they are treated in an NHS hospital, are made aware of the fact that, if they incur charges in excess of £1,000 and do not pay them within three months, the Information may be

5. [2014] EWHC 1532 (Admin).

Box 23.3: *W, X, Y and Z v the Secretary of State for Health and the Secretary of State for the Home Department* (cont.)

passed to the Secretary of State for onward transmission to the Home Office for the stated immigration purpose can have any, still less any reasonable, expectation that the Information will not be transmitted in precisely that way.

The present case is concerned with a particular regime under which patients are usually informed that the limited details contained in the Information may be disclosed to a limited class of persons for a particular reason connected with immigration control. It should not be seen as a Trojan horse which will lead to the dismantling of the principle that information about a person's health and medical treatment is inherently private and confidential."

The case of *Scott v LGBT Foundation*[6] referred to in **Box 23.8** below is another example.

Information that is not confidential

If a patient waives their right to confidentiality or consents to the use of their information, the information will cease to be confidential to the extent of that waiver or consent.

Anonymised information may be used without breaching confidentiality. This is illustrated by the *Source Informatics* case[7] described in **Box 23.4**.

Box 23.4: *R v Department of Health, ex parte Source Informatics Limited*

Source informatics (Source) was a company concerned for commercial reasons to obtain information as to doctors' prescribing habits. Source then sell this information on to pharmaceutical companies so that they may more effectively market their products. The information was derived from prescription forms presented at pharmacies. Source had no interest in the names of patients or information that could identify them. It wanted, in particular the prescribers' names and the products they prescribed. To obtain these details, they paid pharmacies £150 per annum. In return, pharmacies downloaded anonymised information using specially designed computer software. The information was passed to Source which aggregated it in the form of a database. The information would enable pharmaceutical companies to target more precisely promotions and communications regarding their products.

The Department of Health issued a policy document that stated that the provision of anonymised data breached patients' confidence. Source challenged the lawfulness of the policy document in an application for judicial review. The Court of Appeal upheld Source's argument that the policy document did not accurately reflect the law. Lord Justice Simon Brown said:

6. [2020] EWHC 483 (QB).

7. [2001] QB 424.

Box 23.4: *R v Department of Health, ex parte Source Informatics Limited* (cont.)

"The patient has no proprietorial claim to the prescription form or the information it contains. Of course, he can bestow or withhold his custom as he pleases – the pharmacist, note, has no such right: he is by law bound to dispense to whoever presents a prescription. But that gives the patient no property in the information and no right to control its use provided only and always that his privacy is not put at risk ... pharmacists' consciences ought not reasonably to be troubled by co-operation with Source's proposed scheme. The patient's privacy will have been safeguarded, not invaded. The pharmacist's duty of confidence will not have been breached ...

Participation in Source's scheme by doctors and pharmacists would not, in my judgment, expose them to any serious risk of successful breach of confidence proceedings by a patient (any more than were a prescribing doctor, asked by a manufacturer's representative what medicine he ordinarily prescribes for a given condition, to answer candidly on the basis of his current practice)."

There is a legal duty in England and Wales, and a professional duty in Scotland to report female genital mutilation (see **Chapter 24**) and reporting it would not breach any duty of confidentiality.[8]

Lawful disclosure of confidential information

Confidential information may be disclosed without a patient's consent where:

- this is authorised by statute or a court order;
- this is authorised by a warrant issued by a justice of the peace (see **Chapter 2**);
- it is required by a GPhC inspector; (see **Chapter 2**);
- notice has been given by a Coroner to provide evidence or produce documents (see **Chapter 1**);
- health records or information have been requested by a medical examiner (see **Chapter 1**);[9]
- it is in the public interest because it is essential to protect the patient or third parties from the risk of death or serious harm. Notification of an infectious disease may be an example of disclosure in the public interest (See the section on Notifiable diseases in **Chapter 2**). For example, the case of *W v Edgell*[10] (**Box 23.5**) illustrates the balancing of the right to confidentiality against other rights.

---

8. Section 5B of the Female Genital Mutilation Act 2003 imposes the duty on healthcare professionals, and provides that reporting will not breach any obligation of confidence.
9. In the case of information, regulation 25A of the Medical Certification of Cause of Death Regulations 2024 provides that the supply of information does not breach any obligation of confidence.
10. [1990] Ch. 359.

Box 23.5: *W v Edgell*

W suffered from paranoid schizophrenia. He had shot and killed five people and injured two others. He pleaded guilty at his trial to manslaughter on the grounds of diminished responsibility and he was ordered to be detained in a secure hospital. W's responsible medical officer recommended to the Secretary of State that W be transferred to a secure unit with a possible view to W's future release. The Secretary of State refused to consent to W's transfer. In support of an application to a mental health review tribunal, W sought a report from an Edgell, an independent consultant psychiatrist. The report did not support W's application. It disclosed that W had a longstanding and continuing interest in home-made bombs. Edgell did not accept that W was no longer a danger to the public. W withdrew his application and refused to consent to Edgell disclosing the report to the medical officer at the secure hospital. Edgell was concerned that those treating W should know the contents of his report and sent it to the medical officer. It was also sent to the Secretary of State. W sued for an injunction to restrain Edgell from communicating the contents of his report.

The Court held that although W had a personal interest to ensure that his confidentiality was not breached, the maintenance of the duty of confidence by a doctor to his patient was a matter of public interest; and the public interest in maintaining that confidence was outweighed by the public interest in protecting others against possible violence.

Misuse of private information

Separate from the tort of breach of confidentiality, there is also a tort of misuse of private information.[11] Liability is determined by applying a two-stage test: (1) does the claimant have a reasonable expectation of privacy in the relevant information; and (2) if yes, is that outweighed by countervailing interests. To justify a claim, the information that is disclosed must "reach a level of seriousness". In *Underwood v Bounty UK Limited*, the court held that the disclosure by a hospital trust of a patient's name, gender and date of birth to a commercial organisation did not reach the level of seriousness that would enable a claim to succeed.[12]

The right to privacy under the European Convention on Human Rights

Article 8 of the European Convention on Human Rights which is incorporated into UK law through the Human Rights Act 1998 (see **Chapter 1**) says:

> *"Everyone has the right to respect for his private and family life, his home and his correspondence."*

The case of *LH v Latvia*[13] in **Box 23.6** illustrates how the right to privacy has been dealt with in relation to medical records.

---

11. *Vidal-Hall v Google Inc* [2015] EWCA Civ 311.
12. *Underwood v Bounty UK Limited* [2022] EWHC 888 (QB).
13. [2014] ECHR 453.

Box 23.6: *LH v Latvia*

The applicant, LH, gave birth at a state hospital in Latvia. She brought a claim against the hospital, alleging that a tubal ligation had been performed without her consent. In the meanwhile, the Inspectorate of Quality Control for Medical Care and Fitness for Work, at the request of the hospital's director, initiated an administrative inquiry concerning the care given to the applicant over a seven-year period. The Inspectorate received files from three medical institutions and issued a report containing sensitive medical details. The summary of the conclusions was sent to the medical director. In response to LH's complaint, the Latvian Government argued that it was entitled to monitor the quality of healthcare with the aim of protecting the public interest.

The European Court of Human Rights was not satisfied that the collection of the applicant's data was necessary for the purposes of medical treatment or the provision or administration of health services and any public interest the Inspectorate was pursuing had not been identified. The Court noted that the Inspectorate appeared to have collected the applicant's medical data indiscriminately, without any prior assessment of whether the data collected would be potentially decisive, relevant or of importance for achieving whatever aim might have been pursued by the Inspectorate. The lack of an identified justifiable purpose may be contrasted with the *W, X, Y and Z* case referred to above.

The Court upheld LH's claim that her Article 8 rights had been violated. It said:

"It is crucial not only to respect the sense of privacy of a patient but also to preserve confidence in the medical profession and in the health services in general."

The Court awarded her €11,000 by way of compensation.

Where there is a reasonable expectation of privacy, damages can be awarded without a claimant having to prove that distress or material damage has been caused (unlike a claim for breach of the Data Protection Act and the General Data Protection Regulation,[14] as to which, see below).

Confidentiality when a pharmacy is sold

Pharmacies maintain patient records for a variety of purposes. When a pharmacy is sold to a new owner, the question arises whether the seller is able to provide to the new owner the patient records in order to facilitate seamless care for the patients in question. For example, the new owner may need to know about repeat prescriptions that patients may request. In these circumstances, it is not practicable to obtain the consent of patients except possibly on a piecemeal basis.

The transfer of records to a new owner seems to be common practice. Patients may not know that a pharmacy has a new owner. Subject to the requirements of the Data Protection Act and UK GDPR (see below), for example as to how long the seller has held the records (see below), the *W, X, Y and Z* case (see above) indicates that the existence of the duty of confidence depends on what patients may reasonably expect. If a patient reasonably expects that information provided to the owner of a pharmacy from which the patient seeks services will be transferred to a new owner if the pharmacy is sold, in

14. *Lloyd v Google LLC* [2021] UKSC 50.

order for the patient to continue to receive the same services, there would not be a breach of the duty of confidence owed by the seller.

Caldicott principles and the duty to share information

In 1997, the Caldicott Committee recommended six good practice principles to be applied to the use of confidential information in the NHS. It also recommended that a senior person, preferably a health professional, should be nominated in each health organisation to act as a guardian, responsible for safeguarding the confidentiality of patient information. Every NHS organisation has had to have a Caldicott Guardian since 1998, and each local authority with adult social care responsibilities has been required to do so since 2002. Additional principles have since been added to encourage information sharing in the best interests of patients, service users and users of social care services and to increase transparency in the way confidential data are used.

The eight Caldicott Principles are set out in **Box 23.7**.

Box 23.7: The Caldicott Principles

Good information sharing is essential for providing safe and effective care. There are also important uses of information for purposes other than individual care, which contribute to the overall delivery of health and social care or serve wider public interests.

These principles apply to the use of confidential information within health and social care organisations and when such information is shared with other organisations and between individuals, both for individual care and for other purposes.

The principles are intended to apply to all data collected for the provision of health and social care services where patients and service users can be identified and would expect that it will be kept private. This may include for instance, details about symptoms, diagnosis, treatment, names and addresses. In some instances, the principles should also be applied to the processing of staff information.

They are primarily intended to guide organisations and their staff, but it should be remembered that patients, service users and/or their representatives should be included as active partners in the use of confidential information.

Where a novel and/or difficult judgment or decision is required, it is advisable to involve a Caldicott Guardian.

Principle 1: Justify the purpose(s) for using confidential information
Every proposed use or transfer of confidential information should be clearly defined, scrutinised and documented, with continuing uses regularly reviewed by an appropriate guardian.

Principle 2: Use confidential information only when it is necessary
Confidential information should not be included unless it is necessary for the specified purpose(s) for which the information is used or accessed. The need to identify individuals should be considered at each stage of satisfying the purpose(s) and alternatives used where possible

Principle 3: Use the minimum necessary confidential information
Where use of confidential information is considered to be necessary, each item of information must be justified so that only the minimum amount of confidential information is included as necessary for a given function.

Box 23.7: The Caldicott Principles (cont.)

Principle 4: Access to confidential information should be on a strict need-to-know basis
Only those who need access to confidential information should have access to it, and then only to the items that they need to see. This may mean introducing access controls or splitting information flows where one flow is used for several purposes.

Principle 5: Everyone with access to confidential information should be aware of their responsibilities
Action should be taken to ensure that all those handling confidential information understand their responsibilities and obligations to respect the confidentiality of patients and service users.

Principle 6: Comply with the law
Every use of confidential information must be lawful. All those handling confidential information are responsible for ensuring that their use of and access to that information complies with legal requirements set out in statute and under the common law.

Principle 7: The duty to share information for individual care is as important as the duty to protect patient confidentiality
Health and social care professionals should have the confidence to share confidential information in the best interests of patients and service users within the framework set out by these principles. They should be supported by the policies of their employers, regulators and professional bodies.

Principle 8: Inform patients and service users about how their confidential information is used
A range of steps should be taken to ensure no surprises for patients and service users, so they can have clear expectations about how and why their confidential information is used, and what choices they have about this. These steps will vary depending on the use: as a minimum, this should include providing accessible, relevant and appropriate information – in some cases, greater engagement will be required.

Using statutory powers,[15] the National Data Guardian for Health and Social Care has issued guidance about the processing of health and adult social care data in England.[16] A person providing NHS services must have regard to the guidance[17] recommending the appointment of a Caldicott Guardian by public bodies exercising functions relating to the health service, adult social care or adult carer support in England and by other persons or organisations providing services as part of the publicly funded health service. This recommendation thus includes pharmacies and dispensing doctors who provide NHS services.

15. Section 1(2) of the Health and Social Care (National Data Guardian) Act 2018. The Act applies to England and Wales, but the power to publish guidance relates only to England.
16. https://assets.publishing.service.gov.uk/government/uploads/system/uploads/attachment_data/file/1013756/Caldicott_Guardian_guidance_v1.0_27.08.21.pdf (accessed 31 December 2024).
17. Section 1(3)(b)(i) of the Health and Social Care (National Data Guardian) Act 2018.

The role of Caldicott Guardians is to assist with processing of confidential data of patients and service users of publicly funded services. The guidance stipulates that Caldicott Guardians must be afforded the freedom to exercise their judgement and advise or decide in the best interests of patients and service users. The role may overlap with that of Data Protection Officer and the same person could carry out the same roles as long as no conflict of interest arises. The Caldicott Guardian need not be an employee, but the role could be provided by another organisation and/or could be shared with other providers of healthcare services.

According to the guidance, the Caldicott Guardian should:

> *"play a key role in helping to ensure that their organisation(s) satisfy the highest ethical and legal standards for processing patient and service user confidential information. Their main concern is confidential information relating to patients, service users and their care. However, in some circumstances the Caldicott Guardian's judgment may also be needed in relation to the use of information about other individuals, such as staff or relatives of service users."*

Organisations are responsible for including their Caldicott Guardian's contact details on the Caldicott Guardian register, which is maintained by NHS Digital.[18]

Section 251B of the Health and Social Care Act 2012[19] creates a duty to share information about an individual that is held by a relevant health or adult social care commissioner or provider (referred to as the *relevant person*). The relevant person must ensure that the information is disclosed to:

1. persons working for the relevant person; and
2. any other relevant health or adult social care commissioner or provider with whom the relevant person communicates about the individual.

The duty only applies so far as the relevant person considers that disclosure is:

a. likely to facilitate the provision to the individual of health services or adult social care in England; and
b. in the individual's best interests.

The relevant person need not comply with the duty to disclose if the relevant person reasonably considers that either:

1. the individual objects, or would be likely to object, to the disclosure of the information;
2. the information concerns, or is connected with, the provision of health services or adult social care by an anonymous access provider; or
3. for any other reason the relevant person is not reasonably able, or should not be required to, comply with the duty.

The duty does not permit the relevant person to do anything that would be inconsistent with the common law duty of care (see **Chapter 24**) or the common law

18. NHS Digital is part of NHS England, as to which, see below.
19. This section was added to the Act in 2015.

duty of confidence (see above), or which would be inconsistent with the Data Protection Act (see below).

Data protection

Data Protection Act 2018

Data protection is regulated by the Information Commissioner and enforced by the *Information Commissioner's Office* (ICO).[20]

The Data Protection Act 2018 incorporates the UK GDPR (General Data Protection Regulation). This regulates the processing of personal data and imposes legal obligations on data controllers and data processors. The broad definitions include:

- *personal data*, any information relating to an identified or identifiable natural person ("data subject");
- *data controller*, decides what data to process and how;
- *processing*, the collection, recording, organisation, structuring, storage, retrieval, consultation, use and disclosure of data.

Pharmacy owners will, therefore, be data controllers and any pharmacy employee or locum who deals with data will be a processor.

The definition of *processing* does not cover information that is disclosed only verbally. This was confirmed in the case of *Scott v LGBT Foundation*,[21] described in **Box 23.8** below.

Box 23.8: Scott v LGBT Foundation

The LGBT Foundation is a charity which supports the needs of lesbian, gay, bisexual and transgender communities. Its services including counselling and advice in relation to health and wellbeing. The claimant, Mr Scott, completed a self-referral form in order to access the Foundation's services. In the form, he stated that although he had no current plans to "actively kill" himself, he was "seriously considering stopping taking my ... meds because I just don't want to be alive anymore". He also detailed a previous suicide attempt.

The self-referral form included these words:

"Contact with your GP:

We routinely inform GPs when one of their patients has applied to access our talking therapies ... If you do not wish for us to contact your GP please tick this box.

Please note that as part of our confidentiality policy, if there is reason to be seriously concerned about your welfare, we may need to break confidentiality without your consent to help you stay safe. We will try to get your consent first but this may not always be possible.

PLEASE NOTE: we cannot process this referral without GP details ..."

---

20. The Data Use and Access Bill was proceeding through Parliament at the time of going to print. If and when passed by Parliament, the Information Commissioner's Office will be replaced by The Information Commission.

21. [2020] EWHC 483 (QB).

Box 23.8: Scott v LGBT Foundation (cont.)

(Immediately below this section, Mr Scott wrote his GP's contact details).

Mr Scott did not tick the box saying he did not want his GP to be contacted.

Mr Scott saw a Foundation officer for an intake assessment to ascertain what the best support would be and to assess any risks to the service-user's safety.

At the intake session, the officer informed Mr Scott about the Foundation's policy regarding confidentiality, and explained that any information disclosed by him during the intake assessment would be passed on if the Foundation believed that he or a third party was at risk. During the intake assessment, Mr Scott told the officer that he had experienced suicidal thoughts, most recently on the previous evening and that he had attempted to cut his wrists some months earlier. He said that in the past two weeks, he had considered cutting his wrists. Mr Scott said he was currently experiencing suicidal thoughts.

The officer told Mr Scott that due to serious concerns regarding his welfare, she would have to discuss the intake assessment meeting with his GP. Mr Scott did not raise any objections at this point.

The officer telephoned Mr Scott's GP. She informed the receptionist of his disclosure of suicidal ideas and that he had considered slitting his wrists. The communication was only verbal and no documents were shared with the GP by the Foundation. That information was passed on by the receptionist to Mr Scott's GP who tried to contact Mr Scott and then emailed him.

Mr Scott sued the Foundation for breaching the Data Protection Act 1998 (the Data Protection Act 2018 and GDPR were not in force at the time of the disclosure, but the definition of "processing" was not materially different in the 1998 Act) and for breaching his confidentiality.

Mr Justice Saini held that a verbal disclosure did not constitute the processing of personal data and could not give rise to a claim under the Data Protection Act. The judge held that even if Mr Scott's personal data had been processed, the disclosure was necessary to protect Mr Scott's vital interests so that if the disclosure had taken place after GDPR came into force, the disclosure would have been covered by the exemption in Article 9 below.

The judge struck out the breach of confidence claim because the duty of confidence was subject to a qualification in the intake form, permitting the very limited disclosure to his GP and it had also been made clear to Mr Scott before the start of the assessment that information disclosed by him during the intake assessment would be passed on if the foundation believed that he or a third party was at risk. This is exactly the situation that arose.

Data protection principles

All personal data must be processed in accordance with data protection principles, meaning that among other things, the data must be processed fairly and lawfully. Lawfulness is addressed in the following section. In terms of fairness, key requirements are:

- processed data should not exceed what is needed for a specified lawful purpose;
- data must not be processed in a manner that is incompatible with the purpose for which it was collected;
- data must be accurate and kept up to date;
- data must not be kept longer than necessary for the specified purpose;

- appropriate measures must be taken against unauthorised or unlawful processing and against accidental loss; and
- data must not be transferred to a country outside the European Economic Area unless that country has adequate protection arrangements.

As an example of processing data in a manner that was incompatible with the purpose for which personal data was collected, in 2022, the General Optical Council dealt with a case in which a dispensing optician had sent a text message to a patient, saying "if your (sic) interested I am also would you like to take this further". The Fitness to Practise Committee found that the sending of this text was sexually motivated and described the use of the patient's personal data to make his approach was "self-evidently extremely serious".[22]

The *Pharmacy2U* case[23] in **Box 23.9** is an example of a failure to comply with the requirement of fair processing. It was the first case in which the ICO imposed a civil monetary penalty.

Box 23.9: Civil financial penalty imposed by ICO on Pharmacy2U Ltd

In October 2015, the ICO investigated the online pharmacy business Pharmacy2U Ltd. Although GDPR was not in force at the time of the events complained of, fair processing was already one of the data protection principles at that time under the Data Protection Act 1998.

Pharmacy2U had advertised patient details for sale at a cost of £130 per 1000 records. No consent had been obtained from patients. The patient lists it sold included patients with conditions such as asthma, Parkinson's disease and erectile dysfunction, and a breakdown of the data was made available. The information had been sold to a health supplements company and to an Australian lottery company.

The ICO imposed a civil penalty of £130,000.

The GPhC suspended the company's pharmacist commercial director from the register for three months and gave a warning to the pharmacist Chief Operating Officer at a Fitness to Practise hearing in May 2016.

Lawful basis for processing

Anyone who processes personal data (including pharmacists, pharmacy employees and locums) must have a lawful basis for doing so. Article 6 of UK GDPR provides a number of possible bases and those of particular relevance to the data processed in a pharmacy include:

- the data subject has consented to the processing for a specific purpose;
- the processing is necessary for compliance with a legal obligation to which the controller is subject;

22. https://optical.org/media/c2df2rtg/f-21-29-snelgrove-substantive-april-and-june-website.pdf (accessed 31 December 2024); https://www.dailymail.co.uk/news/article-11051787/Veteran-optician-64-suspended-mistaking-female-patients-yoga-moves-sexy-flirting.html (accessed 31 December 2024).

23. https://pharmaceutical-journal.com/article/news/pharmacy2u-fined-130000-for-selling-patient-data (accessed 31 December 2024).

- the processing is necessary for the performance of a task carried out in the public interest; and
- the processing is necessary for the purposes of the legitimate interests pursued by the controller or by a third party.

Pharmacy owners must decide which lawful basis they rely on, and be in a position to demonstrate, that they are entitled to do so. Relying on a patient's consent to process personal data is the least practical option because:

- consent must be explicit and for a specified purpose;
- patients must opt in – they cannot consent by default; and
- when consent is obtained, the controller will be under an obligation to provide information to patients, including their right to withdraw consent.

Withdrawing consent must be as easy as it was to give consent in the first place. Any failure to satisfy these conditions will invalidate the consent.

The processing of patient medication records is necessary for the performance of a task – the provision of health services – carried out in the public interest.[24]

An alternative lawful basis is the necessity of complying with a legal obligation because, in the case of NHS prescriptions,[25] failure to comply with this obligation may result in fitness to practise sanctions being imposed for breaching the terms of service. In the case of private prescriptions, processing patient data is a legal obligation under the Human Medicines Regulations 2012[26] and breaching this requirement is an offence.[27]

As an alternative lawful basis, maintaining patient records is consistent with good patient care, and pharmacy owners who dispense private prescriptions have a legitimate interest in processing patient data in the interests of patient care. Pharmacy owners providing non-NHS services may therefore choose to rely on legitimate interest as the lawful basis for processing data – but this lawful basis is not available in the case of NHS services because pharmacies that provide NHS services come within the definition of public authorities.[28]

Special category data

Personal data concerning health fall into a special category of data (classified under the previous Data Protection Act as *sensitive personal data*). Processing data of this type is prohibited unless one of the following conditions applies:

- the data subject has given explicit consent to the processing for one or more specified purposes; or
- processing is necessary for the purpose of the provision of health or treatment.

---

24. *YSL v Surrey and Borders Partnership NHS Foundation Trust* [2024] EWHC 391 (KB).
25. In the NHS terms of service (in England, for example, in paragraph 10 of the terms of service in Schedule 4 to the National Health Service (Pharmaceutical and Local Pharmaceutical Services) Regulations 2013).
26. Regulation 253 of the Human Medicines Regulations 2012.
27. Regulation 255 of the Human Medicines Regulations 2012.
28. A qualification to Article 6(1)(f) of UK GDPR stipulates that legitimate interest is not available to public authorities as a lawful basis for processing.

Pharmacies can rely on the processing being necessary for the provision of health or treatment on condition that the processing is carried out by or under the responsibility of a health professional or another person who in the circumstances owes a duty of confidentiality.[29] The definition of *health professional* includes pharmacists and pharmacy technicians.[30] A pharmacy employee who is not a pharmacist or pharmacy technician who has a contractual obligation of confidentiality will also be able to take responsibility for processing.[31] Taking responsibility for the processing does not mean that such a person has to do the processing personally.

Exemption for vital interests

Article 9(2)(c) of GDPR permits the processing of "special category" personal data where it is "necessary to protect the vital interests of the data subject or of another natural person where the data subject is physically or legally incapable of giving consent". The ICO explains in its Guidance on the Conditions for sensitive processing[32] that this condition is very limited in its scope, and generally only applies to matters of life and death.[33] However, the exemption was relevant in the case of *Scott v LGBT Foundation*[34] referred to in **Box 23.8**.

Hub and spoke dispensing

At the time of writing, the Department of Health and Social Care intends to amend the Medicines Act 1968 in 2025 to allow a pharmacy that receives a prescription (a spoke) to arrange for it to be dispensed at another pharmacy (a hub) when the spoke and hub have different owners. This will involve special category data (see below) being disclosed by the spoke to the hub. If and when the amendment is made, the position will be as set out in **Box 23.10**.

Box 23.10

At the time of going to press, there were proposals to amend the law. This box sets out what the law will be if those proposals are brought into effect. Readers can check whether the proposals have been brought into effect by checking www.legislation.gov.uk or using a subscription service such as Westlaw for the latest version of [e.g. the Medicines Act 1968/ the Human Medicines Regulations 2012 or searching those sites for the Human Medicines (Amendments relating to Hub and Spoke Dispensing etc.) Regulations *followed by the year].*

---

29. Section 11(1)(a) of the Data Protection Act 2018.
30. Section 204 of the Data Protection Act 2018.
31. *YSL v Surrey and Borders Partnership NHS Foundation Trust* [2024] EWHC 391 (KB).
32. https://ico.org.uk/for-organisations/law-enforcement/guide-to-le-processing/conditions-for-sensitive-processing/ (accessed 31 December 2024).
33. This explanation was upheld by the High Court in *YSL v Surrey and Borders Partnership NHS Foundation Trust* [2024] EWHC 391 (KB).
34. [2020] EWHC 483 (QB).

Box 23.10 (cont.)

Lawful basis
The HMR will provide that the lawful basis for processing by both the hub and the spoke is that it is necessary for the performance of a task carried out in the public interest. If the data is personal data concerning health, the HMR will say that this is necessary for the purposes of preventative medicine, medical diagnosis or for the provision of health care or treatment. To satisfy article 9(2)(h) of UK GDPR, the HMR will impose a duty of confidentiality in respect of that data on any person who is employed or engaged by the hub or the spoke (whether or not that person is a health professional.

Patients' rights

Patients have a number of rights under UK GDPR. These rights must be notified to them at the time their data are collected and must be in language that is clear, concise and easily accessible. Pharmacy owners must consider how the information is to be provided, with options including displaying notices in pharmacies and publishing the information in practice leaflets and on websites.

Among other things, patients have the right:

- to be told their data will be processed;
- to access their data free of charge;
- to the erasure of their data if it is no longer necessary for the purpose for which it was obtained or if there is no legitimate overriding interest in retaining the data; and
- to withdraw consent to processing (if consent is the lawful basis relied on by the controller).

A person whose rights are breached may be able to sue the data controller or data processor for compensation. The Supreme Court has held[35] that a business owner or employer may be vicariously liable for a breach committed by an employee. For further information on vicarious liability, see **Chapter 26**.

Data protection officers

The Data Protection Act 2018 defines any provider of NHS services as a public authority and every public authority must have a Data Protection Officer (DPO). This is an important and potentially onerous requirement.

The contact details of the DPO must be provided to data subjects at the time data are collected (and the name and contact details of the data controller must be provided at the same time). If the data controller is a company, the DPO should have direct access to its board of directors, in order to be able to perform their functions effectively.

DPOs have a number of obligations. Among other things, they must:

- be knowledgeable about data protection law;
- inform and advise employees who process data;
- be a contact point for all data protection issues;

35. *Wm Morrison Supermarkets plc v Various Claimants* [2020] UKSC 12.

- monitor compliance with UK GDPR and internal data protection obligations; and
- ensure non-compliance with UK GDPR is reported to the Information Commissioner's Office within 72 hours.

Websites

The GPhC has published draft guidance on the provision of online pharmacy services (see **Chapter 8**).[36] The guidance includes this advice for the owners of websites through which patients seek medicines:

> *"The digital platform must have secure facilities for collecting, using and storing pharmacy users' details. It must also have a secure link for processing card payments ... Any personal data that you collect via your digital platform should be stored on servers which are hosted in the UK or in another jurisdiction which has equivalent levels of data protection in place."*

NHS guidance and codes of practice

NHS England[37] is required by section 13S of the National Health Service Act 2006 to publish guidance on the practice to be followed in relation to the processing of patient information and other information generated in the course of providing NHS services.[38] Registered persons who carry on an activity connected with the provision of health care must have regard to this guidance. NHS England has published a code of practice[39] on records management, on confidential information and on information security. In Scotland, patients' rights to privacy and confidentiality are set out in *The Charter of Patient Rights and Responsibilities*[40] published pursuant to the Patient Rights (Scotland) Act 2011. In addition, NHS terms of service, for example in Schedule 4 to the National Health Service (Pharmaceutical and Local Pharmaceutical Services) Regulations 2013 – which apply to England – require pharmacies to have a clinical governance system that includes an information governance programme that includes approved procedures for information governance.

Claims for compensation for breach of data rights

UK GDPR itself gives the subject of a data breach the right to claim damages for distress, without having to prove that the breach caused any actual financial loss. However, there

---

36. https://assets.pharmacyregulation.org/files/2025-02/gphc-guidance-registered-pharmacies-providing-pharmacy-services-distance-february-2025.pdf (accessed 6 April 2025).
37. Shortly before going to press, the Prime Minister announced that NHS England would be abolished as a separate body, and its functions will be exercised by the Department of Health and Social Care.
38. https://transform.england.nhs.uk/information-governance/guidance/consent-and-confidential-patient-information/#healthcare_worker (accessed 31 December 2024).
39. https://transform.england.nhs.uk/information-governance/guidance/records-management-code/ (accessed 31 December 2024).
40. https://www.nhsinform.scot/care-support-and-rights/health-rights/confidentiality-and-data-protection/privacy-and-confidentiality-when-using-the-nhs (accessed 31 December 2024).

is no entitlement to damages unless the claimant proves that distress has been caused.[41] As an illustration of the level of compensation a court might award for distress, the supermodel Naomi Campbell was awarded damages of £3,500 against the Daily Mirror in 2004, after it published a photograph of her leaving a Narcotics Anonymous meeting. The decision, based on breach of Ms Campbell's right to privacy, which affected her physical and mental health, was upheld on appeal to the House of Lords.[42]

Financial penalties for breach of data rights

Breaches of data protection will not automatically result in a fine, but the Information Commissioner's Office has power to impose penalties for non-compliance with UK GDPR. There are two tiers of penalty. The higher maximum amount is £17.5 million or 4% of the total annual worldwide turnover in the preceding financial year, whichever is higher. In practice, the higher maximum amount can apply to any failure to comply with any of the data protection principles, any rights an individual may have or in relation to any transfers of data to third countries. If there is an infringement of other provisions, such as administrative requirements of the legislation, the standard maximum amount will apply, which is £8.7 million or 2% of the total annual worldwide turnover in the preceding financial year, whichever is higher.

Financial penalties must be proportionate and take into account all the circumstances. Clearly, inadvertent breaches will be treated less seriously than deliberate breaches, and steps to repair damage and prevent repetition will be taken into consideration when determining the level of any penalty.

The first financial penalty imposed by the ICO for breaching GDPR[43] involved a pharmacy. The details of the case are in **Box 23.11**.

Box 23.11: ICO civil penalty for breach of GDPR

In December 2019, the Information Commissioner imposed a financial penalty of £275,000 for GDPR breaches by a pharmacy owner, Doorstep Dispensaree Limited.[44] The penalty was reduced to £92,000 on appeal to the First Tier Tribunal.[45]

Some 12,491 documents contained personal data and 53,871 special category personal data including names, addresses, dates of birth, NHS numbers, medical information and prescriptions had been found in disposal bags and a cardboard box in a courtyard behind the pharmacy, which was not an appropriately secure area. Most of the data subjects were patients in care homes and likely to be vulnerable. The methods of data storage "did not afford sufficient protection against accidental loss or destruction" and this was a breach of the

44. https://ico.org.uk/media/action-weve-taken/mpns/2616742/doorstop-mpn-20191217.pdf (accessed 31 December 2024).
45. *Doorstep Dispensaree Ltd v Information Commissioner.* Subsequent appeals to the Upper Tribunal [2023] UKUT 132 (AAC) and to the Court of Appeal [2024] EWCA Civ 1515 were dismissed.

41. *Lloyd v Google LLC* [2021] UKSC 50.
42. *Campbell v MGN Limited* [2004] UKHL 22.
43. This pre-dated the UK's exit from the EU, so the breach related to the EU GDPR, rather than UK GDPR, which is equivalent.

Box 23.11: ICO civil penalty for breach of GDPR (cont.)

integrity and confidentiality requirements of GDPR. Some of the personal data was more than two years old, which was a further breach because it indicated that the data had been held for longer than necessary.

The size of the penalty took account of the very large number of seized documents, most of which contained personal data of "highly vulnerable data subjects", which was a "significant aggravating factor".

Data protection offences

The Data Protection Act 2018 creates a number of offences. For example, under section 170, it is an offence for a person knowingly or recklessly:

a. to obtain or disclose personal data without the consent of the controller;
b. to procure the disclosure of personal data to another person without the consent of the controller; or
c. after obtaining personal data, to retain it without the consent of the person who was the controller in relation to the personal data when it was obtained.

In addition to its power to impose civil penalties, the ICO may therefore bring a prosecution in a criminal court. Examples of prosecutions[46] under equivalent provisions in the previous Data Protection Act are included in **Box 23.12**.

Box 23.12: ICO prosecutions

In March 2013, the ICO prosecuted a former receptionist at a GP surgery for unlawfully obtaining sensitive medical information relating to her ex-husband's new wife. She was found to have accessed the information on 15 separate occasions over a 16-month period. The breach became apparent after the receptionist left her job and sent a text message to her ex-husband's new wife, referring to highly sensitive medical information taken from her medical record.

The receptionist was convicted, fined £750 and ordered to pay a £15 victim surcharge. The Deputy Information Commissioner said in an ICO news release:

"This case clearly shows the distress that can be caused when an individual uses a position of responsibility to illegally access sensitive personal information. Ms X knew she was breaking the law, but continued to do so in order to cause harm to her ex-husband's new wife.

The nature of her job meant that she will have been in no doubt as to the importance of patient confidentiality. Despite this, she repeatedly accessed the victim's file without a valid reason."

46. In accordance with the right of individuals to be forgotten, some of the cases referred to in this chapter are no longer accessible on official websites. The authors have decided not to name individuals. The case details may still be found online and are given here solely to provide verification of the details and to assist further research. For example, https://www.bbc.co.uk/news/uk-england-hampshire-21761804 (accessed 31 December 2024) and https://www.wired-gov.net/wg/news.nsf/articles/Pharmacist+who+unlawfully+spied+on+family+and+friends+medical+records+prosecuted+14112014141054?open (accessed 31 December 2024).

Box 23.12: ICO prosecutions (cont.)

In November 2014, a pharmacist working for a Primary Care Trust at three GP surgeries was prosecuted after unlawfully accessing the medical records of family members, work colleagues and local health professionals. The pharmacist had responsibility for handling medication reviews for patients in local residential homes with dementia and other mental health issues. His unlawful access was discovered during a routine audit by the surgery manager at one of the GP surgeries. The audit revealed that the pharmacist was using his security pass to access unrelated medical records.

In a press release, the ICO Head of Enforcement said:

"There is no justifiable reason why [the pharmacist] needed to spy on the medical treatment of all these people. However, he knew he was committing a criminal offence, but he decided to carry on regardless.

The public will be rightly concerned that a medical professional [sic] in a position of trust decided to act in this way. We hope today's prosecution sends a clear message to anyone who may be tempted to do likewise, that unlawful accessing people's medical records is a criminal offence and will result with you being rewarded with a day in court."[47]

47. https://www.wired-gov.net/wg/news.nsf/articles/Pharmacist+who+unlawfully+spied+on+family+and+friends+medical+records+prosecuted+14112014141054?open (accessed 31 December 2024).

In the 2022 case of a health adviser who was convicted of unlawfully accessing the records of 12 patients who were known to him personally, the defendant was ordered to pay £250 compensation to each data subject.[48]

Access to health records

The Access to Health Records Act 1990 provides that a personal representative of a deceased person or anyone who has a claim arising out of a patient's death can also claim access to *sensitive personal data* maintained in health records.

Freedom of Information Act 2000

The Freedom of Information Act 2000 seeks to promote the openness and accountability of public authorities. In Scotland, similar provisions are contained in the Freedom of Information (Scotland) Act 2002. Sections below refer to the 2000 Act.

Whereas the Data Protection Act is concerned to protect the privacy of individuals and their personal data, the Freedom of Information Act gives people the right to seek information from public authorities about how they carry out their duties, why they make the decisions they do and how they spend public money.

48. https://ico.org.uk/about-the-ico/media-centre/news-and-blogs/2022/08/former-health-adviser-found-guilty-of-illegally-accessing-patient-records/ (accessed 31 December 2024). N.B. the report refers to 14 victims, but there is a reference elsewhere to 12 victims and the latter figure is consistent with the total compensation of £3000.

The definition of public authorities and in England and Wales includes:

- NHS England and NHS Health Scotland,
- Integrated Care Boards,
- The General Pharmaceutical Council,
- Special Health Authorities (such as the NHS Business Services Authority – see **Chapter 3**),
- Health Boards (in Scotland) and Local Health Boards (in Wales),
- NHS Trusts and Foundation Trusts,
- Any person who provides NHS pharmaceutical services or local pharmaceutical services,
- Public Health Scotland, and
- NHS Education for Scotland.

Such organisations must adopt and maintain a publication scheme, setting out details of information it will routinely make available, how the information can be obtained and whether there is any charge for it. To manage the cost of meeting requests for prescription data of pharmacies, the NHS Business Services Authority publishes the data on its website.

Requests for information are required by section 10 to be answered promptly and in any event within 20 working days.

There is an exemption from disclosure of personal data in section 40(2) of the Freedom of Information Act if disclosure would contravene any of the data protection principles (see above). Whether the exemption applies involves a three-part test:

- Whether a legitimate interest is being pursued in the request for information;
- Whether disclosure is necessary to meet the legitimate interest in question;
- Whether any legitimate interests override the legitimate interests or fundamental rights and freedoms of the data subject.

In a case where a patient requested disclosure of the revalidation details of a doctor, in connection with a fitness to practice complaint the patient wished to make, it was held that the request did not satisfy the three-part test.[49]

There are also exemptions from disclosure in section 43 of the Freedom of Information Act for information that constitutes a trade secret or information that, if disclosed would, or would be likely to, prejudice the commercial interests of any person (including the public authority holding it). This is subject to a public interest test.

An example of a case in which the ICO adjudicated on whether information could be withheld on the ground that it was a trade secret or would prejudice commercial interests is given in **Box 23.13**.

---

49. *Marcheselli v (1) the Information Commissioner and (2) the General Medical Council* [2023] UKFTT 00076 (GRC).

Box 23.13: ICO adjudication on refusal by Boots to provide information

In 2018, a request was made to Boots Group Plc on behalf of the BBC for information about time standards associated with its dispensing services, and how Boots calculated community staffing needs and associated costs. Boots refused to answer the request on the ground that it was exempt from release as a trade secret and as prejudicial to its commercial interests.

The BBC was producing a programme that was broadcast under the title *Inside Out*, called *Boots – Pharmacists under pressure*. The programme investigated concerns the BBC said had been raised by Boots pharmacists who were worried that work pressures caused by understaffing could have an impact on patient safety, and cause harm.

The BBC complained to the ICO against the refusal to disclose the requested information.

Boots accepted that there is a public interest in community pharmacy being accountable for spending NHS funds, but pointed out that pharmacies are not remunerated based on staffing levels.

Boots responded to the appeal by explaining that it used a unique time standards model to calculate the staffing levels required in store and pointed out that neither the GPhC nor the NHS required any particular staffing level or model. It said as the model was unique, it was a trade secret, and that if it disclosed its model, this would prejudice its commercial interests as other companies could then use or copy the model.

The ICO upheld Boots' arguments. When weighing up whether the public interest outweighed Boots' reasons for refusing to supply the information, the ICO's decision said:

> *"the Commissioner has decided that the public interest in the matter of safe pharmacy and dispensing practices at Boots has been met to a satisfactory degree by the BBC documentary and the GPhC investigation. The Commissioner also notes that Boots has released considerable related information ... during the course of the BBC's investigation. On this occasion the Commissioner therefore considers that there is greater public interest in Boots being able to compete fairly in the pharmacy market, and, as a provider of NHS pharmaceutical services, being able to offer the public a strong and efficient service. She is satisfied that the public interest on this occasion favours withholding the requested information."*

Pharmacies providing NHS services are required to adopt a model publication scheme approved by the Information Commissioner.

SUMMARY

- Patients have a common law right to confidentiality.
- The right to confidentiality does not cease on a patient's death.
- Confidentiality may be overridden if it is in the public interest.
- Confidentiality is a requirement of the GPhC's Standards.
- A patient can waive the right to confidentiality.
- Anonymous information is not confidential.
- There is a right to privacy in the European Convention on Human Rights.
- There is a duty to share information in the NHS and the Caldicott principles deal with information sharing.

SUMMARY (Cont.)

- Data are protected by the Data Protection Act 2018 and UK GDPR. Processing must be fair and lawful. There must be a lawful basis for processing.
- Personal data concerning health is *special category data*.
- Providers of NHS pharmacy services must have a Data Protection Officer.
- Breach of UK GDPR can lead to heavy financial penalties imposed by the Information Commissioner's Office or by prosecution.
- Providers of NHS services are generally required to supply information requested under the Freedom of information Act but there is an exemption in the case of trade secrets or to protect commercial interests.
- Unauthorised access to patient information may lead to fitness to practise proceedings.

FURTHER READING

- Department of Health and Social Care: Confidentiality – *Code of Practice* **https://assets.publishing.service.gov.uk/government/uploads/system/uploads/attachment_data/file/200146/Confidentiality_-_NHS_Code_of_Practice.pdf** (accessed 31 December 2024).
- General Pharmaceutical Council – *In practice: Guidance on confidentiality* (June 2018) **https://assets.pharmacyregulation.org/files/2024-01/in_practice_guidance_on_confidentiality_june_2018.pdf** (accessed 31 December 2024).
- Wingfield J (2007). When confidences should be kept and what constitutes an exception. *Pharm J*, 279: 533–536.

CHAPTER 24

Professional conduct

This chapter deals with the professional conduct of pharmacists, pharmacy technicians and pharmacy students. Amongst other things, it looks at the extent to which the obligation to behave professionally, at all times, may intrude on the private lives of pharmacy professionals.

Introduction

Laws dictate professional conduct, particularly through a series of layers, starting with laws made by the UK Parliament or the parliaments of Scotland or Wales. This is illustrated by a passage in the 2023 consultation paper on the supervision of medicines supplies that was published by the Department of Health and Social Care in England and the governments of Scotland, Wales and Northern Ireland.[1] Under the heading *The role of legislation, regulations and guidance*, the consultation paper said:

"There are 5 layers of pharmacy regulation and governance:

- *government legislation*
- *regulatory rules and standards*
- *professional standards*
- *other standards or professional guidance*
- *local governance policies and procedures*

These underpin the safe and effective provision of pharmacy services and ensure patient and public outcomes and experience. The government's role is to set the overarching legislative framework. The second phase, led by the pharmacy regulators and professional bodies, will set the detail of how this legislation will work in practice."

As an example of these layers, section 72A of the Medicines Act 1968 gives the GPhC power to make rules in relation to responsible pharmacists in respect of premises (see **Chapter 7**); and the proposals to amend the law on supervision (see **Chapter 11**) if implemented, will not spell out detailed requirements as to how supervision should be exercised, but will leave the GPhC to make rules.

Beneath the rules and standards published by the GPhC lies professional guidance published by the Royal Pharmaceutical Society. A joint statement by the two bodies says:

> *"Regulatory standards must be met by all pharmacy professionals and owners of registered pharmacies, otherwise their registration may be at risk.*

1. https://www.gov.uk/government/consultations/pharmacy-supervision/pharmacy-supervision (accessed 31 December 2024).

The professional standards and guidance produced by the RPS provide a framework to support pharmacists and their teams, to develop their professional practice, improve services, shape future services, and deliver high quality patient care.

While professional standards and guidance are not mandatory, they are developed and owned by the profession, and set out what constitutes 'good' in terms of practice, systems of care, and working practices."[2]

It should be explained that in the passage quoted above, although the mandatory standards published by the GPhC are sometimes referred to as professional standards, the Royal Pharmaceutical Society is describing the GPhC's standards as *regulatory standards*; and it is referring to the standards published by the RPS, which is not a regulator, as *professional standards*. Nevertheless, the GPhC's Fitness to Practise Committee may sometimes have regard to the Royal Pharmaceutical Society's *professional standards*. Guidance published by the National Institute for Health and Care Excellence (usually known as NICE – see **Chapter 3**) and guidance published by other regulators, such as the General Medical Council, may also be relevant.

Behaving professionally at all times

In terms of professional conduct, the GPhC's *Standards for pharmacy professionals* (see below) are instructive. Standard 6 says "Pharmacy professionals must behave in a professional manner". An extract from Standard 6 appears in **Box 24.1** below.

Box 24.1: Extract from Standard 6 of *Standards for pharmacy professionals*

People expect pharmacy professionals to behave professionally. This is essential to maintaining trust and confidence in pharmacy. Behaving professionally is not limited to the working day, or face-to-face interactions. The privilege of being a pharmacist or pharmacy technician, and the importance of maintaining confidence in the professions, call for appropriate behaviour at all times. There are a number of ways to meet this standard and below are examples of the attitudes and behaviours expected.

People receive safe and effective care when pharmacy professionals:

- are polite and considerate;
- are trustworthy and act with honesty and integrity;
- show empathy and compassion;
- treat people with respect and safeguard their dignity; and
- maintain appropriate personal and professional boundaries with the people they provide care to and with others.

---

2. https://www.rpharms.com/recognition/setting-professional-standards/statement-on-safe-and-effective-care (accessed 31 December 2024).

Before the Standards came into effect, the Pharmacists' Defence Association (PDA) challenged the lawfulness of the requirement for appropriate behaviour *at all times* and the application of the Standards to non-work related matters.[3] Mr Justice Singh considered that the PDA was unduly concerned about the possible effect on pharmacy professionals. He said:

> *"The Standards need to be interpreted fairly and as a whole. They also need to be interpreted in a way which is rooted in real life and common sense. This is not least because they are intended to guide the conduct of pharmacy professionals in a practical way; they are not addressed primarily to lawyers ... If [registrants] are not polite over a board game, they will not need to lose sleep over whether they can make the relevant declaration that they have complied with the Standards."*

In *Professional Standards Authority for Health and Social Care v General Pharmaceutical Council and Ali* [2021] EWHC 1692 (Admin), the registrant had led a public rally in which he shouted, through a loudhailer, words that were alleged to be antisemitic. A Fitness to Practise Committee had held that they were not, but the Professional Standards Authority appealed against this ruling. In upholding the appeal, Mr Justice Johnson said:

> *"This case does ... engage significant questions of public confidence. It is vitally important that all sections of the community are able to place trust and confidence in advice given by pharmacists ... [T]hat is vividly illustrated by the [COVID-19] pandemic, and the need that all communities are able to have confidence in advice given by pharmacists and other professionals about the risks and benefits of vaccination."*

The European Convention on Human Rights places limits on the obligation to behave professionally at all times, including in a pharmacy professional's private life (Article 8). See, for example, the cases in **Box 24.6** below dealing with the right to freedom of expression, and the decision in *Beckwith v Solicitors Regulation Authority*,[4] in which the High Court overturned a decision that a senior solicitor had acted with a lack of integrity by having a consensual sexual encounter with a junior colleague. The court said:

> *"There can be no hard and fast rule either that [professional] regulation ... may never be directed to the regulated person's private life, or that any/every aspect of her private life is liable to scrutiny. But [professional rules] may reach into private life only when conduct that is part of a person's private life realistically touches on her practise of the profession ... or the standing of the profession ... Any such conduct*

---

3. *The Queen (on the application of Pitt and Tyas) v General Pharmaceutical Council* [2017] EWHC 809 (Admin).
4. [2020] EWHC 3231 (Admin).

> *must be qualitatively relevant. It must, in a way that is demonstrably relevant, engage one or other of the standards of behaviour which are set out in or necessarily implicit from the [professional rules]. In this way, the required fair balance is properly struck between the right to respect to private life and the public interest in the regulation of the ... profession. Regulators will do well to recognise that it is all too easy to be dogmatic without knowing it; popular outcry is not proof that a particular set of events gives rise to any matter falling within a regulator's remit."*

Standards for pharmacy professionals

A report by the Professional Standards Authority in 2022 said:

> *"Declaring and upholding professional standards shows professionals and the public what is deemed unacceptable, which in turn can have a positive impact on other professionals."*[5]

As outlined in **Chapter 2**, the GPhC has a duty to set standards as the basis by which a registrant's fitness to practise may be assessed. The *Standards for pharmacy professionals* are reproduced in full in Appendix 1. The GPhC must also make Rules setting out the criteria to which the Fitness to Practise Committee (**Chapter 25**) is to have regard when considering whether a registrant (pharmacist or pharmacy technician) is fit to practise.[6] The legislation[7] makes it clear that failure to comply with such standards is not, of itself, evidence of misconduct (misconduct is one of the grounds for alleging impaired fitness to practise) but is to be taken into account in any fitness to practise proceedings against a registrant. Registrants must comply with the *Standards for pharmacy professionals,* a summary of which is given in **Box 24.2** below.

Box 24.2: Summary of Standards for pharmacy professionals

All pharmacy professionals contribute to delivering and improving the health, safety and wellbeing of patients and the public. Professionalism and safe and effective practice are central to that role.

Pharmacy professionals must:

1. provide patient-centred care;
2. work in partnership with others;
3. communicate effectively;
4. maintain, develop and use their professional knowledge and skills;
5. exercise professional judgement;
6. behave in a professional manner;
7. respect and maintain the person's privacy and confidentiality;
8. speak up when they have concerns or when things go wrong; and
9. demonstrate leadership.

---

5. https://www.professionalstandards.org.uk/safer-care-for-all (accessed 31 December 2024).
6. The rules are the General Pharmaceutical Council (Fitness to Practise and Disqualification, etc. Rules) Order of Council 2010 and are referred to as the Fitness to Practise Rules.
7. Article 48(3) of the Pharmacy Order 2010.

Standard 6, which refers to behaving in a professional manner, explains that people receive safe and effective care when, amongst other things, pharmacy professionals are trustworthy and act with honesty and integrity. The difference between honesty and integrity is explored further in **Chapter 25**. In the case of *Solicitors Regulation Authority v Wingate Evans*,[8] *integrity* was described as:

> *"a useful shorthand to express the higher standards which society expects from professional persons and which the professions expect of their own members. The underlying rationale is that the professions have a privileged and trusted role in society. In return they are required to live up to their own professional standards."*

Honesty is considered further in **Chapter 25**.

The standards for registered pharmacies are covered in **Chapter 2**.

Guidance to support the Standards for pharmacy professionals

The GPhC has published guidance to support its *Standards for pharmacy professionals*.

Pharmacist prescribers

Pharmacist independent prescribers are responsible for and accountable for the clinical assessment and management of people (with diagnosed or undiagnosed conditions), without needing to consult another prescriber. They are also responsible for the prescribing decisions they make.

This guidance[9] advises:

- the importance of having access to a person's medical records;
- prescribing only within the limits of the prescriber's knowledge, skills and area of competence;
- prescribing in line with local guidelines;
- providing relevant information and deciding what monitoring is needed;
- taking responsibility for the prescriber's practice and working in partnership with other healthcare professionals; and
- keeping the initial prescribing separate from supply.

Two fitness to practise cases in 2022[10] illustrate the importance of prescribing within the limits of the prescriber's competence and the views taken by the GPhC's Fitness to Practise Committee – see **Box 24.3**.

---

8. [2018] EWCA Civ 366.
9. https://assets.pharmacyregulation.org/files/2024-01/in-practice-guidance-for-pharmacist-prescribers-february-2020.pdf (accessed 31 December 2024).
10. It is not possible to give a reference because the cases are no longer accessible on the GPhC's website as a result of its disclosure policy.

Box 24.3: Fitness to practise cases involving pharmacist prescribing

A pharmacist independent prescriber had a contract to write prescriptions for patients who were overseas, transcribing prescriptions written by local prescribers so that the prescribed items could be supplied by a British pharmacy. He wrote prescriptions for dogs, cats and a parrot and wrote prescriptions for humans to treat conditions that included mental health, paediatric epilepsy, HIV, and cancer, all of which were beyond his competence. The Fitness to Practise Committee quoted in its determination the GPhC Standards for the education and training of pharmacist independent prescribers, defining the prescribing role thus:

> *"the prescriber takes responsibility for the clinical assessment of the patient, establishing a diagnosis, and the clinical management required as well as the responsibility for prescribing and the appropriateness of any prescribing ... ; and the Framework makes it clear that 'pharmacist prescribers should assess, consider options, reach a shared decision, prescribe, provide information, monitor and review when prescribing for patients'."*

The Fitness to Practise Committee found the pharmacist's unsafe prescribing amounted to misconduct which impaired his fitness to practise. The pharmacist was suspended from practice for 12 months.

****

A pharmacist independent prescriber was employed by an online pharmacy business. He admitted multiple breaches of professional standards over a six-month period, including prescribing 200 dihydrocodeine 30 mg tablets to a person posing as a patient (who happened to be a journalist). This was in breach of his employer's policy for supplying opioids. The pharmacist's main practice area was the treatment and management of asthma, but he prescribed treatment for dental conditions, hormonal insufficiency and depression without being able to evidence training in those areas. The GPhC's Fitness to Practise Committee found that misconduct was proved and that the pharmacist's fitness to practise was impaired. The Fitness to Practise Committee said:

> *"The deficiencies in the registrant's practice were serious, fundamental and wide-ranging. They went to the core of good pharmacy practice in that his acts and omissions gave rise to potential serious harm to those supplied with prescription only medicines ... the registrant's actions effectively provided a facility for people to apply for prescription only medications without challenge or query as to their proposed use or the context of their administration. The Registrant in effect, gave the applicants the medications they requested. This is in direct breach of his duty as a gatekeeper of prescription only medications."*

When determining the appropriate sanction, the Fitness to Practise Committee considered mitigating factors and aggravating factors. In commenting on the aggravating factors to determine the appropriate sanction, the Fitness to Practise Committee said:

> *"The PIP qualification is an advanced qualification ... It is an autonomous role which requires greater responsibility and care than that of a registered pharmacist without such an advanced qualification. The role of a PIP is an elevated one and the registrant breached the trust of his employer in his claimed expertise and judgment."*

Prescribing by pharmacists gives rise to a number of other professional conduct issues, such as conflicts of interest. Pharmacist prescribers should always prescribe on the basis of what is in a patient's best interests and avoid prescribing on the basis of what would secure the greatest financial benefit to themselves.[11]

For example, in 2023, the GPhC and some other healthcare regulators issued a *Joint statement on meeting regulatory standards during periods of global or national shortage of medicines*. Particular concern arose because of a shortage of Ozempic (a GLP-1 receptor agonist), which prescribed for the treatment of type 2 diabetes. The same drug, under the brand name Wegovy, is also used for weight loss. Weight-loss treatments may be more profitable than diabetes treatments and evidence suggested that prescribing Ozempic off-label for weight loss, was causing a shortage of the product for the treatment of type 2 diabetes. The statement refers to "the need for prescribers to assess the risks and benefits to the patient of taking or not taking a medicine or treatment, and to consider the wider perspective including the public health issues related to medicines and their use and promoting health."[12]

Pharmacist prescribing also widens the scope of the duty of care owed to patients and the potential liability if a patient is harmed by a duty of care. Liability is dealt with in **Chapter 26**.

Consent

The guidance on consent[13] is divided into three main areas; adults, minors below the age of 16, and minors aged 16 and 17.

Adults

It is not normally permissible to treat a patient who has mental capacity without their consent. Indeed, any kind of physical contact, with a patient, however slight, requires consent. Touching a patient without their consent is a tort known as *battery* for which a patient can sue for damages (see **Chapter 26**).

Key features of the guidance include explaining what is meant by consent, the two types of consent (explicit and implied), ways in which consent can be obtained, and capacity or otherwise to give consent (including assessment of capacity).

In terms of capacity, the guidance explains:

- In England and Wales, under the Mental Capacity Act 2005, a person must be assumed to have capacity unless it is established that they lack capacity. A person lacks capacity if, at the time the decision needs to be made, they are unable to make

11. See https://pubmed.ncbi.nlm.nih.gov/30813120/ (accessed 31 August 2024) and https://www.chemistanddruggist.co.uk/CD137350/GPhC-may-look-at-overprescribing-risk-from-IP-contractors-in-future?utm_source=onesignal&utm_medium=web-push&utm_term=CD137350 (accessed 31 December 2024).

12. https://www.pharmacyregulation.org/about-us/news-and-updates/joint-statement-meeting-regulatory-standards-during-periods-global-or-national-shortage-medicines (accessed 31 December 2024).

13. https://assets.pharmacyregulation.org/files/2024-01/in_practice_guidance_on_consent_june_2018.pdf (accessed 31 December 2024).

or communicate the decision because of an impairment or disturbance that affects the way their mind or brain works. If an adult lacks capacity, decisions must be made in their best interests, which must not be made merely on the basis of their age or appearance.

- In Scotland, under the Adults with Incapacity (Scotland) Act 2000, a person lacks capacity if they cannot act, make decisions or communicate them, or understand or remember their decisions because of a mental disorder or physical inability to communicate in any form. If an adult lacks capacity, the medical practitioner primarily responsible for the adult's medical treatment, having certified their opinion about incapacity, has authority to do what is reasonable in the circumstances in relation to medical treatment to safeguard or promote the physical or mental health of the adult. Dental practitioners, ophthalmic opticians and registered nurses also have authority to do so.

The guidance says that if a patient with capacity makes an informed decision to refuse a service or treatment, pharmacy professionals must respect their decision – even when they think that their decision is wrong or may cause the person harm. For a decision to be informed, the patient should be aware of the material risks involved in any treatment[14] and any reasonable alternative treatments. This does not apply when the law says otherwise, such as when compulsory treatment is authorised by mental health legislation. Pharmacy professionals should clearly explain the consequences of a person's decision, but pharmacy professionals must make sure that they do not pressure the person to accept their advice.

Minors below the age of 16

Children below the age of 16 are not presumed to have the capacity to consent. They must demonstrate their competence.

Children under the age of 16 can consent to their own treatment if they are believed to have enough intelligence, competence and understanding to appreciate fully what is involved in their treatment (often referred to as having *Gillick competence* – see below). Otherwise, someone with parental responsibility can consent for them. This could be:

- the child's mother or father;
- the child's legally appointed guardian;
- a person with a residence order concerning the child;
- a local authority designated to care for the child; or
- a local authority or person with an emergency protection order for the child.

14. Unless the disclosure of any risks would be seriously detrimental to the patient's health – see *Montgomery v Lanarkshire Health Board.* [2015] UKSC 11.

Minors aged 16 and 17

Young people aged 16 and 17 are presumed to have the capacity to make their own decisions and give consent for a service or treatment, unless there is enough evidence to suggest otherwise.[15]

All minors

In the case of all minors, their capacity to consent depends more on their ability to understand than on their age. They may have the capacity to consent to some services or treatments but not to others. Pharmacy professionals therefore need to assess the maturity and understanding of the person concerned.

Pharmacy professionals should encourage young people to involve their parents in making important decisions, however, pharmacy professionals should respect a young person's request for confidentiality. The Guidance reflects the outcome of *Gillick v West Norfolk and Wisbech Area Health Authority*[16] (see **Box 24.4** below) and has given rise to the expression *Gillick competence* when referring to a young person or child having sufficient intelligence and understanding to make its own decision about treatment.

The guidance also deals with the situation when young people and children refuse to give consent or lack capacity.

Box 24.4: *Gillick v West Norfolk and Wisbech Area Health Authority*

The Department of Health and Social Security issued to area health authorities a memorandum of guidance on family planning services which contained a section dealing with contraceptive advice and treatment for young children. The guidance stated that clinic sessions should be available for people of all ages. Mrs Gillick, who was the mother of five girls under the age of 16, sought an assurance from her local area health authority that no contraceptive advice or treatment would be given to any of her daughters while under the age of 16 years without her knowledge and consent. The area health authority refused to give such an assurance and stated that, in accordance with the guidance, the final decision must be for the doctor's clinical judgement. Mrs Gillick claimed that the advice was unlawful.

The House of Lords held that:

1. Under NHS legislation, Parliament regarded contraceptive advice and treatment as essentially medical matters and that a girl under the age of 16 years had the legal capacity to consent to medical examination and treatment, including contraceptive treatment, if she had sufficient maturity and intelligence to understand the nature and implications of the proposed treatment.
2. A parent no longer had the right to determine whether a child under 16 should have medical treatment when the child achieved sufficient intelligence and understanding to make that decision itself.
3. Although in the majority of cases parents were the best judges of matters concerning a child's welfare, there might be exceptional cases in which a doctor was a better judge of whether it was desirable to give a girl, in her own best interests, contraceptive advice and treatment, if necessary, without the consent or even the knowledge of the parents.

---

15. Section 8 of the Family Law Reform Act 1969 provides that for the purpose of consent to medical treatment, a person who has reached the age of 16 is to be treated no differently to an adult.
16. [1986] AC 112.

Box 24.4 (cont.)

4. In exceptional cases a doctor will be entitled to give contraceptive advice and treatment to a girl under 16 without her parents' knowledge and consent if the doctor is satisfied that (i) the girl will understand the advice; (ii) the doctor cannot persuade her to inform her parents or to allow the doctor to inform her parents that she is seeking contraceptive advice; (iii) she is very likely to begin or to continue having sexual intercourse with or without contraceptive treatment; (iv) unless she receives contraceptive advice or treatment her physical or mental health or both are likely to suffer; and (v) her best interests require the doctor to give her contraceptive advice, treatment or both without the parental consent.

Parental consent for children with capacity

If a young person or child has capacity to consent, a parent retains the right to consent to the treatment of the young person or child (for example if the child fails to make a decision), though the parent cannot trump – i.e. overrule or replace – the decision of a young person or child who has capacity.[17]

Maintaining clear sexual boundaries

The guidance[18] outlines the importance of maintaining clear sexual boundaries. It describes the power imbalance which normally exist between a patient and a pharmacy professional, identifies that cultural and other reasons can lead to differences in what individuals see as appropriate or inappropriate and also provides guidance on the use of a chaperone. The guidance includes the following advice on avoiding breaches of sexual boundaries:

> *"There are a number of behaviours that may be signs of showing sexualised behaviour towards people receiving care or carers. These include:*
>
> - *when the healthcare professional reveals intimate personal details about themselves to a person under their care during a consultation;*
> - *when the reason behind the following actions is sexual:*
>   - *giving or accepting social invitations (dates and meetings),*
>   - *visiting a home of a person under their care without an appointment,*
>   - *meeting people under their care outside of normal practice, for example arranging appointments for a time when no other staff are in the pharmacy, or*
>   - *asking questions unrelated to a person's health.*

---

17. *AB v CD* [2021] EWHC 741 (Fam) – a case in which the court held that the parents of a 15-year-old had the right to consent on her behalf to her continued treatment with puberty blockers, whether their daughter was Gillick competent or not.
18. https://assets.pharmacyregulation.org/files/2024-01/in-practice-guidance-on-maintaining-clear-sexual-boundaries-february-2020.pdf (accessed 31 December 2024).

If a pharmacy professional finds themselves in a situation where they are attracted to a person under their care, they must not act on these feelings".

A chaperone is a person (usually the same sex as the patient) who is present as a safeguard for the patient and the healthcare professional. They are also a witness to the patient's continuing consent for the procedure. Their role may vary depending on the needs of the patient, the pharmacy professional and the examination or procedure being carried out.

Cases involving inappropriate sexual behaviour are increasingly a feature of fitness to practise cases (see **Chapter 25**). For example, in 2022, the General Optical Council's fitness to practise committee dealt with a dispensing optician who had sent a patient a text, enquiring whether she would like to explore a relationship, motivated by a wish to pursue a sexual relationship. The committee described this as "a clear breach of professional boundaries".[19] In relation to consensual sexual behaviour, see also the case of *Beckwith v Solicitors Regulation Authority* referred to above and in **Chapter 1**.

An example of a 2024 case involving a failure to observe sexual boundaries is given in **Box 24.5**.

Box 24.5: Sexual boundaries – fitness to practise case

The registrant was a pharmacist. While she was supervising Patient A's treatment, she entered into a relationship with Patient A that contained a sexual element. The registrant did not disclose the relationship to her supervisors or other professionals involved in Patient A's care.

The GPhC's Fitness to Practise Committee said:

"The therapeutic relationship between a patient and their healthcare provider is a fundamental cornerstone of healthcare. Breakdowns in this relationship can compromise the treatment they receive and bring serious disrepute to the profession. Additionally, pharmacy professionals must be able to speak to their colleagues and supervisors when issues arise, even if this may cause embarrassment to themselves. This is even more crucial when failure to do so may risk harm to others and compromise the treatment provided to patients."

The registrant was found to have breached the following GPhC standards:

- Standard 5 – Pharmacy professionals must use their professional judgement;
- Standard 6 – Pharmacy professionals must behave in a professional manner;
- Standard 8 – Pharmacy professionals must speak up when they have concerns or when things go wrong.

The registrant was given a warning that, among other things, it is her responsibility to protect the therapeutic relationship, reject any inappropriate advances by patients, or remove herself entirely from such a situation if it is in the patient's best interests.

19. https://optical.org/media/c2df2rtg/f-21-29-snelgrove-substantive-april-and-june-website.pdf (accessed 31 December 2024).

Patient confidentiality

The guidance[20] deals with the duty of confidentiality, protecting confidential information and disclosing information. See **Chapter 23** for more information.

Religion, personal values and beliefs

The guidance document[21] includes guidance for pharmacy professionals and for those who employ them. It includes guidance for those who hold such beliefs on what they should do before (or if) they accept employment as well as what to do when circumstances arise (and see also **Box 24.6** below, which deals with the expression of religious beliefs on social media).

An example of a fitness to practise case involving a refusal to supply emergency hormonal contraception is given in **Box 25.7** in **Chapter 25**.

Raising concerns

Every pharmacy professional has a duty to raise any concerns about individuals, actions or circumstances that may be unacceptable and that could result in risks to people receiving care and public safety. The guidance[22] outlines the importance of raising concerns, how to raise a concern and the legal aspects, including an outline of the Public Interest Disclosure Act 1998, which protects employees who raise genuine concerns in the workplace. The guidance also provides additional guidance for employers. Whistleblowing is also dealt with in **Chapter 2**.

Demonstrating professionalism online

This guidance[23] sets out what should be considered by pharmacy professionals when using social media. Pharmacy professionals have the same responsibilities and obligations when interacting online as they do when interacting face-to-face. Pharmacy professionals are expected to use good judgement and behave professionally when using social media. Pharmacy professionals are reminded that anything they say online can be easily copied and redistributed, and can be taken out of context. This can affect public confidence and trust in pharmacy professionals. Pharmacy professionals should be prepared to challenge poor behaviours and raise concerns with appropriate individuals when needed.

In *The Queen (on the application of Pitt and Tyas) v General Pharmaceutical Council* (see above), Mr Justice Singh considered the requirement in the GPhC's *Standards for*

---

20. https://assets.pharmacyregulation.org/files/2024-01/in_practice_guidance_on_confidentiality_june_2018.pdf (accessed 31 December 2024).
21. https://assets.pharmacyregulation.org/files/2024-01/in_practice-_guidance_on_religion_personal_values_and_beliefs.pdf (accessed 31 December 2024).
22. https://assets.pharmacyregulation.org/files/2024-01/in-practice-guidance-on-raising-concerns-november-2020.pdf (accessed 31 December 2024).
23. https://assets.pharmacyregulation.org/files/2024-01/demonstrating-professionalism-online-february-2020.pdf (accessed 31 December 2024).

pharmacy professionals that the Standards "need to be met at all times, not only during working hours". He said:

> *"there may be occasions which occur outside normal working hours and perhaps in a context which is completely unrelated to the professional work of a pharmacist which may be relevant to the safe and effective care which will be provided to patients. For example, if a pharmacy professional engages in a racist tirade on Twitter,*[24] *that may well shed light on how he or she might provide professional services to a person from an ethnic minority."*

The courts have considered a number of cases in which social media posts led to allegations of misconduct. These cases explore the importance of maintaining professional standards and the tension between this requirement and the right to freedom of expression. Examples of two such cases[25] are given in **Box 24.6.**

Box 24.6: Social media cases

In *Diggins v Bar Standards Board*, Martin Diggins was a non-practising barrister. In 2017, a young black female student posted a message on Twitter that referred to the need for Cambridge University to "decolonize its reading lists and ... not to be so arrogant as to assume civilization began with the writing of white men". Mr Diggins tweeted in reply: "Read it. Now, refuse to perform cunnilingus on shrill negroids who will destroy an academic reputation it has taken aeons to build". A Disciplinary Panel of the Bar Standards Board found that the tweet amounted to misconduct; it reprimanded Diggins and fined him £1,000.

Mr Diggins appealed to the High Court. Mr Justice Warby held that the Panel's task was to decide whether the tweet was likely to undermine the trust and confidence reposed by others in Mr Diggins and the Bar. In order to determine this, the Panel had to follow the principles set out by the Supreme Court in *Stocker v Stocker* ([2019] UKSC 17) which was a libel case:

> *"The judge tasked with deciding how a ... tweet on Twitter would be interpreted by a social media user must keep in mind the way in which such ... tweets are made and read.*
>
> *... it is wrong to engage in elaborate analysis of a tweet ... this is a casual medium; it is in the nature of conversation rather than carefully chosen expression; and ... is pre-eminently one in which the reader reads and passes on.*
>
> *... Twitter is a fast-moving medium. People will tend to scroll through messages relatively quickly. ... The essential message that is being conveyed by a Tweet is likely to be absorbed quickly by the reader."*

In short, words used on Twitter should not be the subject of elaborate over-analysis in "the fast-moving and relatively informal context of social media". On the other hand, this did not mean that a person who is criticised for a tweet can excuse or justify a message merely by saying it was posted casually without thought or inhibition.

---

24. Twitter is now known as "X".
25. *Diggins v Bar Standards Board* [2020] EWHC 467 (Admin) and *The Queen (on the application of Ngole) v The University of Sheffield* [2019] EWCA (Civ).

Box 24.6: Social media cases (cont.)

The judge rejected Diggins' claim that a single tweet could not be misconduct. Moreover, the Panel had found that although the tweet was directed to a particular student and the university, it was published to the world at large and the words were seriously offensive to third parties. It was not a momentary lapse that had been acknowledged and apologised for: Mr Diggins had chosen not to delete his tweet. The judge held that, applying ordinary community standards, the words used were "racially charged".

The appeal was dismissed.

****

In *The Queen (on the application of Ngole) v The University of Sheffield*, Mr Ngole was a studying at the University of Sheffield to become a social worker. He was a devout Christian for whom the Bible is the authoritative word of God. He posted on Facebook in response to a US news story a series of comments such as:

"... [S]ame sex marriage is a sin whether we accept it or not"

"... Homosexuality is a sin, no matter how you want to dress it up"

"... [Homosexuality] is a wicked act and God hates the act"

The University of Sheffield brought fitness to practise proceedings against Mr Ngole. Mr Ngole was told that whilst he was entitled to hold his views about homosexuality being a sin, he was never entitled to express such views on social media or in any public forum because this would undermine the confidence of future potential clients. Mr Ngole was found to have lacked insight and excluded from his course. The University's decision was challenged and the case came before the Court of Appeal which held:

> *"the obligation to maintain confidence cannot extend to prohibiting any statement that could be thought controversial or even to have political or moral overtones. No social worker could be sanctioned for arguing in public that social work was under-funded. The expression of such views in offensive language, however, might well damage confidence. The prevention of the latter would fall within the legitimate aim of the system of professional regulation, prevention of the former would not. The existence of a broad legitimate aim ... cannot extend to preclude legitimate expression of views simply because many might disagree with those views: that would indeed legitimise what in the United States has been described as a 'heckler's veto'."*

On the other hand, the Court held that the

> *"legitimate aim of regulation must extend so far as to seek to ensure that reasonable service users, of all kinds, perceive they will be treated with dignity and without discrimination. Social work service users cannot usually choose their social worker. The use of aggressive or offensive language in condemnation of homosexuality, or homosexual acts, would certainly be capable of undermining confidence and bringing the profession of social work into disrepute. ... [Mr Ngole] had an obligation not to allow his views about a person's lifestyle to prejudice his interactions with service users by creating the impression that he would discriminate against them."*

The Court of Appeal made it clear that the mere expression of religious views about sin does not necessarily connote discrimination against service users; otherwise, no Christian believing as Mr Ngole did would be secure in a healthcare profession, unless they resolved never to express their views on this issue other than in private. Even then, the Court asked rhetorically: what if a private expression of views was overheard and reported?

The right to freedom of expression in Article 10 of the European Convention of Human Rights is not an unqualified right: if Mr Ngole's comments had been abusive, if he had used

Box 24.6: Social media cases (cont.)

inflammatory language of his own, or made a personal attack, such words would fall to be regarded in the same way as would racist views, or inappropriate sexually explicit language. However, the University's stance that any expression of disapproval of same-sex relations (however mildly expressed) on a public social media or other platform which could be traced back to the person making it, was a breach of the professional guidelines was "untenable", disproportionate, and an incursion into Mr Ngole's right to freedom of expression.

With regard to the sanction – expulsion from his course – the Court of Appeal held that this was disproportionate. The University should have considered the possibility of a lesser sanction and tried to give Mr Ngole guidance on what he could and could not say when expressing his beliefs.

The Court concluded by saying

> *"We recognise that a more prolonged exploration of a resolution here might well have proved unpopular with some. However, University authorities have an obligation, as do all regulators, to exercise care and restraint, and to take unpopular decisions, if such represent the just and proportionate result."*

Female genital mutilation: mandatory duty for pharmacy professionals to report

This guidance[26] explains that all pharmacy professionals have a legal duty in England and Wales under the Female Genital Mutilation Act 2003, and a professional duty in Scotland, to report, orally or in writing to the police if:

- they observe physical signs that female genital mutilation (FGM) may have taken place in a girl under the age of 18 at the time of disclosure; or
- a child or young person tells them that they have had FGM.

The guidance refers to local safeguarding procedures, how these obligations align with GPhC standards, and refers to Home Office Guidance that explains that reporting FGM will not breach confidentiality requirements or other restrictions on disclosure which might otherwise apply.

Duty of candour

Following the Francis report into very poor care received by patients at Mid-Staffordshire Hospital Trust (see **Chapter 2**), a legal duty of candour was added to the standards required of sites and activities regulated by the Care Quality Commission. In October 2014, the chief executives of statutory regulators of healthcare professionals (including the GPhC) published as guidance a joint statement on *Openness and honesty – the professional duty of candour.*[27] The statement says that healthcare professionals must:

- tell the patient (or where appropriate, the patient's advocate, carer or family) when something has gone wrong;

---

26. https://assets.pharmacyregulation.org/files/2024-01/female-genital-mutilation-mandatory-duty-to-report-december-2019_0.pdf (accessed 31 December 2024).
27. https://assets.pharmacyregulation.org/files/joint_statement_on_the_professional_duty_of_candour.pdf (accessed 31 December 2024).

- apologise to the patient (or where appropriate, the patient's advocate, carer or family);
- offer an appropriate remedy or support to put matters right (if possible); and
- explain fully to the patient (or where appropriate, the patient's advocate, carer or family) the short- and long-term effects of what has happened.

Moreover, health professionals must be open and honest with their colleagues, employers and relevant organisations, and take part in reviews and investigations when requested. They must be open and honest with their regulators, raising concerns where appropriate, supporting and encouraging each other to be open and honest, and not stop someone from raising concerns.

Conflicts of interest

It is of the essence of professional conduct that a professional person must put the interests of patients or clients ahead of the personal interests of the professional person. A joint statement from the Chief Executives of the statutory regulators of health and care professionals in August 2017[28] gives guidance on what is expected of all healthcare professionals in relation to avoiding, declaring and managing conflicts of interest across all healthcare settings. Among the expectations outlined, the joint statement says that healthcare professionals should:

- put the interests of people in their care before their own interests or those of any colleague or organisation;
- consider where potential conflicts of interest may arise and be open about them;
- be open about, and declare, any conflicts of interest they face;
- reflect on their own learning and CPD needs regarding conflicts of interest; and
- ensure patients have access to visible information on any fees or charging policies for which they are responsible.

Conflicts of interest may arise when prescribing decisions are made. See the section above on Pharmacist prescribers. The GPhC's guidance on providing pharmacy services at a distance, including on the internet, also refers to conflicts of interest (see **Chapter 8**).

Other types of conflict of interest may arise in arrangements to direct prescriptions from GP practices to pharmacies when patients' choice of provider is bypassed.

Equality

This guidance[29] refers to the Protected Characteristics in the Equality Act 2010 and refers to the growing urgency, both in society as a whole and within pharmacy, to tackle all forms of inequality. The guidance sets out the four main types of discrimination:

- direct discrimination (that is, treating one person worse than another person because of a protected characteristic);

---

28. https://assets.pharmacyregulation.org/files/2024-01/conflicts_of_interest_joint_statement_1.pdf (accessed 31 August 2024).

29. https://assets.pharmacyregulation.org/files/2023-02/gphc-equality-guidance-for-pharmacies-december-2022_0.pdf (accessed 31 December 2024).

- indirect discrimination (that is, when there is an organisation's policy that applies in the same way for everybody but disadvantages a group of people who share a protected characteristic);
- harassment (that is, treating people in a way that violates their dignity, or creates a hostile, degrading, humiliating or offensive environment); and
- victimisation (that is, treating people unfairly if they decide to take action under the Equality Act, or if they support someone else who is doing so).

The guidance refers to the legal duty "to make reasonable adjustments to the property [services are provided] from, to meet the needs of disabled people (including ... employees)." This may mean: changing the way services are delivered, providing extra equipment, and removing physical barriers. What is reasonable will depend on the size and circumstances of the pharmacy.

Over and above legal obligations, the guidance says that the GPhC expects pharmacy owners to take whatever steps they need to run their pharmacies in a way that encourages equality of opportunity and respect for diversity. The guidance says that pharmacy owners are responsible for creating and supporting an environment in which pharmacy professionals can demonstrate their professionalism, and deliver person-centred care that takes account of the diverse needs and cultural differences in the communities they serve.

Equality and discrimination also feature in the GPhC's guidance on the outcomes of fitness to practise cases (see **Chapter 25**).

Guidance to support the standards for pharmacy premises

Premises standards are covered in **Chapter 2**. The GPhC has published guidance to support its Standards for pharmacy premises as follows:

Guidance to ensure a safe and effective pharmacy team

The guidance[30] requires pharmacy owners to make sure:

- each pharmacy has enough skilled and qualified staff to provide safe and effective pharmacy services; and
- staff can meet their professional obligations and can raise concerns in an environment which encourages openness, honesty and continuing development.

Pharmacy owners are reminded that they are accountable for making sure the standards for registered pharmacies are met. In a limited or public limited company, the board of directors has a significant role in and ongoing responsibility for making sure people receive safe and effective care from registered pharmacies.

Notably, the GPhC does not suggest minimum staffing levels. Its guidance says that the number of staff and the skill mix needed to provide safe and effective pharmacy services will vary significantly between pharmacies and that owners should consider a

30. https://assets.pharmacyregulation.org/files/document/guidance_to_ensure_a_safe_and_effective_pharmacy_team_june_2018.pdf (accessed 31 December 2024).

range of factors including the volume of dispensing, the changing demands throughout the day, the use of technology, including robotics, the different sets of skills, knowledge and experience within the team and previous incidents and errors and the reasons for them.

Guidance for registered pharmacies providing pharmacy services at a distance, including on the internet

Although this guidance relates to all remote services including, for example, hub and spoke dispensing, it is primarily concerned with online pharmacy which is covered in **Chapter 8**.

Guidance for registered pharmacies preparing unlicensed medicines

The guidance[31] applies to the process of preparing an unlicensed medicine by or under the supervision of a pharmacist under the exemption in the Medicines Act (see **Chapter 5**). Most medicines that are prescribed in Great Britain are licensed by the MHRA. Medicines that are manufactured in a pharmacy are either specials made by companies to whom the manufacture has been outsourced, or extemporaneously dispensed in the pharmacy to which the prescription has been presented. The practice of extemporaneous dispensing and, consequently, the skill involved, has dwindled over the years partly because of the availability of specials manufacturers and partly because of concerns felt by pharmacists in the light of the *Peppermint water case*[32] (see **Box 24.7**).

Box 24.7: The peppermint water case

In 1998 a three-week-old child was prescribed peppermint water to treat colic. The prescription was dispensed at a branch of Boots. It was made up by a pre-registration trainee working under the supervision of a pharmacist. The prescription bore no instructions for dilution or warning that dilution was required. A bottle of concentrated chloroform water was used to prepare the peppermint water. The pre-registration trainee did not appreciate that the concentrated chloroform would need to be diluted. The peppermint water was administered to the child and he died.

Both the pharmacist and the pre-registration trainee were initially charged with manslaughter. Before their trials, the pharmacist and pre-registration trainee agreed to plead guilty to an offence under section 64 of the Medicines Act 1968 of supplying a product that was not of the nature or quality prescribed, in return for which the manslaughter charges were dropped. The pharmacist was fined £1000 and the pre-registration trainee was fined £750.

Prosecutions for manslaughter and under section 64 of the Medicines Act 1968 are dealt with in **Chapter 25**.

The guidance says that patients have every right to expect that when an unlicensed medicine is prepared by, or under the supervision of, a pharmacist in a registered

31. https://assets.pharmacyregulation.org/files/document/guidance_for_registered_pharmacies_preparing_unlicensed_medicines_august_2018_0.pdf (accessed 31 December 2024).
32. *The Pharmaceutical Journal*, March 2000, Vol 264, p390-392.

pharmacy, it is of an equivalent quality to any licensed medicine they will receive, such as those produced by a regulated and licensed manufacturer. Requirements include:

- A risk assessment.
- Regular audit to ensure robust systems enable the owner to demonstrate that the pharmacy continues to be a safe place in which to prepare medicines for patients.
- Reviews reacting to changes of key staff.
- Detailed record keeping so that the method of preparation can be clearly reconstructed in the event of a recall or patient-safety incident.
- Ingredients and starting materials used in the preparation of the unlicensed medicine should be obtained from a reputable source such as a licensed manufacturer or distributor.
- Quality assurance must be in place to make sure a finished medicine is of the quality needed for its intended use.
- Patients should be informed that the medicine is unlicensed and receive an explanation of what this means. Since there will be no patient information leaflet (see **Chapter 18**), appropriate advice should be given to the patient (in writing, if possible) including when there is no direct contact with the patient when the medicine is supplied.
- If the medicine is prepared in line with a British Pharmacopoeia formula or monograph (see **Chapter 20**), there are particular labelling requirements for unlicensed medicines (see **Chapter 18**).
- Specially designed equipment should be available, including accurate measuring scales, cleaning equipment and sterilising equipment.

SUMMARY

- Professional conduct requirements are based on standards and guidance published by the GPhC.
- Non-mandatory guidance is given by the Royal Pharmaceutical Society.
- GPhC standards require pharmacy professionals and pharmacy students to behave professionally at all times.
- Failure to comply with the standards may amount to misconduct.
- The GPhC has published guidance to support its standards for pharmacy professionals and guidance to support its standards for pharmacy premises.

FURTHER READING

- Buerki RA, Vottero LD (2013) *Pharmacy Ethics: A Foundation for Professional Practice*. American Pharmacists Association (written for a North American audience).
- Chemist and Druggist (a weekly publication mostly concerned with community pharmacy): **http://www.chemistanddruggist.co.uk**.
- Elvey R, Hassell K, Lewis P, Schafheutle E, Willis S, Harrison S. Patient-centred professionalism in pharmacy: values and behaviours. J Health Organ Manag (2015) 29 413–430.
- General Pharmaceutical Council (details of pharmacy standards): **http://www.pharmacyregulation.org**.

- General Pharmaceutical Council *Standards and guidance for pharmacy professionals* **https://www.pharmacyregulation.org/pharmacists/standards-and-guidance-pharmacy-professionals** (accessed 31 December 2024).
- General Pharmaceutical Council *Standards and guidance for registered pharmacies* **https://www.pharmacyregulation.org/pharmacies/standards-and-guidance-registered-pharmacies** (accessed 31 December 2024).
- On consent, Govind **https://www.chemistanddruggist.co.uk/CD135648/Flu-vaccinations-and-the-tricky-issue-of-consent--where-do-pharmacy-professionals-stand?vid=PharmaCandD** (accessed 6 August 2024).
- Royal Pharmaceutical Society: **https://www.rpharms.com/**.
- The RPS is a membership organisation for pharmacists and the Pharmaceutical Journal (**http://www.pharmaceutical-journal.com**) is provided free to its members. The RPS also issues annually *Medicines, Ethics and Practice: The Professional Guide for Pharmacists*, which is intended to assist members in interpretation of the law and standards of practice in real life situations.

CHAPTER 25

Fitness to practise

Fitness to practise is about protecting the public. There are processes to ensure pharmacists and pharmacy technicians are fit to practise, for example on first registration, and also to deal with concerns about possible misconduct. There are legal procedures that have to be followed which, in the last resort, may result in removal from the Register.

The role of the General Pharmaceutical Council

The role of the General Pharmaceutical Council (GPhC)[1] is to protect the health, safety and wellbeing of patients and people who use pharmacy services. Its principal functions (Art.4 of the Pharmacy Order 2010)[2] include:

- establishing and maintaining a Register of pharmacists, pharmacy technicians and premises at which a retail pharmacy business is, or is to be, carried on;
- setting and promoting standards (**Chapters 2** and **24**) for the safe and effective practice of pharmacy;
- setting requirements by reference to which registrants must demonstrate that their fitness to practise is not impaired;
- promoting the safe and effective practice of pharmacy by registrants (including, for example, by reference to any code of conduct for, and ethics relating to, pharmacy); and
- ensuring the continued fitness to practise of registrants.

Article 6 of the Pharmacy order says:

> "(1) *The over-arching objective of the Council in exercising its functions is the protection of the public.*
>
> (1A) *The pursuit by the Council of its over-arching objective involves the pursuit of the following objectives:*
>
> (a) *to protect, promote and maintain the health, safety and wellbeing of the public;*
>
> (b) *to promote and maintain public confidence in the professions regulated under this Order;*
>
> (c) *to promote and maintain proper professional standards and conduct for members of those professions; and*
>
> (d) *to promote and maintain proper standards in relation to the carrying on of retail pharmacy businesses at registered pharmacies."*

---

1. The law applicable to fitness to practise is the same across Great Britain, but some other statutory provisions referred to in this chapter apply only to England and Wales.
2. All references to Articles are to the Pharmacy Order 2010 unless otherwise stated.

Fitness to practise also comes under consideration in some NHS processes. These are referred to in **Chapter 3** and are not covered by this chapter.

Fitness to practise

Under the heading *What is fitness to practise?*[3] the GPhC says on its website:

> *"Being fit to practise means a pharmacy professional has the skills, knowledge, health and character to do their job safely and effectively. They must also act professionally and meet the principles of good practice set out in our standards and guidance."*

Elsewhere,[4] the GPhC says:

> *"A pharmacy professional may not be fit to practise for a number of reasons, for example if:*
> - *their behaviour is putting patients at risk,*
> - *they are practising in an unsafe way, or*
> - *their health may be affecting their ability to make safe judgements about their patients."*

Publication of decisions

Decisions of the Fitness to Practise (FtP) Committee are included in this chapter. The FtP Committee was established when the GPhC was created in 2010. Before then, fitness to practise cases (previously referred to as *disciplinary* cases) were heard by the Statutory Committee of the Royal Pharmaceutical Society of Great Britain and, for a short period between the abolition of the Statutory Committee and the creation of the FtP Committee, by a Disciplinary Committee and a Health Committee. Reference to decisions before 2010 will therefore be to one of these former Committees. The GPhC has published a *publication and disclosure policy*[5] in line with which, in the interests of proportionality, it does not publish FtP decisions on its website indefinitely. Where FtP cases are referred to in this chapter, the dates of decisions are given in footnotes as are details of reports in the pharmacy press where available (for the purpose of research), but the registrants in those cases are not named here. The position is different where decisions have been made in a court because those cases often establish or confirm legal

3. https://www.pharmacyregulation.org/patients-and-public/reporting-concerns/how-we-deal-concerns/fitness-practise-faqs (accessed 31 December 2024).
4. Annual Fitness to Practise report 2021-22 https://www.pharmacyregulation.org/about-us/news-and-updates/annual-report-202122 (accessed 31 December 2024).
5. GPhC publication and disclosure policy https://assets.pharmacyregulation.org/files/document/gphc0034v6-publication-and-disclosure-policy-february-2021.pdfhttps://assets.pharmacyregulation.org/files/document/gphc0034v6-publication-and-disclosure-policy-february-2021.pdf (accessed 31 December 2024).

principles to be followed and it is therefore important to be able to find and read those cases. Guidance for finding them is given at the end of this chapter. Transcripts of recent FtP decisions will still be accessible on the GPhC's website until they are removed in accordance with the GPhC's policy.

Specific occasions when fitness to practise will be considered

The Registrar of the GPhC will consider the fitness to practise of a registrant specifically:

- when a prospective registrant first applies for registration (Art.20);
- if it is shown to the satisfaction of the Registrar that a registrant's fitness to practise is impaired as a result of prescribed circumstances (see below) or because of a problem with the registrant's physical or mental health (Art.30) at the time of entry or renewal of an entry in the Register;
- where an allegation is made to the Council that a registrant's fitness to practise is impaired (Art.52); or
- the GPhC has information that calls into question a registrant's fitness to practise, even though no allegation has been made to that effect (Art.52).

Under the FtP Rules,[6] a registrant must notify the GPhC's Registrar in writing within seven days if (Rule 4), amongst other things, they:

a. are convicted of any criminal offence;
b. accept a caution;
c. become subject to an investigation into their fitness to practise by another regulatory body;
d. become the subject of any fraud investigation in relation to the Health Service; or
e. are the subject of a ruling that renders them unable to practise within the NHS on fitness to practise grounds.

When renewing registration annually, registrants are also required to answer questions about, amongst other things, whether they have previously been convicted or cautioned for a criminal offence, or if a determination has been made by a health or social care regulator that their fitness to practise is impaired, or if they have any physical or mental health problems that may impair their ability to carry out their duties in a safe and effective manner. The GPhC informs registrants that they are not covered by the Rehabilitation of Offenders Act 1974. Cautions or convictions for offences contrary to section 67(1) of the Medicines Act 1968 are not protected from disclosure. In most other cases in England and Wales, cautions given to an adult will be protected from the need to disclose them after six years (two years if under 18 at the time of the offence), and most convictions of an adult will be protected from the need to disclose them after 11 years (five and a half years if under 18 at the time of the offence). In Scotland, certain serious convictions must always be disclosed; other convictions cease to be disclosable after

---

6. The Rules are the General Pharmaceutical Council (Fitness to Practise and Disqualification etc. Rules) Order of Council 2010 and are referred to as the Fitness to Practise Rules.

15 years if the registrant was aged 18 or over at the date of conviction and after 7 and a half years if aged under 18 at the date of conviction.[7]

Failure to give disclosure may itself be considered misconduct, and the courts have upheld the serious view taken by regulators of such failure because it strikes at the heart of the registration process and the reliability of the Register; the failure to disclose is highly relevant to whether an applicant is fit to practise.[8]

Grounds for finding impairment

A person's fitness to practise may only be regarded as "impaired" by reason of (Art.51):

- misconduct;
- deficient professional performance (which includes competence);
- adverse physical or mental health which impairs their ability to practise safely and effectively or which otherwise impairs their ability to carry out the duties of a pharmacist or a pharmacy technician in a safe and effective manner;
- not having the necessary knowledge of English
- failure to comply with a reasonable requirement imposed by an individual assessor or an assessment team in connection with carrying out a professional performance assessment;
- a conviction or police caution for a criminal offence,[9] an admonition or absolute discharge ordered by a court in Scotland, accepting a fixed penalty conditional offer by a procurator fiscal, or being bound over to keep the peace;
- having agreed to pay a penalty under the Social Security Administration Act 1992 as an alternative to prosecution;
- inclusion by the Disclosure and Barring Service in a barred list or by the Scottish Ministers in the children's list or the adults' list; or
- a determination of impairment of unfitness to practise by another regulatory body.[10]

Misconduct

Misconduct may relate to professional practice, including dispensing errors (see below), but the meaning of *misconduct* is much wider. In *R (on the application of Remedy UK Ltd) v General Medical Council*,[11] a case concerning alleged misconduct by medical practitioners, Lord Justice Elias said:

---

7. Rehabilitation of Offenders Act 1974, Rehabilitation of Offenders Act 1974 (Exceptions) Order 1975 and Rehabilitation of Offenders Act 1974 (Exclusions and Exceptions) (Scotland) Order 2013. GPhC guidance can be found here https://assets.pharmacyregulation.org/files/2023-06/Fitness-to-practice-declaring-cautions-and-convictions.pdf (accessed 31 December 2024).
8. *Harris v Registrar of Approved Driving Instructors* [2010] EWCA Civ 808.
9. The conviction may occur anywhere in the world but, in the case of a conviction outside the British Islands must be for something that would be a criminal offence in the British Islands.
10. Under the Safeguarding Vulnerable Groups Act 2006.
11. [2010] EWHC 1245 (Admin).

"Misconduct is of two principal kinds. First, it may involve sufficiently serious misconduct in the exercise of professional practice such that it can properly be described as misconduct going to fitness to practise. Second, it can involve conduct of a morally culpable or otherwise disgraceful kind which may, and often will, occur outwith the course of professional practice itself, but which brings disgrace upon the doctor and thereby prejudices the reputation of the profession. Misconduct within the first limb need not arise in the context of a doctor exercising his clinical practice, but it must be in the exercise of the doctor's medical calling. There is no single or simple test for defining when that condition is satisfied. Conduct falls into the second limb if it is dishonourable or disgraceful or attracts some kind of opprobrium; that fact may be sufficient to bring the profession of medicine into disrepute. It matters not whether such conduct is directly related to the exercise of professional skill."

Specifically in relation to pharmacy practice, in a case in which a pharmacist failed to query an ambiguous prescription for a mixture that contained a fatal overdose of pethidine, the High Court held that misconduct is simply to be defined as "incorrect or erroneous conduct of any kind provided that it is of a serious nature judged according to the rules written or unwritten governing the profession".[12]

Directors and superintendents of bodies corporate

If misconduct is alleged to have occurred at a pharmacy, the fact of being superintendent pharmacist[13] of a body corporate that owns a pharmacy, or ownership of a pharmacy,[14] is not sufficient on its own to justify referring an allegation of misconduct against either. In a 2009 case[15] against the superintendent pharmacist of a company at one of whose branches dispensing errors had been made, the former Disciplinary Committee said "before finding misconduct, there must be consent, connivance or neglect by [the superintendent] and it must be of a serious nature – that is to say there must be evidence on which we could find serious fault by the superintendent".

In 2016, the GPhC's FtP Committee held a pharmacist[16] guilty of misconduct in relation to the conduct of a company's online pharmacy business of which she was a director, even though she was not the superintendent or a responsible pharmacist. She had noticed orders for medicines such as codeine linctus and did not take action to stop supplies. The FtP Committee said she "ought to have done more" but was "content to let the business proceed without raising any questions". This failure to make patients her

12. Mr Justice Webster in *The Queen v Statutory Committee of the Pharmaceutical Society, ex parte Sokoh, The Times*, 4 December 1986.
13. *The Queen v The Statutory Committee of the Pharmaceutical Society of Great Britain, ex parte Lewis & Jeffreys Limited, Berg and others* (unreported).
14. *Akodu v Solicitors Regulation Authority* [2009] EWHC 3588 (Admin).
15. 26 January 2009.
16. 29 June 2016.

first concern – described as an abdication of responsibility as a registered pharmacist – had the potential to cause harm to patients and brought the profession into disrepute.

The concept of misconduct is not confined to pharmacy practice. As the GPhC's *Standards for pharmacy professionals* say, (see **Chapter 2**) "The standards need to be met at all times, not only during working hours. This is because the attitudes and behaviours of professionals outside of work can affect the trust and confidence of patients and the public in pharmacy professionals". The standards are reproduced in full in Appendix 1.

Misconduct in pharmacy legislation

There are express statutory references to misconduct in the legislation governing the practice of pharmacy. Specifically, if a registrant fails to comply with standards of conduct, ethics or performance set by the GPhC (see **Chapters 2** and **24**), any such failure is not, of itself, to be taken to constitute misconduct. However, it is to be taken into account in any fitness to practise proceedings (Art.48(3)).

The Medicines Act 1968 imposes certain requirements on responsible pharmacists and superintendent pharmacists (see **Chapter 7**). Section 72B of the Medicines Act says that failure to comply with these requirements may constitute misconduct.

Dispensing errors as misconduct or as deficient professional performance

The question of whether a single dispensing error can be misconduct has been considered by the High Court, which ruled that a single error is capable of constituting misconduct if it is sufficiently serious, although whether it crosses the threshold of seriousness depends on the facts of individual cases. In a dental appeal, the judge, Lord Cooke said:[17]

> *"It is settled that serious professional misconduct does not require moral turpitude. Gross professional negligence can fall within it. Something more is required than a degree of negligence enough to give rise to civil liability but not calling for the opprobrium that inevitably attaches to the disciplinary offence."*

In a 2012 case[18] a pharmacist admitted a series of dispensing errors. The GPhC contended that her fitness to practise was impaired on the alternative grounds of deficient professional performance or misconduct. The FtP Committee followed a ruling of the High Court[19] that where charges of misconduct and deficient professional performance are founded on the same facts, then the Committee can only find impairment on one of those grounds, not on both.

17. *Preiss v General Dental Council* [2001] 1 W.L.R. 26.
18. 16 April 2012 (*Pharm J*, 15 September 2012 p. 307).
19. *Vali v General Optical Council* [2011] EWHC 310 (Admin).

The Committee noted that deficient professional performance was defined in these terms[20] in a GMC case involving a medical practitioner:

> *"It connotes a standard of professional performance which is unacceptably low and which (save in exceptional circumstances) has been demonstrated by reference to a fair sample of the [registrant's] work."*

The Committee went on to rule that "not every instance of deficient professional performance ... will necessarily give rise to impairment". The Committee had regard to the fitness to practise criteria (see below) and concluded that, on the facts of the case, the registrant presented an actual risk to patients and the frequency and gravity of the dispensing errors were such that she might well bring the profession of pharmacy into disrepute. The case was thus dealt with as deficient professional performance, rather than as misconduct.

In a 2022 report, the Professional Standards Authority said:

> *"Health professionals ... are not robots, and by virtue of the high-risk work they do, can make mistakes that lead to permanent injury and even death. These mistakes are more likely to happen when professionals are under pressure, and working in challenging conditions. It is the role of professional regulation neither to punish for past wrongdoing nor to divorce professional failings from the context in which they occurred."*[21]

Convictions and other misconduct

In a criminal case, someone who has been found not guilty of an offence cannot normally be tried again for the same offence. This has been referred to as the *double jeopardy* rule. This rule does not apply to fitness to practise proceedings.[22]

The FtP Committee may find facts proved on the balance of probabilities even though a registrant may have been acquitted of an offence in a criminal court where the burden of proof – beyond reasonable doubt – was higher. In a 2012 case[23] the registrant had been acquitted of rape following a Crown Court trial. Having considered the evidence put forward in the Crown Court and having heard from witnesses, the FtP Committee found the sexual misconduct allegation proved and directed the removal of the registrant's name from the Register. The High Court has ruled[24] that the test in deciding whether to bringing fitness to practise proceedings after an acquittal is not "whether a second bite at the cherry might secure a 'better' outcome, but rather what is in the public

20. *Caelham v General Medical Council* [2007] EWHC 2606, [2008] LS Law Medical 96.
21. https://www.professionalstandards.org.uk/safer-care-for-all (accessed 31 December 2024).
22. *R (Redgrave) v Commissioner of Police for the Metropolis* [2003] 1 W.L.R. 1136.
23. 14 December 2012 (Pharm J, 9 February 2013, p.154).
24. *Ashraf v General Dental Council* [2014] EWHC 2618.

interest, viewing the case through the lens of the obligations placed on the regulator". There may be cases where further investigation by a regulator would be unfair after a registrant has been acquitted, for example, if the allegations do not touch on professional responsibilities to patients or to the NHS, but each case must be considered on its merits.

Convictions and misconduct need not be related to the practice of pharmacy, so there are no limitations on the scope of allegations, including convictions of students,[25] that may lead to consideration of whether fitness to practise is impaired. Examples of cases that have led to fitness to practise proceedings include:

- failure to disclose to the GPhC convictions for theft,[26] for motoring offences,[27] or for drug misuse;[28]
- sexual activity with a 14-year-old girl;[29]
- sexually touching a patient during acupuncture treatment;[30]
- touching a patient in a consulting room[31] (not with a sexual motive, but because the pharmacist lacked appropriate expertise);
- convictions for drink driving or for doing an act to pervert the course of justice;[32]
- theft from an employer;[33] and
- shoplifting.[34]

Students

The General Pharmaceutical Council's Standards for Pharmacy Professionals (see Appendix 1) says:

> *"The standards for pharmacy professionals are relevant to all pharmacy students and trainees while they are on their journey towards registration and practice. The standards explain the knowledge, attitudes and behaviours that will be expected of students and trainees if they apply to join the register.*

---

25. Pharmacy students had been involved in a fracas at the London School of Pharmacy. They were found guilty of unlawful wounding and each given a conditional discharge (which is not classed as a conviction). The High Court held that it was open to the Pharmaceutical Society to bring a case alleging misconduct in disciplinary proceedings, relying on the same facts as were before the criminal court; *R v Statutory Committee of the Pharmaceutical Society of Great Britain and Martin and Shutt Ex p. Pharmaceutical Society of Great Britain* [1981] 1 W.L.R. 886.
26. *Pharm J*, 3 March 2012 p. 284.
27. *Pharm J*, 3 March 2012 p. 283.
28. *Pharm J*, 24 March 2012 p. 395).
29. *Pharm J*, 7 January 2012 p. 14.
30. *Pharm J*, 7 January 2012 p. 14.
31. *Pharm J*, 28 January 2012 p. 122.
32. *Pharm J*, 5 May 2012 p. 570.
33. *Monji v General Pharmaceutical Council* [2014] EWHC 3128 (Admin) (theft of fragrance testers, resulting in a decision to remove the pharmacist's name from the Register).
34. *Pharm J*, 27 June 2012 – repeated shoplifting leading to striking off; Chemist & Druggist, 25 January 2012 – resulting in suspension.

They should be interpreted in the context of education and training and used as a tool to prepare students and trainees for registration as a pharmacy professional.

Pharmacy students and trainees should consider the standards as they move closer to registration and professional practice, and should read them alongside other relevant documents that are provided by initial education and training providers."

University schools of pharmacy are required to have fitness to practise procedures that can be used to deal with allegations concerning students. Similar arrangements are in place for medical students.

The case of *HA v University of Wolverhampton*[35] dealt with important issues concerning the duties of a university, the respective responsibilities of the university and the GPhC, and how to view a conviction of a pharmacy student for serious criminal offences committed when he was 14 years old. See **Box 25.1**.

Box 25.1

HA had been convicted of robbery and assault occasioning actual bodily harm. Both offences were committed when he was 14. He received youth rehabilitation orders.

HA did not declare the convictions when he applied for and was accepted onto the University's MPharm course. When the convictions came to light, the University held fitness to practise proceedings.

HA told the University's Fitness to Practise Panel (FTPP) that the assault was a fight at school in which he knocked another student's tooth out. The robbery was committed when he was part of group which had robbed two youths of a credit card and phone in a park. A letter from his supervising probation officer indicated that he made excellent progress in relation to the youth rehabilitation orders, and they were revoked early.

The FTPP decided to exclude HA from the MPharm course and he challenged the decision in the High Court. Mr Justice Julian Knowles had to decide the following issues:

- Whether the University was entitled to require HA as part of the application process to declare that he had any spent conviction, other than those that would be filtered out.
- Whether the University was entitled to require HA to apply for an enhanced DBS check in respect of his attendance on the MPharm course and associated placements.
- Whether the decision to exclude HA from the MPharm course was a disproportionate infringement of his rights under Article 8 and/or Article 2 of Protocol 1 to the European Convention on Human rights, or otherwise unlawful.

The judge said:

"It is for the [GPhC] to determine what it requires by way of proficiency in order to become a registered pharmacist, and what requirements must be satisfied by those wishing to study with a view to becoming pharmacists. The legislation ensures that the [GPhC's] requirements will be met because those wishing to become pharmacists after university study in Great Britain may only do so if they successfully complete a degree which has been approved by the [GPhC]. That is because of Article 21(1) of the Pharmacy Order, which provides that such a person is appropriately qualified if he has been awarded

35. [2018] EWHC 144 (Admin).

Box 25.1 (cont.)

a qualification in Great Britain that has been approved by the [GPhC] as attesting to a standard of proficiency for the safe and effective practice of pharmacy that, in the [GPhC's] opinion, it is necessary for the person to achieve in order to be entered in the Register of pharmacists. Hence, the [GPhC] has the right to determine which universities may award degrees that educationally qualify students to become pharmacists.

The [GPhC] ensures that its character requirements are met by only accrediting those universities who can prove that they have effective systems in place to ensure that only those students who satisfy those requirements are selected. Universities therefore have a duty and responsibility to operate their systems properly ... in fulfilment of what they have undertaken to the [GPhC] they will do in order to receive the [GPhC's] accreditation, namely, only to select those students whose characters are such that they are fit to begin the course they must pass to become pharmacists. In my judgment, assessing a person's suitability to be a pharmacist means more than just an assessment by the [GPhC] whether an applicant's name is to be entered on the Register under Article 20(1)(a) of the Pharmacy Order. It also includes assessing whether an applicant is suitable to be enrolled on the MPharm course, which is a required step to becoming a pharmacist. If they are not suitable, then by definition they are not suitable to become a pharmacist because they cannot complete the required degree. And ... assessing suitability at that stage can and must include criminal record checks.

In deciding who to admit to an accredited pharmacy course, the University is entitled to have an eye to the future and only to select those candidates which it believes are most likely to successfully enter the pharmacy profession. In making that assessment, the University is not determining that the person will enter the profession: that is a matter for the [GPhC] to determine at the relevant time in accordance with the Registration Rules and the Pharmacy Order ...

The University is entitled to ask itself during the selection process: 'We have been approved to offer a degree which is a required step to enter this profession. Who out of this pool of candidates do we think are most likely to successfully enter the profession, such that we should allocate our limited resources to their education and training, as opposed to another group of applicants?' That, in my judgment, involves an assessment of an applicant's suitability to enter the pharmacy profession ...

... the University's reason for seeking disclosure was in fulfilment of Standard 1 set by the [GPhC], namely, 'Patient and public safety'. The [GPhC] requires character checks to be carried out to ensure that those who enrol on an accredited MPharm course do not have criminal records such as would put the public or patients at risk."

In relation to the proportionality of the University's decision in the light of HA's age at the time of his offences, the judge quoted from an earlier judgment in which the court had said:

"It is important to bear in mind any factors that may diminish the culpability of a child or young person. Children and young people are not fully developed and they have not attained full maturity. As such, this can impact on their decision making and risk taking behaviour. It is important to consider the extent to which the child or young person has been acting impulsively and whether their conduct has been affected by inexperience, emotional volatility or negative influences. They may not fully appreciate the effect their actions can have on other people and may not be capable of fully understanding the distress and pain they cause."

Mr Justice Julian Knowles said it was obvious that the points made in the paragraph he quoted were highly relevant to the question of whether HA's fitness to practise as an adult student pharmacist was impaired by his offences committed aged just 14 to such an extent

Box 25.1 (cont.)

that the protection of the public required that he be removed from the course, or whether his convictions were just the product of childish behaviour which was firmly in the past.

The FTPP's failure to consider the quite considerable mitigation which existed was a fundamental failure which meant the University's decision could not stand. If the FTPP had decided to exclude HA from the MPharm course after considering all the relevant matters, including HA's age at the time of his offending, the exclusion decision might have been upheld.

In another case, a medical student posted on a fellow student's Facebook page a message with the words in capital letters: "I will look for you, I will find you. And I will kill you". These words were viewable by the fellow student's Facebook friends. There was also a private message to the fellow student which was offensive and could be considered threatening. Allegations of misconduct were investigated by a university panel which had guidance that expulsion should be applied if a student's behaviour is considered to be fundamentally incompatible with continuing on a medical course or eventually practising as a doctor. The panel decided that the student was not fit to practise medicine because his fundamental unsuitability for the medical profession could not be corrected. An appeal was unsuccessful, as was a complaint to the Office of the Independent Adjudicator (OIA). An application to the High Court for Judicial Review of the decision of the Adjudicator was dismissed, as was an appeal to the Court of Appeal.[36] The Court of Appeal held that the OIA had a wide power to consider whether an institution's decision was reasonable in all the circumstances, but there were no grounds for interfering with the original panel's conclusion: a decision to expel was consistent with the relevant General Medical Council and Medical Schools Council guidance, which provided that one of the most frequent causes of concern relating to student fitness to practise was aggressive, violent or threatening behaviour, and that expulsion could be appropriate when a student's behaviour was fundamentally incompatible with being a doctor.

Fitness to practise procedures for students do not need to follow the same procedures that apply to registrants, which are set out below, although a structured procedure may be required if misconduct is alleged. This is illustrated by a decision of the Outer House of the Court of Session, described in **Box 25.2** below.[37]

36. *R (on the application of Thilakawardhana) v Office of the Independent Adjudicator for Higher Education* [2018] EWCA Civ 13.

37. *Judicial Review of a decision of the Senate Fitness to Practise Appeal Committee of a Scottish university* [2023] CSOH 52.

Box 25.2: Judicial review of a decision of a Senate Fitness to Practise Appeal Committee of a Scottish university

The petitioner, SM, was in his final year as a dental student. He was initially subject to informal fitness to practise proceedings by the university authorities where the key concerns were high recorded levels of current and historic absences by SM from his course. An investigating officer reported: (i) poor motivation and attendance in his fifth year of study, (ii) low quality and quantity of clinical activity by him recorded on the university's online platform, among other things.

SM was advised by the university that he was being referred for formal fitness to practise proceedings, alleging a failure to satisfy attendance and engagement conditions which had previously been identified to him in informal proceedings. Concerns had been formed about his continuing absences, failure to report illnesses and absences, lack of data to assess his performance, and his failure to engage with a mentoring programme. It was acknowledged that SM had been suffering from certain health conditions which had materially contributed to his perceived failings. The formal fitness to practise proceedings concluded with a decision to exclude SM from his course. SM applied for judicial review of this decision.

SM's barrister argued that the university's fitness to practise procedures were unfair and did not bear comparison with the procedures that would have been followed by the General Dental Council if SM had been on the GDC register.

The judge, Lord Sandison, rejected SM's petition for judicial review, saying:

"[The court] requires to consider whether there is any reason why the law ought to require student fitness to practise proceedings to conform or at least approximate to such proceedings in the context of registered members of a profession which the student aspires to enter. It is difficult as a matter of principle to see why that should be the case. Fitness to practise proceedings against an established member of a profession will generally turn on his or her ability or willingness to behave in a way acceptable to the requirements of the profession in question. In many though not all cases, the lack of such ability or willingness is likely to be demonstrated by misconduct of some kind. In that context it makes sense to proceed in the familiar structured way of fact-finding followed by a determination of whether misconduct has occurred before passing to the question of whether impairment has in consequence been established and then determining sanction. In the context of student fitness to practise procedures, the question in issue is whether the student is meeting various requirements in the course of his or her training which are deemed necessary in order to satisfy the criteria for entering into the relevant profession in the first place. The answer to that question need not, as it did not in the present case, involve any issue of misconduct at all, but rather requires an overall consideration of both matters of fact (for example, how many absences from classes or clinics actually occurred) and matters of impression or opinion (for example, the degree to which the student is engaging with his course of study or demonstrating insight into his position), all feeding together into a rather more wide-ranging and holistic determination of fitness of practise than might typically be the case in fitness to practise proceedings against an established professional. A rigid requirement to proceed in set stages of procedure in that specific context might well hinder or even prevent an appropriate decision being made, and cannot be said to be a legal requirement in the student context. It follows that criticisms made of the [university's] fitness to practise procedures or their outcomes which are based simply on their claimed deviation from what would have been the GDC's procedures or outcomes in the case of fitness to practise proceedings against registered dentists cannot be sustained."

The GPhC has published Guidance on managing fitness to practise concerns in education and training. The Guidance is accompanied by case studies in a separate document. Details are included in the list of further reading at the end of this chapter.

First registration and good character

Before being registered with the GPhC, an applicant must satisfy registration requirements to establish that they are fit to practise the profession.[38] Healthcare regulators are overseen by the Professional Standards Authority for Health and Social Care (PSA). The PSA has published guidance[39] that there are four key elements which form the basis of assessing good character. These are whether an applicant has acted, or there is reason to believe they are liable in future to act:

a. in such a way that puts at risk the health, safety or wellbeing of a patient or other member of the public;
b. in such a way that their registration would undermine public confidence in the profession;
c. in such a way that indicates an unwillingness to act in accordance with the standards of the profession; or
d. in a dishonest manner.

In *Layne v Attorney General of Grenada*,[40] the Privy Council held that Mr Layne, a prospective barrister who had been convicted of murder many years before and who had served his sentence and become rehabilitated, could not satisfy the good character requirement for admission to the bar. Good character has two facets: the candidate's attributes and the risk of damage to public confidence in the profession. The ruling made it clear that the good character requirement was equally applicable to other professions in which the public place great trust. The question to be considered is whether, viewed objectively, the public can reasonably be expected to have confidence in the admission of the candidate. Even if individual members of the public would have confidence in the applicant, this was not sufficient, nor was the fact that Mr Layne was now a man of good character.

The same principles for assessing fitness to practise in the case of someone already registered apply to the case of an applicant for first registration.[41] However, in contrast to the position of an existing registrant, the burden is on the applicant for first registration to satisfy the Registrar that they are fit to practise.

---

38. Rule 10(3)(j) and (k) of the General Pharmaceutical Council (Registration) Rules 2010 are contained in the General Pharmaceutical Council (Registration Rules) Order of Council 2010.

39. *A Common Approach to Good Character Across the Health Professions Regulators*, December 2008, https://www.professionalstandards.org.uk/docs/default-source/publications/policy-advice/common-approach-to-good-character-2008.pdf?sfvrsn=72c67f20_12 (accessed 31 December 2024 – published when the PSA was known as the Council for Healthcare Regulatory Excellence).

40. [2019] UKPC 11.

41. *Jideofo v The Law Society* [2007] EW Misc 3 (31 July 2007).

If the Registrar of the GPhC refuses registration on fitness to practise grounds, the reasons for refusal must be given (Art.24(3)(b)). The applicant has a right of appeal (Art.40) to the Appeals Committee provided the appeal is brought within 28 days of the date on which the written statement of the reasons for the decision was sent. The procedure governing appeals is set out in separate Rules.[42]

Interim orders

Where the Registrar[43] or the Investigating Committee considers that the FtP Committee should consider making an interim order (Art.53(3)) suspending the registrant from practice or making the registrant's practice subject to conditions pending a full (*principal*) fitness to practise hearing, the allegation must be referred to the FtP Committee. The FtP Committee must hold a hearing and give the registrant reasonable notice. The notice period is nevertheless usually very short. The registrant is entitled to attend and be represented at the hearing. Hearings may involve physical attendance or, at the discretion of the chair of the FtP Committee, the hearing may be conducted by teleconference or video link and references to attendance include remote attendance.[44]

The FtP Committee will approach applications for interim orders on the basis of the evidence available so far and the nature of the allegations, and it will make a decision on the basis that the allegation is true, without deciding the facts of the case. It is not the responsibility of the Committee to make findings of fact or to resolve factual disputes, even if the registrant contends that the evidence is weak.[45] Out of fairness to registrants who have not been found guilty of any offence or misconduct, interim order hearings are held in private, so usually the only reported cases are those where there has been an appeal to the High Court or Court of Session.

If it is satisfied that it is necessary for the protection of members of the public or is otherwise in the public interest, or is in the interests of the registrant, the Committee may make an immediate order suspending the registrant from practice, or may impose conditions of practice, for up to 18 months pending a full fitness to practise hearing (Art.56). While 18 months is the maximum length of interim suspension, it should not be regarded as the default period.[46] In deciding whether to impose an interim suspension, the Committee must balance the protection of patients and the public interest against the impact of suspension on registrants who may lose income, home, family, and be on

---

42. General Pharmaceutical Council (Appeals Committee) Rules 2010 which can be found in the Schedule to the General Pharmaceutical Council (Appeals Committee Rules) Order of Council 2010.
43. Rule 6(5) of the FtP Rules.
44. Rule 2A of the FtP Rules.
45. *Abdullah v General Medical Council* [2012] EWHC 2506; the High Court (Mr Justice Lindblom) held that Parliament had entrusted to the GMC's Interim Orders Panel the power to make decisions on a doctor's freedom to practise while his fitness to do so was investigated, using its own experience and expertise and its own knowledge of the public's expectations of the medical profession. The allegations against the doctor were very serious. There was a need to maintain public confidence in the medical profession or the medical regulator, and action would sometimes have to be taken to protect public confidence even where there was no immediate risk to patients.
46. *R (on the application of Scholten) v General Medical Council* [2013] EWHC 173 (Admin).

the verge of bankruptcy, and whose health may be affected.[47] No member of the FtP Committee that has made an interim order may sit as a member of the Committee at a final hearing of the allegation.[48]

If an interim order is made, the GPhC will be expected to prepare its case for a final hearing during the lifetime of the order. If the Council has not been able to bring the case to a final hearing within that time, the Council may apply to the High Court or Court of Session for an interim order to be extended. The Court has power to extend an interim order by up to a further 12 months (Art.56(5)). The Court has generally been willing to grant extensions while the regulator completes the preparation of its case for a final hearing, although not always for the period sought by the regulator. In one of the leading cases,[49] in which an extension was granted, the High Court held that the court could take into account:

- the gravity of the allegations;
- the nature of the evidence;
- the seriousness of the risk of harm to patients;
- the reasons why the case had not been concluded; and
- the prejudice to the practitioner if an interim order were continued.

An example of a case in which the High Court refused an extension of time is given in **Box 25.3**

Box 25.3

In *General Pharmaceutical Council v (1) Kellett and (2) Gamble*,[50] the pharmacists were a husband and wife who were directors of a company that owned three pharmacies and held a wholesale dealer's licence. In 2016, the police found a large number of class C controlled drugs, such as zopiclone, at their premises. They were arrested by the police for unlawful possession and supply of class C controlled drugs. They informed the GPhC of the investigation. They also terminated their wholesale business.

In January 2017, the Fitness to Practise Committee imposed an interim suspension on both pharmacists for the maximum period of 18 months to be reviewed every six months.

In 2017, the Medicines and Healthcare products Regulatory Agency (MHRA) began an investigation, but the MHRA's in-house lawyer did not review the papers until May 2020, only to find that further work was required before a file could be sent to the Crown Prosecution Service (CPS) for a decision on whether to charge the two pharmacists with any offence.

After previous extensions of the interim suspension order, the suspensions were due to run out on 5 July 2020. The GPhC applied to the High Court for a further extension. The MHRA

50. [2020] EWHC 2401 (Admin).

---

47. *R (Scholten) v GMC* (see previous footnote).

48. Paragraph 5 of Schedule 1 of the Pharmacy Order 2010; but where the chair at a hearing of an interim order application heard matters relating to another registrant (Mr Hussain Rasool), the same chair was not required to stand down when Mr Rasool's case later came before him at a principal hearing, and an allegation of bias was rejected by the High Court – *Rasool v GPhC* [2015] EWHC 217 (Admin).

49. *General Medical Council v Hiew* [2007] 1 W.L.R. 2007. This English decision has been followed by the courts in Scotland: see, for example, *IB v General Medical Council* [2024] CSIH 4.

Box 25.3 (cont.)

was still not in a position to send the papers to the CPS. Mr Justice Soole ruled that the court had to take into account two competing questions: whether it would be acceptable not to suspend if, at the end of the day, the pharmacists were found guilty, and whether it would be acceptable to suspend if, at the end of the day the pharmacists were acquitted on all charges. Having considered the evidence and submissions, he found:

- The allegations of supply and conspiracy to supply were grave: serious offences were involved.
- Despite four years having passed, there was still no indication what charges, if any, might be brought.
- Even though the GPhC could not be blamed for delays by the MHRA, the GPhC had to share significant responsibility for the consequences. The GPhC had not been pro-active in pressing the MHRA for updates.
- The GPhC had not provided the court with any evidence as to why an extension should be granted.
- The pharmacists had suffered real and substantial prejudice as a result of the delays.
- No decision whether to bring any charges was likely to be made before October 2020.
- It was no longer proportionate or in the public interest to grant any extension, though this could be considered afresh when the investigation was concluded.

Examples of cases in which registrants have been suspended under interim orders include:

- a pharmacist awaiting trial for a serious sexual offence. When the GPhC applied to the High Court to extend the interim suspension, the judge said "the public would be shocked to know if [the registrant] were to be allowed to continue his practice and while those [criminal] proceedings are ongoing. In my view, the potential risk to the public interest outweighs any prejudice caused to [the registrant]";[51]
- the suspected theft of OxyContin 80 mg and two brands of the human growth hormone, somatropin, and the falsification of pharmacy records to facilitate or cover up the theft;[52]
- a pharmacist accused of taking financial advantage of a vulnerable adult; and
- a number of pharmacists were filmed in a BBC television *Inside Out* programme, selling prescription only medicines without prescriptions. The FtP Committee imposed interim suspensions, stating that a reasonable onlooker with knowledge of the facts would be appalled if no interim suspension was imposed, and the allegations against the registrant were eventually proved. The High Court[53] rejected an appeal in one such case. The judge emphasised that the FtP Committee must scrutinise the unproven allegations with great care to test their cogency. He drew a distinction between cases involving a lack of training, or an honest mistake, or theft, where it

---

51. *General Pharmaceutical Council v Abdullah* [2022] EWHC 180 (Admin).
52. *General Pharmaceutical Council v Khan* [2021] EWHC 3212 (Admin).
53. *Gulamhusein v General Pharmaceutical Council* [2014] EWHC 2591 (Admin).

might be appropriate to impose conditions of practice pending a final hearing, and a case involving "the very important role played by pharmacists in ensuring that drugs for which prescriptions are required are not supplied to those who do not have prescriptions for them".

General Pharmaceutical Council v Mann[54] was a case concerning an interim order imposing conditions that were so restrictive that it was impossible for the pharmacist to find work. Nevertheless, the High Court declined to overturn the conditions. Details of the case are in **Box 25.4**.

Box 25.4

The GPhC had received a report of concerns relating to the possible involvement of a registrant in controlled drug irregularities, in particular suspicious entries concerning methylphenidate 10 mg tablets, at the pharmacy where he had been working. The implication was that the registrant had removed medication from his place of employment for the purposes of self-medication and then created false entries to conceal that fact. The registrant had previous addiction issues relating to methylphenidate.

The FtP Committee imposed conditions requiring the registrant not to work as a sole pharmacist or responsible pharmacist, and to be closely supervised and requiring him to work in a supportive environment. The GPhC applied to the High Court to extend the period during which the conditions would apply. The registrant opposed an extension because he had been clean for a year and because the conditions were so restrictive that he had found it impossible to find work. Alternatively, he asked the court to vary the conditions, for example replacing a requirement for a daily meeting with a supervisor with the less onerous requirement for daily contact with a supervisor. The judge granted the extension, holding that the prejudice to the registrant, significant though it was, was outweighed by the seriousness of the allegations and the significant risk to patients as well as the risk of harm to the registrant himself.

The judge added:

> *"I cannot say that the conditions objected to are inappropriate, disproportionate or unfair ... The requirement not to work as a sole or responsible pharmacist seems to me to be obviously necessary on the facts of this case. No amount of supervision, even daily supervision, would in my judgment be adequate to prevent the risks that lie behind the interim order from actually materialising, if work as a sole pharmacist is permitted, with all of the autonomy that this necessarily involves."*

The judge held that he had no power to vary the conditions, but in any event observed that:

> *"A mere contact requirement might be satisfied, for example, by a single email or by a single text message. That would not be sufficient to achieve the protective purpose for which [the] conditions ha[d] been imposed."*

Freedom of speech

If an interim order is sought that would have the effect of curtailing freedom of speech, for example in restraining the registrant from posting on social media, the order sought should be specific as to what views or opinions the person subject to the order is

54. [2021] EWHC 3217.

precluded from expressing; and section 12 of the Human Rights Act 1998 provides that an interim order curtailing freedom of expression must not be made unless the Fitness to Practise Committee is satisfied that the GPhC is likely to establish at the final hearing that publication should not be allowed. This requires a finding that that success at a final hearing was more likely than not.[55]

Interim orders on public interest grounds

As to whether suspension would be necessary in the public interest, the High Court has held in the case of a dental practitioner convicted of conspiracy to defraud[56] that:

> *"it is ... likely to be a relatively rare case where a suspension order will be made on an interim basis on the ground that it is in the public interest"*

because of the impact on a registrant's ability to earn a living. The Court held that, in the absence of necessity for suspension at an interim stage,

> *"the question of public perception and public confidence could be reflected by an appropriate decision by the Panel, if so minded, at the final hearing when all the facts had been fully explored, all the mitigation fully advanced and the position finally assessed at [the final hearing]".*

Indeed, in a case of non-clinical allegations, it has been held that only something that would impinge more directly on members of the public, such as murder, rape or abuse of children, would justify interim suspension for the purpose of public protection.[57]

An interim order would not be justified on public interest grounds simply because an informed member of the public would be concerned about a healthcare professional was allowed to practise pending an investigation.[58]

The FtP Committee has similar powers of interim suspension in relation to pharmacy premises.[59]

Appeals against interim orders, and reviews

Registrants and pharmacy owners have a right of appeal (Art.56(8)) to the High Court (England and Wales) or the Court of Session (Scotland) against interim orders. Any such appeal must be brought within 21 days of the decision (or such longer period as the court

---

55. *White v General Medical Council* [2021] EWHC 3286 (Admin).
56. *R (on the application of Sheikh) v General Dental Council* [2010] Med. L.R. 323.
57. *Bradshaw v General Medical Council* [2010] Med L.R 323.
58. *Nursing and Midwifery Council v Persand* [2023] EWHC 3356 (Admin).
59. Section 82A of the Medicines Act 1968.

may allow).[60] In the event of an appeal, the interim order will remain in effect pending the outcome of the appeal unless the court orders otherwise.

The FtP Committee must review interim orders within six months and must keep orders under review. Registrants may request an earlier review once three months have passed (Art.56). On a review, the Committee may continue, vary or revoke the interim order.

Initial action in respect of allegations

If the GPhC has information, or receives information or an allegation, that a registrant's fitness to practise is or might be impaired, the Registrar must normally refer the information or allegation to the Council's Investigating Committee (Art.52) unless the allegation falls within the Council's threshold criteria[61] for not making a referral (**Box 25.5**) or unless more than five years have elapsed since the most recent events referred to in the allegation. If more than five years have elapsed, the Registrar may only refer the case if the registrar considers that it is necessary for the protection of the public, or otherwise in the public interest for the allegation to be referred.

Box 25.5: GPhC threshold criteria in fitness to practise allegations

The registrar should not refer a case to the Investigating Committee unless the evidence as a whole suggests that:

Conduct, performance
- it presents an actual or potential risk to patient safety or public safety;
- it undermines, or is likely to undermine, confidence in the pharmacy professions;
- there has been a serious or persistent failure to meet any of the standards for pharmacy professionals;
- the honesty or integrity of the pharmacy professional can no longer be relied on;

Health
- there is adverse physical or mental health which presents a risk to the pharmacy professional's ability to practise safely or effectively; and

Public interest
- it is in the public interest to refer.

---

60. The Pharmacy Order 2012 does not specify a time limit for appealing against interim orders, unlike, for example, appeals against decisions to remove from the register, where Art.58 specifies a 28-day appeal period. Rule 52.12(2) of the Civil Procedure Rules 1998 (in the case of English appeals) specifies a 21-day appeal period. A GPhC guidance note refers to a 28-day appeal period in the case of interim orders, but this appears to be incorrect. https://assets.pharmacyregulation.org/files/document/interim_orders_guidance_on_the_application_process_and_committee_decision-making-july_2019.pdf (accessed 31 December 2024).

61. Art.52 and Rule 6 of the FtP Rules; https://assets.pharmacyregulation.org/files/document/good_decision_making_investigations_and_threshold_criteria_guidance_january_2018. (accessed 31 December 2024).

The Fitness to Practise Rules include provision for bypassing the Investigating Committee and making a referral direct to the FtP Committee in urgent cases, but this provision is only to be used with caution.[62]

In accordance with the GPhC's Publication and disclosure policy registrants are informed that a concern about their fitness to practise has been received unless this would prejudice or adversely affect the investigation. The registrant's employer may also be told if the GPhC considers doing so would be in the public interest.

When making a referral to the Investigating Committee, the Registrar is under an obligation to make any referral to the Investigating Committee within a reasonable time, but failure to do so would not invalidate the referral or provide grounds to set it aside unless a fair disciplinary process is no longer possible.[63]

In practice, some of the Registrar's decision-making is delegated to others, such as Professional Regulation Managers.

The Investigating Committee

In *Professional Standards Authority v General Pharmaceutical Council and R2*,[64] Mrs Justice Lang said: "Formal consideration by the Investigating Committee provides a useful check on the views of officers and lawyers who have undertaken the initial assessment" to refer a case.

The Investigating Committee consists of a lay member who is the chair, two lay members who are deputy chairs, two other lay members, and between three and eleven others who may be lay members or registrants.[65] They have a four-year term of office. The quorum comprises three members and must include a chair or deputy chair, a registrant and a lay member. A legal adviser may be asked to attend any meeting.[66] The legal adviser's function is to ensure that the committee's proceedings are conducted fairly.

The Investigating Committee meets in private. Its primary function is to decide whether an allegation ought to be considered by the FtP Committee (Art.53). The Committee may not hear oral evidence. Instead, registrants will be given at least 21 days in which to make written representations. In relation to a heath allegation, the Committee may require the registrant to agree to be examined by a nominated medical practitioner.

---

62. See *Professional Standards Authority v General Pharmaceutical Council and R2*, referred to below.
63. *R (on the application of Rycroft) v Royal Pharmaceutical Society of Great Britain* [2010] EWHC 2832 (Admin).
64. [2024] EWHC 3005 (Admin).
65. A *lay member* is defined in Rule 2 of the General Pharmaceutical Council (Statutory Committees and their Advisers) Rules 2010 (contained within the General Pharmaceutical Council (Statutory Committees and their Advisers Rules) Order of Council 2010) as a member who is not, and has never been, entered in the Register of any regulatory body and does not hold qualifications which would entitle them to apply for entry in the Register. The Pharmacy Order 2010 (Art.3) defines "regulatory body" as a regulatory body which has the function of authorising persons to practise as a member of a health or social care profession.
66. Rule 21 of the Statutory Committee Rules.

The Investigating Committee will not investigate or determine the facts of a case. In deciding whether to refer an allegation to the FtP Committee, the Investigating Committee will decide whether it considers that there is a real prospect of an allegation being proved at an FtP hearing, and whether the facts, if proved, could demonstrate that the registrant's fitness to practise is impaired. In deciding whether an allegation ought to be referred to the FtP Committee, it will also consider whether referral to the FtP Committee is a proportionate outcome. In making a decision, the Investigating Committee will follow outcomes guidance published by the GPhC. This will involve considering a number of factors including:

- the public interest;
- any aggravating or mitigating factors;
- the circumstances and whether there is any ongoing risk to members of the public;
- the registrant's behaviour, attitude and actions;
- the Registrar's recommendation (which is not binding on the Investigating Committee);
- any written representations from the registrant; and
- any relevant fitness to practise history.

Where the Committee determines that the allegation ought to be considered by the FtP Committee or a registrant has requested a referral, the Committee must refer the case to the FtP Committee. In the event of such a referral, the Registrar must inform the person who made the allegation.

If the Investigating Committee decides that an allegation need not be considered by the FtP Committee, then it may give a warning or give advice (including advice to a person against whom an allegation has not been made, such as a pharmacist's employer). The fact that a warning has been given will appear on the GPhC's online Register for a period, to ensure public confidence in the profession and the regulatory process, and to protect the public.

If the Investigating Committee concludes that the Council should consider exercising any of its powers to bring criminal proceedings, it must notify the Registrar accordingly (Art.53(4)).

Disposal of allegations without hearings

Following a decision of the Investigating Committee to refer an allegation to the FtP Committee, the person responsible for presenting the Council's case may conclude that the case should not proceed to a hearing, for example because there is insufficient evidence to justify a finding that a registrant's fitness to practise is impaired, or the decision to refer was legally flawed because the Investigating Committee failed to take into account a relevant consideration, such as delay. In that event, the Investigating Committee must be informed, and the Committee may rescind the referral,[67] after giving any complainant an opportunity to comment. The Investigating Committee is

67. Rule 38 of the FtP Rules.

not bound to rescind the referral and on occasions has declined to do so. Where a case has been referred by the GPhC Registrar to the FtP Committee, for example, where the registrant has been convicted of a criminal offence, the Registrar considers that he has power to rescind that referral, though there are no words to this effect in the FtP Rules.

The Fitness to Practise Committee

The FtP Committee is to consist of

- a lay member who is the chair;
- between three and eight lay members who are deputy chairs;
- between eight and fifty-one other members who may be lay members or registrants.

Members have a four-year term of office. The quorum for the FtP Committee comprises the chair or a deputy chair and at least two other members, one of whom must be a lay member and one of whom must be a registrant. The registrants must not outnumber the lay members by more than one.[68] A member who has sat on the Committee when granting an interim order may not sit in subsequent proceedings in the case.[69] In most cases, hearings (other than case management meetings) are conducted by a committee comprising a legally qualified chair, a registrant member and a lay member. A chair who does not hold a legal qualification will have a legal adviser present. The function of the adviser includes advising the FtP Committee on questions of law and to intervene to avoid errors of law being made. The legal adviser may be present during the FtP Committee's deliberations, but may not take part in the deliberations.

The Committee may seek advice from a clinical adviser on a health-related issue or any other specialist adviser on issues within their speciality.[70] The Committee may be expected to rely on the specialist knowledge of registrant members, but with the following in mind:[71]

> *"the rules of natural justice preclude expert members from giving evidence to themselves which the parties have no opportunity to challenge and ... where a specialist tribunal drawing on its own knowledge and experience independently identified an important fact or matter which may influence its decision but which has not been the subject of evidence adduced by the parties, it should state this openly and give the parties an opportunity to seek to adduce evidence and/or make submissions on it."*

Indeed, a decision of the former Statutory Committee was quashed by the High Court because, when its members deliberated in private, they consulted *Martindale*[72] without

68. Rule 18 of the General Pharmaceutical Council (Statutory Committees and their Advisers) Rules 2010.
69. Rule 18A(2)(d) of the General Pharmaceutical Council (Statutory Committees and their Advisers) Rules 2010.
70. Rule 23 of the FtP Rules.
71. *Lawrence v GMC* [2012] EWHC 464 (Admin).
72. *Martindale: The Complete Drug Reference*; see: https://www.pharmaceuticalpress.com/products/martindale-the-complete-drug-reference/ (accessed 31 December 2024).

reference to the parties on a point that was not covered by the professional knowledge of the pharmacists on the Committee.[73]

Procedure prior to hearings

As soon as reasonably practicable after an allegation has been referred by the Investigating Committee or the Registrar, the GPhC must serve on the registrant finalised particulars of the allegation, sufficiently particularised to enable them to understand the allegation, together with any witness statements, expert reports or other documents relied on by the Council, and any evidence or documents in the Council's possession that may assist the registrant in the preparation of their defence. As soon as reasonably practicable after service by the Council, the registrant must serve on the Council any witness statements, expert reports and other documents upon which the registrant relies.[74]

There are rules for case management and, if a direction is required any party may request a case management meeting, for example as to compliance with the rules, the disclosure of evidence, issues as to witnesses or to seek a ruling of law. At such meetings, the chair of the FtP Committee, sitting alone, may give directions in order to secure the just, expeditious and effective running of the proceedings before the Committee. Such hearings may take place by video link, teleconference or such other method as is agreed by the parties or, where the parties fail to agree, decided by the chair.[75]

Fitness to practise hearings

Fitness to practise hearings may involve physical attendance or, at the discretion of the chair of the FtP Committee, hearings may be conducted by teleconference or by video link[76] and references to attending hearings include remote attendance. At fitness to practise hearings, both the GPhC and the registrant may be represented by a solicitor or barrister or, in the case of the Council, by an employee.[77] A registrant may also be represented by a person from a defence organisation or trade union. While registrants are not required to attend, not attending, especially when dishonesty has been alleged, virtually invites removal from the Register, if insight is not demonstrated.[78] At the start of any hearing to determine whether a registrant's fitness to practise is impaired (defined as a *principal hearing*), the FtP Committee must determine any preliminary legal arguments. Principal hearings then proceed in up to three distinct stages.

---

73. *Fletcher and Lucas v Pharmaceutical Society of Great Britain*, Pharm J, July 1978 p. 93.
74. Rule 14 of the FtP Rules.
75. Rule 20 of the FtP Rules.
76. Rule 2A of the FtP Rules.
77. Rule 40 of the FtP Rules.
78. *Burrows v General Pharmaceutical Council* [2016] EWHC 1050 (Admin).

Principal hearings, stage 1 – findings of fact

The chair will establish whether the registrant makes any admissions and, if so, will announce that the facts admitted have been found proved. Where facts are in dispute, the case for the Council is then presented to the Committee and evidence will be given in support. The FtP Rules say that subject only to the requirements of relevance and fairness, the FtP Committee may receive documentary evidence and oral evidence from witnesses. A pharmacist, Noor Shaikh, was accused of operating a repeat dispensing service to which patients had not consented, with a view to dishonestly obtaining payment for dispensing. On the evidence of witnesses who did not attend the FtP hearing, the allegations were found proved. Mr Shaikh appealed to the High Court,[79] arguing that the FtP Committee was not entitled to take hearsay evidence into account. Mr Justice Supperstone rejected the appeal, holding that rule 24 did not prevent hearsay evidence being received by the FtP Committee so long as it is reasonable and fair.

After the GPhC's evidence is presented, the FtP Rules[80] permit a registrant to argue that there is no case to answer. Unless the case is dismissed because there is no case to answer, the registrant will then present his or her case and may call evidence. Fitness to practise proceedings are civil (see **Chapter 1**). Unlike criminal proceedings, a registrant has no right to silence in FtP cases and an adverse inference may be drawn if the registrant chooses not to give evidence.[81] The burden of proving disputed facts is on the Council. The standard of proof is the civil one (see also **Chapter 1**): facts must be proved on the balance of probabilities[82] even where what is alleged amounts to a criminal offence. The FtP Rules do not mention that the parties may make submissions as to the findings the FtP Committee should make, but the making of such submissions is accepted practice. The Committee will then deliberate privately before announcing its findings of fact in public (unless the whole case has been heard in private).

When announcing its findings of fact, the Committee will refer to any of the GPhC's Standards which it finds have been breached.

If the GPhC's case has been found proved, the hearing will proceed to the next stage.

Principal hearings, stage 2 – impairment of fitness to practise

After announcing its findings of fact, the Committee must receive further evidence and hear any further submissions from the parties as to whether, on the basis of the facts found proved, the registrant's fitness to practise is impaired (see the section above on Grounds for finding impairment).

---

79. *Shaikh v General Pharmaceutical Council* [2013] EWHC 1844 (Admin).

80. Rule 31(8) of the FtP Rules.

81. *The Queen (on the application of Evgeniy Kuzmin) v GMC* [2019] EWHC 2129.

82. Rule 42 of the FtP Rules.

Fitness to practise criteria and impairment

When deciding whether the requirements as to fitness to practise are met in relation to the registrant, the FtP Committee must have regard[83] to whether or not the conduct or behaviour that has been found proved:

a. presents an actual or potential risk to patients or to the public;
b. has brought, or might bring, the profession of pharmacy into disrepute;
c. has breached one of the fundamental principles of the profession of pharmacy; or
d. shows that the integrity of the registrant can no longer be relied upon.

In cases where it is alleged that a registrant's fitness to practise may be impaired by health factors, the Committee must have regard to whether or not there is evidence of actual or potential self-harm; or harm to patients and/or to the public.

The determination of fitness to practise has been considered by the courts in a number of key cases.[84] The courts have held that the task of the Committee is to take account of any conviction or misconduct of the practitioner and to consider it in the light of all the other relevant factors known to them in answering whether by reason of the registrant's misconduct, conviction, deficient professional performance and so on, their fitness to practice is impaired at the date of the hearing. This is a process of looking forward, as well as back, and taking into account the practitioner's efforts to address their problems and reduce the risk of recurrence. Insight and remediation and the risk of repetition of offending behaviour are all relevant to the assessment. In a case in which a GP was found to have lied about whether he had spoken to a baby's mother, the High Court ruled that "not every act of dishonesty results in impairment".[85] Even if an isolated dispensing error is found to be misconduct, the Committee may conclude that the chance of it being repeated in the future is so remote that a registrant's fitness to practise is not impaired. In a 2012 case involving a series of errors that constituted deficient professional performance, the FtP Committee noted that its "task [was] to determine not whether at some time in the past the registrant's fitness to practise was impaired, but whether it was currently impaired". The Committee took the view that the concept of *remediability* is applicable to cases where impairment might arise from deficient professional performance caused by a consistent tendency to make dispensing errors. On the facts of that case, the Committee found that the registrant's fitness to practise was impaired.

---

83. Rule 5 of the FtP Rules.

84. *Meadow v General Medical Council* [2007] 2 W.L.R. 286; *Cohen v General Medical Council* [2008] EWHC 581 (Admin); *Cheatle v General Medical Council* [2009] EWHC 645 (Admin); *Yeong v General Medical Council* [2009] EWHC 1923; The Queen (on the Application of *Zygmunt) v General Medical Council* [2008] EWHC 2643 (Admin); [2009] LS Law Medical 219; *Professional Standards Authority v General Medical Council and Uppal* [2015] EWHC 1304; *R (on the application of Squier) v GMC* [2015] EWHC 299 (Admin); QBD (Admin); 13 February 2015; *R (on the application of Alami) v Health and Care Professions Council* [2013] EWHC 1895 (Admin).

85. *Professional Standards Authority v General Medical Council and Uppal* [2015] EWHC 1304.

In the case of a doctor who had falsified documents in support of an application that would qualify him for appointment as a consultant, Mrs Justice Lang held[86] that consideration should not only be given to whether the practitioner continues to present a risk to members of the public, but also whether the need to uphold proper professional standards and public confidence in the profession would be undermined if a finding of impairment were not made in the particular circumstances.

In a case[87] in which a doctor training to be a GP had dishonestly falsified timesheets to obtain payment, the High Court overturned a decision of the Medical Practitioners Tribunal that the doctor's fitness to practise was not impaired. Mrs Justice O'Farrell said "it will be an unusual case where dishonesty is not found to impair fitness to practise".

The Committee will retire to deliberate in private before announcing in public its decision on the registrant's fitness to practise and its reasons (unless the whole case has been heard in private).

The FtP Committee may find that the registrant's fitness to practise is not impaired but may nevertheless issue a warning or advice to them or any other involved person. If the FtP Committee decides that the registrant's fitness to practise is impaired, the Committee may then receive further evidence and hear any further submissions as to the appropriate sanction, if any, to be imposed.

Principal hearings, stage 3 – sanction

If a registrant's fitness to practise is found to be impaired, the FtP Committee will hear submissions as to what sanction may be appropriate. These are likely to include reference to the GPhC's *Outcomes Guidance*[88] and may include any mitigating circumstances and any relevant matters in the registrant's history, such as previous adverse findings. The Committee may receive submissions not only from the parties at this stage but also from any other person, perhaps a patient, who has a direct interest in the proceedings.

Decision

After deliberating in private, the Committee will announce its decision and reasons in public (unless the whole hearing has been heard in private). The Committee may:[89]

a. give a warning to the registrant;
b. give advice to any other person or body involved on any issue related to the allegation;
c. give a direction that the registrant's name be removed from the Register (except when impairment is only by reason of health);
d. give a direction that the registrant's entry in the Register be suspended for a specific period up to a maximum of 12 months; or

86. *Professional Standards Authority v General Medical Council and Igwilo* [2016] EWHC 524 (Admin).

87. *General Medical Council v Nwachuku* [2017] EWHC 2085 (Admin).

88. Good decision making: fitness to practise hearings and outcomes guidance published by the GPhC in March 2024.

89. Article 54 of the Pharmacy Order 2010.

e. direct that the registrant's entry in the Register be conditional upon complying with such requirements as the Committee thinks fit. Such conditions may run for up to three years. Examples of conditions[90] include undertaking training, practising under supervision or not holding the position of superintendent pharmacist.

The outcome of hearings will often be case-specific, depending on the Committee's view of the gravity of cases and the insight of the registrant, taking the Outcomes Guidance into account. To ensure that the sanction chosen is proportionate, the possible sanctions are considered in ascending order of seriousness, starting with whether a warning would be a sufficient sanction.

Outcomes guidance

The Committee is required to have regard to the *Outcomes Guidance*.[91] This guidance emphasises that the purpose of sanctions is not to punish the registrant but to protect the public and maintain confidence in the profession of pharmacy and proper standards of behaviour. In the case of a dentist that involved sexual misconduct, it was held that *the public* includes patients, colleagues and visitors.[92]

Aggravating factors

Aggravating factors include dishonesty, sexual misconduct in relation to professional duties, discriminatory behaviour, and lack of insight (dishonesty, sexual misconduct and discriminatory behaviour are referred to in more detail below).

Mitigation

Mitigating factors may include remorse, expressions of regret or apology, genuinely demonstrated insight and remediation, whether the misconduct was a "one-off" incident, and testimonials.

The interests of the public

In reaching its decision, the Committee will attach greater weight to the interests of the public than the interests of the registrant.[93] The Committee will aim to apply sanctions proportionately. In other words, it will impose a sanction that is no more severe than necessary to achieve its purpose. The Committee will therefore usually consider its

---

90. The GPhC has published a "bank" of standard conditions to help the FtP Committee in decision making. Examples relate to registrants putting themselves under the supervision of a GP; undergoing testing for substance misuse; finding a workplace supervisor; naming a mentor; undertaking further training; not working alone; not working as a superintendent pharmacist; and having no involvement in the ordering or dispensing of controlled drugs or lifestyle drugs.

91. Rule 31(14) of the FtP Rules.

92. *Alberts v General Dental Council* [2022] EWHC 2192 (Admin).

93. The consequences of suspension or removal from the Register will often be severe for the registrant and the registrant's family, but the courts have said, for example, in *George v General Medical Council* [2016] EWHC, that personal mitigation has a limited role in fitness to practise cases where the overriding concern is the public interest. The case of *Bolton v Law Society* [1994] 1 WLR 512 is also frequently cited to similar effect.

powers in ascending order of seriousness to determine whether, starting with a warning, this would be sufficient to address the impairment it has found. If the Committee would not consider a sanction appropriate, it will give its reasons before proceeding to consider the next possible sanction. Once the Committee has identified the most appropriate sanction, in cases other than removal from the Register, the Committee will give reasons in its determination as to why the next most severe sanction would not be appropriate or proportionate.

Dishonesty and lack of integrity

The Outcomes Guidance states:

> *"There are some acts which, while not presenting a direct risk to the public, are so serious they undermine confidence in the profession as a whole. The GPhC believes that dishonesty damages public confidence, and undermines the integrity of pharmacy professionals. However, cases involving dishonesty can be complicated – committees should carefully consider the context and circumstances in which the dishonesty took place. Therefore, although serious, there is not a presumption of removal in all cases involving dishonesty ... Some acts of dishonesty are so serious that the [FtP] committee should consider removal as the only proportionate and appropriate outcome. This includes cases that involve intentionally defrauding the NHS or an employer, falsifying patient records, or dishonesty in clinical drug trials."*

According to the Supreme Court decision in *Ivey v Genting Casinos UK Ltd (trading as Crockfords Club)*[94] to find dishonesty, a fact-finding tribunal like the FtP Committee must first ascertain the actual state of the individual's knowledge or belief as to the facts. The question whether the conduct was honest or dishonest is then to be determined by applying the objective standards of ordinary decent people.

A High Court appeal[95] by Elizabeth Burrows sheds further light on the expected approach to sanction in a dishonesty case. Mrs Burrows had been given a police caution for fraud. She had returned dresses to a department store after swapping cheaper price tickets for more expensive ones. The fraud involved less than £100. Mrs Burrows did not attend the FtP hearing, thus depriving herself of the opportunity to demonstrate insight. Mr Justice Kerr said:

> *"not attending the hearing amounts virtually to courting removal ... Cases of dishonesty are always likely to lead to removal. The fact that removal is not inevitable ... does not mean it is necessarily too harsh for a first disciplinary offence."*

---

94. [2017] UKSC 67.

95. *Burrows v General Pharmaceutical Council* [2016] EWHC 1050.

A distinction may be drawn between cases of dishonesty – a basic moral quality which is expected of all members of society involving being truthful about important matters – and a lack of integrity. Integrity refers the higher standards society and professions expected from professionals. It connotes adherence to the standards of one's own profession.[96] In some, but not all cases, a finding of dishonesty is more likely to result in a direction to remove a registrant from the Register than a finding of a lack of integrity.

Sexual misconduct

The GPhC's *Guidance on maintaining clear sexual boundaries* is dealt with in **Chapter 24**. In *Yasin v General Medical Council*[97] Mrs Justice Yip declined to overturn a decision to erase from the medical register the name of a competent doctor following actions that "did not amount to very serious sexual offending", saying:

> *"It may well be that there has been a recent shift in attitudes to sexual misconduct [of that] nature. It is possible that this sort of low level sexual assault is now regarded more seriously than it once was particularly when committed in a work environment."*

Whether a registrant's conduct was motivated by sexual gratification is likely to be irrelevant if, viewed objectively, the conduct was sexual.[98] In *Basson v GMC*[99], the High Court defined *acting with sexual motivation* as conduct done either in pursuit of sexual gratification or in pursuit of a future sexual relationship.

In a case in which a dental practitioner had made inappropriate comments to a dental nurse, including about her eyes, that left her feeling uncomfortable and embarrassed, Mrs Justice Foster rejected a submission that there had been no evidence of harm. The judge said:

> *"a woman is entitled to be protected from sexually-motivated commentary and personalised conversational approaches, particularly in her professional environment. The days have gone by when right-thinking people believed such behaviour was tolerable or, indeed, "just a joke". In my judgment, such behaviour carries with it the notion of harm, absent clear evidence to the contrary."*[100]

---

96. *Wingate v Solicitors Regulation Authority; and Solicitors Regulation Authority v Malins* [2018] EWCA Civ 366.
97. [2018] EWHC 677 (Admin).
98. *General Medical Council v Dr Raied Haris* [2020] EWHC 2518 (Admin).
99. [2018] EWHC 505 (Admin).
100. *Alberts v General Dental Council* [2022] EWHC 2192 (Admin).

Consensual sexual conduct between adults is not likely to give rise to fitness to practise issues – see the case of *Beckwith v Solicitors Regulation Authority*[101] referred to in **Chapters 1** and **22**.

Discriminatory behaviour

In relation to actions or words that had a purpose, at least in significant part, that was referable to race; and in relation to acts showing hostility or a discriminatory attitude to racial groups, the Outcomes Guidance says:

> *"Because of the serious nature of these types of concerns and the impact on public trust and confidence in the profession, the committee should usually consider outcomes at the upper end of the scale. More serious outcomes are likely to be appropriate where a case involves discrimination against patients, colleagues or other people who share protected characteristics, either within or outside their professional life or where there was a pattern of repeated discriminatory behaviour, behaviour was intentional, frequent and with very negative consequences for patients."*

In *Professional Standards Authority v General Pharmaceutical Council and Ali*,[102] a case in which a pharmacist had shouted antisemitic comments through a loudhailer at a public rally in Central London, Mr Justice Chamberlain said "Where a regulated individual makes a comment which, objectively construed, is obviously racist, it will rarely count much in his favour that he did not intend it to be racist. The lack of understanding that or why it was racist may, indeed, give rise to a separate concern."

Duty of candour

Acting with openness and honesty when something has gone wrong is an essential duty (see **Chapter 24**). This is something that the FtP Committee will take into consideration when determining sanction.

Insight and remediation

Insight is a key factor in the choice of sanction. It involves "a recognition and acceptance of what has been done wrong and the implications that flow from it",[103] or, as expressed in the Outcomes Guidance, it means a registrant "can accept and understand that they should have behaved differently". Insight may be demonstrated by an admission of the allegations, but it is possible to maintain innocence and yet

101. [2020] EWHC 3231 (Admin).

102. [2024] EWHC 577 (Admin).

103. *Professional Standards Authority v General Pharmaceutical Council and Onwughalu* [2014] EWHC 2521 (Admin).

demonstrate insight.[104] A lack of insight may be taken to represent a risk that the wrongdoing may be repeated.

Remediation involves steps taken to avoid a recurrence.

Examples of sanctions – Warning

In a case in which a pharmacist became aware that an error had been made in the supply of warfarin, the FtP Committee held that the registrant had not taken urgent and effective steps to check the position because he was reluctant to believe that an error had occurred. The Committee decided to give him a warning, saying "these events have had a profound and devastating effect upon him. In our view, there is nothing that needs to be brought home to [the registrant]. We do not consider that any sanction we impose could serve any useful purpose in that respect".[105]

Examples of cases in which a registrant has been given a warning are given in **Box 25.6**.

Box 25.6: Examples of cases in which a warning was imposed

In a case involving inappropriate sales from an online pharmacy, a pharmacist was given a warning, among other things, to ensure she applied the same high standards of patient care to the supply of medication via an internet pharmacy as to the supply of medication to a patient in a physical pharmacy.

****

In a 2023 case, a patient was prescribed 56 tablets of 20 mg oxycodone hydrochloride. However, the pharmacist supplied 56 tablets of 120 mg oxycodone hydrochloride. The error contributed to the death of the patient.

At the time, the pharmacist had agreed to work in order to help out when there was a staffing crisis at the pharmacy. This was found to be an error of professional judgement. He compounded the error by working without someone to check his work.

The pharmacist admitted that he had failed to carry out any or sufficient checks to ensure that the prescription was dispensed accurately. The Fitness to Practise Committee said:

> *"We weighed in the balance that a suspension would prevent [the pharmacist] from working ... Of greater concern for us was that, as [the pharmacist] is currently serving the public as a locum pharmacist, a suspension would deprive the public of his evidently competent and caring services ... We concluded that, despite the catastrophic results of [the pharmacist's errors], well-informed members of the public would not expect to lose the services of a pharmacist for even a short period, if it were possible to declare Standards and uphold the reputation of the profession by a less severe sanction."*

---

104. *Karwal v General Medical Council* [2011] EWHC 26 (Admin).

105. 4 December 2013.

Examples of sanctions – Conditions

Primarily for the assistance of members of the FtP Committee, the GPhC has published a bank of conditions[106] they might impose in appropriate cases. The conditions include:

- in any type of case, conditions requiring the registrant to tell the GPhC before taking on any position for which the registrant must be registered with the GPhC (for example, taking up new employment as a pharmacy professional) and giving the GPhC the contact details of the employer, superintendent pharmacist and/or pharmacy owner;
- telling certain people in writing about restrictions imposed on the registrant's pharmacy practice;
- not working as a sole practitioner and/or responsible pharmacist and/or superintendent pharmacist;
- in substance misuse cases, the registrant must put themselves under the supervision of a GP/specialist medical practitioner, attend appointments, follow advice and arrange for the GPhC to receive medical reports at specified intervals at the registrant's cost;
- in alcohol and substance misuse cases, undergoing testing for recent and long-term consumption of alcohol and/or specified drugs at specified intervals at the registrant's cost, limiting alcohol consumption in line with the directions of a medical supervisor/GP, or abstaining completely if advised to do so, and not self-medicating;
- in physical and mental health cases, having occupational health assessments, complying with recommendations made by the person undertaking the assessment and arranging for reports to be sent to the GPhC; and
- in performance cases, working with a specified person to draw up a personal development plan, sending a copy to the GPhC, arranging for a named person to provide a report on the registrant's progress towards achieving the aims in the personal development plan, and finding a workplace supervisor.

The conditions will depend on the facts proved and the concern that is required to be addressed, so that the conditions in the bank may need to be adapted or specific conditions may need to be devised to meet the circumstances of a particular case. Examples are given in **Box 25.7**.

Box 25.7: Examples of conditions

A pharmacist told a patient seeking emergency hormonal contraception that she was ending a life and it would be on her conscience. He did not direct the patient to another pharmacy or provide her with other options. The FtP Committee[107] imposed conditions that included notifying all employers or prospective employers of the allegations that had been found

107. 18 July 2013.

106. https://assets.pharmacyregulation.org/files/2023-08/Conditions-bank-and-guidance-July-2023.pdfhttps://assets.pharmacyregulation.org/files/2023-08/Conditions-bank-and-guidance-July-2023.pdf (accessed 31 December 2024).

Box 25.7: Examples of conditions (cont.)

proved, not engaging in the provision of emergency hormonal contraception, and refraining from providing advice or information to patients based on his personal, moral or religious beliefs.

****

In a 2023 case, an employed pharmacist was found to have made sexually-motivated comments to a patient and to a colleague. The FtP Committee took account of the following factors:

- There was a significant age and power imbalance between the pharmacist and his colleague and a significant power imbalance between the pharmacist and the patient.
- The pharmacist's comments were made within earshot of others.
- The pharmacist's conduct left the patient feeling "utterly disgusted" and his colleague feeling "dirty".
- The pharmacist had demonstrated, some, but limited insight into his failings.

The FtP Committee identified the following mitigating factors:

- The registrant has engaged in the regulatory process.
- He apologised to the Committee for any upset his actions may have caused the complainants, which he regretted.
- In the absence of there being any sexually motivated physical contact, the pharmacist's sexually motivated behaviour lay towards the lower end of the scale of seriousness.
- It was momentary, transient and not repeated.
- The comments were fleeting albeit accompanied by other inappropriate behaviour, and, so far as his colleague was concerned, did not result in unwanted sexual contact.

The conditions included:

- You must work with a nominated superintendent pharmacist at a practice where you predominantly work, to draw up a personal development plan, specifically designed to deal with the shortcomings in the following areas of your practice:
  - interpersonal communication skills;
  - sexual boundaries.
- You must within six months undertake training in those two areas.
- The training is to be paid for by you. You must send the GPhC evidence of completion within 10 days of the course.
- You must arrange for the nominated superintendent pharmacist to provide a report on your progress toward achieving the aims set out in your personal development plan every 6 months.
- You must not work as a sole practitioner or superintendent pharmacist.

Examples of sanctions – Suspension

The FtP Committee may decide to impose a suspension of up to 12 months. Typically, a suspension may be given when the Committee considers that a warning or conditions are insufficient to deal with any risk to patient safety or to protect the public or would undermine public confidence. It may be required when necessary to highlight to the profession and the public that the conduct of the registrant is unacceptable and unbefitting a member of the pharmacy profession or when public confidence in the profession demands no lesser sanction.

Habib Khan had been convicted of serious and repeated acts of violence towards his wife and her family. The FtP Committee considered that a suspension of 12 months would be insufficient to reflect the seriousness of the registrant's misconduct and decided that he should therefore be removed from the Register because this was the only available sanction left to them. The Court of Session upheld an appeal on the basis that there was a middle way between a 12-month suspension (that had been considered inadequate) and removal from the Register with no possibility of restoration before the expiry of five years. The Court held that it had been open to the FtP Committee to impose the maximum 12-month suspension and recommend that at a future review by another FtP Committee, a further suspension be imposed. The GPhC appealed to the Supreme Court against the Court of Session's ruling.[108] The Supreme Court held that there was no such middle way. Once the original FtP Committee had concluded that a 12-month suspension would not be adequate, the only appropriate sanction was removal from the Register. However, the Supreme Court also held that because the registrant's conduct did not relate to professional performance and no patient had been, or was likely to be, put at risk, removal from the Register was disproportionate. The Court held that the sanction proportionate to the disrepute into which the pharmacist's conduct had brought the profession was a suspension for 12 months. (This does not necessarily mean that serious domestic violence will not lead to removal from the Register.[109]) Other cases of suspension are given in **Box 25.8**.

Box 25.8: Examples of cases in which suspension was imposed

In the case of a pharmacy technician who had received police cautions for drug offences many years before, the FtP Committee considered that these could not give rise to current impairment, but the failure to declare the cautions when he must have realised that they were required to be disclosed led to a three-month suspension.[110] (It should be noted that there is now a six-year time limit in England after which cautions no longer need to be declared, and that the FtP Committee has not found impairment in cases where a registrant believed he had received a warning from the police, not a formal caution, and the failure to declare was not alleged to have been dishonest.)[111]

****

In a case in which a pharmacist had made dispensing errors that were "comparatively large in number ... and included serious errors in the form of exposure of the patients to risk ...", the FtP Committee considered removal, which not only carries a lasting stigma but would also prevent the registrant from practising for at least five years, would be too severe and

110. *Pharm J*, 21 September 2013 p. 293.
111. 13 November 2016.

108. *Khan (Habib) v General Pharmaceutical Council* [2016] UKSC 64.
109. See *Ibrahim v General Medical Council* [2022] EWHC 2936 (Admin).

Box 25.8: Examples of cases in which suspension was imposed (cont.)

a disproportionate sanction. The Committee considered that the registrant should be given an opportunity to come back to pharmacy and "learn to do the job properly". The Committee directed a suspension for a period of 12 months, saying that in view of her good testimonials she did not deserve to have her name removed, and that the public interest did not demand the removal of her name.

****

A registrant's fitness to practise was found to be impaired because of cocaine use.[112] The chair of the Committee said:

> *"Regular, even if infrequent misuse of drugs, presents a risk to health and might therefore prejudice patients. It is bound to undermine public confidence in the profession, it breaches a fundamental tenet of the profession ...".*

The Committee imposed a 12-month suspension, saying that, when a review took place, the registrant would need to provide evidence that he had kept his knowledge up to date and complied with CPD requirements; proof of attendance at a return to practise course; reports concerning any work he had carried out; and a report from his GP concerning his health, insofar as it might affect his fitness to practise, with particular reference to drug abuse.

****

In a 2023 case, a recently-qualified pharmacist showed a work colleague on his phone an indecent image of a penis. He sent her text messages saying "you still have a really nice figure", if she had a partner he'd be "a lucky man looking at you", and "you look so fit walking around the dispensary". His actions were sexually motivated.

A three-month suspension was imposed. The FtP Committee said:

> *"this was a relatively short period but was justified by the mitigating factors and the registrant's genuine insight and remorse."*

****

A pharmacist had been given a police caution for stealing aftershave, headphones and skin cream to the value of £79.98 from his employer. Mitigation included the isolated nature of the incident, his previous good record, the repayment to his employer of the value of the goods, and the absence of harm to patients or the public. He had made frank admissions to his employer and the police, and referred himself to the GPhC. The FtP Committee found[113] that he had only limited insight and imposed a nine-month suspension.

****

A pharmacist dishonestly enrolled ineligible patients for the Scottish Minor Ailments Scheme (MAS). The Committee was satisfied[114] that his prime motivation was to enhance his reputation at work and to relieve the considerable pressure he was under. He had not set out to defraud the NHS. The pharmacist was suspended for nine months.

112. *Pharm J*, 27 June 2012 p. 795.
113. 5 November 2014.
114. 8 June 2016.

Effect of suspension, and review hearings

When the FtP Committee imposes a suspension, it may conduct a review hearing before the expiry of the extension. It may then allow the registrant to resume practising. Alternatively, it may decide to remove the registrant's name from the Register if there is no evidence of remediation; or it may extend the suspension by up to 12 months; if the registrant has already been suspended for at least two years, the Committee may suspend the registrant indefinitely. At the end of any period of suspension, the Committee may impose conditions of practice.[115]

At a review hearing, the findings of fact made at the principal hearing cannot be re-opened. It will be relevant for the FtP Committee that conducts the review to know whether the registrant now admits the misconduct, but such an admission is not a requirement in order for the FtP Committee to decide that the registrant understands the gravity of the offending and is unlikely to repeat it; it may be sufficient if the registrant demonstrates insight by reassuring the FtP Committee that they know and understand why the conduct previously found proved is unacceptable and cannot be repeated.[116]

There is, in practical terms, a persuasive burden on the registrant to demonstrate that they have fully acknowledged why the past offending behaviour was deficient, and through insight, application, education, supervision or other achievement, have addressed the past impairment.[117] The review committee asks: does the registrant's fitness to practise *remain* impaired?[118]

It has been argued that since a suspended pharmacist must be treated as not being entered in the Register (Art.19(8)) the effect of suspension is to prevent a pharmacist who owns an NHS pharmacy in their own name from providing services and thus put them at risk of removal from the pharmaceutical list (in other words, losing their NHS contract).[119] However, it is thought that the better view is that a suspended pharmacist may continue to own an NHS pharmacy but may not personally provide NHS services during the period of suspension. This view would be consistent with section 132(8) of the National Health Service Act 2006.

Examples of sanctions – Removal from the Register

Removing a registrant's registration is reserved for the most serious conduct. The committee cannot impose this sanction in cases which relate solely to the registrant's health. The committee should consider this sanction when the registrant's behaviour is fundamentally incompatible with being a registered professional.

---

115. The sanction of removal from the register is not available where fitness to practise is impaired only on the grounds of health.
116. *Blakely v General Medical Council* [2019] EWHC 905 (Admin).
117. *Abrahaem v General Medical Council* [2008] EWHC 183 (Admin).
118. *Khan (Habib) v General Pharmaceutical Council* [2016] UKSC 64.
119. Regulation 74(1)(b) of the National Health Service (Pharmaceutical and Local Pharmaceutical Services) Regulations 2013.

Examples of cases in which the FtP Committee directed the removal of the registrant's name from the Register are given in **Box 25.9**.

Box 25.9: Decisions to remove registrants from the register

A pharmacist[120] was accused of selecting a pair of shoes in a store and, pretending she had paid for them, exchanged them for a cardigan worth about £10 or £12. The FtP Committee found she was guilty of a "dishonest scam". Her persistence in denying the allegation was regarded as a lack of remorse and insight that led to her removal from the register.

****

A pharmacy technician employed by the Royal Air Force was convicted of stealing equipment which he ordered. The FtP Committee[121] said that dishonesty "lies at the top end of the spectrum of gravity of misconduct". The Committee noted the severity of the impact on the registrant and his family of removal, but removal from the Register was required. Unusually, the Committee expressed the view that removal need not be the end of the registrant's career and that after a period of reflection, he might apply for restoration to the register.

****

A pharmacist was instrumental in submitting to GlaxoSmithKline 92 apparently valid prescriptions for large quantities of drugs that were extremely expensive and in short supply. The drugs thus obtained were then sold on at a profit. The FtP Committee[122] said that whatever the pharmacist's personal qualities, the sustained dishonesty meant that a suspension could not possibly meet the seriousness of what he did.

****

A pharmacist reported himself to the GPhC because of drug dependency. This did not impair his fitness to practise, but he was found to have stolen drugs over a sustained period from the pharmacy where he worked. Removal from the Register was considered necessary to meet the public interest.[123]

120. 11 July 2013.
121. 3 May 2013.
122. 29 April 2013.
123. 19 November 2012.

In the case of an optometrist[124] who had retired and sold his practice, the High Court overturned a decision to erase his name from the Register because, on the facts of that case, "it was wholly disproportionate to order erasure ... It was not the only means of protecting patients and/or maintaining public confidence in the profession".

124. *Clarke v General Optical Council* [2017] EWHC 521 (Admin).

Interim measures following a decision to suspend or remove from the Register

A suspension or a direction to remove a registrant's name from the Register will not take effect until the 28-day period for appealing has expired or, if an appeal is brought, the conclusion of the appeal. The Committee may impose an immediate suspension if it is satisfied that this is necessary for the protection of members of the public or is otherwise in the public interest or in the interests of the registrant (Art.60). If the FtP Committee has decided that the appropriate sanction is a period of suspension, an immediate suspension to prevent the registrant practising during the appeal period will not count towards the period of suspension imposed as the sanction.[125]

Although there appears to be a tendency for the FtP Committee to decide that if it has found that suspension or removal from the Register are appropriate, there should be an immediate suspension, this must be *necessary* to protect the public or there must be a genuine public interest in immediate suspension. In many cases, the upholding of proper standards of conduct and behaviour may reasonably be said to have been achieved by the sanction the Committee has already imposed without the need for immediate suspension during the appeal period.[126] In one case,[127] for example, a pharmacist was suspended for four months because he had made a dispensing error and then dishonestly tried to conceal what had happened. The FtP Committee held there was no additional public interest that made it appropriate to impose an immediate period of suspension and that, to the contrary, on the basis that the pharmacist's business provided a service to his community, the public interest was served by enabling him to arrange for the smooth transition of his business to enable it to operate during the period of suspension.

Costs

Before a principal hearing or a restoration hearing (see below) takes place, a party may serve on the other party and the secretary to the Committee a schedule of costs and expenses related to or connected with the hearing.[128] This must be done no less than 24 hours before the date of the hearing. After announcing the Committee's decision, the chair may invite representations as to whether costs or expenses should be assessed against either party.

In practice, the Committee does not routinely award costs and there is no principle that costs are paid by the "loser" to the "winner". Costs will usually be awarded only because of the way one of the parties has conducted itself. For example, costs have been awarded against the RPSGB (when it was the regulator) because a case ought not to have

125. *Aga v General Dental Council* [2025] EWCA Civ 68.

126. *Ashton v General Medical Council* [2013] EWHC 943 (Admin); *Davey v General Dental Council* 2015 WL 6757832.

127. 23 August 2013.

128. Rule 46 of the General Pharmaceutical Council (Fitness to Practise and Disqualification etc.) Rules 2010.

been brought against two out of three registrants who were partners in a pharmacy business but who were not alleged to have been involved in the misconduct by a third partner[129] and against the GPhC after a series of procedural errors and unfair treatment in a case in which, amongst other things, a registrant was wrongly informed that his case had been closed with no further action to be taken; he was not told until ten months later that his case was still open.[130]

In another case,[131] a registrant had made false expense claims to an employer. He made admissions of dishonesty when interviewed by the police. When fitness to practise proceeding were brought, he contested the allegations and a hearing was listed for two days. On the first day of the hearing, the registrant accepted that the account he had given to the police was correct and the hearing was completed that day. The expense of arranging the second day was, therefore, wasted. The Committee held that it was unreasonable to have contested the allegations up to the morning of the first day of the hearing, and ordered the registrant to pay the wasted costs.

Where the Committee orders a party to pay costs or expenses, the chair may summarily assess the costs or expenses or require the parties to agree a figure or have them assessed by a person appointed by the secretary.

Disqualification – bodies corporate and their officers

If a body corporate is convicted of a pharmacy-related offence, or if a director, officer or employee of a body corporate is convicted of an offence, or has been guilty of misconduct, then the FtP Committee may disqualify the body corporate and direct the removal from the Register of some, or all, of its premises.[132]

Disqualification – all pharmacy owners

If there is a failure to meet the GPhC's premises standards (see **Chapter 2**), at or from which a retail pharmacy business is carried on, the FtP Committee may disqualify the owner from carrying on the business at all premises or specified premises and direct the removal of premises from the Register.[133]

The powers to disqualify and remove premises from the Register are only exercisable if the owner of the business is found unfit to carry on a retail pharmacy business safely and effectively, so far as concerns the sale or supply of all medicines. Disqualification proceedings have been rare and have been brought where a business has been conducted in wholesale disregard of the rules governing the profession or in flagrant disregard of the need to protect patients and the public.

---

129. *Pharm J*, 1 March 2008 p. 235.

130. *Professional Standards Authority v General Pharmaceutical Council and R2* [2024] EWHC 3005 (Admin).

131. 12 September 2011.

132. Section 80(1)(a) and (b) of the Medicines Act 1968.

133. Section 80(1)(c) and 80(1A) of the Medicines Act 1968.

A direction to disqualify may only be made if the chair of the FtP Committee gives assent.[134]

Disqualification may be for an indefinite period or for a specified period of time. A direction to disqualify will take effect three months after the date of the decision.

Under the Pharmacy (Premises Standards, Information Obligations, etc.) Order 2016, the FtP Committee has power to impose an interim suspension on the use of premises pending a principal hearing, if this is necessary for the protection of the public or otherwise in the public interest.

Appeals

There is a right of appeal (Art.58) to the High Court (in England and Wales) and the Court of Session (in Scotland) against decisions to direct removal from the Register, suspension and the imposition of conditions of practice. A notice of appeal must be lodged at the High Court within 28 days, beginning with the date on which written notice of the reasons for the decision was sent to the appellant. There is no power to extend this period other than in exceptional circumstances where to deny the power to extend time would impair the very essence of the right of appeal, in order to be compliant with the European Convention on Human Rights.[135]

There is a right of appeal against disqualification. Any appeal must be brought within three months from the date of the decision.[136]

Professional Standards Authority for Health and Social Care (PSA)

The fitness to practise role of the GPhC is overseen by the Professional Standards Authority for Health and Social Care (PSA – see **Chapter 2**). If the PSA considers that a fitness to practise decision (including a decision not to take a disciplinary measure) is not sufficient for the protection of the public for the PSA, the PSA may appeal against the decision to the High Court or Court of Session.[137] The question for consideration in such an appeal is whether the GPhC's decision was sufficient:

a. to protect the health, safety and well-being of the public;
b. to maintain public confidence in the profession; and
c. to maintain proper professional standards and conduct for members of that profession.

In *Professional Standards Authority v General Pharmaceutical Council and Onwughalu*,[138] Mrs Onwughalu had been convicted of two counts of cruelty to a child under 16. She received prison sentences for each offence. The FtP Committee decided to suspend her for 12 months. The PSA appealed. Mrs Justice Cox noted that there were

134. Section 82 of the Medicines Act 1968.
135. *Stuewe v Health and Care Professions Council* [2022] EWCA Civ 1605.
136. Section 82 of the Medicines Act 1968.
137. Section 29 of the National Health Service Reform and Health Care Professions Act 2002.
138. [2014] EWHC 2521.

serious aggravating factors and that the applicant had not demonstrated "true insight". The judge held that the Committee had not explained how suspending the registrant would be sufficient to maintain professional standards and to maintain public confidence in the pharmacy profession. She held that the FtP Committee's decision was plainly wrong in view of the registrant's lack of insight, and the offences were directly related to clinical practice and to standards of professionalism. The suspension was quashed and replaced with an order for removal from the Register.

Restoration to the Register and registration following removal

In the case of a person whose name has been removed from the Register at the direction of the FtP Committee, no application for restoration may be made before the expiration of five years from the date of removal or within 12 months from the date of an earlier application.[139] The Registrar will refer any application for restoration to the FtP Committee. The burden of proof in a restoration application is on the applicant, who must prove that they are fit to practise. The approach will be different in clinical error or negligence cases as opposed to cases where the offending behaviour was central to the applicant's functions as a pharmacist such as dishonesty or sexual misconduct. The passage of time since removal from the Register is of considerable importance. Remediation is essential but, even when coupled with the passage of time, these factors do not outweigh the need to maintain public confidence in the profession.[140] In 2013, a pharmacist who had stolen drugs and equipment to the value of more than £400,000 from the pharmacy he managed was sentenced to three years in prison. The FtP Committee directed the removal of his name from the Register. In 2020, the FtP Committee granted his application for restoration to the Register,[141] referring to his "very genuine" remorse, saying it was "satisfied that he is now determined to live within his means and has developed a realistic attitude to material possessions". The Committee went on to say that it was "convinced that there is now very little risk of any repetition, given the very severe consequences which that dishonesty had for the applicant and his family", it also emphasised that "there has never been any question raised about the applicant's professional ability as a pharmacist", adding that the applicant had been on the Register "for some 20 years prior to his removal and no concerns had been raised about his work".

A person whose name was removed from the Register before the GPhC became the regulator will not have been on the Council's Register. As such, an application for restoration cannot be made, and such a person would have to apply for registration to the Registrar. There is no time restriction of the kind that applies to applications for restoration. Initially, the Registrar usually determines such applications without a hearing. If an application is refused, there is a right of appeal to the Appeals Committee.

---

139. Article 57(2) of the Pharmacy Order 2010.

140. *General Medical Council v Shekhar Chandra* [2018] EWCA Civ 1898.

141. Chemist & Druggist, 1 October 2020.

The procedures that have to be followed in order to appeal are set out in Regulations.[142] Appeals take the form of a re-hearing, which may be on paper. The appellant may request a hearing and may give oral evidence. The appellant bears the burden of establishing that the Registrar's decision should be overturned, and the standard of proof is the civil one, i.e. the balance of probabilities.[143]

SUMMARY

- The overarching objective of the GPhC in exercising its functions is the protection of the public.
- Fitness to practise involves suitability to be on the Register without restrictions.
- Fitness to practise decisions are published for a limited period on the GPhC's website.
- The GPhC will consider fitness to practise on an application for first registration and when it receives information or an allegation that fitness to practise may be impaired.
- Registrants are required to disclose convictions and cautions.
- Allegations of impairment are usually based on a conviction, misconduct, deficient professional performance or health.
- Misconduct may relate to professional practice or other conduct that brings the profession into disrepute.
- Dispensing errors may be misconduct or deficient professional performance, but single errors are not usually referred for fitness to practise proceedings unless very serious.
- Deficient professional performance involves a standard of practice that is unacceptably low.
- A superintendent pharmacist or a director of a body corporate may be guilty of misconduct if the body corporate is run in a way that does not protect patients or the public.
- A breach of the GPhC's Standards is not necessarily misconduct but it may be taken into account in any fitness to practise proceedings.
- Acquittal of a criminal offence does not prevent fitness to practise proceedings being brought on the same facts.
- University schools of pharmacy have fitness to practise procedures.
- Allegations may be passed by the GPhC's Registrar to the Investigating Committee, which will decide whether to refer the case to the FtP Committee.
- If the Investigating Committee does not refer a case to the FtP Committee, it may give advice or a warning.
- The FtP Committee may impose an interim suspension or conditions of practise while awaiting a full hearing if it considers this necessary for the protection of the public or the registrant, or is otherwise in the public interest. If premises standards are breached, similar powers exist in relation to premises.
- At a full (or *principal*) hearing, the FtP Committee will decide the facts and whether a registrant's fitness to practise is impaired.

142. The General Pharmaceutical Council (Appeals Committee Rules) Order of Council 2010.

143. Rule 10 of the Appeals Committee Rules.

SUMMARY (cont.)

- Principal hearings proceed in up to three stages – findings of fact, consideration of impairment and sanction.
- If a registrant's fitness to practise is found to be impaired, the FtP Committee can give a warning, impose conditions of practice, suspend for up to 12 months or direct the registrant's removal from the GPhC's Register (but there is no power to remove where impairment is solely on the ground of health).
- In deciding on the appropriate and proportionate sanction, the FtP Committee will have regard to the GPhC's Outcomes Guidance.
- The FtP Committee has power to order the GPhC or a registrant to pay costs.
- A registrant has a right of appeal to a court against certain decisions of the FtP Committee, including suspension or removal from the Register.
- Following removal from the Register, an application for restoration cannot be made before five years have elapsed.
- The GPhC is overseen by the Professional Standards Authority which can ask the High Court to review certain fitness to practise decisions.

FURTHER READING

- *Chemist and Druggist* (a weekly publication for community pharmacy but also publishes short reports of some fitness to practise cases and has links to transcripts on the GPhC website): **http://www.chemistanddruggist.co.uk**.
- Fitness to practise cases: **https://www.pharmacyregulation.org/patients-and-public/reporting-concerns/investigating-concerns/hearings** (accessed 31 December 2024).
- General Pharmaceutical Council; Fitness to Practise FAQs **https://www.pharmacyregulation.org/patients-and-public/reporting-concerns/how-we-deal-concerns/fitness-practise-faqs** (accessed 31 December 2024). The GPhC also publishes an annual Fitness to Practise report which is available on its website.
- Glynn J, Gomez D (2012). *Regulation of Healthcare Professionals*. London: Sweet & Maxwell.
- GPhC (January 2016). *Good decision making: conditions bank.*
- GPhC (January 2019). *Good Decision Making: investigations and threshold criteria guidance.*
- GPhC (March 2017). *Criminal Prosecution policy.*
- GPhC (March 2019). *Good decision making: investigating committee meetings and outcomes guidance.*
- GPhC (March 2024). *Good decision making: fitness to practise hearings and outcomes guidance.*
- GPhC (September 2020). *Guidance on managing fitness to practise concerns in education and training.*
- GPhC (September 2020). Case studies on m*anaging fitness to practise concerns in education and training.*
- Hamer K (2023). *Professional Conduct Casebook.* (4th editioni) Oxford: Oxford University Press.
- *Promoting professionalism, reforming regulation* **https://assets.publishing.service.gov.uk/government/uploads/system/uploads/attachment_data/file/815261/promoting_professionalism_reforming_regulation_-_eds_HW.pdf** (accessed 31 December 2024).

- Temple Bright *A Guide to General Pharmaceutical Council Investigations and Fitness to Practise Proceedings* **https://www.templebright.com/wp-content/uploads/2022/04/Guide-to-GPhC-fitness-to-practise-investigation-2022.pdf** (accessed 31 December 2024).
- The GPhC also publishes every 2 months *Regulate* **https://www.pharmacyregulation.org/regulate** (accessed 31 December 2024); this carries updates on the Council's activities as well as lessons to be learned from selected fitness to practise cases.
- The PSA has a range of material on its website **https://www.professionalstandards.org.uk/** (accessed 31 December 2024).
- What the Fitness to Practise Committee does: **https://www.pharmacyregulation.org/patients-and-public/reporting-concerns/investigating-concerns/what-fitness-practise-committee-does** (accessed 31 December 2024).

CHAPTER 26

Criminal and civil liability

Sources of criminal law

As explained in **Chapter 1**, there are two primary sources of law: law made in legislation or under powers in legislation; and the common law, in which judges declare what the law is. Where the cases referred to in this chapter have been dealt with in England and Wales in the High Court and the Court of Appeal, or in Scotland in the Court of Session, or in the House of Lords or Supreme Court, case references are given in the usual way. However, cases heard in lower courts, such as the Crown Court, are not usually included in recognised law reports because rulings in those cases do not set legal precedents to be followed in later cases. Where available, alternative references are given for those cases.

Criminal procedure and terminology is explained further in **Chapter 1**.

Criminal offences created in legislation

The principal legislation governing pharmacy practice comprises:

- the Medicines Act 1968;
- the Misuse of Drugs Act 1971 (with regulations made under powers in this Act, such as the Misuse of Drugs (Safe Custody) Regulations 1973 and the Misuse of Drugs Regulations 2001);
- the Pharmacy Order 2010; and
- the Human Medicines Regulations 2012 (HMR).

Many breaches of the requirements in this legislation are criminal offences. Breaches of other legislation referred to in this book are also criminal offences. Moreover, as explained in **Chapter 7**, many aspects of pharmacy practice, such as the sale or supply of Pharmacy medicines (**Chapter 11**), Prescription Only Medicines (**Chapter 12**) and controlled drugs (**Chapter 14**) in circumstances corresponding to retail sale[1] are only lawful if the person making the supply is lawfully conducting a retail pharmacy business; and if the person making the supply does not meet the conditions for lawfully conducting a retail pharmacy business, any supply is a criminal offence.

Strict liability and statutory defences

Specific offences are described below. Some offences involve what is known as *strict liability*, which means that an offence is committed whether the person who committed the offences was aware of the true facts or not. Such awareness is referred to by lawyers

---

1. Through a combination of HMR Regs.8, 18(8) and 213, the expression *supply in circumstances corresponding to retail sale* means a supply to someone who does not receive it for the purpose of selling it or supplying it; or administering it or causing it to be administered to one or more human beings. In short, if the sale or supply is a wholesale transaction it does not come within the meaning of *sale or supply in circumstances corresponding to retail sale*.

as having *mens rea*, a Latin term referring to having a guilty mind, and evidence of *mens rea* does not have to be present to prove a strict liability offence has taken place. In the case of other offences, the legislation may provide that the person accused of an offence may have a defence in specified circumstances. The case of *Pharmaceutical Society of Great Britain v Storkwain*[2] (see **Chapter 12**) concerned a pharmacy from which a forged prescription was dispensed. The House of Lords, then the highest court in the UK, held that this was a strict liability offence and that an offence was committed even if the pharmacist did not know that the prescription was a forgery. After this case, the law making it an offence to supply a Prescription Only Medicine except in accordance with a prescription (now in HMR Regs.214 and 255), was amended to provide a defence (now in HMR Reg.245) if the pharmacist, having exercised all due diligence, believes on reasonable grounds that the prescription is genuine. The requirement for due diligence is a common feature of defences in the legislation.

Specific statutory offences and defences

With a view to protecting the public, the Medicines Act 1968 prohibits certain things, and section 67 of the Act says that a person who does any of those things commits an offence. However, there is a current trend to place enforcement in the hands of professional regulators rather than criminal prosecutors.[3] Indeed, in deciding to introduce statutory defences to prosecutions under sections 63 and 64 of the Medicines Act, the Department of Health and Social Care expressed the view that prosecuting authorities should no longer bring prosecutions relating to dealings with medicinal products, saying "By prosecuting under part 12 of the Human Medicines Regulations, prosecuting authorities could be argued to be going against Parliament's intentions to decriminalise dispensing errors. Prosecuting authorities around the UK will no longer be able to bring a relatively simple prosecution for a strict liability offence. This is necessary to help remove the 'fear factor' of an easy to prove prosecution."

The introduction of statutory defences followed the report of a Rebalancing Board and consultations. The defences, which are set out in more detail below, are applicable if certain conditions are satisfied. The defences relate to things done at a registered pharmacy and certain other places (see the definition of *relevant pharmacy service* below), such as hospital pharmacies. The defences will apply even if the pharmacist was both the prescriber and the dispenser. The policy behind the introduction of the defences was to remove the threat of criminal sanctions for inadvertent preparation and dispensing errors, and incentivising an increase in the reporting of dispensing errors, which research suggests will afford greater learning opportunities – translating

2. [1986] 1 WLR 903.
3. https://www.gov.uk/government/consultations/pharmacy-legislation-on-dispensing-errors-and-organisational-governance/outcome/rebalancing-medicines-legislation-and-pharmacy-regulation-programme-consultation-outcome (accessed 31 December 2024).

to a reduction in errors and increased patient safety if the conditions below are met.[4] Among other things, the conditions are based on the duty of candour which healthcare professionals owe.[5]

Adulteration of medicinal products

Section 63 of the Medicines Act prohibits:

1. adding any substance to, or abstracting any substance from, a medicinal product so as to affect injuriously the composition of the product, with intent that the product shall be sold or supplied in that state; or
2. selling or supplying, or offering or exposing for sale or supply, or having in one's possession for the purpose of sale or supply, any medicinal product whose composition has been injuriously affected by the addition or abstraction of any substance.

If a medicine is not sold or supplied in an adulterated state, a person who is charged with an offence ("the defendant") will have a defence (under section 67A) if they prove that:

a. the adulteration took place at a registered pharmacy or in the course of a relevant pharmacy service;
b. if the defendant is accused of the adulteration, the defendant must have been a registrant acting in the course of their profession, or was acting under the supervision of a person who was a registrant acting in the course of their profession; and
c. at the time of the alleged offence, the defendant did not know that the product was being adulterated;
d. if the defendant did not adulterate a medicinal product but is accused of offering or exposing it for sale or supply or it was in the defendant's possession, it is a condition that the person who adulterated the product was a registrant acting in the course of their profession.

If a medicine is sold or supplied in an adulterated state, a person who is charged with an offence will have a defence (under section 67B of the Medicines Act) if they prove that:

a. the adulteration took place at a registered pharmacy or in the course of a relevant pharmacy service;
b. the person who adulterated the product:
    i. was a registrant acting in the course of their profession, or
    ii. was acting under the supervision of a person who was a registrant acting in the course of their profession;

---

4. The Explanatory Memorandum to the Pharmacy (Preparation and Dispensing Errors – Hospital and Other Pharmacy Services) Order 2022 https://www.legislation.gov.uk/uksi/2022/851/pdfs/uksiem_20220851_en.pdf (accessed 31 December 2024).
5. This is a professional obligation – see https://assets.pharmacyregulation.org/files/joint_statement_on_the_professional_duty_of_candour.pdf (accessed 31 December 2024) and see also the Explanatory Memorandum to the Pharmacy (Preparation and Dispensing Errors – Registered Pharmacies) Order 2018 http://www.legislation.gov.uk/uksi/2018/181/pdfs/uksiem_20180181_en.pdf (accessed 31 December 2024).

c. the product was:
   i. sold or supplied in pursuance of a prescription or directions given by a relevant prescriber or a patient group direction, or
   ii. a Prescription Only Medicine that was sold or supplied in circumstances where there was an immediate need for it to be sold or supplied and a prescription could not have been obtained without undue delay; and
d. Condition A or B is met.

Condition A is that before the defendant was charged:

a. the defendant did not know that the product had been adulterated; and
b. if the defendant is the person who adulterated the product, the registrant who supervised the person who adulterated the product or the pharmacy owner, neither the person who adulterated the product nor a registrant who supervised the person who adulterated the product knew that the product had been adulterated.

Condition B is that:

a. before the defendant was charged, an appropriate person, on becoming aware that the product had been adulterated:
   i. promptly ensured that all reasonable steps were taken to ensure that the person to whom the product was intended to be administered was notified that the product had been adulterated, or
   ii. reasonably formed the view that it was not necessary or appropriate to do so, in the circumstances of the case; and
b. the defendant did not know at the time that the product was sold or supplied that it had been adulterated.

Dispensing errors

With a view to protecting the public, section 64 of the Medicines Act prohibits selling or supplying a medicinal product to the prejudice of the purchaser (or patient) which is not of the nature or quality demanded by the purchaser or specified in a prescription. Prosecutions for breach of this section have been brought against pharmacy owners, pharmacists, a pharmacy student and a dispenser.

There is no offence if the medicinal product contains some extraneous matter, the presence of which is proved to be an inevitable consequence of the process of manufacture, nor is it an offence where:

1. a substance has been added to, or abstracted from, the medicinal product which did not injuriously affect the composition of the product and was not carried out fraudulently; and
2. the product was sold having attached to it, or to a container or package in which it was sold, a conspicuous notice of adequate size and legibly printed specifying the substance added or abstracted.

Pharmacists, pharmacy students and dispensing assistants have in the past been convicted of offences under 64 of the Medicines Act because they have made dispensing errors. One example is the case of Mrs Elizabeth Lee, who was a locum pharmacist (see **Box 18.1** in **Chapter 18**).[6] An example of a prosecution of someone who was not a pharmacist is the 2009 case of *Mahoney v Prestatyn Magistrates Court*,[7] a dispenser at a branch of Lloyds Pharmacy handed a patient sertraline when spironolactone had been prescribed. The dispenser argued that the offence could only be committed by a pharmacy owner or a pharmacist. Lord Justice Elias rejected this argument, saying:

> *"one can readily understand why Parliament might have thought it was necessary to impose criminal liability, even on dispensers and others involved in the supply chain, because the consequences of a mistake can be so serious."*

In rejecting an argument that the dispenser had not made a supply, the judge said:

> *"It seems to me that in the normal way she was plainly part of the system of supply. She does not cease to be part of that system because the pharmacist fails properly to comply with the obligations that are imposed upon her. That does not affect the question of who is supplying these goods. Moreover, there is an obvious public interest in ensuring that all those whose failings have led to the selling, wrongly, of a product in this way, should be held accountable."*

Prosecutions have also resulted from errors in a hospital setting. For example, in *R v Guy's & St Thomas' NHS Trust*,[8] a fine of £15,000 was imposed on the Trust because a baby died from an overdose of glucose after a technician transposed glucose and water in parenteral nutrition and the error went unnoticed by a supervisor; and a fine of £45,000 was imposed on the Royal Bournemouth Hospital Trust in a case mentioned below.

The prosecution of Mrs Lee and the concern caused throughout the pharmacy profession at the imposition of a prison sentence for making a dispensing error led to a campaign to decriminalise the making of dispensing errors. Eventually, the Medicines Act was amended; instead of decriminalising dispensing errors, the Act now provides defences if a person is prosecuted under either section 63 (see above) or 64 of the Medicines Act.

Defences in the case of dispensing errors

Section 67C of the Act provides a defence to a prosecution under section 64 if:

a. the product was dispensed at or from a registered pharmacy or in the course of the provision of a relevant pharmacy service;
b. the person who dispensed the product:
    i. was a pharmacist or pharmacy technician acting in the course of their profession, or
    ii. was acting under the supervision of a pharmacist or pharmacy technician who was acting in the course of their profession;

6. *R v Lee (Elizabeth)* [2010] EWCA Crim 1404.
7. [2009] EWHC 3237 (Admin).
8. [2008] EWCA Crim 2187.

c. the product was:
   i. sold or supplied in pursuance of a prescription or directions given by a relevant prescriber or a patient group direction, or
   ii. a prescription only medicine that was sold or supplied in circumstances where there was an immediate need for it to be sold or supplied and a prescription could not have been obtained without undue delay; and
d. Condition A or B is met.

Condition A is that before the defendant was charged:

a. the defendant did not know that the product was not of the required nature or quality; and
b. if the defendant is the person who dispensed the product, the registrant under whose supervision the product was dispensed or the person carrying on the retail pharmacy business or the relevant pharmacy service, neither the person who dispensed the product nor the registrant who supervised that person knew that the product was not of the required nature or quality.

Condition B is that:

a. before the defendant was charged an appropriate person on becoming aware that the product was not of the required nature or quality:
   i. promptly ensured that all reasonable steps were taken to ensure that the person to whom the product was intended to be administered was notified that the product was not of the required nature or quality, or
   ii. reasonably formed the view that it was not necessary or appropriate to do so in the circumstances of the case; and
b. the defendant did not know at the time the product was sold or supplied that it was not of the required nature or quality.

Relevant pharmacy service

A *relevant pharmacy service* is defined in Section 67F of the Act. See **Chapter 9**.

Appropriate person

An *appropriate person* means the person who dispensed the product or the registrant under whose supervision it was dispensed or the person carrying on the retail pharmacy business, or the relevant pharmacy service (or a person acting on that person's behalf).

Relevant prescriber

A *relevant prescriber* means[9] any of the following:

a. a doctor;
b. a dentist;
c. a supplementary prescriber;
d. a nurse independent prescriber;
e. a pharmacist independent prescriber;
f. a community practitioner nurse prescriber;

---

9. HMR Reg.213.

g. a physiotherapist independent prescriber;
h. a podiatrist independent prescriber;
i. a therapeutic radiographer independent prescriber;
j. a paramedic independent prescriber;
k. an optometrist independent prescriber; and
l. an approved country health professional.

When the statutory defences will or will not apply

It will be noted that the defence relates to a medicinal product sold or supplied on prescription in pursuance of a prescription or the direction of a practitioner: the defence will not extend to the sale over the counter of a medicinal product subject to general sale or of a Pharmacy medicine. A dispensing assistant such as Mrs Mahoney, for example, would not be able to rely on a defence under section 67C unless the dispensing assistant could prove on the balance of probabilities that they acted under the supervision of a pharmacy professional. This, in turn, raises the question of what *supervision* means (as to which, see **Chapter 11**). The defences will not apply if the prosecution proves beyond reasonable doubt that, in doing an act in the course of their profession, a person:
(a) used their professional skills for an improper purpose; or
(b) deliberately failed to have due regard for patient safety.

The Explanatory Memorandum[10] that accompanied the Order that introduced the defence to prosecutions contained examples of how the defences may or may not be applicable. These are set out in **Box 26.1**.

Box 26.1: Examples of how defences to prosecution for dispensing errors may work in practice

1. A pharmacist dispenses the wrong dose of a medicine with the potential to cause serious harm on a Friday afternoon. On their way home the pharmacist realises they made an error, telephones the pharmacy service to see if anyone is still there, finds that everyone has gone home or can't talk to a colleague, and then leaves the matter until Monday. The patient is admitted to intensive care over the weekend. In these circumstances, the pharmacist has not discharged their duty of candour "promptly" and so cannot benefit from the defence, even if on the Monday they try to contact the patient before they become aware of the hospitalisation. The availability of the statutory defence means the pharmacist will have a clear incentive to return to the pharmacy on the Friday and take all reasonable steps to contact the patient.
2. Altering the facts slightly but with the same risk of serious harm, the pharmacist is not sure whether or not an error was made and leaves the matter until the Monday. Arguably, because they do not "know" an error has been made, they could still potentially benefit from the defence, albeit that they have clearly behaved unprofessionally. However, if a court determines that they have "deliberately failed to have due regard to patient safety" (section 67D(3)(b)), the court will find that they were not "acting in the course of his or her profession" and so the defence will not be available. Again, even if the pharmacist is unsure, they will have a clear incentive to return to the pharmacy to make sure they discharge their professional responsibilities.

---

10. https://www.legislation.gov.uk/uksi/2018/181/pdfs/uksiem_20180181_en.pdf (accessed 31 December 2024).

Box 26.1: Examples of how defences to prosecution for dispensing errors may work in practice (cont.)

3. Altering the facts slightly again, but still with the same risk of serious harm, this time the error is made by a pharmacy student, who is acting under the supervision of a pharmacist. On their way home, the student realises that they have made an error, and contacts the pharmacy service. The pharmacist is still there. If the pharmacist fails to act, neither of the two – the student or the pharmacist – will be able to benefit from the defence. This may initially seem unfair on the student, albeit that they were the error maker, but if the student has exercised all due diligence to avoid the commission of the offence and the offence is actually due to the default of another person, they have a defence under section 121(2) (Contravention due to default of other person) of the Act and the other person can still be prosecuted by virtue of section 121(1). Thus, all the main protagonists with "duty of candour" obligations will have a clear incentive to ensure that the patient is notified.
4. Many more permutations of these basic facts are of course possible, but this illustrates how the provisions have been designed to incentivise reporting – and not just by the error maker.

The defences to prosecutions for breaching section 64 of the Medicines Act also do not apply to defective medicinal products dispensed on premises of a manufacturer that are not registered as a pharmacy. For example, in a case where a child was prescribed magnesium glycerophosphate to help prevent seizures, Syri Limited, a specials manufacturer supplied a product that contained just 12% of the strength specified on the prescription. The product supplied did not work effectively and the patient was admitted to hospital, suffering from seizures. Syri Limited was convicted and fined £51,000.[11]

Section 64 of the Medicines Act does not apply to supplies made pursuant to a Serious Shortage Protocol because such a supply is not made pursuant to a prescription.[12]

Procuring, supplying and using drugs to cause abortion

The offences under sections 58 and 59 of the Offences Against the Person Act 1861 are dealt with in **Chapter 12**. The use of devices and drugs for contraceptive purposes are not intended to cause abortion, so do not contravene sections 58 and 59 of the Offences Against the Person Act.[13]

Other offences relating to dealings with medicinal products

Part 12 of the HMR concerns dealings with medicinal products, setting out the requirements for selling or supplying medicines subject to general sale, Pharmacy

---

11. https://www.gov.uk/government/news/pharmaceutical-company-fined-for-manufacturing-defective-medicine (accessed 31 December 2024).
12. *The Queen (on the application of The Good Law Project) v Secretary of State for Health and Social Care* [2019] EWCA (Civ) 1211. The ruling is not a binding precedent because the hearing was an application for permission to apply for judicial review, not a full hearing.
13. *R (on the application of Smeaton) v Secretary of State for Health* [2002] EWHC 610 (Admin).

medicines and Prescription Only Medicines (see **Chapters 10, 11** and **12** respectively). HMR Reg.255 states that a person is guilty of an offence if that person breaches any of the following regulations:

a. regulation 214(1) (prohibition on sale etc of prescription only medicine otherwise than in accordance with prescription from an appropriate practitioner);
b. regulation 214(2) (prohibition on parenteral administration of prescription only medicine otherwise than by or under directions of appropriate practitioner);
c. regulation 220 (prohibition on sale etc of medicinal product not subject to general sale otherwise than by or under supervision of pharmacist);
d. regulation 249 (prohibition on sale of a Prescription Only Medicine or Pharmacy medicine by way of wholesale dealing to person not within Schedule 22);
e. regulation 251 (compliance with standards specified in certain publications); or
f. regulation 254 (prohibitions concerning traceability of treatment with advanced therapy medicinal products).

HMR Reg.255 also creates certain other offences which do not provide defences. However, there are some exemptions, setting out circumstances in which an offence is not committed. One example concerns the exercise of all due diligence when a medicinal product is supplied on the strength of a prescription that turns out to be forged (see above). Another example concerns the offence of selling or supplying a Pharmacy medicine or a Prescription Only Medicine unless the sale or supply is made by a pharmacist or the transaction is supervised by a pharmacist[14] and the sale or supply is made from registered pharmacy premises (see **Chapters 11** and **12**). HMR Reg.244 provides that the restrictions do not apply to the sale or supply of a Prescription Only Medicine by a person who has exercised all due diligence and believes on reasonable grounds that the product is subject to general sale, that belief is due to the act or default of another person and the conditions applicable to the retail sale or supply of medicinal products subject to retail sale are met. Further examples of such exemptions are in **Chapter 13**.

Bringing prosecutions for offences under the Medicines Act or HMR

The General Pharmaceutical Council has power in the Pharmacy Order 2010[15] to bring prosecutions for breaching relevant provisions of the Medicines Act and the HMR. It has published a Prosecutions policy[16] the effect of which is that the GPhC is likely to regard Fitness to Practise proceedings (see **Chapter 25**) as a proportionate way to deal with registrants rather than bringing prosecutions against registrants who have broken the law. Prosecutions are therefore rare and usually involve persons who were practising as pharmacists without being registered (see also **Chapter 2**).

---

14. See Chapter 11 regarding proposals to amend the HMR so as to allow pharmacy technicians to supervise transactions.
15. Article 3.
16. https://assets.pharmacyregulation.org/files/gp201489_gphc_criminal_prosecution_policy.pdf (accessed 31 December 2024).

The Crown Prosecution Service has been responsible for bringing prosecutions under section 64 of the Medicines Act in recent years, including the prosecutions of Mrs Elizabeth Lee and Mrs Mahoney (see above). Prosecutions are not limited to community pharmacies. In 2019, following an investigation by the MHRA, the CPS prosecuted Royal Bournemouth Hospital Trust because a leukaemia patient was given five times the required amount of a trial drug.[17]

Offences under other legislation

Corporate manslaughter

The Corporate Manslaughter and Corporate Homicide Act 2007 creates an offence if an organisation such as a corporation causes a person's death where there has been a gross breach of a relevant duty of care owed by the organisation to the deceased. In considering whether there has been a gross breach of a duty of care, a jury may consider, amongst other things, the extent to which the evidence shows that there were attitudes, policies, systems or accepted practices within the organisation that were likely to have encouraged any failure, or to have produced tolerance of it.

In appropriate circumstances, the Act may be used to prosecute companies that own pharmacies, NHS bodies, such as hospital trusts and primary care organisations. Such circumstances may include cases where death occurs through major failures in management arrangements, such as staffing, training or resources. In May 2015, Maidstone and Tunbridge Wells Trust became the first NHS Trust to be charged with corporate manslaughter following the death of a 30-year-old patient. In the event, the Trust was found to have no case to answer,[18] but the case illustrates the possibility of corporate manslaughter cases being brought against trusts or companies that provide health services.

Battery

Any touching of another person, however slight, may be a battery. The touching will be unlawful if it is done without lawful excuse. There will be a lawful excuse if there is actual or implied consent.[19] Battery is described in more detail below in relation to civil liability.

The Consumer Protection from Unfair Trading Regulations 2008

Insofar as the criminal law provides consumer protection, the Consumer Protection from Unfair Trading Regulations make certain misleading actions and aggressive commercial practices an offence. To quote the Explanatory Memorandum accompanying the Regulations, they: "introduce a general prohibition on traders in all sectors engaging

---

17. https://www.independent.co.uk/news/health/patient-safety-death-prosecution-fine-nhs-hospital-bournemouth-drugs-a9241916.html (accessed 31 December 2024).
18. https://www.mtw.nhs.uk/2016/01/no-case-to-answer-in-corporate-manslaughter-trial/ (accessed 31 December 2024).
19. *Marland v DPP* [2023] EWHC 1046 (Admin).

in unfair commercial (mainly marketing and selling) practices against consumers. It ... put in place a comprehensive framework for dealing with sharp practices and rogue traders who deliberately set out to exploit loopholes in existing legislation."

Safeguarding users of health services

Persons working in either health or social care are now subject to several areas of legislation. Before commencing employment, employers of health professionals are required to check with the Disclosure and Barring Service (DBS) to establish their identity, ascertain whether they have a criminal record and whether they are barred from carrying out certain work, usually involving children or vulnerable adults. The DBS covers England and Wales, but similar processes apply in Scotland (see **Chapter 2**).

Employers are legally required to report safeguarding concerns to the DBS and it is illegal for anyone barred by the DBS to work, or apply to work, within the sector from which they are barred. It is also illegal for an employer to knowingly employ a barred person in the sector from which they are barred. Pharmacists and pharmacy technicians are subject to DBS checks but "other staff" such as sales assistants and delivery drivers are not, provided they act under the direction or supervision of a pharmacist or pharmacy technician.[20] Further, certain activities such as using a private taxi (as opposed to a hospital ambulance) to convey a patient to hospital have been exempted in regulations.[21]

It is a criminal offence[22] for an individual who has the care of another individual by virtue of being a care worker (this includes a healthcare worker) or care provider (which includes a provider of healthcare) to ill-treat or wilfully to neglect that individual. The offence focuses on the conduct of the individual, not the outcome; in other words, what the healthcare worker actually did (or failed to do) rather than any harm that resulted. For organisations, the offence focuses on the way their activities are managed and organised and whether an incident amounts to a gross breach of the relevant duty of care to the patient.

Health and Safety at Work etc. Act 1974

The Health and Safety at Work etc. Act 1974 is extremely broad and imposes a duty on every employer to ensure, so far as is reasonably practicable, the health, safety and welfare at work of all their employees. The duty is owed not only to employees but to all workers, including self-employed individuals like locums, and others from risk to their health, safety and welfare. The duties extend to the protection of the health and safety of the public against the risks to health arising from work activities. The Act provides a framework for other health and safety legislation. Detailed requirements are set out in specific Regulations. These Regulations are themselves supported by Approved Codes

---

20. Safeguarding Vulnerable Groups Act 2006 (Miscellaneous Provisions) Order 2012.
21. Safeguarding Vulnerable Groups Act 2006 (Miscellaneous Provisions) Regulations 2012.
22. Criminal Justice and Courts Act 2015, s.20.

of Practice that expand the requirements contained within individual Regulations by providing detailed interpretation and guidance. Approved Codes of Practice are the main working documents for those with health and safety responsibilities.

The principal areas covered are:

- safe plant and machinery (work equipment) and safe operating procedures;
- safe use, handling and storage and transport of articles and substances;
- provision of information, instruction, training and supervision;
- provision and maintenance of a safe place of work with safe means of access and egress; and
- for an employer with more than four employees, provision of a written policy for health and safety and details of the arrangements for carrying out the requirements of the policy.

Others to whom the duty is owed include customers, visitors and the general public. Employees themselves also have a duty under the Act to take reasonable care for their own health and safety and for that of anyone else who may be affected by what they (employees) do or fail to do. There is also a duty to co-operate with their employer on health and safety issues.

Enforcement of health and safety requirements is undertaken by inspectors from the Health and Safety Executive for industrial premises or by officers from local authorities for retail premises. Both regulatory groups have powers to inspect, investigate cases of non-compliance, warn and issue *improvement notices* or *prohibition notices* as well as prosecute offenders.

Among other topics, the Health and Safety Executive has published guidance on:

- using veterinary medicines, including sheep dips;
- safe handling of cytotoxic drugs in the workplace;
- handling cytotoxic drugs in isolators in NHS pharmacies; and
- ergonomics in the pharmaceutical industry.

It is beyond the scope of this book to provide much detail about health and safety legislation. However, it is important to draw attention to the requirement for *risk assessment* as the basic tool for identifying and managing risk. Areas where risks might arise in pharmacy practice include:

- work equipment (Provision and Use of Work Equipment Regulations 1998);
- substances (COSHH Regulations[23]); and
- manual handling (Manual Handling Operations Regulations 1992).

Sharps returned to a pharmacy may pose a particular risk. The Health and Safety (Sharp Instruments in Healthcare) Regulations 2013 are designed to minimise the number of needlestick injuries, focus on risk assessment, and then elimination, prevention and protection. The Regulations do not impose criminal liability directly, but may give rise to criminal prosecution if failure to comply amounts to a breach of the Health and Safety at Work etc. Act. The Regulations require healthcare employers to ensure that:

---

23. Control of Substances Hazardous to Health Regulations 2002 (see also Chapter 21).

a. the use of medical sharps at work is avoided so far as is reasonably practicable;
b. when medical sharps are used at work, safer sharps are used so far as is reasonably practicable;
c. needles that are medical sharps are not capped after use at work unless:
   i. that act is required to control a risk identified by an assessment of the risks to the health and safety of employees to which they are exposed whilst at work for the purpose of identifying the measures the employer needs to take to comply with the requirements of the Regulations, and
   ii. the risk of injury to employees is effectively controlled by the use of a suitable appliance, tool or other equipment;
d. in relation to the safe disposal of medical sharps that are not designed for re-use:
   i. written instructions for employees, and
   ii. clearly marked and secure containers,

   are located close to areas where medical sharps are used at work.

An employer must review at suitable intervals the policies and procedures in place to meet the requirements of the Regulations so as to ensure that those policies and procedures remain up to date and effective.

In addition, the Regulations require an employer to provide each employee who is exposed to a risk of injury at work from medical sharps with information on:

i. the risk of injury;
ii. the legislative requirements;
iii. good practice in preventing injury from medical sharps;
iv. the benefits and drawbacks of vaccination and non-vaccination in respect of blood-borne diseases;
v. the support provided by the employer to an employee who is injured at work by a medical sharp;

and relevant training on:

i. the safe use and disposal of medical sharps;
ii. the correct use of safer sharps;
iii. what employees should do if they are injured at work by a medical sharp;
iv. the health surveillance and other procedures to be conducted by the employer where an employee is injured by a medical sharp.

The duties imposed on employers apply equally to contractors with employees on a healthcare employer's premises, and references to employees include others who work under an employer's supervision and direction.

An injured person must notify the employer of an injury. Employers must record any injury at work from a medical sharp, investigate the circumstances and take any necessary action to prevent a recurrence. Employers must also take immediate steps to ensure that the employee receives medical advice, that treatment is made available and must consider providing the employee with counselling.

The Personal Protective Equipment at Work Regulations 1992 require every employer to ensure that suitable personal protective equipment (PPE) is provided to their employees who may be exposed to a risk to their health or safety while at work except where and to the extent that such risk has been adequately controlled by other means which are equally or more effective; and every self-employed person shall ensure that they are provided with suitable personal protective equipment where they may be exposed to a risk to their health or safety while at work except where and to the extent that such risk has been adequately controlled by other means which are equally or more effective. The legal requirement to provide PPE became particularly significant during the COVID-19 pandemic in 2020 and the HSE updated its guidance on the subject.

Controls on waste

The Department for Environment, Food and Rural Affairs (DEFRA) is the government department responsible for controls on waste and the disposal of medicines and chemicals. Controls on poisons are covered in **Chapter 21**.

Under the NHS terms of service, pharmacies in England must accept and dispose of unwanted drugs.[24] NHS England[25] will arrange for collection and disposal. The terms of service in Scotland and Wales do not require this, but all pharmacies in the ordinary course of their activities will produce and/or need to dispose of pharmaceutical waste. In Scotland, Health Boards are required to arrange collection and disposal. Local Health Boards in Wales have a similar responsibility.

The Environmental Protection Act 1990 introduced a *duty of care* which applies to all persons who import, produce, carry, keep, treat or dispose of controlled waste. This, therefore, applies to pharmacists, who necessarily handle waste or unwanted medicines in the course of their practice. The duty of care lies on all holders of waste at every stage in its history, such that a pharmacist having held controlled waste may only pass it on to an *authorised person*, such as registered carriers, permit/licence holders or someone who is exempt from either being a registered carrier or operating under a permit/licence. Further, they must transfer with the waste such a written description of the waste – a transfer note, setting out the type and quantity of the waste – as will enable others to dispose of the waste appropriately and avoid committing an offence under the Act.

Controlled waste includes household, industrial and commercial waste of any kind, whether conventionally thought of as polluting or not. The Controlled Waste Regulations[26] define *clinical waste* as, among other things, "waste from a healthcare activity (including veterinary healthcare) that (a) contains viable micro-organisms or their toxins which are known or reliably believed to cause disease in humans or other living organisms or (b) contains or is contaminated with a medicine that contains a biologically active pharmaceutical agent ...".

The Regulations also define the type of waste (household, industrial or commercial) based on its source. Under the Environmental Protection Act 1990, permits or licences

---

24. In England, paragraph 14 of Schedule 4 to the National Health Service (Pharmaceutical and Local Pharmaceutical Services) Regulations 2013.
25. Shortly before going to press, the Prime Minister announced that NHS England would be abolished as a separate body, and its functions will be exercised by the Department of Health and Social Care.
26. The Controlled Waste (England and Wales) Regulations 2012.

are required for the storage, transfer, treatment and disposal of waste. A permit or licence is not generally required to store waste on the premises at which it was produced.

Anyone who transports hazardous waste must be registered with the Environment Agency.[27] Movement of hazardous waste is tightly controlled and must be accompanied by a detailed consignment note which describes the waste sufficiently to allow safe ultimate disposal.

Common law offences

Offences that are not created by legislation include, in particular, manslaughter.

Manslaughter

Although negligence is most likely to be considered in the civil courts in an action for compensation for harm caused by the breach of a pharmacist's duty of care, if gross negligence causes or materially contributes to the death of a patient, a pharmacist may be charged with the serious criminal offence of manslaughter.

The leading case in relation to health professionals concerned a hospital anaesthetist.[28] The House of Lords held that the question is whether the defendant's conduct should be characterised as gross negligence and therefore a crime; and whether, having regard to the risk of death involved, the defendant's conduct was so bad in all the circumstances as to amount to a criminal act or omission.

The law of gross negligence manslaughter (sometimes referred to as *medical manslaughter*) has been clarified further in the case of an optometrist, Honey Rose.[29] The Court of Appeal, overturned a conviction and held that to convict:

- there must be a duty of care;
- the duty must have been breached;
- it is reasonably foreseeable the breach gives rise to a serious and obvious risk of death; and
- the breach, in fact, caused death.

In addition:

- the conduct of the defendant must have been so bad in all the circumstances as to amount to a criminal act or omission; and
- the negligence must go beyond a mere matter of compensation and was truly and exceptionally bad so as to justify the conclusion that it amounts to a crime.

Simple *picking* errors are unlikely to result in a pharmacist being prosecuted for manslaughter because there must be something that makes the error *gross*. This might relate to the inadequacy of systems at a pharmacy. However, the circumstances in which a pharmacist is prosecuted for gross negligence manslaughter are limited after the *Honey Rose* case because, however bad an error may be, the prosecution must prove it was reasonably foreseeable that the error gave rise to a serious and obvious risk of

---

27. Waste (England and Wales) Regulations 2011.
28. *R v Adomako* [1995] 1 AC 171.
29. *R v Rose (Honey Maria)* [2017] EWCA Crim 1168.

death. Circumstances where a pharmacist may be guilty of manslaughter include the negligent supply of a product liable to abuse to a patient who takes an overdose and dies. To be guilty of manslaughter, the pharmacist's breach of duty must be a substantial and operative cause of death. If the patient made a fully free, voluntary and informed decision to risk death by taking an overdose, then the pharmacist will not be guilty; but if the patient was acting under any compulsion, whether caused by mental health problems or addiction, the patient's ability to resist feeling compelled to take the product may have been impaired so that the patient's decision was not full, free and voluntary.[30]

Rehabilitation of offenders

Pharmacy professionals and other healthcare professionals (and some others) who have convictions or cautions are treated differently to other members of the public in terms of when convictions and cautions are spent and in terms of their obligations to report and disclose convictions and cautions. Further details are in **Chapter 25**.

Civil liability

Civil law and the terminology used are explained further in **Chapter 1**.

Professional indemnity insurance

Article 32 of the Pharmacy Order 2010 requires all pharmacists and pharmacy technicians to have indemnity arrangements in place to provide appropriate cover in respect of any liabilities that may be incurred in practising. An indemnity arrangement may be an insurance policy or an arrangement made for the purpose of indemnifying a person.

Many pharmacy owners have professional indemnity cover through membership of the National Pharmacy Association or Numark and this will cover liabilities incurred by employees and locums in the course of their work;[31] but many pharmacy professionals choose to take out personal cover, for example through membership of the Pharmacists' Defence Association. Other insurers also provide professional indemnity cover. In other cases, very large pharmacy businesses may choose to self-insure if they regard meeting claims out of their own resources as less costly than paying for commercial insurance.

The Pharmacy Order defines *appropriate cover* as cover against liabilities that may be incurred in practising which is appropriate, having regard to the nature and extent of the risks of that practice. As some of the cases below illustrate, awards of damages may be very large and, without adequate cover, a patient who is entitled to damages may not receive compensation because the pharmacy business or the individual pharmacist does not have the financial means to pay; and the business may face liquidation and the pharmacy professional may face bankruptcy. If patients were not compensated, this would be damaging to the trust that patients and the public place in the profession. In view of this, the Fitness to Practise Committee and its predecessors have dealt severely

---

30. *R v Rebelo* [2021] EWCA Crim 306.

31. If volunteers are used, as they were the 2020 COVID-19 pandemic, pharmacy owners should ensure that their professional indemnity cover extends to volunteers for whose acts or omissions they may be liable (see below).

with pharmacists and pharmacy owners who have be found not to have appropriate professional indemnity cover. In 1997, the High Court described a decision to direct the removal from the register of a pharmacist who had failed to take out professional indemnity insurance for over three years as "amply justified".[32]

Typically, the type of risk to be covered involves injury to a patient as a result of negligence, for example by taking medication incorrectly supplied. Such negligence may give rise to a civil claim for damages (compensation). For reasons discussed below, indemnity insurance should extend to volunteers who assist pharmacy owners.

Whether or not a breach of a duty of care is found, the circumstances giving rise to a claim may also be investigated by the GPhC if there are concerns about a registrant's fitness to practise (see **Chapter 25**). A breach of a duty of care may also lead to NHS proceedings as described in **Chapter 3** or criminal proceedings as described above. It is common for fitness to practise proceedings and other civil proceedings to await the conclusion of any criminal proceedings.

Sources of civil law

Liability under civil law may arise through the common law or through legislation. Liability may arise in contract or in tort. As explained in **Chapter 1**, a tort is a civil wrong. Primarily, it is the common law that dominates issues of civil liability. In addition, certain statutes may now impose civil liability. Examples of these include UK GDPR (see **Chapter 23**) and the Competition Act 1998 (see below).

Contract

Contracts are generally agreements between one person and another to supply goods or services (or a combination of both). The key elements of a contract are:

- there must be an offer by one party and acceptance of the offer by another party;
- there must be consideration – generally, the price to be paid;
- the parties must intend that the agreement will have legal effect.

Except in specific types of contracts (such as contracts for the sale of land), a contract may be oral or in writing (or a combination of both). Whenever a pharmacy sells a product to a customer there is a contract but, as explained in **Chapter 3**, there is no contract when a medicinal product or appliance is supplied on an NHS prescription because there is no consideration: no money is paid to the pharmacy owner. Any prescription charge is in the nature of a tax that is collected on behalf of the NHS.[33]

One of the leading cases on whether there has been offer and acceptance is *Carlill v Carbolic Smoke Ball Co*,[34] In that case, the Defendant was the manufacturer of the carbolic smoke ball, which was designed to prevent users from catching flu. The Defendant placed an advertisement in newspapers which stated that a reward of £100 would be paid to anyone who contracted flu or a cold after using the smoke ball three

---

32. *Whitechurch v Royal Pharmaceutical Society of Great Britain* (1998) 41 BMLR 46.

33. *Pfizer Corporation v Ministry of Health* [1965] AC 512.

34. [1891] 1 QB 256.

times per day for two weeks according to the directions supplied with each ball. The advertisement also stated the Defendant had deposited £1000 with a named bank to show the sincerity of the offer. Mrs Carlill bought a ball in reliance on the advert and used it as directed, but contracted flu whilst using it. She claimed payment of £100. The Defendant argued that the advertisement did not amount to a contractually binding promise because it was directed to the world in general and was too vague. It also argued that if the advert was an offer, Mrs Carlill had not communicated her acceptance. The Court of Appeal held that there was no reason why an offer made to all the world should not form a contract if it was accepted by someone making a purchase. Ordinarily, acceptance of an offer must be communicated to the offeror but the Defendant had shown by the nature of the transaction that it did not expect and did not require notice of acceptance. Anyone who performed the conditions set out in the advertisement had accepted the offer.

Another leading case is *Pharmaceutical Society of Great Britain v Boots Cash Chemists (Southern) Ltd*[35] (see also **Chapter 11**) in which, in a self-service pharmacy, an inspector of the Pharmaceutical Society selected a Pharmacy medicine and put it into a wire basket. The defendant was found not to have made a sale without supervision because the sale had not been made at that point: it would only have been made when the contract was completed by the acceptance of payment for the product.

Although the law of contract has historically been based primarily on common law, the law is supplemented by provisions in legislation, especially in relation to sales to consumers. Amongst other things, the Consumer Rights Act 2015 incorporates into any sale by a trader to a consumer a contractual term that any goods are of satisfactory quality. This will include sales of over-the-counter medicines. If a product is not of satisfactory quality (which includes fitness for purpose), then the consumer has rights against the seller without having to prove that the seller was negligent and regardless of whether the seller created any defect. However, if the purchaser suffers from an abnormality that is not made known to the seller the seller will not be liable to compensate the buyer under the Consumer Rights Act if that abnormality means that the product is not suitable for the particular buyer. In *Griffiths v Peter Conway Ltd*,[36] a customer bought a fur coat. She alleged that when she wore it her neck broke out into a rash. The Court of Appeal held that it was only when the seller had knowledge of the buyer's particular abnormality that the buyer could exercise appropriate care and skill in deciding whether to make a sale.

For completeness, it should be mentioned that legislation giving consumers cancellation rights when ordering goods online do not apply[37] to prescribed medicines.

As well as any entitlement to a refund if goods are rejected, compensation is awarded for a breach of contract. The legal term for compensation is *damages*. The amount of

---

35. [1952] 2 QB 795 and [1953] 1 QB 401.
36. [1939] 1 All ER 685.
37. Regulations 7 and 27 of the Consumer Contracts (Information, Cancellation and Additional Charges) Regulations 2013.

damages is usually what is required to put the injured party in the position that party would have been in if there had been no breach of contract.

Tort

There are a number of types of tort. Below are some of particular relevance to pharmacy practice.

In tort, damages are awarded to remedy any financial loss. Where the tort has caused death the courts in England and Wales will award statutory damages for bereavement. In the case of personal injury, damages will be awarded to compensate an injured person for pain, suffering and loss of amenity. In addition, damages will be awarded to compensate for financial loss caused by the tort.

Negligence

A pharmacy owner, pharmacist, and/or any member of the pharmacy staff may be faced with an action for negligence in the civil courts. The essence of the tort of negligence is that the defendant (*defender* in Scotland) owes a legal duty of care which they have failed to meet, as a result of which, the claimant[38] (*pursuer* in Scotland) has suffered loss or damage. The duty to take care was described by Lord Atkin in the leading case of *Donoghue v Stevenson*[39] as:

> *"The rule that you are to love your neighbour becomes in law, you must not injure your neighbour; and the lawyer's question, Who is my neighbour? receives a restricted reply. You must take reasonable care to avoid acts or omissions which you can reasonably foresee would be likely to injure your neighbour. Who, then, in law is my neighbour? The answer seems to be – persons who are so closely and directly affected by my act that I ought reasonably to have them in contemplation as being so affected when I am directing my mind to the acts or omissions which are called in question."*

Patients and customers to whom professional services (including the supply of medicines) are provided or to whom professional advice is given rely on the care and skill of those who provide such services or advice. Pharmacy owners may owe a non-delegable duty of care to such patients and customers. In other words, this duty is owed by the owner even though a negligent act or omission was committed by an employee or locum.[40] In addition, healthcare professionals owe an individual duty of care to patients or customers to whom they give professional advice. For many years, the leading case in what used to be called *medical negligence* cases (now referred to as clinical negligence) was *Bolam v Friern Barnet Hospital Management Committee*[41] in which it was held that:

38. Prior to 1998, the word *Plaintiff* was used in England to denote a person bringing a claim.
39. [1932] AC 562.
40. See *Hughes v Rattan* [2022] EWCA 107 (Civ) (a case involving negligent dental treatment by associates).
41. [1957] 2 All E.R. 118.

> *"A doctor is not guilty of negligence if he has acted in accordance with a practice accepted as proper by a responsible body of medical men skilled in that particular form of treatment; nor is he negligent merely because there is a body of opinion which would adopt a different technique."*

The *Bolam test*, as it has become known, has been qualified in subsequent cases but it still has some general applicability. In Scotland, the law is broadly the same.[42] A pharmacist occupying a special position in any branch of pharmacy would be expected to have a degree of ability commensurate with that position. Pharmacists are with good reason recognised as experts on medicines. Moreover, as the clinical role of pharmacists widens and the range of services increases, including pharmacists whose role includes prescribing, combined with access to patients' records, liabilities are likely to increase commensurately.

The reported cases involving civil claims against pharmacy owners and pharmacists have involved allegations of negligence. Typically, the cases concern supplying an incorrect product or failing to realise that the product supplied, or the dosage or label, is inappropriate.

In *Dywer v Roderick, Jackson and Cross Chemists (Banbury) Limited*,[43] the court held that, to avoid a finding of negligence, it was not sufficient for a pharmacist to say that they had followed a prescriber's instructions, but that pharmacists owe a duty of care independently of the prescriber. The case is described in more detail in **Box 26.2**. It deals not only with a pharmacist's independent duty of care but also the apportionment of liability when an incorrect prescription is not noticed by a pharmacist and a patient is harmed as a result.

Box 26.2: *Dwyer v Roderick, Jackson and Cross Chemists (Banbury) Limited*

Mrs Dywer was a patient whose GP, Dr Rodrick, diagnosed her as having fairly classical symptoms of migraine. He prescribed Migril, containing ergotamine tartrate. This was a standard treatment for migraine at the time. Dr Rodrick's prescription said:

> *"tabs Migril*
>
> *2 every 4 hours PRN*[44]
>
> *60 tablets"*

44. An abbreviation of the Latin *pro re nata*, meaning "as necessary".

42. *Hunter v Hanley* [1955] SC 200 It must be established that the course the doctor adopted is one which no professional man of ordinary skill would have taken if he had been acting with ordinary care.
43. [1983] Lexis Citation 703.

Box 26.2: *Dwyer v Roderick, Jackson and Cross Chemists (Banbury) Limited* (cont.)

It was common ground that that two tablets every four hours was an excessive dose (described by the trial judge, Mr Justice Stuart-Smith, as "completely and utterly wrong for this particular drug"). He also called it an "appalling blunder". The prescribed dosage was far in excess of the manufacturer's prescribing recommendations. The overdose of ergotamine tartrate had the effect of constricting Mrs Dwyer's blood vessels and arteries, causing gangrene, leading to the loss of both feet.

The prescription was taken to a pharmacy owned by Cross Chemists where it was dispensed. The pharmacist said in evidence about his usual practice:

"The prescription is brought in to me ... I make sure I can read it right through. I judge the whole prescription. I do not just read the product and get the bottle. I then write the label. I put the tablets into the bottle and then stick the label on the bottle."

The bottle was labelled "2 tablets every 4 hours, as required". The pharmacist was aware of the manufacturer's dosage recommendations and he should have appreciated that the combination of two Migril tablets at four-hourly intervals was, in the words of the trial judge, "completely inappropriate and wrong". However, no contact was made with Dr Rodrick. Dr Rodrick and the pharmacist admitted negligence. A partner of Dr Rodrick, Dr Jackson, was also alleged to be negligent because he made a house call on Mrs Dwyer after the prescription had been dispensed, when Mrs Dyer was suffering the effects of ergotamine poisoning. He did not have Mrs Dwyer's notes, did not ask to see the bottle of tablets she had and did not identify ergotamine poisoning as the cause of her symptoms.

The judge said:

"[Counsel for Cross Chemists (Banbury) Limited] likens their position, and indeed that of Dr. Jackson, as a long-stop at cricket. I do not think that that is a correct analogy. It is quite clear on the evidence that the pharmacists, the chemists, have to exercise an independent judgment to ensure that the drug is apt for the patient as well as that it conforms to the physician's requirements. It is an active duty and the evidence is that it is what the chemist writes on the bottle that is the critical thing so far as the patient is concerned. The patient will often forget, or not pay attention to what the doctor may say at the time of prescribing, but he or she relies on the written instructions on the bottle given by the chemist."

The judge held that of the three Defendants, Dr Rodrick's prescription "was the original and fatal error that was the most potent fault and the more serious fault in this case". He apportioned 45% of the liability to Dr Rodrick, 15% of the liability to Dr Jackson and 40% to Cross Chemists (Banbury) Limited. Dr Jackson appealed to the Court of Appeal which overturned the finding of liability against him,[45] leaving Dr Rodrick responsible for 60% of the damages and Cross Chemists (Banbury) Ltd responsible for 40%. This apportionment of 60% to the prescriber and 40% to the pharmacy has been followed in subsequent cases in which a pharmacist has failed to spot incorrect prescribing by a doctor, resulting in harm to a patient.

45. [1983] Lexis Citation 725, *The Times* 12 November 1983, 127 SJ 805.

In *Prendergast v Sam & Dee Limited*,[46] a handwritten prescription was misread (see **Box 26.3**) but the greater fault lay with the pharmacist who should have realised that the prescription was not what he believed it to be. Causation is often a key issue in

46. *Prendergast v Sam & Dee Ltd* [1988] 3WLUK 198; *Pharm J*, 26 March 1988 p. 404 (NB an appeal to the Court of Appeal (1989) 1 Med LR 36 was dismissed).

clinical negligence cases: a claimant must not only show that the defendant has been negligent, but must show that the negligence caused the harm of which the claimant complains. In this case, the doctor argued unsuccessfully that any negligence in the way the prescription was written was overtaken by the subsequent negligence of the pharmacist – breaking the chain of causation.

Box 26.3: *Prendergast v Sam & Dee Ltd*

Mr Prendergast visited his GP on 17 December He was prescribed Amoxil (amoxicillin) for a chest infection. The prescription was handwritten and Amoxil was spelt with a lower case "a". He took the prescription to a pharmacy owned by Sam & Dee Limited where the pharmacist misread Amoxil as a product beginning with the letter "d" and read the name on the prescription as "daonil" (glibenclamide), which is what was dispensed.

Mr Prendergast was not diabetic and taking Daonil caused him irreversible brain damage. A claim was brought against both the GP and Sam & Dee Ltd.

Mr Justice Auld held that doctors had a duty to their patients to write prescriptions sufficiently legibly so as to reduce the likelihood of them being misread by a busy or careless pharmacist. The pharmacist, in turn, was under a duty to give some thought to the prescriptions being dispensed. If there was an ambiguity in the prescription, the pharmacist should not dispense a drug without first satisfying themself that it was the correct one.

The judge said that even assuming that the prescription was unclear, the pharmacist should have been alerted to the fact that if Daonil was being prescribed, the dosage and quantity on the prescription were inappropriate for Daonil. The pharmacist should also have noticed that the man who collected the drugs did not claim exemption from paying an NHS prescription charge for the Daonil, although patients with diabetes were entitled to exemption from prescription charges. It was not enough for pharmacists to blindly dispense drugs without giving thought to what they were doing.

Mr Justice Auld said:

> *"The GP should have taken account of the possibility that a poorly written prescription might be misinterpreted by the pharmacist: Every now and then the competent or tired and/or flustered and/or distracted pharmacist might very well mechanically dispense a prescription which in more alert and quieter moments he would question ...*
>
> *It is accepted that a prescription which is so written as to invite or reasonably permit misreading by a pharmacist under ordinary working conditions (which it is accepted may be less than ideal) falls below the necessary standard ...*
>
> *... it is well-established that the pharmacist, if in any doubt at all, should contact the doctor before [dispensing] ...*
>
> *... Looking at the case as a whole ... the chain of causation from Dr Miller's bad handwriting was not broken and the consequence of his writing a word which could reasonably be read as 'daonil', even with the other factors [which should have caused the pharmacist to realise the prescription was not for daonil] is not enough to make it beyond reasonable foreseeability that daonil would be prescribed."*

Unlike the case of *Dwyer v Rodrick and Cross Chemists (Banbury) Limited* (see **Box 26.2** above) the greater fault in this case lay with the pharmacist and Mr Justice Auld apportioned liability to 75% against the pharmacist and 25% against the doctor.

The case of *Horton v Evans and Lloyds Pharmacy Limited*,[47] (**Box 26.4**) has significance beyond a pharmacist failing to spot that a prescription was or could be an overdose. The judge drew a distinction between a case where a pharmacist knew the patient had previously been prescribed the same medicinal product at a lower strength, and one in which the pharmacist did not know this. This has implications for liability when the patient's summary care record is available for a pharmacist to consult. The case also addressed the question of whether the chain of causation that began when the prescription was written and continued when it was dispensed at a branch of Lloyds Pharmacy, was broken when a different doctor subsequently wrote a prescription for the same strength of the same product, relying on what Lloyds Pharmacy had supplied.

Box 26.4: *Horton v Evans and Lloyds Pharmacy Limited*

Cathy Horton was a successful businesswoman and lawyer. For some years, she had been prescribed by different doctors 0.5 mg dexamethasone tablets to treat a glandular condition. In July 2001, she saw a GP, Dr Evans, as a private patient. Dr Evans gave her a prescription for 28 tablets, dexamethasone 4 mg. The dose was not specified on the prescription. Dr Evans had given Mrs Horton a prescription for dexamethasone once before but, on the earlier occasion, the prescription was for 0.5 mg whereas, in July 2001, the prescription was for eight times the strength of her previous tablets.

The prescription was taken to a branch of Lloyds Pharmacy Limited. The Lloyds pharmacist saw in Lloyd's Pharmacy's computerised patient medication records that Mrs Horton had previously received 0.5 mg tablets from the pharmacy on seven previous occasions. He therefore looked up dexamethasone in the British National Formulary and referred to the usual range for dexamethasone as being "0.5-10 mg daily". The pharmacist did not think it necessary to question the accuracy of the prescription because the strength of tablets was within the "usual range".

Mrs Horton began taking the tablets immediately without reading the label on the bottle. She went on holiday to the United States. While there, she saw a general physician. She showed him the bottle supplied by Lloyds Pharmacy and asked him for a repeat prescription. The US physician prescribed dexamethasone 4 mg for Mrs Horton. The overdose of dexamethasone over a period of time caused Cushing's syndrome with psychiatric disturbance. Mrs Horton's business went downhill.

The trial judge, Mr Justice Keith, drew a distinction between a case in which a patient had not previously had prescriptions for dexamethasone 0.5 mg and one in which the pharmacist knew that she had. He said:

> *"Such a significant increase raised at the very least the possibility that the prescription might be inaccurate. The question was no longer whether the strength of the dexamethasone being prescribed came within its usual therapeutic range, and could for that reason be said to be suitable for Mrs Horton. The question now was whether the prescription really represented what Dr Evans had intended to prescribe, or whether the dramatic increase in the strength was a mistake."*

The judge found support for his finding in the Lloyds Pharmacy Standard Operating Procedures which said:

47. [2006] EWHC 2808 (QB); the assessment of damages reference is reported at [2007] EWHC 315.

Box 26.4: *Horton v Evans and Lloyds Pharmacy Limited* (cont.)

"If the patient already has a patient medication record on the computer, previous medication details on the medication record should be studied in order to check that there has been no change to the strength or dose of the patient's medication. Any changes should be queried with the patient or the prescriber."

The judge found that the Lloyds pharmacist had "fallen below the standards that could reasonably have been expected of a reasonably careful and competent pharmacist".

It was argued that the prescribing by the US physician, relying on seeing the Lloyds Pharmacy tablet container, was negligent and that this negligence broke the chain of causation that began with the writing of the prescription and continued with the supply from Lloyds Pharmacy, so that any harm suffered by Mrs Horton after the US prescription was written was not attributable to the prescription dispensed at Lloyds Pharmacy. The judge rejected this argument because the US physician had not initiated the course of treatment for Mrs Horton's glandular condition. The judge considered that a doctor "who is simply asked to provide a *repeat* prescription is, on the face of it, in a very different position. He is merely replicating what a previous physician has thought to be appropriate".

It should be pointed out that Dr Evans did not dispute liability and evidence was not given on his behalf. In particular, as the learned judge noted, he had not received expert evidence as to what a reasonably competent doctor should have done when asked for a repeat prescription of dexamethasone 4 mg. It may therefore be open to doubt whether the same view would be taken of negligence by the US physician if the case were to come before a court today and if expert evidence was given regarding medical practice. However, Mr Justice Keith also held that even if he had found that the US physician was negligent, this did not break the chain of causation. He said:

"I do not believe that it would be right, when looking at the whole sequence of events which culminated in the devastating deterioration in Mrs Horton's health, to say that [the Lloyd's pharmacist's] failure to question Dr Evans' prescription was so eclipsed by [the US physician's] intervention that [the Lloyd's pharmacist's] conduct could properly be relegated to no more than a mere occurrence in the history of events. Secondly, there was nothing unreasonable in what [the US physician] was subsequently to do. Thirdly, for the reasons which I shall come to later, I think that [the Lloyd's pharmacist] should reasonably have foreseen the reliance which might be placed by a physician other than [the US physician] on the label on the bottle. And fourthly, most important of all … I think that [the Lloyds pharmacist] must bear a real responsibility for why [the US physician] thought that Mrs Horton had been prescribed 4 mg tablets a day … [The Lloyds pharmacist's] breach of duty caused [the US physician] to provide Mrs Horton with the prescription … and these acts [by the US physician] did not constitute independent events. Much of the information which caused [the US physician] to think Mrs Horton was on 4 mg a day was information on the label … That information was only on the label because the [Lloyds pharmacist] had dispensed the prescription … there was therefore a direct causal link between [the Lloyd's pharmacist's] breach of duty in failing to question the correctness of the prescription and [the US physician] providing Mrs Horton with a prescription for a daily dose of 4 mg tablets."

In this case, nearly £1.5 million damages were awarded, apportioned between the Dr Evans and Lloyds Pharmacy Limited.

Another example of the significance of causation can be found in **Box 15.2** in **Chapter 15**.

Negligence by practitioners of alternative medicine

Similar standards to those applicable to pharmacists apply to practitioners of alternative medicine. In *Shakoor v Situ (trading as Eternal Health Co)*,[48] consulted a practitioner of traditional Chinese herbal medicine who prescribed a course of herbal remedy which had been prepared in accordance with a traditional recipe or classic formula. After taking nine doses, S became ill and later died of acute liver failure which was attributable to a rare and unpredictable reaction to the remedy. S's widow alleged that the practitioner had been negligent in prescribing the remedy or had been negligent in prescribing the remedy without warning S of the potential risks of the medicine – risks that were referred to in a number of articles published in orthodox medical journals.

The judge held that it was necessary to consider the standard of care of a practitioner of alternative medicine with regard to that practitioner's knowledge that he was practising his art alongside orthodox medicine. A practitioner was required to take sufficient steps so as to be confident that a remedy had not been reported adversely. In this case, the practitioner's actions had been consistent with the standard of care appropriate to traditional Chinese herbal medicine in accordance with established requirements. It followed that there had been no breach of duty.

Patient records

In England, the NHS Summary Care Record (SCR) is an electronic summary of key clinical information (including medicines, allergies and adverse reactions) about a patient, sourced from the GP record. Pharmacy owners in England are required by their terms of service[49] to have access to the SCR. These terms of service say that the pharmacy owner (referred to as an *NHS Pharmacist*) must access the summary information in a patient's summary care record whenever the owner is providing pharmaceutical services to a patient, to the extent that the owner, in the exercise of the owner's clinical judgement, considers it appropriate to do so. While the terms of service do not place the task of consulting the SCR on individual pharmacists who are not the owner of the pharmacy where they are working, the English NHS terms of service require owners to secure compliance with the terms of service by a registered pharmacist.[50] As the *Horton* case above illustrates (though this was a case in which the pharmacist consulted the pharmacy's patient medication records rather than the SCR), a pharmacist may be negligent in two particular ways: firstly, if the pharmacist fails to consult the available records when the pharmacist should have done so; and, secondly, if the pharmacist does consult the records but fails to act appropriately, based on what the SCR reveals. Similar principles apply elsewhere in the UK, for example where pharmacists in Scotland have access to Patient Care Records, and in Wales where

---

48. [2001] 4 All ER 181.
49. Paragraph 29A of Schedule 4 to the National Health Service (Pharmaceutical and Local Pharmaceutical Services) Regulations 2013.
50. Paragraph 1 of Schedule 4 to the National Health Service (Pharmaceutical and Local Pharmaceutical Services) Regulations 2013.

pharmacists have access to the Welsh GP Record, although the NHS terms of service in Scotland and Wales do not specify circumstances in which patient records should be consulted.

Supervision

At the time of writing, the Department of Health and Social Care (DHSC) had proposed to amend the Human Medicines Regulations to enable pharmacists to authorise pharmacy technicians to supervise the sale or supply of Pharmacy medicines and Prescription Only Medicines (see **Chapter 11**). This gives rise to the question of liability if an error is made when a pharmacy technician supplies or supervises a supply. The DHSC consultation paper offers this answer:

> *"For example, if a pharmacist authorises a pharmacy technician to carry out dispensing activities and something goes wrong, ... in a civil context, where a number of people are arguably at fault - which might include the pharmacy owner - the courts are highly experienced at apportioning blame where it truly lies - potentially in percentage terms. This will already be a live issue where someone acts under the supervision of a pharmacist and the supervised person is at fault, and what changes with authorisation may be the amount of blame that the courts might attach to the various people potentially at fault, but not the principle that the court may have to work out where blame truly lies."*[51]

Hub and spoke dispensing

Hub and spoke dispensing involves a prescription being received at one pharmacy (the spoke) and dispensed at another pharmacy (the hub) with the dispensed medicine being sent from the hub to the spoke for supply to the patient. If a dispensing error is made at the hub, for example because the wrong medicine is dispensed, and the wrong medicine is then supplied from the spoke to the patient because the error is not noticed at the spoke, it is suggested that the pharmacist responsible for supervision at the hub and the responsible pharmacist at the spoke will both owe the patient a duty of care. Therefore, both pharmacists will be liable to compensate the patient, and their employer will be vicariously liable for their negligence (whether they have the same employer under the law at the time of writing or different employers if section 10 of the Medicines Act 1968 is amended to allow one pharmacy business to provide dispensing services for another pharmacy business – see **Chapter 12**). It should be said that the Department of Health and Social Care's consultation paper on hub and spoke dispensing anticipates that the hub and spoke will include in written arrangements between them a provision that specifies which of the hub and spoke will be liable if the wrong medication is supplied to a patient. This may be relevant to any fitness to practise proceedings arising from a

---

51. https://www.gov.uk/government/consultations/pharmacy-supervision/pharmacy-supervision (accessed 31 December 2024).

dispensing error, but an agreement between a hub and spoke would not have the legal effect of removing a duty of care owed to a patient.

Diagnosis and prescribing

Just as medical practitioners may be liable for negligent diagnosis and prescribing, the same applies to all other healthcare professionals including supplementary and independent prescribers who may make an error in diagnosis or in prescribing.

Battery

Deliberate physical contact with a patient without that patient's consent is not only a criminal offence (see above) but is also a tort known as battery and may give rise to a claim for damages. Consent may be implied but, if time and circumstances allow, it would be prudent for a pharmacy professional who wishes to touch a patient or customer, for example with a view to deciding on the most appropriate treatment, to ask the patient for permission to touch the relevant part of the patient's body or at least to tell the patient in advance of the intention to do so. Consent may be specific. For example, a patient who gave her doctor express consent to give an injection in her right arm was held to be entitled to damages because he injected her in her left arm.[52] If there is no express or implied consent, it is not a defence to a battery claim that the practitioner believed they were acting in the patient's best interests or did, in fact, act in the patient's best interests.[53]

Regard should also be had to *In practice: Guidance on maintaining clear sexual boundaries*, published by the General Pharmaceutical Council, including the advice on chaperones.

Breach of statutory duty

Some legislation creates obligations and rights that may give rise to claims.

Health and safety and employers' liability

Employers have legal duties under the Health and Safety at Work etc. Act (see above). There are also various regulations made under powers in the Act. Breaches of the Act or regulations may give rise to a civil claim for damages by an employee who is injured as a result of such a breach. Employers must have insurance for any liability to employees and must display a certificate of insurance.

Occupiers' Liability

The Occupiers' Liability Act 1957 imposes a duty of care on the occupier of premises to a person who visits the premises. This duty is, for example, owed by a pharmacy owner to patients and customers. Claims may arise, for example, if a customer is injured as a result of a slip or trip.

---

52. *Allan v New Mount Sinai Hospital* (1980) 109 D.L.R. (3d) 635.
53. *R v St George's Healthcare Trust, ex parte S* [1998] 3 WLR 996.

Confidentiality and data protection

A breach of the duty of confidentiality or the misuse of private information or a breach of data protection obligations may give rise to a claim for damages. These issues are discussed in **Chapter 23**.

Vicarious liability

Sometimes a claim for compensation is made against an individual pharmacist who is alleged to have been negligent, but as in the cases referred to above, the claim for compensation is almost always made against the pharmacy owner. The term *vicarious liability* in this context signifies the liability which an employer or business owner may incur to a person who suffers loss or damage caused by an employee in the course of their employment, or a locum acting in the course of their engagement. The employer or business owner need not have been at fault in order to be vicariously liable.

The test of whether an employer is liable for the acts or omissions of an employee is whether what the employee did was closely connected with acts the employee was authorised to do. It will be obvious in some cases that an employer is vicariously liable for something an employee has or has not done, such as when an employed pharmacist or a locum makes a dispensing error or when an employed delivery driver negligently causes a road traffic accident in the course of making deliveries. Vicarious liability will be less obvious in other cases. The Supreme Court gave judgments in two cases in 2020, *Wm Morrison Supermarkets plc v Various Claimants*[54] and *Barclays Bank plc v Various Claimants*[55] that shed light on the applicable principles and how they may be applicable in pharmacy practice. The cases are described in **Box 26.5**. Among other things, the *Barclays Bank* case highlights that vicarious liability can extend to the acts or omissions of someone who is not an employee. The question for the court was "whether the tortfeasor is carrying on business on his own account or whether he is in a relationship akin to employment with the defendant". It is unclear whether a court would hold that the relationship between a pharmacy owner and a self-employed locum pharmacist is akin to employment.[56]

Box 26.5: *Wm Morrison Supermarkets plc v Various Claimants* and *Barclays Bank plc v Various Claimants*

The Morrisons case – the facts

An employee of the Morrisons supermarket chain, Andrew Skelton, was a senior auditor in the internal audit team. In July 2013, he was disciplined for minor misconduct. Four months later, Morrisons' auditors requested payroll data. This task was delegated to Skelton who was given

54. [2020] UKSC 12.
55. [2020] UKSC 13.
56. See *Hughes v Rattan* [2022] EWCA 107 (Civ), a case in which a dental practice owner was held not to be vicariously liable for dental associates who were self-employed.

Box 26.5: *Wm Morrison Supermarkets plc v Various Claimants* and *Barclays Bank plc v Various Claimants* (cont.)

access to the names, addresses, gender, dates of birth, phone numbers, national insurance numbers, bank details and salaries of every member of staff. Skelton uploaded the data to a publicly accessible website. He did this from his home. When Morrisons were alerted, they took steps to ensure that the data was removed from the internet, informed all employees and took steps to protect their identities. Morrisons spent more than £2.26m in dealing with the immediate aftermath of the disclosure. Skelton was convicted of a number of offences and sentenced to eight years' imprisonment.

Morrisons faced a claim from over 9,000 employees who contended that Morrisons were vicariously liable for the breaches by Skelton of the employees' confidentiality and of the Data Protection Act 1988 (the current Data Protection Act has similar provisions to those in force at the time – see **Chapter 23**). Cases over the last 20 years, including House of Lords and Supreme Court decisions have clarified when vicarious liability will arise. In particular, the courts have considered what functions or "field of activities" had been entrusted by an employer to an employee and whether there was a sufficient connection between the position in which the employee was employed and the employee's wrongful conduct to make it right for the employer to be held liable under the principle of social justice.

The legal test

Whether Morrisons were vicariously liable for Skelton's wrongful acts depended on whether Skelton's disclosure of the data was so closely connected with acts he was authorised to do, that for the purposes of the liability of his employer to third parties, his wrongful disclosure may fairly and properly be regarded as done by him while acting in the ordinary course of his employment. The mere fact that Skelton's employment gave him the opportunity to commit wrongful acts was held not sufficient to warrant the imposition of vicarious liability.

The outcome

An employee's motivation in committing a wrongful act may sometimes be relevant: Skelton's motive – whether he was acting on his employer's business or for purely personal reasons - was held to be relevant. The Court said that it was "abundantly clear that Skelton was not engaged in furthering his employer's business when he committed the wrongdoing in question. On the contrary, he was pursuing a personal vendetta, seeking vengeance for the disciplinary proceedings some months earlier ... Skelton's wrongful conduct was not so closely connected with the acts which he was authorised to do that, for the purposes of Morrison's liability to third parties, it can fairly and properly be regarded as done by him while acting in the ordinary course of his employment".

Can an employer be vicariously liable for data breaches or breach of confidentiality?

The final question was whether an employer could be held vicariously liable for breaches of the Data Protection Act by an employee as a data controller, or for misuse of private information and breach of confidence. The Supreme Court held that an employer could be vicariously liable although Morrisons were not vicariously liable in this particular case.

The Barclays Bank case – the facts

Barclays appealed against a ruling that they were vicariously liable for the acts of someone who was not an employee. The late Dr Gordon Bates had been engaged by the bank to carry out medical assessments of employees or prospective employees. It was alleged that he had

Box 26.5: *Wm Morrison Supermarkets plc v Various Claimants* and *Barclays Bank plc v Various Claimants* (cont.)

committed sexual assaults on some 126 claimants. It was no longer possible to make a claim against the doctor.

The outcome

In this case, Dr Bates was not at any time an employee of the Bank. Nor, viewed objectively, was he anything close to an employee. He was in business on his own account as a medical practitioner.

Barclays' appeal was allowed.

In a health and social care setting, the High Court[57] has held that when an employee divulged confidential information about the wife and children of a man with whom the employee had a relationship, the employer was not vicariously liable even though the employment gave the opportunity to access and process the information. The disclosure was no part of the work the employee had been engaged to do and she was pursuing her own agenda. Her wrongful conduct was not so closely connected with acts she was authorised to do that, for the purposes of the employer's liability to third parties, it could fairly and properly be regarded as done by her while acting in the ordinary course of her employment.

The question of whether a pharmacy owner is vicariously liable for volunteers is considered below.

Liability for unqualified employees

In *Darnley v Croydon Health Services NHS Trust*,[58] the Supreme Court held that vicarious liability can extend to unqualified employees (see **Box 26.6**).

Box 26.6: Vicarious liability for unqualified staff

In *Darnley v Croydon Health Services NHS Trust*, the claimant, Michael Darnley, had been struck on the head. A friend drove him to the A&E Department at Mayday Hospital in Croydon. The claimant told the receptionist that he thought he had had a head injury and was feeling very unwell. The receptionist said there was a wait of up to four or five hours. The claimant told the receptionist he was feeling too unwell to wait that long. After waiting 19 minutes, he left because he was feeling too unwell to remain and went to his mother's home. The claimant's condition worsened, and he suffered severe and permanent brain damage because he had not been treated when he first attended the hospital. The A&E receptionist had failed to inform the claimant that he would be seen by a triage nurse within 30 minutes of arrival. Had he been told this, he would not have left the hospital.

The Supreme Court held it was not appropriate to distinguish between medical and non-medical staff because the Hospital Trust owed the patient a duty of care and had given the A&E receptionist the role of being the first point of contact for persons seeking medical assistance. As a result, the receptionist was responsible for providing accurate information about the availability of medical assistance and the hospital Trust was vicariously liable for her negligence.

57. Ali v Luton Borough Council [2022] WEHC 132.

58. [2018] UKSC 50.

Volunteers

Pharmacy professionals as volunteers

Pharmacy professionals may act as volunteers, for example by using their professional expertise when coming to the aid of a member of the public where the relationship is not one of healthcare professional and patient. For example, a pharmacy professional who has been trained to give CPR[59] or administer an adrenaline auto-injector (for example, an EpiPen) may use those skills when not on duty to save a member of the public from harm. Nevertheless, the member of the public may suffer injury as a result and make a claim for damages against the pharmacy professional.

Like anyone else, volunteers owe a duty of care to take reasonable steps to avoid causing harm to someone whom it is reasonably foreseeable will suffer harm if reasonable steps are not taken. Claims against healthcare professionals for taking action in emergencies are very rare. One such case was *Cattley v St John's Ambulance Brigade*[60] (see **Box 26.7**).

Box 26.7: *Cattley v St John's Ambulance Brigade*

A 15-year-old boy had had an accident on his motorcycle while taking part in a schoolboy motor scrambling event. He was treated on the track by members of St John's Ambulance Brigade before being taken to hospital. He was found to have suffered an incomplete paraplegia from compression fractures involving the spinal cord. He alleged that his spinal injury was made worse by the negligent way he was treated by the St John's Ambulance men who treated him immediately. His Honour Judge Prosser said:

> *"There can be no doubt … that the St John's Ambulance man, in holding himself out to attend events as he does, owes a duty of care to those to whom he finds he has to render first-aid … In my judgment the test to be applied to determine whether negligence has been proved against the first-aider … is the test set out in Bolam … any … person holding himself out as a [trained] first-aider … would be negligent if he failed to act in accordance with the standards of the ordinary skilled first-aider exercising and professing to have that special skill of a first-aider … the true test for establishing negligence in a first-aider is whether he has been proved to be guilty of such failure as no first-aider of ordinary skill would be guilty of, if acting with ordinary care."*

The judge rejected the argument that the test of negligence should be modified because the ambulancemen were volunteers and he held that the test of negligence should not be altered to cater for an emergency situation, saying:

> *"That again is unnecessary. Anyone confronted with an emergency situation is not to be held to the standard of conduct normally applied to one who is not in that situation. This does not mean that any different standard is to be applied in the emergency. The conduct required is still that of a reasonable person under the circumstances as they would appear to one who was using proper care, and the emergency is to be considered only as one of the circumstances."*

---

59. See, for example, https://www.chemistanddruggist.co.uk/CD011201/Boots-pharmacists-CPR-skills-save-baby-girl (accessed 31 December 2024).

60. [1988] Lexis Citation 1703.

Box 26.7: *Cattley v St John's Ambulance Brigade* (cont.)

An objective standard must still be applied and a person's own judgment or impulse is still not the sole criterion. He may still be found negligent if, notwithstanding the emergency, his acts are found to be unreasonable."

Judge Prosser QC held that there was "a body of evidence and a strong body, of those skilled in first-aiding and of those more highly qualified, which supported the view that [the St John's volunteers] acted in accordance with the ordinary skills to be expected of a trained St John's Ambulance first-aider, exercising ordinary care in what they were doing when dealing with the Plaintiff." He therefore dismissed the claim.

To avoid discouraging so-called Good Samaritans, the Social Action, Responsibility and Heroism Act 2015 (sometimes called the SARAH Act) was enacted. Section 3 of this Act requires a court to consider whether a person, in carrying out the activity in the course of which the alleged negligence or breach of statutory duty occurred, demonstrated a predominantly responsible approach towards protecting the safety or other interests of others. This Act does not prevent a volunteer from being found liable to an injured person, but it places the good intentions of the volunteer in the forefront of the mind of a judge who has to decide whether the defendant has breached a duty of care. In the Public Bill Committee stage before the Act became law, the Minister said in the House of Commons:

> *"In a finely balanced case, if the court's consideration of these provisions tipped the balance in favour of a defendant who had acted for the benefit of society, demonstrated a generally responsible approach towards the safety of others during an activity, or intervened to help somebody in an emergency, we would welcome that outcome. It would be for the courts to decide how much weight to give those factors on a case-by-case basis. We do not consider that there is any risk of the clause being misinterpreted by the courts as somehow granting individuals immunity from civil liability or watering down the standard of care that is generally applicable."*[61]

Other volunteers

During the COVID-19 pandemic in 2020, many volunteers offered to assist pharmacies by, among other things, delivering medicines. Volunteers owe a duty of care and can be liable to someone who is injured as a result of their negligence or who suffer loss or damage because the volunteer commits a tort other than negligence, for example if the volunteer causes a road traffic accident or if the volunteer delivers the wrong medication to a patient or if, the volunteer inadvertently discloses a patient's data to someone who is not authorised to receive it. In the event of a claim, section 2 of the SARAH Act may apply (see above).

If a volunteer who is assisting a pharmacy owner breaches a duty of care or, for example, a duty of confidentiality, the question will arise whether the pharmacy owner

61. https://hansard.parliament.uk/Lords/2014-11-04/debates/14110452000429/SocialActionResponsibilityAndHeroismBill (accessed 31 December 2024).

is vicariously liable for the acts or omissions of the volunteer. This will be decided under the principles discussed above. It is not clear whether a court would find that the relationship between a pharmacy owner and a volunteer is akin to employment. If no payment is involved, that points away from vicarious liability. On the other hand, volunteers are not acting on their own account and, in the *Barclays Bank* case referred to above, the Supreme Court recognised that the traditional link between employment and vicarious liability was broken by recent developments such as the "gig" economy.

Indemnity and contribution

Even if contracts between pharmacy owners and employees or locums do not say so, there is an implied term that employees and locums will exercise reasonable care in carrying out their responsibilities.[62] A person who incurs a loss through being vicariously liable may claim damages against the person who caused the loss.

In addition, the Civil Liability (Contribution) Act 1978 provides that a person who is liable to compensate another person for damage may claim a contribution to that compensation from another person who is liable for the same damage.

These provisions enable a pharmacy owner to claim an indemnity from a negligent employee or locum for damage the latter may have caused.

Immunity from civil liability

For reasons of public policy, regulation 345 of the Human Medicines Regulations provides immunity from civil liability – but not from product liability under the Consumer Protection Act 1987 (see below) – for any loss or damage resulting from the use of a product recommended or required by the licensing authority (the Medicines and Healthcare products Regulatory Agency) even though the product does not have a marketing authorisation, certificate of registration or traditional herbal registration (see **Chapter 5**). The regulation applies to:

a. pathogenic agents,
b. toxins,
c. chemical agents, or
d. nuclear radiation;

which may cause harm to human beings.

The regulation, which was amended during the COVID-19 pandemic in 2020 so as to facilitate the use of a vaccine for which there had not been time to obtain a marketing authorisation, gives immunity to:

a. any holder of an authorisation for the product;
b. if there is no holder of an authorisation for the product but the sale or supply of the product is authorised by the licensing authority on a temporary basis, the person responsible for placing the product on the market;[63]
c. any manufacturer of the product;

62. *Lister v Romford Ice and Cold Storage Limited* [1957] AC 555.

63. As to the meaning of "placing on the market", see Chapter 5.

d. any officer, servant, employee or agent of a person referred to above;
e. any health care professional; and
f. any person, not being a health care professional, who administers the product in accordance with a protocol relating to coronavirus and influenza vaccinations and immunisations.

Product liability

The Consumer Protection Act 1987 implemented EC Council Directive 85/374/EEC ("the Directive"). It creates liability without fault on the part of the producer for damage caused by a defect in their product. Section 1 of the Act says there is a defect in a product if "the safety of the product is not such as persons generally are entitled to expect".

Liability is strict; in other words, someone injured by a defective product does not have to prove that the defect was caused by a failure to take reasonable care. Four classes of person may face liability for a defective product: the manufacturer, the importer, the person who holds themselves out as the manufacturer or, in the event of none of the former being identified, the person supplying the product to the victim. The first three groups have a primary liability; the supplier has a secondary liability based upon their inability to identify a primary producer. When medicines might be the subject of an action in the courts (there have been very few cases under the Act, but see below), the primary producer will normally be the manufacturer. The supplying pharmacist should, therefore, ensure that they have adequate systems and records to ensure that the manufacturer can always be identified with some certainty. Liability probably does not arise from repackaging licensed medicines or from supplying them against a prescription, provided the source is known.

The supplying pharmacist will carry full liability for "own branded" goods in which the pharmacy's name and address are affixed to containers of medicines made up elsewhere and not so identified. The supplying pharmacist also carries full liability when they prepare their own remedies for a patient under section 10 of the Medicines Act (**Chapter 5**). In these circumstances, it is advisable to maintain full manufacturing records so that the producer of the ingredients can always be identified. Claims may be made for up to three years after the "relevant date" – when the victim became aware of the facts – subject to a maximum of 10 years from the date of putting the product into circulation.

There have been a number of claims against manufacturers of medicinal products, alleging that their products were defective and caused harm, but few such cases have been successful. In *Wilkes v Depuy International Ltd*,[64] the claimant had undergone surgery to insert an artificial hip. It was made from metal components, one of which was a steel femoral shaft (C-Stem). Three years after surgery, the C-Stem fractured, causing metal debris to be shed around the joint. Mr Justice Hickinbottom held that the aim of the Directive was to "solve the problem, peculiar to our age of increasing technicality, of

64. [2016] EWHC 3096 (QB).

a fair apportionment of the risks inherent in modern technological production". He gave the example:

> *"one can imagine a pharmaceutical product that is highly beneficial to most patients but, in a minority, causes death or serious injury, for a reason unascertained and unascertainable, may nevertheless be held to lack the appropriate level of safety for the Act, and therefore be defective."*

The judge went on to consider the need to balance risks against benefits when deciding whether a product was defective. He said:

> *"Primary amongst the purposes for which a medicinal product is marketed is the relief of a patient's symptoms and/or betterment of his condition and/or increase in his ability to function. Given that such a product will inevitably have some risks attached ... any assessment of its safety will necessarily require the risks involved in use of that product to be balanced against its potential benefits including its potential utility."*

In the event, the claim was unsuccessful because the C-Stem was held not to be defective. What happened "was rare, unpredicted and unpredictable".

In a case decided by the European Court of Justice (ECJ),[65] an advice column in a newspaper was written by an expert in herbal medicine. According to the article, fresh, coarsely grated horseradish applied to the skin for two to five hours could help alleviate rheumatic pain. However, there was a misprint in the article and the length of time for applying the horseradish poultice should have been given as two to five minutes. An Austrian citizen who applied a horseradish poultice for two to five hours claimed to have experienced severe pain due to a toxic skin reaction. She sued the newspaper owner, claiming that the owners were liable under the Directive. The Austrian court referred the case to the ECJ.

The ECJ held that, for the purposes of the Directive, a "product" meant something "movable" that was industrially produced or which was used in the construction of something immovable. The Directive did not cover services. The ECJ drew a distinction between the newspaper – the physical item – and the advice it contained. Advice was not part of the inherent characteristics of the printed newspaper and inaccurate advice fell outside the scope of the Directive so that neither the publisher nor the printer nor the author could be held liable under the Directive. The ECJ observed that, depending on the applicable domestic law, liability could still arise if there were a contractual obligation such as a warranty, or if there was a relevant tort.

---

65. *VI v KRONE – Verlag Gesellschaft mbH & Co KG* (C-65/20) - this decision is not binding on courts in the UK, but it may have persuasive force.

Intellectual property rights

Medicinal products are often the subject of litigation over intellectual property rights such as patents and trademarks. For example, there have been numerous claims brought by the manufacturers of branded products against the manufacturers of generic medicines, alleging that the launch of generic medicines infringes patent rights. In some of those cases, claims have also been made against pharmacy owners who have bought generic medicines that are alleged to have infringed patent rights.

In *Warner-Lambert Company LLC v Generics (UK) Ltd*,[66] the claimant alleged that the launch of generic pregabalin infringed its patent for Lyrica. The Lyrica patent was originally granted to protect the use of the drug in the treatment of seizure disorders, notably epilepsy. However, Warner-Lambert were later granted a second patent for the treatment of neuropathic pain. The latter patent remained current after the patent for treating seizure orders had expired. If Warner-Lambert was right in asserting that the latter patent was valid, it would mean amongst other things that any pharmacy or pharmacist who supplied generic pregabalin to a patient who had a seizure disorder would have breached the patent and be liable for substantial damages or loss of profits, even if the pharmacist did not know the condition for which pregabalin had been prescribed.

The Supreme Court dismissed Warner-Lambert's claim. Amongst other things:

- The Supreme Court recognised the risk that pharmacists who acted in good faith could be sued for large sums of money for unintentionally breaching a patent. The court also recognised that this risk would stifle the generics market and pharmacists would not be willing to supply the generic version if there was a risk of being sued.
- The Justices gave different reasons for dismissing the appeal. Lord Sumption and Lord Reed were of the view that if the outward appearance (including packaging, labelling and patient information leaflet) was presented as suitable for the patented use, a pharmacist who dispensed it for a non-patented use (such as epilepsy in this case) would not be liable for patent infringement. Lord Mance agreed except to the extent that there might be a rare case in which the context made it obvious that the outward appearance should not be taken at face value.
- The result means that pharmacists are now less at risk of being sued for patent infringement, but there is still some risk if the outward appearance of a patented product suggested a use that was not a patented use.
- It is worth bearing in mind that the case was about "second use" patents i.e. Warner-Lambert already had a patent for Lyrica for the original use, and were seeking to extend it for use in the treatment of neuropathic pain. If there was no second use and the original Lyrica patent was still current for the treatment of seizure disorders, a pharmacist who supplied a generic version could still be sued and the Supreme Court judgment would not remove the liability.

66. [2018] UKSC 56.

Liability under the Equality Act 2010

The Equality Act 2010 bans unfair treatment and helps to achieve equal opportunities in the workplace and in wider society. The Act lists nine *protected characteristics* which may not be used as a reason to treat people unfairly. They are:

1. age;
2. disability;
3. gender reassignment;
4. marriage and civil partnership;
5. pregnancy and maternity;
6. race;
7. religion or belief;
8. sex; and
9. sexual orientation.

The Equality Act sets out the different ways in which it is unlawful to treat someone, such as direct and indirect discrimination, harassment, victimisation and failing to make a reasonable adjustment for a person with a disability (see below). The Act prohibits unfair treatment in the workplace when providing goods, facilities and services; when exercising public functions; in the disposal and management of premises; in education; and by associations (such as private clubs).

Direct and indirect discrimination

The Equality Act defines direct discrimination as follows (s.13):

> *"A person (A) discriminates against another (B) if, because of a protected characteristic, A treats B less favourably than A treats or would treat others."*

Direct discrimination within pharmacy can occur in the way a service is provided to an individual in relation to a protected characteristic; for example, avoiding interaction with a patient who is deaf because the conversation may be harder than it would be with a patient who can hear. Furthermore, in relation to employment, actions may be taken that individuals were discriminated against in relation to offers of employment, promotion, dismissal or redundancy based on one or more protected characteristic(s). To succeed in a claim that there has been a failure to make reasonable adjustments for a disability, the complainant must show that the person against whom the complaint is made either knew or could reasonably have been expected to know of the complainant's disability.

Indirect discrimination is defined by the Equality Act as follows (s.19):

> *"A person (A) discriminates against another (B) if A applies to B a provision, criterion or practice which is discriminatory in relation to a relevant protected characteristic of B's."*

In many cases, it will be obvious that a particular action involves direct discrimination. In other cases, it will be less clear to an individual implementing a provision, criterion or practice within the workplace that actions taken involve indirect discrimination. For example, the provision of health information via the internet may cause issues for individuals with a disability if their requirements are not taken into consideration at the point of design. To assist in combatting issues, since August 2016 all organisations that provide NHS care and/or publicly-funded adult social care are required by law to follow the Accessible Information Standard (AIS), which "sets out a specific, consistent approach to identifying, recording, flagging, sharing and meeting the information and communication support needs of patients, service users, carers and parents with a disability, impairment or sensory loss".[67]

Harassment and victimisation

The Act contains two provisions which provide protection to individuals who take action under the Act, termed *prohibited conduct*. Therefore, the Act provides protection against *harassment* and *victimisation*.

The Act defines *harassment* (s.26) as:

A person (A) harasses another (B) if:

- A engages in unwanted conduct related to a relevant protected characteristic; and
- the conduct has the purpose or effect of:
  violating B's dignity, or
  creating an intimidating, hostile, degrading, humiliating or offensive environment for B.

The Act also defines harassment in relation to unwanted conduct of a sexual nature (s26(2)) and unwanted conduct of a sexual nature or that is related to gender reassignment or sex (s.26(3)).

In relation to harassment, the relevant protected characteristics are: age, disability, gender reassignment, race, religion or belief, sex and sexual orientation.

Victimisation is defined (s.27) as:

A person (A) victimises another person (B) if A subjects B to a detriment because:

- B does a protected act, or
- A believes that B has done, or may do, a protected act.

In relation to a *protected act*, the Act lists the following actions:

- bringing proceedings under this Act;
- giving evidence or information in connection with proceedings under this Act;
- doing any other thing for the purposes of or in connection with this Act;
- making an allegation (whether or not express) that A or another person has contravened this Act.

Reasonable adjustments

Under the Equality Act, anyone who provides services to the public must make reasonable adjustments – at the provider's cost – where the provider's practice puts a disabled person at a substantial disadvantage compared to people who do not have

67. See: https://www.england.nhs.uk/ourwork/accessibleinfo/ (accessed 31 December 2024).

disability. The duty involves taking reasonable steps to avoid the disadvantage or adopting a reasonable alternative method of providing the service. Where a person with disabilities would be at a substantial disadvantage unless an auxiliary aid is provided, there is a duty to take reasonable steps to provide one.

Reasonable adjustments may include providing a free home delivery service to a disabled person who would have difficulty accessing a pharmacy, and an auxiliary aid may include the use of a portable induction loop for hearing aid users, or the supply of medicines in a monitored dosage system. Further guidance is available from the Equality and Human Rights Commission and from NHS England on their respective websites.

Civil penalties

In a regulatory context, some modern legislation now enables financial penalties to be imposed as a first line of enforcement, rather than bringing people before a criminal court (even though regulators usually also have powers to bring criminal prosecutions). These financial penalties are often referred to as *fines*, and the word *fine* is used here for convenience, but they are civil penalties and do not result in the person on whom they are imposed having a criminal record. The sums involved are often very large. Examples of such legislation include UK GDPR (see **Chapter 23** referring to a penalty of £275,000 imposed on a pharmacy owner), the Medicines and Medical Devices Act 2021 (**Chapter 22**), and the Competition Act 1998.

Competition Act 1998

This Act reflects a worldwide trend to open up markets, stimulate competition and establish transparent and fair marketing arrangements. It seeks to do this by outlawing agreements between businesses and decisions taken by businesses on concerted practices that affect trade in the UK. Those decisions are not allowed to have as their object or effect the prevention, distortion or restriction of competition within the UK. An example of such a practice would be people acting together directly or indirectly to fix the purchase or selling process. The rules not only affect retailers but also trade associations or any other group of persons acting together in a way as to distort competition. The fines under the Competition Act can be very high, as the maximum ceiling on the fine is 10% of company turnover.

In December 2013, Lloyds Pharmacy Limited, brought to the attention of the Office of Fair Trading, a cartel agreement with Tomms Pharmacy between May and November 2011 that the two businesses would not supply prescription medicines to care homes in England already supplied by the other. The companies that owned Tomms Pharmacy agreed to pay a fine of over £380,000 (reduced to reflect its admission and agreement to co-operate with the Office of Fair Trading).[68]

As another example of the operation of the Competition Act, the Competition and Markets Authority (CMA - which had taken over the functions of the Office of Fair Trading)

68. https://www.gov.uk/cma-cases/investigation-into-the-supply-of-healthcare-products (accessed 31 December 2024).

found[69] that King Pharmaceuticals Ltd and Auden Mckenzie (Pharma Division) Ltd shared out between them the supply of the antidepressant drug, nortriptyline, to a large pharmaceutical wholesaler in 2014 and 2015. The two companies agreed that King would supply only 25 mg tablets and Auden Mckenzie only 10 mg tablets. They also colluded to fix quantities and prices. King and Auden Mckenzie admitted breaching competition law and were respectively fined £75,573 and £1,882,238. Accord-UK (which had taken control of Auden Mckenzie's nortriptyline business) and Auden McKenzie agreed to make a £1m payment to the NHS. The CMA also fined King, Lexon (UK) Ltd and Alissa Healthcare Research Ltd for illegally sharing commercially sensitive information to try to keep nortriptyline prices up when the cost of the drug was falling between 2015 and 2017. King and Alissa admitted breaking the law and were fined £75,573 and £174,912 respectively. Lexon did not admit to breaking the law and were fined £1,220,383.

In August 2019, following a CMA investigation, Aspen group companies admitted entering into an illegal anti-competitive agreement with two competitors in 2016, paying their competitors to stay out of the market for fludrocortisone, leaving Aspen as the sole supplier of fludrocortisone, with the ability to set prices without facing any competition. To bring the investigation to a close, Aspen agreed to pay £8m to the National Health Service.[70]

The CMA also has a role in preventing predatory pricing. During the COVID-19 pandemic in 2020, the CMA investigated[71] allegations of profiteering by a small number of pharmacies over the price of products such as hand sanitizer though, in the event, it found no evidence to justify taking action against any of them.

SUMMARY

- Breaches of legislation governing pharmacy practice and breaches of other legislation, including health and safety law, are criminal offences.
- Offences may be committed by pharmacy owners, employees, locums and unqualified staff.
- The legislation that creates some offences also provides a defence in certain circumstances if specified conditions are met. The Human Medicines Regulations contain exemptions that avoid an offence being committed in certain circumstances.
- The GPhC has the power to bring prosecutions but seldom does so, usually regarding it as proportionate to use other powers of enforcement.
- As well as offences created by legislation, some offences are part of the common law. These include manslaughter. A healthcare professional who causes death through gross negligence may be guilty of this offence, but the scope for prosecutions in such cases has narrowed as a result of case law.

---

69. https://assets.publishing.service.gov.uk/media/5f115b4dd3bf7f5baab7a5e4/Market_Sharing_Decision.pdf (accessed 31 December 2024).

70. https://www.gov.uk/government/news/cma-pharma-probe-secures-8m-for-the-nhs (accessed 31 December 2024).

71. https://www.gov.uk/cma-cases/hand-sanitiser-products-suspected-excessive-and-unfair-pricing (accessed 31 December 2024).

- Civil liability may arise in contract, tort or as a result of the provisions of some legislation.
- It is a professional requirement to have indemnity insurance.
- Pharmacy professionals owe a duty of care to patients that must be exercised independently of prescribers.
- Torts which may give rise to a claim for damages include negligence, health and safety breaches, occupiers' liability and battery.
- Access to the summary care record, prescribing and hub and spoke dispensing may all lead to an increase in the risk of liability.
- Employers will be liable for the torts of employees and locums when those torts are committed in the ordinary course of the activities of a pharmacy. The position is less clear if a tort is committed by a volunteer.
- There is an implied term in a contract of employment that the employee will exercise reasonable care in carrying out their employment. A pharmacy owner is entitled to claim damages from an employee who breaches the implied term.
- A person who is liable to compensate another person may claim a contribution towards damages or an indemnity from someone who is liable for the same damage.
- If a defective product causes harm, damages may be claimed from manufacturers and others without proving negligence.
- Pharmacies that stock or supply products that infringe intellectual property rights may be sued for damages.
- Some legislation provides that financial penalties may be imposed, often for very large sums. These penalties are civil, not criminal.

FURTHER READING

- Department of Health: Environment and sustainability Health Technical Memorandum 07-01: Safe management of healthcare waste **https://assets.publishing.service.gov.uk/government/uploads/system/uploads/attachment_data/file/167976/HTM_07-01_Final.pdf** (accessed 31 December 2024).
- Health and Safety Executive Approved Code of Practice *Workplace health, safety and welfare* **https://www.hse.gov.uk/pUbns/priced/l24.pdf** (accessed 31 December 2024).
- Langley, C. A. (2014). Pharmacy legislation – public protector or professional hindrance? Medical Law Review. 22 (1), 87-108.
- Ministry of Justice - Guidance on the Rehabilitation of Offenders Act 1974 and the Exceptions Order 1975 - **https://assets.publishing.service.gov.uk/media/653f7e52d10f3500139a6b20/30102023___Guidance_on_the_Rehabilitation_of_Offenders_Act_1974_and_The_Exceptions_Order_1975.pdf** (accessed 31 December 2024).
- Pharmaceutical Journal (31 August 2007) *How to manage the health and safety risks in your pharmacy* **https://www.pharmaceutical-journal.com/news-and-analysis/how-to-manage-the-health-and-safety-risks-in-your-pharmacy/10006919.article** (accessed 31 December 2024).
- Reissner D (2016) The risks of ignoring summary care records, *Chemist & Druggist*, 26 April **https://www.chemistanddruggist.co.uk/CD000954/David-Reissner-The-risks-of-ignoring-summary-care-records/** (accessed 31 December 2024).
- Reissner D (2017). Can pharmacists, or pharmacies, be convicted of manslaughter? *Chemist and Druggist*, 6 November 2017 **https://www.chemistanddruggist.co.uk/CD001187/Can-pharmacists-or-pharmacies-be-convicted-of-manslaughter** (accessed 31 December 2024).

APPENDIX 1

The Standards for pharmacy professionals

Introduction

1. "Pharmacy professionals" (pharmacists and pharmacy technicians) play a vital role in delivering care and helping people to maintain and improve their health, safety and wellbeing. The professionalism they demonstrate is central to maintaining trust and confidence in pharmacy.
2. Patients and the public have a right to expect safe and effective care from pharmacy professionals. We believe it is the attitudes and behaviours of pharmacy professionals in their day-to-day work which make the most significant contributions to the quality of care, of which safety is a vital part.
3. The standards for pharmacy professionals describe how safe and effective care is delivered through 'person-centred' professionalism. The standards are a statement of what people expect from pharmacy professionals, and also reflect what pharmacy professionals have told us they expect of themselves and their colleagues.
4. At the heart of the standards is the principle that every person must be treated as an individual. Pharmacy professionals have an important role in involving, supporting and enabling people to make decisions about their health, safety and wellbeing. For example, what is important to one person managing their short or long-term condition may not be important to another.

The Standards for pharmacy professionals

1. There are nine standards that every pharmacy professional is accountable for meeting. The standards apply to all pharmacists and pharmacy technicians. We know that pharmacy professionals practise in a number of sectors and settings and may use different ways to communicate with the people they provide care to. The standards apply whatever their form of practice. And even when pharmacy professionals do not provide care directly to patients and the public, their practice can indirectly have an impact on the safe and effective care that patients and the public receive, and on the confidence of members of the public in pharmacy as a whole.
2. The standards need to be met at all times, not only during working hours. This is because the attitudes and behaviours of professionals outside of work can affect the trust and confidence of patients and the public in pharmacy professionals.
3. The meaning of each of the standards is explained, and there are examples of the types of attitudes and behaviours that pharmacy professionals should demonstrate. The examples may not apply in all situations.

4. The standards include the term 'person-centred care' and refer to a "person" throughout. This means 'the person receiving care'. The term may also apply to carers or patients' representatives depending on the situation.

The standards and pharmacy students and trainees

1. The standards for pharmacy professionals are relevant to all pharmacy students and trainees while they are on their journey towards registration and practice. The standards explain the knowledge, attitudes and behaviours that will be expected of students and trainees if they apply to join the register.
2. They should be interpreted in the context of education and training and used as a tool to prepare students and trainees for registration as a pharmacy professional.
3. Pharmacy students and trainees should consider the standards as they move closer to registration and professional practice, and should read them alongside other relevant documents that are provided by initial education and training providers. The standards and registration.

The standards and registration

1. The standards are designed to reflect what it means to be a pharmacy professional. They are also at the heart of initial education and training, registration and renewal as a pharmacy professional, and continuing fitness to remain registered. Applying the standards.

Applying the standards

1. Pharmacy professionals are personally accountable for meeting the standards and must be able to justify the decisions they make.
2. We expect pharmacy professionals to consider these standards, their legal duties and any relevant guidance when making decisions.
3. The standards and supporting explanations do not list the legal duties pharmacy professionals have, as all pharmacy professionals must keep to the relevant laws. Relevant guidance is published by a number of organisations, including professional leadership bodies, other regulators, the NHS, National Institute for Health and Care Excellence and Scottish Intercollegiate Guidelines Network, as well as by the GPhC.
4. There will be times when pharmacy professionals are faced with conflicting legal and professional responsibilities. Or they may be faced with complex situations that mean they have to balance competing priorities. The standards provide a framework to help them when making professional judgements. Pharmacy professionals must work in partnership with everyone involved, and make sure the person they are providing care to is their first priority.

Standards for pharmacy professionals

All pharmacy professionals contribute to delivering and improving the health, safety and wellbeing of patients and the public. Professionalism and safe and effective practice are central to that role.

Pharmacy professionals must:

1. provide person-centred care
2. work in partnership with others
3. communicate effectively
4. maintain, develop and use their professional knowledge and skills
5. use professional judgement
6. behave in a professional manner
7. respect and maintain the person's confidentiality and privacy
8. speak up when they have concerns or when things go wrong
9. demonstrate leadership

Standard 1: Pharmacy professionals must provide person-centred care

Applying the standard

Every person is an individual with their own values, needs and concerns. Person-centred care is delivered when pharmacy professionals understand what is important to the individual and then adapt the care to meet their needs – making the care of the person their first priority. All pharmacy professionals can demonstrate "person-centredness", whether or not they provide care directly, by thinking about the impact their decisions have on people. There are a number of ways to meet this standard, and below are examples of the attitudes and behaviours expected.

People receive safe and effective care when pharmacy professionals:

- obtain consent to provide care and pharmacy services
- involve, support and enable every person when making decisions about their health, care and wellbeing
- listen to the person and understand their needs and what matters to them
- give the person all relevant information in a way they can understand, so they can make informed decisions and choices
- consider the impact of their practice whether or not they provide care directly
- respect and safeguard the person's dignity
- recognise and value diversity, and respect cultural differences – making sure that every person is treated fairly whatever their values and beliefs
- recognise their own values and beliefs but do not impose them on other people
- take responsibility for ensuring that person-centred care is not compromised because of personal values and beliefs
- make the best use of the resources available

Standard 2: Pharmacy professionals must work in partnership with others

Applying the standard

A person's health, safety and wellbeing are dependent on pharmacy professionals working in partnership with others, where everyone is contributing towards providing the person with the care they need. This includes the person and will also include other healthcare professionals and teams. It may also include carers, relatives and professionals in other settings – such as social workers and public health officials. There are a number of ways to meet this standard and below are examples of the attitudes and behaviours expected.

People receive safe and effective care when pharmacy professionals:

- work with the person receiving care
- identify and work with the individuals and teams who are involved in the person's care
- contact, involve and work with the relevant local and national organisations
- demonstrate effective team working
- adapt their communication to bring about effective partnership working
- take action to safeguard people, particularly children and vulnerable adults
- make and use records of the care provided
- work with others to make sure there is continuity of care for the person concerned

Standard 3: Pharmacy professionals must communicate effectively

Applying the standard

Communication can take many forms and happens in different ways. Effective communication is essential to the delivery of person-centred care and to working in partnership with others. It helps people to be involved in decisions about their health, safety and wellbeing. Communication is more than giving a person information, asking questions and listening. It is the exchange of information between people. Body language, tone of voice and the words pharmacy professionals use all contribute to effective communication. There are a number of ways to meet this standard and below are examples of the attitudes and behaviours expected.

People receive safe and effective care when pharmacy professionals:

- adapt their communication to meet the needs of the person they are communicating with
- overcome barriers to communication
- ask questions and listen carefully to the responses, to understand the person's needs and come to a shared decision about the care they provide
- listen actively and respond to the information they receive in a timely manner
- check the person has understood the information they have been given
- communicate effectively with others involved in the care of the person

Standard 4: Pharmacy professionals must maintain, develop and use their professional knowledge and skills

Applying the standard

People receive safe and effective care when pharmacy professionals reflect on the application of their knowledge and skills and keep them up-to-date, including using evidence in their decision making. A pharmacy professional's knowledge and skills must develop over the course of their career to reflect the changing nature of healthcare, the population they provide care to and the roles they carry out. There are a number of ways to meet this standard and below are examples of the attitudes and behaviours expected.

People receive safe and effective care when pharmacy professionals:

- recognise and work within the limits of their knowledge and skills, and refer to others when needed
- use their skills and knowledge, including up-to-date evidence, to deliver care and improve the quality of care they provide
- carry out a range of continuing professional development (CPD) activities relevant to their practice
- record their development activities to demonstrate that their knowledge and skills are up to date
- use a variety of methods to regularly monitor and reflect on their practice, skills and knowledge

Standard 5: Pharmacy professionals must use their professional judgement

Applying the standard

People expect pharmacy professionals to use their professional judgement so that they deliver safe and effective care. Professional judgement may include balancing the needs of individuals with the needs of society as a whole. It can also include managing complex legal and professional responsibilities and working with the person to understand and decide together what the right thing is for them – particularly if those responsibilities appear to conflict. There are a number of ways to meet this standard and below are examples of the attitudes and behaviours expected.

People receive safe and effective care when pharmacy professionals:

- make the care of the person their first concern and act in their best interest
- use their judgement to make clinical and professional decisions with the person or others
- have the information they need to provide appropriate care
- declare any personal or professional interests and manage these professionally
- practise only when fit to do so
- recognise the limits of their competence
- consider and manage appropriately any personal or organisational goals, incentives or targets and make sure the care they provide reflects the needs of the person

Standard 6: Pharmacy professionals must behave in a professional manner

Applying the standard

People expect pharmacy professionals to behave professionally. This is essential to maintaining trust and confidence in pharmacy. Behaving professionally is not limited to the working day, or face-to-face interactions. The privilege of being a pharmacist or pharmacy technician, and the importance of maintaining confidence in the professions, call for appropriate behaviour at all times. There are a number of ways to meet this standard and below are examples of the attitudes and behaviours expected.

People receive safe and effective care when pharmacy professionals:

- are polite and considerate
- are trustworthy and act with honesty and integrity
- show empathy and compassion
- treat people with respect and safeguard their dignity
- maintain appropriate personal and professional boundaries with the people they provide care to and with others

Standard 7: Pharmacy professionals must respect and maintain a person's confidentiality and privacy

Applying the standard

People trust that their confidentiality and privacy will be maintained by pharmacy professionals, whether in a healthcare setting – such as a hospital, primary care or community pharmacy setting – in person, or online. Maintaining confidentiality is a vital part of the relationship between a pharmacy professional and the person seeking care. People may be reluctant to ask for care if they believe their information may not be kept confidential. The principles of confidentiality still apply after a person's death. There are a number of ways to meet this standard and below are examples of the attitudes and behaviours expected.

People receive safe and effective care when pharmacy professionals:

- understand the importance of managing information responsibly and securely, and apply this to their practice
- reflect on their environment and take steps to maintain the person's privacy and confidentiality
- do not discuss information that can identify the person when the discussions can be overheard or seen by others not involved in their care
- ensure that everyone in the team understands the need to maintain a person's privacy and confidentiality
- work in partnership with the person when considering whether to share their information, except where this would not be appropriate

Standard 8: Pharmacy professionals must speak up when they have concerns or when things go wrong

Applying the standard

The quality of care that people receive is improved when pharmacy professionals learn from feedback and incidents, and challenge poor practice and behaviours. This includes speaking up when they have concerns. At the heart of this standard is the requirement to be candid with the person concerned and with colleagues and employers. This is usually called the "duty of candour" – which means being honest when things go wrong. There are a number of ways to meet this standard and below are examples of the attitudes and behaviours expected.

People receive safe and effective care when pharmacy professionals:

- promote and encourage a culture of learning and improvement
- challenge poor practice and behaviours
- raise a concern, even when it is not easy to do so
- promptly tell their employer and all relevant authorities (including the GPhC) about concerns they may have
- support people who raise concerns and provide feedback
- are open and honest when things go wrong
- say sorry, provide an explanation and put things right when things go wrong
- reflect on feedback or concerns, taking action as appropriate and thinking about what can be done to prevent the same thing happening again
- improve the quality of care and pharmacy practice by learning from feedback and when things go wrong

Standards 9: Pharmacy professionals must demonstrate leadership

Applying the standard

Every pharmacy professional can demonstrate leadership, whatever their role. Leadership includes taking responsibility for their actions and leading by example. Wherever a pharmacy professional practises, they must provide leadership to the people they work with and to others. There are a number of ways to meet this standard and below are some examples of the attitudes and behaviours expected.

People receive safe and effective care when pharmacy professionals:

- take responsibility for their practice and demonstrate leadership to the people they work with
- assess the risks in the care they provide and do everything they can to keep these risks as low as possible
- contribute to the education, training and development of the team or of others
- delegate tasks only to people who are competent and appropriately trained or are in training, and exercise proper oversight
- do not abuse their position or set out to influence others to abuse theirs
- lead by example, in particular to those who are working towards registration as a pharmacy professional

APPENDIX 2

Specified medicinal products at high dilutions

Schedule 21 to the Human Medicines Regulations 2012 lists the specified medicinal products to which Reg.242 applies.

Part 1: unit preparations diluted to at least one part in a thousand (3×)	Part 2: unit preparations diluted to at least one part in a million (6×)	Part 3: unit preparations diluted to at least one part in ten (1×)	Part 4: unit preparations diluted to at least one part in ten (1×) for external use
Agaricus muscarius	Adonis vernalis	Abies excelsa	Adonis vernalis
Ailanthus glandulosa	Agaricus bulbosus	Abies nigra	Agricus bulbosus
Apocynum cannabinum	Agaricus muscarius	Abies nobilis	Agricus muscarius
Aurum Iodatum	Agnus castus	Acalpha indica	Agnus castus
Belladonna	Ailanthus glandulosa	Agate	Allanthus glandulosa
Bismuth subgallate	Alum	Alisma plantago aq.	Alum
Bryonia alba dioica	Amethyst	Alstonia scholaris	Amethyst
Calcium fluoride	Ammonium iodide	Aluminium	Ammonium iodide
Cantharis	Amygdalae amarae	Amber (Succinum)	Amygdalae amarae
Cerium oxalicum	Apatite	Ambra grisea	Apatite
Chelidonium majus	Apocynum androsaemifolium	Ammonium phosphate	Apocynum androsaemifolium
Chenopodium oil	Apocynum cannabinum	Angostura vera	Apocynum cannabinum
Cina	Argentite	Anthoxanthum	Argentite
Colocynthis	Argentum chloride	Apis mellifera	Argentum chloride
Convallaria majalis	Argentum iodide	Aqua marina	Argentum iodide
Gelsemium sempervirens	Arnica	Aqua mellis	Artemisia cina
Hyoscyamus niger	Artemisia cina	Aralia racemosa	Aspidium filix-mas
Lycopodium	Aspidium filix-mas	Aranea diadema	Aspidium anthelmintica
Manganese acetate	Aspidium anthelmintica	Arum maculatum	Aurum sulphide
Ranunculus bulbosus	Aurum sulphide	Arum triphyllum	Balsamum copaivae
Terebinthinae oleum	Balsamum copivae	Asarum	Balsamum peruvianum
	Balsamum peruvianum	Asperula odorata	Barium citrate
	Barium citrate	Astacus fluviatillis	Barium sulphate
	Barium sulphate	Auric chloride	Bismuth metal
	Bismuth metal	Badiaga	Bismuth subgallate
	Bismuth subgallate	Beech (*Fagus sylvestris*)	Bismuth subnitrate
	Bismuth subnitrate	Bellis perennis	Boletus laricis
	Boletus laricis	Berberis aquifolium	Bovista
	Bovista	Borago officinalis	Cade oil
	Cade oil	Butyric acid	Calcium fluoride
	Calcium fluoride	Calcium metal	Carduus marianus
	Cantharis	Calcium chloride	Cedar wood oil
	Carduus marianus	Calcium oxide	Cerium oxalicum
		Calcium sulphate	

Part 1: unit preparations diluted to at least one part in a thousand (3×)	Part 2: unit preparations diluted to at least one part in a million (6×)	Part 3: unit preparations diluted to at least one part in ten (1×)	Part 4: unit preparations diluted to at least one part in ten (1×) for external use
	Cedar wood oil	Castoreum	Chalcocite
	Cerium oxalicum	Ceanothus americanus	Chalcopyrite
	Chalcocite	Cedron	Chelidonium majus
	Chalcopyrite	Cerato (*Ceratostigma willmottiana*)	Chenopodium oil
	Chelidonium majus	Cherry Plum (*Prunus cerasifera*)	Colocynthis
	Chenopodium oil	Chestnut, red and sweet	Convallaria majalis
	Colocynthis	Cholesterinum	Copper silicate, Nat
	Convallaria majalis	Chrysolite	Crotalus horridus
	Copper silicate, Nat.	Cistus canadensis	Cucumis melo
	Crotalus horridus	Clematis erecta	Cucurbita
	Cucurbita	Conchae vera	Datura stramonium
	Cucumis melo	Conchiolinum	Derris
	Datura stramonium	Corallium rubrum	Diamond
	Derris	Crab apple	Ephedra vulgaris
	Diamond	Crocus sativus	Ferric acetate
	Ephedra vulgaris	Erbium	Ferrous iodide
	Ferric acetate	Erigeron canadense	Ferrous oxalate
	Ferrous iodide	Fuligo	Ferrous sulphide
	Ferrous oxalate	Genista tinctoria	Formic acid
	Ferrous sulphide	Geum urbanum	Gall
	Formic acid	Glycogen	Gelsemium sempervirens
	Gall	Gnaphalium leontopodium	Gneiss
	Gelsemium sempervirens	Gold	Hamamelis virginiana
	Gneiss	Gorse (*Ulex europaeus*)	Hepar sulfuris
	Granatum (Pomegranate) bark	Graphites	Hyoscyamus niger
	Hamamelis virginiana	Gratiola officinalis	Iris florentine
	Hepar sulfuris	Gymnocladus (American coffee tree)	Jaborandi
	Hyoscyamus niger	Haematoxylon campechianum	Juniperus sabina
	Iris florentine	Hecla lava (ash from Mount Hecla)	Kaolinite
	Jaborandi	Hedeoma pulegioides	Lachmanthus tinctoria
	Juniperus sabina	Hedra helix	Lapis albus
	Kalinite	Heliotrope	Lycopodium
	Lachmanthus tinctoria	Heracleum spondylium	Magnesium
	Lapis albus	HerniariaHornbeam (*Carpinus betulus*)	Magnesium acetate
	Lycopodium	Iberis amara	Magnesium chloride
	Magnesium	Impatiens	Magnetite
	Magnesium acetate	Iris germanica	Manganese acetate
	Magnesium chloride	Iris pseudacorus	Nicotiana tabacum
	Magnetite	Jacaranda procera	Nicotiana tabacum oil
	Manganese acetate	Jatropha curcas	Oleander
	Nicotiana tabacum	Juncus communis	Opuntia vulgaris
	Nicotiana tabacum oil	Justica adhatoda	Oxalic acid
	Oleander	Lamium album	Petroleum
	Opuntia vulgaris	Laurus nobilis oil	Phellandrium aquaticum
	Oxalic acid	Laurocerasus	Pix liquida
	Petroleum	Ledum palustre	Platinum
	Phellandrum aquaticum	Lilium tigrinum	Platinum chloride
	Pix liquida		Potassium hydroxide
	Platinum		Potassium silicate
	Platinum chloride		Pyrethrum
	Potassium hydroxide		Pyrolusite
			Ranunculus acris

Part 1: unit preparations diluted to at least one part in a thousand (3×)	Part 2: unit preparations diluted to at least one part in a million (6×)	Part 3: unit preparations diluted to at least one part in ten (1×)	Part 4: unit preparations diluted to at least one part in ten (1×) for external use
	Potassium silicate Pyrethrum Pyrolusite Ranunculus acris Ranunculus bulbosus Ranunculus flammula Ranunculus repens Ranunculus sceleratus Rhodium oxynitrate Rhododendron chrysanthemum Rhus toxicodendron Salicylic acid Scrophularia aquatica Sodium aluminium chloride Sodium auro-chloride Sodium hypochlorite Sodium nitrate Squill Stannum metal Staphisagria Sulphur iodide Tamus communis Tannic acid Terebinthinae oleum Theridion Thuja occidentalis Topaz Uric acid Zinc hypophosphite Zinc isovalerate	Lonicera caprifolium Lysimachia vulgaris Magnesium phosphate Magnesite Magnolia Marum verum Melilotus officinalis Menispermum canadense Mephitis putorius Mercurialis perennis Mimulus (*Mimullis guttatus*) Moschus Myrica gale Myrtus communis Ocimum basilicum Olive Oxalis acetosella Pangamic acid Paullinia cupana Penthorum sedoides Pollen (mixed) Polygonatum multiflorum Polygonum aviculare Polypodium vulgare Primula vulgaris Prunella vulgaris Ptellea trifoliata Ratanhia Robinia pseudoacacia Rubia tinctorum Rumex acetosella Sal marina Sarcolactic acid Sarracenia purpurea Scleranthus (*Scleranthus annuus*) Silica Silphium laciniathum Sodium benzoate Spongia marina Star of Bethlehem (*Ornithogalum umbellatum*) Ulmus campestris Vine Walnut (*Juglerus regia*) Water violet (*Hottonia palustris*) Wild oat Wild rose	Ranunculus bulbosus Ranunculus flammula Ranunculus repens Ranunculus scelerantus Rhodium oxynitrate Rhododendron chrysanthemum Rhus toxicidendron Salicylic acid Scrophularia aquatica Sodium aluminium chloride Sodium auro-chloride Sodium hypochlorite Sodium nitrate Squill Stannum metal Sulphur iodide Tannic acid Terebinthinae oleum Topaz Uric acid Zinc hypophosphite Zinc isovalerate

APPENDIX 3

Patient Group Directions

Taken from the Human Medicines Regulations 2012 (Regs.229-234, and Sch. 16).

Particulars to be included in a Patient Group Direction (PGD)

The following particulars are to be included (HMR Schedule 16, Part 1):

1. the period during which the Direction is to have effect;
2. the description or class of medicinal product to which the Direction relates;
3. the clinical situations which medicinal products of that description or class may be used to treat or manage in any form;
4. whether there are any restrictions on the quantity of medicinal product that may be sold or supplied on any one occasion and, if so, what restrictions (but see note, below);
5. the clinical criteria under which a person is to be eligible for treatment;
6. whether any class of person is excluded from treatment under the Direction and, if so, what class of person;
7. whether there are circumstances in which further advice should be sought from a doctor or dentist and, if so, what circumstances;
8. the pharmaceutical form or forms in which medicinal products of that description or class are to be administered;
9. the strength, or maximum strength, at which medicinal products of that description or class are to be administered;
10. the applicable dosage or maximum dosage;
11. the route of administration;
12. the frequency of administration;
13. any minimum or maximum period of administration applicable to medicinal products of that description or class;
14. whether there are any relevant warnings to note and, if so, what warnings;
15. whether there is any follow-up action to be taken in any circumstances and, if so, what action and in what circumstances;
16. arrangements for referral for medical advice; and
17. details of the records to be kept of the supply, or the administration, of products under the Direction.

Note that the particulars specified in point 4 may be omitted in the case of a PGD relating to administration only, for PGDs constituted under the following Regulations:

- HMR Reg. 230 – Exemption for supply etc under a PGD to assist doctors or dentists;
- HMR Reg. 231 – Exemption for supply etc under a PGD by independent hospitals etc.;
- HMR Reg. 232 – Exemption for supply etc under a PGD by dental practices and clinics: England and Wales;
- HMR Reg. 233 – Exemption for supply etc under a PGD by persons conducting a retail pharmacy business;

- HMR Reg. 234 – Exemption for supply etc of products under a PGD to assist the police etc.

Persons on whose behalf a PGD must be signed, for supply by NHS bodies and local authorities (HMR Schedule 16, Part 2 and Part 3)

Class of person or force or service by whom or on whose behalf the health care is provided or the product is supplied	Person on by whom or whose behalf the Direction must be signed
Common Services Agency	The Agency
Health authority	The health authority
Special health authority	The special health authority
NHS trust or NHS foundation trust	The trust
Local authority	The Chief Executive or Director of Public Health of the local authority
The United Kingdom Health Security Agency	The Chief Executive of the United Kingdom Health Security Agency
A person who supplies medicinal products pursuant to an arrangement made with: a. the Common Services Agency; b. a health authority; c. a special health authority; d. an NHS trust; e. an integrated care board; f. NHS England;[1] g. a local authority; h. the United Kingdom Health Security Agency; or i. an NHS foundation trust.	The Common Services Agency (where the arrangement has been made with the Agency); otherwise the: a. health authority; b. special health authority; c. NHS trust; d. an integrated care board; e. NHS England; f. a local authority; g. Chief Executive of the United Kingdom Health Security Agency; or h. NHS foundation trust; with which the arrangement has been made.
A police force in England and Wales	The chief officer of police for that police force (within the meaning of the Police Act 1996)
A police force in Scotland	The chief constable of that police force (within the meaning of the Police (Scotland) Act 1967)
The prison service in England and Wales	The governor of the prison in relation to which the health care in question is being provided
The prison service in Scotland	The Scottish Prison Service Management Board
His Majesty's Forces	a. the Surgeon General b. a Medical Director General, or c. a chief executive of an executive agency of the Ministry of Defence
Contractor carrying out helicopter search and rescue operations on behalf of the Maritime and Coastguard Agency	Medical Director of the contractor carrying out search and rescue operations on behalf of the Maritime and Coastguard Agency

1. At the time of going to press, the Prime Minister had announced that NHS England would be abolished and its functions taken over by the Department of Health and Social Care.

APPENDIX 4

Schedule 1A to the Poisons Act: Regulated and Reportable Substances

Schedule 1A to the Poisons Act 1972 lists regulated and reportable substances. Part 1 lists regulated explosives precursors and Part 2 regulated poisons. Members of the general public require a licence in order to import, acquire, possess or use one of these regulated substances lawfully. Details of the transaction must be entered on to the licence and the item must bear a warning label (see **Chapter 21**). Part 3 lists reportable explosives precursors and Part 4 reportable poisons. No licence is required to possess these substances, but a supplier must report any transaction, involving the supply, or proposed supply, of a regulated or reportable substance to a customer if the supplier has reasonable grounds for believing the transaction to be suspicious.

Part 1 Regulated explosive precursors

Substance	In concentrations (weight in weight) over (%)
Ammonium nitrate in concentration of 16% by weight of nitrogen in relation to ammonium nitrate or higher	
Hexamine	
Hydrochloric acid	10
Hydrogen peroxide	12
Nitromethane	30
Nitric acid	3
Phosphoric acid	30
Potassium chlorate	40
Potassium perchlorate	40
Sodium chlorate	40
Sulfuric acid	15

Part 2 Regulated poisons

- Aluminium phosphide
- Aluminium sulphide
- Arsenic; its compounds
- Barium, salts of, other than barium sulfate: barium carbonate and barium silicofluoride

- Bromomethane
- Calcium phosphide
- Calcium sulfide
- Chloropicrin
- Fluoroacetic acid; its salts; fluoroacetamide
- Hydrogen cyanide; metal cyanides, other than ferrocyanides and ferricyanides
- Lead acetates; compounds of lead with acids from fixed oils
- Magnesium phosphide
- Magnesium sulfide
- Mercury, its compounds
- Oxalic acid in concentrations over 10% weight in weight
- Phenols (phenol; phenolic isomers of: cresols, xylenols, monoethylphenols); compounds of phenols with a metal in concentrations over 60% weight in weight of phenols or, for compounds of phenols with a metal, the equivalent of over 60% weight in weight of phenols
- Phosphorus, yellow
- Sodium sulfide
- Strychnine; its salts; its quaternary compounds
- Thallium, salts of
- Zinc phosphide
- 2.4 Dinitrophenol and compounds including sodium dinitrophenolate

Part 3 Reportable explosive precursors[1]

- Acetone
- Aluminium powders with a particle size less than 200μm, as a substance or in mixtures containing 70% or more, by weight, of aluminium and/or magnesium.
- Calcium ammonium nitrate
- Calcium nitrate
- Magnesium nitrate hexahydrate
- Magnesium powders with a particle size less than 200μm, as a substance or in mixtures containing 70% or more, by weight, of aluminium and/or magnesium.
- Potassium nitrate
- Sodium nitrate
- Sulfur

Part 4 Reportable poisons

For circumstances where requirements of the Act do not apply to a specified substance or mixture, see regulations made under section 9B of the amended Act.

- Aldicarb
- Alpha-chloralose

---

1. As amended by the Poisons Act 1972 (Explosives Precursors) (Amendment) Regulations 2018.

- Ammonia in concentrations greater than 10% weight in weight
- Barium, salts of: barium carbonate; barium silicofluoride
- Carbofuran
- Cycloheximide
- Dinitrocresols (DNOC); their compounds with a metal or a base
- Dinoseb; its compounds with a metal or a base
- Dinoterb
- Drazoxolon; its salts
- Endosulfan
- Endothal, its salts
- Endrin
- Fentin, compounds of
- Formaldehyde, in concentrations greater than 5% weight in weight
- Formic acid, in concentrations greater than 25% weight in weight
- Hydrofluoric acid; alkali metal bifluorides; ammonium bifluoride; alkali metal fluorides; ammonium fluoride; sodium silicofluoride
- Metallic oxalates
- Metal phosphides
- Metal sulfides and polysulfides
- Methomyl
- Nicotine; its salts; its quaternary compounds
- Nitrobenzene, in concentrations greater than 0.1% weight in weight
- Oxamyl
- Paraquat, salts of
- Phenols (as defined in Part 2 of Schedule 1A) in substances containing no more than 60% weight in weight of phenols; compounds of phenols with a metal in substances containing no more than the equivalent of 60% weight in weight of phenols
- Phosphorus compounds: azinphos-methyl, chlorfenvinphos, demephion, demeton-*S*-methyl, demeton-*S*-methyl sulfone, dialifos, dichlorvos, dioxathion, disulfoton, fonofos, mecarbam, mephosfolan, methidathion, mevinphos, omethoate, oxydemeton-methyl, parathion, phenkapton, phorate, phosphamidon, pirimiphos-ethyl, quinalphos, thiometon, thionazin, triazophos, vamidothion
- Potassium hydroxide, greater than 17% of total caustic alkalinity
- Sodium hydroxide, greater than 12% of total caustic alkalinity
- Sodium hypocholrite
- Sodium nitrite
- Thiofanox

Index

A

B

C

D

E

F

I

J

K

L

M

O

P

Q

R

S

T

U

V

W

X

Y